Global Marketing Management

Global Marketing Management

Changes, New Challenges, and Strategies

Second Edition

Kiefer Lee
Principal Lecturer in Marketing, Sheffield Hallam University

Dr Steve Carter
Professor of Marketing, Leeds Metropolitan University

OXFORD
UNIVERSITY PRESS

OXFORD

UNIVERSITY PRESS

Great Clarendon Street, Oxford OX2 6DP

Oxford University Press is a department of the University of Oxford.
It furthers the University's objective of excellence in research,
scholarship, and education by publishing worldwide in
Oxford New York

Auckland Cape Town Dar es Salaam Hong Kong Karachi
Kuala Lumpur Madrid Melbourne Mexico City Nairobi
New Delhi Shanghai Taipei Toronto

With offices in
Argentina Austria Brazil Chile Czech Republic France Greece
Guatemala Hungary Italy Japan Poland Portugal Singapore
South Korea Switzerland Thailand Turkey Ukraine Vietnam

Oxford is a registered trade mark of Oxford University Press in the UK
and in certain other countries

Published in the United States
by Oxford University Press Inc., New York

The moral rights of the authors have been asserted
Database right Oxford University Press (maker)

First published 2005

Second edition 2009

British Library Cataloguing in Publication Data
Data available

Library of Congress Cataloging in Publication Data
Lee, Kiefer.
Global marketing management : changes, new challenges, and strategies / Kiefer Lee, Steve Carter.—
2nd ed.
    p. cm.
  Includes index.
  ISBN 978–0–19–923942–9
1. International business enterprises—Management. 2. Strategic planning. I. Carter, S. (Steve) II. Title.
HD62.4.L44 2009
658.8'4—dc22
2009005337

Typeset by Macmillan Publishing Solutions
Printed in Italy by L.E.G.O S.p.A
ISBN 978–0–19–923942–9

1 3 5 7 9 10 8 6 4 2

PREFACE

The international dimension increasingly pervades every market and marketing activity, even domestically, as competition grows from both domestic and transnational organizations. Ignoring this trend is a perilous decision. The management task is not only to be alive to this development, but to recognize, plan, and react to some fundamental 'megatrends' in the global marketing environment. These trends are fivefold. First, rapid changes in technology, especially the explosive growth of the World Wide Web which is changing the face of communications, distribution and relationships between buyer and seller. Secondly, the rapid emergence of the global service economy, especially as it has outstripped the manufacturing sector among the three areas which dominate world trade—that is, the USA, Western Europe and Japan. Thirdly, the evolution of the 'Knowledge' economy as a source of competitive advantage, focusing as it does on the 'people' asset in organizations. Fourthly, the increasing importance of managing relationships between suppliers, organizations, customers, and other stakeholders, in order to forge long-term and profitable relationships. Finally, the need for increasing transparency of corporate practices worldwide and the pressure that this puts organizations under to be more socially responsible in their business activities.

These changes, as well as the 'traditional' problems of accounting for cultural differences between nations and the need to select the right strategies of market entry, have brought about new challenges on both strategic and operational levels to organizations of all sizes and at various stages of internationalization. This requires all organizations to openly embrace these contemporary issues and thoroughly examine their implications and applications on the management of their marketing activities in the global context.

The book adopts the strategic marketing management framework, which provides an examination of the key management decisions on developing and executing successful global marketing programmes. In addressing the contemporary issues raised above, this book will integrate and draw on new and existing theoretical insights from other management disciplines, including services marketing, knowledge management, relationship marketing, e-commerce and e-business, and corporate social responsibility. The discussion on these issues seeks to demonstrate how, through adequate management of these issues, an organization can seek to develop and maintain sustainable global competitiveness. While these issues are integrated throughout the book wherever possible, there will be dedicated chapters for the identified issues to enable a focused discussion.

In short, it is the aim of this book to equip students and managers with some of the most current knowledge and practical skills to help them make key management decisions and navigate their organizations in the increasingly dynamic and challenging global business environment. It enables the reader to:

- identify, evaluate and integrate a wide range of management concepts to create and execute highly effective global marketing programmes;
- analyse and remedy management problems in managing global operations;
- decide on appropriate market entry strategies;
- assess and monitor effectiveness; and
- examine the implications and applications of contemporary thinking on global marketing management.

Structure of the book

The book is divided into three parts, which together cover the essential elements of planning and implementing a global strategic marketing plan. The first part, which has six chapters, covers the *analysis* stage in global marketing and looks at the global marketing environment, changes, and new challenges. The second part, which has eight chapters, covers the *strategy development* stage, and the last part, which has two chapters, looks at *implementing and controlling* global operations. Each chapter has an introductory section comprising an overview of the main topics, the learning objectives for the reader, and a section identifying the key management themes. There is a summary of the main points at the end of each chapter.

Success in global marketing management will only be achieved if the marketer is able to translate and apply the concepts, principles, and knowledge of global marketing into achievable and strategic, implementable marketing plans. More than this, the global marketer must be highly aware of the environmental megatrends which could derail any well-laid marketing plan. To this end, each chapter has a series of illustrative cases within it, as well as a longer case at the end, to illustrate the concepts and principles being discussed in the chapter. At the end of each chapter there is a series of end-of-chapter exercises and typical discussion and examination questions to reinforce the materials covered in the text. Every organization cited in the book has a web link when mentioned, so the reader can immediately follow through the illustration or example cited, thus increasing the 'practical' element of the book. In addition, to remind the reader of the emerging megatrends in the global environment and their impact, each chapter includes three illustrations covering the technology, relationship, and social responsibility aspects.

At the end of each part there is a longer, more comprehensive case which focuses on the three elements of strategic marketing planning. The case at the end of Part One covers the analysis part of global marketing planning, the case at the end of Part Two, the strategy development side, and the case at the end of Part Three, the implementation and control side of strategic planning.

Using this book

The aim of this book is to equip students and managers with some of the most current knowledge and practical skills in order to make key strategic management decisions and navigate their organizations through an increasingly dynamic and challenging global trading environment. With its easy-to-follow approach, it makes an ideal text to incorporate into a typical semester for undergraduate or postgraduate programmes, or for students of marketing professional bodies such as the Chartered Institute of Marketing (CIM). It also would be ideal for marketing executives, given the examples of good practice.

Global Marketing Management has been developed to help the reader learn, understand, and practice most of the elements of global strategic marketing planning. The intention is not to cover every single element of the strategic process, nor, certainly, to explore the detail of strategy implementation. It also stresses that there is not one 'right' strategy, but that there are ways of putting a plan together that reduces the risk of failure. It focuses on the effect of the global megatrends on the strategy planning process and shows

Chapters

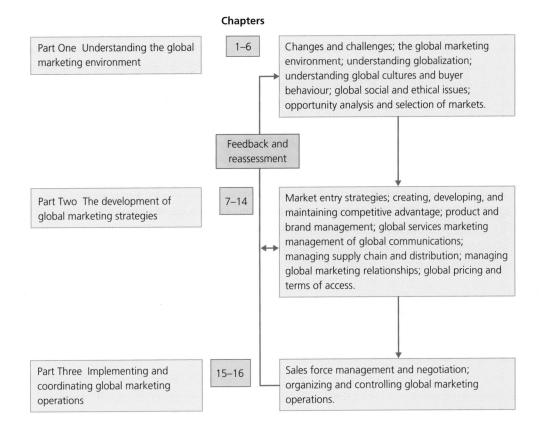

that there are different ways of achieving a chosen strategy. The book is structured as above.

Parts

The three parts of the book focus on the topics of analysis, strategy development and implementation, and controlling global operations. Each part contains a grouping of chapters relevant to that part.

Chapters

The chapters contain an introduction and learning objectives which provide the focus for the study. Also included here is a section on management issues that lists the strategic and practical implications of topics covered in the chapter. Each organizational example or illustration is 'hot linked' to the appropriate website so that the reader can explore the example further. The chapters contain additional aids to learning, such as a chapter summary, an end-of-chapter case study and exercises, discussion and examination questions, and suggestions for further reading. On the companion website, there are also activities for students to explore sources on the internet to prepare for a designated seminar-type discussion.

Illustrations

The illustrations are intended to reinforce the material learning and also to be the starting point for further discussion and an exploration of deeper and wider issues. The illustrations cover all sizes and types of organization as well as less developed and more developed countries. Each chapter has three illustrations covering the global megatrends in technology, relationships, and social responsibility, i.e. The Digital Impact, The Relationship Perspective, and Whose Responsibility Is It? In addition, each chapter is also enriched by relevant mini-case illustrations, to demonstrate the application of theory to practice and to inspire students' imaginations. These illustrations are meant to be provocative discussions and cover such topical areas as obesity, the effect of the 'hero' culture, and piracy.

Case studies

There are two types of case study. The first are short, end-of-chapter cases which are meant to illustrate and provoke discussion on the content of the chapter. Further information can be obtained from the web. The second type is a more integrative case which appears at the end of each part. These cases contain more information and cover the issues explored in the chapters within that part of the book. These cases enable the reader to develop real practical skills in developing strategic international marketing plans. In order to complete these, the reader will need to bring together the various strands and elements included throughout the book.

Web support

This book is fully supported by the accompanying website, which can be found at: http://www.oxfordtextbooks.co.uk/orc/lee_carter2e/. This enables the learner and lecturer alike to access additional resources to explore the topic further.

In this new edition, the website contains, for lecturers, a video case study of Oxford Instruments (www.oxford-instruments.com), featuring an interview with the company's strategic marketing director, Simon Durrant. The video is organized into clips in accordance with the chapters in the book. Each video clip essentially provides the 'practitioner insights' of the company in pursuing each area of its planning for international marketing. The companion website also provides useful resources for planning engaging learning sessions, i.e. a full set of PowerPoint slides, suggested approaches and answers to all the cases, end-of-chapter exercises and discussion and examination questions.

ACKNOWLEDGEMENTS

There are many individuals and organizations that the authors are indebted to for their contributions and involvement in making the writing of this new second edition possible.

First and foremost, the authors would like to express their gratitude to the following contributors for their excellent contributions to the book:

Nick Ellis   Chapter 13: Marketing Global Marketing Relationships
University of Leicester

Jean Barclay   Chapter 5: Understanding Global Social and Ethical Issues
Sheffield Hallam University

The authors would like to thank the team at Oxford University Press, especially Nicki Sneath and Helen Cook, for their help in the creation of this book. Many thanks also to the external reviewers who have greatly assisted in developing this book.

The authors are grateful to the copyright holders for permission to reproduce copyright materials. Copyright holders have been credited in the text where their material appears. While every effort has been made to trace the owners of copyright material, in a few cases this has proved impossible. The authors take this opportunity to offer their sincere apologies to any copyright holders whose rights we may have unwittingly infringed.

Last but not least, the authors would like to thank their families, friends, and colleagues. The journey to completing this new edition would have been a lot more difficult without their understanding, generosity, and support.

BRIEF CONTENTS

PART ONE

Understanding the Global Marketing Environment   1

1	Changes and New Challenges	3
2	The Global Marketing Environment	36
3	Understanding Globalization	70
4	Understanding Global Cultures and Buyer Behaviour	103
5	Understanding Global Social and Ethical Issues	141
6	Opportunity Analysis and Selection of Markets	169
	Part One Case Study: Daimler AG (Mercedes-Benz)—The Place of an Icon in Global Marketing	202

PART TWO

The Development of Global Marketing Strategies   207

7	Market Entry Strategies	209
8	Creating, Developing, and Maintaining Competitive Advantage	245
9	Product and Brand Management	279
10	Global Services Marketing	311
11	Management of Global Communications	343
12	Managing Supply Chain and Distribution	381
13	Managing Global Marketing Relationships	412
14	Global Pricing and Terms of Access	447
	Part Two Case Study: IKEA—A Long March to the Far East	485

PART THREE

Implementing and Coordinating Global Marketing Operations   489

15	Sales Force Management and Negotiation	491
16	Organizing and Controlling Global Marketing Operations	519
	Part Three Case Study: Oxfam International—Famine Relief or Pressure Group?	548
Glossary of Marketing Terms		551
Index		555

DETAILED CONTENTS

List of Vignettes   xviii
List of Figures   xxii
List of Tables   xxiv
A Guided Tour of the Book   xxv
Online Resource Centre   xxviii

PART ONE
Understanding the Global Marketing Environment

Chapter 1: Changes and New Challenges   3

What is Global Marketing?   6
Changes in the Global Market Environment   8
The Need for a New Approach to Global Marketing   20
Organizing for Global Marketing   30

Chapter 2: The Global Marketing Environment   36

The Global Marketing Environment: A Definition   37
Factors within the Global Environment   39
The Political Environment   42
The Legal Environment   45
The Economic Environment   46
The Socio-cultural Environment   56
The Technological Environment   57
The Competitive Environment   62
The Currency Environment   63
Pressure Groups   64

Chapter 3: Understanding Globalization   70

What is Globalization?   72
Opportunity or Threat?   79
Global Migration   89
Environmental Sustainability   92

Chapter 4: Understanding Global Cultures and Buyer Behaviour 103

What is Culture?	105
Understanding Consumer Behaviour	113
Culture and Consumer Behaviour	114
Managing Cultural Differences	118
Conducting Cross-cultural Analysis	120
Commodity Trading	130
Government Buying Behaviour	131
Organizational Buyers or B2B Buyer Behaviour	132
Culture and Ethics	134

Chapter 5: Understanding Global Social and Ethical Issues 141

Global Social and Ethical Issues	142
The Corporate Response to Social and Ethical Issues	153
Corporate Social Responsibility and Competitive Advantage	160

Chapter 6: Opportunity Analysis and Selection of Markets 169

Global Market Selection	170
Marketing Information System	171
International Marketing Research	172
Global Market Segmentation	185
Selecting Markets for Targeting	188
Part One Case Study: Daimler AG (Mercedes-Benz)—The Place of an Icon in Global Marketing	202

PART TWO
The Development of Global Marketing Strategies

Chapter 7: Market Entry Strategies 209

The International Marketing Environment and its Effect on Market Entry Strategies	211
The Process of Internationalization	213
Other Theories of Internationalization	224
International Business Models	226
Market Entry Modes	230
The Electronic Marketplace	235
Marketing Strategy and Mode of Entry	235

Chapter 8: Creating, Developing, and Maintaining Competitive Advantage   245

National Competitiveness and Global Competition   246
Factors Affecting the Growth of Global Competition   248
Strategy and Competitive Advantage   254
The Anatomy of Competitive Advantage   255
Creating Competitive Advantage through Generic Strategies   260
The Resource-based Theory of Competitive Advantage   263
New Sources of Competitive Advantage   266

Chapter 9: Product and Brand Management   279

The Components of the International Product   280
International Product Management   282
Product Strategy   288
Strategic International Branding   293
New Product Development   302

Chapter 10: Global Services Marketing   311

The Significance of Services in the Global Economy   312
The Drivers for Growth in Cross-border Services   314
Defining Cross-border Services   319
The Challenges of Marketing Services Internationally   324
International Retail Franchising   328
The Strategic Considerations for Marketing Services Globally   330

Chapter 11: Management of Global Communications   343

Changes and Issues in Marketing Communications   344
Moving beyond the 'Standardize or Localize' Debate   344
The Drive towards Integration   347
Advertising   350
Public Relations   359
Direct-response Marketing   362
Sponsorship   366
Exhibitions and Trade Fairs   368
Planning for Online Communications   371

Chapter 12: Managing Supply Chain and Distribution — 381

A New Approach to Managing Supply Chains and Distribution — 383
Factors Affecting Global Supply Chain Decisions — 386
Collaboration in the Supply Chain — 391
Developing Market-responsive Supply Chain Strategies — 397

Chapter 13: Managing Global Marketing Relationships — 412

What is a Marketing Relationship? — 413
Managing Marketing Relationships — 419
Relationships and Networks — 424
Customer (Vertical Downstream) Relationships — 425
Supplier (Vertical Upstream) Relationships — 428
Lateral (Horizontal) Partnerships — 430
Internal Partnerships — 434
Strategic Challenges in Managing Relationships — 436

Chapter 14: Global Pricing and Terms of Access — 447

Factors Affecting Global Pricing Decisions — 449
Pricing Strategy — 452
Specific Price Approaches — 455
Price Adaptation — 458
Price Changes — 464
Special Issues in Global Price Setting — 465
The Export Order Process — 475
Terms of Access — 475
Special Trade Terms in Exporting — 477
Export Documentation — 478
Part Two Case Study: IKEA—A Long March to the Far East — 485

PART THREE
Implementing and Coordinating Global Marketing Operations

Chapter 15: Sales Force Management and Negotiation — 491

The Changing Nature of Sales Management — 493
International Sales Management Decisions — 495
Cultural Impact on International Sales Force Management — 498
Developing Customer-oriented Personal Selling — 502

Sales Negotiations and the Effect of Culture   503

Preparing for Selling and Negotiating   504

Preparation for Sales Negotiations   505

The Transactional Sales Negotiation Process   507

The Relationship Approach to Sales Negotiation   507

Ethical Considerations in Global Negotiations   510

The Role of Training   512

Chapter 16: Organizing and Controlling Global Marketing Operations   519

Philosophy of Management   521

Planning for Global Marketing   521

Global Control Mechanisms   525

Organizing for Global Marketing   535

Issues in Global Organizational Structures   540

Part Three Case Study: Oxfam International—Famine Relief or Pressure Group? 548

Glossary of Marketing Terms   551

Index   555

LIST OF VIGNETTES

MINI-CASE ILLUSTRATIONS

Chapter 1

Facing up to the challenge   14
Samsung: at the cutting-edge of home entertainment   20
How Microsoft stays ahead of global competition   27

Chapter 2

Maize to Africa: the great famine of 1992   41
A typical SLEPT analysis   42
China's entry into the WTO   55
Sony's Group Code of Conduct   65

Chapter 3

The global success of Starbucks   73
The business of managing waste disposal   96

Chapter 4

The consequences of getting it wrong culturally   105
Cultural differences, West vs. East   123

Chapter 5

Honeywell International   146
The World Bank   148
UN Draft Norms—new standards for corporations
and human rights   151
Codes of practice and child labour   152
The Sialkot football programme   153
Dell Computers: moving towards environmental
sustainability   154
The Texas Instruments Ethics Office   160
The Co-operative Bank's Ethical Policy   161

Chapter 6

The Nissan Cube   176
Second homes in Europe   177
Data collection in less developed countries   183
International failures   185
VALS as a segmentation method in international marketing   188
Experian and Mosaic UK customer segmentation   195
Market segmentation and personas   197

Chapter 7

Nu Skin Enterprises   227

Chapter 8

The changing fortunes of Royal Selangor   248
Ariel's Clean Water Campaign   252
Electrolux develops its people to their full potential   269

Chapter 9

Product Attributes: the case of ISO 9000   282
McDonald's—a case of global product adaptation   284
The melting pot: holiday homes in the sun   285

Chapter 10

Competing for the best talents   316
Upholding the world-class service standards   326
The Louis Organization   335

Chapter 11

Global guidelines drive local marketing   351
The BT Global Challenge   363
Monster.com   372

Chapter 12

Factors driving increased partnerships in Toys 'R' Us   392
Green Isle Foods   400
The 'real' costs of offshore manufacturing   402

Chapter 13

Cutting it in the world of fashion   415
Making waves in the swimwear market   418
Relationships management in NGOs   433

Chapter 14

Low cost/no-frills airlines, easyJet and Ryanair   457
Solace   462
The case of fair trading: Oxfam   466
Price cooperation in global markets   481

Chapter 15

The need to optimize sales force efficiency   496
Ethics in global marketing   512

Chapter 16

BP's management structure   537
How technology can help to bypass 'formal'
organizational structure   540

@ **THE DIGITAL IMPACT**

Chapter 1
Telemedicine: delivering twenty-first-century
medical services to consumers   15

Chapter 2
Music and the 'grey consumer'   59

Chapter 3
Putting the 'e' into commerce   84

Chapter 4
Mobile text messaging and imaging:
a global phenomenon   112

Chapter 5
Shell's dialogue with stakeholders   163

Chapter 6
Customer specific segmentation with the internet   187

Chapter 7
Trading on eBay   218

Chapter 8
Managing the flow of information around the globe   259

Chapter 9
New (and old) products for all   293

Chapter 10
The development of e-tailing   329

Chapter 11
The marriage of direct marketing and interactive media   364

Chapter 12
Supply chain management and e-commerce   390

Chapter 13
'E-relationships'   438

Chapter 14
Empowering customers   463

Chapter 15
Using multimedia to help increase sales force effectiveness   495

Chapter 16
Westpac—technology and global operations and control   533

? **WHOSE RESPONSIBILITY IS IT?**

Chapter 1
Making trade free and fair for all   17

Chapter 2
Ethics and the internet   61

Chapter 3
Does globalization work for everyone?   87

Chapter 4
Role models—heroes or villains?   117

Chapter 5
Sharing concerns   164

Chapter 6
Ethics in marketing research   184

Chapter 7
Euro 2004 and China   236

Chapter 8
Promoting decent working conditions   267

Chapter 9
Obesity—the new sword of Damocles   286

Chapter 10
Codes of ethics and international franchising   329

Chapter 11
Climate change? Or is it just bad weather?   355

Chapter 12
Corporate social responsibility—is it any of your business? 396

Chapter 13
Assuming social responsibility in managing
international relationships — 429

Chapter 14
The great summer holiday 'rip-off' — 454

Chapter 15
Does nationality affect people's ethical perceptions
and behaviours? — 500

Chapter 16
The aftermarket in less developed countries — 531

Chapter 12
Managing supplier relationships in China — 394

Chapter 13
Fabric of relationships — 428

Chapter 14
Outsourcing — 462

Chapter 15
The 'Pink Cadillac' phenomenon — 508

Chapter 16
Downsizing and outsourcing — 541

THE RELATIONSHIP PERSPECTIVE

Chapter 1
Partnership for strategic advantage — 29

Chapter 2
Radio frequency identification (RFID) — 62

Chapter 3
The merger of Sony and BMG in the music business — 83

Chapter 4
Business ethics at work in China — 130

Chapter 5
Cross-sector partnerships and human rights — 149

Chapter 6
The world travel and tourism industry — 196

Chapter 7
Zambian high-value horticultural exports — 221

Chapter 8
Mixing business with pleasure — 272

Chapter 9
Hollywood and branding — 285

Chapter 10
Strategic outsourcing—the new collaborative structure — 337

Chapter 11
Collaborate to innovate — 361

END-OF-CHAPTER CASE STUDY

Chapter 1
Time to face the music — 32

Chapter 2
Scenario planning in a rapidly changing global
marketing environment — 66

Chapter 3
The making of a global fast food giant — 98

Chapter 4
The evolution of the Chinese middle class — 136

Chapter 5
Fairtrade — 166

Chapter 6
The challenge of retailing British wine — 198

Chapter 7
The Samsung Group — 239

Chapter 8
Proton: The challenge to survive in the global market — 274

Chapter 9
Formula One and Bernie Ecclestone — 306

Chapter 10
Heathrow Terminal 5: the making of a world-class service — 339

Chapter 11

Think globally, act locally—the case of Jack Daniel's   376

Chapter 12

Re-enginering supply chain to achieve global
competitive advantage   408

Chapter 13

The evolution of customer loyalty schemes   442

Chapter 14

The (s)cents of the perfume business   482

Chapter 15

Developing an effective sales force structure   515

Chapter 16

Anglo American—a global mining conglomerate   544

LIST OF FIGURES

1.1	Changes in the global market environment	9
1.2	The new challenges facing global businesses	22
1.3	Organizing for global marketing	30
2.1	Reasons for accounting for international environmental factors	38
2.2	Models of environmental analysis: PEST vs. SLEPT	39
2.3	The global marketing environment	40
2.4	World Bank classification of economies, 2003	49
2.5	Global economic facilitators	53
3.1	The discourses of globalization	73
3.2	Global economic disparities	88
3.3	Components of global climate change	93
3.4	Energy consumption and economic income	95
4.1	The 'Iceberg Model' of culture	106
4.2	The four layers of culture	107
4.3	The components of culture	108
4.4	The interaction of culture and consumer behaviour	115
4.5	Lee's four-step approach to avoiding the dangers of the self-reference criterion	119
4.6	The contextual continuum of cultures	122
4.7	Schwartz Value Inventory (SVI)	128
5.1	Why corruption matters?	145
5.2	The ten principles of the UN Global Compact 2000	150
5.3	The Johnson & Johnson Credo	156
5.4	Unilever's Code of Business Principles	157
5.5	Corporate social responsibility and competitive advantage	160
5.6	Body Shop International plc's mission statement	162
6.1	Global market selection process	171
6.2	Marketing information system	171
6.3	Market profile analysis	172
6.4	The international marketing research process	173
6.5	'Rough' market screening	175
6.6	Techniques for assessing incipient markets	176
6.7	'Fine' market screening process	178
6.8	The ranking of markets (attractiveness and ability to compete)	179
6.9	Ability to compete vs. market attractiveness	180
6.10	Market expansion possibilities	191
6.11	The 'waterfall' vs. 'shower' approaches to market entry	192
6.12	Steps to achieve strategically equivalent market segments in international marketing	193
7.1	The effects of the international market environment on the market entry decision	211
7.2	Market entry strategy	213
7.3	Internationalization process of organizations	214
7.4	The network effect	219
7.5	Factors influencing the choice and importance of market entry mode	230
8.1	Factors driving increased global competition	249
8.2	Superior vs. inferior perceived values	255
8.3	The anatomy of competitive advantage	256
8.4	Generic competitive strategies	261
8.5	Creating and leveraging capabilities	264
9.1	Components of a product or service offer	281
9.2	Standardization vs. adaptation in international markets	283
9.3	Product life cycle	290
9.4	The BCG matrix	290
9.5	Product growth strategies	292
9.6	The themes of a brand as differentiators	295
9.7	Branding strategies	296
9.8	Dimensions of global brand	299
9.9	Architecture of a global brand	300
9.10	Process of new product development	302
10.1	Cumulative services export growth, 1994–2003 (%)	314
10.2	Drivers for growth in cross-border services	315
10.3	The services and intangibility continuum	319
10.4	The consumer–producer interaction	320
10.5	Six-sector service taxonomy	322
10.6	Lovelock and Yip (1996): categories of service	323
10.7	Intangibility vs. environmental sensitivity	325
10.8	The development of effective knowledge management	331
10.9	Strategic options for cross-border services marketing	333
11.1	Factors preventing standardization of marketing communications	346
11.2	Consumer-driven communication process	349
11.3	Development of a creative plan	352
11.4	Development of a creative plan: determining creative 'positioning'	352
11.5	Considerations of public relations planning in a cross-cultural context	362
11.6	Types of sponsorship and associated values	368
11.7	Planning for a promotional event	370

12.1 An international supply chain 383

12.2 Fundamentals of effective supply chain management 384

12.3 Supply chain relationships and approaches 385

12.4 Influential factors in international supply chain 387

12.5 Considerations in developing an international supply chain 389

12.6 Internationalization of the procurement process 398

13.1 The shift from 'transactions' to 'relationships' 417

13.2 The stages of relationship development 419

13.3 Alternative approaches to inter-organizational interaction 422

13.4 Criteria for evaluating the value of strategic relationships 427

13.5 How internal relationships add value across conventional functions 436

13.6 Strategic challenges in managing relationships 437

14.1 Steps involved in an international pricing strategy 448

14.2 Cost reduction strategies 451

14.3 Pricing policy options 454

14.4 The global price-setting decision process 463

14.5 Special issues in global pricing 465

14.6 Example of price escalation 465

14.7 The export order process 476

15.1 The forces affecting the nature of selling and sales management 493

15.2 International sales management decisions 497

15.3 Determinants of sales personnel international staffing decisions 499

15.4 The traditional vs. the new model of personal selling 502

15.5 The selling mix 503

15.6 Factors affecting successful preparation for sales negotiations 505

15.7 Factors affecting successful sales preparation 506

15.8 Differences in sales training: Northern vs. Southern Europe 513

16.1 The global planning and control process 522

16.2 Benefits from planning global operations 523

16.3 Factors affecting marketing control 527

16.4 Components of a global marketing audit 529

16.5 Traditional and non-traditional methods of international marketing control 530

16.6 The balanced scorecard 532

16.7 Screening strategies for implementation problems 534

16.8 The factors that determine the most appropriate global organizational structure 535

16.9 Function-based organizational structure 536

16.10 Area- or region-based organizational structure 536

16.11 Product-based organization structure 538

16.12 Matrix organizational structure 539

16.13 The 'hub and spoke' organizational structure 539

LIST OF TABLES

1.1 Estimated and projected population of the world, major development groups and major areas, 1950, 2000, and 2050, according to the different fertility variants 9

1.2 Median age by major area, 1950, 2000, and 2050 (median variant) 10

1.3 World exports of merchandise and commercial services, 2006 (US$ billion, percentage of change) 16

1.4 Overview of approaches in marketing theory 21

2.1 Percentage share of world merchandise and commercial services 47

2.2 The nature of economies and their organizational implications 50

2.3 Different forms of market agreement 51

2.4 Internet usage statistics (estimated) 58

2.5 The global challenges of changing electronic communications technology 60

3.1 Frequency of core non-tariff barriers of selected countries 80

3.2 Transport costs, 1930–90 82

3.3 Communication and computer costs, 1960–2000 82

5.1 Transparency International's Corruption Perceptions Index 2007 143

5.2 Bribery in business sectors 2002 144

5.3 Institute of Business Ethics Guide to Good Practice in the Implementation of Codes of Conduct 159

6.1 Market research required at the internationalization decision stage 174

6.2 Bases for international market segments 186

6.3 Factors affecting choice of market concentration vs. market diversification 191

7.1 International marketing environmental factors to be considered in international market entry decisions 212

7.2 Principal market entry modes, involvement, risk, and control 231

7.3 Comparison of the various entry modes 234

7.4 Entry modes and different marketing strategies 236

9.1 International strategies 288

9.2 The top ten global brands, 2007 294

9.3 Most admired international brands 294

10.1 World trade in commercial services by category, 2006 313

12.1 Comparison of transactional and collaborative relationships 393

14.1 Factors to be considered in pricing products and services globally 450

14.2 Key features of pricing strategy 453

14.3 Pricing objectives 455

14.4 Factors affecting currency fluctuations and rates of exchange 467

14.5 Export documentation 479

14.6 Finance for exports 480

16.1 International marketing activity checklist 524

16.2 Planning problems, headquarters, and subsidiary levels 525

A GUIDED TOUR OF THE BOOK

Part Openings

Title pages designed to provide an introduction to each main area of study, giving a brief overview of the chapters to follow.

PART ONE

Understanding the Global Marketing Environment

Part One addresses global marketing issues concerning the process involved in planning for global marketing. It stresses that, without careful consideration of the contemporary developments in the emerging global market environment involved in the planning for global marketing, the chances of

Chapter Overviews

A page referenced summary of the main topics of the chapter, allowing quick and easy navigation.

Chapter overview

Chapter Introduction	382	Collaboration in the Supply	
A New Approach to Managing Supply		Types of buyer–supplier rela	
Chains and Distribution	383	The scope of collaboration	
Effective management of risk	384	Developing Market-respons	
Effective management of trade-offs	384	Chain Strategies	
Effective management of strategic relationships	385	Global sourcing	

Learning Objectives

A bulleted list describing what the student should learn from the chapter, providing structure and context for learning.

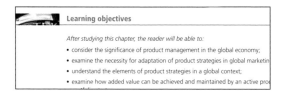

Learning objectives

After studying this chapter, the reader will be able to:

• consider the significance of product management in the global economy;
• examine the necessity for adaptation of product strategies in global marketin
• understand the elements of product strategies in a global context;
• examine how added value can be achieved and maintained by an active pro

Management Issues

This feature identifies the strategic and practical implications of topics covered in the chapter, encouraging students to consider the real-life application of theory.

Management issues

The management issues that arise include:

• What are the important discourses of globalization and how are they shapin environment?
• In what ways is globalization creating business opportunities and new challe

Chapter Introduction

Each chapter begins with a short introduction identifying the key topics covered in the chapter.

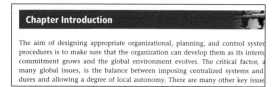

Chapter Introduction

The aim of designing appropriate organizational, planning, and control system procedures is to make sure that the organization can develop them as its intern commitment grows and the global environment evolves. The critical factor, a many global issues, is the balance between imposing centralized systems and dures and allowing a degree of local autonomy. There are many other key issue

Mini-Case Illustrations

Each chapter is enriched by a number of mini-case illustrations to illustrate the application of theory to practice, with a well-balanced coverage of MNCs and SMEs in the manufacturing and services sectors operating in various parts of the world, including Africa and Asia.

MINI-CASE ILLUSTRATION Cultural differences, West vs. East

The West, particularly the USA, is transactional in its negotiations. The objective is to work towards closure based on mutual understanding and a legally binding agreement. The Chinese prefer not to view the process as one of 'negotiation' as the word suggests the disagreeable notion of conflict which must be avoided at all costs. 'Negotiation' for the Chinese means working towards an ongoing relationship or problem-solving process rather than a one-off agreement. In working towards an agreement to provide ventilation equipment to China, the UK company Xpelair, found that its Chinese partner wished the company to make adaptations to one of its standard household ventilation products in order to meet the requirements of the Chinese market. This ongoing process lasted for several months, involving a number of visits to China, in order to arrive at a mutually acceptable product solution.

Diagrams and Tables

Diagrams and tables are used to help students understand and absorb key concepts.

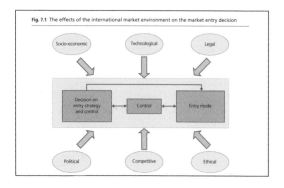

Fig. 7.1 The effects of the international market environment on the market entry decision

Photo Illustrations

Coloured photos, images, and advertisements throughout the book help to illustrate the application of marketing concepts and to inspire students' imaginations.

Web Links

Each organizational example or illustration is 'hot-linked' with the relevant URL for the reader to explore the example further.

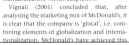

The Relationship Perspective

This boxed vignette provides a short illustrative case study of how an organization can leverage its business relationships to achieve global strategic advantage.

The Digital Impact

This boxed vignette provides a short illustrative case study of how an organization has harnessed the power of new technology to implement successful global marketing programmes.

Whose Responsibility Is It?

This boxed vignette provides a short illustrative example of social or ethical issues confronting organizations in global marketing operations.

Chapter Summary

At the end of each chapter a summary provides a quick reminder of key points in the chapter.

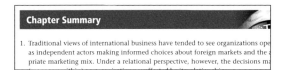

End-of-Chapter Case Study

Each chapter concludes with a short case study designed to help students apply their learning into a real marketing problem.

End-of-Chapter Exercises

Suggested exercises to enable students to test their understanding.

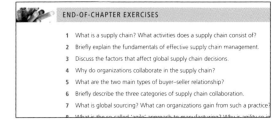

Discussion and Examination Questions

A list of short-answer study questions and essay-type questions found in exams which can be used for revision or as a focus for group discussion.

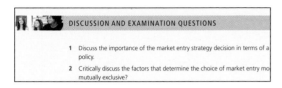

Further Reading

A list of suggested resources for further research.

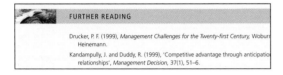

References

A complete listing of all referenced publications used in the chapter.

End-of-Part Cases

Each part concludes with a long case study to consolidate the themes covered in the preceding chapters.

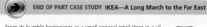

ONLINE RESOURCE CENTRE

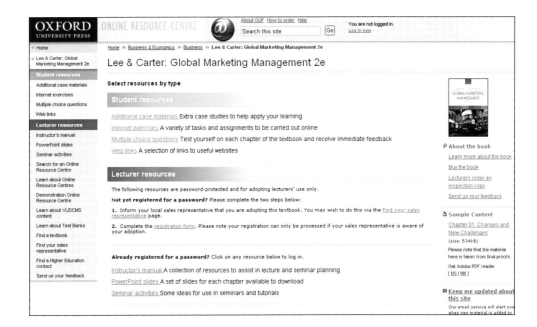

Visit the *Global Marketing Management* online resource centre at
www.oxfordtextbooks.co.uk/orc/lee_carter2e/
to find an extensive range of teaching and learning resources, comprising:

For students and lecturers

- Multiple-choice quiz bank to test students' understanding of the concepts covered in each chapter.
- Internet exercises providing activities for students to carry out online.
- Additional case studies with accompanying questions for further study.
- A list of annotated URLs 'hot-linked' to web sites of relevant organizations and Internet sources for each chapter.

For lecturers

- PowerPoint slides to accompany the book for lecture presentations.
- Additional case studies with accompanying questions to be used at the lecturer's discretion.
- Instructor's manual comprising teaching notes for all end-of-chapter case studies in the book, guide solutions to all end-of-chapter exercises and discussion & examination questions in the book, and guide solutions for all Internet exercises on the student part of the site.
- Seminar activity for each chapter.
- An accompanying DVD is available to lecturers who adopt the text for use in teaching to offer students an enhanced learning experience. The DVD comprises a suite of clips based on an interview conducted with Oxford Instruments, filmed specifically to accompany the text. Please ask your sales representative for further details.

PART ONE
Understanding the Global Marketing Environment

Part One addresses global marketing issues concerning the process involved in planning for global marketing. It stresses that, without careful consideration of the contemporary developments in the emerging global market environment involved in the planning for global marketing, the chances of survival for any organizations are minimal. The emphasis is on the changes and new challenges that the marketing environment poses to the global marketer. Then, Part Two and Part Three address the decisions and concepts which associate with strategy development, the marketing mix decisions, and implementation and control issues in global marketing management.

This Part begins with an introduction in Chapter 1 giving an overview of today's marketing environment. In doing so, it seeks to highlight the important changes and new challenges, and their implications for organizations operating internationally. A summary follows of the scope of global marketing strategy and management within this rapidly changing environment.

Subsequent chapters address three important areas. First, we consider the dynamic nature of the global marketing environment within which organizations review, reflect, and respond to emerging opportunities and operational complexities. The topics under close examination here include: (a) the changes in the political, economic, social, and technological environments; (b) the current discourses of globalization; and (c) the global social and ethical issues. Secondly, and importantly, cultural influences and their effects on buyer behaviour, consumers, business-to-business and government are discussed. Finally, the identification and the process of market selection are considered. This part concludes with a discussion on the importance of an active intelligence system and the process of segmenting and choosing target markets. In each chapter, established and contemporary theories are explored as well as numerous examples and cases illustrating this important area of global marketing management.

CHAPTER ONE
Changes and New Challenges

Chapter overview

Chapter Introduction	4
What is Global Marketing?	6
Domestic marketing	6
International marketing	6
Global marketing	7
Changes in the Global Market Environment	8
The emergence of new economic powerhouses	8
A new direction in global engagement	11
The changing consumer demographics and expectations	12
The changing nature of competition	13
The emergence of a global services economy	16
The advent of new technologies	18
The growing transparency of corporate practices	19

The Need for a New Approach to Global Marketing	20
The new rules of global engagement	22
The new global economic architecture	23
Matching the needs of the new global consumers	24
Achieving global competitiveness	25
Marketing using new technologies	26
Knowledge as a source of global competitive advantage	26
The importance of managing relationships	28
Corporate social responsibilities and ethics	28
Organizing for Global Marketing	30
Chapter Summary	32

Learning objectives

After studying this chapter, the reader will be able to:

- define the meanings and scope of global marketing;
- consider the changes in the market environment which impact on the management of global marketing;
- discuss the new challenges that global marketers face in responding to the new global environment;
- present an overview of the different levels of decision-making involved in the process of global marketing planning, and the competences that can be developed to respond creatively to the changing global environment.

Management issues

The management issues that arise from this chapter include:

- What are the current developments and changes in the market environment which may impact on the organization's operations globally?
- How and to what extent do these market changes present new challenges to the global marketing management of the organization?
- In the light of market changes and new challenges, on what basis can the organization develop new sources of global competitive advantage?

Chapter Introduction

Global marketing has become a popular subject, which is reflected in the burgeoning number of publications in this area. In the light of increasing globalization of the world economy, global marketing is a necessity for the survival of all organizations, big or small, rather than a luxury traditionally reserved for the multinational corporations (MNCs). As consumers and citizens, we live in an era when almost everything can be made and sold anywhere. The phrase 'global village' is such an integral part of the international vocabulary that it is difficult to conceive of a place which is not touched by something 'international'. Climbing Mount Everest, for instance, once an awe-inspiring achievement for the brave few, is no longer an expedition but a commoditized package tour. Growth in the total volume and value of world trade now exceeds any other period in history. The World Trade Organization (WTO, www.wto.org) puts the global trade in goods today at an estimated US$11.76 trillion per annum, while services at some US$2.71 trillion per annum.

Reflecting back to the early 1980s, few would have guessed that the world economy would change so dramatically. Cars were not very different from what they had been in the 1960s. Grocery stores (rather than 'supermarkets') in 1980 still had no electronic inventory or point-of-sale systems. No one could even have imagined the widespread use of home computers or the burgeoning use of the internet. Although there has always been a continuum of improvement, even medical research and treatment had hardly made any fundamental leaps forward. While the global economic framework had expanded, changed, and drawn in new and different players, such as Japan and Taiwan, the basic features remained the same: economic dominance by the USA, with the irrepressible ascent of Japan and a rehabilitated Germany combining with other European Economic Community countries to form a single trading bloc. The massive potential of China, India, Brazil, and Russia, not to mention the so-called Third World nations, were relatively untapped (Neef, 1999).

Dramatic changes began to occur after the 1980s. Medical and drug research achieved enormous breakthroughs—genetic engineering, for example, revolutionized the investigation and treatment of previously intractable diseases. In less than a decade, computing shifted from heavy and cumbersome mainframes to personal computers and then to laptops with thousands of times the power of their ancestors. The internet began to develop in the 1990s, with organizations learning to face the challenges of electronic commerce and competing in the 'virtual marketplace'. Well-known giants, including Westinghouse (www.westinghouse.com) and RCA (www.rca.com), suddenly found themselves in trouble and began stripping valuable assets to maintain efficiency. Once large and redoubtable organizations such as IBM (www.ibm.com) and AT&T (www.att.com) started to 'de-layer' by shedding their workforce. Thanks to a shift towards the outsourcing of 'non-core' operations, there is a return to focus on 'what we do best', i.e. the 'core business'. Due to the increasing reliance upon external parties to deliver those 'non-core' operations, the management of relationships (especially those external to the organization) has become a vital management skill. Small and medium-sized companies are suddenly springing up and flourishing. Nations that few in the West have spoken of since World War II have emerged as the 'Tiger Economies', attracting huge amounts of foreign investment as their growth rates double and treble those of the advanced economies (Neef, 1999).

Globalization appears to be resolving itself into the growth of trading blocs, with the inevitable tensions of individual nations having to cede power to supranational governments. The next few decades may see attempts to resolve a number of tensions created by the growth of powerful trading blocs, for example between winners and losers and between falling wages costs and social policies. The issue of social change due to the changing demographics of world population has a significant impact on the world economy. While the world population is forecast to grow from its present 5.7 billion to 8.5 billion by 2030, the increase will be in countries where the average daily earnings are less than US$2. Already 80% of the poorest countries of the world, with 40% of the world population, are short of the most basic resources, such as fresh water, food, and medicine, while having to cope with alarming rates of infection with HIV and AIDS. The impact on the environment, coupled with the desire to sustain and improve lifestyles, is likely to create tension between the world's rich and poor. The world population is also getting older. Over 65-year-olds today account for between 13% and 20% of the population. By 2025, it is estimated that in Japan the elderly will account for one in four. For businesses this has extreme implications. In the USA today there are 4.5 workers for every pensioner; by 2030 it will be 1.7 (Sanderson, 1998). The emergence of these 'grey consumers', who are (and will be) considerably better off financially than the previous generation, will mean demand on organizations to cater for their every possible need from day-to-day consumables, financial services, and high-quality healthcare.

Products and services offered in the marketplace have become highly sophisticated as organizations today offer not one product or service but a 'complete solution'. As the costs in production fall in physical products, it is the service package that augments the value of the organization's market offer. In particular, it is the specific configuration of the different components in the organization's service package that communicates added value to the customer (Kandampully and Duddy, 1999). In response to the increasing importance of services, the competitiveness of organizations will become more and more dependent upon 'intellectual' power as opposed to 'resource' power. The classical economist's theory of comparative advantage, as Sanderson (1998) argues, may well become redundant due to the falling price of raw materials and the increased importance of intellectual capital. Any cursory glance at the industries of the twenty-first century, such as microelectronics, biotechnology, robotization, and telecommunications, amply demonstrates that any new theory of comparative advantage will be based on 'brain power' rather than physical resource.

From what is primarily a debate confined to environmental scientists to becoming one of the most hotly discussed contemporary and pervasive issues, climate change is now widely viewed as one of the most urgent issues of our time. In just 200 years, the amount of carbon dioxide in the atmosphere—the major gas that causes climate change—has increased by 30%. Concentrations of greenhouse gases are now higher than at any point in the past 800,000 years. Over the past century, average near-surface global temperatures have risen by 0.7°C. The ten warmest years on record have all been since 1990. Six of the ten warmest years on record in the UK were between 1995 and 2004. In Europe, the August 2003 heatwave was probably the hottest for at least 500 years. During August 2003, the hottest temperature ever recorded in the UK was taken in Brogdale in Kent. It was 38.5°C. Between 4 and 13 August 2003, over 2,000 people in the UK died as a result of the heat. The autumn and winter floods in 2000 in the UK were the worst for 270 years in some areas. Flooding on farmland cost the farming industry nearly £500 million (source: www.climatechallenge.gov.uk).

So, what do these developments mean for business? How do they affect the management of global marketing operations? The clear implication is that these developments will shape the nature of competition, the source and scope of competitive advantage as well as the physical environment in the immediate future. It is the aim of this chapter to consider these environmental changes and the ways in which they will impact on the management of global marketing. We will then examine the new challenges that marketers face in responding to the new global business environment. We begin with an introduction to the term 'global marketing', the role it plays, and the significance it has on the survival of today's organizations.

What is Global Marketing?

Global marketing is expansive, extensive, and complex. It can be seen as both a business strategy and an operation, as a force for good and/or as the 'new imperialism'. It can be embodied in companies or perceived as a phenomenon (e.g. business globalization, the internet, etc.). One view of global marketing is as a giant supply chain management system or an added value system. Global giants such as Toyota (www.toyota.com), VW (www.vw.com) and DaimlerChrysler (www.daimlerchrysler.com) source their raw materials, semi-processed and processed materials, finance and human inputs from all over the world and deliver the results of the combination of these, i.e. vehicles, to numerous market segments, adding value as they do so.

Defining terms in the global marketing arena is a complex issue. Marketing across political and cultural boundaries raises many questions, problems, and juxtapositions, rendering precise definitions difficult. Typical issues centre on the standardization–adaptation argument; locus of control—central or devolved; and when exactly a multinational corporation focus becomes a global one. How does global marketing differ from domestic and international marketing? While there are no universal definitions, the following are those that we suggest for use throughout this text.

Domestic marketing

The focus of domestic marketing is primarily marketing carried out within a defined national or geographic boundary where the marketer is relatively free to plan, implement, and control marketing plans, including decisions on the marketing mix (i.e. the 'controllables'), within a relatively known and easily researchable marketing environment (i.e. the 'uncontrollables'). Over time, the marketer learns to anticipate the needs and wants of his/her market. There is little need to attend to the demands of the across-boundary markets, other than to monitor and meet the threat of imports. Focus and control are firmly on the domestic market.

International marketing

International marketing takes place when the marketer explores markets outside the national boundaries of the domestic market. This often begins with direct or indirect exporting to a neighbouring country. The focus is to find markets which have needs similar to those in the domestic market and can be satisfied with similar products and services. Typical of these are standard product parts and computers. While the marketing environment may be different and some adjustment may have to be made to the marketing mix elements, exporting in economic terms is basically the movement of surplus production overseas. Once again, planning, implementation, and control of the marketing mix are based in the exporting organization.

When organizations begin operating across a number of national/political boundaries, they need a more cohesive and constructive approach to their engagement with their international markets. As they progress in their internationalization, organizations would increasingly recognize the importance of accounting for country-to-country differences in their international marketing planning decisions. Because they value these differences, there is the recognition that there are many distinct marketing systems, leading to the notion that international marketing can be viewed as 'a collection of more or less coordinated domestic marketings' (Perry, 1999: 45). In this sense, the characteristics of international operations are the differing effects of, and the emphases on, the uncontrollable marketing elements and hence the need for differing marketing mixes to address those differences. However, international operators may wish to minimize the effect of these differences by operating a standardized marketing mix policy by appealing to global market segments. The emphasis may still be on central production, planning, implementation, and control, with deference paid to different market conditions. When organizations begin to produce in different countries and market according to the demands of local or regional markets, with the resultant devolution of production, planning, implementation, and control ('think global, act local'), then they are evolving into a 'multinational'. Despite this devolution, most multinationals have a corporate base from which to operate through a network of subsidiaries. The media company BSkyB (www.sky.com) is a typical example.

Global marketing

The concept of global marketing begins with the notion that the world has no centre. The 'borderless' global marketplace encompasses the participation of all countries—not only the industrialized and the newly industrialized nations, but also the emergent economies such as China and India—in international competition. This new 'market internationalism' is coupled with more integrative global structures, including free trade areas, common markets, and multilateral agreements (e.g. World Trade Organization) which link international markets more closely, even though protectionism and conflicts coexists with it. It rests upon 'the dynamic premise that consumer preferences can be, and are, constantly being reshaped by *common exogenous* (rather than *endogenous*) forces, resulting in the convergence of many consumers' wants and desires' (Perry, 1999: 48). The growing availability and spread of communication and transportation technologies are making consumers more homogeneous and foreign markets more accessible. National borders are no longer effective barriers against external influences. For instance, the internet has made it possible for foreign companies to get around local advertising restrictions. Global marketing organizations would strive exclusively to 'maximize standardization, homogenization, similarity, concentration, dependence, synchronization, and integration of marketing activities across markets' (Svenssen, 2002: 581).

On the other hand, the truly global marketing organizations would also have an enlightened recognition that global consumers differ in their consumption behaviour from culture to culture. Markets are about people, not products. There may be global products, but there are not global people. There may be global brands but they are no global motivations for buying those brands (De Mooij, 1998). Global organization seeks to lever its resources across political and cultural boundaries to maximize opportunities and exploit market similarities and differences in search of competitive advantage. There is a proactive willingness to adopt a global perspective instead of a country-to-country or region-by-region perspective in the development of a marketing strategy. It will move its resources from country to country to achieve its goals and maximize stakeholders' value by globalizing marketing activities in the organization of worldwide efforts, the research of domestic and foreign markets, the pursuit of international partnerships, the sourcing of raw materials and support services, and the managing of international transactions. Organizations would operate as if the world were one large market, ignoring superficial regional and national differences while making sure that marketing activities fit the products and services to the practices and cultural characteristics of different markets.

Changes in the Global Market Environment

The events of 11 September 2001 at the World Trade Center in New York, will be remembered for generations to come. The USA and its allies, in retaliation for 9/11, devastated Afghanistan because they believed that the Taliban was harbouring the terrorists responsible, and Iraq for possessing weapons of mass destruction. More than seven years since 9/11, the so-called 'war against terror' continues to dominate the American agenda and that of its allies. This war will last a long time. Tackling terrorists who want to continue their mission until victory or martyrdom is an awesome task. The cost in purely business terms was real and immediate. Like the Middle East oil crisis of the early 1970s, the effect on global business has been enormous. No one could have foreseen this event yet it changed the way countries and organizations trade internationally.

The French poet Paul Valéry might have been forecasting for today's multinational corporation when he muses that 'the trouble of our times is that the future isn't what it used to be'. The internet and new communications technologies are revolutionizing the way businesses are conducted. For instance, mobile technology is changing the way businesses interface with customers, and the way customers interface with one another. In China, home to the world's largest mobile network, this is particularly true. 'On New Year's Day, we had about 5 billion SMS New Year's greetings', said the man who runs the network, Wang Jianzhou, Chairman and Chief Executive, China Mobile Communications Corporation (www.chinamobile.com). The hitherto economic might of the West is increasingly being challenged as many economies in other parts of the world are emerging as new champions. The world is currently undergoing a demographic shift that amounts to an earthquake for business. With much of the planet experiencing a youth bulge, rates of mortality and fertility are falling in the developed world, with average life expectancy projected to reach 100 by the end of the century. In Europe, talent is increasingly mobile and thus tough to retain: employees between the ages of 25 and 34 spend an average of just 2.9 years in a job. In Africa, a surplus of workers is driving immigration to the north (World Economic Forum, 2008). To survive and prosper in the rapidly evolving global marketplace, companies must win the war for talent, innovate rapidly, but also, where appropriate, collaborate effectively. Good corporate citizenship will also attract customers, especially if such citizenship underpins business models themselves. In short, worldwide markets reward swift and agile companies, and those that win the race for talent and customers must be responsive to both. To be truly responsive, corporations must be good as well as great.

These developments have tremendous political, economic, social and technological implications on the global marketing environment. Essentially, they become the new market realities with which all marketers need to contend. Any global marketing strategy, that is—in the words of Peter Drucker (1999: 50)—'any commitment of present resources to future expectations', has to start with taking stock of these changes. It would be impractical to list them all. The following changes are those which we believe present the most immediate and significant challenges for organizations operating in the global business environment. This is illustrated in Fig. 1.1.

The emergence of new economic powerhouses

According to the United Nations, 60%—approximately 3.7 billion people—of the world population today live in Asia (see Table 1.1). By 2050, this population will grow to about 7.4 billion—two-thirds of the world population. With a median age of 26.2 in 2000 (see Table 1.2), Asia also accounts for some of the world's youngest and most

Fig. 1.1 Changes in the global market environment

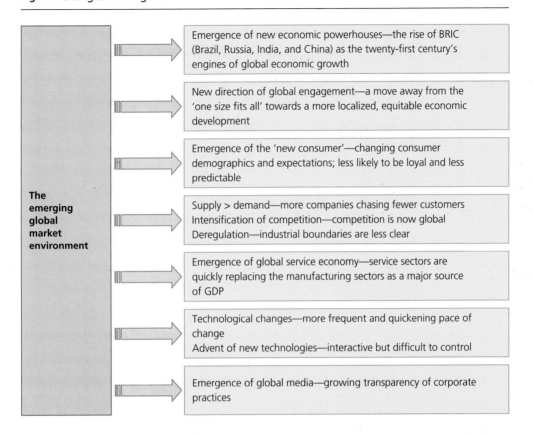

<table>
</table>

Table 1.1 Estimated and projected population of the world, major development groups and major areas, 1950, 2000, and 2050, according to the different fertility variants

Major area	Estimated population (millions)		Estimated population (millions)
	1950	2000	2050
World	2519	6057	13049
More developed regions	814	1191	1162
Less developed regions	1706	4865	11887
Least developed countries	197	658	3150
Other less developed countries	1508	4207	8738
Africa	221	794	3566
Asia	1399	3672	7376
Latin America and Caribbean	167	519	1025
Europe	548	727	580
Northern America	172	314	446
Oceania	13	31	56

Source: Based on data sourced from United Nations World Population Trends 2000 (www.un.org).

Table 1.2 Median age by major area, 1950, 2000, and 2050 (median variant)

Major area	Median age (years)		
	1950	2000	2050
World	23.6	26.5	36.2
Less developed regions	21.4	24.3	35.0
More developed regions	28.6	37.4	46.4
Least developed countries	19.5	18.2	26.5
Africa	19.0	18.4	27.4
Asia	22.0	26.2	38.3
Europe	19.2	37.7	49.5
Northern America	29.8	35.6	41.0
Latin America and Caribbean	20.1	24.4	37.8
Oceania	27.9	30.9	38.1

Source: Based on data sourced from United Nations World Population Trends 2000 (www.un.org).

highly educated working population, who will make significant contributions to the region's rapid economic development.

All these figures confirm that the Asia Pacific region will again become the focus of global marketers. It is believed that significant economic potentials in the region will be driven by the enormous development possibilities in China. As observed by Heinrich von Pierer (2002), Chairman of the Managing Board at Siemens AG (www.siemens.com), the country and its some 1.3 billion inhabitants already possess considerable economic clout. The age structure of the Chinese population suggests that it has the youngest population in Asia and is the seventh-largest economy and the eighth-largest trading nation in the world. According to the World Bank (www.worldbank.org), the Chinese economy will account for 25% of the total world GDP by 2025—ahead of America (20%) and India (13%). In the next few years, the distribution of power within the world economy will clearly shift towards China.

India, with its population rapidly reaching 1 billion, is projected to become another emerging economic powerhouse. Indeed, India is projected in the next decade to surpass China to become the world's most populous nation. Like China, India offers significant global marketing opportunities due to its population size and its growing urbanized middle-class which has considerable purchasing power. While the problem of illiteracy is still widespread, India enjoys a disproportionately large and highly educated workforce, especially in computer science and engineering. It already has the second largest software development industry outside the USA. It is clear that economic growth in India will accelerate and it will become a major global economic entity.

Among the economies in transition, Russia has maintained a strong economic growth rate in recent years, largely owing to the high international prices of, and strong external demand for, oil and gas. Rising export revenues have also spilled over into strong domestic demand in many of these economies. Private capital inflows have further contributed to the strong economic performance in the Russian Federation and Kazakhstan, while official financing and remittances remain an important source of funding of domestic spending for smaller economies, such as Georgia and Moldova. Robust regional growth is expected to continue in 2007 and beyond.

It is perhaps easy to neglect some of the emerging economies in the Latin American region, i.e. Brazil, Argentina, Chile. These economies experienced high rates of economic growth in the past but, according to the Economic Commission for Latin America at the United Nations (www.un.org), the severe slowdown in the world economy in 2001 cut short the recovery that had begun in 2000 and dashed hopes that Latin America was about to embark upon a new growth cycle. In Latin America and the Caribbean, export revenues have increased by 20% during 2006, boosted largely by a continued improvement in commodity prices, while the volume of exports has increased at about 8%. Chile and Peru have benefited the most from increases in the value of basic metals and minerals exports. Similarly, Bolivia and the Republic of Venezuela have been favoured, respectively, by higher prices of natural gas and oil. Meanwhile, the two largest exporters of the region, Mexico and Brazil, expanded their export volume in 2006.

The Latin American economies are making notable macroeconomic advances, although much remains to be done in order to improve the long-term growth rate, which is far lower than required, in order to reduce the high level of unemployment. The international business conditions are set to improve due to strong economic fundamentals and further economic cooperation within the region.

Among less developed economies, growth in Africa has maintained a strong pace, reaching almost 5.6% in 2006. Many countries in Africa have sustained a relatively strong recovery since 2003, driven by increasing hydrocarbon export earnings, vibrant global demand for, and favourable international prices of, some non-oil commodities, vigorous domestic demand, and markedly growing foreign direct investment (FDI) flows and donor support. This contrasts with a much poorer performance in the African countries suffering from protracted civil unrest and political disturbances, adverse weather conditions, and/or decreased tourism revenues. The region's gross domestic products (GDP) is expected to expand by 5.6% in 2007.

While the financial crisis in the early years of the twenty-first century severely dampened the economic boom and the current global slowdown has a negative impact on development in the Asia Pacific and Latin American regions, it is widely predicted that the emerging markets in these regions will fuel much of the world economic (GDP) growth in the immediate future.

A new direction in global engagement

The term 'globalization' has acquired considerable emotive force. Some view it as a beneficial process—a key to future world economic development—and also inevitable and irreversible. Others regard it with hostility, even fear, believing that it increases inequality within and between nations, threatens employment and living standards, and thwarts social progress.

The concept of economic globalization is not new. The breaking down of economic barriers, for instance, took place in the laissez-faire era of the nineteenth century (Mohamad, 2002). According to the International Monetary Fund (IMF, www.imf.org), economic globalization is a historical process, the result of human innovation and technological progress. It refers to the increasing integration of economies around the world, particularly through trade and financial flows. The term sometimes also refers to the movement of people (labour) and knowledge (technology) across international borders. It refers to an extension beyond national borders of the same market forces that have operated for centuries at all levels of human economic activity—village markets, urban industries, or financial centres. Markets promote efficiency through competition and the division of labour—the specialization that allows people and economies to focus on what they do best. Global markets offer greater opportunity for people to tap into more and larger markets. It means they have access to more capital flows, technology, cheaper imports, and larger export markets.

The concept of globalization seems deceivably simple. It suggests that globalization will liberalize the world economy from unnecessary bureaucracy and trade barriers. When nation states remove all barriers to global competition, the movements of goods and services, capital, multinational operations, and financial institutions will bring greater efficiency to and better utilization of the world's resources. In short, globalization will bring good for every citizen, greater wealth creation, and prosperity.

For most of the latter half of the twentieth century, this concept of globalization was enthusiastically embraced by a number of developing nations, especially in East Asia and Latin America. For many, it brought new opportunities for wealth creation and prosperity. However, it also brought hidden risks arising from volatile capital movements and poverty, discovered by many in the Asian and Latin American financial crises of the late 1990s.

The Mexican crisis of 1994–95 was the first in what became a long series of financial crises affecting developing economies in the late 1990s. It demonstrated the potential for sharp changes in investor sentiment, triggered in this case by an unsustainable external imbalance, an overvalued exchange rate pegged to the US dollar, a fragile financial system, and a tightening of financial conditions in the USA (long-term interest rates rose sharply in the first half of 1994 amid fears of rising inflation and following a tightening by the Federal Reserve). The Asian crisis, starting in Thailand, was triggered by similar problems (external imbalances, financial fragilities, and exchange rate overvaluation) in an environment of further exchange rate appreciation through links to the US dollar, weakening export growth, and excessive short-term foreign borrowing. The more recent Russian and Brazilian crises both erupted following concerns over domestic policy and the sustainability of exchange rate pegs.

If there was a lesson to be learned from these experiences, it was that while globalization could accelerate the development of an economy, it could take it away just as easily. These recent negative experiences have set off a new direction in global engagement for many developing nations. For instance, while many Asian political leaders and thinkers seem to accept that globalization is still a positive necessity, they no longer see the existing 'one size fits all' economic globalization, where free markets are allowed to function without interference, as the only way to global engagement. The current global economic slowdown has made it clear to these nations that it is also no longer wise to base their future economic growth on the export-led foreign direct investments which are largely driven by the interests of the USA and Western Europe.

The changing consumer demographics and expectations

In order to be able to develop successful customer-driven global marketing strategies, organizations need to take into account changing consumer demographics and expectations. Changes in global consumer demographics, especially in terms of their increasing life expectancy and wealth, are constantly shaping the expectations of how consumers' needs should be served.

According to the UN *World Population Prospects* (United Nations; 2000), the number of older people (60 or over) will more than triple, increasing from 606 million today to nearly 2 billion by 2050. The increase in the number of the *oldest old* (80 or over) is expected to be even more marked, passing from 69 million in 2000 to 379 million in 2050,

The increasing number of so-called 'grey consumers' has significant implications on patterns of demand and expectations in the global markets.

more than a fivefold increase. The population aged 60 or over in the more developed regions currently constitutes about 20% of the population and by 2050 it will account for 33%. The older population of the more developed regions has already surpassed the child population (persons aged 0–14) and by 2050 there will be two older persons for every child. In the less developed regions, the proportion of the population aged 60 or over will rise from 8% in 2000 to close to 20% in 2050.

As the projection for the ageing population increases, life expectancy is also set to increase. In 2000, the *octogenarians* (aged 80–89) outnumbered *nonagenarians* (aged 90–99) by a wide margin, i.e. 88% of the 69 million people over the age of 80, and the proportion of *centenarians* (aged 100 and over) is small, i.e. 0.3% or 180,000. However, octogenarians are projected to increase to 314 million in 2050, 5.2 times the number in 2000, while the number of nonagenarians will reach 61 million, an eightfold increase. But the number of centenarians will grow the fastest, so that by 2050 it will be 18 times as large as the number in 2000. As world fertility continues to decline and life expectancy rises, the world population will age faster in the next 50 years than during the past half-century.

However, the world population as a whole in terms of growth in per capita GDP is becoming wealthier. The World Bank's Development Indicators in 2002 showed a consistent trend that the number of people living in developing countries on less than US$1 a day fell from 1.3 billion to 1.2 billion between 1990 and 1999, and people living in extreme poverty fell from 29% to 23% over the same period. In terms of regional patterns of long-term economic growth, all trading regions sustained a reasonably positive growth rate between 1960 and 2000, ranging from East Asia (which grew faster than any other developing region with GDP per capita growth of 5.3% a year) to the more moderate 1.6% a year in the Latin American and Caribbean region.

The changing consumer demographics in life expectancy, declining fertility, and increased wealth have significant implications on consumer demand and expectations. Consumers will live and work longer (improved healthcare and diet), consume more products/services per capita (family units are smaller), have a higher disposable income and sophistication (they are likely to be working longer and are more knowledgeable than previous generations), and be more demanding (they have more experience in comparing products/services over a longer life span). The new breed of consumers will have even higher expectations of how their wants and needs are to be fulfilled. Many companies are becoming more customer-driven in catering for the needs of consumers. However, the better they serve these consumers and provide higher values, the further they fuel consumer expectations. The proliferation of privatization in the public sectors to improve efficiency and provide choice for consumers will also enhance this trend.

The changing nature of competition

In the era of global business, when goods and services can be marketed and sold in ways that were unimaginable in the past, organizations need to compete for survival not only within their domestic market but globally, and also be prepared to fight for market share.

MINI-CASE ILLUSTRATION **Facing up to the challenge**

In 1983, Loo Leong-Thye, the founder of Challenger Technologies (www.challenger.com.sg), started his first computer products retail business with a little shop at the Sim Lim Tower in Singapore. Today, Challenger Technologies is a S$60 million business and has grown from one small outlet to two IT superstores and four small-format outlets.

The first Challenger Superstore was opened approximately fifteen years ago at the Funan IT Mall (www.funan.com.sg). It has since expanded from a retail outlet of 430 sq ft in floor area to two superstores occupying a combined retail space of approximately 66,000 sq ft. The Superstore offers the latest and largest selection of IT products, including personal computers, notebooks, printers, scanners, digital imaging solutions, personal digital assistants, mobile and wireless connectivity solutions, audio-visual and projection equipment, and related peripherals. Customers are also given the widest choice of brands, such as Acer (www.acer.com), Fujitsu (www.fujitsu.com), Symantec (www.symantec.com), Adobe (www.adobe.com), Canon (www.canon.com), Palm (www.palm.com), Logitech (www.logitech.com), and Iomega (www.iomega.com). To cater for the budget-conscious customers, Loo has created another chain of smaller IT outlets, called the Matrix IT Gallery, which are conveniently situated at four of Singapore's IT-hotbed areas.

The company's achievement in managing its growth in the competitive IT industry in Singapore is widely regarded as nothing less than extraordinary. The company counts among its customers well-known corporate clients as well as walk-in customers. Challenger Superstore has become a household name among IT enthusiasts and customers with a diverse need in IT.

Like many other businesses, Challenger suffered major financial losses when the Asia financial crisis hit in 1997. Sales dropped by one-third in a year, forcing the company to implement immediate drastic actions to save the business. Having lost confidence in the economy, businesses and consumers alike were busy cutting back their costs and daily expenditure. For the first time since 1983, Loo wondered if his business would survive the economic recession. Facing up to an economic downturn with little sign of improvement for the foreseeable future proved to be the greatest challenge that Loo had to face. He made the tough decision to pull out of Thailand, Indonesia, and Brunei in 2001 when it incurred some S$5.5 million in losses. The company disposed of a small number of its assets to keep its short-term finance afloat.

As the Asian economy recovered in 2004, the company saw its sales begin to rise again for the first time since 1997. After years of cut-back and retrenchment, the company have opened numerous Challenger Superstores and Matrix outlets, taking advantage of the economic recovery in Singapore and the surrounding countries. Apart from its core retail business, Challenger has developed its IT service business by setting up a regional franchise scheme. The changing fortune of Challenger provides an excellent example of how a company can benefit from, as well as be adversely affected by, the volatile international economies. Even the close monitoring of the macro and micro environments may often not be able to completely shield the company from political and economic catastrophes.

Sources: www.challenger.com.sg; www.challengerasia.com; and www.theedgedaily.com.

The nature of global competition is and will be shaped by the following realities:

The size of the (usually foreign) competitors is increasing and they have more resources (i.e. more people and capital) to compete
In today's global marketplace, many sectors are characterized by the growing dominance of a small number of giant multinationals. When we look at Glaxo-Smith-Kline (www.gsk.com) and Pfizer (www.pfizer.com) in drugs, Microsoft (www.microsoft.com) and Apple (www.apple.com) in computer operating systems, General Motors (www.gm.com) and VW in cars and commercial vehicles, Disney (www.disney.com) and Warner Bros (www.warnerbros.com) in entertainment, and Shell (www.shell.com) and BP (www.bp.com) in the oil and its derivatives business, the reality for many organizations of having to compete with the invincible competitors is all too real.

While competitors can seemingly access any international markets and compete freely, they are protected by government in their own domestic market
In a global market environment, it is assumed that organizations compete by the same rules using the same tools (i.e. people, knowledge, and resources) available to all. The concept of global competition seems deceptively simple: in a fully globalized marketplace where all players can access markets free from protectionism and operate under similar market forces conditioned by a set of universal rules, organizations that reign are those which are most efficient and offer superior competitive advantage. However, the global

THE DIGITAL IMPACT Telemedicine: delivering twenty-first-century medical services to consumers

Telemedicine has been defined as the use of telecommunications to provide medical information and services over distance and it is improving healthcare for people every day. It allows doctors and healthcare specialists to diagnose and treat patients whether that span is across a street, a city, a region, or an ocean. It may be as simple as two health professionals discussing a case over the telephone, or as sophisticated as using satellite technology to broadcast a consultation between providers at facilities in two countries, using video-conferencing equipment. Telemedicine can prevent uncomfortable delays, high travelling expenses, and family separation by bringing specialized medical care directly to the people who need it, when they need it.

Telemedicine typically involves doctors using one of two types of technology. The first is called 'Store-and-Forward', which is used for transferring digital images from one location to another. The Store-and-Forward techniques typically involve sending pictures, X-rays, and other patient information directly to the computer of a specialist. After reviewing that information, the specialist sends the diagnosis back to the local doctor, who treats the patients and provides follow-up care. This is typically used for non-emergency situations, when a diagnosis or consultation may be made in the next 24–48 hours.

There are many programmes worldwide using a variety of technologies to provide healthcare. For instance, at the University of Kansas Telemedicine Programme (www2.kumc.edu/telemedicine), telemedicine technology has been used for several years for oncology, mental healthcare to patients in rural prisons, hospice care, and most recently, to augment school health services by allowing school nurses to consult with doctors. Several telemedicine programmes are being initiated where the costs and danger

of transporting prisoners to health facilities can be avoided. The University of Texas Medical Branch at Galveston Center for Telehealth and Distance Education (www2.utmb.edu/telehealth) was one of the original programmes to begin providing services to prison inmates, and sees over 400 patients per month. Home healthcare is another booming area of telemedicine. A programme in Japan has home-bound patients communicating daily with a doctor, nurse, or physical therapist.

Telemedicine does not have to be a high-cost proposition. Many projects are providing valuable services to those with no access to healthcare using low-end technology. The Memorial University of Newfoundland telemedicine project (www.med. mun.ca/pdcs/) has been using low-cost Store-and-Forward technology to provide quality care to rural areas in under-developed countries for many years.

Source: http://trc.telemed.org.

marketplace is not a level playing field. Even the USA, the number one perpetrator of 'free trade', recently resorted to protectionism when its steel industry came under threat from cheap imports. The European Union continues to spend half of its entire budget on subsidizing its agricultural produce, and there seems to be little sign of reform. Japan, while under enormous pressure to reform its declining economy, is slow to remove many of its non-tariff barriers.

Competitors will not be limited to those that currently operate in the same industry

It has often been a misconception of many organizations that their competitors are those operating in the same industry. Many well-established organizations are surprised by new entrants to the market which are not identified in their sophisticated competitor analysis—because it focuses only on existing competitors in the same industry. In the UK, for instance, many new entrants to the financial services market are high-street retailers. When we take a broader perspective, every organization is a potential competitor as every player in the market is fighting for a larger share of the consumer's disposable income.

The *new competition* is between networks rather than single organizations

The intensity of today's competition, the increasing expectations of consumers, and the quickening speed of technological change are leading to shorter product life cycle. This means that the window for recuperating investments in research and development, and pursuing global dominance, is narrowing. In order to compete organizations form alliances with other market players, either on a temporary project-based footing or through something more permanent, such as a joint venture. The new competition is and will be increasingly between networks rather than single organizations.

The emergence of a global services economy

The trading of 'invisibles'—services—plays a vital role in today's world economy. Infrastructural services (e.g. transportation, communications, financial services), education, health, recreation, and other professional services now represent approximately 28% of world trade. Services make up a major portion of many national economies, ranging from 39% of GDP in a country such as Nigeria, to 89% in economies such as Hong Kong (China). In the US economy, 77% of its GDP is generated from the services sector, which employs 80% of its workforce. The UK economy shares a similar pattern with 70% of its GDP generated from services and only 18% from manufacturing.

On average, the services sectors produce 45% more revenue per capita than manufacturing and other sectors. The services sector is already increasing in importance in most developing countries and particularly in less developed countries (LDCs), and usually contributes to at least 45% of the GDP. In general, the services sector is expanding faster than sectors such as agriculture or manufacturing. For most efficient value-added primary industries, services usually make up one-quarter of inputs too. Increasingly, even in goods production, the major portion of value-added (up to 70%) comes from services inputs: upstream (such as feasibility studies and research and development activities); on stream (such as accounting, engineering, and administrative services); and downstream (such as advertising, warehousing, and distribution).

The world trade in services is currently estimated to be worth US$2.71 trillion compared to US$11.76 trillion in merchandise. Trade in services has been growing at approximately 16% a year for the past ten years as opposed to 7% growth for merchandise during the same period. With reference to Table 1.3, the export of commercial services in both value and share of world trade has steadily increased every year between 2000 and 2006. Among the three broad commercial services categories—transportation, travel, and other commercial services—the latter is by far the largest and also the fastest-growing category. In 2006, other commercial services categories, which include software services, expanded by 13%, while transportation and travel services were up by 9% and 7% respectively.

Table 1.3 World exports of merchandise and commercial services, 2006 (US$ billion, percentage of change)

	Value	Annual percentage of change			
	2006	2000–06	2004	2005	2006
Merchandise	11762	11	22	14	15
Commercial services	2710	10	20	11	11
Transport	626	10	25	12	9
Travel	737	7	18	8	7
Other commerical services	1347	12	19	12	13

Source: Based on data sourced from *WTO's, World Trade Report* (2007: 10).

WHOSE RESPONSIBILITY IS IT? Making trade free and fair for all

Globalization has made the world a much smaller place. It has facilitated the buying and selling of goods and services between countries. Today these goods and services can travel further and faster so that, for instance, products from all over the world can be found at your corner shop. This can be anything from fruits and vegetables, to cars, banking services, clothing, and bottled water. The scale and pace of this kind of trade has increased over time and has become a powerful tool. International trade is considered a prime driver of how well a country develops and how well the economies of different countries perform.

World trade could also reduce poverty. For instance, if Africa, East Asia, South Asia, and Latin America were each to increase their share of world exports by 1%, the resulting gains in income could lift 128 million people out of poverty. In Africa alone, this would generate US$70 billion—approximately five times the amount the continent receives in aid.

In practice, however, the set-up of global trade rules and the way in which they are administered by the World Trade Organization works best for those countries which are already rich. This inevitably increases the gap between the rich and poor countries, which are already struggling to compete. Part of the problem is that trade is not always equal. When countries put restrictions such as tariffs on goods from other countries, imported goods become more expensive and less competitive than goods from their own country.

In addition, the so-called rich countries continue to subsidize heavily their domestic businesses. This means that governments give money or other forms of support to local or domestic businesses, to make sure that they are cheaper than imported products and services. This can allow unsuccessful and inefficient businesses to prosper. The resulting surpluses are dumped on world markets, undermining the livelihoods of millions of small-holder farmers in poor countries. And while these businesses continue to grow, smaller or local producers, especially in many poorer countries—those that need support the most—are being

destroyed. Such measures are called 'protectionist', as they have the effect of closing off a country's markets to goods from other countries. Many wealthy countries in Europe, as well as the USA and Japan, use these tactics to support their own domestic economies, making it impossible for smaller or less developed countries to gain a foothold in the global marketplace. Many of these countries are creating double standards by forcing other countries to open up their markets. When developing countries export to rich-country markets, they face tariff barriers that are four times higher than those encountered by rich countries. Those barriers cost them US$100 billion a year—twice as much as they receive in aid.

Reform of world trade is only one of the requirements for ending the deep social injustices that pervade globalization. Action is also needed to reduce inequalities in health, education, and the distribution of income and opportunity, including those inequalities that exist between women and men. However, world trade rules are a key part of the poverty problem and fundamental reforms are needed to make them part of the solution.

Sources: www.greenpeace.org and www.maketradefair.com.

As the services sector is quickly replacing the manufacturing and agricultural sectors as a major source of GDP in most of the developed economies (especially the USA, Western Europe, and Australasia, which, when combined, account for approximately 80% of world trade), the volume and value of world trade in services are set to become even more dominant in the world economy. In addition, of the top 100 companies worldwide (by revenue), more than half (55%) are services organizations. It is little wonder that in the latest rounds of World Trade Organization meetings, governments paid special attention to a consensus on fair trade practices with regard to services, especially for protecting intellectual property rights, issues of barriers to trade in services, regulation of international data flows, etc. The strategic management of services in the global context is obviously of increasing significance to marketing managers.

For further discussion on the growth of services trade and the implications on global marketing, see Chapter 10.

The advent of new technologies

The advent of new technologies (e.g. the internet and the World Wide Web, mobile devices, digital TV) has opened up business and marketing opportunities in the development of innovative products and services, and the creation of new values to consumers. For instance, conventional marketing and targeting techniques allow an organization to reach hundreds, thousands, or even tens of thousands of potential customers. But with a personal computer and a modem the organization can reach a community of millions at a fraction of the cost. By 2012, eMarketer (www.emarketer.com) projects that over 1.7 billion people worldwide (24.5%) will access the internet at least once per month. Nearly 50% of the world's internet population will live in the Asia Pacific region. China has overtaken the USA as the most populous internet nation in the world and the Asia Pacific region will top 500 million internet users. The share of the world's internet users in Europe and North America will fall, though absolute numbers will continue to rise in both regions, as the share of users in Latin America and the Asia Pacific region both grow. The Netherlands and the Scandinavian countries lead the world in terms of internet penetration, and reached something of a saturation point around 80% of the population in 2007. Countries such as China, Russia, India, Brazil, and Mexico are relatively immature internet markets and will be the primary drivers for worldwide internet user growth over the next five years.

Of growing significance is digital TV, the take-up rate for which has exceeded internet usage for the first time in the UK, and other internet-enabled mobile devices such as mobile phones, PC notebooks, and palmtops. More than 8 million people worldwide today have access to television delivered by internet protocol (IPTV) services. IPTV will be used in 38.4 million homes worldwide by 2012 (source: www.informatm.com). It is estimated that IPTV subscriptions and video-on-demand would generate an estimated US$14.7 billion in worldwide revenue by 2012, up from US$1.5 billion in 2006. That revenue will come from a mere 3.1% of the world's TV households. More importantly, IPTV has become a major source of internet television advertising for companies seeking to reach customers globally. The revenue for this form of advertising will hit US$10 billion worldwide by 2011, which would equal 18% of all internet advertising spending, which is forecast at US$57 billion.

The size of the online market is impressive, but size alone is merely the beginning of its attraction for the commercial sector. New technologies can provide a competitive edge because they give businesses a leverage over its time and investment, allow them to target prospective consumers easily, and level the playing field between them and their competitors, no matter how large or well financed.

The rapid adoption of these technologies as a commercial medium has led to businesses experimenting with innovative ways of marketing in the electronic environment. As a commercial medium, new technologies offer opportunities as a powerful delivery channel, a medium for marketing communications, and a market in and of themselves. Those opportunities are associated with the interactive nature of the medium.

First, there is significant potential to reduce distribution costs. This can be seen in the cases of publishing, information services, and software. Organizations are able to target customers directly, thus eliminating some of the marketing costs and constraints imposed by conventional methods such as terrestrial television. This may also make distribution more efficient due to reduced overhead costs resulting from uniformity, automation, and integration of management processes.

Secondly, online businesses are able to transfer more of the selling function to the customer, through online ordering and the use of e-commerce. This also benefits the business in the form of capturing customer information on buying preferences and behaviour.

The interactive nature of new technologies is conducive to developing customer relationships. This potential for greater customer interaction facilitates relationship marketing and customer support to a greater degree than has been possible with traditional media. This has provided unprecedented opportunities to customize communications precisely to individual customers, allowing them to request as much or as little information as they wish, when they wish, and how they wish.

Finally, the new technologies also bring operational benefits, especially for industrial suppliers, which include reduced errors, time, and overhead costs in information processing; reduced costs to suppliers by electronically accessing online databases of bid opportunities, online abilities to submit bids, and online review of awards.

The growing transparency of corporate practices

Globalization brings businesses into contact with countries which conduct business by different rules. Until recently, businesses had relative freedom to exercise a different set of practices in different countries. Due to the lack of transparency in what businesses got up to in other countries, many businesses had been able to exploit those differences in the legal frameworks or conditions between countries to maximize profits.

The emergence of global media and internet technologies means that businesses are now confronted with a much greater level of transparency of their international practices than ever before. The advent of modern, truly global communications technologies has brought about an avalanche of new debates on issues ranging from the exploitation of cheap and child labour, environmental pollution and global warming to genetically modified organisms (GMOs) and privacy on the internet. Added to this is the unprecedented scrutiny by non-governmental organizations (NGOs) and the increasing global consumers' demand for the right of access to information. Over 60 countries have passed legislation that recognizes and protects the right to access information held by public bodies. In Europe, Africa, and the Americas, countries have adopted human rights treaties—i.e. European Convention on Human Rights (ECRH); African Charter on Human and Peoples' Rights; and American Convention on Human Rights—all of which recognize the right to freedom of opinion and expression, including the right to seek, receive, and impart information. The right to access information held by public bodies is a key piece of the wider right to freedom of opinion and expression. The exercise of this right enables consumers to keep their businesses as well as governments accountable for unethical or socially irresponsible practices in developing countries.

The growing transparency of corporate practice worldwide has put pressure on organizations not just to be more ethical in their business operations but also to assume greater social responsibility towards a range of global social issues, including combating climate change, minimizing the abuse of human rights in employment practices, and elevating global poverty. These pressures may come from an organization's own ethical values, its home-country government, or constituencies which threaten to boycott its products or to spread adverse publicity about it. Many companies, including Nike (www.nike.com), with its alledged sweatshops in Indonesia, Nestlé (www.nestlé.com), with the ways in which it marketed its milk powder in Africa, and Shell (www.shell.com), over criticism of its perceived failure to oppose the Nigerian government's abuse of human rights, have learned the hard way. Bad behaviour in one country can be seized on by the NGOs and the media, and then broadcast in the home country. Many organizations now believe that socially responsible behaviour not only helps to avoid negative consequences from perceived irresponsibility but can also lead to strategic and financial success.

The Need for a New Approach to Global Marketing

Organizations of the twenty-first century are confronted with many new marketing challenges. These challenges are inexorably linked with global developments in the increasingly dynamic and volatile global business environment. The clear implication is that they will shape the nature of global competition and the source of competitive advantage. So, the question that every organization competing in this environment needs to ask is: what does it take to compete?

Being competitive in the twenty-first century, in the words of Zairi (1996: 54–5): requires an unprecedented set of extraordinary strengths. For one thing, the dynamics of the market are more turbulent where there is parity in terms of product/service technological capability and intense competition in less tangible, 'soft aspects', such as customer service, quality and responsiveness.... For another thing, successful competitiveness often is the result of the ability to determine rational capability (through strengths and weaknesses) and a rigorous attack to fulfil customer needs that are well defined through closeness to the market (voice of the customer). Finally, winning comes through innovation, uniqueness (differentiation), teaching rather than following, a culture of continuous improvement and learning.

Approaches to global marketing have evolved as the marketing environment demands. Judging by the many and varied approaches put forward over the years, there has been no shortage of new ideas in the evolution of marketing theory. Table 1.4 presents an overview of approaches, ranging from the 'transactional' to the 'relational', their period of origin, and some proponents of the approach.

MINI-CASE ILLUSTRATION Samsung: at the cutting-edge of home entertainment

Consumers often experience confusion at the prospect of buying a quality home cinema system. Even the most technical consumers can end up in a frenzy when faced with the vast number of options and brands available.

The world of home entertainment is rapidly evolving. Within a few short years the industry has gone from analogue Pro-Logic amps, laser discs, and clunky CRT TVs to digital surround-sound, DVD, and hang-on-the-wall displays. The proliferation of budget all-in-one systems, LCD projectors, and separate components, in parallel with the growth in internet sales, are quickly driving prices down. The revolution in home entertainment is set to continue for some time.

Samsung (www.samsung.com), the Korea-based multinational, is at the cutting edge of this revolution. In recent years, it has been prolific in providing consumers with high-quality, affordable home entertainment systems. The company recognizes that, to stay ahead in this highly competitive market, it is vital to maintain good investments in product innovation and brand-building marketing to capture the imagination of consumers. Without a steady stream of new products, Samsung would risk losing its hard-earned share of the global market.

To showcase its latest extensive range of home entertainment products in the UK, Samsung recently took over the first floor of the Old Truman Brewery in East London to launch its 'Sport TV Event 2004' campaign. Latest products range from the mighty 80-inch plasma screen television, the world's largest LCD 54-inch high definition television (HDTV), and the latest innovation in picture-processing called Digital Natural Image Engine (DNIe). Samsung claims that DNIe is able to produce the clearest, most detailed, and natural images by including a fifth picture enhancer, i.e. the Image Optimizer.

Samsung is working diligently to create sustainable, distinctive market advantages, with an ambitious mission to become the dominant player in the global LCD industry. It has embarked on a truly global approach to its LCD business for the immediate future. First, it seeks to expand the market share of four key products: high value-added Notebook PCs, large-scale monitors (greater than 17 inches), LCD TVs (greater than 26 inches), and mobile devices by expanding their application areas. Secondly, it seeks to improve cost competitiveness by drastically reducing the number of required parts by investing in innovative manufacturing to minimize raw material costs and defects. Thirdly, it has invested heavily in the creation of a global brand as the basis for a clear differentiation of its innovative, well-designed products.

Sources: www.whathomecinemamag.com; www.samsung.com.

Table 1.4 Overview of approaches in marketing theory

Transactional	Corporate re-engineering— 'the Lopez era'	Resource-based	Relationship	Organizational learning	Expert systems/ database	Interactive, bench-marking
Keegan (1960), Townsend (1971), etc.	Peters (1987), David (1986), etc.	Prahalad and Hamel (1990)	Grönroos (1994)	De Gues (1999)	Chaffey (1999)	Zairi (1996)
1960s & 1970s	1980s	1990s	1990s & 2000s	1990s & 2000s	1990s & 2000s	1990s & 2000s

The modern history of marketing can be traced back to the 1960s, often referred to the era of scale and specialization, which typified the aspirations of organizations up to the 1970s. Relentless efforts to pursue 'vertical integration' drove many companies, including Ford (www.ford.com), IBM, and Unilever (www.unilever.com) to acquire the key channel resources and to internalize, via large specialized departments, the skills needed to run the business effectively. The relationships between a company and its external stakeholders (including customers) were, by and large, characterized by a series of contracts and financial transactions. Increased competition in the 1980s sharply eroded gross margins, thereby forcing many companies into programmes of asset disposal and elimination of large specialized departments and support activities. The subsequent downsizing and delayering in the name of corporate re-engineering or restructuring were inevitable as companies found decision-making, especially at the frontline, too cumbersome and bureaucratic. Many sought to boost profits by exploiting their monopoly power in the supply chain. For instance, in the 1980s, General Motors, under Lopez, the then CEO, confronted its suppliers with demands for 30% discounts to maintain the business. These exploitative strategies proved unsustainable as core capabilities and relationships (both internal and external) were neglected. Carefully developed business and social networks—the very bases of an organization's competitive advantage—were sacrificed for short-term gains. Organizations which survived into the 1990s realized that competence in managing strategic relationships was essential for successful businesses in dynamic environments. They sought to move from a traditional transactional to a collaborative culture in which members of the supply chain work together and learn from one another to reduce total system waste for the benefit of all parties. Further, there was a renewed sense of urgency to acquire and manage the organization's capabilities as core competence is dependent upon its ability creatively to combine unique capabilities. Collaborations enable the organization to extend its capabilities and substantially enhance its capacity for innovation (Doyle, 1995).

The rapid evolution of approaches in the 1990s, fuelled partly by the revolution in digital technology and most certainly by research and practice, struggled to keep pace with the rapidly changing environment. For instance, relationship marketing was supposed to be the answer to the shortcomings connected to transactional approaches. This proved not to be the case. While the business-to-business market may have found this approach significant in the management of the supply chain and in outsourcing goods and services, it had a mixed reaction in the consumer world. For instance, many UK banks saw the advent of the internet as positive in their quest to get closer to the customer. However, apart from some notable examples, e.g. Smile (www.smile.co.uk) and Egg (www.egg.co.uk), banks have shied away from adopting the technology, not only due to cost, but also through fear of a backlash from the traditional over-the-counter customers. As a cost-cutting tool,

Fig. 1.2 The new challenges facing global businesses

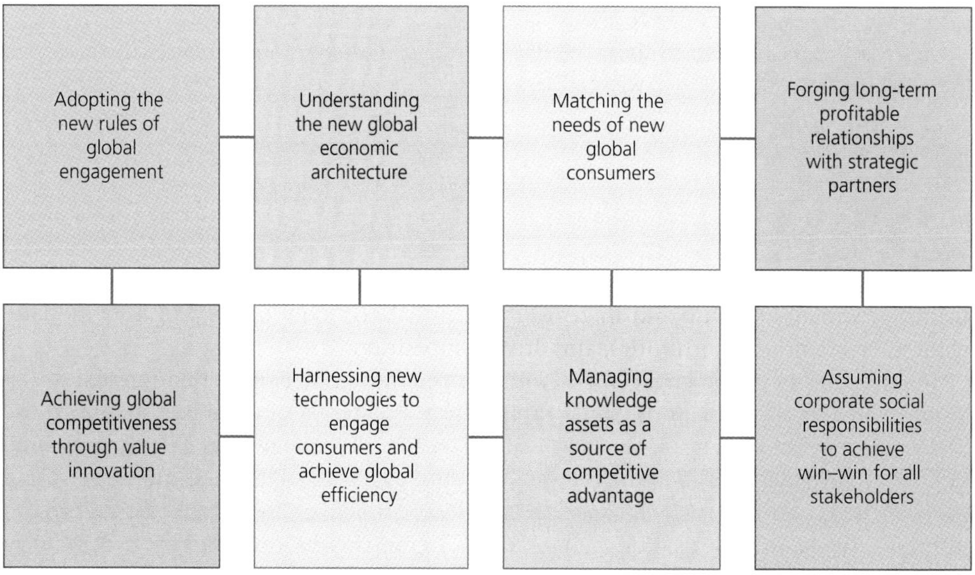

Adopting the new rules of global engagement	Understanding the new global economic architecture	Matching the needs of new global consumers	Forging long-term profitable relationships with strategic partners
Achieving global competitiveness through value innovation	Harnessing new technologies to engage consumers and achieve global efficiency	Managing knowledge assets as a source of competitive advantage	Assuming corporate social responsibilities to achieve win–win for all stakeholders

banks have found the internet invaluable but have lost customers, who dislike this form of transaction, in the process.

There can be little doubt that pressure to innovate and to find new approaches to managing successful marketing operations will continue for many years. However, new thinking in global marketing management should not negate the merit of old theories. Organizations in the twenty-first century recognize that effective management of relationships and core capabilities will continue to be crucial to the success of an enterprise. The whole notion of a universal approach which could provide the solution for every organization must be abandoned. As organizations and consumers become more diverse, the search for a 'one size fits all' marketing solution will prove self-defeating. The search for solutions to the new marketing problems must begin by asking the right question. To find answers, organizations must consider the following challenges confronting them in their response to the new global environment (see Fig. 1.2).

The new rules of global engagement

The financial crises in the late 1990s in Latin America and the global economic downturn of the early twenty-first century in East Asia ruined economic prosperity and caused many businesses to fold. With it came arguments for the decoupling of state interests with business (e.g. South Korea and the Chaebols), the necessity to adopt good governance (e.g. Malaysia, Thailand, Indonesian Central Banks) and the adoption of a Western-style market orientation (despite the 'family' approach of many Asian countries).

Many of the affected nations have since undergone new beginnings. Of significance is the new direction in global engagement put forward by Asian leaders. Many now believe that globalization should become more introspective and regionalized, and accept 'globalism' only as an added impetus to national development. Alternative sources of growth will come from making conditions more conducive to local investments and production, building up the strength of domestic markets and increasing regional trade and investments. Regional cooperation in trade, investment, and finance should be intensified, while actively reducing excessive dependence on developed countries for growth (Mohamad, 2002). The most significant of these is the latest consideration by the East Asian Vision Group—set up in 1999 by the leaders of ASEAN 3 (China, Japan and Korea) to formulate agendas for East Asian cooperation—of the establishment of an East Asian Economic Community. A free trade arrangement is envisaged within ten years (Panitchpakdi, 2002). This was followed by the proposal of the Japanese government in January 2002 for a comprehensive economic partnership between Japan and ASEAN to widen cooperation in trade and investment, human resource development, science and technology, and tourism.

The new challenge for global businesses, especially those operating in Asia, arises from their ability to adapt to the changing nature of market opportunities, which are shaped by the new rules of global engagement. These nations would welcome and support global businesses which stimulate and increase the regional economy by helping to stimulate business, create new opportunities, and drive competition.

The new rules of global engagement will also be affected by issues of nation state (e.g. Latvia), ethnic movements (e.g. the Balkans), ethnic conflict and the nation state (e.g. Afghanistan), peasant revolt and resistance (e.g. Burundi, Chechnya), which all bring challenges to the global marketer in so far as they directly affect trade and have knock-on effects. Threats of conflict may have far-reaching effects. The aftermath of war with Iraq and the consequential destabilizing effects of oil supplies in the Middle East saw the world facing an increase in fuel prices by almost 50% within four years and caused a slowdown in air travel, affecting the oil and travel industries respectively.

Issues of human nature—health, disease, hunger, and poverty—affect global business operations. The devastating effect of HIV/AIDS has implications for the use, training, and replacement of expatriates and local staff in multinational organizations as well as an affect on demand for products and services. With infection rates at 30% in some African countries, and among affluent consumers, there is an effect on the demand and supply of goods and services and the balance between them. These factors, plus those above, may be both a blessing and a curse for the insurance industry globally. On the one hand, premiums are welcome but, on the other, payouts can be enormous, which in turn affect premiums leading to slowdown in demand.

It is important for organizations to consider how these new rules of global engagement affect the planning of global marketing operations. Chapter 3 tackles the issues relating to globalization and the implications they have on the management of global marketing operations.

The new global economic architecture

The emergence of new economic powerhouses has real implications for the future of the global economic architecture. A major challenge to marketers, especially those based in the West, will be the emergence of new economic blocs and superpowers. Currently, with no real challengers, the USA dominates the global scene, both in terms of world GDP (23%) and politically. For the last 15 years, the USA has 'led the world', especially since the break-up of the USSR and the continued decline of the Japanese economy. However, that is due to change. The World Bank estimates that India will be the next emergent superpower within a decade and that by 2025 China, which at present has only 3% of world GDP, will have 25% of world GDP. The question is what this will do to the balance of trade. China's 2002 accession to WTO and its efforts to increase regional trade via the enhanced ASEAN will greatly enhance Asian trade liberalization. Many companies are already investing heavily in China. It seems increasingly likely that Asia will become the production hub and the West the service hub.

Added to this is rising global instability. Since the end of the Cold War, the world has been increasingly unstable. The Middle East has long been a concern, as are Iraq, Iran, North Korea, Indonesia, the Philippines, South America, Africa, and the former Soviet States. This brings into focus the need for a more vigorous risk-assessment process. Some would argue that the 2003 conflict with Iraq was about saving the global operations of the Exxon Oil Company and not with saving the world from a dictator. The events in New York of 11 September 2001 had far-reaching effects on global marketers. Some airlines never recovered (e.g. American Airlines, www.americanairlines.com, Swissair, www.swiss.com), and travel and tourism suffered an estimated 25% loss to and from the USA in the immediate aftermath, affecting thousands of employees. Many global disruptions are unforeseen and cause instant chaos. This has spawned a whole business in crisis and catastrophe planning and management. The challenge for global marketers is to be ready for the unexpected.

Chapter 2 discusses in greater detail the latest developments, challenges, and opportunities, e.g. trading blocs, new industrialized nations, emerging markets, and China's participation in WTO etc., and the driving forces of globalization.

Matching the needs of the new global consumers

From a business perspective, changing demographics and expectations of consumers globally present implications on the nature of market opportunities. Drucker (1999: 49) observes that 'in all developed countries older people have become the most prosperous group in the society, with their post-retirement incomes in many cases substantially higher than their pre-retirement incomes. Their numbers will continue to increase.' Shrinkage in the number of young people—especially those under 18—means that parents concentrate a larger proportion of their disposable incomes on their children, especially in education and leisure. It is conceivable that consumption behaviours and patterns of these consumer groups will largely shape the global consumer market and with it the world economy. Judging from the evidence, this is already happening.

The challenge and opportunity afforded by the ageing population (the 'grey market') has not yet been fully explored by global marketers. Most advertising and promotion are still aimed at the young and the thirtysomethings. Yet simple arithmetic reveals at least 2.5 billion of the world population in this grey market, many having no family commitments but a high income to spend on holidays, cars, second homes, and eating out. The challenge is not only to find products and services which appeal to this market, but also to make contact with it through appropriate communication. Those organizations which do so will reap the rewards—witness the successful Saga

Saga is an exemplary UK service provider which targets specifically at the grey consumers.

The new breed of consumers expect more customized products and services to cater for their needs.

organization (www.saga.co.uk) in the UK which provides holidays, insurance, and many other products and services specifically to the grey market.

Thanks to advances in communication and transport, consumers around the world are converging in their consumption patterns. It is estimated that of the world's six billion people today, five billion are already consuming at the level of developed countries like Western Europe, Japan, and the USA. Multinationals such as Microsoft, McDonald's (www .mcdonalds.com), Nike, and Coca-Cola (www.coke.com) are reaping the benefits of this convergence of behaviour. Added to this is the growth of urbanization. Witness the mega-metropolis of Tokyo with 30 million inhabitants and Mexico City with 15 million. The implications are enormous. These city dwellers have lifestyles which require information, communication, and specific points of purchase. The opportunities for global marketers are undoubtedly great but diversity brings its own challenges.

This new breed of consumer will seek goods and services which conform to their needs. They look for products and services which serve their patterned needs. World branding will, therefore, become more and more important—Disney, IBM, Nintendo (www .nintendo.com), PlayStation (www.playstation.com), BSkyB, etc. This trend is likely to grow, with the emergence of new giants, who are likely to be linked to the communications and interface (e-commerce) industries.

This global consumer development or 'emulation', bringing with it the resultant opportunities and challenges to global marketers, will also have far-reaching environmental consequences. This relentless drive to emulate Western lifestyle with its demand-driven growth in consumption, waste, energy use, and emissions will offer a different type of challenge. Wilk (1998) offers some fascinating insights: Are we witnessing the growth of cultural imperialism? Is the cultivation effect of Western media very strong? Many case studies suggest that these worries are unfounded and that most groups emulate their local elites. Yet more recently, we have witnessed a move away from class competition models of consumer behaviour towards a focus on communication, nationalism, advertising, and the growth of markets and retailing.

How does the global marketer cope with the challenge of diversity and subculture and yet, on the other hand, the global consumer? Wilk (1998) offers some answers. This lies in honing those skills that determine consumer behaviour and having a healthy scepticism of the so-called models of global consumer behaviour. No single tool (or tools) exists for establishing a global consumer and marketers have few truly comparative cross-cultural databases. What we know is that globalism is on the increase but we do not know why the consumer culture in developing countries is vectored differently from that of developed countries. There is no general model of consumer behaviour and, while we know consumption rises as income rises, we are still unsure which products or services that increased income will be spent on. As an example, McDonald's appeared to have a global formula yet, for the first time in its history, at the end of 2002, it made a quarterly loss. Why? The answer lies partly in the competitive arena but also in the consumer behaviour arena. Tastes have swung to the perceived more healthy forms of food on an increasingly global scale.

Chapter 4 furthers the discussion on the changes in today's consumers by examining the social and cultural influences on consumer behaviours in different parts of world.

Achieving global competitiveness

It is too much of a truism to say that the world is becoming a more competitive marketplace. For the last three decades authors have been predicting the convergence of competition to such a degree that by the turn of the twenty-first century it was predicted that 200 organizations would dominate world trade. When we look at Microsoft, General Motors, Disney, and

Shell or BP, we could be forgiven for thinking that the predictions are coming true. However, if we broaden the marketing arena to cover banking, insurance, service industries, government procurement, and so on, the predictions seem far from true. What is not in dispute is the dominance of certain market sectors by a few operators, and certainly the examples above are cases in point in their respective industries. Equally true is the fragmentation of certain markets, including food production and processing, and small-scale specialist retailing. This has given rise to the phenomena of market dominance and 'hyper-competition' as bipolar extremes, with many markets falling between the two. The challenge to global marketers is how to seek an operational, if not lasting, competitive advantage, and new and different ways to add value. With ever-shortening product life cycles, demands for high quality at low prices, care for the environment, changing rules of the competitive game via mergers and acquisitions, and an increasingly demanding customer wanting 'instant gratification' rather than long-term satisfaction, the challenge of the competitive environment is huge.

Being competitive requires an unprecedented set of extraordinary strengths. The discussion in Chapter 8 considers the meaning and implications of several key competitive principles underpinning the success of global organizations. It also examines the specific strategies, processes, and techniques which global marketers may employ to seek and retain competitive advantage.

Marketing using new technologies

The development of the internet and other new technologies is still at the very early stage. We may be even earlier on the learning curve for harnessing these technologies to create a truly unique advantage in the global marketplace. Even as businesses try to absorb the revolution of the internet, teenagers in Europe and Asia are already shaping the next revolution in mobile communication and commerce. This revolution will play out differently in different parts of the world, and will probably play out differently from what we expect, unless we understand the new hybrid consumers. The demand for customization means that the process of developing products and going-to-market has been transformed. The establishment of physical and virtual communities means that the nature of the interaction of companies with customers has changed. The creation of new channels means that companies need to manage across complex webs of marketing and distribution. The rise of new pricing models and value equations means that traditional approaches to pricing and revenue models need to be reconsidered. Technology creates greater interactivity and transparency, and has transformed the entire supply chain.

Of course, it is not just e-commerce that is encompassed by the umbrella of new technologies. We must include interactive media, electronic databases, EPOS (electronic point of sale), and a host of other technological wizardry. Therefore, the new challenge for global marketers is not just to catch up with and stay ahead of new technologies but also to learn and benefit from how consumers interact with the technologies.

The development of the new media and the ways in which they may be applied for global marketing planning and operations are now an integral part global marketing management. This is an important theme which is discussed throughout this book.

Knowledge as a source of global competitive advantage

Intensive global competition, the economic transition from manufacturing to services, technological changes, and the dynamic process of globalization itself have stretched organization capabilities to the limit. With the world economy set to rely heavily on the services sector and with a much higher level of information and intelligence to respond

MINI-CASE ILLUSTRATION **How Microsoft stays ahead of global competition**

For many years, Microsoft never seems to get the respect for being a real market innovator. The global software giant consistently plays second fiddle to other high-tech companies, such as Apple and Google (www.google.com). In its attempt to win over critics and stay ahead of global competition, Microsoft has been sowing the seeds of innovation in the last 15 years by investing heavily into Microsoft Research (MSR), which is one of its most distinguished research and development (R&D) units. MSR has spawned innovations seen today in products from Windows Vista to Exchange Server to Xbox 360.

Founded in 1991, MSR is dedicated to conducting both basic and applied research in computer science and software engineering. Its goals are to enhance the user experience on computing devices, reduce the cost of writing and maintaining software, and invent novel computing technologies. Researchers focus on more than 55 areas of computing and collaborate with leading academic, government, and industry researchers to advance the state of the art in such areas as graphics, speech recognition, user-interface research, natural language processing, programming tools and methodologies, operating systems and networking, and the mathematical sciences. With a budget of more than US$250 million, MRS currently employs more than 800 people in six R&D laboratories located all over the world, from the Silicon Valley in California to Beijing in China and Bangalore in India. MSR collaborates openly with colleges and universities worldwide to enhance the teaching and learning experience, inspire technological innovation, and broadly advance the field of computer science. MSR incubates not only futuristic ideas but young minds, having hired 700 interns worldwide this year, including 250 computer science PhD candidates in Redmond alone, which is roughly 21% of all the computer science PhD candidates in the USA. Microsoft officials claim it is the world's largest PhD internship programme for computer science. The MSR staff, however, are not just computer scientists; it includes psychologists, sociologists, anthropologists, and medical doctors who are tasked with pushing the envelope on state-of-the-art technology as much or more than transferring their technology into new and existing Microsoft products.

While technology transfer is only one aspect of MSR, which has a dozen people working on that issue alone, the lab does have a long list of technology innovations that are part of the Microsoft product portfolio, including systems used to support the backend of Microsoft's Windows Live Mail service (formerly HotMail), Vista's SuperFetch feature that monitors the company's most-used applications, interactive voice response technology, such as Exchange 2007, and the TrueSkill ranking feature that is key to Xbox Live's online gaming.

To compete for the future in a fast-changing software technology global market, Microsoft firmly believes that it needs to plant the seeds of innovation within the company and its networks of business partners by investing heavily into long-term R&D projects. There are no products Microsoft produces today that have not either taken technology from research, come directly out of research, or been built using the tools and technologies it has created in research. What is happening in its laboratories today projects what might be possible in another five to ten years. MSR and similar projects are what the company believe will ensure not merely its survival but its future global market leadership.

Source: Based on materials sourced from www.networkworld.com.

effectively, it follows that organizations of all sizes increasingly need strategically to manage their most valuable assets—people and information (i.e. the knowledge base). It is argued that effective management of knowledge will provide the basis for developing the ability to thrive through creating a source for competitive advantage. To retain talent, management must demonstrate empathy for its needs and create attractive workplaces. Corporate boards must be diverse, and CEOs must be able to manage across political and cultural boundaries. Increasingly, this means recruiting leadership from countries outside Europe and North America.

Knowledge management has occupied an important part of contemporary management thinking. As observed by Sanchez (2003: 3):

> there appears to be no agreement among managers or management academics as to what exactly we mean by terms like 'organizational knowledge', nor is there any generally accepted

methodology for managers to use in managing knowledge. It is in fact often the case that these ideas either fall into the category of abstract theoretical schema with no clear connections to the realities of managers and their organizations, or belong to the category of 'practical' action-oriented steps that ignore insights into human cognition and organizational behaviour that have been developed in psychology, sociology and other disciplines in recent years.

So, the real challenge for global marketers is to derive practical and implementable ways to support, improve, and stimulate the creation and use of knowledge to enhance organizational competences and bring strategic benefits to organizations.

The current thinking on knowledge management and its implications on global marketing management are discussed in Chapter 10 within the context of services marketing and management. The discussion seeks to demonstrate how knowledge may be used to provide a new source of competitive advantage, especially in service delivery.

The importance of managing relationships

In the light of increasing global competition, accelerating technology, and costs in reaching new customers, most organizations no longer have sufficient skills, resources, and time to operate their core processes and pursue global market dominance on their own. Acquiring a new customer can cost up to five times more than retaining an existing one. It is a known quantity that the cost of acquiring new customers will become even higher. If the Pareto 80/20 rule (i.e. 80% of revenue is generated from 20% of customers) is valid, and loyal customers spend a larger share of their disposable income with their trusted suppliers, the new challenge for global marketers is to devise strategies which go beyond building superficial customer relationships and engage customers in a meaningful and sincere manner.

The world's top 1,000 companies spent 10% more on research and development in 2006 than they did in 2005; but most innovation now comes through collaboration with employees, customers, and business partners. As new competition will increasingly be driven by inter-organizational collaboration rather than single organizations, the challenge for global marketers is to find innovative ways to forge long-term, profitable relationships with other players within the economic chain, including competitors, employees, customers, suppliers, retailers, and business partners. The formalization of these relationships will take the form of a strategic network, which organizations can use to develop new product innovations by pooling resources, rationalizing processes by cooperating on common business operations, and, more importantly, creating new ways to satisfy customers.

Managing marketing relationships has become increasingly important as businesses realize the need to build and sustain relationships with their customers as well as other stakeholders. The discussion in Chapter 13 reflects this growing trend and explains global marketing within this context. It seeks to define the key concepts of relationship marketing and to explain why this has become an important issue in today's global marketplace. Also discussed are strategies for planning and developing relationships and how relationship marketing may be used to provide global competitive advantage for companies.

Corporate social responsibilities and ethics

Corporate social responsibility and the ways organizations discharge their moral and ethical responsibilities are vital issues concerning all businesses in today's global environment. As organizations grow larger in both size and economic power, the external scrutiny into their behaviour in terms of use (and/or abuse) of their power and their economic impact on a wide range of stakeholders and the environment is also becoming more penetrative.

THE RELATIONSHIP PERSPECTIVE Partnership for strategic advantage

In April 2002, the Coca-Cola Company (www.coke.com) and Groupe Danone (www.danonegroup.com), the owner of the Evian brand, formed a partnership for Groupe Danone's retail bottled spring and source water business in North America (USA and Canada). Under the agreement, Coca-Cola is to manage the marketing, sales, and distribution of Evian. Distribution will continue through the Coca-Cola system, including Coca-Cola Enterprises, Coca-Cola Bottling Company United, Swire Pacific Holdings, Philadelphia Coca-Cola Bottling Company, and Coca-Cola Bottling Company of Northern New England, as well as other existing distributors of Evian. Danone will continue to undertake all global product development.

Both Coca-Cola and Danone see this partnership as a deal that can offer substantial strategic advantages for their respective beverage brands. Aligning Danone's interests in North America with Coca-Cola and its extensive distribution system would advance Danone's access to the biggest market in the world.

For Coca-Cola, the partnership offers the company the opportunity to add what is already a leading premium water brand to its portfolio. Over the long term, it would enhance Coca-Cola's ability to realize more fully the growth opportunity in the water category.

Sources: atlanta.bizjournal.com; www.bottledwaterweb.com.

This raises a serious challenge and calls for ingenious solutions from the global marketer. While a number of organizations clearly take their responsibilities seriously, and have adopted appropriate strategies and policies, an organization's approach to its moral and ethical responsibilities requires constant monitoring and adaptation to respond to the many and varied global market developments. In practice, this will involve regular risk assessment, improved sophistication of market analysis, market entry and withdrawal strategies, appropriate marketing mix combinations, expatriation of funds, and implementation and control strategies.

The current concern that all businesses and the general public have ethical behaviours and social responsibilities is not restricted to the domestic marketplace. In the era of the global economy, multinational companies (MNCs) need to be concerned with how they carry out their business as well as their social role. Many shareholders today respond to socially responsible corporate global citizenship as well as outstanding financial performances. By partnering with governments and civil societies and working within core competencies, organizations can greatly benefit societies and improve their bottom lines simultaneously. According to an Edelman[1] (www.edelman.com) study of 5,000 consumers in nine countries, 70% would pay more for a socially or environmentally responsible brand. But such responsibility must be integrated into the essence of the companies—and emblazoned in the hearts of its employees—for it to resonate with consumers. 'It's not what you do with your money after you've earned it that matters,' said HM Queen Rania Al Abdullah of the Hashemite Kingdom of Jordan, a Member of the Foundation Board of the World Economic Forum, 'but it's how you've earned the money that determines your success and your value added to society.'

[1] Edelman claims to be the world's largest independent public relations firm, with 2,000 employees in 43 offices worldwide.

Chapter 5 examines some of the major ethical issues confronting MNCs. It seeks to demonstrate how organizations are able to use corporate social responsibility (CSR) and ethical practices not only to increase trade but to provide a competitive advantage in the global marketplace.

Organizing for Global Marketing

This book approaches global marketing in the way the manager of an organization does, reflecting the different levels of decision-making involved in the planning process. It is important to recognize that organizations differ in their international activities according to their needs, resources, capabilities, and international experience. To be successful at global marketing, all organizations, whatever their size, need to develop the competences and respond creatively to the changing global environment or even contribute to shaping the environment itself. It is the aim of this book to equip students (as emerging practitioners) and managers with some of the most current knowledge and practical skills in order to navigate their organizations through an increasingly dynamic and challenging global business environment . It is structured around the fundamental requirements for making sound global marketing decisions. Global marketers must have the competence in dealing with a number of strategic and day-to-day decisions on various level of complexity. These decisions are grouped into three areas, as illustrated in Fig. 1.3.

Fig. 1.3 Organizing for global marketing

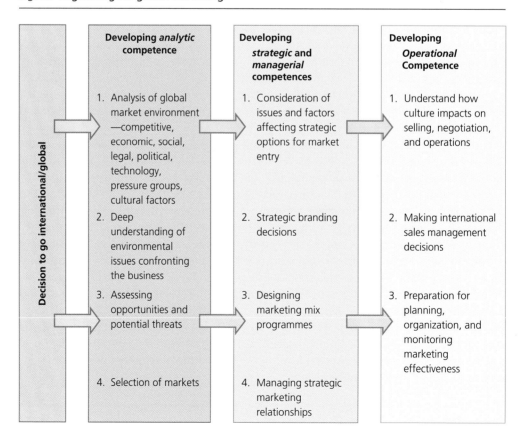

The following table provides an outline of how this book is organized and the way in which it is structured to take readers through their development of decision-making competence in each of the decision areas.

Decision Areas	Chapter	Development of Decision-making Competence
Understanding the Global Marketing Environment	1: Changes and New Challenges 2: The Global Marketing Environment 3: Understanding Globalization 4: Understanding Global Cultures and Buyer Behaviour 5: Understanding Global Social and Ethical Issues 6: Opportunity Analysis and Selection of Markets	To compete successfully in today's global marketplace, managers first need to develop the *analytic competence* in assessing opportunities and selecting markets for entry. Chapter 1 aims to equip managers with an understanding of the global market environment by providing an overview of the contemporary issues in global marketing, and how they present new challenges to the management of global marketing operations. Chapters 2, 3, 4 and 5 are devoted to help develop a deeper insight into the global market environment by examining the current discourses of globalization, global cultures and buyer behaviour, and the global social and ethical issues. Chapter 6 provides managers with the grounding for decisions on information needs, conducting analysis of market opportunities, and selecting the right markets to do business.
Development of Global Marketing Strategies	7: Market Entry Strategies 8: Creating, Developing, and Maintaining Competitive Advantage 9: Product and Brand Management 10: Global Services Marketing 11: Management of Global Communications 12: Managing Supply Chain and Distribution 13: Managing Global Marketing Relationships 14: Global Pricing and Terms of Access	Once opportunities are identified, managers need to develop the *strategic competence* to develop global marketing strategies to ensure successful market entry and ongoing marketing management. Chapters 7 and 8 aim to equip managers with the knowledge and skills to consider the various factors and issues affecting the choice of different market entry strategies. In doing so, managers would be able to arrive at decisions on what strategies to adopt in order to maximize competitive advantage. Chapters 9, 10, 11, 12, 13 and 14 aim at developing managers' *managerial competence* in designing global marketing programmes consistent with the chosen market entry strategy. These chapters cover the four key marketing mix decision areas as well as strategic branding and managing marketing relationships.
Implementing and Coordinating Global Marketing Operations	15: Sales Force Management and Negotiation 16: Organizing and Controlling Global Marketing Operations	To ensure successful implementation of global marketing strategies, managers need to develop *operational competence* to manage and coordinate the global marketing effort. Chapter 15 is intended to equip managers with an understanding of the important considerations in making international sales management decisions and how culture impacts on selling and negotiation. Chapter 16 aims to help managers prepare for planning, organization, and monitoring marketing effectiveness.

Chapter Summary

1. Defining global marketing is not an easy task as marketing across political and cultural boundaries raises many questions, problems, and juxtapositions, rendering precise definition difficult. The truly global marketing operation is one which seeks to lever its assets across political and cultural boundaries, looking to maximize opportunities and exploit market similarities and differences in the search of competitive advantage.

2. Global marketing strategy has to start with taking stock of market changes in the global market environment, especially those that present the most immediate new challenges for today's global organizations.

3. The challenges and responses can be categorized as either external or internal. External forces include the evolution of the global consumer, an increasingly destable world, rapidly changing technology, emergent demographics, the call for global governance and an ethical approach to doing business, an increasingly competitive environment, and a combination of these which is challenging the ways of doing business. Internally, the demand to maximize all stakeholder values, find new ways of adding value, capture and retain customers, all in a lean and cost-efficient resource environment, is a challenge of huge proportions.

4. Many approaches to global marketing planning have been put forward in response to the evolution in the global marketplace. Mere tinkering with the marketing mix is no longer sufficient to address the challenges. Paradigm shifts are often the only answer. These often require the development of new organizational mindset, knowledge and competences, and will require the organizations to engage in long-term planning and sustainable implementation.

 END-OF-CHAPTER CASE STUDY **Time to face the music**

Western pop music is produced, marketed, and consumed throughout the world. It has grown over the last 50 years to become a truly global industry worth US$30 billion. Since 1960s, the pop world has played a large part in cultural shifts. As the industry and its companies grew, the public became as interested in the artists as celebrities, putting them on a par with Hollywood's idols. As MTV and its associated media channels popularized pop music in the 1980s, endlessly broadcasting the big hits, the pace of change in pop music increased as more artists became instant big sellers.

The music industry market is concentrated in the USA and the UK. A third of all recorded music is bought in the USA, where most of the major labels are based, and 89% of recorded music is bought in the top ten markets in the world. In the UK, every member of its population buys an average of four CDs every single year, more than any other country in the world. Across Europe, artists see the UK as being a major breaking-ground for success, while UK acts and labels spend vast amounts of time and money attempting to break into the US market.

Despite its market potential, it is a tough business to succeed in the global music industry. It is estimated that 90% of album releases fail to break even. The 10% of releases that do become profitable need to make enough money to write off those failed investments. With the reward for success so high, there are far more people willing to attempt to take their chances at being part of the industry. It is perhaps this lack of predictability that makes the pop world so alluring, attracting new generations of fans, artists, and investors willing to put up the money to support it.

The global music market is dominated by EMI Records, SonyBMG, Vivendi Universal and AOL Time Warner. The so-called 'Big Four' have 90% share of the global music market and operate in all of the major markets in the world. Each operates in a variety of fields, incorporating publishing, electronics, and telecommunications. In achieving their dominance in music sales, the Big Four each own a large portfolio of labels, from formerly independent labels to large regional operators in different territories. The biggest exception to their domination of the market is in India, where the large film music market has so far defied these corporations. Africa has also proved to be a difficult market for the American-owned corporations, largely because the economic situation outside South Africa means a lack of profitable markets. In South Africa, Gallo Records is one of the biggest record labels, not only because of its representation of African music, but also from being exclusive licensee for Warner Music International.

Although sales of CDs over the past decade have risen by 150%, year-on-year worldwide sales are starting to fall. Along with decreasingly favourable world economic conditions and competition from other leisure products, the reasons for this decline emerge from the increased availability of free and pirated music. One of the biggest problems for record companies is that CD recorders such as CD-R and CD-RW have become widely and cheaply available. In 2001, the value of CD-R sales overtook recorded music sales for the first time. Although these sales include CD-Rs sold for use as computer data storage as a large storage medium to replace floppy disks, this is often viewed by music industry associations as a key reason for the decline in music CD's sales.

Pirated CDs have been valued at US$4.3 billion each year at the expense of legal global music sales. Today, CD-R piracy is considered to be at its highest levels in Latin America, Western Europe, and North America. In China, an estimated 90% of the CDs sold are pirated copies. The problem of music piracy is exacerbated by the proliferation of music download sites on the internet. With digital copies of CDs and single tracks available to download and copy on to other CDs, the problem is considered to be far greater than that of cassettes in the 1970s and 1980s, as music was difficult to share and exchange without the internet.

The global music industry has been complacent in catching on to the potential and danger posed by the internet and digital technologies. In the past, the music industry has been able to dominate format changes and dictate to the public what it can buy. It now faces the prospect of having to compete in a changing market where consumers have become accustomed to acquiring music in digital formats for free. Thanks to these new communication technologies, the bargaining power has shifted dramatically away from the music companies towards the music consumers as they can now get around paying to buy expensive CDs in the shops. The ratio of unlicensed tracks downloaded to legal tracks sold is about 20 to 1. There is a growing community of people willing to share their music files, whether from recording their own CDs on to their computers or by downloading from other online users. Despite efforts by the industry to stop it from happening, online peer-to-peer sharing of music files appears to be here to stay, at least for the foreseeable future.

It is perhaps understandable why many music lovers prefer to access and enjoy their music digitally. Apart from being able to acquire music at a much lower cost or even free, consumers want to 'pick and choose' exactly which tracks they want and decide how they wish to experience music. This change in consumer preference has fuelled a growth in the so-called global digital music, with sales totalling an estimated US$3 billion in 2007—a roughly 40% increase on 2006 (US$2.1 billion). Single-track downloads, the most popular digital music format, grew by 53% to 1.7 billion (including those on digital albums). Digital sales now account for an estimated 15% of the global music market. In the world's biggest digital music market, the USA, online sales now account for 30% of all revenues. The growth in digital music sales has surged ahead despite the tens of billions of illegal files that are swapped every year.

The growth rate of around 40% in digital sales, however, does not offset the sharp fall in CD sales globally. It is clear that the industry needs to do something to combat this threat to their revenue, and it is with this in mind that some recent CDs have included copy protection technology to prevent them from being copied. This approach has angered many legitimate music consumers as making a back-up copy of a music CD for personal use is not illegal. For an industry used to dictating how its consumers listen to its products, it is clear that it is still some way from offering a solution that is palatable to its consumers as well as its shareholders.

Sources: Based on and adapted from the BBC World's Special Report on Global Music Industry (http://www.bbc.co.uk/worldservice/specials/); and IFPI's Digital Music Report 2008 (www.ifpi.com).

Case discussion questions

1 What do you think are the factors that make the global music industry so successful?

2 In your analysis, what are the major market changes that contributed to the troubles of the global music industry? Could the music companies have better prepared themselves for these changes? If so, how?

3 In what ways do the music companies respond to resolve the music piracy problem? To what extent are they effective in curbing the problem?

4 What do you think are the new challenges confronting the future of the global music industry?

END-OF-CHAPTER EXERCISES

1 What is the definition of global marketing? How does it differ from international and domestic marketing?

2 Identify and discuss the important changes in the global market environment.

3 Describe the new challenges which are faced by today's and future global marketers.

4 Summarize the various approaches to global marketing planning.

DISCUSSION AND EXAMINATION QUESTIONS

1 Discuss how changing consumer demographics globally will impact on consumers and their expectations of products and services.

2 Any global marketing strategy, that is—in the words of Peter Drucker (1999)—'any commitment of present resources to future expectations', has to start with taking stock of the changes in the global marketing environment. Discuss.

3 After the financial crisis in the late 1990s and early 2000s, critically evaluate how likely it is that much of the world's economic growth in the immediate future will be fuelled by the emerging markets in the Asia Pacific and Latin American regions, and why.

4 In the light of rapid global market changes, discuss the changing nature of global competition and the ways in which it will present new challenges for organizations which operate globally.

5 Why do you think the issues of corporate social responsibility and ethics are of tremendous significance for global marketers today?

FURTHER READING

Drucker, P. F. (1999), *Management Challenges for the Twenty-first Century,* Woburn, MA: Butterworth Heinemann.

Kandampully, J. and Duddy, R. (1999), 'Competitive advantage through anticipation, innovation and relationships', *Management Decision,* 37(1), 51–6.

Mohamad, M. (2002), 'Globalization: Challenges and Impact on Asia', in Richter, F.-J. and Mar, P. C. M. (eds.), *Recreating Asia: Visions for a New Century,* Singapore: John Wiley & Sons (Asia), pp. 5–11.

Von Pierer, H. (2002), 'Asia—A Region Oriented Toward the Twenty-first Century', in Richter, F.-J. and Mar, P. C. M. (eds.), *Recreating Asia: Visions for a New Century,* Singapore: John Wiley & Sons (Asia), pp. 71–80.

REFERENCES

Chaffey, D. (1999), *Business Information Systems: Technology, Development and Management,* London: FT/Prentice Hall.

David, F. R. (1986), *Fundamentals of Strategic Management,* Englewood Cliffs, NJ: Prentice-Hall.

De Gues, A. (1999), *The Living Company,* London: Nicholas Brealey Publishing.

De Mooij, M. (1998), *Global Marketing and Advertising: Understanding Cultural Paradoxes,* Thousand Oaks, CA: Sage.

Doyle, P. (1995), 'Marketing in the new millennium', *European Journal of Marketing,* 29(12), 23–41.

Drucker, P. F. (1999), *Management Challenges for the Twenty-first Century,* Woburn, MA: Butterworth Heinemann.

Grönroos, C. (1994), 'From marketing mix to relationship marketing: towards a paradigm shift in marketing', *Management Decision,* 32(2), 4–20.

International Monetary Fund (IMF), 'Globalization: Threat or Opportunity?' www.imf.org (accessed on 22/07/2004).

Kandampully, J. and Duddy, R. (1999), 'Competitive advantage through anticipation, innovation and relationships', *Management Decision,* 37(1), 51–6.

Keegan, W. (1960), *Marketing Management: Policies and Decisions,* Boston, MA: Houghton Mifflin.

Mohamad, M. (2002), 'Globalization: Challenges and Impact on Asia', in Richter, F.-J. and Mar, P. C. M. (eds.), *Recreating Asia: Visions for a New Century,* Singapore: John Wiley & Sons (Asia), pp. 5–11.

Neef, D. (1999), 'Making the case for knowledge management: the bigger picture', *Management Decision,* 37(1), 72–8.

Panitchpakdi, S. (2002), 'Asia's New Scenarios', in Richter, F.-J. and Mar, P. C. M. (eds.), *Recreating Asia: Visions for a New Century,* Singapore: John Wiley & Sons (Asia), pp. 239–48.

Perry, A. C. (1999), 'International versus domestic marketing: four conceptual perspectives', *European Journal of Marketing,* 24(6), 41–54.

Peters, T. J. (1987), *Thriving on Chaos,* London: Pan Books.

Prahalad, C. K. and Hamel, G. (1990), 'The core competence of the corporation', *Harvard Business Review,* May/June, 79–91.

Sanchez, R. (2003), *Knowledge Management and Organizational Competence,* Oxford: Oxford University Press.

Sanderson, S. M. (1998), 'New approaches to strategy: new ways of thinking for the millennium', *Management Decision,* 36(1), 9–13.

Svensson, G. (2002), 'Beyond global marketing and the globalization of marketing activities', *Management Decision,* 40(6), 574–83.

Townsend, R. (1971), *Up the Organization: How to Stop the Company Stifling People and Strangling Profits,* Philadelphia, PA: Coronet.

United Nations (2000), *World Population Prospect: The 2000 Revision,* Population Division Department of Economic and Social Affairs, New York. (www.un.org).

Von Pierer, H. (2002), 'Asia—A Region Oriented toward the Twenty-first Century', in Richter, F.-J. and Mar, P. C. M. (eds.), *Recreating Asia: Visions for a New Century,* Singapore: John Wiley & Sons (Asia), pp.71–80.

Wilk, R. R. (1998), 'Emulation, imitation, and global consumerism', *Organization & Environment,* 11(3), 314–33.

World Economic Forum (2008), *World Economic Forum Annual Meeting 2008: The Power of Collaborative Innovation,* Davos Report, Davos, Switzerland 23–27 January (www.wef.org, accessed on 24/02/2008).

World Trade Organization (2007) *WTO's World Trade Report 2007. Six Decades of Multilateral Trade Cooperation: What Have We Learnt?* Geneva: WTO.

Zairi, M. (1996), 'Competition: what does it mean?', *The TQM Magazine,* 8(1), 54–9.

online resource centre

Visit the companion website to this book for lots of interesting additional material, including self-assessment questions, internet exercises, and links for each chapter:

http://www.oxfordtextbooks.co.uk/orc/lee_carter2e/

CHAPTER TWO
The Global Marketing Environment

Chapter overview

Chapter Introduction 37

The Global Marketing Environment:
A Definition 37
   The importance of accounting for the global
   environment 38

Factors within the Global Environment 39
   The intermediate environment 39
   The macro environment 42

The Political Environment 42
   The role of the government in the economy 43
   Political stability and risk 43
   International relations 44

The Legal Environment 45

The Economic Environment 46
   The role of socio-economic blocs and global
   interdependence 50
   Economic facilitators 53
   China's accession to the WTO 55

The Socio-cultural Environment 56
   Approaches to the study of culture 57

The Technological Environment 57

The Competitive Environment 62

The Currency Environment 63

Pressure Groups 64

Chapter Summary 66

Learning objectives

After studying this chapter, the reader will be able to:

- define the meaning and scope of the global marketing environment;
- consider the factors in the marketing environment and their effect on global marketing planning and management;
- examine the challenges of the global marketing environment and how marketers respond to these.

Management issues

The management issues that arise from this chapter include:

- What are the current factors and challenges in the marketing environment and how do they impact on global planning and marketing?
- How does marketing management in an organization capture these factors and challenges, and how often? Assess their impact and plan an appropriate response.
- How can a marketing organization turn these challenges to global competitive advantage?

Chapter Introduction

To speculate on the trends and developments of the global business environment is a hazardous business, despite the growth of techniques such as risk analysis designed to minimize those hazards. For example, before the Asian financial crisis in the late 1990s, it was a widely held view that Asia, the most dynamic trading region in the world, would dominate the global economic landscape of the twenty-first century. When the Thai national currency collapsed on 2 July 1997, no economist foresaw that this would be the beginning of a crisis which would derail the region's economic 'fairytale' and eventually affect the world. During the crisis, the national currencies of Malaysia, South Korea, Indonesia, and the Philippines went into freefall as a result of prolonged currency speculations which threatened to bankrupt the region's financial institutions, stock exchange markets, and businesses. In 2006, this region suffered another human calamity of global significance, a tsunami which killed thousands of people. Thankfully, with the help of massive global assistance, Thailand, the Philippines, and Malaysia recovered remarkably quickly. In 2006–07 Russia began to flex its considerable gas and oil 'muscle' to such a degree that economies could be almost 'held to ransom'. This was unheard of since the oil crisis of the 1970s.

In many ways these crises were a warning sign for the global business environment. Apart from the short-term problems over the stability of some Asian economies and governments, the financial crisis exposed longer-term anxieties: prolonged pessimism in consumer confidence; the widening gap between rich and poor, both within and between countries; and concern that foreign companies would help to erode traditional cultures. Such concerns are now widely shared and have been given expression through the anti-globalization movement. The rise of this movement, combined with the events of 11 September 2001 and their aftermath, the tsunami, and the global recession (Ellis, 2002), gave the century a sobering start. Pockets of recession remain, e.g. Japan. However, a cautious optimism on the global outlook now dominates despite the continuing threats of the Middle East and global terrorism.

These events present a unique challenge for businesses all over the world and there is a new sense of uncertainty about future developments. Businesses are beginning to understand how their markets are intertwined and to realize that 'they operate in a fragile global environment, in which markets, suppliers, and finance are subject to violent shocks' (Ellis, 2002: 60). Global events can be unpredictable and catastrophic but at the same time can be planned for in global business operations. A problem arises when organizations do not take account of the environment in which they conduct business.

This chapter will first examine the meaning, importance, and scope of the global marketing environment followed by a discussion on the factors or forces within the global marketing environment which marketers need to account of, and the approaches to conducting environmental analysis. The chapter also considers the challenges in today's global environment and how marketers can respond to them.

The Global Marketing Environment: A Definition

We can define the global marketing environment as:

Those variables, largely out of the organization's control but which it must account for, within which it conducts its business globally.

Some authors describe these variables as 'uncontrollables', unlike decisions on, and implementation of, the marketing mix variables, over which an organization has full or, to a greater or lesser extent, more control. However, this is not strictly true since many global operators have varying degrees of control over the so-called 'environmentals'. Depending on the type of regime, there are considerable variations between countries in the laws governing business conduct. This can give rise to practices which may be unacceptable in other cultures. As we shall see in the section on 'political factors', some governments view the offer of financial inducements by potential suppliers as acceptable, whereas others view them as bribery. Governments offering favourable tax regimes and other incentives, such as soft loans to inward investors, may be operating a global standard practice, but others may see these as equally inequitable. Faced with such a situation, some global operators may be in a strong position to influence the buy decision, rendering the political factor far from 'uncontrollable'. Failure to account for the environment may expose global planning and operations to high risks.

The importance of accounting for the global environment

Kelloggs (www.kelloggs.com) found that pitching their products as a healthier alternative to the traditional Indian breakfast did not succeed in that market and they now aim at a Westernized niche market. This illustrates the importance of culture, which is just one of the important environmental variables which cannot be ignored.

There are numerous reasons for taking the marketing environmental factors into account. These include the following (shown in Fig. 2.1):

- they reduce the risk of failure;
- they isolate the most important environmental variables so that businesses can concentrate on those which are most significant and not those that need little or no attention;
- they aid international/global strategy planning decision-making;
- they aid decision-making on strategy implementation—which markets to enter and the appropriate marketing mix—hence saving time and money;
- they enable potential global businesses to assess the riskes of conducting business between and within different countries.

Fig. 2.1 Reasons for accounting for international environmental factors

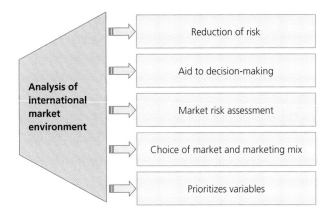

Fig. 2.2 Models of environmental analysis: PEST vs. SLEPT

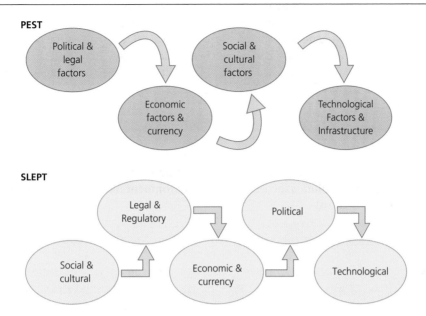

A global environmental analysis can be conducted in a similar way to a SLEPT (Social, Legal, Economic, Political, and Technological factors), or PEST (Political, Economic, Socio-cultural, and Technological factors) analysis or other matrix analysis (see Fig. 2.2). The factors need to be assessed both in terms of importance and impact. For example, currency fluctuations are not regarded as an important issue in most countries of the EU today as most have adopted the Euro. Ironically, this could be important for UK businesses and potential inward investors because of the UK's continued insistence on the pound.

Factors within the Global Environment

The global marketing environment comprises the *intermediate environment* and the *macro environment*. The intermediate environment contains those factors which are semi-controllable through contract, e.g. suppliers and banks. The macro environment is made up of those factors which are generally uncontrollable, e.g. cultural and economic factors. These factors are summarized in Fig. 2.3. We will now consider each factor in turn.

The intermediate environment

The intermediate environment is semi-controllable by organizations in the sense that most goods and services are provided on a contractual basis. The types of goods and services provided depends on the type of organization and for the purposes of this text the providers will be categorized as *suppliers, distributors, partners, stakeholders,* and *customers.* In organizational terms, these providers are part of an organization's 'stakeholders', along with customers, employees, interest groups (e.g. Greenpeace, www.greenpeace.org), and government. Stakeholders are defined as any constituent body having a direct or indirect interest in the organization, and all have to be taken into account if an organization is to

Fig. 2.3 The global marketing environment

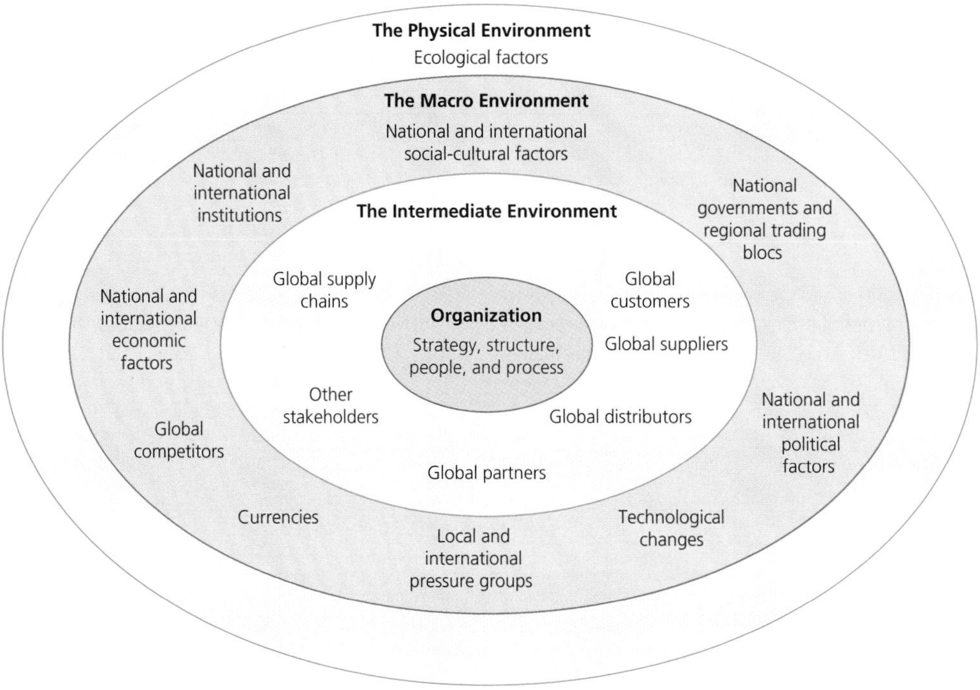

prosper. Interest groups and government are less controllable than factors in the intermediate environment and are discussed later in this chapter.

Suppliers are any provider of goods and services used by an organization to add value. These include suppliers of original equipment, e.g. machinery or office furniture. Others include commodities (e.g. vegetables); semi-finished goods (e.g. gear boxes); and consumables (e.g. heat, light, water, and stationery). Whilst most of these providers form part of the supply chain (and therefore are interlinked to the organization), they are not necessarily owned by the organization and as such cannot be controlled. Organizations minimize the risk of breakdown of supply by working closely with suppliers, often undertaking joint research and development. Networking has become a feature of the supply chain environment, and this has led to even closer cooperation between supplier and customer. It was the Japanese who pioneered the 'Just in time' supply relationship, necessitating a move from an arm's length to a relationship approach to suppliers. This movement has been a feature of the business-to-business market as well as the consumer market. This is an important development in international marketing and is explored in Chapter 13. While networking is common to both domestic and global marketing, the logistics of crossing national boundaries make networking a more risky activity. Not only is there a possibility of breakdown in supply, but currency fluctuations, political factors, and even weather, in the case of foodstuffs, can add to the risks.

Distributors are those logistical and institutional providers of transport, warehousing, and order fulfilment. They will be covered in detail in later chapters, but they usually work closely with organizations but are not wholly controllable, unless owned by the organization, and therefore have to be carefully monitored and planned for. A number of airlines temporarily ceased operation in the wake of 9/11, e.g. Air New Zealand (www.airnz.com), leaving some tour operators to find alternative carriers.

MINI-CASE ILLUSTRATION **Maize to Africa: the great famine of 1992**

The colonialists introduced maize (corn) to Eastern and Southern Africa as a cheap, easily grown foodstuff. Over the years, milled maize (or maize meal) has become the staple diet of the indigenous peoples of Eastern and Southern Africa. From Kenya in North Central Africa to South Africa, small-scale and commercial farmers grew maize for sale to state-owned maize boards. These in turn stored the grain for sale to domestic millers and/or for export. This arrangement ended in the 1980s and 1990s when, encouraged by the World Bank, most state-owned maize marketing regimes were deregulated and privatized under the 'Economic Structural Adjustment' programmes. One element which remains is the buffer maize stock—the Strategic Grain Reserve—mainly owned by government. The reserve is kept in case of crop failure and until imports are mobilized from sources outside the region. In 1992, the rains failed, rendering even the reserve inadequate to cope with the crisis. What followed was one of the biggest and most complex international relief operations ever mounted in Eastern and Southern Africa.

Some 30 million people were at risk. Zimbabwe, the bread-basket of Africa, was down to producing 400,000 tons of maize. Normally it would produce 2 million tons. Some 9 million tons were needed, from as far away as the USA, as food relief agencies like the World Food Programme, obtained donations worldwide. The logistics problem was equally large. With few trains and railway lines in the region, hundreds of trucks were mobilized.

The South African ports of Port Elizabeth and Durban were supplemented by Beira in war-torn Mozambique as shiploads of maize were rushed to Southern Africa. Lorry loads of maize had to travel thousands of kilometres across the borders of South Africa, Zimbabwe, Zambia, Malawi, and Tanzania, negotiating poor roads, the risk of bandits, and the notoriously dangerous Beira corridor between Mozambique and Zimbabwe. Many border formalities were not waived due to the risk of opportunists using 'relief trucks' to transport illegal contraband. Despite the problems, in less than a year, the situation was brought under control with relatively few deaths from starvation.

Partners are the huge range of mainly service providers who provide services necessary to make international operations run smoothly and more efficiently. These include banks, freight forwarders, market research agencies, insurers, cold store operators, government agencies, accountants, commodity brokers, etc. They can also be partners in joint ventures and alliances. These facilitators usually operate in a highly competitive market. The international organization therefore needs to be aware of those providing the knowledge, skills, and service at the most effective price and in the most efficient way. A number of large multinationals (e.g. Ford, www.ford.com) operate these services 'in-house', finding them cheaper and easier to control.

Stakeholders, among whom are shareholders, as well as providing capital, play an increasingly important role in global operations. These days, short-term expectations are high among shareholders. As a result, large investment institutions, whose actions are accountable to shareholders, look for quick financial returns. The threat and/or reality of flights of capital from a public-quoted global institution are sufficient to focus the mind of the corporate executives. For example, in 2004 Marks and Spencer (www.marksand-spencer.co.uk) shareholders, particularly institutional ones, were not satisfied with the company's performance and demanded something be done. The executives at Marks and Spencer were instructed by its shareholders to take quick and drastic actions to restore its former annual £1 billion profit. Sometimes organizations are powerless to stop the flight of capital as many Thai and Malaysian companies found in 1997–98 after the financial crisis. Worried investors moved their capital elsewhere.

Customers are the reason why all profit-making organizations exist. It can be argued that customers are the most important 'factor' in global marketing, yet the most complex. Chapter 4 gives the detail of 'customers', explaining their behaviour and the complexity of cultural factors influencing their behaviour. Research is vital to an understanding of the nuances of the global customer, so Chapter 6 provides detail of how to conduct the appropriate research and, from that, assess the potential of markets.

MINI-CASE ILLUSTRATION A typical SLEPT analysis

A company manufacturing and selling a food product wishes to invest in a developing country of great potential. It assesses five relevant marketing environmentals in the table below. It realizes that the product has to be adjusted to market tastes but believes it will sell well. This is rated as a critical factor to success, so gets a high rating. All five factors are given a weighting, which when combined must equal '1'. The score for each factor is the rating multiplied by the weighting (the 'score' column). All factors are scored similarly and management decides that a total score greater than '2' will be acceptable. While the judgements on weightings and ratings may be subjective, this analysis enables a more informed 'go/no go' decision.

(1) Factor	(2) Rating (out of 5) 1 = Very important 5 = Very unimportant	(3) Weighting	(4) Score (2 x 3)
Product culture bound	1	0.3	0.3
Joint venture a necessity for entry	1	0.3	0.3
State of economy	4	0.1	0.4
Political stability	4	0.2	0.8
Technology available	3	0.1	0.3
TOTAL		1.0	2.1

Acceptable total score for investment 2; in this example, score is 2.1 so 'invest'.

The macro environment

International marketers must compete in 'different' or 'like' environments. The ability to interpret the environment and take appropriate action is the key to success. The environment often changes rapidly in the critical gap between planning to market and implementation. Wireless Application Protocol (WAP) technology phones are a classic example of this. Some mobile phone companies invested heavily to develop WAP technology. Unfortunately, it was only an intermediate technology which was rapidly overtaken by a simultaneously developed, advanced technology in third generation (3G) mobile communications. However, instability may bring rewards. For example, a rapid depreciation of currency can aid exports, especially if inputs to these exports are locally sourced.

There are a number of approaches to analysing the environment for planning purposes. The SLEPT analysis allows the global marketer to analyse the major environmental factors and examine the effect of these factors on global marketing planning and implementation. The Illustration gives an example of such an analysis.

In addition to the SLEPT factors, it is also important for global marketers to analyse the *competitive environment*, the *currency environment*, and *pressure groups*, which respectively influence an organization's global marketing operations. We shall examine each of these factors in turn, and the effect of these variables on global marketing planning and implementation.

The Political Environment

The political environment includes any national or international political factors which may affect an organization's decision-making, planning, implementation, and control mechanisms. Marketers have to work within the framework of each country's ruling party. Pepsi (www.pepsi.com), for instance, was forced to withdraw from India because the then Indian government wanted to protect its own soft drink industry. Factors involved are attitudes to sovereignty, taxes, expropriation of profits, equity dilution, and political risk.

Ideologies can affect the way in which governments behave. Cuba, for instance, is still ostensibly communist, but the development of tourism and its infrastructure is signalling a move to a limited form of capitalism.

There are a number of aspects to the political environment and these are as follows:

The role of the government in the economy

One important question to be answered is what role the government plays in the targeted country. One of its roles is to exercise sovereignty, which is defined as supreme political authority. Two factors govern a nation state's activity: its economic development and the political and economic system. Government can play either a participatory role or a regulatory role depending on the level of economic development. For example, over the last 30 years many developing countries, like those in Africa and South East Asia, have been undertaking World Bank-supported 'structural adjustment programmes'. This entailed a change from a 'command' (state-controlled) to a 'market' (capitalist or market forces) economy, examples of which include Argentina and Tanzania. This has meant that these governments have changed their stance from 'participation' (directly involved in commerce and trade) to 'facilitator/regulator' (not directly involved but providing a conducive environment through appropriate infrastructural and legislative developments). These changes are not immediate. The physical change is one thing, achieving practical change is another. Some governments see globalization as the 'new colonialism' and are wary of the aims of the World Trade Organization (WTO, www.wto.org). Malaysia, for example, in recent times, has been vociferous in its stance against the new economic order. The continuing trend of applications to join the European Union (EU) suggests that some countries are willing to trade sovereignty for economic gain. Yet, on the other hand, there has been a trend to 'nationalism', the recent Bosnian conflict being a prime example.

Political stability and risk

A change in government or policy may affect global marketing substantially. 'Level of involvement' in an economy and 'attitude to risk' are important variables to consider. Low perceived risk means that involvement is more attractive than high perceived risk. Exporting is low-risk and so political stability is not high on the agenda. A more rigorous analysis of political risk may be warranted if the organization is considering longer-term or greater financial involvement. For example, potential investors are more likely to favour stable investment destinations like the EU and the USA to politically uncertain areas like Russia, South Africa and Indonesia.

Three types of political risk can be identified:

- **Ownership risk**: where lives, property and 'intellectual property' are exposed, e.g. in war-torn countries such as Iraq and Afghanistan.

- **Operating risk**: where political activities can interfere with the ongoing operations of a firm, e.g. the 2007 Kenya political riots which interfered with the tourist industry operations.

- **Transfer risk**: which occurs mainly when companies wish to transfer profits or other forms of capital between countries, e.g. Zimbabwe.

Typical political risks, and consequent action, can be many. These include *import restrictions, exchange controls, tax controls, expropriation of property, labour restrictions, market controls*, and *price controls*.

Wrongly assessing the political environment can be costly. If the host government and organization experience a serious communications breakdown, local officials may have the power to confiscate company assets, expropriate them, or simply increase governmental controls over them. Dilution of equity (seizure of assets or adverse government controls, such as taking a stake in the organization) is a serious threat, especially in developing countries. Faced with equity dilution, organizations have four major courses of action:

(a) follow the law of the land;

(b) take pre-emptive action;

(c) negotiate under the new law; or

(d) leave the country.

Many international organizations were faced with this scenario in India in the 1970s and 1980s. The threat of dilution has also led many organizations to seek joint ventures in host countries such as Malaysia and China.

Similar action can be taken over taxation. It is not unusual for international organizations to be incorporated in countries outside those of residence and business. This may be a serious economic cost in terms of lost revenue to a country. Sometimes governments have come down hard on organizations they believe are avoiding payment of local taxes. Others have negotiated bilateral tax treaties. In 1997, the Organization for Economic Cooperation and Development (OECD, www.oecd.org) passed the model Double Taxation Convention for Income and Capital to guide countries in bilateral negotiations. This convention means that income or capital gains is not taxed twice. As long as two countries or more agree to this, the effect of transferring a taxpayer from one country to another evens out.

Expropriation is a particularly virulent form of nationalization. Ethiopia, Nigeria, India, and the Philippines have all imposed forms of expropriation, be it partial remittance of profits, quotas for national employment, increased local content, etc. Johnson and Johnson (www.jnj.com) is one of many firms which had to submit to a host of regulatory conditions in India in the 1970s. Recently, Bosnia, Serbia, and Indonesia have also experienced political intervention and suffered the consequences in terms of loss of investment and trade.

There are a number of procedures which can be followed to assess the type of political risk and avoid overestimating or underestimating it. One procedure is a three-step process:

1. **Determine issues relevant to the firm**: this is a prioritized assessment of the crucial economic and business issues.

2. **Determine political events**: this requires as assessment of relevant political events, their probability of occurrence, their impact and the willingness/ability of the government to respond to them.

3. **Determine probable impacts and responses**: this requires an impact assessment of probable scenarios and possible responses to initial and ultimate risks.

Another procedure would be to consult the BERI (Business Environment Risk Index, www.beri.com). BERI is extremely comprehensive and, for a fee, provides numerous reports. For example, the Financial Ethics Report (www.beri.com/qlm.asp) rates each country on 11 weighted criteria, (e.g. taxation constraints and convertability for principal, interest, and fees), with each criterion rated on a scale from 5 (best case) to 0 (worst case). Therefore, a 'perfect' country would receive a score of 100 (20×5).

International relations

International trade can be affected by how governments behave towards each other. France, Germany, and Belgium's refusal to aid the USA, the UK, and Spain in the war with Iraq in early 2003 put temporary constraints on relationships between the countries and also in post-war Iraq reconstruction. French companies, hoping to win contracts after the war, found themselves behind those of the USA and the UK in the rebuilding process. This occurred at the same time as 12 countries, mainly ex-Iron Curtain countries, signed the treaty of accession to join the EU. The EU showed signs of solidarity with the accession but there was deep division over the Iraq affair. These divisions have now subsided.

One country's, or economic bloc's, system of law-making can have a serious effect on another's. The EU has passed some strict laws and regulations which have had a serious economic effect on some countries with which it does business. For example, its phyto-sanitary regulations (i.e. regulations on types and dosages of pesticides/insecticides and pest/disease incursion) have forced exporters of high-value horticultural products (e.g. mangetout, baby sweetcorn) to European markets to invest in appropriate pack houses, packaging, and pesticides. This can add thousands of pounds to production and marketing costs, making it more difficult for producers such as Zimbabwe, Zambia, Kenya, and Thailand and, eventually, forcing up prices for consumers. Since the accession of the Eastern European countries and former Balkan states to the EU in 2006 onwards, the UK has experienced unprecedented worker migration from these countries (some unaudited figures suggest close to 2 million additional immigrants by the beginning of 2008). Although adding economically to the UK, this also brings with it issues of acculturation, expatriation of wages, and strain on welfare and educational services.

Since the Iraq conflict in 2003, the USA, under the Bush administration, has been strengthening its influence on world politics. Not only did it intervene in Iraq, but its influence is spreading throughout the region as it puts in place the Middle East 'Road Map' to secure peace. This involves Israel as well as Palestine. The regime change in Iraq is a classic example of the effect of sudden and violent uncontrollable changes in the world's marketing environment. From virtually no trade with Iraq, since the 2003 war, international marketers have had opportunities for trade and development opened up. The final months of the Bush administration in 2008 were increasingly taken up with attempts to obtain a settlement in the Middle East to the so called 'Palestinian' issue.

The role of the United Nations (www.un.org) cannot be underestimated. The Security Council is a major source of international law and is likely to play an ever-increasing role globally.

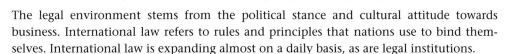

The Legal Environment

The legal environment stems from the political stance and cultural attitude towards business. International law refers to rules and principles that nations use to bind themselves. International law is expanding almost on a daily basis, as are legal institutions.

There are a number of key aspects to the international legal environment:

- **Local domestic law**. It is best to employ a local expert for local domestic law or an international organization with specialist knowledge. The organization's home market laws are important because, for example, they may limit what can be exported.

- **International law**. There are a number of international laws that affect an organization's activity. There are laws on patents, trademarks, and copyright piracy (CDs, software, etc.), and others deal with international conventions, e.g. the WTO. The EU is attempting to harmonize legal systems across regional boundaries and bind member states to a common legal system.

Further issues remain over *case* versus *code* law (the former takes a case-by-case approach rather than the latter, which is based on precedent), the scope of jurisdiction, intellectual property rights and patents, licensing and trade secrets, and issues of bribery and corruption. Product and corporate liability is growing, particularly in the USA and UK.

Countries vary in their approach to conflict resolution, dispute settlement, and litigation. This can involve exorbitant and prolonged legal battles in court but there are alternatives, such as international arbitration courts, some of the oldest of which are in London and Zurich. The United Nations Conference on International Trade Law (UNCITRAL, www.uncitral.org) has also been a significant player in arbitration.

Political and legal considerations are obvious and challenging. Not only do they set 'the rules of engagement' but they are particularly relevant in planning and implementing the marketing mix. The degree to which an organization can expatriate profits affects price, laws on advertising, labelling and packaging, and marketing communications. Patents, trademarks, and trade secret laws affect product development and marketing policies. Intel (www.intel.com), the multinational computer chip manufacturer, jealously guards its name against any imitators or copycats. It is prudent to seek legal advice during the planning and implementation of the marketing mix as subsequent litigation can be costly.

The rapid development of internet and communication technologies (ICTs) has raised serious challenges to global marketing operations. These challenges include issues of data protection, property rights, especially intellectual property, patents and trademarks, and copyright. The WTO is trying to sort out protocols for international property rights. Companies like Microsoft (www.microsoft.com) and Disney (www.disney.com) believe they are losing millions of dollars per annum to illegal copying, as do designer-label clothing companies. Imitators abound in Thailand and Malaysia, although the authorities in both countries have been taking action against them. Piracy is difficult to trace at source, to police, and to stamp out. Perhaps the solution is cooperation from the authorities of countries affected, and hefty fines and prison terms for those offenders convicted. But it is the demand side, not the supply side, which needs most education. No demand means no supply. At the end of 2007, it was estimated, based on surveys, that UK consumers had changed their attitude to 'copy cat, and fake designer goods since 2003. In 2003, it is estimated that only 5% of UK citizens would consider buying fake goods, but in 2007, that figure had risen to 45%. This is of great concern to manufacturers. Dealing with piracy and abuse of copyright may not be straightforward in countries confronted by issues such as poverty and poor consumer education, which demand a more constructive solution to the problems.

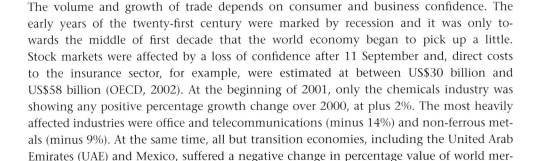

The Economic Environment

The volume and growth of trade depends on consumer and business confidence. The early years of the twenty-first century were marked by recession and it was only towards the middle of first decade that the world economy began to pick up a little. Stock markets were affected by a loss of confidence after 11 September and, direct costs to the insurance sector, for example, were estimated at between US$30 billion and US$58 billion (OECD, 2002). At the beginning of 2001, only the chemicals industry was showing any positive percentage growth change over 2000, at plus 2%. The most heavily affected industries were office and telecommunications (minus 14%) and non-ferrous metals (minus 9%). At the same time, all but transition economies, including the United Arab Emirates (UAE) and Mexico, suffered a negative change in percentage value of world merchandise trade over 2000, with Asia suffering the most at exports of minus 9%, North America minus 7% and Western Europe at minus 1%. Transition economies achieved a positive (plus 5% change in exports) but this was counter-balanced by an 11% change in imports. This reinforces the view that the developing world is dependent on imports, especially of finished goods, and exports of agricultural, mining, and travel products and services.

According to the IMF (*World Economic Outlook Report*, April 2007) it was metals and oil which were taking the commodity limelight. The year 2006 was dominated by surges in metal prices and sharp movements in oil prices. Metals were a major contributor to a 22% increase in the IMF commodities and energy index in 2006. Oil prices rose more sharply in 2006 onwards, reaching a record US$134 a barrel in June 2008. These dramatic movements led to much hedge-buying in the world oil market. Food prices also strengthened. Commodities such as coal, copper, cotton, and coffee also showed quite sharp movements in price. While economies had shown signs of some recovery in the middle years of the first decade of 2000, an OECD report (www.OECD.com, 11 January 2008) on a November 2007 report of Composite Leading Indicators suggested changes in the later years (OECD, 2008). There was a downsizing (slowdown) in all major seven OECD economies except the USA, Germany, and the UK, where only a downturn was indicated. Latest data from major non-OECD countries point to a continued steady expansion of the Chinese and Brazilian economies, improved performance in Russia, but a worsening outlook in India. Table 2.1 illustrates the dominance of developed countries in world trade. The table shows that less developed and heavily indebted countries have only a fraction of the world's trade. Ironically, though, according to the CIA *Factbook* (CIA, 2004), it is the developed economies which have the largest current account deficits. Yet, as a percentage of GDP, it is insignificant compared to the debt burden being carried by the underdeveloped and emergent economies. For example, the USA had a current account deficit of US$668 billion and the UK US$42 billion, less than 5% of GDP, whereas Mauritania, with a debt of only US$2.5 billion, represented 45% of GDP and Nicaragua, with a debt of US$12.34 billion, represented 38% of GDP. Even further irony is provided by the World Bank, which suggests that, in counter-balance to the rather negative prospects predicted for the OECD economies, as outlined above, developing economies are likely to cushion the rich country slowdown in 2008, primarily through commodity exports and discoveries, strengthening demand and further assistance in pursuit of the Millennium Goals (World Bank, 2008).

Table 2.1 Percentage share of world merchandise and commercial services

Country	Merchandise (%)		Commercial services (%)	
	Exports	Imports	Exports	Imports
North America	15	22	17	17
South and Central America	3	3	3	3
Europe	44	43	52	48
Commonwealth of Independent States	3	2	2	2
Africa	3	2	2	3
Middle East	5	3	2	3
Asia	27	25	22	25
Total	100	100	100	100

Source: Based on data from WTO (2006: Chart 5, World Trade by Region).

The unprecedented market growth in economies such as China, and in the wealth of the oil-rich states of the Gulf, led to a growing concern in the West over what these economies would do with their new-found wealth, the so-called 'Sovereign Wealth Funds' (SWF). As at January 2008, the biggest players were Abu Dhabi Investment Authority with £316 billion in funds (with a holding in Citigroup Bank), China Development Bank with funds of £160 billion (with a holding in Barclay's bank), and GIC, Singapore with funds of £11 billion (with a holding in UBS and Citigroup Banks). Together, these largely secretive government-controlled investment vehicles have funds of £1 trillion, giving them enormous economic firepower. Incidentally, China has accumulated reserves of some £750 billion, which it is looking to invest abroad. Some countries, such as Switzerland, have generally resisted investment from these fundholders, while other countries, such as the UK, have embraced them. On the plus side, these SWFs have shored up many enfeebled Wall Street banks, caught short by ill-advised investments. On the negative side, some countries believe that they are little more than political weapons used by cynical foreign regimes. Other negatives include the fact that the funds could be used to attack currencies, as George Soros did to the pound sterling in 1992. Others claim the investment is merely to steal technology or intellectual property. With China and Russia hardly enjoying good relations with the West, the suspicions are not easily allayed. The way ahead seems to be for both sides to adopt a more transparent approach, and to this end the IMF is currently drawing up a SWF code of practice. Drawing it up is one thing, making it acceptable to, and enforceable by, all sides is another matter.

The economic environment is an important factor when considering global operations. It is made up of the international economic structure that affects marketing between nations and the economy of the nations in which it conducts trade. Therefore, it is important that the global marketer analyse his/her own economic environment as well as that of the markets in which he/she wants to conduct business.

Market potential can be gauged by assessing the population size, growth, density, distribution, and age distribution, as well as disposable income and its distribution. Questions to be answered by this analysis include:

(a) How big is the population and at what rate is it growing?

(b) Where is the population located and how dense is it?

(c) What is the population age and distribution?

(d) What is its disposable income and distribution?

Answers to these questions will reveal the likely current and future demand, the distribution strategy needed, the product strategy, the marketing opportunities available to different segments of the population, whether the population can afford the goods and services on offer, and which segments offer the most potential.

Many attempts have been made to classify economies for the purpose of analysing market potential. The World Bank, using the Atlas Method, classifies economies in terms of gross national income (GNI) into low income, middle income (subdivided into lower middle and upper middle) or high income. It also uses geographic region and levels of external debt as other analytical groups. Fig. 2.4 is a representation of GNI groupings.

For purposes of analysis, economies can be classified also as:

• *less developed* or *lesser developed*, in the earlier stages of industrialization, growing domestic market with increasing competitive threat (e.g. Malawi);

• *newly emerging*, with decreasing dependence on agriculture, industrialization, rising wages, rising literacy rates, formidable competitors (e.g. Botswana);

• *emergent*, where industrialization is advanced (e.g. Mexico); and

• *post-industrial*, marked with a knowledge economy, information processing where new products opportunities are in innovation (e.g. Japan).

Fig. 2.4 World Bank classification of economies, 2003

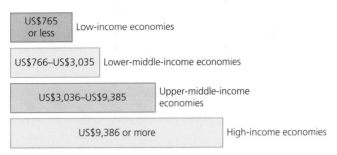

Source: Based on World Bank data, 2003 (www.worldbank.com).

The latter can be called the 'resource economies' and the former categories the 'production economies'. Up to now, the resource economies have been the countries where value has been added from the production economies. This has led to a global search by the resource economies for ever cheaper sources of production (e.g. global car manufacturers), moving from country to country, seeking out low-cost production. This classification essentially gives an indication of the potential demand in an economy. For instance, demand in less developed economies is likely to be for the essentials of everyday life at an affordable price, although there will be pockets of wealth and an opportunity for luxury goods. Developed economies are more likely to be consumers of services and luxury or discretionary goods. However, these are likely to be markets where there are many sub-segments and opportunities, for example, the grey market.

Economic analysis also has implications for the pattern and incidence of consumption. Developed economies may have short replacement cycles, for example, cars are changed every three years in the UK on average, whereas in less developed economies, such as Bangladesh, they may be kept longer and recycled. The political stance is also likely to be 'hands off' as countries move through the lesser developed to post-industrial economic stage spectrum.

Many of these classifications are simplistic and do not capture the characteristics and diversity of markets. The second classification is based on the so-called natural evolution of economies, but economies can leapfrog economic stages. For example, Botswana has been able to progress rapidly based on its resources of diamonds, coal, minerals, cattle, and high-value tourism. The same can be said of oil-rich countries.

As well as market size, the international organization should understand the nature of the economy in which it proposes to operate. Table 2.2 shows the relevant factors and their implications to the organization and global marketers.

Over the last few years, the BRIC economies (Brazil, Russia, India, and China) have rapidly become the new economic 'powerhouses'. Brazil, the twenty-third largest exporter in world merchandise trade at US$118 billion (WTO, 2005), is rapidly becoming a force to be reckoned with in South America and beyond. Once well known as the custodian of the Amazon rainforest, it is becoming more than that now. Tracts of the rainforest are giving way to coffee, cattle, fruit, and other commodities, as well as a thriving manufacturing sector. Oil and gas finds are adding to economic development. Russia, with US$244 billion of exports in 2005 (WTO, 2005), increased its trade by 33% from 2004 and is the world's thirteenth largest exporter of merchandise. Founded on its abundant gas and oil wealth, Russia is rapidly emerging as an economic force. Its new-found wealth has encouraged the investment by leading brand names as well as a source for Russian investment overseas. India, the twenty-ninth largest exporter in world merchandise trade (WTO, 2005), with US$95 billion, is predicted to be the world's second largest economy by 2015, although this might be somewhat ambitious. It has a growing reputation in computer

Table 2.2 The nature of economies and their organizational implications

Factor	Implication
Natural resources, climate, and typography	What are the natural and human resources for use in production and marketing? For example, in Singapore there are no natural resources but a highly skilled and resourceful labour pool
	Physical characteristics, e.g. mountains, which may form logistical problems. For example, Malaysia is physically divided into West and East Malaysia by the Timor Sea
	Typography may require adaptations to products and services, for example, Toyota 'tropicalizes' its vehicles for Africa
Power and communications	Are they available and if so are they reliable? They may affect production and marketing operations. For example, Zimbabwe, Ethiopia, and Indonesia experience power cuts regularly
Economic activity	What is the basic economic activity of the country? Agricultural, industrial, or service? Depending on the activity, this can be a good indicator of likely demand, lifestyles, and product/service requirements. For example, Uganda is mainly agricultural and so its importation of 'services' is limited
Population distribution	Is the population mostly urbanized or rural? This will affect product and service decisions, communications, and logistical operations. For example, Egypt's population is mainly concentrated in the cities of the Nile Delta whereas the Indonesian population is dispersed throughout its numerous islands
Economic indicators	What is the level of inflation, education, balance of payments situation, level of employment, and social security? This has an effect on all marketing activities. For example, the current status of Zimbabwe, Iraq, and Afghanistan make it very difficult to do business there

software as well as manufacturing. For example, Mittal Steel (www.Mittal.com) is one of the largest steel conglomerates in the world and Tata (www.tata.com) recently bought Land Rover and Jaguar from the Ford Motor Company. However, its reputation as a hub for call centres has somewhat declined due to less then predicted performance, resulting in a number of companies relocating back to the UK and the USA. India's rapidly burgeoning middle classes (some 400 million), with their new-found wealth, are, like the Chinese middle classes, set to be the engine of global economic growth over the next ten years. The BRIC economies are somewhat dependent on their respective emerging 'middle class', however, all four countries still have a large percentage of their populations living in poverty. The issue, therefore, is how well these countries will be able to address this problem and spread the economic prosperity beyond the 'middle class'. Without this, the economic miracle will not be sustainable. As China is predicted to be the world's number one economy by 2025, and has the majority of the world's population, this chapter and the next concentrates on this example as one of the emerging BRIC economies.

The role of socio-economic blocs and global interdependence

Since the end of World War II, nations have been creating distinctive socio-economic blocs to preserve and advance their self-interest. The three key trading regions of the world are the EU, the North American Free Trade Area (NAFTA), and the Asia Pacific Region (ASEAN). Between them they account for 85% of world trade. There are differences between forms of market agreement. Doole and Lowe (2004: 50) identify nine forms, as outlined in Table 2.3.

In each of the forms shown in Table 2.3, there are varying degrees of harmonization and cooperation between countries. The EU is an example of full economic and political cooperation, with a centralized bureaucracy to administer it. Bilateral agreements are 'weak' but these are important forms of cooperation where the degree of harmonization is low and there is no free movement of factors of production. Developing countries usually begin cooperation with weaker forms of cooperation and move towards a more integrated form. This is typical of Southern and Eastern Africa, which has been cooperating in some form or another for the last 20 years but is yet to achieve anything like a common market form.

The following is a brief description of the major blocs:

The **European Union** is probably the most developed in terms of regionalism, starting in the early 1960s as an iron and steel union between France and West Germany. It has four main institutions. The Commission, which acts independently of national governments, although its members are appointed by EU member countries, and is responsible for making proposals to the Council of Ministers and executing the decisions of the Council. The Council of Ministers is the main decision body of the EU and consists of foreign ministers of EU states. Heads of government meet three times a year as the European Council. The presidency of the Council rotates between member states. The European Court of Justice consists of judges and advocates generally appointed for a fixed period by governments of member states. The Court is responsible for deciding on the legality of decisions made by

Table 2.3 Different forms of market agreement

Type of market agreement	Example
Free trade area: different countries agree to remove all tariffs between its members	NAFTA (North American Free Trade Agreement), EEA (European Economic Area), EU, and EFTA, COMESA (Eastern and Southern Africa)
Customs union: different countries agree to abolish tariffs between them and impose common external tariffs	Mercusor (Brazil, Paraguay, Uruquay, Argentina, Bolivia, and Chile)
Common market: different countries agree to abolish tariffs between them, impose common external tariffs and permit a free flow of all factors of production between themselves	CACM (Central American Nations)
Economic union: Common Market conditions plus harmonization of economic, fiscal, and monetary policy	EU
Political union: economic union conditions plus full political harmony	USA, Canada
Bilateral or multilateral trade: trade regulation or possible liberalization in one or more sectors	Zimbabwe and China in construction
Sectoral free trade: removal of internal tariffs in a specialized sector	Multi-fibre Agreement
Economic cooperation: consultation on and possible agreement on economic trade policies	APEC (Asia Pacific Economic Cooperation)
Trade preference agreement: preferred trade terms leading, possibly, to a free trade area	SADC (Southern African Development Conference)

the Council of Ministers and the Commission, and for adjudicating between states in the event of dispute. The European Parliament consists of members elected for five years by the voting public in the member states. Members (MEPs) have the right to be consulted on legislative proposals submitted by the Council of Ministers or the Commission and have the power to reject or amend the budget of the EU. The Parliament meets in Strasbourg, its committees are in Brussels, and its secretariat is in Luxembourg.

The EU is now a union of 27 countries, 12 new member states (mainly former iron-curtain countries, e.g. Poland, the Czech Republic) having signed the treaty of accession in May 2003. It has 480 million people and accounts for 44% of world trade. The aim of the Union is a complete political and economic convergence, however contentious that may be. The challenge for organizations is one of keeping up with developments. Organizations are anticipated to merge or create joint ventures, or other forms of cooperation, to compete in this enlarged market. The Union, however, creates various challenges for countries which are not members but which wish to trade with it.

The role of the old COMECON countries is an emerging issue, as many have recently joined the EU. Their economies are potentially low cost but require rapid development. One emergent trend is the migration of labour from the new member states to the more developed EU countries. The challenge to the old-established EU, countries such as France and the UK, will be how to compete and yet help to develop these economies. For further detail on how these Central European economies are dealing with 'marketization' see Hooley et al. (2000).

NAFTA comprises the USA, Mexico, and Canada. It is broadly similar to, but more loosely organized than, the EU. It has an agenda of expansion and consolidation and so forces the interdependence of Central and Southern America. NAFTA has as its aims the elimination of tariffs on manufactured goods, the elimination of tariffs on 57% of Mexican agricultural produce, the harmonization of customs procedures and bureaucracy, the liberalization of finance, textiles, and telecommunications, and the establishment of a trade commission to settle disputes (for further details, see www.nafta-sec-alena.org).

ASEAN includes countries such as Malaysia, Indonesia, Thailand, the Philippines, Brunei, and Singapore. They have some joint planning agreements but their major worry is the effect of the latest round of WTO talks, which they see as 'new colonialism' and a major benefit to the West. By 2005, the ASEAN states, along with Vietnam, Myanmar, Cambodia, and Laos, have agreed to form a free trade area—AFTA. This will create a tariff-free market of some 500 million people. Given the diverse cultures and fierce competition between them, AFTA has its sceptics. The members of ASEAN are largely members of APEC, the Asia Pacific Economic Community, which includes Australia among its 23 Asia Pacific countries. It is a forum to discuss ways to build closer economic and trade cooperation. The USA is supportive of APEC and wishes to see it evolve beyond a forum as it intends to invest further and deeper in the Pacific, it being the prime market for US products, (for further details, see www.aseansec.org).

There are many other groupings, including SADC (Southern and Eastern Africa Development Community), UEMOA (West African States in an Economic and Monetary Union), and the Andean Pact (Venezuela, Colombia, Ecuador, Peru, and Bolivia), but these, while regionally important, are small in terms of world trade and are dogged by inter-country disputes.

Creating interdependence is not simply a pursuit of self-interest. The bargaining power of these trading blocs is such that they can conclude favourable bilateral and trilateral arrangements. The path, though, may not be smooth. We have recently witnessed the 'banana war' between the USA and the EU concerning preferential treatment by the EU for Caribbean producers. We have also seen an iron and steel war between the same two countries in 2002–03, with the USA accusing the EU of dumping cheap steel while it imposes tariff barriers to the import of steel, the 'Buy America Bill', and the 2006–07 GM modified crops debate.

Economic facilitators

While trading blocs have encouraged the volume of world trade, this growth has not been incidental. It could not have happened without the help of a number of facilitators which have, and still are, creating a climate for liberalizing trade-reducing regulations and helping less developed nations to join the ranks of the trading nations (Fig. 2.5).

- **The World Trade Organization**
  The WTO was the successor to GATT (General Agreement on Tariffs and Trade formed in 1948 as a Treaty) and came into being in 1995. GATT was founded in line with many of the other international organizations, following World War II. The reasoning behind GATT was far-thinking—to prevent unnecessary trade wars and economic ruin. The purpose of GATT was to reduce tariffs and other obstacles to trade via a series of regular meetings between member countries (called 'rounds', numbering nine so far). Evidence of its action includes the reduction of tariffs between member nations. For example, between 1950 and 2000 tariffs as a percentage of manufactured value fell from 25% to 4% between the USA, UK, Japan, and Germany. Gains in trade as a result of these rounds are evidenced by increases in trade (1948 US$10 billion, 1993 US$1 trillion) and the fall of tariffs from an average of 47% in 1947 to less than 5% in the 1980s. The WTO also overseas the settlement of trade disputes between nations. With China's recent accession to the WTO, the results are awaited as both Western and Eastern economies jostle for a share of the huge Chinese market as well as relocating production, and taking advantage of relatively cheap labour. However, the 'cheap Chinese' labour syndrome is rapidly disappearing as Chinese consumer incomes increase and they chase more and more goods and services, often of international quality and 'designer label' status. As China, in 2008, stands as the world's fourth biggest economy, with vast financial reserves, the 'West' is becoming somewhat worried by China's capacity to invest in world economies. China, currently, is the biggest investor in Africa with a US$ 20 billion 'footprint'.

  The eighth round, begun in 1986 in Uruguay and concluded in 1995, saw a reduction in tariffs by a further third and the establishment of new rules for trading between industrialized nations. Moreover, its power to force nations to comply with new trading is dramatically increasing and it continues to expand its membership. The Doha round,

Fig. 2.5 Global economic facilitators

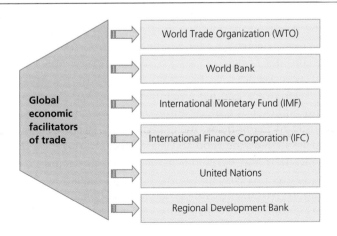

post 1995, witnessed some spectacular failures, primarily the failure to reduce US and EU farm subsidies, thus making access to these markets more difficult for outsiders. For further details visit www.wto.org.

- **The World Bank**
  The role of the World Bank, or the International Bank for Reconstruction and Development (IBRD) plus International Development Assistance (IDA) is multifunctional but it is best known as the provider of 'soft' loans to governments to assist economic development. This usually takes the form of major project development (e.g. dams), turnkey agricultural assistance (e.g. information systems for farmers) and road building. There are some 130 countries 'signed up', with the USA being the largest shareholder, opening it up to accusations of being a US 'puppet' organization. The billions of dollars and other currencies (US$19.5 billion in 2002 to 100 developing countries and the US$42 billion pledged by donors over three years at the Berlin Conference in December 2007 to aid the world's poorest countries) provide development of both local and international business. However, it is important to recognize that the methods employed by the World Bank are not always in line with national thinking. For instance, during the 1980s and 1990s World Bank-sponsored Economic Adjustment Programmes were viewed by some African countries as 'a medicine too strong', especially as competition and free trade have resulted in unemployment and social unrest. For further details visit www.worldbank.org.

- **The International Monetary Fund and International Finance Corporation**
  The International Monetary Fund (IMF) is frequently referred to as the 'bank nations love to hate'. Its remit is simple:

  - to establish orderly foreign exchange arrangements;
  - to encourage the creation of convertible currencies; and
  - to stabilize and reduce balance of payments disequilibrium.

  It helps those countries with balance of payments problems and offers financial support to economies in deficit. It acts, therefore, like a bank offering businesses help with a cash-flow crisis. Obviously, for global marketers its activities can create conditions for favourable trade. A bonus is the devaluation which sometimes accompanies IMF activities, giving a boost to exports. Whereas the IMF focuses on the 'public' sector, the International Finance Corporation (IFC) focuses more on investment in financial instruments and institutions. For further details visit www.imf.org.

- **The United Nations**
  The United Nations (UN) is the best-known worldwide organization, although its credibility has been called into question in recent years, for example over Iraq. Headed by a Secretary General, elected for a term of five years from and by the member states, it emerged out of the old League of Nations. Based in New York, its high-profile role is international peacekeeping. It has been involved in the Balkans, Cyprus, and Afghanistan in recent years, and has a role in fostering and developing projects in less developed countries (LDC). It undertakes projects, provides consultancies and physical technology transfer in many fields, including health, agriculture, and education. The specialized agencies include the Food and Agriculture Organization (FAO), dealing with agricultural cooperation and development mainly in developing countries, the High Commission for Refugees (UNHCR), the World Food Programme (WFP), and the World Health Organization (WHO). The United Nations Conference on Trade and Development (UNCTAD) is responsible for the dissemination of knowledge and technical expertise. The United Nations Development Programme (UNDP) is one of the main arms for

economic and social development, with support programmes as diverse as developing an information system for crop early warning situations, e.g. in Ethiopia, to AIDS education programmes in Zimbabwe. The FAO is currently focusing on poverty reduction through food security. The UN obtains its funding from annual subscriptions from member countries. It also administers multilateral or bilateral funding for projects from outside its own funds, for example, Japan's support for an Agricultural Marketing Training project in Eastern and Southern Africa. For further details visit www.UN.org.

• **Regional Development Banks**
There are a number of regional development banks, supported partly by funds from member states. The European Bank for Reconstruction and Development, the African Development Bank, and the Asian Development Bank are just a few. One of the best known is the European Bank for Reconstruction and Development (EBRD). Created in 1990, its initial remit was to assist the former communist economies of Eastern Europe to adjust to the market-led trading environment. It has now extended that remit to international development, including intervention in Africa and Bosnia.

The role of these multilateral agencies in the development of world trade is undoubted. Without them, the world would not have developed as rapidly as it has. Although they have their detractors no one has any credible suggestions for replacing them.

China's accession to the WTO

China formally became a WTO member on 11 December 2001. With 1.3 million inhabitants and the resulting economic clout, it is not only the world's most populous country but also the fastest growing economy in the world. It is now the fourth largest world

---

MINI-CASE ILLUSTRATION China's entry into the WTO

The 1990s witnessed some of the world's most miraculous but sustainable growth in China's national economy, which averaged approximately 7% per annum. In 2001, as reported by Shi Guangshen (2002), China's Minister of Foreign Trade and Economic Cooperation, fixed asset investment increased by 13.7% and the total retail sales of social consumption surged by 10.1%. Imports and exports amounted to US$509.77 billion, an increase of 7.5%. In the breakdown, exports stood at US$243.61 billion, and imports at US$266.15 billion, 6.8% and 8.2% higher, respectively, than the previous year. Approvals for setting up of foreign-invested enterprises totalled 26,139, an increase of 16.01% over the corresponding period of the previous year. The contractual value of foreign investment grew by 10.4% to US$69.19 billion, and the utilized value climbed by 14.9% to US$46.85 billion (Shi, 2002: 55). In short, the economic achievements for the past decade in China are nothing short of a miracle.

China's entry into the WTO and its anticipated influential role are set to make a significant contribution to the recovery and development of the Asian and the wider global economies. While the US, Japanese, and European economies struggle at the end of the global recession, China has maintained steady economic growth (some 10% average over 2000–08) and brought much needed business opportunities to the industrial and commercial sectors. In 2005, 70% of China's GDP was in the private sector and China's foreign trade grew faster than the GDP over the last

25 years. As at 2006, China's GDP stood at US$10.17 trillion, about 16% of that of the USA, and in the first nine months of 2007 GDP grew at 10.7%, the best in 11 years. It is estimated that there are currently more than 1 million Chinese *dakuans* or dollar millionaires, and over 5% of the population are declared affluent by Chinese standards. It is a country that is fast transforming into a market-based economy from one that

http://www.wto.org/

was centrally planned and controlled by its communist government. As at 2006, China was the world's fourth largest economy. The Chinese economy, according to the World Bank, 'will account for 25% of the total world economy by the year 2025, ahead of the US (20%) and India (13%), the distribution of power will clearly shift toward China' (Pierer, 2002:73). Accession to the WTO has provided China with the opportunity to get 'in shape to become, perhaps, the world's most important economic engine in the not-so-distant future' (ibid.).

economy and currently attracts the most foreign direct investment. Its accession to the WTO will undoubtedly add to the country and provide an impetus to the political, economic, cultural, and technological developments in the global context. China has benefited enormously from accession. While there are large differences in incomes regionally, and areas of real poverty, many provinces, with their 'economic development zones', have grown wealthy. Cities like Shanghai and Beijing are very modern, and Shanghai in particular is a shopping and tourist paradise, with its many ultra-modern shopping malls selling a vast array of 'designer' labels. Chinese consumers are getting more sophisticated, incomes and education levels are rising, demand is booming, and so the emphasis is now on satisfying the latent demand rather than viewing China as a 'cheap labour' market. The price of progress, though, can be high. With its voracious appetite for raw materials and booming construction and production industries, China will continue to face real environmental 'issues' in the foreseeable future.

The Socio-cultural Environment

The complexity of the global socio-cultural environment is manifested in a number of ways. For instance, social class and income have a significant effect on purchases of consumer goods and services. Food is a basic need but what we eat depends on income and culture. Spain and Portugal are the highest consumers of fish in the EU, while the Scandinavians consume most bread and cereals. Switzerland is the largest consumer of coffee in the world and Greece the smallest. The French are the largest consumers of mineral water and the Germans of beer. Today, the British drink more champagne than the French. The socio-cultural environment is changing so rapidly that it is hard for marketers to keep up. The French company Danone (www.danone.com) is consistently producing products in demand, especially yoghurts (its health-conscious Actimel range) and cheese-based products, to follow global health trends.

Differences in social and cultural environments differ from culture to culture. The USA may see business conducted in 'black and white' terms, based on objectivity and written and unambiguous contracts, while others may see more a 'grey' area, allowing for flexibility and subjectivity. For example, managers in the Far East require 'friendship' and cultural sensitivity before doing business, and the 'word' may supercede the need for a written contract. Marks and Spencer are finding that the role of the international manager is becoming more demanding as it seeks to globalize its business into culturally more diverse markets. Workshops, case studies, role-playing, etc. are all ways to become culturally aware. Many companies, such as the Centre for International Briefing (www.farnhamcastle .com), based in Surrey (UK), specialize in intercultural briefing.

One aspect of 'culture' playing an increasing role in global marketing planning is the ageing global population and the drift from rural to urban cities. World population is now 5.7 billion and is likely to be 8.5 billion in 2030. Where? In countries where average daily earnings are less than US$2 a day. Already 80% of the poorest countries with 40% of the world's population are short of basic resources such as water and food and are ravaged by disease. The result? Tension between rich and poor countries. Also, the population is getting older, with 20% of the world's population aged 65+. In the USA today, there are 4.5 workers to every pensioner; in 2030, it is predicted that the figure will be 1.7 workers to every pensioner. According to the UN world population prospects, people over the age of 60 will triple from 606 million now to 2 billion in 2050. In developed countries the number of older people has overtaken the child population. With this growth of an ageing population, life expectancy is increasing. Octogenarians (80–89) number 314 million and are set to increase fivefold by 2050, and nonagenarians (90–99) are set to increase 8 times to 1 billion. Coupled with declines in world fertility rates, the world will be composed of an older population in 40 years time. But, on the other hand, the world is getting wealthier; those in severe poverty fell in the last five years from 29% to 23%. The net effect will be increased expenditure on healthcare and consumer living, and people working longer. The 'grey customers' effect will be considerable, with organizations having to cater for their every need and whim. One remarkable fact is that the 'silver-haired surfers' are rapidly emerging as the largest demographic using the internet. In the UK, one in five of internet users is over 55 years of age. It is the largest group of internet users in the country, with women in that age group the biggest users of all (over 40 hours per month). They are surfing, chatrooming and U-tubing far in excess of any other age group. This has meant that advertisers have had to review their communications to the 'silver haired' rather rapidly. The consumer is now truly 'sovereign' and dictating needs to the producer.

Coupled with these changing demographics is the drift from 'rural' to 'urban' dwelling as more and more people seek better incomes, living conditions, salaries, and education. By 2010 it is estimated by the UN Statistics Division that 50% of people will be living in urban areas. By 2015, it is estimated (again by the UN Statistics Division) that the world's top five cities will be Tokyo with 26.4 million, Mumbai with 26.4 million, Lagos with 23.2 million, Dhaka with 21.1 million and Sao Paulo 20.4 million people (United Nations, 2008). The implications for global marketers of this 'urban drift' is that a rethink will have to be made on target markets, distribution (both physical and institutional), type and volumes of goods and services, communications, and research methods. Competition is likely to be more intense as more and more goods and services are concentrated into a smaller geographical area.

Approaches to the study of culture

There are many analytical approaches to the study of culture. Maslow's (1970) hierarchy of needs model hypothesized that people's needs can be arranged into a hierarchy of five levels, from the basic psychological needs to the highest order needs—self-esteem. Lee (1966) developed the concept of the self-reference criterion (SRC) and how this can get in the way of cultural empathy. Hall (1977) developed the concept of 'high'- and 'low'-context culture: low-context cultures place an emphasis on writing (e.g. the USA) while high-context cultures emphasize the verbal and contextual (e.g. China). Hofstede (1997, 2001) developed a cultural typology based on four dimensions: power distance, individualism, masculinity, and uncertainty avoidance. Hampden-Turner and Trompenaars (1998) take the cultural typology further. These approaches will be expanded in Chapter 4 where culture is linked to consumer behaviour. For a more detailed discussion on culture and some excellent comment of Hofstede's work, see Bakacsi et al. (2002).

The Technological Environment

Two of the principal drivers to global development have been the speed of communications and the reduction in the cost of technology. According to a World Bank report, *Global Economic Prospects 2008: Technology Diffusion in the Developing World* (World Bank,

2008), the convergence of communications and technology has accelerated the process, as has the universality of technology or, as Anderson Consulting called it, 'the ubiquity of technology'. The explosive growth and use of the internet has been at the heart of developments. In some less developed countries, such as Bangladesh, access to computers and the integrity of the system may not be as good as in other low-income economies. Table 2.4 shows the incredible penetration of internet users in the developed world (over 50% on average) and the fact that one in five of the world's population are now 'wired up'.

E-commerce is one of the revolutions of the technological era. Starting with electronic data interchange (EDI), where data was merely transferred between organizations, it has grown into electronic commerce and other interactive forms of business, including interactive television and new telephony mobile devices. Global marketers have now had to become cognizant with, and comfortable in using, new forms of marketing. Phrases like 'viral marketing', 'search engine marketing' and 'online database marketing' have become practical realities.

There has been a 150% increase in the use of the internet globally since 2000 (407 million users). Latin America, the Middle East, and Africa have shown the largest increases, and the USA and Canada less so. The latter is accounted for by a number of Americans no longer using the web. The continued, rapid upward rise of the internet is giving global marketers more opportunity for widening their communications, research, and distribution facilities.

We now have virtual shopping malls. Amazon.com (www.amazon.com) is the classic example of online marketing, but superstores are rapidly entering the field. It is estimated that almost £10 billion of goods and services were bought online for Christmas 2007 in the UK. Some 4 million people shopped online on Christmas Day alone, generating £84 million. The boom was mainly due to the fact that high street giants such as Marks and Spencer, Comet, and Dixons launched their sales online on that day. In fact during 2007, UK consumers spent £46.6 billion on internet shopping, a 54% increase over the previous year (Interactive Media in the Retail Group, 2008, see www.imrg.org). That equates to 15p in every £1 spent on retailing in the UK. According to IMRG boss, James Roper, 'the internet has now become the dynamo of retail—it is where all the growth is now' (*Daily Mail*, 18 January 2008). Yet it is in business-to-business (e-business/marketing) services, particularly financial services, that online activity has really come of age (e.g. General Electric purchases most of their components online). One of the most successful sites is e-Bay. com. Founded by a Frenchman in the mid-1990s, it is now an industry worth £30 billion. The site receives 121,500 hits per minute, 175 million searches and 10 million bids per day. There are, on average, 21 million items on sale with 3 million new ones added every day. In 2006, 700,000 US citizens gave up their day jobs to become e-Bay traders.

Table 2.4 Internet usage statistics (estimated)

Regions	Population (2007)	Population (%of world)	Internet usage (latest data)	Population (penetration) %
Africa	941,249,000	14.2	44,234,000	4.7
Asia	3,733,783,000	56.5	461,703,000	12.4
Europe	801,820,000	12.1	343,787,000	42.9
Middle East	192,755,000	2.7	33,510,000	17.4
North America	334,659,000	5.1	237,168,000	70.9
Latin America/Caribbean	569,133,000	8.6	122,384,000	21.5
Oceania/Australia	33,568,225	0.5	19,243,000	57.3
World total	6,606,970,000	100	1,262,032,000	19.1

Source: Based on www.Internetworldstats.com/stats.htm (accessed on 17/01/2008).

However, the late 1990s and the 2000s saw hundreds of dot com companies fold as the e-future failed to deliver on its promise. The demise of Boo.com, the UK online retailer, was a classic example of this.

In addition, questions still remain over security of monetary transactions on the internet, especially in developing countries. The aforementioned e-Bay is employing hundreds of people to help prevent fraud. For a discussion on the effects of e-crime on e-commerce and e-business, see Philippsohn (2003). Invasions of privacy, unsolicited e-mail, piracy, and/or illegal download-loading can be a problem. Napster, the online music company, had problems with the music industry when it put downloadable music on the web, thus depriving record companies and, by extension, artists of millions in lost revenues. Eventually it was forced off the web by a court action but is now back (The Digital Impact). Vivendi Universal (www. vivendiuniversal. com), on the other hand, was a legal version of Napster and is very profitable.

The Computer Misuse Act 1990 provides, among other penalties, for imprisonment of up to six months for using the web for illegal purposes. The Reed Elsevier Information Security Breaches Survey (ISBS, 2001) and the Computer Security Institute survey (2001) give facts and figures of security breaches, the former showing internal and external unauthorized access, theft, and viruses as the main security breaches. There is some evidence that consumers are coming offline, some 25 million in the USA in 2002. It is estimated that by 2008, despite all the hype, internet trading will only account for 5% of world trade.

New technologies are changing strategic marketing thinking. The day of the truly 'sovereign' consumer is rapidly arriving. Organizations are faced with the need to secure a dominant market position yet start-up costs can be vast. Companies are forming joint ventures to get started and seeking synergies, some of which have been more successful than others. The merger of TimeWarner and AOL (www.timewarner.com), now de-merged, is an example. AOL alone spent US$500 million in advertising and start-up costs before it reached its position of dominance. But the need constantly to innovate is paramount.

THE DIGITAL IMPACT Music and the 'grey consumer'

The internet has 'infected' our culture and affected it ways never dreamed of, both positively and negatively. Two examples of its positive effect include 'music' and the 'grey consumer':

First there was the iPod (www.apple.com/ipod), Apple's digital music store no bigger than a Walkman, but capable of storing hundreds of tunes digitally. Then, in mid-June 2004, the same company launched the iTunes online music store in the UK. A week after launch its sales rivalled those of CDs, more than 450,000 songs were sold online compared to 500,000 CD sales. The success is dwarfed by the USA, where 85 million songs have been downloaded from iTunes on to PCs, iPods, and CDs. Napster (www.napster.com), once banned from the internet for pioneering online music, has now made a legitimate comeback in a similar guise to Apple. The phenomenon could lead to the demise of the CD, which, in its time, caused the demise of the tape cassette and vinyl record.

One remarkable fact emerging in the UK is the phenomenon of the 'silver-haired surfers'. They are the largest demographic users of the internet. In 2007, one on five of the UK population using the internet were over 55 years old. They are surfing, chatrooming and U-tubing in excess of any other user, forcing the communications industry to rapidly review its media effectiveness in reaching this group.

Despite the high cost of start-up, the internet is an ideal medium for small businesses and basic websites need not be that costly to construct.

The implications of changing electronic communications and technological developments on global marketing, especially the communications industry, are enormous. These are summarized in Table 2.5. The key is to visit exhibitions, take the relevant trade press, and alert sales staff. Also, the internet has spawned the development of new ways of marketing, in particular, permission marketing. Consumers are invited, maybe via more traditional communications media, to send their e-mail address to obtain information. That triggers a chain reaction of communication until the recipient requests a halt. As the information is only given to the consumer on request, then 'permission' has been granted. This is less intrusive than unsolicited e-mail and more effective. Team Domino (www.teamdomino.com) in the UK, with their 'Tempus' e-mail-based database system, is typical of a permission marketing organization.

The internet is having a profound effect on the global communications industry (advertising, public relations, personal selling, and so on). The paradigm of 'talking' to selected consumers via a medium of company choice is a rapidly disappearing concept. Consumers are now, via the internet, reversing the process, and they are choosing how and when they will talk to companies, not the other way round. Blogging and social networking websites such as Facebook are powerful ways in which consumers can influence the choice of products and services of other consumers by posting testimonials and comments which can rapidly escalate into a powerful 'purchase/non-purchase force'. Companies will ignore this phenomenon at their peril.

The early years of the twenty-first century revealed another potentially huge breakthrough in technology which could affect global marketing, especially in product development.

Table 2.5 The global challenges of changing electronic communications technology

Challenge	Response
The speed of change	Shorter planning cycles, more effective planning processes, faster product innovation and marketing
Technology and communications convergence (ICT)	More market entry possibilities, new ways to communicate with the market and distribute goods and services
The internet and interactive media	E-commerce and e-business ventures, interactive media, changing the ethos of the business and planning, organizing and implementing the new technology. Changes to the marketing mix
Market and organizational structure	Ability to come to terms with, and respond to, electronic markets, virtual markets, blurring of organizational boundaries, virtual organizations, outsourcing, flatter organizational hierarchies, symbiotic alliances with external partners
High start-up and innovation costs	Partnering and alliances
Rules of competition	Be in 'first', form alliances, innovate to defend market position
Disintermediation	Either 'go with the flow' or find new ways to compete
High risk of failure	Do 'homework' well. Devise a marketing strategy then an electronic strategy. Have a long-term horizon
Monetary transaction security, piracy	Ensure 'electronic key' and appropriate legalities are in place
Possible transaction breakdown	Ensure e-marketing strategy is in place, including fulfilment requirements

WHOSE RESPONSIBILITY IS IT? **Ethics and the internet**

While the internet has been a technological marvel, it has also been a source of abuse by unscrupulous people trying to make money in an illegal way. The early 2000s saw a rise in global-wide child pornography and internet 'grooming' chatrooms, leading to arrests, conviction, and, for example, placement on the UK's Sex Offenders' Register. Other internet crimes include selling internet addresses to organizations without the consent of the web address owners. Recently, one UK offender was convicted for selling a list of some 2 million addresses. Other abuses include stealing credit card numbers and SPAM. A global initiative on an international scale was launched by police in June 2004 to crack down on paedophiles. It is targeting 'grooming' sites. Police will monitor chatrooms and those caught will receive, on screen, a flashing icon to indicate police presence. Pay-per-view sites will also be targetted through cooperation with credit card companies. An initiative between global police forces was also announced following a summit in London of the International Virtual Global Taskforce, which aims to make the web a safer place for children.

Another example of the virtual world, with both positive and negative possibilities, sprung up in the UK in 2005–08—'Second Life'. This website allows visitors to live a virtual life of their choice, be it a multi-millionaire or a pensioner. In fact, visitors can now buy or sell property on the site or indulge in very sinister, morally questionable activities. This development raises significant ethical questions which need to be answered soon. These include who is allowed on to the site? Everyone? Does it encourage undesirable and sometimes immoral behaviour? Who is monitoring the site and policing it against questionable activity? What is and is not allowable on the site?

The breakthrough is in molecular rearrangement called *nano-technology*, which is basically the ability to rearrange molecules. The German car manufacturer Audi (www.audi.com) has appointed a project director to develop the technology and its application. For example, on the Audi TT sports model the inside driving mirror is capable of dimming in two seconds and is non-reflective so the driver never sees a double image. Audi are also working on the technology to allow the driver to change the colour of a car at the press of a button. The ability to 'chameleonize' and, as Audi are predicting, to make products almost invisible, opens up opportunities and challenges hitherto unseen. In 2004, Mercedes-Benz (www.mercedes-benz.com) launched an updated version of the C-class saloon which came, Mercedes claimed, with scratch resistant paint. This was based on nano-technology.

'Technology' (or the innovations associated with it) as an environmental factor has been recognized as one of the most important global marketing 'environmentals'. Technology can either be 'sustainable' or 'disruptive'. 'Disruptive technologies' (i.e. those technologies that can unexpectedly replace a current one, often with dramatic results) can devastate the best laid strategic plans. The new Boeing Dreamliner, with its use of carbon fibre technology (as opposed to more costly and heavier aluminium or titanium technology), is about to revolutionize the aircraft building industry. This brings 'strength with lightness' to the aircraft, aiding reductions in fuel usage and carbon emissions.

Information Week (www.informationweek.com, 17 January 2008) suggests that there are five disruptive technologies that Chief Information Officers (CIOs) and IT managers need to look out for: radio frequency identification, web services, server virtualization, graphics processing, and mobile security. *Washington Technology* (www.washingtontechnology. com, 17 January 2008) suggests that government systems integrators need to watch out

THE RELATIONSHIP PERSPECTIVE Radio frequency identification (RFID)

Radio frequency identification (RFID) is destined to takeover from bar coding as the new way to monitor and control product as it moves through the logistics chain. The technology involves a small radio wave-emitting chip which can be attached to products and can be 'active' (i.e. called into use at any time in the supply chain) or be 'passive' (i.e. used for a specific purpose). The technology offers manufacturers and suppliers many benefits, including the ability to check the movement of the product at any stage in the supply chain, who is using the product and when, the stock position, and when the product ceases to be in use. Its advantage over the bar code is that it can make available much more information than can be contained in a bar code and can enable a manufacturer or supplier to 'get closer to the customer'. It does raise a few ethical considerations, however, such as 'Big Brother watching you,' because the chip can be 'alive from cradle to grave' and it can track who is using the product throughout its lifetime. And yet, it looks as if the technology is here to stay. Wal-Mart (www.walmart.com) has embraced the technology, and is obliging suppliers to use it. This has already affected the American wine industry as giants like Julio Gallo, who supply Wal-Mart, have introduced it into the supply chain, affecting the supply process from producer to customer.

for open-source software and nano-technology. These last two technologies are potential 'dynamite', the former having a potentially huge effect on global giants such as Microsoft and the latter in a multitude of applications, including those which can be used in the car industry. One sure thing about 'technology' in a global world is that, as more and more organizations share and adopt similar technologies, (e.g. the design software for automotive engineering) the more the world becomes 'flatter'. This means that organizations will enjoy a less 'technologically competitive edge' than in previous years, making it more essential that they compete on other dimensions, such as the unique skills, quality of the workforce, and other means of reducing costs.

The Competitive Environment

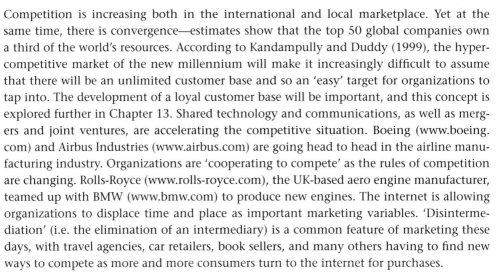

Competition is increasing both in the international and local marketplace. Yet at the same time, there is convergence—estimates show that the top 50 global companies own a third of the world's resources. According to Kandampully and Duddy (1999), the hyper-competitive market of the new millennium will make it increasingly difficult to assume that there will be an unlimited customer base and so an 'easy' target for organizations to tap into. The development of a loyal customer base will be important, and this concept is explored further in Chapter 13. Shared technology and communications, as well as mergers and joint ventures, are accelerating the competitive situation. Boeing (www.boeing.com) and Airbus Industries (www.airbus.com) are going head to head in the airline manufacturing industry. Organizations are 'cooperating to compete' as the rules of competition are changing. Rolls-Royce (www.rolls-royce.com), the UK-based aero engine manufacturer, teamed up with BMW (www.bmw.com) to produce new engines. The internet is allowing organizations to displace time and place as important marketing variables. 'Disintermediation' (i.e. the elimination of an intermediary) is a common feature of marketing these days, with travel agencies, car retailers, book sellers, and many others having to find new ways to compete as more and more consumers turn to the internet for purchases.

More companies are using outsourcing and value chain analysis to source components from all over the world to gain competitive advantage. Toyota (www.toyota.com) and VW (www.vw.com) use components from France, Spain, South America, and a host of other countries in the manufacture of their automobiles. 'Like' and 'substitute' competition is on the increase as less developed nations begin to leverage their low-cost production base and access global technology. The need for a more high-tech and effective competitor intelligence system is driving many organizations to sophisticated database intelligence systems such as Oracle (www.oracle.com).

Porter (1985) suggests that in order to be an effective player, organizations must understand competitive patterns in their industry. Hence he developed his five-force model of competitive analysis. His five forces include:

- the threat of new entrants;
- the bargaining power of buyers;
- the threat of substitutes;
- the bargaining power of suppliers; and
- the intensity of rivalry.

In global marketing, Porter's model would suggest that organizations should balance these forces in a series of strategic moves or re-position the organization so that it is in the best position to defend itself against competitive forces.

An assessment of competitors should be through a series of steps. Kotler (2003) describes these steps as follows:

1. Identifying the organization's competitors.

2. Determining the competitors' objectives.

3. Identifying the competitors' strategies.

4. Assessing the competitors' strengths and weaknesses.

5. Estimating the competitors' reactions.

6. Selecting competitors to attack and avoid.

The key to understanding competitors is to obtain competitive intelligence. This can come from internal sources such as the sales force, suppliers, and distributors, or from external sources such as market research companies and published data (e.g. government statistics). All these sources have to be checked for reliability and validity. Smaller businesses may not be able to afford to set up a formal intelligence system so personnel, especially senior executives, should be aware of any sources they should access. The internet and search engines such as Google (www.google.com) are a useful starting point for accessing competitor's information. The internet, coupled with other external competitive information (newspapers, company newsletters, and other professional magazines such as *Fortune* magazine, www.fortune.com), can produce a large amount of competitive information.

The Currency Environment

The world currency environment is worth billions annually. The derivatives market alone is estimated at some US$88 billion per annum. Worldwide trading and foreign exchange dealing complicate the issue further. Foreign exchange fluctuations are unpredictable and can be far-reaching and catastrophic in effect. The financial meltdown in South East Asia, ruined many businesses in that region as currencies lost value and capital fled the markets. Such changes can be stimulated by a number of factors, most of which are out of the control of the international marketing organization.

Variations in exchange rates can easily escalate costs, erode profit margins, and make investments look vulnerable. In 2004, drinks giant Diageo (www.diageo.com) stated that currency fluctuations in Nigeria, Venezuela, and Korea would knock £200 million off profits over two years. However, currency increases can bring unexpected windfalls. Some regimes have pegged their economies to the US dollar to try to avoid rapid fluctuations; others, such as the EU, have created a common currency as a means of avoiding fluctuations. However, the Euro has its problems and it remains to be seen if the Euro succeeds in its aims.

In an increasingly globalized and interconnected world, dramatic events in one country can radically affect another. Such is the case in the 'currency' environment. In 2007, the US sub-prime market (mortgages based on short-term borrowings by the mortgage providers) went into crisis as confidence was lost in this form of borrowings. It is estimated that loses could be as much as £250 billion (American Federal Reserve Chairman, speech in 2008, www.federalre-serve.gov/newsevent/speech/2008speech.htm). The ripple effect reverberated to the UK, where immediately, £25 billion was wiped off the London Stock Exchange. Further, a building society in the UK, Northern Rock (www.northernrock.co.uk), which provided mortgages based on the same type of mechanism as its US counterparts, suffered an enormous run on withdrawals, as savers, worried by the US scenario, rushed to remove their funds. Northern Rock could not cope, resulting in the Bank of England (www.bankof England.co.uk) bailing it out to the tune of £25 billion in guaranteed loans of taxpayers money. The building society was the subject of two private bids by the management and Virgin (www.virgin.com), but in the end, the government decided that these bids were not fully in the interest of the taxpayer and so nationalized it. As a result of the continuing crisis of confidence in the US financial markets, the unthinkable happened in the USA. A major bank, Bear Stearns (www.bearstearns.com) had to ask its US equivalent of the Bank of England, the Federal Reserve (www.federalreserve.gov), to bail it out. It did, but almost immediately J.P. Morgan-Chase (www.jpmorgan.com) stepped in and took over Bear Stearns at a 'bargain' price. This was the beginning of the great global financial collapse of late 2008, pushing countries into recession and companies into bankruptcy.

Pressure Groups

Pressure groups have grown considerably since the days of the pioneering Ralph Nader in the 1960s. This has resulted in many organizations producing ethical statements about their operations and incorporating them into their mission and values statements. Fair trading is a universal notion and is based on an honourable attempt to give producers and manufacturers, many of whom are emergent world economies, a fair price for their labours. Oxfam (www.oxfam.com), the relief organization based in the UK, is an excellent example. It purchases products to sell in its retail outlets from a number of emergent suppliers and makes sure that a guaranteed percentage of the price is returned to them.

Pressure groups can be vociferous. Recent trends have been to boycott organizations, and even countries, which appear to be contravening human and customer rights or acting in an unethical manner. Oil companies such as Shell (www.shell.com) and Exxon (www.exxon.com) have been subjected to such action over their perceived unethical business practices in Nigeria and over environmental concerns, respectively, leading to an attempted consumer boycott in the latter case. This has led some organizations to embark on a public relations campaign or even to employ specific staff to handle their corporate social responsibilities. Also, shareholder pressure groups are increasingly making their voices heard in the boardroom, especially over the terminal bonuses and salaries paid to departing under-performing chief executives, e.g. Kingfisher (www.kingfisher.co.uk) and Glaxo Smith-Kline (www.gsk.com). The pressure groups are not to be ignored, as adverse publicity can be damaging and costly. Such a case, in 2008, led to a 'stand off' between Japan, the UK, and Australia. In late 2007, Japan decided to resume whaling of a depleted and threatened whale species, arguably for 'research' purposes. The Japanese whaling fleet was pursued by environmentalists into the Antarctic waters, where two environmentalists, one British and one Australian citizen, boarded a whale boat. The Japanese crew 'restrained'

Consumers and pressure groups such as Greenpeace (www.greenpeace.org) and Friends of the Earth (www.foe.org) want to see companies switch to cleaner energy. Many countries including China still depend heavily upon less clean energy sources such as coal.

the two men, threatening to put them through the courts for 'piracy', counting the deed as an 'act of terrorism'. The UK and Australian governments protested to the Japanese government and the crisis was resolved when the two men were released to an Australian vessel.

Consumers and pressure groups such as Greenpeace and Friends of the Earth want to see companies switch to cleaner and renewable energy sources. Many countries, including China, still depend heavily upon less clean energy sources such as burning coals. Often maligned, ex US Vice President, Al Gore's film of 2006 (*An Inconvenient Truth*) brought home the realities of global warming.

Most organizations take a positive approach to the environment, while the legislation against environmental pollution has become very strict. Anti-pollution laws, large fines, and environmental summits like the one in Kyoto, Japan, are all having the effect of focusing the corporate mind on social and ethical responsibilities.

MINI-CASE ILLUSTRATION Sony's Group Code of Conduct

Sony (www.sony.com) is one of many multinationals which has taken corporate social responsibility *seriously*. It established a Group Code of Conduct in May 2003. The Code is applicable to the Sony Corporation, companies that are 50% owned by Sony, and other companies as determined. It applies to all Sony Group directors, officers, and employees. The Code covers:

- General Standards—Compliance with laws, relationships with stakeholders, appreciating diversity, avoiding structural conflicts and communications, and concerns and alleged violations.
- Respect for Human Rights—Equal employment opportunities, no forced/child labour, sound labour and employment practices, and a safe work environment.

- Conducting Business with Integrity and Fairness—Product and service safety, environmental conservation, fair competition, advertising, public disclosure, intellectual property, confidential and proprietary information, fair procurement, gifts and entertainment, and recording and reporting of information.
- Ethical Personal Conduct—Insider trading, personal conflicts of interest, corporate assets and media relations, and public statements.

Source: Based on Sony's Code of Conduct (www.sony.com).

Chapter Summary

1. The global marketing environment is defined as those variables, largely out of the organization's control but which it must account for, within which it conducts its business globally. Assessing and planning for the global marketing environment is a complicated, risky but essential activity for global marketers because getting it wrong can be very costly.

2. The global environment is made up of the intermediate environment, including suppliers, distributors, partners, stakeholders, and customers, and the macro environment, comprising technology, the economic, legal, political, and socio-cultural environment, the competitive and currency environments, and pressure groups.

3. An assessment of the global environment is essential for every aspect of marketing, from evaluating market opportunities to marketing planning, implementation, and control, especially the elements of the marketing mix, thus reducing global marketing risk.

4. The factors in the environment can be multifaceted, interdependent, independent, and may advance at different paces. Advancements in the technical field, especially in ICT and the political/legal front, are not to be underestimated. The key is to stay attuned to the key environmental signatures, assess their impact, and take appropriate action as quickly as possible.

5. Pressure groups have become increasingly influential in the global political environment as climate change and ethics are widely regarded by the international media and consumers as important global social issues. Multinational corporations are expected to assume greater social responsibility towards the resolution of those issues.

 END-OF-CHAPTER CASE STUDY Scenario planning in a rapidly changing global marketing environment

Three events took place between 2001 and 2003 which changed the world. One was the attack on the World Trade Center in 2001, the second was the war waged on Iraq by coalition forces in March/April 2003, and the third was the outbreak of severe acute respiratory disease (SARS) in China and Hong Kong at the same time. The shockwaves of these events went round the world.

Stunned by an attack in its own backyard, in 2001 the US government decided to make global terrorism a foreign affairs priority. With the UK and other forces, it attacked Afghanistan, a country it believed was supporting terrorism, and removed the Taliban government. In 2003, the USA and its allies, with overwhelming technological efficiency, attacked Iraq, as the UN stood by, powerless. Ostensibly, the USA was seeking to remove weapons of mass destruction, but it also wished to accomplish regime change, freeing the Iraqi people from the reign of Saddam Hussein. This paved the way for the USA to introduce their 'road map for peace' in the Middle East, an attempt to resolve the Israel/Palestine conflict. The action by the allies in Iraq split the EU. Some countries, such as France, Germany, and their ally Russia, were against the conflict whereas Spain and Italy supported the action. Fence-building took a long time, especially

as at the same time the EU had signed a treaty of accession to enlarge the Community by ten members.

The SARS epidemic started in southern China and rapidly spread to Hong Kong, Canada, and other parts of the world as travellers infected by the virus carried it worldwide. The removal of the Mayor of Beijing and the Health Minister were the result of an initial cover-up by the Chinese.

The three events had a significant and long-running effect on global marketing and trade. In the wake of 11 September, air travel and tourism fell dramatically. Passenger travel from Europe to the USA dropped by 30%. This resulted in the 'snowball' effect. World airlines faced severe passenger downturns, resulting in 30,000 layoffs in the industry. Some 1,000 aircraft were taken out of service. Some airlines did not survive, including Swissair. Suppliers to the airline industry suffered a downturn as global demand for new aircraft declined. Rolls-Royce had to plan for a reduction in the workforce of some 5,000 people involved in aero-engine manufacture.

The fallout did not stop there. The tourism industry was equally hard hit as the effects of a reduction in global travel began to bite. It was estimated that in the UK alone, up to the beginning of 2002, travel revenues fell by 12%. Up to 2,000 hotels and restaurants were affected, and a number of West End theatres closed. In 2001, 16 tour operators and 20 travel agents went bankrupt. The falling number of tourists added to the UK's growing balance of payments gap, standing at £12 billion compared to £9.3 billion over the same period in 2000. Curiously, as the main air carriers struggled, the cut-price airlines, such as UK-based easyJet and Ireland-based Ryanair, serving mainly European destinations, experienced a boom in travel as holiday-makers and businessmen alike switched to them.

As the airlines and the travel industry saw signs of recovery in late 2002, the Iraq conflict began, sending the same shock waves through the travel and tourism industries and their suppliers. Carriers like American Airlines and US Airlines experienced huge financial losses, the former opting for administration to avoid bankruptcy. The outbreak of the SARS virus had the same effect. With the World Health Organization declaring Beijing, Hong Kong, and Toronto as unsafe places to which to travel, airline passenger numbers fell again. Businesses and tourists shunned air travel, especially as it was revealed that air travel was responsible for spreading the virus. Cathy Pacific, the Hong Kong-based airline, saw its revenues fall by some 20% and the company made contingencies for total closure if the trend continued. Chinese restaurants faced ruin in Chinatown, Toronto, and even Chinese residents were shunned by fellow Toronto residents as possible sources of the disease. The

International Labour Organization (ILO) estimates that the threat of terrorism and the SARS outbreak have cost the tourism industry 11 million jobs worldwide (ILO, www.ilo.org, accessed May 2003).

But tourism and the airline industry were not the only victims. Before these events, in the case of the Iraq conflict, millions of dollars were wiped off the world's stock market values. Wall Street and London saw the value of stocks and shares hit their lowest in 2002–03, and remain at a sustained low. Incomes and profits were affected in many organizations—not just air carriers, but also insurance companies, which faced massive compensation claims. The effects were not purely economic and financial. Political relations between nations changed. The EU was split over the war in Iraq and the USA was in no mood to aid those countries or firms which opposed the allies. But countries like France and Russia had invested heavily in the Iraqi oil industry and were owed millions of dollars. Relations between France and Washington reached an all-time low.

A climate of suspicion reigned in the Middle East. Many countries, including Syria, were warned by the USA not to harbour fleeing Iraqi leaders, and were left wondering who might be next to receive the treatment. Collateral nations were hauled into the conflicts, e.g. Pakistan and Turkey, experiencing upheaval at home as political factions took differing views. Even at grassroots level, many countries experienced a racial tension as 'backlash' racism crept into societies with citizens whose ethnic origins lay in China, Iraq, and Afghanistan. Even in liberated Afghanistan and Iraq, not every citizen saw the allies as liberators. The world also witnessed some of the largest anti-war demonstrations ever seen. These nearly resulted in a split in the ruling UK Labour Party and a number of cabinet ministers resigned over the issue. The world in 2003 was not a stable place in which to plan global marketing operations.

Case discussion questions

1 Quoting examples, identify the factors of the global intermediate and macro marketing environment in this case.

2 How should either the airline industry or the tourism industry plan their global marketing operations for 2004–05, given the global scenario in 2003?

END-OF-CHAPTER EXERCISES

1 What is the definition of the marketing environment? What are the factors within it and why is a study of them important for global marketing planning?

2 How do global marketers capture, evaluate the importance of, and effect a response to changes in the global marketing environment?

3 What are the pitfalls of misjudging the elements of 'culture'? How can these be avoided?

DISCUSSION AND EXAMINATION QUESTIONS

1 Discuss the importance of the global marketing environment to a global marketing organization.

2 Culture is one of the most important global environmental factors. How can global marketers capture and account for the nuances of culture in planning their marketing operations?

3 How can astute handling of the marketing environmental factors give a global marketer a competitive advantage?

4 What are the advantages and disadvantages of the growing power of economic blocs (e.g. the EU and nations like the USA) in today's global marketing landscape?

5 How can developments in technology give a service supplier a competitive edge in a global context?

FURTHER READING

Doole, I. and Lowe, R. (2008) *International Marketing Strategy: Analysis, Development and Implementation*, 5th edn., London: Thomson Learning, Chapters 2 and 3.

Hollensen, S. (2007), *Global Marketing*, 4th edn., Harlow: FT/Prentice Hall, Chapters 4, 6 and 7.

Jeannet, J. P. and Hussey, H. D. (2004), *Global Marketing Strategies*, 6th edn., Boston, MA: Houghton Mifflin, Chapter 2.

REFERENCES

Bakacsi, G., Sándor, T., András, K., and Viktor, I. (2002), 'Eastern European cluster: tradition and transition', *Journal of World Business*, 37, 69–80.

CIA (2004), *Factbook*, http://www.cia.gov/library/publications/the-world-factbook/index.html (accessed on 17/01/2008).

Computer Security Institute (2001), *CSI Computer Crime and Security Survey 2001*, Computer Security Institute (www.gocsi.com).

Doole, I. and Lowe, R. (2004), *International Marketing Strategy: Analysis, Development and Implementation*, 4th edn., London: Thomson Learning.

Ellis, V. (2002), 'Regaining Stability and Growth in Asia', in Richter, F.-J. and Mar, P. C. M. (eds.), *Recreating Asia: Visions for a New Century*, Singapore: J. Wiley and Sons (Asia).

Gore, A. (2006), *An Inconvenient Truth*, Los Angeles: Paramount Home Entertainment.

Hall, E. T. (1977), *Beyond Culture*, New York: Anchor Books.

Hampden-Turner, C. and Trompennaars, A. (1998), *Riding the Waves of Culture: Understanding Diversity in Global Business*, 2nd edn., New York: McGraw-Hill.

Hooley, G., Fahy, J., Cox, A., Beracs, J., Fonfara, K., and Snoj, B. (2000), 'Market orientation in the transition economies of Central Europe', *Journal of International Business Studies*, 31(1), 63–81.

Hofstede, G. (1997), *Cultures and Organizations: Software of the Mind*, New York: McGraw-Hill.

—— (2001), *Culture's Consequences: International Differences in Work-related Values*, 2nd edn., Thousand Oaks, CA: Sage.

IMF (2007), *World Economic Outlook*, April, Geneva: IMF.

Information Week (2008), www.informationweek.com/nes/showArticle.html?articleID=196800208 (accessed on 17/01/2008).

ISBS, (2001), *The Reed Elsevier, Information Security Breaches Survey 2001: Technical Report UK*, Axent: ISBS.

Kandampully, J. and Duddy, R. (1999), 'Relationship marketing: a concept beyond the primary relationship', *Marketing Intelligence and Planning*, 17(7), 315–23.

Kotler, P. (2003), *Marketing Management, 11th International Edition,* London: Pearson Education International.

Lee, J. (1966), 'Cultural analysis in overseas operations', *Harvard Business Review*, March–April, 106–14.

Maslow, A. H. (1970), *Motivation and Personality*, 2nd edn., New York: Harper & Row.

OECD (2002), *Economic Outlook of the OECD*, June. Paris: OECD.

OECD (2008), *Composite Leading Indices*, 11 January. Paris: OECD.

Philippsohn, S. (2003), 'What is Fraud and How to Track it Down', www.bettermanagement.com (accessed on 17/01/2008).

Pierer, H. V. (2002), 'Asia—A Region Oriented toward the Twenty-first Century', in Richter, F.-J. and Mar, P. C. M. (eds.), *Recreating Asia: Visions for a New Century*, Singapore: J. Wiley and Sons (Asia).

Porter, M. E. (1985), *The Competitive Advantage: Creating and Sustaining Superior Performance*, New York: Free Press.

Shi, G. (2002), 'Deepening Cooperation and Achieving Common Prosperity', in Richter, F.-J. and Mar, P. C. M. (eds.), *Recreating Asia: Visions for a New Century*, Singapore: J. Wiley and Sons (Asia).

United Nations (2008) Statistics Division, www.un.org (accessed on 17/01/2008).

Washington Technology (2008), www.washingtontechnology.com/print/17_20/19859-1. html?topic=cover-stories (accessed on 17/01/2008).

World Bank (2008), *Global Economic Prospects 2008. Technology Diffusion in the Developing World*, January, Washington, DC: World Bank.

World Trade Organization (2006), *International Trade Statistics*, Geneva: WTO.

online resource centre

Visit the companion website to this book for lots of interesting additional material, including self-assessment questions, internet exercises, and links for each chapter:

http://www.oxfordtextbooks.co.uk/orc/lee_carter2e/

CHAPTER THREE
Understanding Globalization

Chapter overview

Chapter Introduction — 71

What is Globalization? — 72
  An economic reality? — 72
  A political reality? — 75
  A technological reality? — 77
  A cultural reality? — 77

Opportunity or Threat? — 79
  The opportunities of globalization — 79
  The threats of globalization — 84

Global Migration — 89
  Migration and economic growth — 90
  Migration and humanitarian crises — 91

Environmental Sustainability — 92
  Climate change — 93
  Climate change and food security — 94
  Energy security — 94
  Assuming social responsibility towards
  sustainable development — 95

Chapter Summary — 97

Learning objectives

After studying this chapter, the reader will be able to:

- develop an understanding of globalization and how it is shaping the economic, political, technological, and cultural realities of the global business environment;

- consider the market opportunities and threats of globalization for organizations which seek to operate within the global marketplace;

- explain the social-economic impacts of migration on global economic growth;

- identify and review the impact of global business activities on the physical environment, and discuss how organizations can assume greater social responsibility towards sustainable development.

Management issues

The management issues that arise include:

- What are the important discourses of globalization and how are they shaping the global business environment?

- In what ways is globalization creating business opportunities and new challenges?

- What are the available approaches to further deepen our business involvement and operations in the global marketplace?

- How do the emergent global social, ethical and green issues affect our business? How should we address them?

Chapter Introduction

Although the term 'globalization' has become a cliché in daily usage, the concept is not new. The first wave of globalization took place between 1870 and 1914. This was triggered by a combination of falling costs in transportation and a reduction in trade barriers, which opened up the possibility for a productive use of land and the flow of goods, capital, and people. According to World Bank estimates, export relative to world income at that time nearly doubled to about 8%, while foreign capital more than tripled relative to income in the developing countries of Africa, Asia, and Latin America. There was a massive human migration—as many as 60 million people migrated from Europe to the so-called New World, e.g. America and Australia. The wave of migration from densely populated China and India to less densely populated Sri Lanka and South East Asia probably shared the same magnitude. The total migrants during the period were estimated as nearly 10% of the world's population.

While technology continued to reduce transport costs, this wave of globalization ground to a halt in 1914. Despite unprecedented growth in the economy and the reduction in poverty, the impact of globalization on inequality within countries deepened due to incompetent economic policies, unemployment, and social instability. Between 1914 and 1945, governments were driven to protectionism and pursued inward-looking economic and nationalist policies. Governments mistakenly thought that they could protect their citizens from an economic downturn abroad by raising tariffs and restricting imports. In fact, this worsened the global depression and led to sharply reduced trade, plunging output, and pervasive unemployment. This is a standing proof that globalization is not an irreversible process as global economic integration clearly took several steps backwards during this period.

The years from 1950 to 1980 were seen as the second wave of globalization, one that focused on integration among the industrial countries by restoring trade relations, economic growth, and stability after World War II. Europe, North America, and Japan erected a series of multilateral trade liberalizations under the auspices of the General Agreement on Tariffs and Trade (the predecessor of the WTO). Most developing countries were isolated from this and concentrated on exporting primary commodities and pursuing inward-oriented policies. The Organization of Economic Cooperation and Development (OECD, www.oecd.org) economies surged with unprecedented growth rates. Within most OECD countries there was a modest trend towards greater equality, aided by social welfare policies and programmes. Growth in developing countries also recovered but less strongly, so the gap between rich and poor countries widened and the number of poor people increased (World Bank, 2002).

The current wave of globalization began in the early 1980s and gained unparalleled momentum throughout the 1990s and the early twenty-first century. It has been driven in many cases by significant technological advances in computing, communications, and transportation, and perhaps also the internationalization of business corporations in search for new customers, cheaper resources, and skilled labour. Many see this wave as the *golden era* for developing countries, which for the first time have been able to harness the potential of their labour and land to break into global markets for manufactured goods and services. Their share of world export in manufactured goods rose from less than 25% in 1980 to over 80% in 1998. With reference to Dollar and Kraay's (2001) data, within many developing countries (including China, India, Brazil, Thailand, and Indonesia), the per capita growth rate throughout the 1990s substantially exceeded that of the rich countries. While references to the previous waves of globalization are made throughout this chapter, it is the current wave and its implications for the global business environment that we focus on.

We first explore the meanings of globalization and its associations and, in doing so, the term 'globalization' is used in a broader and more general context to incorporate the cultural, political, and technological as well as the economic discourses. We then consider the market opportunities and threats of globalization and weigh up the benefits and challenges for organizations. Here we restrict our usage of the term 'globalization' to a more narrow context of global business and trade. Finally, we consider the social, ethical and green issues and their impact on the global market environment.

What is Globalization?

Globalization is a complex phenomenon that affects many aspects of our lives. There is no straightforward or accepted consensus as to what exactly the term represents. Some view it as an inevitable and irreversible process fundamental to the future of world economic development—that is, the growing integration of national economies around the world which is the key to rapid economic growth and poverty reduction in developed and developing countries. Some regard globalization as the outcome of development in new technologies, especially in the areas of communication and transportation. These technologies enable people to 'rapidly traverse the globe physically, transmit information almost instantaneously, and send goods around the world in hours or days. The speed of transmission and the mobility of capital mean that both space and time seem to have been truncated, or to have collapsed entirely' (Schirato and Webb, 2003: 46). For others, the term 'globalization' is treated with distrust and fear, believing that it exacerbates poverty and inequality between rich and poor (both between and within countries), cultural convergence and the disappearance of many indigenous cultures, the spread of deadly diseases (e.g. AIDS, tuberculosis) and global terrorism (e.g. the Bali bombing), and global warming and environmental degradation.

There is no single definition that could accommodate the disagreements over its meanings and applications, but it is perhaps possible to understand it by examining some of the discourses which have been grouped under the term. Those we will examine are the economic, political, technological, and cultural changes that associate with globalization, as illustrated in Fig. 3.1.

An economic reality?

There seems to be plenty of evidence of the existence of globalization, especially in the so-called 'global marketplace'. The global presence of giant multinational corporations such as Coca-Cola, Sony, McDonald's, Nike, Starbucks Coffee (see mini-case illustration) is perhaps strong evidence that verifies its existence, at least from an economic perspective. From this viewpoint, globalization is perceived as:

> the decline in transaction costs or barriers to doing business or otherwise interacting with people of other nations around the world. Its effect is to enhance the integration of markets for goods, services, technology, ideas, capital, and labour, reducing the differences in prices for those products and factors across space. (Anderson, 2000: 9–10)

Fig. 3.1 The discourses of globalization

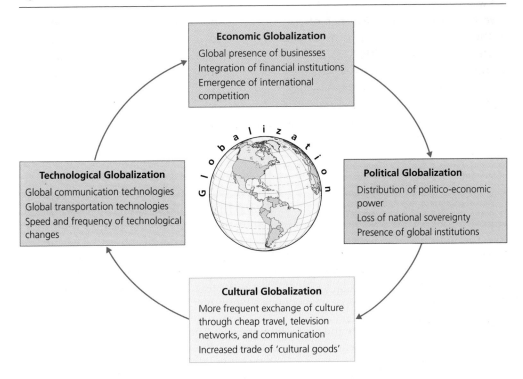

The extent of the acceleration in economic globalization is evident in the statistics of global trade. For instance, export volume in merchandise has grown faster than output for all periods except between the two world wars. More than one-fifth of global output is now destined for export, which is double the proportion in the 1950s. In addition, annual outflows of foreign direct investment (FDI) grew more than sixfold between 1983 and 1990 and have continued to grow more than twice as fast as merchandise trade in the 1990s. In terms of cross-border mergers and acquisitions, the annual value has trebled and amounted to over US$300 billion by the end of the twentieth century (Anderson, 2000).

MINI-CASE ILLUSTRATION **The global success of Starbucks**

With over 7,500 retail outlets worldwide, Starbucks Coffee (www.starbucks.com) must be one of the most familiar sights in the high streets of international cities. When Starbucks originally opened in 1971 in Seattle's Pike Market Place, it was a coffee house with little or no difference from any other local coffee houses. This changed in 1982 when Howard Schultz, then director of retail operations and marketing, fell in love with Italian coffee and introduced it at Starbucks. The first café latte was served in 1984.

The secret behind Starbucks' success lies in its recognition that going global is not about setting up indistinguishable stores which are 'identical copies', but making adjustments to cater for the local customer tastes and lifestyles. The idea is to make every outlet blend into the local community just like a local store. Some elements are (inevitably) standard but a lot of efforts are put into localizing the menu and service needs. In China, for instance, coffee-flavoured *mooncakes* (a cake normally eaten during the Mooncake Festival) and Green Tea Frappuccino cater for the Chinese palate. In Malaysia, the local Starbucks has a Raspberry Cream Frappuccino made to appear like an *air bandung* (a sweet syrup drink) smoothie. Nine of its outlets in this country are fitted with Wi-Fi (wireless high-speed internet access) connections, allowing customers to go about their business. Students are known to stay and study all day, and even all night, at outlets with 24-hour opening.

Sources: www.theedgedaily.com; www.starbucks.com.

The evidence of economic globalization is evident in almost all corners of the globe. Transnational companies make their presence felt by using eye-catching advertisements in the world's major cities.

The present discourse of globalization seems to be dominated by a highly general idealization of capitalism and market fundamentalism. Globalization, accordingly, is a conceptualization of the international political economy, which suggests that all economic activity, whether local, regional, or national, must be conducted within a perspective and attitude that is constantly global in its scope. In this view, since 'everything is global these days', decision-making by businesses or governments cannot be effective without consciously incorporating global-level thinking and concerns. In the globalization perspective of international political and economic reality, it suggests that the multinational organization is the central actor with an 'objective agenda' of creating wealth through the transfer of technology, market making, and global managerialism. Government should generally be restricted to a supporting, supplementary and secondary role to the needs of the organization (Spich, 1995). Spich (1995: 8) summarized this:

> The world is changing rapidly and really getting smaller. The internationalization of domestic economies, the interdependence of issues and nations, the opportunity to think and act globally have forced us all to note that a new political-economic regime is at hand. Technology has created opportunities for the movement of information, goods, services and techniques as never before. To fight these changes is folly and madness. Barriers to exchange, trade and investment must be lowered so that all may benefit from increased access to markets and resources. Even though this will create some dislocations and costs, in the end the ever-rising tide of prosperity will make everyone better off!
>
> The way to get the most out of this new world context is to foster free-market institutions and practices while simultaneously limiting government to the important role of protecting and guaranteeing free-market activity. In this new world the dynamics of competition, through the agency of the corporate form of enterprise, will be the objective determinant of rank and success. Only by creating lean, responsive corporate 'fighting machines' will the nest of firms be able to survive and thrive. The new competition suggests that nations, via their strong economies, will be at war in the battlefields of the marketplace. It is in their interests to create strong business sectors via responsible monetary and fiscal policies, limited regulation and maximization of private incentives to grow beyond national borders. There will be winners and losers in the economic war. The winner will be the *globalizers*. The rest will be *localizers* lost in their limited concerns for the here and now. The 'prize' economic development, high standards of living and freedom from want, goes to those who take the chance of letting competition be the game, who open their doors to foreign goods and investment and who think globally now!

For the anti-globalization protestors in Seattle, Melbourne, and Genoa (see 'the threats of globalization' section below for a detailed discussion on anti-globalization sentiment), it is these narrowly defined economic aspects of globalization that are the subject of controversy. To these protestors, there is little doubt that it is the ruthless pursuit of Western capitalism that is 'responsible for most of the misfortunes of the world, from environmental degradation and vandalism, to the worldwide exploitation of workers. For them, it is a reality which has changed the world, with negative consequences for their lives' (Schirato and Webb, 2003: 9).

In short, Western capitalism is at the heart of the economic discourse of globalization, whether we take the perspectives of the capitalist or the anti-globalization protestors. In the eyes of the capitalist, it is 'the closer integration of the countries and peoples of the world which has been brought about by the enormous reduction of costs of transportation and communication, and the breaking down of artificial barriers to the flows of goods, services, capital, knowledge, and (to a lesser extent) people across borders' (Stiglitz, 2002: 9). It is accompanied by three main institutions that govern (and dominate) the development of globalization: the International Monetary Fund (IMF, www.imf.org), the World Bank (www.worldbank.org), and the World Trade Organization (WTO, www.wto.org). The anti-globalization protestors may regard globalization 'in terms of the power and influence of global capitalism, embodied in the practices of transnational corporations, the World Bank, and the IMF; or characterize it as the various political, economic and cultural ways in which American hegemony has imposed itself upon the world; or point to the ways in which the International Monetary Fund (IMF) and the World Bank, operating as *de facto* arms of American free-trade policies, have effectively undermined the sovereignty of developing nations' (Schirato and Webb, 2003: 9). Understanding the current workings (and controversy) of economic globalization is particularly important for global marketers as any changes in this discourse—either brought about by the international institutions or the anti-globalization protestors, or both—can effect new marketing challenges in the global business environment.

A political reality?

Globalization is not just an economic phenomenon. It is also a powerful force that radically changes the political reality of the world in ways that are unprecedented. We can analyse the political changes that associate with globalization at two levels: (1) the international distribution of power between developing and developed countries; and (2) the domestic power of nation states.

In terms of the international distribution of power, economic power is shifting away from the developed countries for the first time towards the developing countries, i.e. countries that strongly increased their participation in global trade and investment, including Brazil, China, Malaysia, Hungary, India, and Mexico. According to World Bank development statistics, some 24 developing countries—with approximately 3 billion people—have doubled their ratio of trade to income over the past two decades. The economies of these countries are growing more rapidly (average of 5%) than those of the OECD economies (average of 2%) during the 1990s. With their enormous population and economic potentials, countries such as China and India are set to become major economic powers which will enable them to flex their political muscles with greater force. The emergence of these new economic powerhouses has implications on the future of the global political architecture.

At the level of domestic politics, globalization changes the power relations between government, business, and civil society. One of the main transformations is that of the domestic power of nation states. The increasing significance of a global economy seems to restrict the choices open to a government, hence limiting its influence on national policies

China is quickly becoming one of the world's largest economies due to its rapid and continuous economic growth over the past 20 years.

and the daily lives of its citizens. The argument, according to Schirato and Webb (2003), is that the throng of trans- and multinational corporations, international bodies of jurisdiction and management, and the congeries of regional and international blocs means that the power to determine national policies is increasingly being denied to the governments of nation states, which will perhaps eventually lose their reason-to-be and wither away. As a result, most governments are less free to intervene in the business cycle of their economies through fiscal and monetary policies, e.g. to prevent the economy from overheating.

We see how the sovereignty of a nation state can give way to the demand of an international institution in the immediate aftermath of the Asian financial crisis in the late 1990s. Threatened with the possibility of the resulting withdrawal of international capital, the governments of South Korea, Thailand, and Indonesia bowed to the demand of the IMF to take drastic contractionary actions to restrict spending and raise interest rates, which have the undesirable effects of inhibiting economic growth and prolonging the crisis. The governments of these nation states felt powerless to resist despite the fact that they knew what they needed to do to prevent the crisis worsening and to minimize damage (Stiglitz, 2002). The Malaysian government was brave enough to risk the wrath of the IMF and openly questioned the logic of its policies. During economic downturns when consumer demand is sluggish, taking contractionary (rather than expansionary) fiscal policies was widely perceived to be inappropriate because it could lead to falling consumer demand and hence stifle economic growth. Malaysia subsequently rejected the IMF's financial bailout but 'paid the political price' in widespread criticism from the (mainly Western) international community.

The decline of state sovereignty fits well with the general idealization of the contemporary perspective of globalization discussed above, which favours a limiting role for national government to that of supporting the needs of a free market economy. Since multinational corporations (MNCs) are the main actors in a free market economy, the locus of sovereignty is conceivably being shifted from the nation states into the hands of these MNCs (Brinkman and Brinkman, 2002). The capital of MNCs can now flow into a country and create thousands of jobs just as easily as it flows out of it and jobs are taken away. As a result, governments find themselves competing against each other by providing a 'favourable investment climate' in the form of special tax concessions and lax pollution laws at the expense of the local people and the environment. The sovereignty of nation states is frequently compromised to keep the MNCs happy.

The advent of new communication technologies (especially those related to telecommunications, computing, and the internet) also play a role in the erosion of nation states' sovereignty. In the past, exchange of information, ideas, research, sound, and images across borders were usually achieved in the forms of objects—books, letters, and films. A government could exercise control and censorship over the content by restricting the movement of these objects within its national border (Brinkman and Brinkman, 2002). Technological breakthroughs in communication have robbed the government of this power by enabling the seamless flow of data and images across borders making them difficult to police and censor.

The current wave of globalization is accompanied by profound changes in the global political architecture. Globalization has empowered the governments of some developing countries (e.g. China and India) at the expense of the governments of developed countries. In other respects, globalization weakens the power of the nation states—that is, the ability of the government to control events around them and determine domestic policies.

A technological reality?

The development of new technologies has been responsible for many changes, especially in the nineteenth and twentieth centuries. Indeed, all waves of globalization in modern history have been, in one way or another, fuelled by technological inventions or innovations in transport and communications. In the late nineteenth century, the advent of the steam engine, which created the railway and steamships, shortened the time required to travel long distance and dramatically lowered the cost of transportation, making it possible for the first time to transport goods and people with ease. The second technological revolution took place in the mid-twentieth century when the mass production of cars and telephones brought down the costs of technology to a level that most people (who lived in the Western world) could afford. It is therefore unsurprising that technology is one of the prominent elements associated with globalization.

The invention of digital technology is central to the third technological revolution and the current wave of globalization. Aided by the deregulation of telecommunications markets, the digital revolution has lowered long-distance communication costs, and especially the cost of rapidly accessing and processing knowledge, information, and ideas (Anderson, 2000). The technology is versatile and its applications broad, which include computers, the internet, mobile telephones, satellite technology, and video conferencing. It enables the circulation of data, sound, and/or images at greater speed across communication technologies and not just within them. It is also central to the networking potentialities because it is characterized by growing convergence and thus brings together different media (Schirato and Webb, 2003).

The speed and frequency of technological change are accelerating at a rate unseen in history—old technologies are being phased out and new technologies invented almost on a daily basis. As the world continues to globalize, the force of technology is 'reshaping the way we communicate with each other, the way we gets things done and the way we fit ourselves to time and space' (Castells, 2000: 1).

A cultural reality?

Globalization can be understood simply not just as a set of economic, political, and technological processes but an exchange of cultures, which involves interaction between people. Essentially, it is the 'real' people and the ways they live, work, and act that bear the effects of globalization on a daily basis.

Globalization has brought people of different cultures from all corners of the world closer together—thanks to the accelerating, although uneven, diffusion of radio, television, the internet, satellite, and digital technologies which have made instant communication possible across large parts of the world. The cost reduction in transportation, especially air travelling, has enabled more people (as agents of their cultures) to engage in cultural exchanges.

Although it is impossible to quantify the magnitude of cultural exchange between nations, the United Nations Educational, Scientific and Cultural Organization (UNESCO, www.unesco.org) suggests that an overview of world trade in cultural goods could perhaps provide an indication of patterns of production and consumption of culture, which are embedded in *cultural goods* and *services*. Music, books, crafts, films, and many other cultural goods and services move across international borders creating a complex tapestry of cultural trade flows. According to UNESCO statistics (2005), the global market value of industries with strong creative and cultural components is estimated at US$1.3 trillion with an annual growth rate of over 7%. Globally, these industries are estimated to account for more than 7% of the world's GDP (World Bank, 2003). These statistics may not report the true size of international cultural trade flow as these statistics only present trade which is quantifiable. It is extremely difficult to measure those cultural products whose special nature makes them endlessly available and reproducible at insignificant costs. For instance, a single master copy of a copyrighted work, e.g. a blockbuster movie valued at a few dollars, according to national export statistics, may be electronically transferred to another country where copies are reproduced under a licence and generate millions of dollars through sales.

Cultural products consist of both tangible goods and intangible services (see Fig. 3.2). The tangible cultural goods include all consumer goods which convey ideas, symbols, and ways of life, such as books, magazines, multimedia, software, recordings, films, videos, audiovisual programmes, crafts, and fashion design (Alonso Cano et al., 2000). Cultural services, as defined by UNESCO (2005), are those activities aimed at satisfying cultural interests or needs. They facilitate the production and distribution of tangible cultural goods. Examples of cultural service include the licensing of copyrighted audiovisual materials, the promotion of performing arts and cultural events, and the preservation of books, recordings, and artefacts in libraries and museums.

The growing international trade in cultural products ensures that people are becoming increasingly exposed to the values of other cultures. The question is whether the so-called 'global culture' increases in diversity as the diffusion of cultures accelerates, or reduces in diversity as dominant (Western) cultures displace local ones? The answer is inconclusive—we see evidence that globalization both increases and reduces the diversity of cultures.

On the one hand, there seems to be evidence that globalization leads to the homogenizing of culture due to the convergence of global media, whose ownership are increasingly concentrated in a small number of (Western) media conglomerates. For instance, the world's production of films is monopolized by a handful of film companies in Hollywood (e.g. Walt Disney, www.disney.com; Warner Bros, www.warnerbros.com) where they are produced and distributed. The production and broadcast of global media are, therefore, understandably highly Westernized and directly reflect (and promote) the so-called Western cultures. Both developing and developed countries see a danger of cultural homogenization and the subsequent loss of identity. The perception of the danger is real and strongly felt (World Bank, 2002). For instance, the French government subsidizes its film and culture industries for fear of increasing 'Americanization', especially among its young people. In an attempt to preserve its language and cultural traits from extinction, the devolved government of Wales now enforces domestic policies to ensure the continuity of its traditions.

Conversely, globalization increases social diversity as foreign cultures enter a society and coexist with the local culture. For example, in countries where there is a sizable population of multi-ethnic groups, e.g. the USA, where approximately 30% of its population are non-white, different cultures coexist and add to the diversity of (rather than being driven out by) the local culture. An example of what this implies is the variety of food available in all major international cities where Chinese takeaway, Indian curries, Italian pizzas, and Japanese sushi, among others, are enjoyed alongside the local cuisine. Far from facing the threat of extinction, 'the networking of the globe may regenerate traditional practices, languages and forms of cultural production' (Schirato and Webb, 2003: 157). Smith (1990: 175) argues that the new communication technologies 'make possible a denser, more intense interaction between members of communities who share common cultural characteristics, notably language which can re-energize ethnic communities and their nationalisms'. In other words, a culture can evolve or hybridize into another richer (and possibly more sophisticated) form by amalgamating elements from a number of foreign cultures. The evidence of this is overwhelming when we look to modern music, interior design, and arts in the society in which we live.

Globalization is producing a significant impact on the global cultural environment, whether we believe it enriches or displaces local cultures. There is no easy solution for this concern. Under the WTO exceptions for products with high cultural content, nation-state governments are permitted to devise strategies to preserve traditions and subsidize cultural products.

In summary, the interconnectedness of computers worldwide, the convergence of cultures and consumer tastes, the unparalleled growth in international trade of merchandise and services, and the proliferation of institutions concerned with or involved in global governance have meant that nation states, organizations, and individuals are becoming 'increasingly enmeshed in worldwide systems and networks of interaction, and relations and networks of power, so that distant occurrences and developments can come to have serious domestic impacts while local happenings can engender significant global repercussions' (Held and McGrew, 2000). The forces of globalization are very real and responsible for many changes that could impact upon the political, economic, social, and technological aspects of the global business environment, and the patterns of our lives as both citizens and consumers.

Opportunity or Threat?

Global marketing is about widening business horizons to encompass the world in the pursuit of new market opportunities by putting available resources to the best possible use in order to create values for customers and other stakeholders. It is globalization, with the help of global marketing, that gives companies such as Coca-Cola (www.coke.com), McDonald's (www.mcdonalds.com), Gap (www.gap.com), and Microsoft (www.microsoft.com) the phenomenal global success and recognition they enjoy today.

From a marketing perspective, globalization presents organizations with unlimited opportunities to grow and transform, not only to become larger but more competitive and efficient. In order to exploit these opportunities, organizations realize that they not only need to face the hidden risks and new challenges, but also adopt a new approach to ensure survival and compete successfully.

The opportunities of globalization

Market access

In a market economy, the creation of an efficient global market environment has to be 'embedded in a framework that enables its productive potential to flourish and to be used for socially and ecologically sustainable development' (Streeten, 2001: 9). The fact that globalization is proceeding rapidly is, to a great extent, the consequence of increased integration and interdependence of trade, capital, direct investment, technology, information, and labour across national borders. It implies the adoption of a common set of policies by all participating countries as if they were one economic entity.

The two major international initiatives responsible for globalization, and the subsequent widening of market access for all participating countries, are the General Agreement on Tariffs and Trade (GATT, www.gatt.org) and its successor, the World Trade Organization (WTO). GATT made significant achievements in the liberalization of trade

Table 3.1 Frequency of core non-tariff barriers of selected countries

(a) Developed countries

	1993	1996
Australia	0.7	0.7
Canada	8.3	7.3
European Union	22.1	13.0
Iceland	3.0	0.5
Japan	11.4	9.9
Mexico	2.0	14.1
New Zealand	0.4	0.8
Norway	5.9	2.6
Switzerland	3.6	0.2
Turkey	0.4	0.6
USA	23.0	16.7

(b) Developing countries

	1969–94	1995–98
Argentina	3.1	2.1
Brazil	16.5	21.6
Chilew	5.2	5.2
Colombia	55.2	10.3
Hong Kong, China	2.1	2.1
India	99	93.8
Indonesia	53.6	31.3
Korea, Rep. of	50.0	25.0
Malaysia	56.3	19.6
Morocco	58.3	13.4
Nigeria	14.4	11.5
Singapore	1.0	2.1
South Africa	36.5	8.3
Thailand	36.5	17.5
Uruguay	32.3	0.0

The definition of core non-tariff barriers used in Michalopoulos (1990) is similar to the one used in OECD (1997). The main difference is that Michalopoulos does not include anti-dumping measures and countervailing actions.

Source: www.worldbank.org/research/global

by means of reduction in tariffs on no less than 50,000 products, which was equivalent to two-thirds of the trade value of its participating members. By the time GATT was replaced by the WTO in 1995, tariffs had been reduced from an average of 40% in 1945 to about 5%.

The WTO also makes good progress in the reduction of non-tariff barriers (NTBs), which are notoriously difficult to define. Table 3.1 shows the pervasiveness of core NTBs in both the agricultural and industrial sectors for a sample of countries. The figures show a clear decline in the use of core NTBs in a majority of countries between the early 1990s and the years following the entry into force of the WTO Agreement (World Trade Organization, 2001).

Within Western Europe, the widening of market access has been especially progressive following the Treaty of Rome and the formation of the European Free Trade Area (EFTA). At the same time, many non-OECD countries began moving away from inward-looking to outward-oriented trade and investment policies. Many previously inaccessible markets, such as China, India, and the former Soviet Union countries, have now opened up their markets following political changes. The more countries open up and reform, the greater is the gain to other countries from doing likewise. The implications of trade liberalization for any organizations that operate in the global environment are significant. They expand the opportunities for consumers, organizations, and governments to access markets of a much wider range of goods and services, investment funds, and technologies. Small companies which have previously been unable to export because their access to foreign markets was restricted, or because the cost of overcoming red-tape or technical barriers was too high, can now market their products and services abroad. The enlargement of their markets means that they are able to produce more and benefit from economies of scale therefore making them more competitive.

On the other hand, trade liberalization also opens up the internal markets for foreign competition. High-cost and less-productive producers find themselves no longer able to compete. Nonetheless, the higher turnover of businesses is an important benefit in a market economy. Aw et al. (2000) find that within a five-year period in Taiwan, the replacement of low-productivity businesses with new, higher productivity entrants accounted for half or more of the technological advances in many industries. Globalization rewards businesses that are innovative and competitive, regardless of their size and country of origin. As global companies enter local markets, local companies are entering global ones. The resulting competition drives up product quality, widens the range of available goods and services, and keeps prices low.

Financial integration

The liberalization of trade, which promotes the movement of goods and services, needs to be facilitated by the movement of financial capital to enable the exchange or transaction to take place between individuals, organizations, or governments. The movement or flow of financial capital is central to the process of economic growth because it provides the means by which organizations make possible the investment into a variety of projects for financial returns wherever they may be located. These basic theoretical propositions have been put to work through two types of cross-border financial flow to the advantage of many organizations which seek to do business globally.

The first type of cross-border financial flow, so-called *portfolio capital*, consists of investments that are potentially short-term in nature, including loans between banks and investments in traded bonds and equities. According to the Bank for International Settlements in its September 2003 *Quarterly Review,* the global flow of foreign exchange has reached the incredible figure of over US$2 trillion per day, which exceeds some 60 times the level of world exports (BIS, 2003).

In contrast, *foreign direct investment* (FDI), the second type of financial flow, consists of long-term holdings of equity where the aim is to control or exercise influence over local firms. FDI has become increasingly linked to trade as it is no longer sufficient simply to ship products across borders to customers waiting in 'foreign lands'. Customer and business products often require local servicing operations, as well as research and development and marketing enterprises, if they are to be sold effectively in other countries. Moreover, financial and professional services typically can only be supplied by a presence in other countries in order to service the client 'on the ground' (Litan, 2000).

This process of integration began in the 1980s, when many emerging (and mature) markets began to liberalize their financial systems, opened their capital accounts, and implemented other market-oriented reforms. In general, the period from the mid-1980s to the mid-1990s was characterized by the removal of many government restrictions on financial market activities.

Overall, there has been a steady and significant volume of net private capital flows (i.e. bank loans, portfolio investment, and direct investment) into these emerging countries, amounting to an average of US$94 billion a year in 1995–96 (WTO). Although the current net private capital flows to emerging markets as a group remain far below the peak reached in the mid-1990s, they still amounted to US$44 billion in 2002. Flows to central and Eastern Europe have held up better than those to other regions, supported by the process of accession to the European Union (Litan, 2000). The inward flows of financial capital, especially in the form of FDI, made significant contributions to the phenomenal economic growth in Latin America and East Asia in the latter half of the twentieth century.

The reduction in communication and transportation costs

The reduction in communication and transportation costs is a major force for increasing the integration and interdependence between countries, thus fuelling globalization. In terms of transportation, the advent of commercial aircraft and the introduction of containerization have benefited the physical transportation of goods from one location to another—a process that was once labour-intensive, time-consuming, and expensive. Due to these developments, the average transportation cost per passenger mile has effectively dropped from US$0.68 in 1930 to US$0.11 in 1990 (see Table 3.2). This reduction has made it more economical to ship goods over long distances, thereby driving the globalization of business operations and production.

Costs of telephone communication and computers have also plummeted exponentially since 1960, which lowers the cost of coordinating and managing a global organization (see Table 3.3). Further, the increasing technological sophistication in communications and computing have brought about a more integrated global trading system, a global capital market, and more international transactions that formerly took place via national financial institutions are now being internalized within single organizations or corporate alliances. The increasing mobility of the productive assets of organizations enables them to minimize their corporate income tax exposure by strategically locating their headquarters and using transfer pricing in their intra-organization international trade (Anderson, 2000).

The decreasing cost and increasing sophistication in communication technologies have also revolutionized the ways in which organizations communicate and maintain relationships

Table 3.2 Transport costs, 1930–90

Year	Ocean transport Wheat, % of production costs 1920 = 100	Average air transportation Revenue per passenger mile (in 1990 US$)
1930	100	0.68
1950	38	0.30
1990	30	0.11

Source: Based on data sourced at Baldwin and Martin (1999); World Economic Outlook, www.imf.org, May 1999, Table 11. The full table is accessible via www.imf.org.

Table 3.3 Communication and computer costs, 1960–2000

Year	Cost of a 3-minute phone call from New York to London	Price of computers relative to GDP deflator (2000 = 1000)
1960	60.42	1,869,004
1980	6.32	27,938
2000	0.40	1,000

Sources: Based on data sourced at World Economic Outlook, www.imf.org, May 1997, Table 11, updated to 2000; US Commerce Department, Bureau of Economic Analysis. The full table is accessible via www.imf.org.

THE RELATIONSHIP PERSPECTIVE The merger of Sony and BMG in the music business

In June 2004, the EU gave the go ahead for the 50/50 merger between BMG (www.bmg.com) and Sony Music (www.sonymusic.com). The merger made Sony Music the world's second-largest music company after Vivendi's Universal Music (www.umusic.com), with combined revenue of approximately US$5 billion. The new company is to be named Sony BMG and will include a wide array of ownership and distribution of recording labels, such as Arista Records, Columbia Records, Epic Records, J Records, Jive Records, RCA Victor Records, RCA Records, Legacy Recordings, Sonic Wave America, and others.

Global music market share, 2007

Music label	Market share (%)
Universal	25.7
Sony BMG	21.2
Warner	13.8
EMI	12.8
Independents	26.5

The global music industry has faced a number of difficulties in recent years due to increasing competition from DVDs and other media, declining sales of CDs, and illegal downloading. Both Sony Music and BMG saw the merger as an appropriate and necessary response to current market conditions. It is estimated that the merged company has saved up to US$350 million a year in annual costs.

The initial proposition for the merger was fiercely resisted by the EU and the wider global music industry. After the merger, 80% of the global music market is in the hands of only four companies. According to some critics—including Apple Computers (www.apple.com), keen to protect its iTunes online music store—Sony's strong position in consumer electronics would give the combined entity too much power over the way the sale of online music evolves. While small labels will continue to exist, they become increasingly unable to grow without becoming part of one of the Big Four music giant corporations. This pattern looks set to continue into the future as the larger companies continue their strategy of acquisition, and potentially merge among themselves in an attempt to dominate the market even further.

Sources: www.reuters.com; www.bbc.co.uk; www.sonymusic.com.

with customers. Global communications such as satellite, cable TV, and the internet, have made it possible for organizations to reach a wider audience and develop 'global brands' that are consistent and recognizable worldwide. The interactive nature of these technologies is conducive to developing customer relationships as they are not only capable of improving the accessibility to customers but facilitating highly personalized and effective two-way communication. This potential for greater customer interaction enhances relationship marketing and customer support to a greater extent than has been possible with traditional media.

Global sourcing, purchasing, and production

The globalization of markets has heightened the tendency among organizations—often MNCs—to source goods and services from different locations in response to country-differentials in the cost of labour, tax regimes, business regulations, and the overall investment climate. Gone are the days when manufacturing companies obtained inputs only from domestic sources. With the increasing complexity in product design, production process, and logistical infrastructure, companies need global sourcing and purchasing practices. For example, global automobile manufacturers, such as Ford (www.ford.com) and Toyota (www.toyota.com), now manage a complex global network of sourcing, purchasing, and production. A Ford car can be designed by a Japanese company based in Tokyo with components manufactured in South East Asia, Western Europe, and the USA, then shipped to the Czech Republic for assembly before shipping to the US market for sale. The network of sourcing, purchasing, and production can be re-configured to support the marketing and logistical needs of a different car model.

Locating production facilities in strategic target markets can help to overcome market entry and trade barriers. In a country or region that imposes high trade barriers for

THE DIGITAL IMPACT Putting the 'e' into commerce

Dagang Net (www.dagangnet.com) is Malaysia's leading e-commerce service provider that specializes in managing port, logistics, and customs-related e-transactions. It owns and operates a national e-commerce trade and business exchange that handles some 40 million electronic trade transactions and RM1.8 billion customs duty payments annually from 2,000 corporate customers. In 1995, the company was given a 15-year government concession to roll out the infrastructure for e-commerce nationwide. The concession would allow Dagang Net to run an exclusive electronic linkage to the Malaysian customs on matters involving import and export declaration and clearance. The aim was to develop an electronic clearing system which would enable Malaysia's sea ports to benefit from the faster turnaround time, lower document error rate, and reduced document processing time which could translate into significant cost savings for many businesses.

When the Royal Customs Malaysia first mandated the electronic submission of customs declarations from manual processing at Port Klang in January 2005, forwarding agents staged a protest outside the Kedai EDI (Electronic Data Interchange), the subsidary of Dagang Net Technologies Sdn. Bhd. The initial resistance was deemed to be inevitable as the new system was seen by many Malaysian companies as an 'expensive gamble' that required substantial investment. Much of the initial investment would go towards acquiring new software, hardware, and for setting up a disaster recovery centre, as well as a sizeable allocation for training.

It appears that the 'gamble' worked. For instance, in Port Klang, Malaysia's largest sea port, the new system developed by Dagang Net has reduced documentation error rates from 40% to 5%. The paperless customs clearance system has resulted in total cost savings of more than RM100 million annually in terms of manpower, paper, and time. Cargo turnaround time in Port Klang has also been halved from four to two days and document processing time has been reduced by 12 hours to 15 minutes.

The system has been expanded beyond the management of sea ports. It is already driving the electronic trade facilitation of the maritime and aviation activities in Port Klang, Kuala Lumpur International Airport (KLIA), Port of Tanjung Pelepas (PTP), Pasir Gudang, Tanjung Kupang (as the second link to Singapore), Tanjung Puteri, Penang, Kuantan and Kemaman.

direct imports, it may be necessary to establish a production facility within the country or regional trading bloc. A number of car manufacturers set up assembly facilities in Malaysia to avoid heavy tariffs imposed on direct imports, and access other key emerging markets, including Vietnam, Indonesia, and Thailand, that operate within the ASEAN Free Trade Area. For a more detailed discussion on the issues of supply chain, refer to Chapter 12.

The threats of globalization

Macroeconomic volatility

One of the major problems of globalization which poses a significant threat to the stability of the global business environment is the increasing vulnerability of national economies to global macroeconomic volatility. As previously discussed, a succession of financial crises in the 1990s and the early twenty-first century—Mexico, Thailand, Indonesia, Korea, Russia, Brazil, and Argentina—have brought catastrophic economic repercussions to the global economy. Although the countries initially affected have impressive records of economic performance, they were not fully prepared to withstand the shocks that came through the international financial markets—i.e. erratic speculations, sudden shifts of investor sentiments, and the rapid movement of capital (especially short-term finance) into and out of countries (International Monetary Fund, 2003). Approximately 95% of the capital that flows internationally is now purely speculative, e.g. using expensive high-speed computers to buy and sell currencies a split second after their exchange rates have changed (Trainer, 2000). As the world economy becomes more interdependent and interlinked, it is less likely that any economy would be able to resist an adverse global or regional shock from the so-called contagion effects. An economic crisis could quickly spread to other economies as a result of a decline in the demand for foreign imports, therefore causing businesses in neighbouring countries to suffer. It seems clear that the financial crises in the late 1990s would not have developed as they did without exposure to the volatile and unpredictable global capital market.

In addition, the increased economic integration, particularly in the global financial sphere, and the erosion of national government sovereignty make it more difficult for governments to manage domestic economic activity, for instance by limiting governments' choices of tax rates and tax systems or their freedom of action on monetary or exchange rate policies. Yet, at the global level, the lack of regulations to restrict unscrupulous speculation and the absence of global governance to promote macroeconomic stability only serve to exacerbate the problem.

Macroeconomic volatility does not promote a global business environment that enables world trade to grow and businesses to flourish. The massive economic contraction and the resulting sluggish global consumer demand in the aftermath of the crises forced many global companies into cutting back their investments and enduring financial hardships. Volatility of short-term capital flows leads to large fluctuations in foreign exchange and interest rates, making it difficult for global companies to manage long-term borrowing and financial risks, and implement wage increases and international pricing.

Globalization of competition

An inevitable consequence of the globalization of markets and marketing activity is the growth of competition on a global basis. Being able to compete successfully in the global marketplace is now a critical factor for survival in many industries. In some industries, global companies have virtually excluded all other companies from their markets. An example is the detergent industry, in which three companies—Colgate (www.colgate.com), Unilever (www.unilever.com), and Procter and Gamble (www.pg.com)—dominate an increasing number of detergent markets worldwide, including Latin America and Asia Pacific. Because some companies make a quality product, it is imperative for all companies to be able to harness their strength in establishing a global brand name and leveraging the scale and scope economies on a global basis in order to compete successfully (Keegan, 2002).

Liberalization, deregulation, and privatization—the three forces that closely associate with economic globalization—are transforming the global business environment. The dynamics of the market are more turbulent and unpredictable as globalization brings a greater number of competitors and more intensive competition. While global market opportunities have increased and market access is easier due to the liberalization of world trade, organizations are also finding it harder to fence off foreign competitors operating in their domestic markets. Organizations which succeed in this environment are often adept at leveraging their core competences to become more responsive to customer demands. To do so involves a relentless need to increase the pace of technological change which in turn leads to the shortening of product life cycles. As a result, the window of time in which an organization recuperates its investment in research and development and pursues market dominance worldwide is becoming smaller.

The Old Economy, with an emphasis on the physical factors of production of capital, land, and labour, is quickly giving way to the so-called New Economy, which is characterized by information, knowledge, and technology. Two intertwined strategic forces are compelling organizations to reconsider their business assumptions: the intensification of global competition and the digitization with connectivity brought about by revolutions in information processing, telecommunication, and internet technologies. These two forces translate into competition that is increasingly knowledge-based (Lang, 2000). The economic transition is a particular issue in developed countries—so much so that the recent WTO trade negotiation rounds in Doha (2001) and Cancun (2003) were scheduled to focus on topics of the New Economy, e.g. copyright, patent, and trademark protection.

Lang (2000: 540) argues that:

> this increasingly knowledge-based nature of competition is driving change in how value chains are being managed within and across firms. It also signals a demographic shift in the workforce to knowledge work, whose mobile exponents demand a different type of work environment and executive leaderships. There are also heightened demands from more knowledgeable customers, whose bargaining power in the marketplace is enhanced by knowledge.

In particular, businesses are being transformed, as they change focus to an aggressive strategy of real-time supply chain collaboration using the internet and telecommunication technologies. World-class organizations such as Dell (www.dell.com), Fedex (www.fedex.com), and Amazon.Com (www.amazon.com) are accelerating their efforts to align processes and information flows throughout their entire value-added supply chains. It is no longer appropriate to see suppliers and customers as though they are managed in isolation. Suppliers and customers are inextricably linked through a sequence of events that brings raw material from its supply source through different value-adding activities to the ultimate customer (Lang, 2000). This presents organizations with unprecedented challenges as they will have to abandon familiar but obsolete business practices and develop the ability to manage diversity, complexity, and ambiguity in employee, supplier, and customer relationships in the New Economy.

The growing anti-globalization sentiments

For the majority of the second half of the twentieth century, the concept of globalization was enthusiastically embraced by many developed as well as developing countries, especially in East Asia and Latin America. Opening up to international trade has helped many countries to grow more quickly than they would otherwise have done and has brought the people of those nations new opportunities for wealth creation and prosperity. See, for example, the dramatic increase in per capita income that has accompanied the expansion of trade in South Korea, China, Ghana, and Mexico. Foreign aid, another aspect of the globalized world, has brought relief to millions who live in war-torn and impoverished regions. And irrigation and education projects have brought literacy and higher standards of living to the very poor.

At the Seattle meeting of the WTO in 1999 there were huge anti-globalization demonstrations. Since then the movement has grown and many meetings of the IMF, the World Bank, and the WTO are now scenes of conflict. The death of a protester in Genoa in 2001 was the beginning of the trend against the development of globalization (Stiglitz, 2002). So, why has globalization—a force that was once so enthusiastically embraced—become the subject of such hatred?

Many anti-globalization protesters see the concept of globalization as (mis)used to 'justify and legitimize the neo-liberal global project—that is, the creation of a global free market and the consolidation of Anglo-American capitalism within the world's major economic regions. In this respect, the ideology of globalization operates as a "necessary myth" with which politicians and governments discipline their citizens to meet the requirements of the global marketplace' (Held and McGrew, 2000: 4) in order to facilitate the global reach and domination of multinational corporations. The growing dominance of MNCs in the political economy is clearly illustrated in the US government's refusal to

WHOSE RESPONSIBILITY IS IT? Does globalization work for everyone?

During the fiercest clashes between the police and anti-globalization protesters in Cancun, Mexico, Lee Kyung-Hae, a Korean farmer, was among a group of about 150 Koreans in the frontline trying to pull down the security fences separating the protesters from the resort where the latest round of WTO negotiations were in progress in September 2003. Climbing to the top of the fence, he turned to his compatriots and said: 'Don't worry about me, just struggle your hardest.' He then stabbed himself in the chest with a knife and severed the left atrium of his heart. He died a few hours later in hospital.

Who was Lee Kyung-Hae, and more importantly, what drove him to commit suicide? The answer lies near Jangsu in South Korea, a town of 30,000 farming households in North Cholla Province. This is the land where Lee attempted to realize an idealistic vision of a modern model farm. But he also experienced the pain of losing his farm because of a sudden opening of markets to foreign trade.

Born to a relatively wealthy family of rice traders and landowners in 1947, Lee was described as a quiet and kind man. As the eldest son, he inherited the family's mountain land while his siblings left for the city for more profitable undertakings. He studied agricultural science at university where he met his wife. After his graduation in 1974, they returned to work at his family home where he put what he had learned into practice. His experiment eventually paid off: 30 hectares of grazing pastures, paddy fields, and buildings, housing and sheds that the Lees built from scratch on the steep wooded slopes of his family's land. He spent five years preparing the land and his determination eventually prevailed.

His world was turned upside down when the Korean government opened the market to imports of Australian cows and encouraged Korean farmers to expand their stocks with cheap loans. The combination of cheap imports and domestic over-supply led to a collapse in the price of beef. The herd, paid for by the loans, was almost worthless. To meet interest repayments, Lee had to sell dozens of cows every month. When he ran out of cattle, the banks repossessed the land. He mastered the testing environment in farming but lost his land to the bigger forces of globalization. From then on he became an ardent anti-globalization activist, dedicating his efforts into organizing unions, influencing government policy, and opposing trade liberalization, in particular, the WTO. He was always in the frontline of the often bloody street demonstrations that characterize the recent WTO meetings or G8 summits. He said the multinationals and big gov-

© Photodisc

ernments that control the WTO were pursuing a form of globalization that is inhumane, farmer-killing, and undemocratic. It was believed that he sacrificed himself to tell the world about the reality of today's Korean farmers, who are heavily in debt and live miserable lives under the auspices of globalization.

Source: Based on Watts, J., 'Field of Tears' published in *The Guardian*, G2 Supplement, on 16 September 2003.

© Courtesy of Greenpeace

sign the Kyoto Protocol on Climate Change in 1997. This was widely seen as the result of a US$13 million campaign financed by US car manufacturers, oil companies, and some trade unions in these industries (Francisco, 2002). Through the WTO, US and other Western drug companies could now stop drug companies in India and Brazil from 'stealing' their intellectual property, despite the fact that these companies (often with the support of their governments) are making life-saving drugs available at a fraction of the price at which the drugs are sold by the Western drug companies. Thousands have been condemned to death because they are deprived of these drugs at prices they cannot afford to pay. In the case of

Fig. 3.2 Global economic disparities

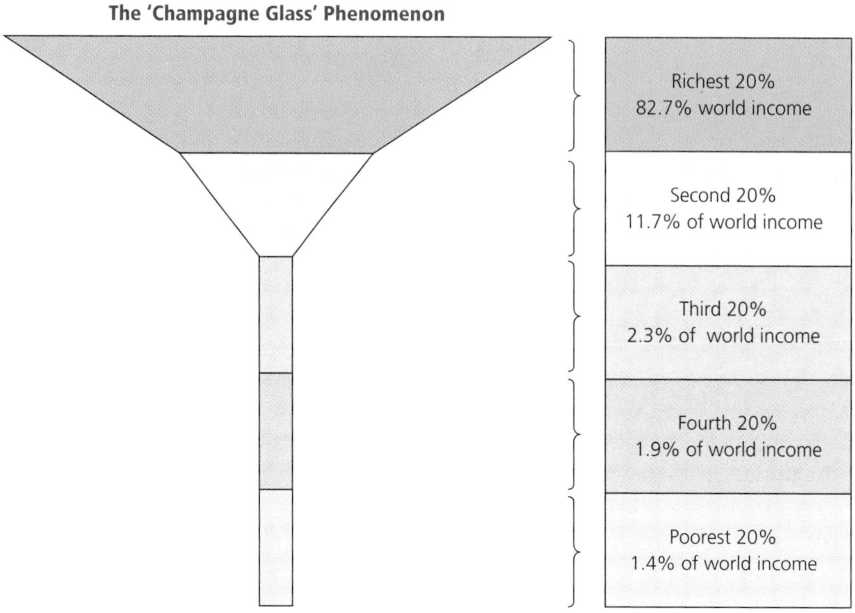

The 'Champagne Glass' Phenomenon

	Richest 20% 82.7% world income
	Second 20% 11.7% of world income
	Third 20% 2.3% of world income
	Fourth 20% 1.9% of world income
	Poorest 20% 1.4% of world income

Source: Based on Wade (1992). By permission of Oxford University Press.

AIDS, the international outrage was so great that drug companies had to relent, eventually agreeing to lower their prices to sell the drugs at cost in late 2001 (Stiglitz, 2002).

The growing divide between the rich and the poor has left an increasing number of people in the Third World living in dire poverty. Despite global attention to poverty alleviation, the number of people living in poverty has increased. In 2002, it is estimated that 1.2 billion people—one-fifth of world's population—survive on an income of less than US$1 dollar a day (Francisco, 2002); more than 45% of the world's population (2.8 billion people) live on less than US$2 a day (World, Bank, 2002). Moreover, the income gulf between the rich and the poor has become wider than ever before. In 1960, the income of the richest 20% of the world's population stood at about 30 times that of the world's poorest 20%; by 1997 the corresponding figure was 74 times (UNDP, 1997). While the top 20% of the world's population now possess 87.7% of world income, 80% of the world population have 17.3%. This is clearly illustrated in Wade's (1992) 'champagne glass' pattern of inequality between the world's rich and poor (see Fig. 3.2).

The hypocrisy of many rich countries in the pursuit of self-interest at the expense of the poor countries has enraged many anti-globalization protesters. For instance, while many developing countries have eliminated trade barriers, they continue to confront protectionism in the rich countries. Average tariff rates in rich countries are low, but they maintain barriers in exactly the areas where developing countries have comparative advantage: agriculture and labour-intensive manufactures (e.g. textiles), by erecting non-tariff barriers such as heavy subsidies, complicated technical standards, and anti-dumping legislation. According to World Bank estimates, protectionism in rich countries costs developing countries more than US$100 billion per year, denying these countries desperately needed export income.

Finally, the growing discontent over globalization also derives from the environmental degradation which continues across the globe. Mining and, oil and gas extraction by big businesses are taking place in sensitive ecological areas, including protected areas, often with financial support from the World Bank and governments. Intensive farming and manufacturing practices with high chemical and toxic inputs still abound, despite the call for environmentally friendly and sustainable agricultural and production methods. Notwithstanding the existence of the precautionary principle and the worldwide campaign on bio-ethics, many members of the scientific community continue to cooperate in the field testing of genetically modified plant and crop varieties, with massive financial support from corporations like Monsanto (Francisco, 2002). The emerging issues of corporate social responsibility (CSR), and ethical behaviour are discussed in Chapter 5.

Accelerating global inequality, unethical and irresponsible MNCs' practices, and the worsening environmental degradation do not promote a stable or sustainable global business environment conducive to growth and prosperity. New thinking on business, markets, and sustainable development is, as Ellis (2001: 17) argues, desperately needed to address the horrific dimensions of poverty and exclusion. Without access to the opportunities and benefits of global economic change, 'existing inequalities will be exacerbated and many developing countries will be forced deeper and deeper into the margins of global society, with all the dislocations that can bring—for example, mass migration, political instability or even regional conflicts'.

More importantly, sustainable development that enables the developing economies to grow will bring substantial benefits, not least in financial terms, to all businesses. The world's population is projected to grow by 2 billion in the next 25 years and most of this growth will concentrate in developing countries. The exclusion or marginalization of these new people will prevent them from becoming the new producers, new consumers, new savers, and new investors (Ellis, 2001). The opportunity costs that the global community will bear from the loss of these economic as well as social potentials are hard to estimate. It is self-destructive if the world community continues to ignore these issues and fails to address them constructively.

Global Migration

Migration is a global social issue which has long been regarded as something that 'could be addressed only gingerly because the right to exclude has traditionally been considered the essential defining aspect of national sovereignty, it has now taken on dimensions and legitimacy that put it alongside the more conventional international phenomena such as trade, macroeconomics, development, and health' (Bhagwati, 2004:208). Economics and the social impact of migration are inseparable in the way we consider international flows of humanity.

Cross-border human migration is not a new phenomenon. Throughout history, periods of growing international trade have been corresponded by flows of international migration. For instance, an estimation of 60 million Europeans migrated to the New World countries (e.g. the USA, Canada, Brazil, and Australia) between 1850 and 1910 in what Hatton and Williamson (1998) refer to as 'the age of mass migration'. This was also a period of rapid growth of international trade, boosted by a decline in transport and communication costs associated with the development of the railway infrastructure, steamships, electricity, and the telegraph.

Today, the United Nations estimates that 175 million persons reside outside the country of their birth, which is about 3% of world's population. The number of migrants has more than doubled since 1975. Sixty per cent of the world's migrants currently reside in the more developed regions and 40% in the less developed regions. Most of the world's migrants live in Europe (56 million), Asia (50 million), and Northern America (41 million). Almost one in every ten persons living in the more developed regions is a migrant. In contrast, only one in every 70 persons in developing countries is a migrant.

It is perhaps interesting to note that most of the migrants in the nineteenth and early twentieth centuries to the main receiving countries of the New World were Europeans, i.e. 91% in the period 1820–70; and 88% in the period 1870–1920 (Solimano, 2002). In contrast, the majority of migration in the post-World War II period and early twenty-first century are non-Europeans from poor into rich Western countries. The composition of foreign population in OECD countries reveals the importance of factors such as distance and, to some extent, language and cultural affinities in the decision to migrate. For instance, 75% of Japan's foreign population was from Korea, China, and the Philippines; 25% of the USA's foreign population is from Mexico and Canada. In addition, we have also witnessed large flows of illegal migration in the last two decades, from the poor to the rich countries, to escape dire poverty at home and in search of better economic opportunities. It is precisely because (legal and illegal) migration from the poor countries to the rich ones, instead of from the old to the new, is on such a large scale that the international flows of humanity today carry with them new seeds of discord. These present concerns that must be confronted (Bhagwati, 2004).

In response, to restrict migration, the main recipient countries, such as the USA and the UK, have introduced significant changes in the legislation on migration since the 1960s, as a result of growing concerns about the economic, social, political, and demographic consequences of immigration. At present, about 40% of the countries in the world have policies aimed at lowering immigration levels. For example, a preference system was set up in the USA to favour immigrants with settled family members already in the country and those with skills in short supply. In Europe, there is a dual EU immigration regime in which every EU citizen (with the exception of the newly joined member states) has full rights to reside and work in any country of the Union. Non-EU citizens, on the other hand, face several restrictions to immigration and need working permits to reside and work legally. This evolving notion of European citizenship is closely connected to an increasingly racialized sense of European identity.

Migration and economic growth

In contrast to the basic premise of market fundamentalism, which favours the free movement of all means of production, global capitalism in the twenty-first century favours the free flow of goods and capital across national borders but restricts the movement of people. This paradox makes for a worthy phenomenon to be understood and explained. In his studies of globalization, Bhagwati (2004) observes three types of 'human flow' which have promoted corresponding concerns and policy actions worldwide. First, there is a clear distinction between the poor and rich counties. Migrations from poor to rich nations are very different in their implications from those that are the other way around. Secondly, it is important to differentiate the flow of skilled from unskilled migrants. The former can exacerbate 'brain-drain' problems for poor countries, while the latter can be treated as an opportunity for them. Thirdly, there is a difference between voluntary migrations and those that reflect involuntary movements prompted by political conflicts, climate change, and persecution.

As Solimano (2002) contemplates, the interaction between long-term economic growth and migration is a complex issue. What are the economic impacts of migration on the economic growth of both receiving and sending countries? In the receiving countries, international migration can help ease labour market shortages, therefore relaxing a labour constraint for growth. As the ageing population in most rich countries continues to rise, the demand for immigrant workers has increased to supplement the dwindling domestic labour force and provide their struggling social security systems with the much needed tax collectables to support the retired population.

On the other hand, the demand for skilled workers has increased exponentially world-wide as the information technology revolution has created a huge need for computer experts, electronic engineers, and programmers. To enable these industries to flourish, other types of knowledge worker, such as venture capitalists, lawyers, accountants, management consultants, and academics, have also become the prime targets of many rich countries, which tempt them with favourable immigration rules for them and their families, opportunities to work with the world's best companies and so on.

However, the transfer of young, able, and talented human capital from one country to other can have a significant negative growth effect in the sending countries, which are often poor and can ill-afford to lose scarce talented key workers. Less developed countries cannot afford modern professionals or the economic rewards or the social conditions they seek, making them powerless to stem the negative 'brain-drain'. For instance, Bhagwati (2004) estimates that more than 70% of foreign-born PhDs graduates in the USA remain in the country, many eventually becoming citizens. Most of these students come from the best higher education institutions in their home countries. For example, graduates of the Indian Institute of Technology (IIT, www.iitd.ac.in) accounted for 78% of US engineering PhDs granted to Indians in 1990. Over half of all Taiwanese awarded similar PhDs attended the National Taiwan University and the National Cheng Kung University. From the market fundamentalist perspective, the level of total world output increases as people (as means of production) move from countries with lower labour productivity to countries with higher labour productivity, where they have the technology and infrastructure to more efficiently utilize labour inputs. This, however, occurs at the expense of the less developed countries.

Migration and humanitarian crises

The rise of humanitarian crises globally is a major cause of international migration in recent years. According to the United Nations High Commission for Refugees (UNHCR, www.unhcr.org), there were 2.4 million asylum applications in Europe between 1991 and 1995, of which 11% were granted full refugee status and a similar number were given leave to stay on other grounds. The number of refugees in the world at the end of twentieth century stood at 16 million. The largest number of refugees are found in Asia (9 million), followed by Africa (4 million). Three million refugees are located in developed countries.

History is filled with instances in which people have been forced by violence to flee from their homes. Indeed, the humanitarian principle of offering refuge to them was well established before the seventeenth century, when the term 'refugee' was coined for the Protestants fleeing France to avoid forced conversion. The political upheaval in Europe in the nineteenth century gave rise to the term '*émigrés*' to refer to political revolutionaries who fled persecution. In the twentieth century the forced expulsion of people who were then denied their nationality brought in the concept of the 'stateless'. These three terms were largely subsumed within the modern definition of 'refugee' (Zolberg et al., 1989).

Today, refugees have a special status within international law and with it the rights and privileges stay in a receiving country and entitlement to humanitarian aid. In industrialized nations, where refugees used to arrive in relatively small numbers, the states were generally happy to accommodate the new arrivals. During the Cold War refugees from communist states arriving in the West were in fact welcomed as they offered propaganda opportunities. Today, there is a widespread perception that many people who claim refugee status in developed nations are actually purely economic migrants. A lot of effort has been invested into restricting access to claim refugee status in order to weed out those who are not entitled. As countries look to restrict access to asylum, there is a tendency to highlight the numbers of refugees and asylum seekers as a justification for ever more stringent measures. Distinctions are frequently blurred between asylum seekers, economic migrants, and illegal immigrants, and the focus is often on the numbers of asylum applications rather than the small numbers who are actually granted refugee status.

In reality, the majority of refugees are found in the poorest countries of the world today. Due to their low average incomes, and often inadequate healthcare and education systems, the arrival of large number of refugees in need of immediate assistance can create an impossible burden for such states, which struggle to meet the needs of their own people. Confronted with such situations, these countries often appeal to the international community for assistance. However, there is no standard global agreement to determine what and how assistance is provided. The response often depends on the donor countries' relationship with the refugees' country of origin, the receiving countries, and the level of global media coverage.

Large flows of migration due to humanitarian crises are becoming commonplace today. It is a contemporary and pervasive global social issue that clearly deserves more analysis both in its magnitude and composition. Discussions at the global level which have so far privileged globalization of trade must now include the design of institutional settings to manage massive migration flows.

Environmental Sustainability

Over the past 20 years, concern has been growing about the impact of business activity on the environment and socially responsible companies have had to address a growing set of environmental demands from their stakeholders. Unlike other problems of globalization, global environmental problems affect both developed and developing countries. Customers and shareholders are becoming increasingly sensitized to environmental issues and pressure groups have a strong voice in shaping attitudes to environmental practice. Current concerns with respect to environmental protection cover a wide range of issues. For instance, multinational companies are seen to have a major impact on climate change, particularly with regard to direct emissions of 'greenhouse' gases as a by-product of industrial processes. The UN has estimated that transnational companies are directly responsible for half of all emissions of greenhouse gases. There are concerns about deforestation, including the impact of the loss of rainforest in the Amazon on the planet's ability to absorb greenhouse gases, the human rights of indigenous peoples, and impacts on biodiversity in terms of species extinction. The creation of waste and its management have become major issue, as many modern processes have hazardous and toxic waste as their by-products and as consumer incomes rise, both the packaging and replacement of products create new waste management problems. There are also increasingly concerns over food security, e.g. overfishing by large factory fleets owned by global companies, the effects of pesticide use on rivers and other water resources, and the potential impacts of genetically modified crops on local environments.

Climate change

Climate change is perhaps the least quantitatively understood global issue. The Intergovernmental Panel on Climate Change (IPCC, 2001) claims that most of the observed global warming over the last 50 years is likely to have been due to the increase in greenhouse gas concentrations. About 75% of the cumulative greenhouse gas emissions are produced by industrialized countries. Their per capita emission is on average five times higher than those of developing countries. The USA has the highest emission per capita at 20 times higher than the developing countries.

There is now a consensus in the global scientific communities that human activities are interfering significantly with the global climate, with potentially devastating consequences for economic growth and sustainable development. Fig. 3.3 shows the impact of climate change on the environment as mean temperature increases. From an economic perspective, Furtado and Kishor (1997) at the World Bank Institute estimate that the costs associated with climate change are at 1.5–2% of gross domestic product (GDP) in industrial countries, and as high as 9% of GDP in developing nations. For countries that have a specialized and natural resource-based economy, e.g. countries heavily dependent on agriculture or forestry, and with a poorly developed and land-tied labour force, estimates of damages are several times larger. The warming of the globe of 2–3° Celsius can cause damage of up to US$500 billion per year, which is more than four times the combined net private capital flows to middle-income economies. These estimates are believed to capture only part of the impact of climate change as they do not reflect damages from possible large-scale catastrophes, severe floods, and hurricanes. Also not included in these estimates are the costs that are difficult to quantify financially, e.g. the loss of rainforests that entails loss of biodiversity, the degradation of ecological functions such as coastal watershed protection, and human health impact due to diseases and loss of life.

Fig. 3.3 Components of global climate change

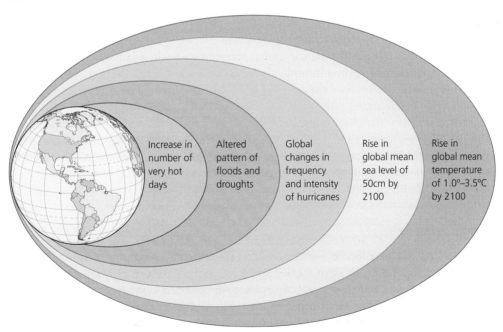

Source: Based on studies published by World Bank Institute of the World Bank (2002: 1).

Dealing with the climate change problem will require a global effort to control greenhouse gas emissions. To stabilize atmospheric concentrations of carbon dioxide, emissions must be brought below the level of natural absorption of greenhouse gas emissions in the Earth's carbon cycle, which is equivalent to a 90% cut in the level of today's emissions (Feinstein, 2002). The fundamental question for the global community is: How do we reconcile the requirement for economic development to meet basic human needs with the need to protect the environment? Developing countries, due to their relatively small cumulative contribution to the increase in atmospheric concentrations of CO_2, would be unwilling and unable to invest their scarce resources to combat climate change as they need to cater for more urgent domestic needs to provide food, energy, and other vital services for the poor. For that reason, industrial countries will need to shoulder the main responsibility to provide the required new resources to tackle the pressing problem of climate change.

Climate change and food security

Hunger and malnutrition are (and continue to be) persistent and widespread problems in many developing countries. The effects of global climate change can quickly exacerbate these problems and stiffle economic growth. Adverse weather conditions, such as floods and droughts, which pose significant threats to agricultural production, are likely to increase in the near future as the climate changes. The consequential unproductive or lost days of agricultural production, constrained mental abilities, and persistent vulnerability to disease and illnesses can substantially reduce these countries' ability to feed themselves.

The rise of mean global temperature and the rise of sea levels as a result of global warming are putting the world's delicate ecosystems under enormous strain. The progressive loss of productive agricultural lands, the degradation of coastal areas, and the shortage of fresh water are affecting people living in parts of the world already suffering from food insecurity. The area of productive land for food agriculture is also constantly diminishing because of population growth and increased land conversion for lucrative biofuel cultivation.

The problem of food security caused by climate change is laden with both ethical and equity issues. It is uncertain how the global communities will adapt to climate change. Simple extrapolation of existing information based on the impact of past disasters on social systems is inadequate because the scale of global climate change is so much greater. For example, the destabilizing effects of the impoverishment and displacement of a large number of environmental refugees, including the potential for destructive conflicts over diminishing resources, are not known. Quantifying the socio-economic impact of climate change is a complex process. Nevertheless, no matter how these impacts are viewed, they are likely to be large and unequally distributed across geographical areas of the world (Furtado and Kishor, 1997).

Energy security

There is a strong correlation between energy consumption and economic income, as clearly illustrated in Fig. 3.4. In modern society, most economic developments would be impossible without reliable and easy access to large supplies of energy. In other words, economic growth that creates employment and consumerism relies upon additional or more efficient use of energy. For this reason, many governments make provision for substantial budget expenditures to support various direct or indirect subsidies in their domestic economy.

Fig. 3.4 Energy consumption and economic income

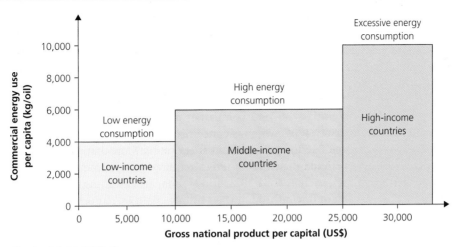

Source: Based on Feinstein (2002: 1).

For the first time in recent history, the world is confronted with the prospect that the production of crude oil, which is the main energy source today, will peak in the immediate future. The International Energy Agency (IEA) forecasts—traditionally regarded as conservative by the markets—put current demand at around 90 million barrel per day. At a rate of 3% increase in demand per year and annual finds of 10 billion barrels, it has been estimated that as early as 2013 the world will reach 'the time of maximum production'. The demand for oil has increased much quicker than previously estimated mainly due to the fast growth of new emerging markets, in particular, China and India. Meeting the costs of oil demand presents a significant challenge to the global economy. The cost of extracting current known reserves is estimated to be in the region of US$900 billion between 2006 and 2013. This massive cost can double as new investments need to be made to explore new oil deposits in order to secure future production from 2013 to 2030. This can mean that an added US$250 billion a year will need to be spent.

For the world's 2.5 billion truly poor people (i.e. those who live on less than US$2 per day), the main energy issue is access to modern energy for: (a) domestic consumptive uses, such as cooking and basic lighting; (b) socially productive uses, such as education and healthcare delivery; and (c) economically productive uses, such as irrigation, small industries, and computing. Modern energy plays a crucial role in empowering business development, employment, income generation, and more productive social services that lift populations out of poverty and enable economic growth (Feinstein, 2002). In the light of the world's dwindling oil reserves, developing countries have good reason to harbour concerns about the vulnerability of their energy security. Any major fluctuations in oil prices due to natural or man-made events can spell disaster to their domestic economy. For instance, the recent extensive losses of electric transmission in the earthquake in Gujarat (India) and the deliberate terrorist targeting of power stations and oil pipelines in Iraq stand as powerful testimony to this fact.

Assuming social responsibility towards sustainable development

Although the behaviour of companies is regulated by national legislation in the markets in which they operate, this regulation is largely seen as setting minimum standards rather than as benchmarks of best environmental practice. Companies with a claim to social responsibility are expected to exceed these standards and generate innovative approaches to environmental management.

Rather than seeing environmental protection as a business cost, socially enlightened companies are coming to see environmental management as an essential business tool in gaining and sustaining competitive advantage. The mini-case illustration below lists a number of benefits, noted by Business for Social Responsibility (www.bsr.org), which businesses have gained from taking the environment into account in the design of their products, services, and operations, leading to the overall reduction of operating costs.

In addition to in-house initiatives, more companies are registering their production plant to the industry standard ISO 14001, which is concerned with environmental issues and for which there is evidence that its adoption decreases energy costs. More than 10,000 companies have registered for this standard, which specifies required environmental management systems. Major companies, such as Ford, IBM, and Honda, are cascading their approach to environmental management down through their supply chain by requiring their suppliers to be registered to ISO 14001 or to develop environmental management systems which are compatible with ISO 14001 (Albaum et al., 2002).

 MINI-CASE ILLUSTRATION **The business of managing waste disposal**

New revenue streams. Waste disposal managers at Los Angeles airport needed a way of managing the 19,000 tons of food scraps produced on their premises each year. They formed a programme with a nearby sewage and utility plant to process the scraps and send the resulting methane on to the utility plant. The airport now saves US$12 a ton in disposal costs and receives US$18 a ton for the energy generated by its scraps. In addition, the sewage digesters produce reusable water and nutrient-rich slurry which can be sold as fertilizer.

Improved product design. By applying environmental principles to product design, companies can spur innovation internally and among their suppliers. This may lead to more efficient practices or new products and market opportunities. ITT International produce night-vision devices for military purposes which use an inert, non-toxic gas in their production. It was decided that this gas should be replaced on environmental grounds and one of the company's plants tried nitrogen as a replacement. They discovered not only that nitrogen worked, but that it cost US$500,000 less to buy and handle.

Greater asset retention. In its initiatives to recapture around 1.5 billion pounds of material waste and eliminate hazardous waste from its products, Xerox has saved US$2 billion over the past decade.

Reduced material use. In the early 1990s, GM began a 'Shared Savings' partnership with its primary chemical supplier at a Wisconsin plant. This partnership changed the traditional supplier–customer relationship into a chemical service model, in which the supplier is paid for managing chemicals, and the supplier's profit is based on performance rather than sales volume. In its first three years, this programme yielded a 50% decrease in chemical use.

Increased worker productivity. When Verifone, an electronic equipment manufacturer and subsidiary of Hewlett-Packard,

incorporated environmental features into a warehouse and manufacturing plant in California, including energy efficiency measures, increased worker access to natural light, and the use of non-toxic building materials, it resulted in an annual estimated saving of US$110,000 in energy costs, a 40% reduction in absenteeism, and a 5% improvement in productivity.

Enhanced brand. In 2002, BP gained the approval of a number of NGOs when the company met its goal for reducing greenhouse gas emissions by 10% from a 1990 baseline, and to ensure 50% of the company's pump sales worldwide came from clean fuels.

Expanded market share. Whirlpool reported a 20% per share increase in core earnings when it introduced the Duet washing machine which uses 68% less water and 67% less electricity than conventional models.

Source: www.bsr.org.

Although socially responsible companies pay heed to the environmental consequences of their activities, companies are now being challenged to go beyond this and engage with the concept of 'sustainable development'. This term comes from the wider global debate led by the United Nations in respect of environmental issues and was first put forward in the Brundtland Report (1987), which was the initial product of the UN World Commission on Environment and Development. The focus of the global environmental debate is how to achieve sustainable development—development that meets the needs of the present generation without compromising the ability of future generations to meet their own needs. It has as its main consideration the maintenance of the continuing ability of the environment to supply raw materials and assimilate waste while maintaining biodiversity and quality of life. This concept was further developed by the First International Earth Summit held in Rio de Janeiro in 1992, which adopted Conventions on Climate Change and Biological Diversity, and later summits held in Kyoto (1997) and The Hague (2000).

The adoption by companies of a sustainable development approach to environmental issues can be seen as the third stage in an evolutionary process of responses to concerns about the environment (Stigson, 1999). The first stage is reactive compliance with environmental legislation. The second stage is where companies have come to see business advantages in good environmental practice, especially those of lower costs and greater resource efficiency, and have focused on improving products and processes to gain these advantages. The third stage involves the integration of environmental performance into business development to become a key contributing factor to the strategic positioning of companies, creating value and new sources of competitive advantage. Sustainable development practice requires a holistic approach, including changes to management systems and company philosophy and marketing practices, as well as maintaining efforts to reduce pollution and to improve waste management and resource efficiency. Although many companies have adopted practices which enhance 'the bottom line' through the cost savings gained by waste reduction and energy efficiency, a full sustainability model aims to enhance the 'triple bottom line', involving the measurement of performance against not only economic efficiency, but also environment, economy, and equity—the components of the 'triple bottom line'. In practice, this means that companies not only look for ways to improve economic efficiency, but also ways for 'protecting and restoring ecological systems and the enhancement of the well-being of people' (Business for Social Responsibility, www.bsr.org). An example of a company seeking to incorporate sustainable development into its business practice is Design Tex, a subsidiary of Steelcase Inc (www.steelcase.com), which manufactures textiles for commercial use.

Companies attempting to integrate sustainability into their business practice often publish sustainability reports, in addition to company reports, and environmental performance reports, which outline their approach to sustainability and provide an overview of how these practices are adding value to company business.

Chapter Summary

1. Globalization is a complex phenomenon that affects many aspects of our lives. There is no straightforward or accepted consensus as to what exactly the term represents. It is, however, possible to understand it by examining some of the discourses (e.g. political, economic, technological, and cultural) which have been grouped under the term.

2. The interconnectedness of computers worldwide, the convergence of cultures and consumer tastes, the unparalleled growth in international trade of merchandise and services, and the proliferation of institutions concerned with or involved in global governance are responsible for many changes that could impact upon the global business environment, and the patterns of our daily lives as citizens and consumers.

3. Globalization presents organizations with unlimited opportunities to grow and transform to become not only larger but more competitive and efficient. These opportunities are accompanied by hidden risks and organizations which seek to compete successfully need to face up to new challenges and continue to evolve.

4. At policy levels, the discourse of globalization today is more favourable to the movements of goods and capital than the movement of people across the globe. Global migration can have a positive effect on the long-term growth of receiving countries by keeping labour costs down, increasingly profitability of investment, and rising national savings. In labour-abundant, low-income sending countries, the emigration of low-skilled people has little depressing effects. In contrast, large outflows of highly-educated professionals and talented entrepreneurs from poor developing countries can produce a detrimental effect on the long-term growth of these countries.

5. The effects of global climate change can exacerbate poverty in poor developing countries and threaten food security. The adverse impacts of severe floods and droughts, increasing mean global temperature, and the inundation of coastal areas can bring significant damage to ecosystems and threats to agricultural production. Successful initiatives to mitigate global climate change can only be achieved by fostering international cooperation, strengthening institutional regimes to combat global warming, and deep commitment from industrial countries in providing resources and technical assistance.

6. Multinational companies are increasingly under pressure to assume social responsibility towards sustainable development. Companies with a claim to social responsibility are expected to exceed minimum legal requirements and generate innovative approaches to environmental management. Rather than seeing environmental protection as a business cost, socially enlightened companies are coming to see environmental management as an essential business tool in gaining and sustaining competitive advantage.

 END-OF-CHAPTER CASE STUDY **The making of a global fast food giant**

With 30,000 restaurants in 120 countries and a total of 46 million customers everyday, McDonald's is undoubtedly the largest and best known fast-food brand in the world. For many people, the brand has come to symbolize the hopes and the fears of the Americanization of global culture.

With its slogan 'One World: One Taste', McDonald's has revolutionized the food industry by changing the way food is produced, marketed, serviced, and consumed. McDonald's slogan articulates its ambitious corporate vision of dominating the global fast-food market. When McDonald's Pushkin Square opened in the heart of Moscow on 31, January 1990, it broke all opening-day records for the number of customers served, and is still the busiest branch in the world. The former Soviet Union now has 79 restaurants. The largest

McDonald's in the world opened in 1992 in Beijing, and there are now almost 800 McDonald's with 50,000 staff in mainland China. Outside the USA, visiting McDonald's fast-food restaurants offers a bite of the American Dream. It is little wonder that its golden arches are often branded by free market capitalists as a symbol of the success and the benefits of globalization to businesses.

So, how did it all begin? Ray Kroc, the founder of McDonald's, was a humble salesman selling paper cups and milk-shake mixers for over 30 years before he started his first fast-food restaurant. At the age of 52, he developed a vision and its endless possibilities when he saw the McDonald brothers' hamburger restaurant selling tasty food to big queues in San Bernardino, California in 1954. He was attracted by the cleanliness, simplicity, efficiency, and profitability of the McDonald brothers' operation. They had applied the assembly-line concept synonymous with a manufacturing factory by stripping fast-food service down to its essence, eliminating choices and fussy waitresses. The result is a swift, no-frill restaurant at reasonable prices: 15 cents for a burger, 10 cents for fries, and 10 cents for a soft drink. The McDonald brothers applied automation to food, just as Henry Ford had to car manufacture.

Ray Kroc struck a deal with the McDonald brothers to buy out their business and retained the friendly Scottish sound of their name and the golden arches in their restaurant. The first McDonald's opened in Des Plaines, Illinois, in June 1955. In five years it became a chain of 200 restaurants. After ten years the company went public, and the share price doubled to US$50 in the first month. By 1995 there were over 18,000 restaurants worldwide. The McDonald's Corporation surpassed US$1 billion in total revenue in just 22 years. By comparison, Xerox took 63 years to make its first billion dollars; IBM took 46 years.

In the formative years in the US market, McDonald's understood that having high visibility for its brand and easy accessibility to its products were crucial to its success. One way of achieving this was by making its restaurants easily accessible on the US highway system. Through its franchise system, it was able to vastly increase the number of its restaurants in every corner of the USA within a very short period of time. Today, over half of the US population live within three minutes' drive of a McDonald's, and Ray Kroc, the founder of the restaurant chain, made sure they did so. He used the company aeroplane in the 1960s to spot from the air the best locations and road junctions for new restaurant branches.

In his search for suitable locations, Kroc often used church steeples as his guide because he wanted to attract church-going families to his temples of efficiency and nourishment, which always had clean toilets. He supported the expansion of his restaurants by investing heavily in targeted advertising. 'Give Mom a night off' was an early advertising slogan, which worked really well for traditional, family-centred, churching-going American families. His 'godly' strategic pursuit paid off as more people in the USA today eat in McDonald's than go to church or synagogue. Surveys have shown that the golden arches are better known than the Christian cross.

After decades of unprecedented global expansion, the wind of change is blowing through the empire of fast food. The vision of endless growth through new markets across the planet for fast-food companies now looks unsustainable when it is not what people want any more. In the old days, no franchise holder anywhere in the world could deviate from the 700-page McDonald's operations manual known as 'the Bible'. But that policy has changed as the company realizes that it needs to adapt to local sensitivities in order to ensure successful market entry. For instance, McDonald's caused a public outcry in India when their Hindu customers learned that the french fries were precooked in beef fat in the USA, as cows are sacred creatures to Hindus. The Big Mac has been replaced by the Maharaja Mac, which is made of mutton and served in all its restaurants in India. Likewise, McDonald's in Pakistan offers three spicy McMaza meals—Chatpata Chicken Roll, Chicken Chutni Burger, and

Spicy Chicken Burger. All three are served with Aaloo fingers and a regular drink. Even in the USA, what the customers want today are more choices, not less. For instance, in Evansville, Indiana, there is now a 'McDonald's With the Diner Inside', where 100 combinations of food are served with full table services. In Britain, McDonald's has been redesigning outlets with a more contemporary look, removing strip lighting and immobile seats. A total of 140 British outlets have recently been refurbished, with a further 200 to follow.

Apart from dealing with changes in customer demands, McDonald's has had to endure public criticism from the global media and NGOs. It has become the global symbol associated with being American, authoritarian, abusive of animals, exploitative of workers, unhealthy, ecological unsound, and ruthlessly profiteering. For animal rights activists, or those who dislike industrial corporate capitalism or US foreign policy, the local branch of McDonald's, with its big bright windows, becomes an easy target. In recent years branches of McDonald's have been attacked in America, Australia, Belgium, Canada, China, Finland, France, Holland, India, Indonesia, Lebanon, Poland, Russia, Saudi Arabia, Sweden, and the UK.

Other protests against McDonald's have captured the public imagination. For instance, when the European Union refused to accept imports of American hormone-enhanced beef, the USA responded (under World Trade Organization rules) by putting tariffs on *foie gras*, Roquefort cheese, and other European farm products. Ten French farmers drove their tractors through and destroyed a half-built McDonald's in protest. Other farmers filled a McDonald's branch with apples, another with chickens, geese, turkeys, and ducks.

These attacks on McDonald's in recent years have undoubtedly taken some of the shine off the company's global success. McDonald's has, so far, weathered all of these problems, and has continued to expand into more and more countries. There is little doubt that McDonald's will continue to grow, finding ever more remote locations to expand its fast-food empire. Only time will tell if they continue to adhere to Ray Kroc's four guiding principles of quality, service, cleanliness, and value.

Source: Based on selected extracts from BBC World Service on Globalization, www.bbc.co.uk/worldservice.

Case discussion questions

1 In what ways do you think political, economic, cultural, and technological discourses of globalization have enabled McDonald's to become the largest global fast-food company?

2 Using the information provided in the case and your personal knowledge, discuss the various criticisms which have been directed towards McDonald's. Do you think those criticisms are justified?

3 What are the changes that McDonald's has been undertaking in order to reinvent its business? What are the potential benefits and risks associated with those changes for the future of the business?

END-OF-CHAPTER EXERCISES

1 Identify the three waves of globalization and briefly describe the factors that contributed to these developments.

2 What is globalization? How would you go about making sense of this highly complex and contentious phenomenon?

3 Identify and briefly explain the different discourses that are closely associated with globalization.

4 Is globalization an opportunity or threat? Briefly discuss the opportunities and threats of globalization for an organization that seeks to operate within it.

5 What are the major drivers of global migration? Explain what the economic and social impacts are of global migration.

6 What are the main global issues which are posing a threat to environmental sustainability?

DISCUSSION AND EXAMINATION QUESTIONS

1 'Globalization is a highly complex and contentious phenomenon. There is simply no straightforward or accepted consensus as to what the term represents.' Discuss.

2 With appropriate examples, examine the economic, political, technological, and cultural discourses associated with globalization.

3 To what extent does globalization present market opportunities for businesses, or is it a threat?

4 The anti-globalization protestors have accused the current wave of globalization as the source of accelerating global inequality, MNC's exploitation, and environmental degradation. How valid is this accusation? Discuss with examples.

5 What are the reasons why there have been growing concerns about the impact of business activity on the environment? In what ways can multinational companies assume socially responsible in addressing these concerns?

FURTHER READING

Bhagwati, J. (2004), *In Defence of Globalization*, New York: Oxford University Press.

Stiglitz, J. E. (2002), *Globalization and its Discontents*, Harmondsworth: Penguin Books.

Usunier, J. -D. (2000), *Marketing Across Cultures*, 3rd edn., Harlow: FT/Prentice Hall.

REFERENCES

Albaum, G., Strandskov, J., and Duerr, E. (2002), *International Marketing and Export Management*, 4th edn., London: FT/Prentice Hall.

Alonso Cano, G., del Corral, M., and G. Poussin, (2000), *Culture, Trade and Globalisation: 25 Questions and Answers*, Paris: UNESCO Publishing.

Anderson, K. (2000), 'Globalization, the World Trade Organization and Development Strategies of Poor Countries', in Yusuf, S., Wu, W., and Evenett, S. (eds.), *Local Dynamics in an Era of Globalization*, Oxford: Oxford University Press for the World Bank.

Aw, B. Y., Chung, S., and Roberts, M. J. (2000), 'Productivity and the decision to export: micro evidence from Taiwan and South Korea', *World Bank Economic Review*, 14(1), 65–90.

Baldwin, R. E. and Mastin, P. (1999), *Two Waves of Globalization: Superficial Similarities, Fundamental Differences*, NBER Working Paper No. 6904, January.

Bhagwati, J. (2004), *In Defence of Globalization*, New York: Oxford University Press.

Bis (2003), *Quarterly Review: International Banking and Financial Market Developments*, September, Geneva: Bank for International Settlements.

Brinkman, R. L. and Brinkman, J. E. (2002), 'Corporate power and the globalization process', *International Journal of Social Economics*, 29(9), 730–52.

Brundtland, G. (ed.) (1987), *Our Common Future: The World Commission on Environment and Development*, Oxford: Oxford University Press.

Castells, M. (2000), *The Rise of the Network Society*, 2nd edn., Oxford and Malden, MA: Blackwell.

Dollar, D. and Kraay, A. (2001), *Trade, Growth, and Poverty*, World Bank Research Working Paper No. 219, Washington, DC: World Bank.

Ellis, V. (2001), 'Can global business be a force for good?', *Business Strategy Review*, 12(2), 15–20.

Feinstein, C. (2002), *Economic Development, Climate Change, and Energy Security—The World Bank's Strategic Perspective*, Energy & Mining Sector Board Discussion Paper Series, Paper No. 3, September, Washington, DC: World Bank.

Francisco, G. (2002), 'The Threat of Globalization and the World Crisis', *The Trade and Sustainable Development Conference Proceedings*, 4–5 June, Bali.

Furtado, J. I. and Kishor, N. (1997), *Global Climate Change and Biodiversity: Challenges for the Future and the Way Ahead*, World Bank Institute, Washington, DC: World Bank.

Hatton, T. J. and Williamson, J. G. (1998), *The Age of Mass Migration: Causes and Economic Impact*, Oxford: Oxford University Press.

Held, D. and McGrew, A. (2000), *The Global Transformations Reader: An Introduction to the Globalization Debate*, Malden, MA: Polity Press.

International Monetary Fund (2003), *Globalization: Threat or Opportunity?*, IMF Issues Brief, 28 August. Washington, DC: IMF.

IPCC (2001), *Climate Change 2001: An Assessment of the Intergovernmental Panel on Climate Change*, available at: www.ipcc.ch.

Keegan, W. (2002), *Global Marketing Management, 7th International Edition*, Englewood Cliffs, NJ: Prentice-Hall.

Lang, J. C. (2000), 'Managing in knowledge-based competition', *Journal of Organisational Change Management*, 14(6), 539–53.

Litan, R. E. (2000), 'Toward a global financial architecture for the twenty-first century', in Yusuf, S., Wu, W., and Evenett, S. (eds.), *Local Dynamics in an Era of Globalization*, Oxford: Oxford University Press for The World Bank.

Schirato, T. and Webb, J. (2003), *Understanding Globalization*, London: Sage.

Smith, A. D. (1990), 'Towards a global culture?', in Featherstone, M. (ed.), *Global Culture: Nationalism, Globalisation and Modernity*, London: Sage.

Solimano, A. (2002), *International Migration and the Global Economic Order: An Overview*, Washington, DC: World Bank (www.worldbank.org).

Spich, R. S. (1995), 'Globalization folklore: problems of myth and ideology in the discourse on globalization', *Journal of Organisational Change Management*, 8(4), 6–29.

Stiglitz, J. E. (2002), *Globalization and its Discontents*, Harmondsworth: Penguin Books.

Stigson, B. (1999), 'Sustainable development for industry and society', *Building Research & Information*, 27(6), 424–30.

Streeten, P. (2001), *Globalization: Threat or Opportunity?*, Copenhagen: Copenhagen Business School Press.

Trainer, T (2000), 'Two common mistakes about globalization', *International Journal of Sociology and Social Policy*, 20(11), 46–58.

UNDP (1997), *Human Development Report 1997*, New York: Oxford University Press.

UNESCO Institute of Satistics (2005), *International Flow of Selected Cultural Goods and Services, 1994–2003: Defining and Capturing the Flows of Global Cultural Trade*, UNESCO Sector for Culture (www.unesco.org).

Wade, R. (1992), *Human Development Report 1992*, New York: Oxford University Press for the United Nations.

World Bank (2002), *Globalization, Growth and Poverty: Building an Inclusive World Economy*, Policy Research Working Paper No. 23591, Oxford: Oxford University Press for the World Bank.

World Bank (2003), '*Urban Development Needs Creativity: How Creative Industries Affect Urban Areas. Development Outreach*', Washington, DC: World Bank, (www.worldbank.org).

World Trade Organization (2001), *Market Access: Unfinished Business: Post-Uruquay Round, Inventory and Issues*, Special Studies, Economic Research and Analysis Division, Geneva: WTO.

Zolberg, A. R. Suhrke, A., and Aguayo, S. (1989), *Escape from Violence: Conflict and the Refugee Crisis in the Developing World*, New York: Oxford University Press.

For more details on the history of modern globalization see *Globalization, Growth and Poverty* (*2002*), World Bank Policy Research Report No. 23591; and the excellent and downloadable collection of research publications on the World Bank website: www.worldbank.org/research/global.

online resource centre

Visit the companion website to this book for lots of interesting additional material, including self-assessment questions, internet exercises, and links for each chapter:
http://www.oxfordtextbooks.co.uk/orc/lee_carter2e/

CHAPTER FOUR

Understanding Global Cultures and Buyer Behaviour

Chapter overview

Chapter Introduction	104
What is Culture?	105
Language	109
Religion	109
Values and attitudes	110
Education	110
Social organization	111
Aesthetics	111
Adoption of technology	112
Political discourse	112
Understanding Consumer Behaviour	113
Culture and Consumer Behaviour	114
Cultural value system and consumer behaviour	116
Types of need and consumer behaviour	117
Managing Cultural Differences	118

Conducting Cross-cultural Analysis	120
Hall: high vs. low context approach	120
Hofstede: dimensions of culture	122
Hampden-Turner and Trompenaars: behaviour and value patterns	125
Schwartz: value inventory	127
Fang: cross-cultural theory	127
Applying cross-cultural frameworks	129
Commodity Trading	130
Government Buying Behaviour	131
Organizational Buyers or B2B Buyer Behaviour	132
B2B buying models	132
The effects of culture on B2B buyer behaviour	133
Culture and Ethics	134
Chapter Summary	135

Learning objectives

After studying this chapter, the reader will be able to:

- develop an understanding of what culture is and how the main components of a culture impact on a culture's way of life;
- explain the intimate relationships between cultural influences, consumer needs, and consumer behaviour;
- discuss the approaches which can be used to conduct cross-cultural analysis;
- examine the nature of business-to-business marketing and buyer behaviour;
- examine the effect of culture on ethical decision-making.

Management issues

The management issues that arise from this chapter include:

- How do the influences of culture determine if a product or service fits in with the culture's way of life? What level of adaptation may be necessary?
- How does the complexity of culture affect the analysis, strategic development, and implementation of marketing planning?
- What are the available approaches that an organization can use to manage cultural differences and analyse the cultural effects on buyer behaviour?

Chapter Introduction

Understanding the cultural diversity of the global marketplace requires a great deal of effort from global marketers. According to Pukthuanthong and Walker (2007), everyone who does business in a foreign country has to be aware of, and responsive to, that nation's culture. In the West, cultural differences between countries tend to be comparatively minor and businessmen and women can typically adjust to another nation's culture without major difficulties. This is particularly important in Asia where cultural sensitivity is essential to business success. While there is no shortage of examples of successful foreign companies' business operations, there is also considerable evidence of companies failing to gain fruitful market entries. For instance, the number of aborted expatriate overseas assignments in China alone is estimated at between 20% and 50%. The accompanying costs to businesses from these failed overseas assignments have been estimated at billions of dollars. The causes of these failures are, typically, due to a combination of the inability to reconcile management disagreements with local partners, technical and/or infrastructural failures, and more importantly, a lack of insight into how cultural factors affect consumers' patterns of behaviour as well as ways of doing business.

Since satisfying the culturally learned needs of target customers is a fundamental objective of marketing, gaining an intimate knowledge of the social and cultural influences of customers and the determinants of their purchase behaviour are vital to the success of marketing across cultures.

It is perhaps impossible for a 'cultural outsider' to know everything about a foreign culture, but the important gain from being able to empathize with other cultures is, as suggested by Bowman and Okuda (1985: 21), to create a climate of understanding and respect:

> People of goodwill can manage to reach agreements and to develop friendship in spite of difficulties encountered in the communication process. The willingness to accept differences, to suspend cultural prejudices, and to preserve in the face of misunderstandings can overcome even great differences in perceptions and expectations.

Having respect for, and an understanding of, another culture as well as the ability to set aside one's own cultural mores generally distinguishes successful global marketers from their less successful counterparts. Perhaps the biggest problem faced by multinational organizations is learning how best to market products and treat customers in emerging global markets (Miles, 1995). Global marketers will only be successful if they rise to the challenge of understanding culture and how it impacts on global market planning and implementation.

This chapter begins with a discussion of what we mean by culture and how the influences of a culture impact on the way of life of its people. We highlight the complex nature of culture and how it presents the global marketer with the challenge of dealing with its implications. We then move on to examine the intricacy of cross-cultural consumer behaviour and present a model that helps to explain the interaction between cultural influences,

MINI-CASE ILLUSTRATION **The consequences of getting it wrong culturally**

In Richard Gesteland's (2000) 'Do's and taboo's: proper etiquette in the global market place', there are fascinating examples of why billions of dollars are lost every year because executives do not understand the customs and traditions of their guest countries. For instance, on getting it right culturally, Gesteland tells the story of a Canadian company which thought it was on the verge of signing its first deal with an Egyptian company. The Egyptian executive flew to Canada where he was chief guest at a banquet. The Canadian company thought it had been astute in providing a range of non-alcoholic drinks for its Arab guest and introducing him to a number of the other guests. But the Egyptian businessman complained of the 'rude and offensive treatment' he had received and said he would not do business with 'such discourteous people'. This was because he had been offered food and drink only once and his Canadian host had spent too much time speaking to other banquet guests.

consumer needs, and consumer behaviour. This is followed by an exploration of how, when faced with the challenge of conducting cross-cultural analysis, the global marketer may endeavour to develop methods to compare and contrast consumers and buyers across cultures. Finally, we turn our attention to examining the nature of business-to-business marketing and buyer behaviour.

What is Culture?

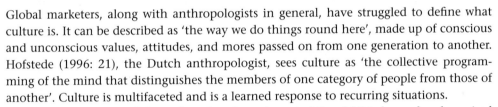

Global marketers, along with anthropologists in general, have struggled to define what culture is. It can be described as 'the way we do things round here', made up of conscious and unconscious values, attitudes, and mores passed on from one generation to another. Hofstede (1996: 21), the Dutch anthropologist, sees culture as 'the collective programming of the mind that distinguishes the members of one category of people from those of another'. Culture is multifaceted and is a learned response to recurring situations.

It is generally accepted that culture has three characteristics: (a) it is learned and acquired over time as members interact in a group; (b) it is interrelated, one part of culture is connected to another, e.g. religion and attitudes to marriage; and (c) it is shared, group members pass values on, e.g. parents to children. It also can be viewed as having two other layers: visible and hidden, as illustrated in Fig. 4.1. Visible, overt behaviour, like the clothes worn and eating habits, can be easily seen. Values and morals, like family values, are not so visible and basic cultural assumptions, such as 'ethnicity' and 'national identity', are not always overt, but can be the subject of, sometimes, wrong assumption. Malaysia, for example, has three main ethnicities—Malay, Chinese, and Indian. The physical differences between them are not always apparent and neither are the 'ethnic' values. An example of different cultures in Malaysia and their effect in the workplace is given later in this chapter. The 2008 bloody riots in Kenya, ostensibly in protest over the alleged rigged presidential elections, gave rise to deep-seated (less visible) tribal differences rising to the surface once again. Attitudes can differ as a result of culture. The status of the Mercedes Benz (www.mercedes-benz.com) may alter depending on where you are. In many parts of Africa it is a symbol of status and power, but in Cyprus or Spain it can be a useful taxi. The global appeal of many convenience foods and soft drinks suggests that global consumers have similar values when it comes to products, for example Coca-Cola (www.coke.com). Although culture may define boundaries between people, it does not limit the global operator.

Fig. 4.1 The 'Iceberg Model' of culture

The search for cultural universals is an important activity for global marketers. Sport, art, education, and music are global phenomena. Such universals account for the success of the Beatles and Madonna, Levi Strauss (www.levi.com) and IBM (www.ibm.com). However, marketers must not lose sight of culture seen from a local point of view. The fact that some may stereotype Americans as both 'gung ho' and 'narrow minded' and the British as 'conservative' may be because they are being looked at from the standpoint of an 'outside' culture and not from a local perspective. Global marketers should learn to take an objective perspective.

Culture can affect communication and negotiations. For example, the people from the subcontinent of India shake their head from side to side when they mean 'Yes', whereas in many other cultures this means 'No'. Knowledge and understanding of verbal and nonverbal communications is vital when negotiating. Translation from one language to another can be a minefield, and is particularly important when it comes to packaging and advertising. Endless languages on a label may seem tedious but may be necessary. In Japan, English labels give a stylish image and Western look. In Zimbabwe, the phrase 'export quality' was important psychologically—prior to opening the economy to imported goods in the 1990s, Zimbabweans were used to poor quality, domestically produced goods.

Social behaviour is an essential ingredient in successful business relationships. Showing the soles of one's feet in Thailand is anathema, and shaking hands is not always advisable. In Japan, a handshake followed by a bow is acceptable. Awareness of intercultural socialization pays dividends. Although the EU is now a 'common' market, many cultural differences exist—none so striking as the French and the British who are just 40 kilometres apart. The French, in general, are a hierarchical and status-conscious society, the British less so. This is reflected in the way the French and British dress, greet each other, and do business. Ambler and Styles, in *The Silk Road to International Marketing* (2000), stress the need to be 'biologically' attuned to the culture, and cite the dominant success of Procter and Gamble (www.pg.com) in Vietnam as a result of the immersion by a senior executive in the culture of that country long before it decided to enter the market. Ethnocentricity and cultural myopia are similar terms, and both are a key to success. They refer to the inability to see or act other than from the standpoint of your own cultural experience.

Being able to rise above this is the key. Educational partnerships around the globe are an interesting example of this. In linking up deals with other educational establishments, British universities are constrained by the 'rules of engagement' imposed on them by the UK Quality Assurance Agency (QAA). This means that in signing agreements, the UK institutions impose their own cultural interpretation of quality on foreign educational establishments. A good example is the issue of plagiarism. In some cultures, copying from the internet and/or journals without acknowledging sources may be perfectly acceptable but not in the UK, where educational institutions take a serious view of this practice. In some cultures, issues such as these may be seen as cumbersome and detrimental. The spirit of the law may be seen as more realistic and workable than the letter of the law.

We can define the culture as:

> Patterned ways of thinking, feeling and reacting, acquired and transmitted mainly by symbols, constituting the distinctive achievements of human groups, including their embodiments in artefacts; the essential case of culture consists of traditional ideas and especially their attached values.
>
> Kluckhohn (1951: 86)

Like an onion, culture can be viewed as consisting of different layers: (a) national culture, giving a cultural context in which business operates; (b) business culture, where businesses operate within a specific environment ('market' or 'centrally planned', for example) and where the 'rules of the game' are known; (c) organizational culture, where employees may have different individual cultures but adopt a common set of values or beliefs; and (d) individual behaviour, where individuals, through interaction with others, 'learn' culture and adopt their own 'culture'. This is illustrated in Fig. 4.2. There have been many studies linking the two variables organizational culture to organizational financial performance, but in a study on Malaysian business, Yeo and Carter (2005) examined the effect of three variables—culture strength, managerial competences, and their effect on corporate

Fig. 4.2 The four layers of culture

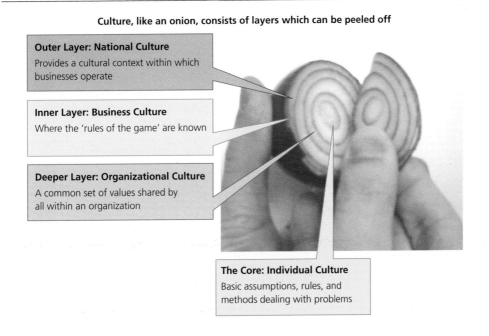

Culture, like an onion, consists of layers which can be peeled off

Outer Layer: National Culture
Provides a cultural context within which businesses operate

Inner Layer: Business Culture
Where the 'rules of the game' are known

Deeper Layer: Organizational Culture
A common set of values shared by all within an organization

The Core: Individual Culture
Basic assumptions, rules, and methods dealing with problems

performance—as measured by return on investment and return on equity. The study looked at the questions of whether there are corporate cultures which can be classified as strong; is there a relationship between strong culture and managerial competences, and how would these factors (strong culture and managerial competences) affect corporate performance. The cases used in the study comprised ten diversified public listed companies, which, being Malaysia, had a variety of individual behaviours and corporate cultures as a result. The study found that there was a relationship between 'strong' corporate culture and managerial competences and that both strong corporate culture and managerial competences had a significant impact on corporate effectiveness. There was a fit between the right elements of corporate strength (e.g. teamwork, rewards, and hard work) and the competency domains such as 'emotional involvement and 'build' orientation. This finding has important implications for managers as globalization increases the pace of communication, resulting in intense mobility of human capital. This has led to organizations operating in diverse geographic locations, stimulating the flow of human capital across borders. The findings of the study enable managers to, firstly identify culture strengths which might be context- and culturally-specific; secondly, provide appropriate training for employees to match the culture; and thirdly, emphasize the competency domains to boost performance.

It is only in recent years that socio-cultural influences have been identified as critical determinants of marketing behaviour. Culture is so pervasive yet so complex that it is difficult to define in short, simple terms. It is often assumed that because nations appear to be similar, e.g. the UK and the USA, the cultures must be the same. This is far from the case as the USA, for example, has infinitely more cultural diversity than the UK. The key components of culture in the global marketing environment are shown in Fig. 4.3. We shall consider each of these components (sometimes also known as cultural influences) in turn.

Fig. 4.3 The components of culture

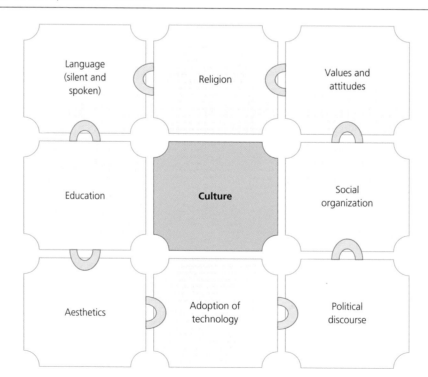

Language

Foreign markets may differ from the domestic in terms of the language. 'Language' can be both 'verbal' and 'non-verbal'. The ability to speak the language of the country targeted or operated in, enables companies to gather information on which to plan, operate, and control their businesses, 'access' society, communicate effectively, and 'contextualize', (i.e. see 'language' nuances). In some markets, such as Canada, there are a number of languages and the official one may differ from the one in common use. Countries with more than one official language sometimes are easy to spot (e.g. Malaysia has three official languages). Other countries with widely differing dialects are sometimes more difficult (e.g. people in Zimbabwe speak English and a number of native dialects). This can cause problems, both domestically and internationally. Malaysia, until recently, insisted that all primary school teaching must be in Bahasa Malay (the national language) but soon realized the limited usage outside Malaysia, so reverted to the universal language of trade and commerce, English. Non-verbal language (e.g. body language) is equally important. For instance, the use of hand gestures and facial expression are vital elements of verbal communication in the Indian culture. The importance of non-verbal communication is more important in 'high context' countries than 'low context' countries. People in 'high context' countries are more sensitive to different message systems than in 'low context' ones. See later discussion on Hall and Hall (1987).

Different languages pose challenges to global marketers and are best tackled by using a native speaker or a specialist organization such as the Document Company (www.fujixerox.co.jp). Instances abound of differences in linguistic nuance and it is easy to get it wrong. For example, the British luxury car manufacturer Rolls-Royce (www.rolls-royce.com) found that the name of its Silver Cloud model did not translate well into German—directly translated, it becomes a very rude word. Particularly affected are marketing communications, packaging, labelling, technical manuals, and face-to-face communications. American Motors' 'Matador' brand car meant 'Killer' in Spain, Pepsi's slogan, 'Come alive with Pepsi', meant 'come out of the grave' when translated into German.

Religion

Religion is a major cultural variant. There are over 100 different religions in the world, the predominant ones being Christianity, Islam, Hinduism, Buddhism, and Judaism. Religion can be the basis for transcultural similarities. Religion brings with it a number of symbols, colours, rituals, holidays, taboos, philosophical systems, numbers, etc., which have profound implications on consumer behaviour. The number '8' in Chinese stands for prosperity and long life; while the '4' is to be avoided as it has sinister connotations. Property developers are able to charge buyers a premium for a flat on the eighth floor, and the fourth floor is often missed out so that it becomes the fifth. Crown Cork and Seal (www.crowncork.com), the US-based bottle sealing company,

Religion often has significant impact on consumer behaviour. For example, in most Islamic countries, alcohol consumption is either prohibited or actively discouraged.

has found its crown logo unacceptable universally and scantily clad ladies advertising products or services are not well received in Islamic societies.

Religion can have a real effect on an organization's products and services. Not only does it affect the obvious, such as packaging and communications, but also the way business is conducted. Holidays or holy days can interrupt business as well as shape the ways in which it is conducted. Islamic culture is adverse to usury and so the banking systems are quite different from those of the West. Consumption patterns, like fish on Friday for Catholics, can be affected. Attitudes to gender differences may affect who is contactable in an organization and by whom. In the Middle East, women are restricted in their capacity as consumers and this might affect the ability to carry out research on them.

Religion has become ever more important after 9/11 and 7/7 (the UK Underground bombings). Concern, real or apparent, has been raised in the UK over the non-integration of cultures, based on religion. Pakistan, Iraq, and the Middle East are witnessing an increasing instability based mainly on factions of religion. This increasing uncertainty has led to global marketers having to reconsider their operations in affected areas. For example, Dubai has rapidly diversified its economy by offering opulent living to mainly the world's richest people. However, in modernizing itself in this way, Dubai has created an interesting variety of cultures, including different religious beliefs, which potentially, at least on the surface, appear to be in conflict. Attracting the world's 'rich' is a fine strategy, but often the 'rich' bring with them many cultural mores which are at odds with Dubai's Muslim culture (e.g. the consumption of alcohol). Balancing the need to attract new industries and consumers to Dubai while preserving its traditions, including its religious ones, is no easy task.

Values and attitudes

Achievement, work, attitudes to wealth, change, and risk-taking are all universal characteristics but their interpretation may vary from country to country. In some areas, for example Africa, lateness may be universal due to infrastructural difficulties or poor time-keeping. Some executives think it a symbol of importance if you are kept waiting for an appointment.

The effects of local culture, practice, values, and attitudes affect the way in which work is conducted and other organizational issues, such as personnel and staff motivation. Global organizations may find it difficult to enforce their values and culture universally. If attitudes and standards are not maintained or enforced, an organization may lack global credibility. This affects many organizations. For instance, in Southern Africa, Toyota (www.toyota.com) wished to maintain a global world-class standard of servicing for their vehicles but this was not deliverable in the early 1990s. Lack of foreign currency to purchase parts, poor training locally and a less than professional attitude mitigated against it.

Another complicating factor is the 'fad attitude' to products and services. There is growing evidence that consumers, especially in post-industrial societies, want to be satisfied in different and constantly changing ways. This is evidenced by shorter product life cycles and the incidence of innovation in many product and service categories, e.g. cars, music, clothes, financial services, and holiday destinations. The challenge for the global marketer is to gauge whether it is a fad or a lasting phenomenon and invest accordingly.

Education

While primary, secondary, and tertiary education may be treated as a given in the Western world and in countries such as Japan, it is not a universal phenomenon. In Southern Africa, for example, literacy rates are considerably different. Primary literacy rates in Zambia are only 40%, whereas in Malaysia they are as high as 90%. The higher the educational levels, the more opportunities there are for marketers to be more sophisticated. This has a direct effect on segmentation, communications, packaging, and labelling. But low levels of literacy may mean that consumers are unable to read labels. Also, the more educated the market, the less consumers are likely to be 'accepting'. Soap powder packed only in plastic bags may be acceptable in some cultures, but not all.

There is an increasing trend to Westernization among the world's educated young. The effect of popular music and artistes as well as television characters should not be underestimated. Almost everyone has heard of Mickey Mouse and this has led to the Disney theme park phenomenon (www.disney.com), the latest being the possible construction of one in Johor Bahru in Malaysia. Similarly, the success of Universal Studios (www.universalstudios.com) with characters like Donald Duck and Spiderman.

The Beatles, Michael Jackson, the Red Hot Chilli Peppers, Scissor Sisters, Robbie Williams, Madonna, Coldplay, The Killers, Kaizer Chiefs, Artic Monkeys, Keane, James Blunt, and the Rolling Stones appear regularly in the diet of young (and not so young) people. In Japan, there are public places set aside in some cities where the young can dance with their digital music players. Global communications and the evolution of global 'youth culture' segments have been a driving force. Global marketers, therefore, can take advantage by seizing on the possibilities presented by this globally aligned segment. Products like music are obvious, followed by clothes, sport, travel, and cosmetics to name but a few examples.

Social organization

Social organization is the way society organizes itself. Factors to be considered include interest groups, status systems, the role of the different sexes, caste systems, and social institutions. Social systems are useful bases for segmenting markets. An example is the role of women in Islamic societies or India, where they are usually expected to be traditional and submissive. In the light of increasing multi-racialism and multiculturalism in modern societies, it can be dangerous to make generalizations about the factors of social organization in a society. The stereotypical view of Americans being an individualistic and materialistic people who champion equal opportunity for all is often inaccurate for a nation with more than 30% of its population made up of the most diverse range of cultures and social systems.

Aesthetics

Aesthetics are the way local cultures perceive things like design and beauty. Colours mean different things in different cultures and local knowledge is a must. What pleases the eye of a Westerner may not be acceptable in some countries. Benetton (www.benetton.com), the Italian clothing maufacturer, found its fortunes flagging in the mid-1990s, due in part, according to some observers, to Benetton's highly controversial shock advertising based on the theme 'The United Colours of Benetton'. The adverts were designed to centre on social and political issues and used shocking images based on the environment, terrorism, and sexually transmitted diseases. One set of adverts on sexuality used AIDS as a theme in some images. In France it caused a controversy. One AIDS victim took out an advertisement with his own face on it with the tagline 'during the agony, the sales continue'. The images were not well received in the USA either. Eventually, Benetton paid compensation to some victims and in other instances, such as parts of Germany, the products were banned. American cars are virtually non-existent in the UK. Bikinis are seldom seen in Muslim countries.

THE DIGITAL IMPACT Mobile text messaging and imaging: a global phenomenon

In November 2007, there were one billion text messages sent every week in the UK. (Mobile Data Association, www.text.it, 21 January 2008). Mobile text messaging and imaging is common to all cultures. It is used in nearly every context and business situation. In the Far East and southern Africa, for example, texting is a fashionable activity for any self-respecting youngster. In business and service situations, imaging can be used for finding solutions to problems, displaying samples, and a host of other activities. Buyers searching for new sources of clothing anywhere in the world can send sample images back to headquarters, along with price, delivery details, etc. But it is the power to communicate to certain segments that has made mobile texting and imaging a prime medium for some advertisers. Setting aside potential ethical considerations for the moment, mobile service companies can specifically target certain age groups, sub-cultures (music lovers), or any other categories of buyers, and directly send advertising messages, products, or services to their mobile phones. Products and services sold in this way include night clubs, phone services, and educational products. For example, those linked to the Vodafone (www.vodafone.com) mobile network, on entry to South Africa receive a mobile text message of welcome and a reminder of Vodafone's services. In 2004, iTouch (www.itouchplc.com) concluded a licensing agreement for the animated film *Shrek 2*. The deal gives the mobile services company the right to distribute *Shrek 2*

Mobile Data Association

games, video clips, wallpapers, picture greetings, and ringtones in the UK, Spain, Ireland, Portugal, and South Africa.

Avoiding offence may have implications for packaging, labelling, product design, communications, distribution, and organizational personnel issues such as the clothes and demeanour of employees. Learning to empathize with local cultures and understanding the aesthetics are crucial to successful market penetration.

Adoption of technology

Technology in the cultural sense refers to how people adopt and adapt to the technology in a material sense. Depending on a country's state of economic development, technology may have to be made simpler to avoid costly repair. A good example of appropriate technology is that of the locally built AVM buses in Zimbabwe. Based on an extremely strong chassis and engine, and with simple mechanics, they are more suited to the rough rural conditions than any sophisticated imported bus. Global marketers need to be aware of what will and what will not 'fit' the local conditions and make adjustments accordingly. A more detailed discussion on 'Technology' and its effects is given in Chapter 2.

Political discourse

Political discourse as a component of culture is a growing phenomenon. It refers to discussion among group(s) of people who have a vested interest in influencing the political agenda or establishing a dialogue with politicians, within countries. This can take the form of merely voicing an opinion via the media or more active forms of discourse via street demonstrations. Zimbabwe is a classic modern-day example of groups of people (the Movement for Multi Party Democracy, MMD) who have engaged in political discourse to change the one-party regime of Zanu PF. Other examples include the demonstrations which brought an end to the split of Germany, and the constant dialogue between the activists opposed to globalization and leaders of the G7 countries.

In conclusion, there is little doubt that culture can make or break international operations, hence the need to study its components and identify its impact on strategic planning and implementation. There has been, and continues to be, much research into the effects of culture, particularly cross-cultural studies, in an attempt to discover similarities and differences to aid in market selection and entry, and marketing mix selection and operation.

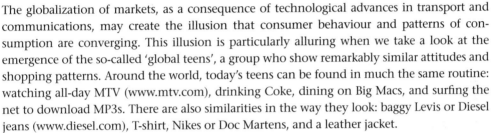

Understanding Consumer Behaviour

The globalization of markets, as a consequence of technological advances in transport and communications, may create the illusion that consumer behaviour and patterns of consumption are converging. This illusion is particularly alluring when we take a look at the emergence of the so-called 'global teens', a group who show remarkably similar attitudes and shopping patterns. Around the world, today's teens can be found in much the same routine: watching all-day MTV (www.mtv.com), drinking Coke, dining on Big Macs, and surfing the net to download MP3s. There are also similarities in the way they look: baggy Levis or Diesel jeans (www.diesel.com), T-shirt, Nikes or Doc Martens, and a leather jacket.

The assumption that using standardized marketing strategies can target consumers across cultures is, however, preventing the marketer from appreciating the differences in consumers' ability and motivation to buy. Cultural differences can be demonstrated by different brand choices, consumption habits, and purchase behaviour. A French consumer is expected to differ greatly in his or her wine choices from, say, an American or Australian consumer. The French have a long tradition of wine consumption and, in France, wine is an everyday product. For the USA and Australia, the so-called 'new world' in wine production and consumption, wine-drinking starts later in life and concerns a smaller proportion of the population. Vintage plays a lesser role and wine type or variety is more important—a French consumer would normally identify a wine first as a Bordeaux or Burgundy, while an Australian might identify the wine first by its grape variety, e.g. Sauvignon, Chardonnay (Aurifeille et al., 2001). In addition, the consumption situations and patterns also vary across cultures. The Chinese, in general, would normally only consume alcohol when celebrating with esteemed hosts and are therefore more likely to spend significantly more per purchase. Any generalization of this kind, as pointed out by Hill and Still (1984), could expose marketers to the danger that a competitor may identify and exploit these differences in order to make their marketing mix more appealing to segments identified within each national market.

As these examples show, it is difficult to generalize about consumer behaviour because consumption patterns vary. Even if there are similarities in demands for a given product between countries A and B, the ability to pay may differ due to socio-economic difference. For example, Thailand's socio-economic conditions are more advanced than China's, with the former possessing a higher per capita GDP (i.e. US$3251) than the latter (i.e. US$2055) in 2006 (United Nations Statistics Division, 2008, www.un.org). The socio-economic conditions of markets significantly affect consumer behaviour (Tse et al., 1989) due to variances in ability to pay. When the ability to pay is low, consumers may focus more heavily on price and performance attributes in making product evaluations on purchase decisions. Consumers with a higher ability to pay are able to choose luxury products and brands.

South Koreans have the opportunity to travel abroad and sample foreign consumer products as a result of their higher income and standard of living, as well as earlier liberalization policies for travelling abroad. Compared to China, South Korea's exposure to foreign cultures and brands through travel, as well as the imports of Western goods into its markets, is more extensive (Kim et al., 2002), although in 2008, this is beginning to change rapidly due to China's advancing economy and the fact more Chinese are travelling extensively.

Meeting consumer needs in different countries by providing the right products and services is an ongoing challenge for businesses. Consumers may choose particular products not only because these products provide the functional or performance benefits expected, but also because products can be used to express consumers' personality, social status, or affiliation, or to fulfil the need for change or novelty (Kim et al., 2002). The needs, choice, and preference of the consumer for a particular product are generally affected by complex social and cultural influences. The consumer's value system, which reflects the social influences and cultural environment, could be influential in shaping the needs to be fulfilled through purchase and consumption decisions, and therefore, consumer behaviour (Yau, 1994).

A question occupying global marketers more and more is the 'convergence' and/or 'divergence' of cultures. Driven by ever-widening mass communications (e.g. Sky Television, www.sky.com), increasing global travel, and more available education, one argument suggests a convergence of culture epitomized by McDonalds (www.mcdonalds.com), KFC (www.kfc.com), Nike (www.nike.com), and MTV. The other argument, based on various characteristics of culture, such as 'religion' and 'ethnicity', suggests a more divergent globe. What is certain is that generational barriers are getting more blurred. Sport and music 'role models' whatever their age, seem able to bridge the generations. This blurring has made the cross-border 'same product-same message' or 'different product-different message, strategies more difficult to assess and implement. Segments are not so easily categorized, as the example given in Chapter 2 on 'technology' showed, where the 'silver-haired' generation was more internet-savvy than face value would give them credit. This blurring makes it all the more difficult for global marketers to manage their market operations internationally.

When emerging economies around the world adopt the free enterprise system of the West, they also take on board the values assumed in the West to be a part of a capitalistic system (Bond and King, 1985). The argument that exposure to Western ways of engaging in business will result in the adoption of Western values suggests that the demands, opportunities, and management leadership styles of a technologically advancing society shape value systems that respond to industrialization rather than to indigenous cultural forces (Garg and Ma, 2006). In contrast is the argument that culture is sufficiently powerful to ensure that managerial values will continue to remain different despite the Western style of industrialization (Lincoln et al., 1978). Organizations typically must consider, either directly or indirectly, the influence of foreign as well as domestic economic and socio-political systems (Tung and Miller, 1990). However, in the case of Chief Operating Officers, economic and socio-economic political systems are encouraging speedy adaption to foreign organizational systems and management styles (Garg and Ma, 2006).

Culture and Consumer Behaviour

As the world economy becomes increasingly cross-cultural, marketers are confronted with the challenges of marketing and managing in multicultural marketplaces. In the coming decades, as businesses 'enter new international markets, an understanding of how culture influences consumer behaviour will be crucial for both managers and consumer research-ers' (Luna and Gupta, 2001: 45). 'Culture' affects motivation which in turn impacts on customer needs and wants. It leads to different patterns of behaviour (e.g. circumstance and type of product purchased, for instance Christian New Year and Jewish New Year), different values attached to products (e.g. bottled water in Europe as a 'designer' drink ver-sus water as a necessity in the Gobi Desert), different decision-making (e.g. 'pester power' of children in the West versus family survival in Sierra Leone), different forms of commu-nication (e.g. ban on cigarette TV advertising in the UK versus no ban on TV advertising in the USA), and different forms of retailing and other intermediaries (e.g. the souk in (Morocco versus the shopping mall in Malaysia).

The model in Fig. 4.4 depicts the mutual influence of culture, consumer needs, and consumer behaviour. It suggests that consumers' behaviour is a result of the cultural value system in a particular context. An individual's cultural value system is developed over time as he/she is socialized into a particular group. Societal culture as well as regional sub-culture and familial values all influence the formation of the cultural value system. Thus, the system includes cultural elements that individuals have in common with the group(s) to which they belong, as well as the idiosyncratic values unique to the individual (Luna and Gupta, 2001). As the model suggests, culture affects consumer behaviour by influ-encing behavioural and consumption decisions, hence creating desires and driving the consumer to select products or brands that fulfil specific needs. In other words, individual consumers' needs and desires are shaped by values which are influenced by the society they belong to (Kim et al., 2002). Marketing communication is represented in the model as a moderator of the effect of culture on consumer behaviour by acting as the vehicle to transfer meanings or values from the culture's value system to consumer goods and services. It is the mechanism which is used by organizations to transmit marketing mes-sages of products or brands in ways that are culturally relevant and/or appealing to that target consumer. As depicted in the model, marketing communications can also affect consumer behaviour independently of culture (Luna and Gupta, 2001). For instance, the advertisements for Müller yoghurt (www.muller.co.uk), where a mother deprives her child of the yoghurt with the caption ('There is motherly love, and there is Müller love . . .') and McCain's (www.mccain.com) Oven Potato Chips, where family members are shown fighting over who gets a larger portion of the potato chips, are promoting self-centred behaviours and personal indulgence.

Fig. 4.4 The interaction of culture and consumer behaviour

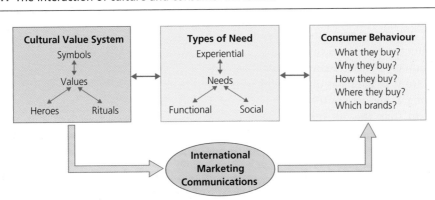

Source: Based on Luna and Gupta (2001: 47).

Cultural value system and consumer behaviour

According to Hofstede (1996), culture influences behaviour through its manifestations: values, heroes, rituals, and symbols. It is a widely accepted view that values are central to the notion of culture, and the underlying determinant of consumer attitudes and consumption behaviour. *Values* have been described by Rokeach (1973) as a centrally held, enduring belief which guides actions and judgements across specific situations and beyond immediate goals to more ultimate end-states of existence. Values are structured in a society's cultural value system, an enduring organization of beliefs concerning preferred ways of living and behaving. Since the composition of a value system is unique to a culture, it is possible to map values of a culture through research and distinguish the value systems of one group of consumers from another.

Every culture is governed by a unique set of values passed from one generation to the next. For example, relating sex to ice cream, as in the Häagen-Dazs (www.haagendazs .com) advertisements (where a pair of lovers is shown engaging in foreplay with the aid of a tub of Häagen-Dazs), would not be acceptable in the Chinese culture. The message of the product being 'dedicated for personal pleasure and indulgence' would cause offence to the family-centred population as 'good things' are supposed to be shared among family members. In Malaysia, many Chinese believe that the accumulation of wealth and material possessions is the most desirable goal and the source of happiness. In contrast, many Malays, while acknowledging the need to work hard, place more emphasis on spending time with families and socializing with friends. It is important for global marketers to identify the prevalent set of values in the targeted international consumer markets and to understand how these values affect purchase behaviours.

Heroes, as defined by Hofstede (1996: 8) are 'persons, alive or dead, real or imaginary, who possess characteristics which are highly prized in a culture, and who thus serve as models for behaviour'. Examples of heroes may range from political leaders, members of the royal family, rock stars, scientists, intellectuals, and religious leaders to comic characters. Heroes may have a profound influence on consumer behaviour through their association with certain products and brands. Indeed, products or brands 'promoted' within blockbuster movies or associated with a famous personality have been proven to yield considerable profits, sometimes irrespective of their quality.

A *ritual* can be defined as 'an expressive, symbolic activity, comprising a number of behaviours occurring in a fixed order, frequently repeated over time' (Antonides and van Raaji, 1998: 71). While religious rituals are the most obvious type of ritual, ritualistic behaviour also occurs in relation to ordinary behaviours such as eating, going on holiday, personal care, sports, and gift-giving (Rook, 1985). Rituals are important for consumer behaviour because they involve the consumption of goods and services. For instance, gift-giving is universal, especially during cultural festivals although the ritualistic behaviours of gift-giving and gift-receiving may vary across cultures. In most Western cultures it is polite for the gift-receiver to unwrap the gift in front of guests and express gratitude. In a number of East Asian cultures it is considered rude for a gift-receiver to unwrap gifts in front of guests as unwrapping gifts is a 'private affair'. In countries such as Japan and Hong Kong, where the presentation of a gift is often seen as equally(if not more) important than the gift itself, it is not unusual to see a gift being boxed and wrapped in numerous layers to convey the goodwill and sincerity of the gift-giver. Consumers in these cultures are willing to pay a premium for goods and services that are presented in a perceptively better way.

Symbols refer to a broad category of processes and objects that carry a meaning unique to a particular group (Geertz, 1973: 89). Symbols and their associated meanings are

WHOSE RESPONSIBILITY IS IT? Role models—heroes or villains?

Every child has a hero. For some, heroes are cartoon characters like Scooby Doo, the Sonics, the Hulk, Spiderman, or Superman. For others, it may be all-action heroes like the Terminator, Jackie Chan, The WWEs, The Game, or Lara Croft. Yet others may find their role models in football, (e.g. Christiano Ronaldo or Stephen Gerrard) or other sports. Heroes make for big business and profits. In recent years there has been growing concern that the boundary between healthy fantasy-hero worship and reality may have crossed over.

In 2004, research in the USA suggested that young children were watching television five hours per day on average, and that they were definitely being influenced by it. In the example of the shootings of teachers and children at Columbine School, USA, and other similar gun-related incidents at schools by school children, researchers were sure that a link could be established between these events and violent TV heroes, or other heroes, admired by the perpetrators. Graham Tibbetts, writing in the *Daily Telegraph* (2 October 2007) and quoting research, said that even two hours of TV viewing per day for children aged 2–5 years could be harmful. The research showed that 16% of children (in the research group of 2–5 years) watched TV for two hours or more per day only when 2 years old, 15% watched more than two hours per day when 5 years old, and 20% maintained their viewing habit when 3 years plus.

Children's games are another source of gratuitous violence and sex. This time, it is not only comic characters or sporting heroes that are characterized but other heroes, such as US Marines and British troops, fuelled by TV and newspaper coverage of the Iraq war. In 2007, a particularly violent computer game, marketed by Sony, depicted scenes uncannily like the inside of Manchester Cathedral in the UK. Such was the outcry that Sony withdrew the game and apologized, contesting that no offence or intention to replicate the inside of the cathedral was intended.

Why, in parts of the world where such television programmes and films cannot be seen, are children not carrying out these copycat crimes? As television and films, and their global presence, begin to spread further, is it time to consider their effect on children and do something, or does global commercialism take precedence?

Source: Tibbetts (2007).

inherently unique to a given culture. They normally rely on objects or natural elements (such as colours, shapes, locations, materials, animals, and gestures) to express or transmit their meanings. For instance, as illustrated by Usunier (2000 and Usunier and Lee, 2005), the colour white symbolizes birth or a happy life event in the West, whereas in China it symbolizes death and mourning. The colour red can be related to blood or caution in the West, but in China it is the colour of prosperity and vigour, and is used as the colour of important events and celebrations.

Types of need and consumer behaviour

The goal of marketing is to fulfil consumer needs in a manner better than the competition. Therefore, the primary focus of a marketing-oriented organization is to get close to its customers so that they understand their needs and problems. Much research has been dedicated to understanding and classifying human needs. Perhaps the most influential model is Maslow's 'hierarchy of needs' (Maslow, 1970). According to this model, an individual will satisfy basic needs first, and will only move up the hierarchy of categories as 'lower' needs are fulfilled. The categories include lower level physiological needs (warmth, shelter, food) at the bottom, then higher physiological needs (safety, belongingness), then needs to satisfy the 'ego', and finally to 'self-actualization'. The hierarchical nature of Maslow's model implies that the order of development is fixed, i.e. a certain level must be attained before the next, higher, one is activated.

In marketing, consumer needs can be more simply categorized into *functional*, *social*, and *experiential*. Every product or service exists to satisfy a *functional need*. For example, a car is a means of transport designed to satisfy the functional need of getting from A to B. Functional needs are 'considered fairly low-level motivator[s], encouraging consumers to focus on the intrinsic advantages of the product' (Kim et al., 2002: 486).

Products or services are also consumed to satisfy *social needs* such as social approval, affiliation, or personal expression (e.g. status, prestige) and outward-directed self-esteem (ibid.). Consumers who have higher social needs normally value a socially accepted and visible product or brand that symbolizes the desired status or prestige. In India, for instance, the possession of Western or imported goods is associated with the prestige, wealth, and exclusive lifestyles of the elite classes in society.

Finally, the consumer's choice and preference of products are also reflected in his/her intention to satisfy the *experiential needs*, such as novelty, variety, and sensory gratification or pleasure (ibid.). In the light of increasing consumer demands and expectations, experiential needs are an important aspect of consumption in today's modern societies. In most Western societies, burgeoning wealth and income have provided consumers with the means to indulge in luxurious and novelty goods and services to satisfy their experiential needs—a phenomenon not unfamiliar in many developing nations.

Consumer needs, to be fulfilled through consumption of particular products or brands, vary considerably with the socio-economic and cultural differences among consumer markets. In their study of the relationship of consumer needs and purchase behaviour in China and South Korea, Kim et al. (2002) found that the types of consumer needs to be satisfied when purchasing and consuming clothing products were different between the two countries' consumers. For instance, Chinese consumers, who were brand loyal, were more likely to satisfy their experiential needs with fashion statements or their social needs with prestige. By contrast, Korean female consumers' brand loyalty seems to be attributed to the fact that their loyal brands fulfilled more of their social needs and performance expectations (i.e. functional needs) than their experiential needs. In short, consumers' general purchase behaviour reflects the utilization of different consumer needs, which are conditioned by culture and social values.

Managing Cultural Differences

Most people 'have an automatic and unconscious tendency to refer to our own thought framework, which is mainly tied to our national culture, to interpret situations, evaluate people, communicate, negotiate or decide which attitude to take' (Usunier, 2000: 432). This often unconscious attempt to compare other cultures through one's own culture is referred to by James Lee (1966) as the 'self-reference criterion' (SRC). This may present problems when seeking new markets, assessing how consumers may behave in them, and in deciding on the elements of the international marketing mix. In order to avoid this, Lee suggests a four-step approach, illustrated in Fig. 4.5. To use the model effectively, marketers need to know their own cultures and that of the target countries. This is not an easy task.

Fig. 4.5 Lee's four-step approach to avoiding the dangers of the self-reference criterion

Step One	Define the problem or goal in terms of home country traits, habits, and norms
Step Two	Define the problem or goal in terms of foreign culture traits, habits, and norms
Step Three	Isolate the SRC influence in the problem and examine it carefully to see how it complicates the problem
Step Four	Redefine the problem without the SRC influence and solve for the foreign market situation

Source: Based on Lee (1966).

An interesting illustration is in purchasing a well-known brand of Japanese vehicle in southern Africa in the early 1990s before many economies in the region were opened up to international trade through World Bank-sponsored Economic Structural Adjustment Programmes (see Chapter 2). In domestic (UK) terms, one of the primary concerns of a car purchaser is after sales of parts and service. This is taken for granted in the West, and the temptation is to think that this applies throughout the world (Step One in Lee's framework). In Southern Africa, where sourcing foreign currency was a problem, it could not be taken for granted that dealers would have spare parts over the life of the vehicle (Step Two). This was a problem because car owners might have had to take their vehicles off the road until currency became available, revert to 'pirate parts', or even stolen parts (Step Three). The solution was to understand that in Southern Africa spare parts were a problem. This led the Japanese company to identify the most likely parts needed over the life of the vehicle (e.g. exhausts, points, filters), and to advise customers to source enough foreign currency to buy the vehicle and these essential parts at the same time (Step Four).

Companies such as Toyota (www.Toyota. com), Nissan (www.nissanmotors.com), and Guinness (www.guinness.com) know the importance of avoiding the SRC, hence they have local management as well as international personnel in all their in-country operations.

However, the process of 'enculturation' (i.e. learning about one's own culture through society, education, or informally via peer groups) comes over time and may affect consumer behaviour in different ways over a person's life-span. This is different from 'acculturation', which is an understanding of other cultures in order to empathize with them. This requires the ability to empathize with the culture and to exercise cultural neutrality by recognizing that

Food is often the easiest way for many consumers to identify and relate to a culture. What a people eats can often provide insights into their traditions, way of life, taste and preferences.

differences exist without making judgements. In Africa, for example, timekeeping is not a prerequisite, often exasperating British executives. The Chinese trait of making friends before doing business is again alien to the attitude of Western businessmen. In a study by Cao (2008), observing a potential business tie-up between a Chinese and UK ventilation company, the UK company had to rapidly learn that the Chinese were as interested in 'trust' and 'long-term' relations as in short-term contractual issues. Many Malay children have rice for breakfast, Americans have fried eggs, and Indian children hot and spicy Sambal curry. To health-conscious Western mothers, these may seem anathema. It is this cross-cultural toleration and understanding which is the basis for successful global marketing.

Conducting Cross-cultural Analysis

The discussion so far has concentrated on understanding culture and identifying its components and its influence on consumer behaviour. We have established that culture is a complex issue and a generic term that plays host to more specific variables such as language, education, and religion. Given such 'complexities, often market analysts use *country* or *nationality* as a surrogate for culture' (Doole and Lowe, 2004: 67). It is, however, inaccurate to simply place individuals under an umbrella represented by the cultural values of their nationality. Marketers who take a generic portrait of culture may end up adopting a mass-market approach which does not allow consideration to sub-cultures, market segmentation, and consumer profiling. Any attempt to equate culture directly with the nation state or country would be misguided as nations are made up of sub-cultures and are often explicitly multicultural. The complexity of culture therefore creates a challenge to the global marketer in conducting cross-cultural analysis.

Cross-cultural analysis has been defined as the systematic comparison of similarities and differences in the material and behavioural aspects of cultures. Many approaches have been put forward in an attempt to provide a framework or structure in order to achieve a meaningful cross-cultural understanding. While there is not yet a universally recognized approach, some of the approaches (Hall, 1977; Hofstede, 1984) are widely accepted as important in this area. In the following sections we will examine some of these works and the ways in which they are applied to analysing consumer behaviour across cultures.

Hall: high vs. low context approach

Edward T. Hall was author of *The Silent Language* (1959) and *The Hidden Dimension* (1966). The foundation for his lifelong research on cultural perceptions of space was laid during World War II when he served in the US Army in Europe and the Philippines. When he was Director of the Foreign Service Institute training program for technicians assigned to overseas duty, Hall observed the many difficulties created by failures of intercultural communication. His main contribution to the culture debate was that he observed basic differences in the way that members of different cultures perceived reality and how these were responsible for miscommunications of the most fundamental kind

Hall (1977) stressed the fact that cultures differ in the ways in which people understand and communicate, i.e. language is one of the most important components of culture. Language differences between cultures can be vast, so there will be marked differences in cultures. For example, English and Japanese are two very different languages, and so are their cultures. However, Spanish and Italian have Latin as their base, so Spaniards and Italians have similar cultural norms and beliefs. Central to this approach is the concept of context or silent language—that is, the level of importance different cultures place on the situational factors involved in the encoding and decoding of communication.

Hall contributed two dimensions to the context of culture: 'high vs. low' and 'monochronic vs. polychronic time'. For the first dimension, Hall suggested that all 'information transactions' can be characterized as 'high', 'middle' or 'low' context. High context transactions feature pre-programmed information that is in the receiver and in the setting, with only minimal information in the transmitted message—Implicit. For low-context transactions, most of the information must be in the transmitted message in order to make up for what is missing in the context—Explicit. The context of a culture can be identified as either high or low depending on the clarity of the spoken word and/or the way communications were influenced by the surroundings or context in which they were spoken. Low-context cultures rely on spoken or written language for their meaning. High-context cultures rely on the elements or context surrounding the message to develop understanding of the message. The greater the contextual difference between those trying to communicate, the greater the difficulty organizations will have in communicating accurately. The Japanese, for example, surround their communications with context, depending on whether they are talking to different genders or age groups. This is not always easy to spot. The following examples illustrate the difficulty in language and translation:

- Japanese hotel notice to hotel guests:
  'You are invited to take advantage of the chambermaid.'
- Acapulco hotel notice regarding drinking water:
  'The manager has personally passed all the water served here.'
- Visitors to a zoo in Budapest were asked:
  'Not to feed the animals. If you have any suitable food, give it to the guard on duty.'
- A Bangkok dry cleaner to potential customers:
  'Drop your trousers here for best results.'
- An Italian laundry innocently suggested:
  'Ladies leave your clothes here and spend the afternoon having a good time.'

Hall's second dimension, 'monochronic vs. polychronic time' deals with the ways in which cultures structure their time in relation to interpersonal relations, activity coordination, personal time, and organizations. 'Monochronic' means dealing with 'one thing at a time'. It is more structured and rigid than 'polychronic', which means being able to deal with 'multiple tasks all at once', and so is less structured and flexible.

Hall's work finds practical significance in the fact that most 'tips for trips overseas' leaflets issued by national foreign trade organizations are based on his work. This is because it is easy to offend hosts in other cultures, especially in terms of 'high-' and 'low-context' matters.

Hall's approach assumes that language differences exist between cultures which, in turn, distinguish one culture from another. Fig. 4.6 is an illustration of Hall's approach to culture and shows that the Swiss, for instance, can be identified as having a low-context culture, where communication relies on spoken and written language for meaning. In comparison, Japan is a high-context culture due to its highly complex methods of communication

Fig. 4.6 The contextual continuum of cultures

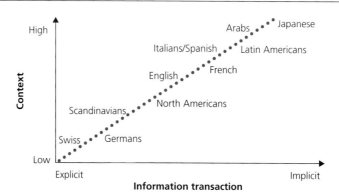

in relation to age, gender, and social standing. The greater the contextual difference between those cultures trying to communicate, the more complex it becomes to accomplish accurate communication.

Language plays a significant role in describing and conveying consumer benefits, suggesting product qualities and convincing potential buyers. It must use words that represent local worldviews (Usunier, 2000) to make a positive impact on consumers in their purchase behaviour. In a low-context culture such as Germany (the Germans have a reputation for talking literally, with explicit messages and low context), consumers prefer clarity and precision in what they pay for. For instance, they are more likely to insist on precise and detailed labelling that describes the ingredients and/or the process of production. In business negotiations, there is a tendency to schedule meetings precisely, an unspoken commitment to punctuality, and attention to every detail in any business contract or agreement.

In contrast, in a high-context culture such as China, consumers pay less attention to the small print but more to the social value of the product or brand. As social approval is important, the purchase decisions are, to a large extent, influenced by the perceived social acceptance and meaning associated with the product or brand. In business negotiation, there is less likelihood of placing undue attention on details while more efforts are usually made to get to know the business partner, as long-term relationships are highly valued.

Hofstede: dimensions of culture

The work of Geert Hofstede, a Dutch organizational anthropologist, is perhaps the most widely used and accepted approach to cross-cultural analysis (www.geert-hofstede.com). Hofstede describes culture in the following way: 'Culture is more often a source of conflict than of synergy. Cultural differences are a nuisance at best and often a disaster' (Hofstede, www.geart-hofstede.com).

Hofstede provided a universally applicable framework for classifying cultural patterns. He derived his culture dimensions from examining work-related values in IBM employees in 40 countries during the 1970s. Subsequent studies, validating the earlier results, were conducted on commercial airline pilots and students in 23 countries, civil service managers in 14 counties, 'up-market' consumers in 15 countries, and 'elites' in 19 countries.

Hofstede's original groundbreaking research, which was intended to uncover differences in work-related issues, was carried out on a sample of 116,000 IBM employees. The findings concluded that the cultures of different nations can be compared in terms of four dimensions: *power distance*, *uncertainty avoidance*, *individualism*, and *masculinity*. Later work revealed a fifth dimension, *Confucian dynamism*. This dimension assessed culture on the basis of whether it was universalistic or specific. 'Universality' means that what is true and good can be defined and applied everywhere, whereas 'specific' means it is unique and relationships are more important in determining what is right or wrong. The original four dimensions, according to Hofstede (1984, 1996, 2001), account for the cross-cultural differences between behavioural patterns around the globe.

Power distance (PD) refers to the way societies deal with human inequality. Some societies are divided on physical and intellectual capability differences, others are not. France and the Philippines have relatively high scores in power distance, whereas Denmark and Sweden share a much lower score. Combining PD and individualism (IDV) reveals some interesting combinations. Collectivist countries seem to display high power distance, while the opposite is true of individualistic societies. Nearly all developing countries have a tendency to rate highly on both collectivism and power distance.

The process of decision-making tends to be different between cultures with high PD and those with low PD. These differences are easily highlighted in the nature of organizational decision-making. In high PD cultures, the power of decision-making is concentrated among a few people at the top of the hierarchy, while those at the bottom have little say. In contrast, the power of decision-making tends to be more equally shared among all participants in low PD cultures.

Uncertainty avoidance (UA) refers to how societies deal with the uncertainty of the future. At one end of the spectrum, weak UA cultures tend to accept uncertainty, take risks easily, do not work too hard, and live a day at a time. Examples are Denmark and Sweden. At the other end of the spectrum, strong UA cultures, such as Belgium and France, try to beat the future, resulting in nervousness, aggression, and emotionalism.

Having a high level of UA translates into a cultural identity that does not take risks and is more sensitive to the consequences of risk-taking. Not being able to predict an outcome of a purchase makes a consumer less likely to try a new product. This relates to the psychological risk and negative connotations of something outside the safety net of normal life. The challenge for the global marketer is to identify and empathize with this

MINI-CASE ILLUSTRATION **Cultural differences, West vs. East**

The West, particularly the USA, is transactional in its negotiations. The objective is to work towards closure based on mutual understanding and a legally binding agreement. The Chinese prefer not to view the process as one of 'negotiation' as the word suggests the disagreeable notion of conflict which must be avoided at all costs. 'Negotiation' for the Chinese means working towards an ongoing relationship or problem–solving process rather than a one-off agreement. In working towards an agreement to provide ventilation equipment to China, the UK company Xpelair, found that its Chinese partner wished the company to make adaptations to one of its standard household ventilation products in order to meet the requirements of the Chinese market. This ongoing process lasted for several months, involving a number of visits to China, in order to arrive at a mutually acceptable product solution.

risk and aim to dilute it, using effective communication in their promotional activities. It will be important to educate the consumers in order to create a positive perception of the brand or product, thus reducing the perceived risk associated with the purchase.

Individualism (IDV) describes the relationship between an individual and his/her fellow in society. At one end of the spectrum is the society with loose individual ties where people are expected to look after themselves (i.e. high IDV). At the other end is the society with strong ties between individuals, where each member is expected to look after others (i.e. low IDV). This explains the extended family syndrome.

A key area of consumer behaviour closely associated with IDV is the decision-making unit (DMU)—those involved in the process of purchase and the level of influence they have on the purchase decision. In a highly individualistic culture, people are mostly concerned with their own goals and that of their immediate family. The DMU for a purchase decision is small and restricted to the individual and immediate family. In contrast, the purchase decision of consumers who belong to a highly collectivist culture tends to be influenced not only by immediate family but also by the extended family, making the composition of the DMU a much bigger entity. Marketing communications designed to appeal to either of these audiences need to be refined to reflect these differences in the process of decision-making in purchases.

Chen et al. (1998) noted that in order to achieve mutual benefits in inter-organizational culture, a partner in an individualist culture will only stay in the relationship as long as the mutual benefits are compatible with the individual interest. In the event that one partner feels that the other partner is using power to force him/her to comply with the other's demands, the affected partner may cease or exit for fear of being exploited. By contrast, the partner in the collectivist culture is more likely to concentrate on the mutual goals and benefits, and, as long as these are maintained, it may comply with attempts to influence the other partner. On the basis of the above, it is better to be 'collectivist' rather than in a highly 'individualistic' culture (Terawatanavong and Quazi, 2006).

The Chinese culture, in particular, places strong emphasis on the maintenance of so-called *quanxi* networks, under which harmony with and within organizations is frequently favoured over information disclosure and shareholder rights (Bruton et al., 2004). This is a form of 'collectivism' rather than 'individualism'. While Western business culture emphasizes profit maximization, shareholder rights, and transparency, Chinese business culture typically has a high tolerance for information asymmetry between the firm's insiders and external investors as well as outside board members (Bruton et al., 1999; Pukthuanthong and Walker, 2007). However, as documented in a case study by Mann (1997), having a handful of top executives and government officials in one's *quanxi* network is not enough. Many of the first Western venture capitalist who entered China failed because they believed that *quanxi* with a few top officials in the Chinese government would be sufficient to guarantee their success. But this is not what *quanxi* is all about. The network has to be broad-based to be beneficial.

Another characteristic of *quanxi* is that it is driven by unwritten social rules. Unlike the West, contracts that go sour in China have little legal protection. As a result, Chinese business partners rely more heavily on the social responsibilities that come with well maintained *quanxi* relationships (Pukthuanthong and Walker, 2007).

However, in 'encouraged' industries in China, the role of *quanxi*, has lost ground to a different set of market-driven competitive rules, which now tend to determine winners and losers. Moreover, the number of restricted industries within which it still plays a dominant role has been reduced because of government deregulation and market development. Thus, it is the particular conditions that have precipitated he change, not any general diminution in the importance of *quanxi* in the Chinese culture (Liu and Roos, 2006).

Masculinity (MAS) deals with the degree to which societies display stereotypical male and female differences. *Masculine* societies stress making money and so admire individual brilliance and achievement. This applies equally to the women in those societies, which include Japan and Italy. In more *feminine* cultures, both males and females value feminine traits such as endurance and are more people-oriented. Sweden, Norway and the Netherlands rank among the most feminine societies.

In a highly masculine culture, products that accentuate individual achievement or status tend to be appealing as they enhance the perceptions of masculinity and 'greatness'. Consumers find it easy to relate to advertisements that encourage materialistic possessions and promote personal indulgence. On the other hand, consumers in feminine cultures, which value relationships and harmony, tend to find advertisements that promote individualistic (and narcissistic) behaviour selfish and unacceptable.

Confucian dynamism was added as another dimension of the cross-cultural framework in Hofstede's later work (1996), after conducting an international study on Chinese employees and managers. It relates to whether a culture is universalistic or particularistic. Universalistic cultures believe what is true and good can be applied everywhere, whereas particularistic cultures believe circumstances and relationships are more important in determining what is right and good. Chinese culture is full of Confucian philosophy stressing obedience and hierarchies and the need for smooth social relationships. After applying 'Confucian dynamism' to 23 countries, Hofstede came up with the term 'long-term orientation' (LTO), based on Confucian dynamism. A high LTO score equals persistence, ordering relationships by status, and observing this order, whereas a low LTO score equals personal steadiness and stability.

There are many studies which find their roots in the works of Hofstede. In the negotiation process, Fletcher and Fang (2006) reports on the 'Chinese Gentleman [sic],' the Chinese negotiator who behaves on the basis of mutual trust, seeking cooperation and 'win-win' solutions. The Chinese see the cultivation of righteousness as far more important than the pursuit of profit, and views contracting as an ongoing relationship or problem-solving process rather than a 'one-off' legal package. The Chinese disagree with the Western notion of 'negotiation' as it connotes a somewhat disagreeable idea of conflict, which must be avoided at all costs. Confucian negotiation strategy is characterized by cooperation. The Chinese may be less developed in technology and industrial organization, but they have few peers when it comes to negotiation, and often Western negotiators fall far short in this skill when matched together. This skill comes from deep-seated Chinese culture and tradition, and to understand the nature of the Chinese negotiating style it is necessary to look at the philosophical foundation of Chinese thought. Whereas Western managerial style is very much process-driven, the Chinese managerial style is very much situationally driven.

Hampden-Turner and Trompenaars: behaviour and value patterns

Dahl (2004) provides a useful description of the work of Hampden-Turner and Trompenaars. Hampden-Turner and Trompenaars (1998) classified culture along a mix of behavioural and value patterns. Their research was conducted among business executives from a number of organizations. They identified seven value dimensions:

1. **Universalism vs. particularism**: The degree to which a culture emphasizes rules and consistency in relationships, or accepts flexibility and the bending of rules to fit circumstances. Universalist cultures prefer clear rules and believe that personal relationships should not interfere in business decisions, whereas particularist cultures accept flexibility of rules and believe that institutionalized obligations to friendship and kinship are considered 'moral' requirements.

2. **Communitarianism vs. individualism**: The degree to which a culture emphasizes individual freedoms and responsibilities in relationships, or focuses more on group interests and consensus. It is almost identical to Hofstede's dimension of individualism vs. collectivism.

3. **Neutral vs. emotional**: The degree to which feelings are openly expressed. Neutral cultures emphasize objectivity and reserved detachment in relationships, whereas emotional cultures allow more opened emotionality and the expression of feelings. Southern countries, e.g. the Mediterranean countries and Central and South America, are more emotional, whereas Anglo-Saxon cultures, e.g. the USA, the UK, and Northern Europe, are more neutral.

4. **Diffuse vs. specific cultures**: The degree to which a culture emphasizes focused and in-depth relationships or displays broader and more superficial ones. Diffuse cultures (e.g. Germany, France, China) are concerned with keeping people's face—this is why people in diffuse cultures take so much more time to get to the point. It is about avoiding private confrontations so others will not feel offended and will not take disagreements personally. Specific cultures are those that separate the role of each party or transaction, and less time is spent on building relationships. It is about getting straight to the point and focusing on 'getting the job done as soon as possible.'

5. **Achievement vs. ascription**: The degree to which a culture emphasizes earned or performance-based status, or status based on social standing and non-performance factors. In cultures that emphasize achievement, status is accorded on the basis of performance, and promotion is on merit and outcome, regardless of age. In ascriptive cultures, status is accorded on the basis of durable characteristics, such as age. Achievement in ascriptive cultures is less about individuals and is more of a collective concern. Organizations in these societies have a high power distance relationship and the resulting hierarchy is requisite. This dimension is almost identical to Hofstede's power distance dimension.

6. **Human–time relationship**: Different attitudes towards time (past, present, and future) are reflected by the contrast between notions of time—linear and sequential, or circular and synchronic. Pressures to resolve problems quickly so that time will not be 'lost' are more likely in synchronic than sequential cultures and cultures which are synchronic are more collectivist and particularist.

7. **Human–nature relationship**: This is about how a culture sees the natural environment and the extent to which it should be controlled. Inner-directed cultures wish to subdue nature. These cultures are self-motivating, e.g. the USA and, to a lesser extent, France. The development of such cultures may be related to their history. The great inducement for the USA was to fight against nature and forge out a new nation. The French see themselves as the 'Grand Nation' with a centralized state. They have fought many battles and wars, and resisted natural forces. *Outer-directed cultures*, however, feel more dependent upon the environment and live in harmony with nature (e.g. Japan).

As we have seen, two of these dimensions, communitarianism vs. individualism and achievement vs. ascription, are close to Hofstede's collectivism/individualism and power distance dimensions (Hofstede, 1984). The dimension universalism vs. particularism describes a preference rather than a 'trusting' relationship. Most of the other dimensions reflect the extent to which feelings are expressed rather than the value itself. The human–time dimension is close to Hall's work on time-related perceptions.

Hofstede and Hampden-Turner and Trompenaars obtained their data from business professionals using questionnaires. However, Hofstede's work is focused more towards values, whereas Hampden-Turner and Trompenaars asked respondents to report on their behaviour in a number of work and leisure situations. Both pieces of research attempted to derive values from a series of questions. This approach gives a practical bias, but the conclusions are derived from a limited number of questions. This can affect 'predictability' from the research and interpretations of the data may have been affected by the context of the questioning.

Schwartz: value inventory

Schwartz (1992, 1994; see also Dahl, 2004) takes a different approach, using the 'SVI' (Schwartz Value Inventory). Schwartz asked 60,000 respondents from 63 countries to assess 57 values as 'guiding principles of one's life'. Unlike Hofstede (1984) and Hampden-Turner and Trompenaars (1998), Schwartz separated the 'individual-level' analysis from the 'culture-level' analysis, and distinguished between value types and value dimensions. A 'value type' is a set of values that can collectively be given one description, such as 'power'. Values in the value type have other values, which are located in a different direction from the opposing value type. A 'value dimension' can consist of different value types.

Schwartz identified ten individual value types: power, achievement, stimulation, self-direction, universalism, benevolence, tradition, conformity, tradition, and security. A detailed description of these value types is provided by Dahl (2004). Each of these individual-level value types represent a number of values which can be combined to form a joint 'idea'. Dyadic dimensions can then be constructed, for example, the 'universalism' value type represents social justice and tolerance, whereas the 'benevolence' domain represents promoting the welfare of others (see Fig. 4.7).

Fang: cross-culture theory

Studies such as Hofstede (1984) and Hall (1977) were conducted before the recent revolution in cross-border communication, the internet, the accelerated movement of people between countries, and the rising level of globalization. National cultures have become more fluid, fuzzy, complex, and paradoxical than before. Fang (2003) provides a critique of the philosophical and methodological foundations of Hofstede's fifth dimension, 'Confucian dynamism', and the yin–yang perspective to cross-cultural theory building. Although quite 'China-specific', the study does have 'other cultural implications.' Fang (2003, 2006) models the business culture of China on the basis of three forces: conditions in the People's Republic of China (PRC), Confucianism, and Chinese stratagems. Regarding the first of these forces, conditions in the PRC, Fang suggests that it is necessary to examine the prevailing political ideology; the extent of socio-economic planning and government involvement; the existing legal framework; the state of technology in the market and the attitude towards innovation; the nature, equity, and average level of income distribution; the magnitude of resource endowment, including infrastructure and capital; exposure to international influences; and the rapidity of change of values and lifestyles in the society in a broader context of globalization. According to Fang, these factors are a reflection of underlying culture.

The second force, Confucianism, can be described as both a philosophy and a religion. It comprises: underlying religious and/or philosophical underpinnings, such as morality and trust; the role of, and obligations on, self in interpersonal relationships; the strength

Fig. 4.7 Schwartz Value Inventory (SVI)

SVI	A high SVI score indicates...
Power	Individuals who value social status and dominance over people and resources
Achievement	A high priority is given to personal success and admiration
Hedonism	A preference is given to pleasure and self-gratification
Stimulation	A preference for an exciting life
Self-direction	Individuals who value independence, creativity, and freedom
Universalism	A preference for social justice and tolerance
Benevolence	Values that promote the welfare of others
Tradition	A respect for traditions and customs
Conformity	Values that represent obedience
Security	Values relating to the safety, harmony, and welfare of society and of oneself

of family orientation; respect for age and hierarchy; and the requirement to avoid conflict and create harmony, dignifying rather than diminishing the other party (face).

The third force, Chinese stratagems, is all about strategy and tactics. These can also apply to other cultures as all cultural groups have culturally influenced negotiation tactics and approaches to strategic thinking in life as a whole. In some societies this might mean 'winning' by subtle means, and in others, by confrontation. In all these cases, strategic and tactical moves influence relationship creation and network formation. In most books on negotiation, generally Western research-based negotiation strategies are based either on game theory (which result in 'win-lose' or 'zero-sum game' outcomes) or on social exchange theory (which aims to achieve a 'win-win' outcome). Fang (2003) argues that in China, both strategies ('win-win' vs. 'win-lose') are employed jointly, whereas in the West the use of one strategy usually precludes the other. Hence, managers doing business in emerging Asia need to go beyond traditional national cultural stereotypes to capture cultural diversities and paradoxes within politically defined and artificially created boundaries. According to Fang (2003), understanding ethnic culture, regional culture, professional culture, and emerging global culture, within and across national boundaries, and the interplays between them, provide a better basis for predicting underlying cultural differences and similarities in managing relationship creation and network formation with business partners in emerging Asian markets.

Applying cross-cultural frameworks

The complexity of culture creates a challenge to the market analyst as each approach aims to take a 'slice' or a single variable of culture to use as its focus, thereby representing culture only from that single perspective. An example is Hall and Hall (1987), who identified language as the most important factor in the analysis of culture. In support of the idea of using language as a basis for cross-cultural analysis, Terpstra and Sarathy (1994: 13) concede that language is the most obvious cultural component that provides the link to all other components of culture: where 'words of a particular language are merely reflecting the culture from which it derives'. Using language as a mirror image of culture therefore highlights as many differences in a given culture as it shows similarities.

Although his framework of cultural analysis draws strength from its ability to offer insights into the way in which different cultures communicate, Hall's framework is nonetheless a simplistic approach that fails to offer a complete picture of what culture is—i.e. often complex and multidimensional.

Hofstede's dimensions of culture are probably the most influential approach to cross-cultural analysis. Although his work was developed in relation to organizational issues at the corporate level, it is transferable and can be applied to infer behavioural patterns in society as a whole, which includes the consumers. The schematic nature of this approach is an advantage to the cultural analyst—the ability to plot dimensional scores against each other and against other countries is an extremely powerful visual aid as well as a practical tool for comparing and contrasting cultures.

There are many critics of Hofstede's methodology (Bakacsi et al., 2002) and the claims which he and others have made for the results. There are questions about what constitutes a 'national' culture. In discussing Hofstede's analysis, it is important to realize that his four cultural dimensions are represented through the grouping of national cultures. It would be naïve to think that cultural diversity, complexity, and sensitivity can be encapsulated into one generic framework. The USA, for example, has made deliberate attempts to 'homogenize' its diverse population through education and reinforcing key national values; the UK has not. Hofstede also collected his data from a work-related situation and questions arise over whether they can be transferred to other non-work situations, such as consumer behaviour. Many economies today simply do not fit easily into Hofstede's framework, e.g. Malaysia, with its mix of three different but complementing cultures—Malay, Chinese, and Indian. The UK is another example. While 94% of the population is white European, the other 6% is made up of Indian, Pakistani, Chinese, African, Caribbean, Bangladeshi, Greek, Italian, Polish, and countless other nationalities. These different groups bring with them diversity of language, religious beliefs, mores, and customs. Hence the thriving sub-markets in Chinese and Indian food. Cultural strata may even go further than this. Within these primary nationality or 'country of origin' cultures there are even more layers of sub-cultures. Young people may adopt a transient hero culture (e.g. pop stars), presenting global marketers with global merchandizing opportunities. This takes the discussion back to the original

THE RELATIONSHIP PERSPECTIVE Business ethics at work in China

As international trade and business opportunities grow in China, Western firms are being attracted to the Chinese market in ever increasing numbers. Working in a global environment necessitates constant negotiations with suppliers, customers, and other stakeholders. One of the major challenges of participating in a global economy is to understand and manage the ethical practices and behaviours of international partners (Volkema, 2004). To take advantage of the emerging opportunities in China, it is imperative that global executives understand the ethical mindset of their negotiation counterparts in order to develop effective relationships (Al-Khatib, 2007). Western standards and norms of ethical behaviour have not yet been established in China. Therefore, to succeed, it is necessary to focus on building trust and managing it. Western investors who focus on building personal trust that emulates healthy family and friend relationships will find that such an approach will promote a more congenial and productive atmosphere than formal, arm's length contacts and contracts (Al-Khatib, 2007).

The current Chinese environment is the result of a difficult and somewhat disappointing transition to a free market economy. This, coupled with the absence of a well-defined legal system, has resulted in a relaxed and consequence-free attitude among Chinese towards ethical negotiation. This situation makes it imperative that multinational managers operating in China codify the desirable and undesirable behavioural activities of the Chinese negotiating partner, host country staff, workers, customers, and suppliers. Moreover, such as effort to codify behaviour is bound to fail if it does not take into account Chinese culture, economic challenges, and China's past

history. Chinese and Western joint venture partners must agree on a middle ground of firm-specific policies and codes of ethics. For example, *guanxi* is still acceptable behaviour in China, so Western firms operating in China may adapt their policies by allowing some acceptable level of nepotism (Robertson et al., 2003; Al-Khatib, 2007). One factor worrying the West somewhat is China's current trading partners, some off whom (e.g. Zimbabwe) may be questionable. However, what the West needs to understand is the cultural traditions and mores. The Chinese tend to be more relativistic decision-makers and so reject absolute moral philosophy and tend to be more 'situationists'. So, in engaging in ethical decision-making, the Chinese tend to rely less on idealistic concerns and more on economic or self-interest-driven concerns.

argument about placing individuals into groups based upon their nationality or country. This view is shared by Usunier (2000: 14), who describes nationality as a 'variable [that] is too artificial to avoid the traps of cliché and stereotype', as cultural identity is something that extends beyond the labels attached to the country of residence or origin of birth.

Given the complex nature of culture, the challenge to the global marketer is to intelligently use, either singularly or together, the relevant aspects of these frameworks and distill them into a usable framework pertinent to their own organization. We have seen the effect of culture on consumer buyer behaviour earlier in the chapter and the chapter now concludes with a brief look at organizational buyer behaviour, involving numerous buying influences. The forms of organizational buying behaviour considered are commodity trading, government procurement, and business-to-business or B2B buying behaviour.

Commodity Trading

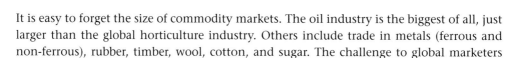

It is easy to forget the size of commodity markets. The oil industry is the biggest of all, just larger than the global horticulture industry. Others include trade in metals (ferrous and non-ferrous), rubber, timber, wool, cotton, and sugar. The challenge to global marketers is when to buy and sell these commodities. Most commodity marketing is governed by supply and demand and is priced accordingly. This can lead to production and marketing cartels, such as the Organization for Petroleum Exporting Countries (OPEC), which can be powerful in fixing prices. Witness the action and reaction when OPEC decided to raise prices by 25% in 1972—it brought world economies to a standstill and caused massive inflation around the world. Most commodities are traded 'spot' or 'future' (see Chapter 14 for more discussion) and fortunes can be won and lost by so doing.

Of recent interest is the trend to fair and ethical trading. Diamonds are mainly produced for industrial applications (e.g. drill bits) and, recently, there has been an outcry over diamonds sourced from economies in conflict (e.g. the Democratic Republic of Central Africa), so-called 'conflict diamonds'.

The Exploration of new sources of raw materials may involve organizations singly or jointly. BHP (www.bhpbiliton.com), the Australian mining giant, invested some US$275 million in opening up the Hartley platinum mine in Zimbabwe, only to close it a few years later. Such costs mean that to develop new supplies of commodities, companies, like governments, must often 'cooperate to compete' by forming an affinity group like a joint venture to explore a market opportunity.

As shown in Chapter 2, the price of commodities, including food, gas, oil, copper, gold, and platinum, has rocketed by up to 35% in the period 2006–08. Not only has this had a knock-on effect in terms of an increase in consumer prices, but it has made the buying of them increasingly difficult as it has become a 'seller's market'. As these commodities, except processed food, are often bought and sold on the futures or forward markets, estimating the forward price is not easy. The buy/sell situation is also being compounded by countries such as China and India, which are scouring the globe in search of commodities to fuel their burgeoning economic growth, thus pushing prices higher than anticipated.

Government Buying Behaviour

Governments are usually the major procurers in a country. In the USA, the government accounts for 30% of all purchases. Only the government can afford to provide a national health service, transport infrastructure development, and national insurance.

In order to provide services or products to government, there are two types of tender: open and selective (or limited). The former is self-explanatory; the latter not so obvious. For national security reasons, only nationals may bid, and in the case of limited tender, bids are accepted only from 'recognized' suppliers. For example, the British government probably has a very limited list of acceptable bidders for the supply of nuclear reactors.

Recently, the EU has attempted to break down this 'closed shop' approach. In the quest for 'best value', the British government, for example, has broken supplier monopoly on its Navy dockside facilities and is considering placing orders for its new generation of aircraft carriers with the French company, Thales (www.thalesgroup.com). Government buying is complex. For example, if British Airways (www.ba.com) were to place an order with Boeing (www.boeing.com), the American plane manufacturer, the British government would look for 'buy back', that is, it would hope that the engine supplier would be British, in this case Rolls-Royce. Similarly, doing business with governments whose economies are less stable can be risky. The size of order versus potential non-payment needs careful consideration and astute contracting. Governments can cooperate with other governments in major capital projects where the initial capital investment is beyond the means of any one or several companies, e.g. the Channel Tunnel and Concorde involved both French and British governments. Of course there is always the question of 'gifts' or 'commission'. In some countries, government contracts would not be available without resort to these methods, but how far should a company go to obtain an order? Some may argue that the giving of gifts is not only restricted to developing countries, but to developed ones as well.

Organizational Buyers or B2B Buyer Behaviour

In contrast to consumer behaviour, where middlemen or manufacturers sell direct to consumers, business-to-business (B2B) buying is where one business sells to another business before the product goes on to a third party, which, indeed, may be yet another business. Take a product like a modern passenger aeroplane. The ultimate buyer of the service might be the passenger (because without the passenger there would be no point in making the plane), however the immediate customer might be British Airways. When British Airways take an option on an Airbus (www.airbus.com), the order may go to Toulouse in France where the plane is assembled. An extremely complicated logistical buying and delivery process is initiated before the aeroplane reaches British Airways. It is this complexity which differentiates the B2B buying process from that of consumer buying.

As we have seen, organizational buying can be complex. Not only are financial decisions important, but so are technological and company motivational factors. Getting to the decision-making unit (DMU), i.e. the personnel who make the buying decision, is complex enough in domestic marketing, but even more so in organizational marketing. For example, in many multinational conglomerates, such as Inchcape (www.inchcape.com), Hyundai (www.hyundai.com), Anglo American (www.angloamerican.com), or Daimler Chrysler (www.daimler-chrysler.com), there are so many subsidiary companies that it is very time-consuming to find the purchase decision-maker.

The 'make' or 'buy' decision is a complex one. Japanese companies rely on a network of suppliers with whom they work to produce a solution to their supply needs. The practice of 'cooperate to compete' is growing among a number of organizations. Bombardier (www.bombardier.com), the Canadian rail transport solution company, and Rolls-Royce are typical examples. Culture can have a bearing on the organizational buying process. Italian and Spanish decision-making is perceived to be autocratic, German decision-making is based on respect, especially in engineering, and Japanese decision-making is built on trust and respect for elders.

Another aspect of organizational buying is the 'source of funds' syndrome. As discussed above, many international opportunities require funding, often from unlikely sources. Governments, anxious to explore strategic opportunities, may provide funds. For example, the British government provided funds to BAe Systems (www.bae.co.uk) to help maintain its stake in the Euro Fighter. Similarly, and controversially, it is subsidizing rail operators in the UK. GE Capital (www.gecapital.com) is one of the largest providers of finance to charge card institutions, and provides capital to many car hire firms to purchase fleet acquisitions.

B2B buying models

There exist several models of buying behaviour, from the straight re-buy, modified re-buy, or *new task* model of Robinson et al. (1979), the DMU analysis model of Webster and Wind (1972), to the more relationship-based (e-business) and database models of recent years (see Chaffey, 2002; Chaffey et al., 2003). For example, the 'three task' model approach of Robinson et al. (1979) proposes that the purchase decision involves three decisions:

- **Straight rebuy**: where goods and services are routinely purchased on a replenishment basis without the need to search for new buyers, e.g. paper consumables.

- **Modified rebuy**: where goods and services may undergo specification changes but the current supplier is retained. There are many situations where this takes place in the B2B world, especially as companies innovate. For example, when car manufacturers update their models, they work with component suppliers to adjust the specifications of the component parts.

- **New task**: here the purchase is completely new and may involve a big information search on potential suppliers, evaluation, negotiation, and choice of new suppliers, e.g. a made-to-order cruise liner.

Whatever the model, culture will play an important part in the buying decision process. If we take the Robinson et al.'s model (1979), a culturally *ethnocentric* organization will favour national suppliers, while the greater risk-takers will look elsewhere. Today, China is becoming a favoured source of supply, although the supplier is often a factory set up by a previously high-cost-based country company. Sony (www.sony.com), for example, is sourcing hi-fi components from Malaysia and China.

Relationship marketing, often coupled with technology, is a major trend in buyer behaviour. General Electric (www.ge.com), a large supplier of electrical switchgear, transformers, components, and aircraft engines, sources the bulk of its components via the internet. Such is the sophistication of the internet that manufacturers can design and 'test' components without seeing or handling them. Internet procurement and customer relationship marketing is also probably more prevalent in B2B situations than in consumer buying behaviour.

The effects of culture on B2B buyer behaviour

Culture and organizational buyer behaviour provide a challenge. 'Conventional' international marketing views the role of culture as having a fundamental influence on marketing. While not downplaying the effect of 'culture' in international considerations, organizational buying behaviour can be very different from consumer purchase behaviour. For instance:

- Cooperating to compete between organizations is a global reality. For example, British Petroleum (www.bp.com) has a joint venture in Russia and in the second quarter of 2004 BP's profits hit £74,000 per second on the back of its soaring Russian output. Cost profit for BP in 2006 was US$22.253 billion compared to US$19.314 billion in 2005.

- Governments are major procurers and often cooperate to provide services and products, e.g. EU cooperation to produce the Euro Fighter.

- Technology, specifically the internet (e-business), is providing global design in manufacturing, supply chain management, and marketing opportunities, e.g. the car industry.

- It is assumed that organizational buyers are more 'rational' than consumer buyers, due to the relatively higher purchase values of products and services bought, the complexity of the buying situation, and the source of finance (e.g. new military equipment).

- Increasingly, major international projects are joint ventures in manufacturing, marketing, and financing between private organizations, governments, and sources of funds, e.g. the new Hong Kong International airport.

- Components and services are becoming globally standardized, e.g. the 'CE' kitemark.

- There is increasing attention to business ethics, corporate responsibility, and fair trading, e.g. the Virgin Group and diamond trading.

Culture and Ethics

'Culture' has an effect on ethical decision-making within and between organizations. Increasingly in the twenty-first century, consumers and other stakeholders are looking for a more 'ethical' approach to business. Traditionally, the pursuit of profit has been the key driver in business. However, with a move towards sustainability, business firms are looking towards a more holistic perspective, i.e. the interconnection between economic growth and environmental and social sustainability. Also they have to shift their thinking from the conventional way of viewing 'impact' on the environment and society to that of creating a long-term vision of environmental and social sustainability (Setthasakko, 2007). Companies are looking more and more at both external (e.g. civil societies) and internal (e.g. leadership of top management) key determinants driving companies towards a more responsible attitude towards the environment and society. Governments have a key role to play in passing rules and regulations to enhance sustainable development in society (e.g. emission levels, environmental taxes). In the West, governments have the power to enforce and punish those companies which are purely economically driven and to force them to adopt more environmentally-friendly strategies. Not so in South East Asia, for example, where weak law enforcement and inconsistent regulations have made the legal instruments rather impotent. Studies (e.g. Bergstrom et al., 2005), however, show inconsistencies between the West and East in this regard. Price and quality take precedence over environmental issues, as exemplified by the USA, where consumers are environmentally conscious but their concerns are not necessarily illustrated by their purchase decisions (e.g. 'gas guzzling' cars and cheap petrol).

Past studies (e.g. Petroni, 2001) have concentrated more on the positive aspects of corporate environmental responsibility, such as cost reduction, customer satisfaction, and improved corporate image. However, Setthasakko (2007) claimed that the government, local communities, and top management leadership are key determinants of corporate sustainability.

Culture is a determinant of ethical decision-making. However, cultures have different values and attitudes to morality, so the interpretation of what is and what is not ethical may differ considerably across nations. Folklore (and reality) suggests that Nigeria's Customs, for example, require extra financial incentive to allow goods to enter the country. They are by no means the only country that does so. When does 'commission' become a bribe? In 2007, even the UK government was being closely scrutinized over a huge arms deal with Saudi Arabia, on the question of alleged improper conduct.

Many global operators have a code of ethics under which they do business (e.g. the Virgin Group, www.virgin.com/RBP) (see Chapter 5). An organization's ethical commitment can be considered on a continuum, ranging from 'not ethical' to 'most ethical'. 'Not ethical' is seen as not even following the law and 'most ethical' requires the company to have a code of ethics which addresses eight major issues: competition, strategic alliances, local sourcing, equity participation, local reinvestment, transfer prices, taxation, and financing. This set of standards is supposed to govern business behaviour and influence decision-making within it. Virgin's code, for example, states that it will do business with those organization's which give their employees at least one day off work per week.

As with all codes of practice, 'policing' every company's code would be an administrative impracticability, and the reality of behaviour may be somewhat different from the rhetoric. Nike, for example, has often been accused of using Far Eastern 'sweat shop' labour, an allegation it has been quick to defend factually.

Chapter Summary

1. Culture is made up of conscious and unconscious values, attitudes, and mores that are passed from one generation to another. Culture can make or break international operations, hence the need to study its components and identify its impact on strategic planning and implementation. Language, religion, values and attitudes, education, social organization, aesthetics, technology, and political discource are the main components or influences of culture.

2. It is dangerous to generalize about consumer behaviour in different countries because consumption patterns vary considerably. Even where similarities exist in the demands for a product between two countries, the *ability to pay* may differ due to socio-economic difference.

3. Meeting consumer needs in different countries by providing the right products and services is an ongoing marketing challenge for businesses in competitive global marketplaces. Culture affects consumer behaviour by influencing behavioural and consumption decisions, hence creating desires and driving the consumer to select products or brands that fulfil specific needs.

4. Cross-cultural analysis is the systematic comparison of similarities and differences in the material and behavioural aspects of cultures. Many approaches have been put forward in an attempt to provide a framework or structure to achieve a meaningful cross-cultural understanding. While there is not yet a universally recognized approach to conducting cross-cultural analysis, Hall's and Hofstede's approaches are among the most widely recognized and accepted.

5. In contrast to consumer behaviour, where middlemen or manufacturers sell direct to consumers, business-to-business (B2B) buying is where one business sells to another before it goes on to a third party. Types of B2B buying include commodity trading, organizational buying, and government procurement.

6. Culture and ethics are interconnected. While companies are seeking to take a more ethical and socially responsible stance, different cultures may result in different ethical behaviour with, and within, organizations across national boundaries.

END-OF-CHAPTER CASE STUDY The evolution of the Chinese middle class

Shanghai in the 1970s was a grim place in the midst of the Mao Tse-Tung era. Now it's a sea of glass towers, clean streets, and dozens of shopping malls selling thousands of Western-branded goods to well-dressed and sophisticated people, rivalling Singapore and Hong Kong. Many of today's Chinese young don't even remember Chairman Mao. If current trends continue, China will be the new superpower of the late 2020s, with a per capita income matching the USA and consuming more oil than the entire world uses today. And, of course, it will have some 1.2 billion consumers, enjoying their new-found wealth. The masses of newly educated Chinese care more about their stability and material gains, very much like their Hong Kong and Malaysian cousins, than they care about those things that seem to obsess the West—human rights and democracy. Why change the system if achievements can be gained without it? Things will no doubt change, albeit slowly, but they will.

The growing sophistication of the middle classes will be one catalyst to change. Many have been educated abroad, exposed to both the good things in life and the bad, such as drugs and vice. They are inculcated with material ambition and the energy that feeds China's success. They want to have their own houses (many couples live in rented apartments or still with their parents), travel, watch TV, speak English, and go out. In Hangzhou, a lovely small (only 7 million people!) holiday city near Shanghai, nearly 9,000 new cars are licensed per month. And these are not your average runabout, but include many Chryslers, Volkswagens, Porches, and Bentleys. However, with free education ceasing at 9 years old and with everything being geared to 'economics', life is still not that easy. Rich couples might, at a price, be able to break the one child per family rule.

The West will probably still lead in innovation and services, while China continues to manufacture, but the future lies in the middle classes being able to design and innovate. That's where the real money can be made. Chinese middle-class views of the West vary dramatically. England is perceived as both charming and conservative, the USA as very rich and successful but seeking to exercise world control. Many of the Chinese middle class work for the government, where steady work has its bonus-earning business commissions—for which some in the UK may have another name. The men of the middle classes work hard and long, maybe to get a bigger apartment, or several apartments, and have more children. But economic progress comes at a price. Vast swathes of factory and housing developments were 'scars' on the landscape, not to mention the resultant pollution. How long can China's reputation for spiritual peace and culture survive? Older Chinese often see the emergent middle-class young as privileged. They did not endure the rigours of the previous generation. They are interested in what people outside China think of their country rather than what they are told from within. Some wonder, having not travelled, if the USA is really as it is portrayed in the movies. Surfing the net has become a pasttime as the thirst for knowledge grows.

Abroad, the middle classes see their government scouring the world for energy and raw materials to fuel the exploding economic growth. Sometimes China's foreign policy of non-intervention (e.g. operating in countries like Sudan and North Korea) can be misconstrued. While China and Russia are not bosom buddies, China is determined to balance the power of the USA. Certainly, China's vast foreign reserves and sovereign value assets for investment causes some to shudder in the West. Will China use them to 'buy into' technologies it does not yet possess? Does it matter? After all, the Japanese have done it for years, and before that so did the UK and the USA. Militarily, the West has little to fear, but it well may economically. For example, for every £5 the UK spends on Chinese imports, only £1 goes the other way.

The educated middle classes stand to benefit from China's economic 'gold rush', and eventually, so will the millions of others in China less well placed. In fact, in a strange way, the educated Chinese seem closer to the West than many other countries—they are hardworking, ambitious, not given to confrontation at a personal level, and they enjoy the fruits of their labours and the fact that they are now 'show cased' to the world.

Case discussion questions

1 Identify the reasons why the middle classes in China are emerging as 'global consumers'. Classify the factors as 'internal' and 'external.'

2 Given the continuous growth of markets in China, how useful are concepts like 'market segments' and 'competitive positioning' to the Chinese middle classes? On what basis might organizations successfully segment the market.

END-OF-CHAPTER EXERCISES

1 What is culture? Briefly explain the main components of a culture.

2 Why is it so important to understand how culture influences consumer behaviour? With reference to the Model of Interaction of Culture and Consumer Behaviour, discuss how consumer behaviour is affected by culture.

3 What is a self-reference criterion? Why is it considered dangerous when seeking to understand another culture?

4 What is cross-cultural analysis? Describe Hofstede's and Hall's approaches to cross-cultural analysis.

5 Explain how the following approaches can be used to conduct cross-cultural analysis:

(a) Hampden-Turner and Trompenaars' behaviour and value patterns

(b) Schwartz's value inventory (SVI) model

(c) Fang's cross-cultural theory

6 What are the important considerations of B2B buying in an international context? Identify and describe the three types of B2B buying.

DISCUSSION AND EXAMINATION QUESTIONS

1 What are the main components/influences of culture? Discuss, with examples, the marketing implications of cultural influences on consumer behaviour.

2 How would you define your own culture? Using relevant examples, discuss how language can obstruct effective communication.

3 'It is dangerous for the marketer to make any generalizations about consumer behaviour in other countries'. Discuss the validity of this statement.

4 Cross-cultural analysis is the systematic comparison of similarities and differences in the material and behavioural aspects of cultures. Discuss and evaluate the approaches to cross-cultural analysis.

5 Define values, heroes, rituals and symbols. How do these elements influence consumer behaviour in an international context?

FURTHER READING

Brennan, R., Canning, L. E., and McDowell, R. (2007), *Business to Business Marketing*, London: Sage.

Doole, I. and Lowe, R. (2008) *International Marketing Strategy: Analysis, Development and Implementation*, 5th edn., London: Thomson Learning, Chapter 3.

Hall, E. T. (1959), *The Silent Language*, New York: Anchor Books.

_____ (1966), *The Hidden Dimension*, New York: Anchor Books.

Hofstede, G., website, http://feweb.uvt.n/center/hofstede/index.htm.

Hollensen, S. (2007), *Global Marketing*, 4th edn., Harlow: FT/Prentice Hall, Chapters 3 and 7.

REFERENCES

Al-Khatib, J. A. (2007), 'Business-to-business negotiating in China: the role of morality', *Journal of Business and Industrial Marketing*, 22(2), 84–96.

Ambler, T. and Styles, C. (2000), *The Silk Road to International Marketing: Profit and Passion in Global Business*, Harlow: FT/Prentice Hall.

Antonides, G. and van Raaij, W. F. (1998), *Consumer Behaviour: A European Perspective*, Chichester: J. Wiley & Sons.

Aurifeille, J.-M., Quester, P. G., Lockshin, L., and Spawton, T. (2001), 'Global vs. international involvement-based segmentation: a cross-national exploratory study', *International Marketing Review*, 19(4), 369–86.

Bakacsi, G., Sándor, T., András, K., and Viktor, I. (2002), 'Eastern European cluster: tradition and transition', *Journal of World Business*, 37, 69–80.

Bergström, K., Solér, C., and Shanahan, H. (2005), 'Professional food purchasers' practice in using environmental information', *British Food Journal*, 107(5), 306–19.

Bond, M. H. and King, R. T. O. (1985), Coping with the threat of westernization in Hong Kong' *International Journal of Intercultural Relations*, 9, 351–64.

Bowman, J. P. and Okuda, T. (1985), 'Japanese–American communication: mysteries, enigmas and possibilities', *The Bulletin of the Association for Business Communication*, 4, 18–21.

Bruton, G., Ahlstrom, D., and Yeh, K. (2004), 'Understanding venture capital in East Asia: the impact of institutions on the industry today and tomorrow', *Journal of World Business*, 39(1), 72–88.

——, Dattani, M., Fung, M., Chow, C., and Ahlstrom. D. (1999). 'Private equity in China: differences and similarities with the Western model', *Journal of Private Equity*, 2(2), 7–14,

Cao, L. (2004), 'Optimizing the International Business Relationship: The Case of the Ventilation Industry in China and Europe', Unpublished PhD thesis, Leeds Metropolitan University, Leeds.

Chaffey, D. (2002), *E-Business and E-Marketing Management*, Harlow: FT/Prentice Hall.

——, Mayer, R., Johnston, K., and Ellis-Chadwick, F. (2003), *Internet Marketing: Strategy, Implementation and Practice*, 2nd edn., Harlow: FT/Prentice Hall.

Chen, C. C. Chen, X., and Meindl, J. R. (1998), 'How can cooperation be fostered? The cultural effects of individualism–collectivism', *Academy of Management Review*, 23(2), 285–304.

Dahl, S. (2004), *Intercultural Research: The Current State of Knowledge*, Middlesex University Discussion Paper No. 26, January.

Doole, I. and Lowe, R. (2004), *International Marketing Strategy: Analysis, Development and Implementation*, 4th edn., London: Thomson Learning.

Fang, T. (2003), 'A critique of Hofstede's fifth national culture dimension', *International Journal of Cross-Cultural Management*, 3(3), 347–68.

—— (2006), 'Negotiation: the Chinese style', *Journal of Business and Industrial Marketing*, 20(1), 50–60.

Fletcher, R. and Fang, T. (2006), 'Assessing the impact of culture on relationship creation and network formation in emerging Asian markets', *European Journal of Marketing*, 40(3/4), 430–46.

Garg, R. K. and Ma, J. (2005), 'Benchmarking culture and performance in Chinese organizations', *Benchmarking: An International Journal*, 12(3), 260–74.

Geertz, C. (1973), *The Interpretation of Cultures*, New York: Basic Books.

Gesteland, R. (2000), 'Do's and taboo's: proper etiquette in the global market place', *Management News, Zimbabwe Institute of Management*, 1st Quarter.

Hall, E. T. (1959), *The Silent Language*, New York: Anchor Books.

—— (1966), *The Hidden Dimension*, New York: Anchor Books.

—— (1977), *Beyond Culture*, New York: Anchor Books.

—— and Hall, M. R. (1987), *Hidden Differences: Doing Business with the Japanese*, New York: Anchor Press.

Hampden-Turner, C. and Trompenaars, A. (1998), *Riding the Waves of Culture: Understanding Diversity in Global Business*, 2nd edn., New York: McGraw-Hill.

Hill, J. S. and Still, R. R. (1984), 'Adapting products to LDC tastes', *Harvard Business Review*, 62 (March/April), 91–101.

Hofstede, G. (1984), *Culture's Consequences: International Differences in Work-related Values*, Thousand Oaks, CA: Sage.

—— (1996), *Cultures and Organizations: Software of the Mind*, New York: McGraw-Hill.

—— (2001), *Culture's Consequences: International Differences in Work-related Issues*, 2nd edn., Thousand Oaks, CA: Sage.

Kim, J.-O., Forsythe, S., Gu, Q., and Moon, S.-J. (2002), 'Cross-cultural consumer values, needs and purchase behaviour', *Journal of Consumer Marketing*, 19(6), 481–502.

Kluckhohn, C. (1951), 'The Study of Culture', in Lerber, D. and Lasswell, H. D. (eds.), *The Policy Sciences*, Stanford, CA: Stanford University Press.

Lee, J. (1966), 'Cultural analysis in overseas operations', *Harvard Business Review*, March–April, 106–14.

Lincoln, J. R., Olson, J., and Hanada, M. (1978), 'Cultural effects of organizational structures: the case of Japanese firms in the United States', *American Sociological Review*, 43, 829–47.

Liu, H. and Roos, L.-U. (2006), 'Managing strategic planning paradigms in China', *Marketing Intelligence and Planning*, 24(5), 432–45.

Luna, D. and Gupta, S. F. (2001), 'An integrative framework for cross-cultural consumer behaviour', *International Marketing Review*, 18(1), 45–69.

Mann, J. (1997), *Beijing Jeep: The Short, Unhappy Romance of American Business in China*, 2nd edn., New York: Simon & Schuster.

Maslow, A. H. (1970), *Motivation and Personality*, 2nd edn., New York: Harper & Row.

Miles, G. L. (1995), 'Mainframe: the next generation', *International Business*, August, 14–16.

Petroni, A. (2001), 'Developing a methodology for analysis of benefits and shortcomings of ISO 14001 registration: lessons from experience of a large machinery manufacturer', *Journal of Cleaner Production*, 9, 351–64.

Pukthuanthong, K. and Walker, T. (2007), 'Venture capital in China: a culture shock for Western investors', *Management Decision*, 435(4), 708–31.

Robertson, C. J., Gilley, K. M., and Street, M. D. (2003), 'The relationship between ethics and firm practices in Russia and the United States', *Journal of World Business*, 38(4), 375–84.

Robinson, P. J., Faris, C. W., and Wind, Y. (1979), *Industrial Buying and Creative Marketing, Boston*, MA: Allyn and Bacon and the Marketing Science Institute.

Rokeach, M. (1973), *The Nature of Human Values*, New York: Free Press.

Rook, D. W. (1985), 'The ritual dimensions of consumer behaviour', *Journal of Consumer Research*, 12, 251–80.

Setthasakko, W. (2007), 'Determinants of corporate sustainability: Thai frozen seafood processors', *British Food Journal*, 109 (2), 155–68.

Solomon, M., Bamossy, G., and Askegaard, S. (2002), *Consumer Behaviour: A European Perspective*, 2nd edn., Harlow: FT/Prentice Hall.

Swartz, S. H. (1992), 'Universals in the Context and Structure of Values: Theoretical Advances and Empirical Tests in 20 Countries,' in M. Zanna (ed.), *Advances in Experimental Social Psychology*, San Diego, CA: Academic Press.

—— (1994), 'Beyond Individualism/Collectivism: New Dimensions of Values,' in U. Kim, H. C. Triandis, C. Kagitçibasi, S. C. Choi, and G. Joon (eds.) *Individualism and Collectivism: Theory Application and Methods*, Newbury Park, CA: Sage.

Terawatanavong, C. and Quazi, A. (2006), 'Conceptualizing the link between national cultural dimensions and B2B relationships', *Asia Pacific Journal of Marketing and Logistics*, 18(3), 173–83.

Terpstra, V. and Sarathy, R. (eds.) (1994), *International Marketing, Forth Worth*, TX: Dryden Press.

Tibbets, G. (2007), 'Two hours' TV a day harms children', *Daily Telegraph*, 2 October, www.telegraph.co.uk.

Tse, D. K., Belk, R. W., and Zhou, N. (1989), 'Becoming a consumer society: a longitudinal and cross-cultural content analysis of print advertisement in Hong Kong, the PRC and Taiwan', *Journal of Consumer Research*, 15, 457–72.

Tung, R. L. and Miller, E. L. (1990), 'Managing in the twenty-first century: the need for global orientation', *Management International Review*, 30(1), 5–18.

Usunier, J.-C. (2000), *Marketing Across Cultures*, 3rd edn., Harlow: FT/Prentice Hall.

Usunier, J.-C., and Lee, J., (2005), *Marketing Across Cultures*, 4th edn., Harlow: FT/Prentice Hall.

Volkema, R. J., (2004), 'Demographic, cultural, and economic predictors of perceived ethicality of negotiation behavior: a nine-country analysis', *Journal of Business Research*, 57(1), 69–78.

Webster, F. E. Jr. and Wind, Y. (1972), 'A general model of organizational buyer behaviour', *Journal of Marketing*, 36(2), 12–19.

Yau, O. H. M. (1994), *Consumer Behaviour in China: Customer Satisfaction and Cultural Values*, New York: Routledge.

Yeo, C.-M. A. and Carter, S. (2005), 'Linking Culture Strength and Managerial Competencies to Corporate Performance: The case of Malaysia', *Global Business Anthology*, Worcester: Business and Economics Society International, 408–28.

online resource centre

Visit the companion website to this book for lots of interesting additional material, including self-assessment questions, internet exercises, and links for each chapter:

http://www.oxfordtextbooks.co.uk/orc/lee_carter2e/

CHAPTER FIVE

Understanding Global Social and Ethical Issues

Chapter overview

Chapter Introduction 142

Global Social and Ethical Issues 142
    Corruption 143
    Human rights 147
    Labour practices 150
    Environmental protection 153

The Corporate Response to Social and Ethical Issues 153
    Codes of ethics 155
    Making codes effective 158
    Ethics training 158

Corporate Social Responsibility and Competitive Advantage 160
    Reputation management 160
    Risk management 163
    Employee satisfaction 163
    Innovation and learning 164
    Access to capital 164
    Improved financial performance 165

Chapter Summary 165

Learning objectives

After studying this chapter, the reader will be able to:

- acquire an understanding of the major social issues that companies need to address in the global marketplace in order to be considered socially responsible business practitioners;
- consider the use of codes of ethics by global companies to address issues relating to social responsibility;
- demonstrate how corporate social responsibility and ethical practice can provide competitive advantage in the global marketplace.

Management issues

The management issues that arise from this chapter include:

- What are the main issues that socially responsible companies need to take into account when transacting business in the global marketplace?
- How and to what extent can codes of ethics help to address issues relating to social responsibility?
- How can corporate social responsibility and ethical practice provide competitive advantage in the global marketplace?

Chapter Introduction

The current concern that business and the general public have for ethical behaviour and social responsibility is not restricted to the domestic marketplace in the era of the global economy. The increasing transparency of corporate practices worldwide has put pressure on companies to be more socially responsible in all their activities. These pressures can come from a company's own ethical values, its home country government, or constituencies that threaten to boycott its products or spread negative publicity about it. Against this background, many companies now believe that socially responsible behaviour not only helps to avoid negative consequences from irresponsible business practice, but that it also leads to strategic and financial success.

This chapter demonstrates how companies can use corporate social responsibility and ethical practices not only to increase trade, but also as a source of competitive advantage in the global marketplace. It looks at some of the issues which companies operating in the global marketplace need to address if they are to be considered as socially responsible business practitioners. Although many of the issues are not unique to international activity, international companies are perceived to have a key role as change agents in wider globalization processes, and this means that participating in the global marketplace raises important issues concerning the wider impact of business on social development and the growth of individual economies, particularly with respect to conducting business with countries where governance structures are weak or non-existent.

The chapter looks at what might be considered to constitute ethical practice in the global context and examines the role of corporate codes of practice in implementing social responsibility, as well as the ethical guidelines available to companies to formulate such codes. This has become a critical area for many companies which are increasingly being held responsible not only for the activities of their own employees, but also for those of their sub-contractors and strategic alliance and joint venture partners, not all of whom will necessarily share the same values, operate under the same legal systems, or have the same ethical priorities. The chapter concludes by looking at social responsibility and ethical practices as sources of competitive advantage and examines how companies are changing their behaviours in order to gain significant advantage in markets around the world.

Global Social and Ethical Issues

Over the past decade a consensus has developed among businesses, academics, governments, international institutions, and the general public that there are a number of social issues in the global marketplace with which companies have to engage in order to be considered socially responsible business practitioners. Foremost among these are concerns about corruption and corrupt practice in international activities, human rights, labour practices, and environmental protection. Although, at first sight, these concerns may be thought to be largely internal matters for countries themselves to deal with, they are issues which have been shown to have a detrimental effect on individual economies and to be major impediments to the growth and development of the world economy. Companies, therefore, have to take a stance on such issues—whether, for example, to take advantage of weak governance under the guise of a 'when in Rome, do as the Romans do' approach to global markets, and thereby add to the problems of individual countries, or whether to adopt more socially responsible practice in their business transactions. These issues will be discussed in order to consider what is meant by socially responsible practice on a global scale.

Corruption

Corruption can be defined as 'the abuse of public office for private gain' (Lasserre, 2003) and covers a wide range of local practices, including bribery, fraud, money laundering, cronyism, extortion, and embezzlement. Although this definition refers largely to government officials, a similar definition can be applied to employees of private companies and to others who abuse a position of trust for personal gain. Corruption in all its forms is widespread, varying in extent both between countries and across industries. One of the major sources of information on the extent of corruption is Transparency International (TI), a non-governmental organization dedicated to combating all forms of corrupt practice. The information published by Transparency International provides annualized snapshots of perceptions of corruption from both a country perspective and an industry perspective by means of two indices—the Corruption Perceptions Index (CPI) and the Bribe Payers Index (BPI).

The Corruption Perceptions Index (CPI)

The TI Corruption Perceptions Index ranks countries in terms of the degree to which corruption is perceived to exist among public officials and politicians. The 2007, CPI ranked 180 countries by their perceived levels of corruption, as determined by expert assessments and opinion surveys. Scores range between 10 (highly clean) and 0 (highly corrupt). Table 5.1 shows a selection of the results of the 2007 survey for the 180 countries included in that year's index.

Table 5.1 Transparency International's Corruption Perceptions Index 2007

Rank	Country	CPI score	Rank	Country	CPI score
1	New Zealand	9.4	56	Greece	4.6
	Denmark	9.4	61	Poland	4.2
	Finland	9.4	64	Turkey	4.1
4	Singapore	9.3	72	China	3.5
9	Australia	8.6		India	3.5
12	United Kingdom	8.4		Mexico	3.5
14	Hong Kong	8.3		Brazil	3.5
16	Germany	7.8	105	Argentina	2.9
17	Japan	7.5		Egypt	2.9
19	France	7.3	143	Indonesia	2.3
20	USA	7.2		Russia	2.3
22	Chile	7.0	162	Bangladesh	2.0
28	Estonia	6.5		Venezuela	2.0
34	Taiwan	5.7	172	Chad	1.8
41	Czech Republic	5.2	177	Haiti	1.6
	Italy	5.2	178	Iraq	1.5
43	Malaysia	5.1	179	Somalia	1.4
	South Korea	5.1		Myanmar	1.4

Source: Transparency International Corruption Perception Index 2007, www.transparency.org.

Table 5.2 Bribery in business sectors 2002

Business sector	BPI score
Public works/construction	1.3
Arms and defence	1.9
Oil and gas	2.7
Real estate/property	3.5
Telecoms	3.7
Power generation/transmission	3.7
Mining	4.0
Transportation/storage	4.3
Pharmaceuticals/medical care	4.3
Heavy manufacturing	4.5
Banking and finance	4.7
Civilian aerospace	4.9
Forestry	5.1
IT	5.1
Fishery	5.9
Light manufacturing	5.9
Agriculture	5.9

Source: Transparency International Bribe Payers Index 2002, www.transparency.org

The Bribe Payers Index (BPI)

The Bribe Payers Index records perceptions of the extent of bribery by multinational firms based on surveys of the views of business executives, commercial banks, law firms, Chambers of Commerce, and chartered accountancies. It was conducted by Gallup International Association in 15 emerging market economies. The 2002 index was based on responses to the question: 'How likely is it that senior public officials in this country would demand or accept bribes, e.g. for public tenders, regulations, licensing, in the following business sectors?' (www.transparency.org). Table 5.2 shows the outcome of the 2002 survey. In the same way as the Corruption Perceptions Index, a score of 0.0 represents very high perceived levels of corruption and a score of 10.0 represents very low perceived levels of corruption.

The impact of corruption

For many companies, corruption has traditionally been viewed as an 'awkward but necessary' part of doing business in international markets and considered to be an everyday aspect of the general global business environment. Increasingly, however, businesses are becoming aware of the corrosive impact of corruption on the growth and development of individual countries and their markets, and businesses which participate in corruption are being seen by a growing number of important stakeholders not so much as victims of corruption, but rather as key actors in perpetuating it. Additionally, the true costs of corruption are now becoming apparent and whereas engaging in foreign corrupt practice may bring financial benefits to the few, corruption itself distorts the marketplace and prevents growth of business opportunities for the many (see Fig. 5.1). The World Bank (www.worldbank.org) has singled out corruption as the greatest obstacle to economic development today in that it 'distorts the rule of law and weakens the institutional foundation on which economic growth depends' (World Bank, 2003).

Fig. 5.1 Why corruption matters?

Corruption and Business
- Increases the costs of doing business
- Erodes competitive advantage
- Blocks access to international markets
- Damages market efficiency
- Loss of reputation
- Credit restrictions and blacklisting

Corruption and Development
- Reduces government tax revenues
- Limits government ability to invest in public health and education
- Weakens the public infrastructure on which growth depends
- Increases construction projects costs
- Increases susceptibility to financial crises
- Damages future business potential

Corruption and development

Countries with high levels of corruption generally have low levels of GDP and depressed rates of investment. Corruption reduces government tax revenues and thereby can limit government ability to invest in public health and education. It can weaken the public infrastructure on which business growth depends, leading to inadequate, expensive, and intermittently provided services such as electricity, transport, and telephone services (Doh et al., 2003). Construction projects may cost more due to construction companies marking up bids for contracts in order to include kickbacks both for public officials making the award and for bribes being paid throughout the construction process. Evidence has accumulated to suggest that corruption may increase an economy's susceptibility to financial crises. In particular, evidence concerning the Asian financial crisis of 1997, the collapse of the Russian rouble in 1998, and a number of financial crises in Latin American countries in the 1980s and 1990s suggests that corruption may have been a contributory cause (Boatright, 2000). Corruption may damage a country's future business potential by directing scarce entrepreneurial talent away from the leading of growth and development activities into unproductive activities of little benefit to the countries concerned (Doh et al., 2003).

A major cause of concern with respect to longer-term projects that can lead to the development of business and economic growth potential is that corruption weakens courts and regulatory agencies, with international investors and donors becoming reluctant to lend funds to countries lacking adequate rule of law or transparency and accountability in government administration (UNODC, www.bsr.org, 2004). The harmful effects of corruption are especially severe on the poor, who are hardest hit by economic decline and are most reliant on the provision of public services, and where corruption diverts funds which have been supplied for essential services and development, this effectively 'sabotages policies and programmes that aim to reduce poverty' (World Bank, 2003: 1).

Corruption and business

Although some commentators have attempted to make a case for corruption as a means of 'greasing the wheels of business' and speeding up business transactions, the overall impact is overwhelmingly negative. Companies participate in corruption largely for two reasons: first, because of a misguided respect for local norms; and, secondly, because of fear that if they do not, they may find themselves at a disadvantage in respect of competitors and lose business because of this. This fear is not shared by all companies as the mini-case illustration below demonstrates.

Corruption, by its very nature, is an inefficient way of doing business. At the very least it increases the costs of doing business; at its worst it impedes the development of fair and efficient markets, erodes genuine competitive advantage, and blocks access

MINI-CASE ILLUSTRATION Honeywell International

In its code of business conduct, Honeywell (www.honeywell.com) lists integrity as the first of a dozen workplace behaviours required by the company, explaining that 'integrity is a bedrock principle of all our behaviours'. In a landmark case, Honeywell declined to bid for a major airport contract in Asia because it was asked for a bribe as the price of entry. When a subsequent scandal revealed that all 11 bidding companies had paid bribes, they were disqualified and Honeywell won the contract. In its code, the company states that, 'Honeywell strictly prohibits bribes, kickbacks or any other form of improper payment, direct or indirect in order to obtain a contract, some other commercial benefit or government action. The Company also strictly prohibits any employee from accepting such payments from anyone.'

All Honeywell employees, as well as all agents, consultants, and independent contractors, are held responsible for knowing and complying with the code. Supervisors and those identified to be at higher risk because of the nature of their work must affirm on an annual basis that they have complied, brought it to the attention of those they supervise, and know of no violations. To encourage employees to share their concerns, Honeywell has a freephone international ethics advice line with calls that go directly to an outside agency for review. Employees can call this agency to follow up concerns they have raised. In addition, Honeywell has a confidential electronic advice line that can be accessed through its ethics and compliance website. The company also has local advice lines in each region in which it operates.

Source: Adapted from www.bsr.org.

to markets (Boatright, 2000). The costs of doing business can rise significantly due to corruption—one major study conducted by *The Economist* in 1999 estimated that bribery payments in Indonesia accounted for 20% of business costs.

The costs of bribery are also recurring, since companies known to pay bribes are often asked to pay more bribes at each stage of the contracting process, and the size of payments demanded tends to increase as companies engage in a form of 'competitive bribery' (www.bsr.org). Bribery is essentially a secret act and this means that redress cannot be sought for breaches of contract through normal legal channels.

Market efficiency is damaged by bribery because companies no longer compete on the grounds of price and quality, but compete merely to gain access. Companies whose competitive advantage is based on innovation and efficiency may find that they cannot enter certain markets because entry is controlled by bribery. The shareholders who invest in companies which bribe may find they are basing their investment decisions on information that bears little resemblance to the true competitive position relative to comparable companies. They run the risk of significant loss if the company reputation suffers due to accusations of corruption and any resulting fines, litigation, or civil and criminal sanctions. These risks are becoming more prevalent as companies begin to face the increasing likelihood of prosecution due to a tightened global regulatory environment.

Bribery increases the costs of doing business. Companies involved in bribery run the significant risks of being fined, civil or criminal sanctions and loss of reputation.

Legislation

Although most countries have enacted legislation to deal with corruption within their own borders, this legislation has tended to apply only to corruption within that country rather than corrupt practices by home companies abroad or bribery of foreign public officials. An exception is the US Foreign Corrupt Practices Act, which, since 1977, has prohibited US companies and foreign companies listed on the New York Stock Exchange from giving bribes to foreign officials to gain contracts abroad. Prosecutions under this Act have resulted in fines of up to US$69 million, with firms being banned from government contracting or having to operate under 'intrusive consent agreements' (www.bsr.org). Senior managers have also been fined up to US$50,000.

More recently, however, a number of new initiatives have led to changes in national legislation in order to criminalize corrupt practice outside the jurisdiction of home governments. Key to these developments has been a number of conventions which signatory countries integrate into national law and which are binding on companies' activities in the global marketplace. Foremost among these conventions in the scale of its global reach is the OECD Convention on Combating Bribery of Public Officials in International Business Transactions (1999) which, to date, has been ratified by 35 countries, including all the major European countries as well as Argentina, Australia, Brazil, Canada, Japan, Korea, Mexico, and the USA (OECD, www.OECD.org). This Convention prohibits bribery of foreign officials and requires countries which adopt it to pass national legislation which incorporates this into all national law relating to corruption and corrupt practices. The Council of Europe Criminal Law Convention (1999) aims to harmonize national laws on corruption and criminalizes both domestic and international bribery, and other forms of corruption, and applies to the private sector as well as to civil servants, judges, and members of parliament. The European Convention on Corruption (1997) provides for the prosecution of corruption involving officials of the EU or member states of the EU (www.bsr .org). Other Conventions include the Organization of American States (OAS) Inter-American Convention against Corruption (1997), which requires signatories to criminalize bribery of domestic and foreign officials, and to assist in the investigation and prosecution of such acts. More than 25 countries have ratified the Convention, including Argentina, Brazil, Canada, Chile, Mexico and the USA (www.bsr.org).

Credit restrictions and blacklisting

In addition to tightening legislative controls, companies which engage in foreign corrupt practices also face restrictions on credit and blacklisting for contracts by international institutions. Approaches taken by major international institutions are covered in the mini-case illustration below.

Although corruption remains widespread and is endemic in a number of national marketplaces and industries around the world, frameworks such as these provide not only clear statements that corruption is damaging both to national economies and to business globally, but also guidance as to where the social responsibility of business lies in the global marketplace with respect to these issues. However, companies considered as socially responsible go far beyond mere compliance with national legislation and international agreements, and are proactive in developing management systems which ensure that corrupt practices have no place in internal corporate cultures and external behaviours.

Human rights

Human rights are the standards of treatment to which all people are entitled. The most widely recognized definition is the Universal Declaration of Human Rights adopted by the United Nations in 1948. Although human rights, as considered in the benchmark of the Universal Declaration, were originally intended to guide the activities of governments,

MINI-CASE ILLUSTRATION **The World Bank**

In addition to national laws and international agreements, many lending institutions take corruption and bribery into account when giving credit. The World Bank includes fraud and corruption provisions in its procurement and consultancy guidelines. Companies that have been found to have infringed the provisions are placed on a public blacklist which is used by the World Bank and some credit agencies when considering loans and contracts.

Nearly 70 firms have been permanently banned in this way from competing for World Bank contracts. Regional development banks have taken a similar approach. Export credit agencies from OECD countries require companies applying for credit to include explicit anti-corruption guarantees.

Source: www.bsr.org.

the increasing globalization of business has brought more companies into contact with human rights issues through their operations in countries whose governments do not respect the principles of the Declaration. The activities of numerous pressure groups and non-governmental organizations, such as Amnesty International (www.amnesty.org) and Human Rights Watch (www.hrw.org), have heightened public and corporate awareness of human rights abuses and media coverage of human rights issues is extensive.

Companies are usually implicated in human rights issues through involvement with governments using abusive methods to protect the interests of the company. This can involve complicity with governments in these activities or by ignoring the activities taking place. Companies have been associated with this form of human rights abuse when local demonstrators protesting at their activities have been beaten, detained without trial, tortured, or executed by local police and security forces. Complicity arises in that where companies are aware that such practices are the norm within a society, they are considered to be involved by this knowledge when hiring local security forces or seeking the protection of local police. Companies are also implicated when they contribute to political regimes that abuse human rights. This can include contributions to political funds, the payment of bribes to political leaders, and money laundering. Complicity also extends to sub-contractors, and there are many cases where the human rights of ethnic minority indigenous people have been abused in the form of forced labour sanctioned by government and tacitly accepted by companies hiring these contractors.

The pressures on companies to abandon such practice come mainly from the activities of human rights organizations which publicize company activities and the resulting influence this has on consumer and investor behaviour. Such activities, for example, resulted in the boycott of Shell petrol stations in Europe and elsewhere in protest at Shell's presence in Nigeria. Investors can choose to invest in companies which are listed on socially responsible stock indices such as the FTSE4Good and the Dow Jones Sustainability Index. Although there is no formal legislation concerning complicity in human rights abuses, a further avenue of publicity has been generated by cases submitted to US courts under the Aliens Tort Statute (1789). This grants original jurisdiction to US federal courts for any civil action brought by an alien for a tort committed in violation of international law. Although, to date, no case against a private company has gone as far as trial, the resulting publicity and the judgments in court rulings put significant pressure on companies and redefine social responsibility. For example, in the case against Unocal (www.unocal.com), a company involved in building a natural gas pipeline in southern Burma in 2002, a California court ruled that villagers from Burma (Myanmar) who claimed that the company should be accountable for torture, rape, slave labour, and executions committed by Burmese military authorities in connection with the construction could sue Unocal for violating their human rights (Schrage, 2003). Other companies facing criticism concerning their presence in Burma, which is acknowledged to have one of the world's most oppressive regimes, have chosen to abandon their operations, including Levi Strauss (www.levistrauss.com),

Liz Claiborne (www.lizclaiborne.com), Macy's (www.maceys.com), and Eddie Bauer (www.eddiebauer.com). Texaco (www.texaco.com), and Amoco (www.bp.com) have also left, even though six months earlier Amoco's president had described Burma as one of the most promising new regions for exploration (Spar, 1998).

In the absence of legislation governing human rights abuses, combinations of companies, non-governmental organizations, international institutions, national governments, and other groups have begun to engage in partnership to create new relationships in order to address human rights concerns within industries which are particularly susceptible.

The United Nations Global Compact

The UN Global Compact further builds on the idea of partnership as a means of combating human rights abuse, as well as other areas of social concern, by inviting companies to join with UN agencies and labour and civil society in support of ten principles governing responsible business practice in the areas of human rights, labour issues, and the environment (Fig. 5.2). The Compact was initiated in an address to the World Economic Forum in 1999 by the Secretary General of the United Nations, Kofi Annan, who challenged business leaders to join this new initiative aimed at seeking to advance the concept of global corporate citizenship. The Compact was formally launched in July 2000.

Participating in the Global Compact is now seen as a benchmark for socially responsible practice and as such has been generally welcomed by business, with most major companies and many others utilizing the Compact as a framework for internal and external statements on their business practice. Although concerns have been raised that there are no monitoring or enforcement mechanisms contained in the Compact to assure compliance to the ten principles, it can be argued that the Compact reinforces the concept of social responsibility as a matter of self-regulation rather than compliance. Companies signing up to the Global Compact are required to set in motion changes to business operations so that its ten principles become part of strategy, culture, and

---

THE RELATIONSHIP PERSPECTIVE Cross-sector partnerships and human rights

Diamonds

The Kimberley Process Certification Scheme involves more than 30 governments, the European Union, the diamond industry, and civil society to establish minimum acceptable standards for national certification schemes relating to trade in rough diamonds. The aim of the scheme is to stem the flow of rough diamonds from rebel-held conflict areas, which have been linked to human rights violations.

Energy and Extractives

The USA, UK, Dutch, and Norwegian governments, in collaboration with non-governmental organizations and companies in the energy and extractives industries (including Chevron (www.chevron.com), Texaco, Freeport McMoRan (www.fcx.com), Conoco (www.conocophi;lips.com), Shell, BP, and Rio Tinto (www.riotino.com), have embarked on a programme to promote the maintenance of safety and security of business operations while ensuring respect for human rights and fundamental freedoms. The focus of the 'Voluntary Principles on Security and

Human Rights' is on risk assessment, company relations with public security forces, and company relations with private security forces.

Source: www.bsr.org.

Fig. 5.2 The ten principles of the UN Global Compact 2000

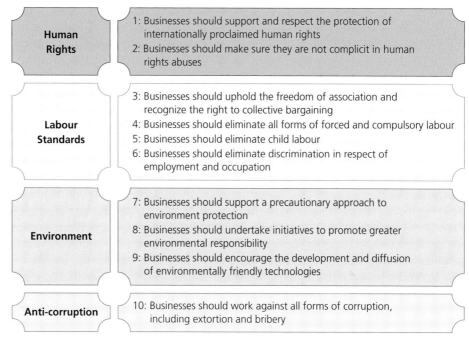

Source: www.unglobalcompact.org.

day-to-day operations. They are also expected to become public advocates for the Global Compact as well as publishing a description of the way in which they are supporting it in their business activities. A further UN initiative which has received positive support from human rights organizations is the UN Draft Norms on the Responsibilities of Transnational Corporations and Other Business Activities with Regard to Human Rights, approved in August 2003. This document sets out the responsibilities of companies for human rights and labour rights and provides guidelines for companies operating in conflict zones as well as prohibiting bribery and activities that harm consumers, including polluting the environment.

Labour practices

Concern about labour practices as a social issue is based on the activities of companies which take advantage of lower labour standards than they face at home, in order to achieve lower costs and hence profit from labour conditions which would be unacceptable within their own domestic environment. The focus of attention has been the use of sweatshop and child labour—not by multinational organizations in their factories but by sub-contractors producing their products in overseas plant. Companies which have attracted attention with respect to their alleged activities in this area include Nike (www.nike.com), Gap (www.gap.com), Walt Disney (www. disney.com), and Reebok (www.reebock.com). The negative publicity which these activities generate has led many companies to fear for their corporate reputation. 'When local producers in Vietnam, Pakistan or Honduras exploit their workforce, few in the West hear of it, especially if the products are not exported to Western markets. But when those same producers become suppliers to Reebok, Levi Strauss or Walt Disney, their actions make headlines' (Spar, 1998: 7). Such fears have led to the promulgation of codes of practice

MINI-CASE ILLUSTRATION UN Draft Norms—new standards for corporations and human rights

'This is now the world's most comprehensive and authoritative standard on corporate responsibility,' said Arvid Ganesan, Director of the Business and Human Rights Program of Human Rights Watch. 'These norms have come to fill an important gap in the protection of human rights worldwide.'

Historically, voluntary standards and initiatives for companies have been limited to specific industries, such as the Fair Labor Association for the clothing and footwear industry or the Voluntary Principles on Security and Human Rights in the Extractive Industries.

The Norms are not a binding set of standards but can be adopted by governments or companies. Their analysis and commentary could provide the conceptual case of a binding instrument on corporate responsibility since the Norms are an authoritative interpretation of the responsibilities of corporations under human rights law. The Norms also close a loophole because they apply to all forms of business and not only transnational corporations.

Source: Extract from *Human Rights Watch Press Release,* 13 August 2003. The full document can be found at hrw.org/press/2003/08/un081303.htm.

with respect to relationships with suppliers and sub-contractors coupled with external monitoring in order to demonstrate good labour practice, as illustrated in the mini-case below. However, such has been the outcry against the worst excesses of major companies, that compliance with codes of practice is often insufficient to address the concerns of pressure groups and other key stakeholders in these issues, and companies now need to be seen to be taking a more proactive approach in addressing structural conditions which give rise to poor labour practice by suppliers and others.

Where companies have faced criticism concerning labour practices by suppliers, withdrawal from a country has been seen as socially irresponsible because, for some commentators, a key issue has been that of the contribution that child labour makes to family income in the poorest areas of the world. This argument was long held as a rationale for exploiting labour practice on the basis that global companies were contributing to the local economy and providing jobs. Without such activities, the argument ran, regions would become poorer by having to rely on local employment. Companies must now address this issue if they do not wish to be accused of causing greater poverty by closing down factories and leaving the country.

Sweatshops

There is no formally recognized definition of the term 'sweatshop', however it has come to mean conditions which are considered exploitative of workers in a number of industries. Generally, these conditions include concerns about acceptable working practices, including health and safety systems, wage levels, working hours and working conditions, and freedom of association. As with child labour, companies seek to act in a socially responsible manner by incorporating required standards into codes of practice governing the activities of their suppliers and sub-contractors. However, where pressure groups remain unconvinced of the good faith of companies in adopting these

MINI-CASE ILLUSTRATION **Codes of practice and child labour**

Wal-Mart Stores Inc

Wal-Mart (www.wal-mart.com) does not tolerate the use of child labour in the manufacture of the products it sells. Wal-Mart will not accept products from suppliers who use, in any manner, child labour in the manufacture of their products. Suppliers must assure that their factories, or the factories of their direct or indirect sub-contractors, do not employ persons younger than 15 years of age, or 14 where the laws of the country allow. If egregious violations are noted—those relating to child labour, human rights abuses, discrimination, or unsafe working practices—for which there may be extenuating circumstances (e.g. worker falsified documents, required additional overtime) the factory is assessed as 'pending fail'. The factory has 10 days to demonstrate that the extenuating circumstances are being addressed. No merchandise may be shipped from factories with an assessment of 'pending fail'. A full re-inspection must be completed within 30 days, even if the factory has demonstrated that extenuating circumstances existed.

A supplier factory is failed when egregious violations are noted and no extenuating circumstances can be documented at the time of the audit. Wal-Mart will not accept products made in factories that fail inspection, or are assessed as 'pending fail'. Should a supplier again place Wal-Mart purchase orders in another failing, or pending fail factory, all orders through that supplier in that country are cancelled. Wal-Mart will terminate the relationship with a supplier on a global basis on the third such occurrence. (Report on Vendor Standards, 2001)

Procter & Gamble

Child Labour and Worker Exploitation Policy: P & G does not use child or forced labour in any of our global operations or facilities. We do not tolerate unacceptable worker treatment such as the exploitation of children, physical punishment or abuse, or involuntary servitude. We expect our suppliers to uphold the same standards. Should a pattern of violation of these principles become known to the Company and not be corrected, we will discontinue the business relationship. For purposes of implementing the above policy, we will employ the following definitions:

Child labour: We will look first to the sovereign laws of the country in which we are doing business. In the absence of any national or local law, we will define 'child' as less than 15 years of age. If local minimum-age law is set below 15 years of age but is in accordance with International Labour Organization (ILO) Convention 138, the lower age will apply. Forced labour is any work or service extracted from any person under the menace of any penalty and for which said person has not offered themselves voluntarily.

Supplier or contractor is someone who has a 'direct' business or contractual relationship with P & G. We will urge our suppliers and contractors to promote the application of these principles by those with whom they do business.

Source: www.bsr.org.

Nestlé

Nestlé is against all forms of exploitation of children. The company does not provide employment to young people before they would have completed their compulsory education and expects its business partners and industrial suppliers to apply the same standards. In all countries where we operate, the Head of Human Resources has confirmed that our practices comply with our principles on human resources and the workplace and child labour. Nestlé abides by national laws in all countries where it operates, and Nestlé complies with the United Nations Convention on the Rights of the Child as well as ILO Conventions 138 and 182.

Even though we do not own agricultural land, and raw materials are primarily bought from processors or traders, we are currently working with the UK, US and Cote d'Ivoire governments, NGOs, process traders and other chocolate manufacturers to assess and eliminate forced child labour in cocoa farming where it may exist. (Nestlé Sustainability Review, May 2002.)

Source: www.bsr.org.

codes of practice and the monitoring systems accompanying them, negative publicity can continue as a result of the company appearing to behave in a reactive rather than a proactive manner. This has allegedly been the case with Nike. In spite of responding to pressure group criticisms of the labour practices of its suppliers, by raising minimum age limits and instituting codes of practice, audits, and monitoring procedures, Nike's approach is perceived to be defensive in that little appears to have been done to address the issue of minimum wages which conform to national law but which are acknowledged to be below subsistence levels in countries such as Indonesia and Vietnam, as well as criticisms of the value of its auditing arrangements. The company's auditors, PricewaterhouseCoopers (www.pwtc.com), allowed an independent observer to accompany their auditors in factory inspections in China, South Korea, and Vietnam. The observer's report concluded that although the auditors found a number of minor violations of

MINI-CASE ILLUSTRATION **The Sialkot football programme**

In 1996, when the International Confederation of Free Trade Unions (ICFTU) launched a campaign against child labour in football production in the Sialkot region of Pakistan, 7,000 children—17% of the region's football manufacturing workforce—were sewing balls full-time. Beginning in 1997, more than 50 sporting good brands, including Adidas, Nike, and Reebok, local manufacturers and the Sialkot Chamber of Commerce and Industry joined with several international organizations to eliminate child labour in Pakistan's football industry. Under the programme, the brands agree to buy footballs only from manufacturers certified as child labour free by independent monitors from the ILO's IPEC. As of April 2002, IPEC was monitoring over 2,600 factories, covering almost 95% of Sialkot's football production, and had found no instances of child labour in the previous nine months.

The companies also fund social programmes for former child workers and their families, including non-formal education centres and micro credit. A Reebok facility in the region uses external monitoring to ensure that no worker is less than 15 years old. Reebok also supports child-focused initiatives in the region, such as a school for former child workers, and healthcare and employment for adult family members of former child workers.

The Sialkot programme has become a model for Pakistan's carpet industry and the football industry in India.

Source: www.bsr.org.

codes of conduct, major violations had been missed. In addition, there was a reliance on factory managers for information, and questions with respect to freedom of association, collective bargaining, child labour, and forced labour were not asked (Florini, 2003). For pressure groups, the issue has not been that Nike has not attempted to address concerns about the labour practices of some of its contractors, but rather that this appears to have been done in an attitude of defensive compliance and as such cannot be guaranteed to fully address the issues.

Environmental protection

Over the past two decades concepts of corporate responsibility towards environmental protection have changed dramatically. As explained in Chapter 3, the concept of 'sustainable development' has come to be seen as a key feature of socially responsible business practice. As concerns about climate change and environmental protection rise in importance to stakeholders, international companies are responding by adopting a number of initiatives, including voluntary industry guidelines; product takeback; and adherence to environmental standards set by international and voluntary bodies; and publication of detailed sustainability reports in order to demonstrate their commitment to tackling environmental protection issues. The mini-case below is an extract from Dell's 2007 Sustainability Report outlining a range of achievements with respect to environmental protection and a number of environmental responsibility goals.

The Corporate Response to Social and Ethical Issues

As seen above, companies wishing to be viewed as socially responsible business practitioners have sought a variety of means to address the challenges of global social issues. In this, the process of social reporting has become a major instrument in demonstrating active commitment to corporate social responsibility. Much of this social reporting focuses

MINI-CASE ILLUSTRATION Dell Computers: moving towards environmental sustainability

	Environmental accomplishments	Environment responsibility goals
Climate protection	Increased customer awareness of carbon emissions by introducing the 'Plant a Tree for Me' carbon dioxide offset programme.	Reduce overall transportation requirements by 25% by using rail trailers to increase capacity of flat railroad cars, more multi-pack configurations, and shipping efficiencies.
	Reduced greenhouse gas emissions from Dell operations and products.	Reduce greenhouse gas (GHG) emissions of Dell's freight operations by increasing the percentage of freight shipped through SmartWay Transport Partnership carriers.
	Reduced emissions from shipping products by optimizing shipping routes, instituting customer delivery notification process, and opening more facilities to assemble products closer to the customer.	Reduce greenhouse gas emissions from Dell supplier operations by requesting applicable data and working with suppliers on emissions reduction strategies once data is collected.
	Reduced electricity usage rate in US office buildings by 5% from previous year.	
Product design	Introduced PCs and servers based on processors that consume less power, helping to reduce the overall power consumption.	Implement server-managed power management for customers worldwide to avoid 40,000 tons of carbon dioxide emissions between 2008 and 2012.
	Introduced Energy Smart programme to provide customers with the ability to optimize performance and efficiency.	
	Enabled power management settings at the factory for PCs and notebooks.	
	Accelerated the date (by six years) to phase out brominated flame retardants in new product designs.	
Materials	Met the EU Restriction on Hazardous Substances by eliminating, for example, lead cable insulation and other lead substances.	Avoid 100,000 tons of lead and 60,000 tons of brominated flame retardants (BFRs) by 2012.
		Eliminate all remaining BFRs and polyvinyl chloride (PVC) by end of 2009 as acceptable alternatives are identified that will not compromise product performance and will lower product health and environmental impacts.
Facilities and manufacturing	Increased waste recycled to 94%.	Recycle or reuse 99% of waste from manufacturing operations by 2012.
		Further reduce carbon intensity by 15% by 2012.
		Improve our average score from the LEED (Leadership in Energy and Environmental Design) Green Building Rating System by 2012.
Product stewardship	Introduced no-charge recycling of Dell computers for consumers worldwide.	Recover 125 million kilograms of discarded product by 2010 through asset recovery programmes.
	Expanded product recovery programme for commercial customers to decommission obsolete equipment in China.	

Source: Dell Sustainability Report, 2007 (www.dell.com).

on the key principles of the UN Social Compact and takes the form of corporate social responsibility audits issued alongside corporate annual accounts or is embedded within wider sustainability reports. By these means, companies take the opportunity to demonstrate that they have adopted codes, standards, and principles that facilitate the building of a global corporate culture which fosters social responsibility. This approach recognizes that whereas corporate social responsibility is concerned with the impact of business on the societies in which they operate, there is also a need to integrate within this the concept of corporate ethics in order to address the issues of individual decision-making and the development of ethical conduct (Boatright, 2000).

Codes of ethics

Corporate codes of ethics attempt to express an organization's values and culture and create guidelines for employees to work by (Sanyal, 2001). Although corporate codes of ethics vary widely, there are generally considered to be two main forms—integrity-based codes and compliance-based codes. Compliance-based codes are designed to ensure compliance with the law and with the company's policies and procedures. Integrity-based codes are based on the values of the organization and stress the responsibility of each employee for ethical behaviour (Boatright, 2000). There are three major types of corporate code adopted by international companies. The first is a code of conduct which is normally completely compliance-based and typically sets out guidelines on a range of issues which form the basis for relationships with suppliers, contractors, and licensees. Such codes set out company policies on issues such as labour practices, including company standards respecting child labour, forced labour, wages, freedom of association, health and safety practice, and other related issues. These codes are normally audited externally to assess compliance. The second type of code is a statement of business principles, which includes reference to essential values while stating company standards and practices. The third type is a statement of the values of the company, emphasizing the responsibility of each employee for ethical conduct. The Credo of Johnson & Johnson (www.jnj.com) is a primary example of this (Fig. 5.3).

Adopting a code of practice is no guarantee that it will be effective. In order to influence behaviour, codes need to provide specific guidelines on company policies and practices, and to explain why the company has adopted these principles and how they support and further the company's business performance. They also need to provide guidance on what to do if employees consider that they are being breached or if they are uncertain how to behave under any given circumstance. Unilever's Code of Business Conduct (Fig. 5.4), for example, provides a statement on the values of the company in carrying out its business transactions, and its approach to relationships with key stakeholders, including employees, customers, shareholders, and business partners. It states company policy and procedures with respect to bribery and conflicts of interest. The code also explains the monitoring and reporting mechanisms adopted.

The use of codes of ethics is not without its critics, especially in regard to codes of conduct. These codes are often criticized for the costs of verification which are seen as business costs, the development of a code verification industry involving largely financial auditing companies, the lack of publication of verification reports, and the thoroughness with which such external verification is carried out. Moreover, the proliferation of guidelines, codes, principles, and standards issued by industry bodies, professional associations, international institutions, and NGOs has been criticized on the basis of confusion over which standards to uphold.

Fig. 5.3 The Johnson & Johnson Credo

Our Credo

We believe our first responsibility is to the doctors, nurses and patients,
to mothers and fathers and all others who use our products and services.
In meeting their needs everything we do must be of high quality.
We must constantly strive to reduce our costs
in order to maintain reasonable prices.
Customers' orders must be serviced promptly and accurately.
Our suppliers and distributors must have an opportunity
To make a fair profit.

We are responsible to our employees,
the men and women who work with us throughout the world.
Everyone must be considered as an individual.
We must respect their dignity and recognize their merit.
They must have a sense of security in their jobs.
Compensation must be fair and adequate,
and working conditions, clean, orderly and safe.
We must be mindful of ways to help our employees fulfil
their family responsibilities.
Employees must feel free to make suggestions and complaints.
There must be equal opportunity for employment, development
and advancement for those qualified.
We must provide competent management,
and their actions must be just and ethical.

We are responsible to the communities in which we live and work
and to the world community as well.
We must be good citizens—support good works and charities
And bear our fair share of taxes.
We must encourage civic improvements and better health and education.
We must maintain in good order
The property we are privileged to use,
protecting the environment and natural resources.

Our final responsibility is to our stockholders.
Business must make a sound profit.
We must experiment with new ideas.
Research must be carried on, innovative programs developed
And mistakes paid for.
New equipment must be purchased, new facilities provided
And new products launched.
Reserves must be created to provide for adverse times.
When we operate according to these principles,
The stockholders should realize a fair return

Source: www.jnj.com/our_company/our_credo/index.htm.

However, companies have found that corporate codes have proved invaluable in answer to stakeholder concerns and in many cases the quality of the code and its effectiveness in implementation have led to improved reputation and increased potential
shareholder interest via the growing ethical investment industry. Johnson & Johnson
found that their code was an essential tool in crisis management when one of its products was tampered with, resulting in several deaths. The strength of its ethical code was
instrumental in the vindication of the company (Boatright, 2000). For socially responsible

Fig. 5.4 Unilever's Code of Business Principles

Standard of conduct: We conduct our operations with honesty, integrity and openness, and high respect for the human rights and interests of our employees. We shall similarly respect the legitimate interests of those with whom with have relationships.

Obeying the law: Unilever companies and our employees are required to comply with the laws and regulations of the countries in which we operate.

Employees: Unilever is committed to diversity in a working environment where there is mutual trust and respect, and where everyone feels responsibility for the performance and reputation of our company. We will recruit, employ and promote employees on the sole basis of their qualifications and abilities needed for the work to be performed. We are committed to safe and healthy working conditions for all employees. We will not use any form of forced, compulsory or child labour. We are committed to working with employees to develop and enhance each individual's skills and capabilities. We respect the dignity of the individual and the right of employees to have freedom of association. We will maintain good communications with employees through company based information and consultation procedures.

Consumers: Unilever is committed to providing branded products and services which consistently offer value in terms of price and quality, and which are safe for their intended use. Products and services will be accurately and properly labelled, advertised and communicated.

Shareholders: Unilever will conduct its operations in accordance with internationally accepted principles of good corporate governance. We will provide timely, regular and reliable information on our activities, structure, financial situation and performance to all shareholders.

Business partners: Unilever is committed to establishing mutually beneficial relations with our suppliers, customers and business partners. In our business dealings we expect our partners to adhere to business principles consistent with our own.

Community involvement: Unilever strives to be a trusted corporate citizen, and, as an integral part of society, to fulfil our responsibilities to the societies and communities in which we operate.

Public activities: Unilever companies are encouraged to promote and defend their legitimate business interests. Unilever will cooperate with governments and other organisations, both directly and through bodies such as trade associations, in the development of proposed legislation and other regulations that may affect legitimate business interests. Unilever neither supports political parties nor contributes to the funds of groups whose activities are calculated to promote party interests.

The environment: Unilever is committed to making continuous improvements in the management of our environmental impact and to the longer term goal of developing a sustainable business. Unilever will work in partnership with others to promote environmental care, increase understanding of environmental issues and disseminate good practice.

Innovation: In our scientific innovation to meet consumer needs we will respect the concerns of our consumers and of society. We will work on the basis of sound science, applying rigorous standards of product safety.

Competition: Unilever believes in vigorous yet fair competition and supports the development of appropriate competition laws. Unilever companies will conduct their operations in accordance with the principles of fair competition and all application regulations.

Business integrity: Unilever does not give or receive, either directly or indirectly, bribes or other improper advantages for business or financial gain. No employee may offer, give or receive any gift or payment which is, or may be construed, as being a bribe. Any demand for, or offer of a bribe must be rejected immediately and reported to management. Unilever accounting, records and supporting documents must accurately describe and reflect the nature of the underlying transactions. No undisclosed or unrecorded account, fund or asset will be maintained.

Continued

Fig. 5.4 (*Cont.*) Unilever's Code of Business Principles

Conflicts of interest: All Unilever employees are expected to avoid personal activities and financial interests which could conflict with their responsibilities to the company. Unilever employees must not seek gain for themselves or others through misuse of their positions.

Compliance—Monitoring—Reporting: Compliance with these principles is an essential element in our business success. The Unilever Board is responsible for ensuring these principles are communicated to, and understood and observed by, all employees. Day-to-day responsibility is delegated to the senior management of the regions and operating companies. They are responsible for implementing these principles, if necessary through more detailed guidance tailored to local needs. Assurance of compliance is given and monitored each year. Compliance with the Code is subject to review by the Board supported by the Audit Committee of the Board and the Corporate Risk Committee. Any breaches of the Code must be reported in accordance with the procedures specified by the Joint Secretaries. The Board of Unilever will not criticise management for any loss of business resulting from adherence to these principles and other mandatory policies and instructions. The Board of Unilever expects employees to bring to their attention, or to that of senior management, any breach or suspected breach of these principles. Provision has been made for employees to be able to report in confidence and no employee will suffer as a consequence of doing so.

Source: www.unilever.com.

global companies, codes of practice provide a means to manage the conduct of a vast number of employees, suppliers, and contractors worldwide to ensure that their aims are met.

Making codes effective

Codes of ethics cannot guarantee ethical behaviour and without further support are unconvincing to key stakeholder groups. This means that socially responsible companies have to proactively engage in inculcating ethical behaviour throughout their operations. There is no shortage of advice available to companies on good practice to make these codes effective. All organizations involved in the promulgation of sound ethical practice provide guidance and blueprints for their design and strategies for effective implementation. The advice provided by the Institute of Business Ethics for good practice in making codes of conduct effective is shown in Table 5.3.

No matter what the source of advice and guidance, all blueprints for making codes effective stress the importance of ethics training for all staff.

Ethics training

Most companies conduct their ethics training in-house, although there are an increasing number of training consultants who provide these services. Most ethics training programmes of international companies centre on both the dissemination and communication of their ethical codes and the discussion of ethical dilemmas that their staff may face in day-to-day operational activities. Many companies include participative training sessions which share ideas, approaches, and methods as to how such dilemmas may be resolved. Initial training sessions often involve consideration of the elements of the codes to ensure that all employees are aware of the ethical implications. Companies hold workshops to introduce their managers to the concept of ethical dilemmas and sensitize staff to ethical issues through exploration of their own values and those of the company, as well as considering situations which involve those dilemmas and discussing the appropriate methods of dealing with them. At Boeing (www.boeing.com), for

Table 5.3 Institute of Business Ethics Guide to Good Practice in the Implementation of Codes of Conduct

Making Codes of Conduct Effective

Good Practice	Poor Practice
Root the code in core ethical values	Pinning the code to the noticeboard
Give a copy to all staff	Failing to obtain board commitment to the code
Provide a way to report breaches in a confidential manner	Leaving responsibility for its effectiveness to HR or any other department
Include ethical issues in corporate training programmes	Failing to find out what concerns the staff at different levels
Set up a board committee to monitor the effectiveness of the code	Not to feature the code in induction training and management development activities
Report on the code's use in the annual report	Not to have a procedure for revising the code regularly
Make conformity to the code part of a contract of employment	Make exceptions to the code's application
Make the code available in the language of those staff located overseas	Fail to follow up breaches of the code's standards
Make copies of the code available to business partners, including suppliers	Fail to set a good example to corporate leaders
Review the code in the light of changing business challenges	Treat the code as confidential or a purely internal document

Source: www.ibe.org.uk/effective.html.

example, line managers hold training sessions in ethics with other employees to consider various ethical dilemmas and how best to handle them. There is also a web-based interactive training programme which integrates a number of scenarios with the company's codes and which teams are encouraged to use. ING (www.ing.com) trains all its staff worldwide using an interactive CD-ROM and the internet so that employees gain experience of the same ethical scenarios and then discuss them with their local managers (Sanyal, 2001). Most companies evaluate their ethics training programmes on a regular basis to take account of new ethical dilemmas and to review the means of delivery. They require ethical training to be ongoing in order that staff can refresh their training and have the opportunity to share experiences. Some companies cascade their training via the reporting line, with managers training their immediate teams who then cascade this throughout their teams.

In order that staff have support, many companies use freephone facilities for managers to talk to ethical advisers either internal to the company or external ethical advisory services, as well as interactive company websites which offer advice and support. It is also vital that ethical conduct is seen as important, and here it is necessary both to involve senior management and to demonstrate the importance the company places on ethical conduct by its staff. Many companies have instituted Ethics Boards and have senior management who take direct responsibility for ethics training and ethical matters. Texas Instruments (www.ti.com), for example, have established an Ethics Office and have appointed an Ethics Director—see mini-case illustration.

MINI-CASE ILLUSTRATION The Texas Instruments Ethics Office

The TI Ethics Office has three primary functions:

- to ensure that business policies and practices continue to be aligned with ethical principles;

- to clearly communicate ethical expectations; and

- to provide multiple channels for feedback through which people can ask questions, voice concerns, and seek resolution to ethical problems.

Source: www.ti.com/corp/docs/company/citizen/ethics/index.shtml.

Courtesy of Texas Instruments.

Corporate Social Responsibility and Competitive Advantage

Over the past decade, more companies have engaged in the concept of corporate social responsibility. From initial reactive stances largely concerned with responding to stakeholder pressures and the activities of pressure groups and NGOs, many companies now have a proactive stance towards corporate social responsibility, based on their experience and practice, providing positive impacts on business economic performance. Although there is no exhaustive list of benefits to be gained from socially responsible practice, Arthur D. Little and *Business in the Community* in 'The business case for corporate responsibility' (2003) identify six 'commonly recognized' benefits that companies may gain. As illustrated in Fig. 5.5, these benefits are: reputation management, risk management, employee satisfaction, innovation and learning, access to capital, and improved financial performance (*Business in the Community*, January 2004).

Reputation management

For all companies associated with socially responsible practice, there are considerable competitive gains in respect of enhanced reputation. In general, reputation management

Fig. 5.5 Corporate social responsibility and competitive advantage

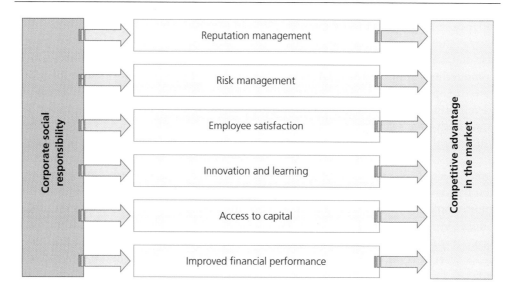

MINI-CASE ILLUSTRATION The Co-operative Bank's Ethical Policy

Business does not operate in a vacuum. Activities inevitably lead to a series of ecological and social impacts. Some industries, by their very nature, have a huge and obvious impact on the environment and society, whilst the impact of others, such as the financial services industry, is not always so apparent. At The Co-operative Bank, we recognise that our impact is, through the provision of finance and banking services to a wide variety of business customers, more far-reaching and profound than the direct impact of our actual operations, so we have put measures in place to ensure that this impact is managed.

The bank's Ethical Policy was introduced in 1992 to set out precisely what ethical standards would govern the types of businesses we would and would not offer services to. We base our Ethical Policy on the concerns of our customers, on the basis that it is their money and they should, therefore, have a say in how it is used.

When we launched the Ethical Policy, more than 80% of customers thought that it was a good idea to have a set of ethical principles guiding our investments. By 2001, this support had grown to 97% of the customers who participated in the review. As well as indicating their overall support for the principle of a policy, customers have the opportunity to indicate their level of support for each of the statements it contains. Statements range from positions on the arms trade and human rights to animal welfare and ecological impact. Customer views do not remain constant over time and new issues emerge as areas of ethical concern, so we periodically review the policy to ensure it continues to reflect customers' concerns; an exercise we are repeating again this year. This far-reaching consultation provides the bank with a clear mandate to implement the Ethical Policy.

The resulting policy sets out those types of business activities that are of such concern to our customers that they don't want the bank to provide business services to them. The policy also contains a number of positive statements that commit the bank to pursue business opportunities with customers engaged in socially or environmentally beneficial activities, such as those involved in recycling, fair trade and the co-operative sector.

To ensure that the bank's Ethical Policy is implemented effectively, Ethical Policy compliance systems are integrated into our everyday bank procedures. On applying for banking services with The Co-operative Bank, all business customers are required to complete an Ethical Policy questionnaire. These questionnaires are passed to a

The **co-operative** bank
good with money

Business Relationship Manager, and/or a member of the bank's new business centre, who undertakes an assessment of the proposal against our Ethical Policy.

If an issue of concern or potential policy conflict is identified, the business is referred to the bank's Ethical Policy Unit for further investigation. The Ethical Policy Unit reviews the acceptability of the business application against the policy statements and against the 1,700 plus case studies held on file. Where appropriate, further in-house research will be carried out and appropriate external sources consulted before a decision is taken.

Only where no conflict with the policy is identified, is a business offered banking facilities. This means that the bank will decline investment opportunities for ethical reasons, regardless of any potential financial gain — the bottom line is ensuring that customers' expectations, as expressed through the Ethical Policy, are upheld.

Since our customers entrust us with the implementation of the Ethical Policy, it is essential that this process is carried out in a transparent fashion.

That is why, every year, we invite an independent auditor to comment on the implementation of the policy and publish his findings, along with details of policy implementation in our Sustainability Report.

In the 2006 Report, the auditor commented as follows:

'The processes and monitoring systems in place to ensure the ongoing, effective implementation of the bank's Ethical Policy have reached a mature state and are producing consistently reliable results. We believe that the work done and evidence acquired by the Ethical Policy Unit (EPU), in respect of bank Ethical Policy implementation, justify the decisions made. This reflects not only the excellent quality of work in the EPU, but also an effective level of awareness across the bank's corporate and commercial departments and the bank network.'

Source: Extracts from The Co-operative Bank's Ethical Policy statement. The full statement can be found at goodwithmoney.co.uk/ethicalpolicy.

by means of socially responsible practice enables companies to build up relations of trust with their stakeholders, making it possible to attract capital and trading partners and increasing sales (www.bsr.org). It is this stakeholder trust that constitutes the competitive advantage that companies may gain from effective reputation management. Some companies have made reputation for ethical behaviour the cornerstone of their business activities. One such company is the Co-operative Bank (www.co-operativebank.co.uk), which refuses to invest in companies involved in tobacco, the arms trade, and the fur trade and animal testing, as well as governments or businesses that fail to uphold human rights and

Fig. 5.6 Body Shop International plc's mission statement

Mission statement

- To dedicate our business to the pursuit of social and environmental change.

- To creatively balance the financial and human needs of our stakeholders, customers, franchisees, suppliers and shareholders.

- To courageously ensure that our business is ecologically sustainable: meeting the needs of the present without compromising the future.

- To meaningfully contribute to local, national and international communities in which we trade, by adopting a code of conduct which ensures care, honesty, fairness and respect.

- To passionately campaign for the protection of the environment, human and civil rights, and against animal testing within the cosmetics and toiletries industry.

- To tirelessly work to narrow the gap between principle and practice, whilst making fun, passion and care part of our daily lives.

Source: www.thebodyshop.com. Reproduced with permission.

businesses whose links with oppressive regimes are a cause of concern. In addition, the Bank has adopted social reporting mechanisms and is an active advocate for causes such as fair trade. It also participates in campaigns seeking to ban trade in conflict diamonds and the financing of land mines. Some major features of the Bank's ethical policy are considered in the mini-case illustration.

Another major company which has gained competitive advantage through its ethical behaviour is The Body Shop International plc (www.thebodyshop.com), which has built an international reputation for its natural cosmetics and the 'greening' of its supply chain. The Body Shop now has over 2,000 outlets in over 60 countries. As with the Co-operative Bank, The Body Shop champions a number of social issues, such as human rights, animal rights, and environmental protection. It clearly states its dedication to social goals in its mission statement (Fig. 5.6).

However, companies which seek to use their reputation as a source of competitive advantage are continually under public scrutiny and may suffer damage if their practices are not considered to fully support the statements they make about themselves. The Body Shop International plc has been challenged on a number of issues, including the use of animal testing in the preparation of ingredients from which its products are made, as well as their impact on local communities around the world. However, The Body Shop has been able to retain its reputation for ethical practice through its response to such unfounded allegations.

Credibility

A key element in managing reputation is that of credibility. If companies seek to enhance their reputations through activities which are perceived as out of step with their other business operations, they may be accused of attempting to use socially responsible practice as a PR exercise and lacking real commitment to change. Brady (2003) identifies three forms of this activity. The first is that of 'greenwashing', where companies generally considered to be socially and environmentally destructive attempt to create a new and

THE DIGITAL IMPACT Shell's dialogue with stakeholders

Companies such as Shell have sought to enhance their reputation by creating dialogue with their stakeholders. In the mid-1990s Shell's reputation suffered as a result of negative publicity concerning its activities in Nigeria and the Brent Spar platform. In April 1998, Shell published its first special report, 'Profits and Principles—does there have to be a choice,' and many key stakeholders saw this report as a positive new course for the company in that it emphasized the company's commitment to accountability and stakeholder contact (Lewis, 2004). This was further substantiated through shell setting up an interactive website in order that stakeholders might discuss issues of concern. Since 1998, Shell has initiated a number of stakeholder dialogues and produced reports identifying key targets it aims to achieve within a social responsibility framework.

false impression of themselves as socially and environmentally friendly. The second is 'bluewashing', where companies state their commitment to humanitarian causes but do little beyond this as a commitment. And the third is 'sweatwashing', where companies associated extensively with sweatshop labour practices attempt to divert attention away from their activities. Companies which seek to enhance their reputations in this way may find that rather than gaining competitive advantage, their corporate image is diminished. McDonald's (www.mcdonalds.com) ran the risk of being perceived in this light when it negotiated a partnership to raise money in association with UNICEF (www.unicef.org.uk). Faced by protests from doctors, academics, and pressure groups, the partnership collapsed largely because of concerns that association with a fast-food company was inappropriate for a charity concerned with promoting good nutrition for children (Brady, 2003).

Risk management

Socially responsible practice has an important role in the competitive advantage available to companies through effective risk management. It not only signals to financial institutions that the company takes the concept of ethical risk seriously, but also that it is a safe custodian in that it seeks to reduce avoidable losses.

Risk management from this perspective also alerts companies to emerging issues which may threaten their social responsibility credentials and encourages active engagement in dialogue and partnership with governments, NGOs, and others in order both to pre-empt and address issues which may appear to challenge the integrity of their operations.

Employee satisfaction

There is a growing body of evidence to suggest that socially responsible practice is a key element in generating employee satisfaction. Companies which are seen to behave with social responsibility can thereby gain competitive advantage through the attraction and retention of talented staff. Various studies have shown that employees tend to be more loyal to companies perceived to be socially responsible. It is significant in this regard that one of the triggers for Shell's new approach to stakeholder engagement was its finding that it was becoming less favoured as an employer of choice by high-flying graduates (Lewis and Bollen, 2004). That this is an important issue for graduates and others can be seen by the compilation of lists of 'best companies to work for' published by business magazines, such as *Fortune*. Competitive advantage can also be gained through increased employee productivity arising from socially responsible practice often through incorporating green design into factories and other buildings. Boeing, for example, found that it experienced increases in productivity of up to 15% from this practice (www.bsr.org).

WHOSE RESPONSIBILITY IS IT? Sharing concerns

Following criticism of some of its activities, Starbucks (www .starbucks.com) has become actively involved with the work of Conservation International's Conservation Coffee programme to support sustainable agricultural practice. It has also formed a partnership with a division of the Environmental Defence Fund to develop environmentally preferable disposable coffee cups (www. bsr.org). Many companies now form partnerships with NGOs in order to understand the issues with which these organizations are concerned and also to work with them to create new sustainable business opportunities.

Innovation and learning

Socially responsive practice may lead companies to design new products and processes as well as identifying market opportunities which enable them to develop new sources of competitive advantage. Unilever, for example, has gained competitive advantage by including social needs in its product design strategies for emerging markets. In Brazil, Unilever created the Ala brand of detergent to meet the needs of consumers who wanted an affordable and effective product for washing clothes by hand in river water. In India, Unilever has developed products such as low-cost tooth powder and fortified staple food stuffs as well as smaller, more affordable pack sizes; and in Tanzania, products such as Key soap are also sold in small units at affordable prices (Hilton, 2004). Both Ben & Jerry's Ice Cream (www.ben/jerry.com) and Body Shop International plc gained competitive advantage through pioneering innovative, socially responsive practice with respect to both ingredients and manufacture (Mirvis, 1994). Ben & Jerry's led the field in the use of natural ingredients in ice cream, working with a dairy cooperative to ensure the quality of its milk ingredients and developing manufacturing practices which included treating its waste water using hydroponics pools. The Body Shop pioneered the use of natural ingredients in cosmetic and toiletry products as well as encouraging the use of refillable bottle schemes and instituting in-house plastics recycling (Mirvis, 1994). NEC (www.nec.com) has pioneered the first 'green computer', which is made with recyclable plastic, eliminates load soldering from its motherboard, and includes a special processor to minimize power use (www.bsr.org).

Access to capital

Companies which have a demonstrated commitment to corporate social responsibility are beginning to gain wider access to sources of capital than companies which do not. Growing numbers of investors are keen to invest in socially responsible companies. In the USA, the market for ethical investment has grown significantly from around US$40 billion in 1984, to US$639 billion in 1995, and reaching US$2.3 trillion in 2001 (Florini, 2003). Many financial providers now use screening services to eliminate specific investor concerns, such as the tobacco industry, animal rights, environmental management, and concerns regarding labour practices. Companies such as Morgan Stanley (www .morganstanley.com), Credit Lyonnais (www.creditlyonnais.com), and Citigroup (www .citigroup.com) all offer screened investment and a number of new stock market indices have been developed, such as the FTSE4Good and the Dow Jones Sustainability Index, which provide information for the ethical investor in the same way as more traditional indices. These indices show that ethical investment normally matches or outperforms traditional investment, giving further impetus to the development of the market in ethical investment.

International institutions are also increasingly taking account of social responsibility in their lending and credit policies, with institutions such as the World Bank and regional development banks refusing access to companies whose records do not show appropriate ethical practice.

Improved financial performance

The pursuit of socially responsible practice has enabled a number of companies to reduce their operating costs and thereby improve their competitive position. Much of the reduction in costs has come through improved environmental management strategies. Companies have found that by reducing their impact on the environment they have benefited from increases in productivity, less material usage, lower power costs, lower waste disposal costs, and lower packaging costs. Companies which have adopted the ISO 14001 standard as an environmental management system have found that their costs have significantly improved. S. C. Johnson (www.scjohnson.com), over the five years from 1990 to 1995, cut effluent from its manufacturing operations by half, reducing its waste management costs, virgin packaging use by 28%, and solvent use by 15%. It eliminated 420 million pounds of waste from products and processes. The company has saved over US$125 million since 1992 (www.bsr.org).

In conclusion, building competitive advantage in the marketplace is the focus of all business activity and as more and more companies gain the knowledge and experience of how to build competitive advantage through socially responsible means, for these companies, socially responsible practice becomes not only better business but smarter business. Seeing corporate social responsibility and ethical practice as a source of competitive advantage is a far cry from the long-held view of corporate social responsibility as a business cost, a matter of compliance with legislation, or a means to ward off negative publicity. Over the last 30 years, business has begun to make this transition and many companies now view social responsibility and ethical conduct as a necessary investment in order to secure financial and business success.

Chapter Summary

1. There are a number of key social issues with which companies have to engage in order to be considered as socially responsible business practitioners. These issues are corruption, human rights, labour practices, and environmental protection.

2. Corruption in all its forms is widespread across industries although it varies in extent both between countries and across industries. Corruption is defined as the abuse of public office for private gain. It includes bribery, fraud, money laundering, cronyism, extortion, and embezzlement.

3. For many companies, corruption is conventionally viewed as an 'awkward but necessary' part of doing business in international markets and is considered to be an everyday aspect of the general global business environment. However, businesses are becoming aware of the corrosive impact of corruption on the growth and development of individual countries and their markets.

4. Countries with high levels of corruption generally have low levels of GDP and depressed rates of investment. Corruption reduces government tax revenues and thereby can limit government ability to invest in public health and education. Businesses which participate in corruption are seen by a growing number of important stakeholders as key actors in perpetuating it.

5. Human rights are defined as the standards of treatment to which all people are entitled. The most widely recognized definition is the Universal Declaration of Human Rights adopted by the United Nations in 1948. Increasing globalization of business has brought more companies into contact with human rights issues through their operations in countries whose governments do not respect the principles of the Declaration.

6. Companies are usually implicated in human rights issues through involvement with governments using abusive methods to protect the interests of the company. Concern about labour practices is based on the activities of companies which take advantage of lower labour standards than they face at home in order to achieve lower costs. They therefore profit from labour conditions which would be unacceptable within their own domestic environment. The focus of attention has been the use of sweatshop and child labour.

7. Although there is increasing legislation to govern company responses to these issues, companies seeking to fully address issues of social responsibility are behaving more proactively. Many have adopted codes of conduct to ensure that social responsibility becomes part of intrinsic in-company values and have instituted appropriate ethics training throughout their worldwide operations.

8. Socially responsible practice and ethical behaviour are no longer merely an active response to stakeholder pressure and the activities of pressure groups. They are now a source of advantage generating major benefits in terms of reputation and risk management, employee satisfaction, innovation and learning, access to capital, and improved financial performance within the intensely competitive global marketplace.

END-OF-CHAPTER CASE STUDY Fairtrade

The fair trade movement aims to guarantee a better deal for producers in the developing world, ensure that a guaranteed price is paid for produce or goods from developing countries, and encourage long-term relationships and trading commitments. Focusing on commodities that constitute a large share of a developing country's economy, such as coffee, tea, cocoa, bananas, and sugar, it encourages farmers to form fair trade cooperatives which eliminate the middleman and establish a system under which the product is produced and distributed. The integrity of the production and distribution chain is guaranteed by certification agencies which authorize a fair trade label for producers. Fairtrade labelling was created in 1986 in response to the request of coffee farmers in southern Mexico. Working in partnership with the farmers, the first Fairtrade label was created in the Netherlands in 1988.

Under the Fairtrade system, importers must pay a guaranteed minimum base price that represents a living wage for the farmer, regardless of world prices, and covers production costs, along with a premium that their organization is able to reinvest. Reinvestment can be either in business or social projects, such as medical care or schools, or in environmental schemes among the wider community. The cooperatives grant members credit and operate advance payment schemes to deal with emergencies. Cooperatives are also encouraged to adopt production methods which protect the environment and the health of consumers.

All products carrying the Fairtrade label have to meet standards set by an international body, the Fairtrade Labelling Organization (FLO) International (www.fairtrade.net). There are two sets of producer standards reflecting the different problems experienced by poor producers and workers in developing countries. Products such as tea and cocoa, for example, are mostly grown by independent small farmers working their own land and marketing their produce through a local cooperative. Most tea is grown on large plantations. The main concern of the independent farmers is receiving a fair price, whereas that of workers employed on tea plantations is receiving fair wages and decent working conditions. The producer standards for small farmers apply to smallholders organized in cooperatives and other organizations with a participative structure. The producer standards for organized workers apply to employers who pay fair wages, guarantee the right to join trade unions, and provide good housing when appropriate. On plantations and in factories, minimum health and safety standards and environmental standards are to be complied with, and no child or forced labour is allowed. Trading standards stipulate that traders must pay a price to producers that covers the costs of sustainable production and living; pay a premium that producers can invest in development; make partial advance payments when requested; and sign contracts that allow for long-term planning and sustainable production practices.

Today there are 360 Fairtrade certified producer groups in 40 producer countries. They sell to hundreds of Fairtrade registered importers, licensees, and retailers in 17 countries, including initiatives in the UK, the Netherlands, Germany, Switzerland, the USA, and Japan. In the majority of these countries, Fairtrade products are now mainstream products and are available in major supermarkets as well as independent shops. They are beginning to gain market share. In the UK, for example, sales of products with the Fairtrade mark had an estimated value of over £490 million in 2007. Fairtrade bananas are the best-selling Fairtrade product with sales topping £150 million. One in four bananas sold are now Fairtrade bananas with 3 million Fairtrade bananas being eaten a day. In 2007, Fairtrade coffee sales rose 24% to over £117 million and items made from Fairtrade cotton increased from over half a million to

just under 9.5 million units. Recent commercial developments should mean Fairtrade tea should account for a tenth of tea sold in the UK by the end of 2008.

Source: www.fairtrade.org.uk. Reproduced with permission.

Case discussion questions

1 What are the main global social issues that Fairtrade seeks to address? To what extent can Fairtrade's approach to social issues be considered to be furthering sustainable development?

2 Why do you think that Fairtrade products have made such inroads into traditional consumer markets? Does this imply that there is an untapped ethical consumer market?

3 Can major food-processing companies safely ignore the success of Fairtrade products? What courses of action would you recommend to such companies?

END-OF-CHAPTER EXERCISES

1 Identify the main global social and ethical issues. Briefly explain how each of these issues is impacting on the operations of transnational organizations.

2 In what ways does corruption negatively affect the economic development of developing nations?

3 What are the methods which can be used by organizations to manage the social and ethical issues that arise from their international operations?

4 The CEO of a clothing manufacturing company has discovered that its suppliers in India are employing child labour in their factories. What advice would you give to the CEO?

5 Prepare a short presentation explaining how socially responsible practice may provide competitive advantage in the global marketplace.

DISCUSSION AND EXAMINATION QUESTIONS

1   Discuss the view that corruption is 'an awkward but necessary' part of doing business in international markets.

2   Given that corruption is widespread around the world, why should companies refuse bribes?

3   What are the main pressures companies face for behaving in a socially responsible manner? Is it sufficient for a company to adopt a code of conduct to be considered a socially responsible company?

4   What contribution do you feel the UN Social Compact can make to fostering socially responsible business practice?

5   Is social responsibility good for business? Discuss with relevant examples.

FURTHER READING

Crane, A., Matten D., and Spence, L. (2007), *Corporate Social Responsibility: Readings and Cases in a Global Context,* London: Routledge.

Hawkins, D. E. (2006), *Corporate Social Responsibility: Balancing Tomorrow's Sustainability and Today's Profitability,* Basingstoke: Palgrave Macmillan.

Kakabadse, A. and Morsing, M. (2006), *Corporate Social Responsibility: A 21st Century Perspective,* Basingstoke: Palgrave Macmillan.

REFERENCES

Boatright, J. R. (2000), *Ethics and the Conduct of Business*, 3rd edn., London: Prentice Hall.

Brady, A. K. O. (2003), 'How to generate sustainable brand value from responsibility', *Brand Management*, 10(4–5), 279–89.

Business in the Community (2004), *Business in the Community*, January, Boston: Beacon Press.

Doh, J., Rodriguez, P., Uhlenbruck, K., Collins, J., and Eden, L. (2003), 'Coping with corruption in foreign markets', *Academy of Management Executive*, 17(3), 114.

Florini, A. (2003), 'Business and global governance: the growing role of corporate codes of conduct', *Brookings Review*, 21(2), 4–8.

Hilton, S. (2004), 'Brands thinking positively', *Brand Strategy*, 178 (Dec.–Jan.), 28.

Lasserre, P. (2003), *Global Business Strategy*, Basingstoke: Palgrave Macmillan.

Lewis, S. (2004), 'The end of the invisible company', *Strategic Communication, Management*, 8(1), 5.

____ and Bollen, A. (2004), 'Brand conduct unbecoming' *Brand Strategy*, 78 (Dec.–Jan.), 34.

Little, Arthur D. (2003), 'The business case for corporate responsibility', *Business in the Community*, December, Boston: Beacon Press.

Mirvis, P. H. (1994), 'Environmentalism in progressive businesses', *Journal of Organizational Change Management*, 7(4), 82–100.

Sanyal, R. N. (2001), *International Management*, London: Prentice Hall.

Schrage, E. (2003), 'Emerging threat: human rights claims', *Harvard Business Review*, 81(8), 16.

Spar, D. (1998), 'The spotlight and the bottom line', *Foreign Affairs*, 77(2), 7.

World Bank (2003), *Commitment to Promoting Good Governance*, Washington, DC: World Bank.

online resource centre

Visit the companion website to this book for lots of interesting additional material, including self-assessment questions, internet exercises, and links for each chapter:

http://www.oxfordtextbooks.co.uk/orc/lee_carter2e/

CHAPTER SIX

Opportunity Analysis
and Selection of Markets

Chapter overview

Chapter Introduction	170	Estimate the value of information	182
Global Market Selection	170	Research design	183
Marketing Information System	171	Data collection	183
International Marketing Research	172	Preparation and data analysis	184
Screening international markets	175	Report writing and presentation	184
Information sources	180	Global Market Segmentation	185
Primary data	181	Selecting Markets for Targeting	188
Research process agreement	181	Chapter Summary	197
Establish research objectives	182		

Learning objectives

After studying this chapter, the reader will be able to:

- consider the role of marketing research and the marketing information system in identifying global market opportunities;
- examine the methodology of global marketing research for identifying global market opportunities;
- describe and discuss the different global market segmentation strategies and methods;
- examine the role of global marketing research and segmentation strategies in evaluating global opportunities and the selection of markets.

Management issues

The management issues that arise from this chapter include:

- What types of information can marketing research uncover to aid the decision on which global market opportunities to pursue?
- What are the ways in which to segment markets globally and what are the strategic implications of segmentation?
- How does marketing research and market segmentation aid the evaluation of global market opportunities and the decision on which markets to enter?

Chapter Introduction

Previous chapters have identified the dangers of the international marketing environment. Technological change, miscalculations of cultural nuances, and the inability to keep up with competitive change are some of the potential dangers which can ruin the best laid international plans. The ill-fated WAP technology-based mobile phone is one of many examples where failure to take account of global technological advances and consumer taste led to its costly demise.

The key to making successful strategic decisions on which market opportunities to take is 'knowledge', either implicit or explicit knowledge. However, 'knowledge' is not enough. Success lies in the astute interpretation and application of knowledge. The explicit gathering of, and the resultant application of, 'knowledge' through the process of marketing research is one way to help reduce the risks and uncertainties of global market opportunities. Another way is through the gathering of implicit data (via the 'knowledge management' process). It is through the latter that organizations like Skandia insurance (www .skandia.com) have been able to grow and prosper globally.

In this chapter we will examine the way in which international market opportunities can be identified, evaluated and a choice made on which one(s) to enter. This will involve a discussion on the role of marketing research and the marketing information system. Many marketing academics would argue that the key to market success lies in the 'market segmentation' process, so the chapter will also examine this concept. Finally, the chapter will show how both marketing research and market segmentation can aid the evaluation and choice of which global markets to enter.

Global Market Selection

The Uppsala School of Internationalization suggests that there are several potential determinants of the choice of foreign market opportunities (Johanson and Vahlne, 1990). These can be classified into two groups: environmental and firm characteristics. The analysis of the environment involves looking at the international market as a country, group of countries, or group of customers displaying the same characteristics. The latter may span several countries. The evolution of the global consumer is a growing phenomenon. Examples include the 'hedonistic tourist', the 'Manchester United fan' (www.manutd.com), or 'Ferrari Man' (www.ferrari.com). The global consumer phenomenon is making it increasingly difficult to segment the market on traditional lines based on individual in-country statistics or distribution/media management that is traditionally based on in-country consumer characteristics. Environmental characteristics that must be identified and researched include traditional global environmentals such as politics, competition, and economics, and other factors including the international industry structure, host-country characteristics (e.g. market potential), and the degree of internationalization of the market. Firm characteristics are those factors internal to the organization and include the degree of international experience, resources, type of business, existing international networks, and the objectives for internationalization. All of this requires information, most of which is gained by explicit or implicit means. This process is summarized in Fig. 6.1.

Fig. 6.1 Global market selection process

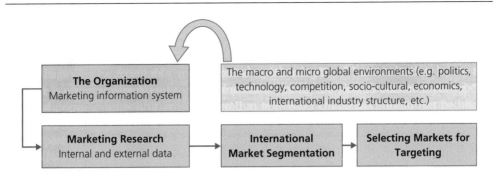

Marketing Information System

An effective marketing information system (MKIS) can be the repository for analysis and the communications arm of an organization's intelligence-gathering function, linking the environment to the organizational decision-makers (Fig. 6.2). The MKIS would include: (a) a data bank into which both environmental and internal company data would be deposited; (b) a statistical function, by which the data would be analysed to inform management decision-making; and (c) a communications function, which would be human, machine, or a combination. Before constructing an information system, the purpose should be made clear. Fig. 6.2 indicates the steps involved in gathering information, and the detail, which follows in this chapter, is based on this approach.

Information can be of two types: (a) continuous, where the company is routinely scanning the environment for useful data; and (b) special problem data, where the organization might instigate a specific piece of research. Such a situation might be where a routine scan of sales of a certain product shows that sales appear to be rising, as was the case with Apple's iPod (www.apple.com/ipod) digital music player at Christmas 2003. After noticing this trend, a company in the same business may instigate special problem research to assess if it is an indication of real incipient demand or a mere sales aberration over the Christmas period. Routine data scanning may also be carried out on published secondary data, again to identify possible sources of demand.

Fig. 6.2 Marketing information system

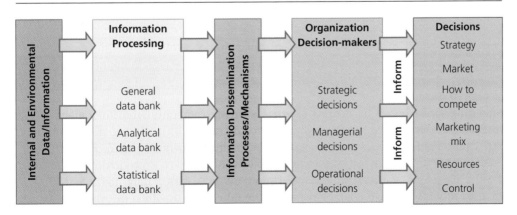

Fig. 6.3 Market profile analysis

Factor	Strategic Objectives	Market Entry	Product Mix	Promotion Mix	Distribution Mix	Pricing Mix	People Mix
SLEPT							
SWOT							
Competition							
Tariff and non-tariff barriers							
Ethics							
Rules of engagement							

Doole and Lowe (2004: 113) have developed a 12 Cs framework (country, concentration, culture/consumer behaviour, choices, consumption, contractual obligations, commitment, channels, communications, capacity to pay, currency, and caveats) for analysing international markets. They suggest that all the data gathered under these categories should be part of the MKIS. However, this is a generalized framework. Research by Scheuing and Carter (1998) suggests that organizations need, to tailor their own MKIS to fit organizational needs, which by no means contain all the generic data Doole and Lowe suggest. Indeed, global giants such as Rolls-Royce (www.rolls-royce.com) and ASEA (www.aseapower.com) have MKISs which include both hard and soft data, often of a surprising nature. In their businesses, where teaming arrangements among competitors is a major factor in gaining contracts, this is closely monitored, as are the movements of staff on leaving the company due to the highly technical nature of the organizations. The suggestion from Scheuing and Carter's research is that individual MKISs are the order of the day. These may contain some generic data. The MKIS may be used to draw up a market profile analysis which will enable the organization to identify potential market opportunities and problems. This enables strategic decisions to be made on market entry modes, building on their competitive advantage, and operational decisions on the most appropriate use of the marketing mix. An example is shown in Fig. 6.3 Such a profile enables the company to assess the competitive advantage it might have after entering a market, the most appropriate marketing mix, and any problems that may be encountered.

International Marketing Research

Marketing research can be defined as the systematic gathering, recording, analysis, and interpretation of data to aid the reduction of uncertainty in marketing decision-making. Fig. 6.4 shows the sequence in conducting the international marketing research process.

The ability to produce fast, yet accurate, results is the key to strategic decision-making. Online databases, the World Wide Web and CD-ROM-based data, such as Dun and Bradstreet (www.dnb.com) data, has transformed the speed at which information is made available. Data warehousing is a well-known phenomenon in the retail industry and any

Fig. 6.4 The international marketing research process

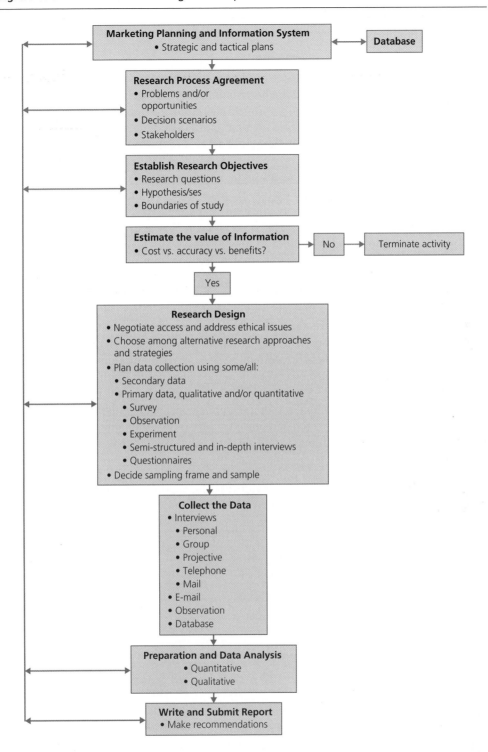

large-scale retailer has access to such facilities. Look at the following sources of data and suggest how these may be used to gather information to assess market opportunities:

- www.euromonitor.com;
- www.web.iderect.com/-tiger/supersit.htm;
- www.europe.eu.int;
- www.mintel.com;
- www.ciber.bus.msu.edu/busrea.htm.

The marketing research industry is large. In 2008 it is estimated that the top 25 market research agencies' turnover was in excess of US$10 billion. Much of the research budget is spent in three areas: cross-cultural research, spanning nations or culture groups; foreign research in another country to that of the researcher; and in multi-country research, conducted in countries where the organization is represented. Nestlé (www.nestle.com) is an example of the latter. It has research facilities in Vevey, Switzerland, its corporate headquarters, but also research facilities in the UK, South Africa, Australia, and elsewhere. However, this general categorization does not reflect the enormity of the research task, where environmental and a host of in-country factors make the unearthing of market potential difficult. International market research should assess market demand globally, evaluate potential markets and the risks and costs of entry, and provide detailed information on which to base effective marketing strategies. In order to do this the researcher has to carry out three functions: (a) scan international markets to identify and analyse opportunities; (b) build a marketing information system to monitor environmental trends and developments; and (c) carry out primary market research to input into the development of marketing strategies and detailed, testable marketing mix options.

The decision to enter international markets can be considerably helped by engaging in market research at every stage of the decision-making process (see Table 6.1). The information in Table 6.1 is required either from secondary or primary sources in order to inform the global marketing decision.

Table 6.1 Market research required at the internationalization decision stage

Decision Stage	Market Research Required
1. Go global?	Marketing environmentals—competitive, economic, social, legal, political, technology, pressure groups, cultural factors SWOT—internal strengths and weaknesses, external opportunities and threats
2. Markets to enter?	Market potential, trade barriers, local marketing environmentals, internal strengths and weaknesses, physical, ethical, and geographic factors
3. How to enter?	Size of market, size and ability to reach segments, behaviour of incumbent market intermediaries and players, logistical costs, risks, and product necessities
4. Marketing mix?	Product line, range, etc., promotion and distribution availability, price expectation and accepability, physical evidence required, and processes required
5. Implementation/control	Type of expected control procedure, sales, marketing share, consumer/business-to-business acceptance, contribution, and profit margins.

Fig. 6.5 'Rough' market screening

Criteria	Purpose
Accessibility	To determine accessibility Can we serve the market effectively and efficiently? What might be preventing us from doing so?
Profitability	To determine profitability Can the market afford us? Can we get adequate profits? What is the likely return on investment and timescale of payback?
Market Size	To determine market size and growth potential What is the existing market size? Is there a latent market? If no demand currently exists, what is the potential for emerging demand?

Screening international markets

Deciding which international market to enter is no easy process. Market research might be used to 'rough' screen markets for initial identification of potential, which is then subject to more 'fine' screening for the actual choice. In the initial stages ('rough' screen) countries are scanned for attraction and prioritization. Although many may be scanned, three criteria help in the process (see Fig. 6.5):

- Accessibility: Can we get there? What might be preventing us?
- Profitability: Can the market afford us? Can we get adequate profits? What is competition? What is the likely payback and timescale?
- Market size: Existing, latent and incipient?

Gilligan and Hird (1985) identified three types of market opportunity:

- Existing markets—markets already covered by existing products/suppliers, making market entry difficult without a superior offering.
- Latent markets—evidence of potential demand but no product offering yet, making market entry easier.
- Incipient markets—no current demand exists but condition and trend suggests future latent demand.

Future competition can be viewed in a similar way with three product types: competitive products, improved products, and breakthrough products. The level and nature of future competition can be analysed by combining the three types of market with the three types of product. In terms of strategy, the greatest challenge is the incipient market–breakthrough product scenario. On the other hand, it is easier to plan a strategy for the existing market–competitive product combination, it being a case of outperforming the competition in terms of operational marketing mix or in positioning terms. The greatest potential lies in the incipient market–breakthrough product category, but this is also difficult to assess. Knowing that 'first to market' often means the biggest payback, researchers employ various techniques to assess market potential. These are shown in Fig. 6.6.

Fig. 6.6 Techniques for assessing incipient markets

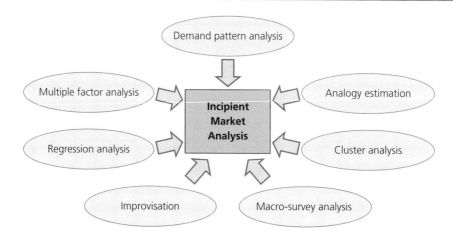

- Demand pattern analysis—the assumption is that countries at different stages of development have different levels of demand and consumption. A comparison is made with another country with similar demand patterns on product release. It is assumed that the country under study will follow suit.

- Multiple factor indices—this assumes that the demand for one product is correlated with another, e.g. the purchase of washing machines and sales of soap powders.

- Analogy estimation—has many detractors due to cost and time in gathering data. Cross-sectional approaches link the ratio of an economic indicator to a product demand, e g. disposable income and car purchase. This ratio is then applied to the country under study to estimate demand. Time-series approaches depend on the assumptions of the international life cycle. What occurs in one country will eventually occur in another.

MINI-CASE ILLUSTRATION The Nissan Cube

Japan's favourite car is not a Toyota, Jaguar, or Mercedes-Benz, but an 'odd'-shaped car, the Nissan Cube (www.nissan.com). Shaped like a cube on wheels, it is powered by a Nissan Micra engine, has more internal lockers and spaces than almost any other car, and looks different from one side to the other. One rear corner has a pillar, the opposite corner, glass. It has high mileage per gallon, is not particularly fast, but is very roomy. Currently it is available only in Japan. However, car manufacturers like Peugeot and Citroën have found that the UK has a latent demand for this 'odd'-shaped car since two years ago both manufacturers launched their own versions of the genre and they both sold well. In 2008, a new, small, novel car called 'Nano', made in India by Tata Motors, made its debut. Costing just £1,200, it's the cheapest car in the world. This is not the only example where a product that is well-established in its own manufactured environment may well sell elsewhere when market conditions are right.

- Regression analysis—complements the analogy approach where multiple factors are used in the equation, e.g. disposable income and taxation levels.

- Cluster analysis—a popular technique using macroeconomic and consumption data to identify market demand, e.g. health expectancy using numbers of doctors and life expectancy to estimate the demand for drugs, or the need for economy and space and the demand for cars, as in the mini-case illustration below.

- Improvisation—extrapolation of data between broadly similar countries and second-guessing demand, e.g. the number of government buildings and the demand for photocopiers and computers.

- Macro-survey analysis—based on social anthropology. The bigger the community grows, the more likely it is to demand more products (see mini-case illustration on second homes in Europe).

These techniques highlight the need for comparative research and constant market screening if incipient markets are to be unearthed. However, they are all based on the assumption that economic development follows the same pattern globally. There is a strong view that global commonality does not exist and that companies need to group countries for the purposes of this type of comparison.

Although marketers have developed their own means, as a 'rough' screening, to assess risk in the choice of international market, there are various proprietary packages which also enable them to assess political, commercial, financial, country-specific, financial, and institutional risk. These have their roots in finance. Long-established methods include the Business Environment Risk Index (BERI, www.beri.com) method and the Goodnow and Hanz temperature gradient. The BERI provides forecasts for 50 countries and is updated every three years. The index assesses 15 environment factors, including political stability, labour productivity, etc. Factors are rated on a scale 0 to 4 where 0 equals unacceptable conditions to 4 equals superior conditions. The factors are also weighted to take account of the importance of the factors. The final score is out of 100; any score over 80 is assessed as a favourable environment and an advanced economy. Scores of less than 40 indicate a high-risk economy. The Goodnow and Hansz temperature gradient assesses a country's environmental factors. Countries are rated on a scale from as hot (USA) to moderate (South Africa) to cold (Zimbabwe). These techniques are not in universal use and there are other commercial screening tools. PricewaterhouseCoopers (www.pwc.com) have specialist risk assessment divisions available to organizations on a consultancy basis.

 MINI-CASE ILLUSTRATION Second homes in Europe

A good example of incipient or latent demand for products or services is the case of Europeans buying second homes in other parts of Europe or choosing to retire abroad. For the British, in particular, Spain is a popular destination. As the British (and Irish) have moved in, so have businesses that cater for their needs. Britons and the Irish like to drink in pubs, hence, the rising number of 'genuine' Irish pubs along the coast of Spain. Similarly, fast-food (there are 80 Chinese restaurants in the small town of Torrevieja on the Costa Blanca alone, for example), bars, and other traditionally non-Spanish food outlets have blossomed. This latent demand has resulted from the influx of foreign customers with their own eating and drinking culture.

Fig. 6.7 'Fine' market screening process

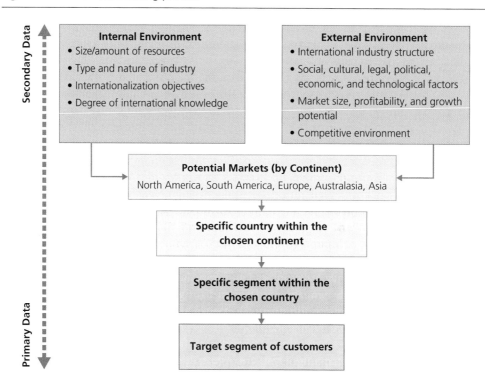

Although 'rough' screening may reveal potentially good markets to enter, more is needed (fine screening) before the decision is made on which specific market to enter. One such process is illustrated in Fig. 6.7.

The first step in the process is for the organization to conduct its own strengths and weaknesses analysis. The appropriate market data used in this process could be mainly from secondary sources like company accounts and documents and cover issues like those identified in the first stage of Table 6.1 above. The second step would be to identify through a 'rough screening' those parts of the globe which would seemingly be the most accessible and show the greatest potential, matched to the organization's identified strengths and weaknesses and environmental analysis. For this stage, secondary data alone may not suffice, so primary data may be required. The third step would be to identify a specific country (or countries), within the chosen part of the world and a specific segment and market within that segment. The appropriate data for this stage would be that identified in stages 2 and 3 of Table 6.1. Increasingly, primary data would be most appropriate for this stage. The final step would be for the organization to develop specific marketing plans, a marketing mix, and an implementation and control process for a specific group of customers, and for this, the data identified in steps 4 and 5 of Table 6.1 would be the most appropriate. At this stage, the organization is likely to be using data of its own making.

This is very much like a 'narrowing down' process, where, at each stage depicted in Fig. 6.7, an elimination process is going on until the actual potential customer group emerges. At each stage, risks are being analysed and steps put in place to identify the serious risks and make contingencies to minimize them.

In order to assess markets with the most attractive potential, a number of techniques can be employed. The most common technique is a matrix. For example, let's say an organization is considering entering three markets A, B and C. Using the matrix approach, it can utilize two dimensions to assess their suitability, market attractiveness, and ability to compete. These dimensions can be made up of a number of sub-factors, including:

- Market attractiveness: market size, market growth, ease of access, economic/political stability, the state and type of competition, ease of reaching customers, customer buying power, stage of development of marketing institutions, and 'entry' regulations.
- Ability to compete: technology, market share, brand/image strength, extent to which marketing institutions are monopolized, market acceptance, ethical stance, and price.

Having identified the relevant sub-factors of the two dimensions, these can be rated using an appropriate numeric scale. For instance, each of these factors can be scored on a scale 1–10, with 1=very poor to 10=very good, and then weighted according to the importance attached to each of the sub-factors. The weighted factors, for one of these dimensions, say market attractiveness, can then be put against each of the three markets. The market with the highest weighted score would be the most attractive to enter (see Fig. 6.8). Further, using two dimensions this time, market attractiveness and ability to compete, a two-dimensional matrix can be constructed. Where the two weighted average scores for each of the two dimensions intersect, this point indicates the strategic implications on potential

Fig. 6.8 The ranking of markets (attractiveness and ability to compete)

	Weighting	Market A	Market B	Market C
Market size	40%	8 (3.2)	6 (2.4)	7 (2.8)
Market growth	10%	3 (0.3)	5 (0.5)	6 (0.6)
Risk of investment	20%	6 (1.2)	4 (0.8)	6 (1.2)
Internal considerations	30%	9 (2.7)	7 (2.1)	3 (0.9)
Total score	100%	26 (7.4)	22 (5.8)	22 (5.5)
Product fit to market demand	50%	9 (4.5)	2 (1.0)	7 (3.5)
Market presence	10%	1 (0.1)	2 (0.2)	3 (0.3)
Resources	20%	3 (0.6)	3 (0.6)	3 (0.6)
Obtainable market share	20%	5 (1.0)	2 (0.4)	4 (0.8)
Total score	100%	18 (6.2)	9 (2.2)	17 (5.2)

Fig. 6.9 Ability to compete vs. market attractiveness

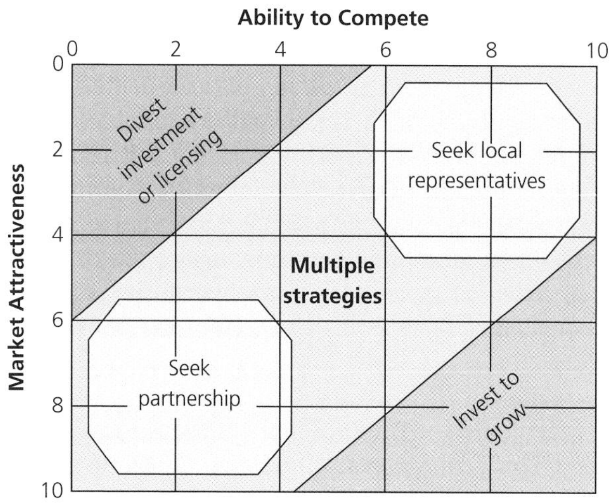

Source: Based on Hollensen (2007: 252).

market entry (see Fig. 6.9). In this case, as opposed to the single dimension matrix, the organization not only can identify the most potentially attractive market to enter, but the strategic implications of so doing.

All, or some, of these techniques aid marketers to 'fine screen' global markets in order to make a decision on the most appropriate one to enter. Of course, these techniques are not all-inclusive. Many organizations have their own ways of both 'rough' and 'fine' screening markets they wish to enter. These are often based on their own intelligence systems and in-country contacts.

Information sources

There are many sources of readily available secondary data. These include written (e.g. UN Year Books) and electronic (e.g. online databases) sources. Data may be *internal* to the organization, such as sales and accounting records, or *external*, such as information from government departments or university libraries. Saunders et al. (2006) give an excellent review of available data sources. Sources of data include:

- Department for International Development UK (DFID);
- the World Bank;
- the United Nations;
- the Chartered Institute of Marketing (UK) and the American Marketing Association;
- university and city libraries;
- Chambers of Commerce;
- embassies;
- banks (both domestic and foreign);
- trade associations;
- export councils;
- foreign trade organizations (e.g. the UK Foreign Office, USAID, the EU);
- international business resources (e.g. http://ciber.bus.msu.edu/busres.htm);

- the World Trade Organization (www.wto.org);
- Euro Monitor (www.euromonitor.com);
- the Global Export Marketing Information system;
- Google (www.google.com).
- Independent research organizations such as MINTEL (www.marketresearch.com.)

Online databases, like Lexis-Nexis (www.lexixnexis.com), coupled with the use of the World Wide Web, have enabled organizations to obtain rapid, up-to-date information which can be accessed around the clock. Not all are free of charge and may require a subscription. However, these sources of data often cost less than a fraction of the cost of commissioned research.

Secondary data has its drawbacks, especially when drawn from government sources. Disadvantages include how recent the data are different base years, differing data systems (e.g. the USA vs. Germany), whether it is analysed in the same way across all sources, and whether it is specific enough for the organization's needs. Problems in the accuracy and collection methods of government data can be particularly acute in less developed countries. To attract inward investment, governments may overstate the true situation. In the Far East it is extremely difficult to assess the authenticity of data, except in Singapore and Japan. Despite these difficulties, secondary data can be a good source of information.

Primary data

One of the truisms of marketing research is that 'companies are often inundated with data but starved of information'. Secondary data may give the company much interesting data but does it provide the information required to make informed decisions on which market opportunity to pursue? The answer is likely to be 'No'. Hence the need to develop a MKIS which gives information that is relevant and actionable. Market scanning can be a useful activity to identify possible market opportunities and the MKIS can be a useful function in helping to build a market profile. However, it is unlikely that these activities alone will be all that an organization needs to select a market segment. Primary research may be required to access the current and vital detail which will augment and hone the information collected (see Fig. 6.1). Further details on the international marketing research process can be obtained from texts such as Churchill (2002). The steps, outlined in Fig. 6.4 are as follows.

Research process agreement

Before any research is carried out it is essential that all stakeholders are in agreement on the purpose and use of the research. This can involve discussions on the problems and/or the opportunities the research is to address. A number of decision scenarios may be identified. While China may appear to be a lucrative market and, indeed, is proving to be for some, it may be better to prospect a more well-known market first, or to use a third party or partnership to spread the risk in the early stages of market launch. All stakeholders, including company executives, parent company, network partners, etc., should be involved in this stage of the research, and improvisation and flexibility are often a necessity. In the early stages companies may call upon informal means of gathering data and this is particularly true for small and medium-sized enterprises(SMEs), which have neither the finance nor expertise to carry out large-scale, sophisticated research (see Rundh, 2003). Often the only way to see the potential in a market is to visit the relevant region. For instance, ascertaining the potential exports of horticultural products from Zambia will necessitate visiting numerous growers, and government and export agencies, as published information is often unreliable. Companies may call on their networks—agents, joint venture partners, licensees or other companies—to join the research process. Consortia may be also used, e.g. the East European Omnibus (www.mrweb.com), which is a monthly research exercise in the Czech Republic, Slovenia, and Hungary. These offer many advantages, such as 'visibility', home support, and economies through joint cost-sharing.

Other decisions taken at this stage will be whether the research will be carried out centrally or decentrally, or by in-house staff or an outside agent. If a centralized decision is taken, then it has to be clearly identified as to who will be responsible for carrying out the research, and communication lines and responsibilities must be established with the subsidiaries. If decentralized, then it must be clarified who is to do what and who will disseminate the findings to other subsidiaries and/or to headquarters. Someone also needs to be appointed in a coordinating role.

Whether the activity is carried out in-house or by an agency depends on company resources, market expertise, and market and product complexity. Whether the company is a business-to-business enterprise or a business-to-consumer one also influences the decision. A highly complex B2B company, with fewer customers, may find it easier to handle the research in-house, whereas a consumer organization may not. There could be a compromise if the organization strategizes and manages the study but uses agencies with specialist experience to carry out the detail (e.g. fieldwork). Companies like Nestlé, Levi, and British Airways adopt this approach.

The research budget, ease of briefing, supervision, coordination of the agency, the standard of competence, and the requirements of the market will dictate the type of agency chosen. It may be local in the market under investigation, a domestic agency with an overseas office, a global agency or a domestic one that sub-contracts fieldwork. Research International (www.research-int.com) is typical of a global agency with branches in countries around the globe. The choice may not be easy. For example, it would be difficult for a Western-based agency, using Western researchers to interview Muslim women in Saudi Arabia. This requires a complex series of sub-contracts and contacts. All these decisions should be part of the research process agreement stage, but not exclusively. Some steps, for example, the networking activity, may be essential in carrying out the fieldwork.

Establish research objectives

Specific research questions and the subsequent research objectives and hypotheses are difficult to couch in the domestic marketing situation. In the international environment, with the environmental uncertainty and varying cultures, it is an even more difficult task. It is also important to define the boundaries of the study. It is far too easy to expand the budget, therefore it is necessary to make a distinction between what is interesting and what is relevant.

Estimate the value of information

At this stage an estimate of the cost versus the value of the primary information should be made. Attempts to make the information more accurate could incur a great deal of extra cost. In order to achieve accuracy, sample sizes, for example, may have to be increased, and this could add to the cost, especially if the topography is difficult to negotiate or the population is more rural than urban. In many places in Africa the population is spread over great distances and much of it is only accessible in the 'dry' season. This can lead to distortions in data estimation. A decision has to be made to terminate the research if the cost of obtaining the data outweighs the benefits it will bring.

Research design

The research design involves a series of elements. This includes negotiating access to respondents, identifying and addressing potential ethical issues, deciding on research philosophies (e.g. positivist or phenomenologist), and determining the research strategy (e.g. quantitative, qualitative, or a combination of both). Following this comes the data collection method (including the collection of secondary data, qualitative and quantitative primary data using surveys, observation, experiments, semi-structured and in-depth interviews and questionnaires) and a decision on the sampling frame and sample, and finally the analytical interpretation. Inevitably, these activities run the risk of cultural misinterpretation. Therefore a study of social values and ways of conducting research is essential. Negotiating access to respondents may be difficult, such as interviewing foreign politicians and company executives. Obtaining reliable and valid secondary data, and even primary data, is a key issue. Where socio-cultural issues are important, qualitative methods of data collection may assume increasing importance. In many developing countries, such as Malaysia and India, there is a suspicion of officialdom and often the best means of collecting the data is by informal interview. In the Easter cattle census in Ethiopia, the government thought that by visiting the cattle markets in Addis Ababa on one day and counting the cattle it would, by estimation, give a good idea of the number of cattle being sold in the markets at Easter. But what about evening cattle movements, informal markets, and enumerator bias?

It is essential that any questionnaires are translated into the vernacular. Unstructured questions may be suitable where there are social cultural interpretations, but they make analysis difficult. It is also important to avoid bias in the wording of questionnaires. For example, 'payment' is a transactional word that is not appropriate to Shariah law, where anything concerning 'debt' is unacceptable.

Observation as a research design may also be difficult, especially where this could be misinterpreted as 'spying'. This is not an interpretation wholly applicable to developing countries. Greece, for instance, has a strict interpretation of what may be classified as 'observation'.

Data collection

This refers to the collection of data in the field and usually takes the form of interviews—personal, group, telephone, mail, electronically, observation, and projective. All these techniques have their problems in international research. Hollensen (2007) provides a

 MINI-CASE ILLUSTRATION Data collection in less developed countries

Collecting data in less developed countries can be challenging. Potential sources of bias are legion. Low literacy levels, lack of physical access, limited technical availability, lack of personal safety, technical skills, and cost are just some of the problems. Many developing countries have low literacy levels (in Mozambique it is as low as 30%), and this makes it difficult to carry out any form of research other than personal interview, which itself can lead to interviewer bias. Rainy seasons are a feature of less developed countries as is poor infrastructure, e.g. Malawi, Bangladesh, Brazil, and Ethiopia. This may mean that research can only be carried out in the 'dry' season. This inevitably hinders the collection of statistics and leads to an under-estimation of results. Lack of the internet and computers for access to databases, the design of questionnaires, and data-processing facilities can limit questionnaire design to hand-written forms and non-web-based data-gathering instruments. In places like parts of Zambia, the Democratic Republic of the Congo, India, the Phillippines, Sudan, and Ethiopia, personal safety can be an issue. Lack of technical training can severely limit the type of research, accuracy of data collected, and data analysis. Cost is always a factor in less developed countries, restricting budgets, and this has a knock-on effect on sample sizes and the use of highly trained personnel. The lack of facilities, both natural, technical, and human, can also hinder activities, hence the use of 'estimation' measures for market potential appraisal.

detailed comparison of the types of contact method—mail, internet/e-mail, telephone, and personal—outlining their advantages and disadvantages. Not everyone has access to a telephone, e.g. in India. In Africa, some parts of Asia, and South America the mail is unreliable. And although people are wary of SPAM, e-mail is a useful technique in B2B marketing. In fieldwork, sources of bias abound. Different cultures will produce a varying response to questionnaires and interviews. If Germans say they will purchase a product, they probably will; not so Italians, who often overstate their intentions. Interviewer bias may be a result of communication difficulties, simply not doing the interviews or poor supervision. It is essential that good training and supervision are put in place to overcome such bias. Local, skilled fieldworkers are sometimes difficult to find and expensive if available, and so substitution with untrained workers is a regular phenomenon. For example, in Ethiopia government funds are at a premium and fieldwork for government research projects is often carried out by local sixth-form students after only a few hours of training. It is essential for good research that adequate training and supervision is carried out.

Preparation and data analysis

Preparation for, and actual analysis, has to be carried out on both qualitative and quantitative data. It is essential that there is a clear protocol both for the method for dealing with 'abnormal' data and to ensure comparability between and across cultures. Data has to be collected according to the same 'unit of analysis' to make any comparison meaningful. Issues can occur with the interpretation of qualitative data, especially where different cultures are concerned.

Report writing and presentation

In international research the danger of the 'self-reference criterion' is always present. The report must be written with this in mind. If the report is written in the foreign language, then it should be accompanied by a translation. Face-to-face debriefings with the researchers are a useful way to deal with any interpretative or other problems.

 WHOSE RESPONSIBILITY IS IT? Ethics in marketing research

It has long been held that, in conducting marketing research, the individual or organization conducting it must act in an ethical way. For this purpose, the British Market Research Society (www.mrs.org.uk) produces a code of conduct. The activities covered range from the rules and ethics when interviewing children to the correct way to conduct street research. There are ample opportunities to be 'fake'. Examples include falsification of sample respondents, data collectors completing questionnaires themselves, cheating on quota samples, and falsifying data analyses. Problems in international marketing include using other research questionnaire responses rather than the one designed, not completing sample quotas, particularly where the terrain or access is difficult, assuming responses if there are language difficulties, or substituting others who are more articulate. This can lead to falsified results. It is therefore essential that market research activities are strictly monitored and checks and balances are put in place.

MINI-CASE ILLUSTRATION International failures

Examples of international marketing failures, in which the lack of marketing research and failure to find out the relevant and significant customer attitudes and motives played a significant part, include the following (Kashani, 1989; Valentine, 1989):

- A large US-based carbonated soft-drink firm set up bottling facilities in Indonesia in an attempt to sell to the 176 million people. The judgement of management proved incorrect as sales of the product fell substantially below expectations. Later, marketing research revealed the reasons why. First, demographic data revealed that there was little disposable income to support purchase of the product. Secondly, the consumption of the product was mainly by tourists and expatriates in the major cities. Thirdly, most Indonesians preferred non-carbonated, coconut-based drinks.

- Vic Tanney's franchised health club tried to implement its US-based marketing strategy in Singapore. Its US-style facilities and exercise equipment drew few customers. Basically, only expatriates were served. Later, marketing research revealed that to be successful the club would need to appeal to Singapore

residents' preference for Western-style competitive sports, Chinese calisthenics, and traditional Asian exercise.

- Lego A/S, the Danish toy company, implemented a Western-style consumer promotion in Japan. This consisted of bonus packs of Lego and gift promotions which had led to sales increases in the USA and Europe when implemented there. It seemed to have no impact in the Japanese market. Marketing research later revealed that Japanese consumers considered the promotion to be wasteful and expensive.

- Coca-Cola launched a new brand of bottled water in the UK, Dasani, in 2004, utilizing a heavy promotional campaign. The company was using the mains supply in its factory in Kent and purifying it, as the company said, using a 'highly sophisticated purification process'. Not only was there an outcry against using tap water, but the water industry was worried that the marketing campaign implied tap water was not pure. The product was withdrawn later in the year. (For a full case on this example, see http://idenet.bth.se/servlet/download/news/22102/ Dasani.pdf.)

Just as with secondary data, primary data can have its problems too. These include the fact that primary research can be very expensive, and there can be problems of identification of sample frames, possible small sample sizes, commercial secrecy, cultural problems, literacy levels, language difficulties and nuances of language, a lack of infrastructure, and a lack of monitoring and control facilities.

This brief description of the primary market research process is intended only as an overview. These data, along with secondary data and market scanning, are intended to inform the market segmentation process. The segment then selected forms the market opportunity.

Global Market Segmentation

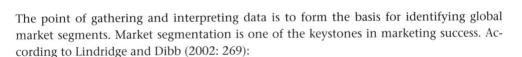

The point of gathering and interpreting data is to form the basis for identifying global market segments. Market segmentation is one of the keystones in marketing success. According to Lindridge and Dibb (2002: 269):

> segmentation is attractive because it helps companies to improve their marketing effectiveness and can lead to more satisfied customers, improved competitiveness, increasingly efficient resource allocation and better designed marketing programmes . . . the underlying principle of segmentation is that customers can be grouped using variables that help to discriminate between product needs and buying behaviour.

In their research on culture, they concluded that it was important not to underestimate the potential buying power of different ethnic cultures. Their study in the UK on the effect of culture on the purchase of 'brown' goods (e.g. televisions, music systems, etc.), found that there was a difference between British Indians and British Caucasians, but not significant enough to warrant culture being used as a segmentation variable. So, although the communications element of the marketing mix may need fine-tuning when promoting to different groups, core marketing strategies and marketing propositions used by manufacturers and retailers need not differ in order to reflect the buying power of both groups.

In general, approaches to international segmentation can be on either a geographic, transnational, or hierarchial country/consumer segmentation basis:

- **Geographic**. Markets segmented on the basis of geography, (north, south, east and west), continent, region, or economic bloc.

- **Transnational**. Markets segmented on the basis of demographics (age, sex income, etc.), psychographics (lifestyles), milieu (a combination of lifestyle and social factors), or behavioural factors (brand loyalty).

- **Hierarchial country/consumer segmentation**. Markets segmented on the basis of identifying 'globally equivalent segments'. This entails: (a) identifying countries that are easily accessible; (b) using criteria to select countries; (c) developing microsegments; (d) looking for similarities across the segments; and (e) using cluster analysis to identify meaningful global segments across boundaries.

In fact, there are two underlying bases to make segmentation work: one is to identify a set of variables or characteristics which will assign potential customers to homogeneous groups; and the other is to find a way so that the groups found are sufficiently different heterogeneously. For example, one might classify wine drinkers as those who prefer red or white, but within this classification there are those who prefer certain types of white and those who prefer certain types of red. Are the types large enough segments to treat as separate? In this example, the answer is 'Yes'. Table 6.2 gives examples of the three main bases for segmenting international markets: product-based, customer-based and psychographics.

Most elements in the table are self-explanatory. Product-based segmentation methods relate to the features of the product or service. Cars are in different colours, sizes, and shapes to appeal to different segments, e.g. the saloon, executive, sports, or commercial vehicle market. Products may be segmented by classification—consumer, B2B, or service. Within these categories may be more sub-categories, appealing to sub-segments of the market. Sports cars may be 'hard' or 'soft' tops, consumer goods maybe 'white' or 'brown', a description differentiating electrical goods from furniture. Customer-based segmentation methods are many and varied. Clothes may be segmented by age—children, young adults, and adults. Demographics are classic ways to segment markets as are geodemographics. The latter are used a lot in global marketing, e. g. Western versus Eastern cultures. Markets may be segmented on the basis of time, e. g. 'off peak' versus 'peak' use of train services. Recently, technology has enabled the use of computer-based relational databases to segment markets, e. g. Experian's EuroMosaic software.

Table 6.2 Bases for international market segments

Product-based	Customer-based	Psychographics
Size, shape, colour, technology, features, product application, consumer, B2B, original equipment, service, length of life, brand, season, 'colour', e.g. 'white goods', goods	Demographics: age, gender, religion, colour, culture, education, social class height Geodemographics: geographical location, urban, non-urban, lowlands, plateaux, highlands, EuroMosaic Other: Behavioural, e.g. product in use, consumption patterns occasion of use, place of use, time of use, loyalty	Lifestyle: Attitudes, Interest Opinions (AIO), perceptions, Value Analysis of Lifestyles (VALS) personality, persona Milieux: combination of lifestyle and social factors

THE DIGITAL IMPACT Customer specific segmentation with the internet

The internet offers the possibility of online market research and customer profiling. It offers organizations on opportunity for exploring customers' needs and characteristics in order to develop a basis for selective planning, design, and control. Customer profiling enables companies to target customers and provides global marketers with new and abundant opportunities to target segments and individuals. It also brings global segmentation into a reality for SMEs, which usually cannot afford the cost of market research.

Satisfying individual customer needs has a positive impact on the perceived attractiveness of product offerings. The internet allows an organization to obtain detailed customer information and to enable sellers to personalize the offering. This can be the basis of a long-lasting relationship with customers. This process is called 'personalization'. When a person logs on to the internet, he/she leaves a range of tracks. Such tracks, if systematically collected and recorded, can be used to formulate a customer profile representing the user's habits and interests and can be used to support one-to-one marketing concepts in e-commerce. Customer profiles can easily be generated at little cost. When suitably processed, they can be transferred to a data warehouse and can be added to over time. Data is collected 'non-reactively' (Janetzko, 1999), i.e. the internet user has no idea it is being collected. In 'normal' market research, data is collected from the individual 'reactively', i.e. with the person's knowledge. Non-reactive data resulting from a customer's usage of the website is usually collected by log files, via Common Gateway Interface (CGI). Log files come in various guises but the most common format is the Extended Common Log Format (ECLF). The basic data on the file include the IP address (internet address of the computer with which the user communicates with the server), the user ID, the time the client retrieves data from the server, the request (shows what data was retrieved for the server), status (whether the data exchange between client and server was successful, Bytes (number of bytes sent in response), referrer (the URL), and the agent (the client's operating system and browser software). Other non-reactive data recorded can include 'environment variables' such as the user's access patterns and the time users spend with the service. Other non-reactive data that can be obtained include 'cookies' (software agents that providers can use for data collection), 'special browsers', 'packet sniffing', and 'web bugs' (invisible images that produce usage information). (For more detail, see Buxel and Walsh, 2003.)

Reactive data collection is collecting data on consumer characteristics that cannot be revealed by using non-reactive data collection technologies. Data useful for building consumer profiles include identification data (user name, address, e-mail address, etc.), descriptive data, such as consumers' basic goods and services preferences, basic sociographic and psychographic data, and communications data which can be obtained when a consumer enters into dialogue with a seller, e.g. via e-mail.

Combining the two sets of data involves analysing data in data warehouses and sifting customers into 'known' and 'anonymous'. Data can be then subjected to rule-based procedures to identify 'anonymous' or 'known customers' and an appropriate communication mix can be developed. Grouping customers into like 'personalities' based on 'reactive' and non-reactive' data can be the basis of global segments.

A good example of a 'known' global customer segment using internet technology is the British Airways Club and BA's Air Miles (www.ba.com) scheme. This scheme is intended to build up a long-term relationship with the customer. When a customer fills out an Executive Club Membership application form, the form asks for detailed data, such as identification data (physical address, e-mail address, etc.). British Airways now has a lot of reactive data. The collection of 'non-reactive data is relatively easy. BA already knows from the application form that the customer has an e-mail address. By using the ECLF procedure, the customer's use of the internet can be ascertained. By combining the reactive and non-reactive data, BA regularly use the internet to communicate with their Executive Club Class members, as well as using direct mail.

An example of an anonymous global segment using rule-based procedures would be banner advertising on the internet. For example, based on your browsing of car specifications for information prior to purchasing a car the procedure described may identify you as a potential purchaser of insurance because of the likelihood is that you will need car insurance. As you browse for car advertisements, a banner may appear from Churchill car insurance (www.churchill.co.uk). If you respond to the banner car insurance advertisement you will be converted from an anonymous customer into a known one. The so-called 'e-tailers' can use the internet, harnessed to database technology, to create a new range of global segments based on ingenious web-based technology.

The corollary to this is that an increasing number of customers and institutions are showing concern about the invasion of privacy and SPAM. This has led the European Union to pass legislation in 2004 that prohibits keeping electronic addresses without the owners' consent.

MINI-CASE ILLUSTRATION **VALS as a segmentation method in international marketing**

The VALS lifestyle system divides consumers into eight sub-groups: Actualizers (sophisticated with high esteem), Fulfilleds (mature, satisfied, and comfortable), Believers (traditionalists), Achievers (career-oriented who like to feel in control), Strivers (seeking self-esteem and motivation), Experiencers (adventurous and enthusiastic), Makers (self-sufficient, working-class), and Strugglers (cautious consumers who seek security). In her research on positioning organizations involved in the coffee/café culture, Woolley (2004) put the VALS analysis together with Aaker's (1997) Brand Personality Framework to produce the following current international segments:

Café retailers	Starbucks	Caffè Nero	Costa	Coffee Republic
Brand Personality	Sophistication Competence	Sincerity Excitement	Excitement Competence	Excitement Competence
The VALS Lifestyle Segment	Actualizers Fulfilled Achievers	Strivers Achievers	Actualizers Fulfilleds Achievers Strivers	Strivers Achievers Makers

Based on this research, Woolley suggested that all retailers were similar, as perceived by her sample, except Coffee Republic, because they are all targeting the same consumer segments. Woolley suggested that the need was for organizations involved in the coffee culture to understand the consumer better, and the resultant branding strategies, in order to identify a position of competitive advantage.

As we shall see, demographics have proved to be poor predictors of behaviour, especially in international marketing. In recent years there has been a tendency to augment these methods with techniques based on 'attitudes', 'interests', 'opinions', and 'perceptions' of consumers, particularly in consumer marketing. Advances in analysing and classifying market research data, especially social research data, has enabled the development of some promising new segmentation techniques. Stanford Institute's (quoted in Schiffman and Kanuk, 2004), Value and Lifestyle System (VALS, see http://www.sric-bi.com/VALS/types.shtml) is widely known and used, for example by coffee/café organizations such as Starbucks. The mini-case illustrates this.

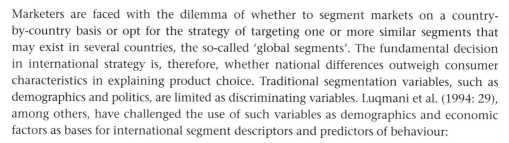

Selecting Markets for Targeting

Marketers are faced with the dilemma of whether to segment markets on a country-by-country basis or opt for the strategy of targeting one or more similar segments that may exist in several countries, the so-called 'global segments'. The fundamental decision in international strategy is, therefore, whether national differences outweigh consumer characteristics in explaining product choice. Traditional segmentation variables, such as demographics and politics, are limited as discriminating variables. Luqmani et al. (1994: 29), among others, have challenged the use of such variables as demographics and economic factors as bases for international segment descriptors and predictors of behaviour:

> The intricacies of consumer marketing are greatest in international markets, where companies invariably have to deal with diverse cultural, political and economic conditions. To grapple with this complexity, multinational forms attempt to group countries into seemingly homogeneous segments on the bases of economic, geographic, political, cultural, religious or

resource variables. This segmentation approach commonly clusters countries according to discrete environmental factors such as GNP, political system. . . . The effectiveness of this method, however, is influenced by such micro variables as the nature of the product, and perhaps more important, the purchase orientations of consumers. . . . Hence macro segmentation must be complemented by consideration of specific micro variables that directly influence consumers' product preferences and which are useful in the delineation of international markets. Furthermore, Whilst the macro approach is helpful in assessing the world market opportunities and formulating business plans, it has been less successful in finding common elements among seemingly disparate international markets. Such linkages are essential for facilitating the effective and orderly coordination of specific global business strategies directed at not only cross-country segments, but also particular customer groups which transcend national boundaries. . . . To accomplish this, countries need to be viewed on a continuum rather than as entirely similar or dissimilar.

Their research, the basis of which has not been yet been fully validated, suggested 'convenience' as a common factor in consumption worldwide and, as such, may provide useful insights for global strategic planning. They suggest that their continuum framework may be useful in planning an integrated approach to world markets. Their approach is dynamic, where countries placed along the continuum need to be evaluated periodically for their shift in convenience. At the time of writing, Luqmani, et al. (1994) classified countries into Innovator, Utopian, Latent, and Traditional, with suggested global strategies to match this categorization.

In a similar vein, the Hartman's Group's (www.hartman-group.com) traditional segmentation is based on environmental concerns and activities, which strike a universal chord:

- True Naturals—express deeply-felt environmental-based concerns and tailor their actions and purchases to these beliefs.

- New Green Mainstream—are concerned about the environment, but alter their actions and purchases only when it is convenient.

- Affluent Healers—are most concerned about the environmental issues that relate to their personal health. They are less inclined to consider the environment when shopping, but can be persuaded with the right message and product attributes.

- Overwhelmed—feel too caught up in life's demands to worry about the environment. They are unlikely to favour a product for environmental reasons.

- Unconcerned—simply do not pay attention to environmental issues or do not feel that the environment is seriously threatened (source: www.demographics.com/publications/ad, accessed on 27/01/2001)

A good example of segmentation based on environmental concerns and activities is the late Anita Roddick's Body Shop (www.thebodyshop.com), which sources its ingredients for its health and beauty products from as many natural and environmentally-friendly producers as possible. More recently, with the rapid growth of 'environmentalism' and the adoption by businesses and governments of 'greener' policies, more and more of these are insisting that their suppliers conduct their businesses with due regard to the environment. For instance, the EU is passing a myriad of regulations of the reduction of carbon dioxide emission and this is affecting all manner of businesses from power generation to car manufacturing.

Such a segmentation base, with its global appeal, may be a better way of segmenting the market for, say, environmentally-friendly products than simple demographics which do not address the environmental issues. Previously, to describe the 'greens', environmental categories would have been linked to demographics. However, this segmentation base has been constructed on a gradual 'core to periphery' lifestyle model, placing consumers on a scale of health and wellness activities. Hartman (see website, www.hartman-group.com) believes that such a model is more useful to marketers as it does not place consumers into strict categories of behaviours and demographics. So, while environmental segmentation may be useful, those wishing to reach the much larger wellness market are better served by the lifestyle model. This comes back to the premise at the beginning of the chapter that it is all well and good to segment markets, but how much 'distance' (heterogeneity) can be put between segments to make them more accessible and profitable? The better you can pinpoint the segment which responds best to your offering, the better it will be.

Malhotra et al. (1998) suggest that regional trading blocs may be a good basis for describing global markets. But while these approaches are not yet fully empirically validated, the evidence is growing. If consumers across cultures show similar behaviour, a global standardized approach to segmentation may be implementable. In products such as consumer electronics, cars, and fashion, despite the problems of distribution standardization, such is the global power of corporations operating in these markets that standardization becomes more of a reality (Hasan and Katsanis, 1994). Fuat Firat and Scultz (1997) took the debate further when they suggested that the world was experiencing such change that how to make sense of it in a way that enabled marketers to seize the opportunities presented by the change was a source of continuing debate. They suggested that the 'postmodern' phenomenon in marketing has the potential to reframe thinking about social trends and business practices in an increasingly global but, they contend, fragmented world. They further suggested that a better understanding of the underlying macro social forces and micro human behaviour associated with postmodernism could, ultimately, be leveraged by marketers to obtain competitive advantage. However, we still await the postmodern breakthrough promised by these and other 'postmodern' marketers.

Aurifeille et al. (2002) looked at an exploratory study into 'involvement' (in the product) as a basis for segmentation globally. In a study of wine, they set out to test whether nationality was a factor in creating segments for retailers. Wine has a range of characteristics likely to be affected by the country where it is sold. While the findings are mixed, they found that there was scope for global wine segmentation, even in countries like France and Australia. They concluded, given the limitations of the size and convenience of the sample, that more global opportunities existed in countries sharing similar wine cultures. This was borne out in the UK, one of the biggest importers of wine in the world. Australia, in particular, has segmented the UK market successfully by introducing 'fun' wine labels, such as Cudgee Creek, Porcupine Ridge, and Zonte's Footstep, in the 35–64 year-old age category, which is by far the largest buyers of wine in the UK (Perez, 2004: 75). Aurifeille et al. (2002) found that using 'involvement' profiles to drive the clustering process was useful when working across cultures, because it removed the problems inherent in using standard demographics, such as poor predictability, due to differences in national structure and behaviour. These are examples of the growing body of evidence to suggest a better way to describe and predict global segment behaviour than segmentation based on traditional geodemographics and environmental variables.

Hollensen (2007) suggests a four-step process for international market selection:

Step 1: Selection of the relevant segmentation criteria.

Step 2: Development of appropriate segments.

Step 3: Screening of segments to narrow down the list of markets/countries. Choice of target markets/countries.

Step 4: Micro segmentation: the development of segments in each qualified country or across countries.

Fig. 6.10 Market expansion possibilities

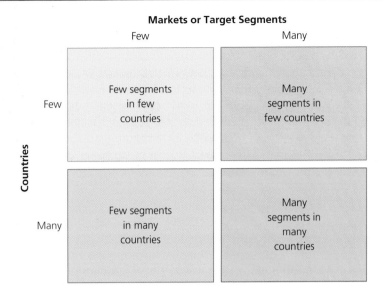

The 'company' and the 'environment' factors will inform the four steps. At the end of the process a decision will be made on marketing entry/expansion—how many markets to enter, when, and in what sequence. The alternatives are shown in Fig. 6.10.

'Few segments in few countries' is typified by high-value tourism (e.g. Botswana), 'few segments in many countries' is typified by children's clothes and shoes, 'many segments and few countries' is typified by nuclear electricity generation, and 'many segments in many countries' is typified by food retailing. The decision to concentrate on a few countries or diversify into many countries, according to Hollensen (2007), is informed by 'company' and 'environmental factors', in addition to 'product' and 'marketing' factors. This is illustrated as in Table 6.3.

Table 6.3 Factors affecting choice of market concentration vs. market diversification

	Favouring country diversification	Favouring country concentration
Product factors	Limited use, low volume, non-repeatable, standard, 'disruptively' innovative, in growth or decline stage of life cycle	General use, high volume, repeat purchase, requires adaption to market, incrementally innovative, in mature stage of life cycle
Company factors	High risk, growth by market development, little market or competitive intelligence	Low risk, growth through market penetration, selecting best markets through market and competitive intelligence
Market factors	Small, unstable, many similar markets, low growth, long-standing competitors with large share, low loyalty, countries synergistic	Large, stable, limited number of markets, high growth, few competitors with limited share, high loyalty, countries low synergistic
Marketing factors	Low communication costs and standardization, low logistical costs, low price	High communication costs and non-standardization, high logistical costs, high price

Source: After Hollensen (2007: 26).

Fig. 6.11 The 'waterfall' vs. 'shower' approaches to market entry

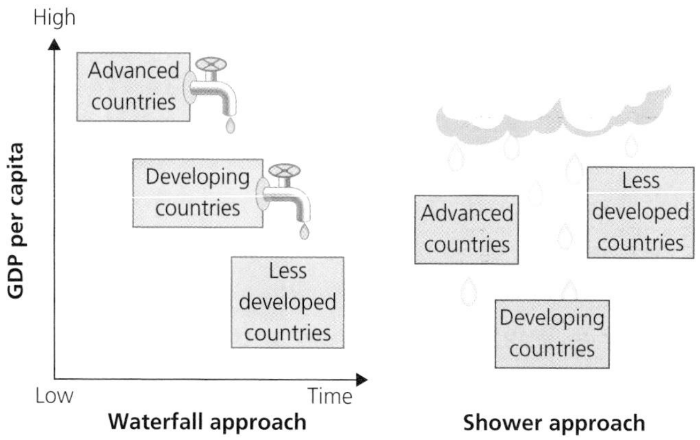

Source: Based on Keegan (1989: 30–1).

Hollensen uses the traditional bases of international segmentation, e.g. demography, economy, geographic, and lifestyle factors. He acknowledges the need for a 'coarse-grained' and 'fine-grained' screen of the market based on general criteria such as GNP and government spending as a percentage of GNP for the former, and market-size calculations and a 'market/country attractiveness and competitive strength matrix' for the latter. Much of Hollensen's model is based on traditional methods of market segmentation. As we have already seen, these bases are poor at predicting behaviour (see Hofstede et al., 1999).

Keegan (1989) suggests an alternative to the 'market concentration'/'market diversification' approach of Hollensen (2007). Keegan uses the incremental strategy approach, which he called the 'waterfall' approach, and the simultaneous approach, which he called the 'shower' approach. The incremental ('waterfall') approach is almost an experimental approach, where organizations enter a single market first, build up experience, and then enter other markets based on this experience. On the other hand, the simultaneous ('shower') approach is where the organization feels confident enough to enter several markets simultaneously to leverage its core competences and resources. An example of the former is the expansion overseas by Tesco supermarkets and an example of the later is Microsoft, with its software. Both approaches are illustrated in Fig. 6.11.

Doole and Lowe (2004) suggest that market segmentation may be a process carried out after the scanning stage. The partitioning of markets into segments which respond to the same marketing stimuli is the basis of their argument. This approach allows the organization to concentrate its resources strategically rather than to attempt a market penetration approach based on a 'market spreading' exercise. They contend that pareto analysis (the 80/20 rule) is a good way of clustering countries, the former receiving greater attention than the latter. They argue that the two bases for segmenting international markets are geographical (countries) and transnational criteria (individual decision-makers). Based on the business portfolio matrix of Harrel and Kiefer (1993), the authors divide the geographical criteria into primary, secondary, and tertiary markets based on country attractiveness and the company's compatibility with each country. This approach is particularly useful for companies operating in a portfolio of markets and wishing to prioritize market opportunities. Ford tractors took such an approach, looking at market size, growth rate, government regulations, and economic and political stability, coupled with competitive strength and company compatibility with the market. After so doing, Ford chose Kenya, Pakistan, and Venezuela as primary markets. While the primary segmentation may be by country, the secondary base may be by within country variables such as demographics and lifestyles. As we have seen, these may not be easy to identify and may be difficult to apply across all markets once identified. Demographics, for example, may not be good predictors of behaviour. Hence recent research has concentrated on identifying other bases for segmentation, based on global universals rather than 'blunt' instruments such as demographics.

Doole and Lowe (2004) suggest that a country as a unit of analysis may be too large to be of operational use and that an alternative approach based on the 'decision-maker' may be better. Key bases for segmentation using this analysis include variables such as demographics, psychographics, and behavioural criteria. Demographics include sex, age, and social class, but are poor at predictive ability. Psychographics include lifestyle factors such as activities, interests, and opinions (see Hartman example above).

Behavioural variables include patterns of consumption or loyalty to products as well as the context for usage. When linked to technology, some methods of segmentation offer a powerful tool for strategic decision-making (see mini-case illustration on Experian and Mosaic UK below). Although offering a powerful segmentation tool, changes in lifestyles and differing patterns of consumer behaviour among the segments make this method a device with limitations. However, the internet, linked to the information that a 'connection' gives about an individual, offers a potentially powerful, targeted segmentation technique. The mini-case illustration on Experian is a good example.

Kale and Sudharshan (1987) suggest a process to formulate strategically equivalent segments (SES) to transcend national boundaries. Segmentation based purely on geographical

Fig. 6.12 Steps to achieve strategically equivalent market segments in international marketing

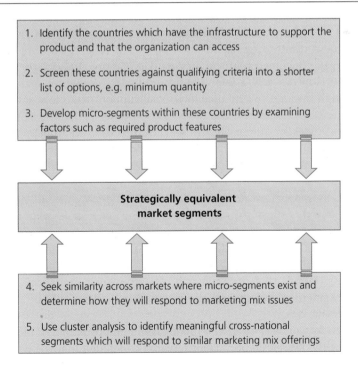

factors leads to national stereotyping and ignores the fact that segments may exist across national boundaries. These similarities should be identified (see the Hartman example above) and so should the way in which they differ from other segments. Kale and Sudharhsan (1987) suggest a series of steps to achieve SES segmentation, which is illustrated in Fig. 6.12.

This approach places consumers at the heart of the international segmentation process and enables managers to design strategies aimed at cross-national segments. It also enables strategists to develop global segmentation strategies which may be more effective and lucrative than an approach that segments the market on a country-by-country basis. An interesting example is the travel and tourism industry. (see the Relationship Perspective box).

The debate is whether traditional macro environmentals are good predictors of behaviour or not. Although the evidence is that they are not, it would be unwise to dismiss them out of hand. Burt and Gabbott (1995), in an article looking at the elderly consumer and non-food purchase behaviour, concluded that there was evidence of some form of segmentation in the shopping behaviour of elderly consumers in their sample. Their research showed that Marks and Spencer (www.marksandspencer.co.uk) had a very clear role in the minds of elderly people. Writing much later, Carrigan (1998), in an article on the grey market (the elderly aged over 50), furthered the theme and related it to an international ageing context. Carrigan identified that this market raised a new opportunity for companies engaged in travel, healthcare, security and leisure. The growth of companies such as Legal and General and Prudential Insurance (www.prudential.com), with healthcare plans for the over 50s, are examples of this phenomenon. Carrigan blamed lack of understanding of the needs for the over 50s for the failure to capitalize on the spending power of this segment. She offered some statistics to substantiate the market size claims of this segment. By 2000, there were 390 million people worldwide aged 65 or over. In the UK alone, it is predicted that by 2024 over 40% of the population will be over 50, with 18.7% of the population retired. By 2040, 20% of the US population will be aged over 50. Japan, Canada, and Australia all face ageing populations. By 2000 over 400 million people in developing nations were aged 60+. The over 50s of the future may wear more jeans and drink more Coke than their predecessors as their buying habits grow with them. While concentrating her research on the sports and health centre market in particular, Carrigan concluded that the grey market is more challenging than any other segment. She developed a 4 × 2 50+ 'life group' matrix, based on finance high/social support needs high through to a finance low/social support needs low, intrinsic/extrinsic motivation dimensions to describe the greys as good timers, affluents, companiables, independents, health seekers, affluent health seekers, directeds, and independent directeds. The overriding conclusion was that the grey market should be treated in a targeted rather than a shotgun approach, and that the market was a universal rather than a national phenomenon.

Demographics as a global macro segmentation variable may have its limits, but when harnessed to a lifestyle or other descriptor, can reveal new market opportunities. As far back as 1986, Lesser and Hughes were arguing that lifestyle and psychographic dimensions may have added to the predictive ability of demographics, but, at the time of the authors' research, their relationship with consumer behaviour had been far from impressive. The authors claimed that their research, despite several limitations, indicated that psychographic segments developed in one geographic market could be generalizable to other geographic markets.

Recent research by Gonzalez and Bello (2002) asserts the construct of lifestyle in market segmentation for the tourist market. Their research concluded that the demand for tourism was increasingly less well explained by socio-demographic and economic criteria but better by the use of general lifestyle variables in order to segment the market and predict the behaviour of leisure travellers. In a well-researched and informative article, based on Spanish destinations, they provided a set of key predictor variables for use in segmenting the market for holidays. These were self-realization at work, enterprising attitude, fashion, independence, concern for the environment, conformism, value for money, responsibility at work, emancipation, novelty, liberalism, hedonism, safety on the streets, development of society, pragmatism, solidarity, caution, attachment to home, familiarity, materialism, ambition and conservatism. The segmentation of the market that emerged made a division into five clusters: home-loving, idealistic, independent, hedonistic, and conservative. While the labels and characteristics were contextually bounded in Spain, the methodology could be extrapolated to other locations.

 MINI-CASE ILLUSTRATION Experian and Mosaic UK customer segmentation

Experian (www.experian.co.uk), the Nottingham-based UK research organization, is famed for its 'credit ratings', particularly for the consumer market. When a customer applies for credit to purchase goods, he/she may well be referred, by the seller, to Experian, which runs a credit check to establish credit worthiness. If that customer has a poor record of payment, or has a County Court judgment against him/her, Experian will inform the seller and credit may be refused. Experian are an effective direct marketing operation, based on their ability to create and marry databases, some of which are external to the company. Experian's Mosaic UK and Euro Mosaic classifies some 380 million people into neighbourhood types. Ten Euro Mosaic types have been identified: elite suburbs, average areas, luxury flats, low-income inner city, high-rise social housing, industrial communities, dynamic families, low-income families, rural agricultural, and vacation retirement. Mosaic UK identifies groupings of consumer behaviour for households and postcodes. All UK consumers are grouped into 61 distinct lifestyle types and 11 groups, which comprehensively describe their socio-economic and socio-cultural behaviour. The Mosaic UK has both a quantitative and qualitative element to the field data. The quantitative component has developed 400 variables over 20 years of existence. The qualitative component comprises a number of experts who have interpreted the classifications and provided a detailed understanding of each of the Mosaic groups and types. All the data are combined with information from higher levels of geography and Census Output Areas.

Linked to postcodes and addresses, this enables the identification of UK and pan-European geodemographic segments. Based on the principle that similar neighbourhoods attract people with similar social and professional leanings, for example footballers, doctors, and blue-collar workers, Experian has developed a system for direct marketers to target a segment of the market for goods and services which the company believes will be attracted

to them. By tapping into other databases, such as credit card records, membership records, etc., organizations are now able to offer a wide range of potential client contacts, even to multinational marketers such as European lottery organizations. For a 182-page detailed description of Mosaic UK, refer to the source document below.

Source: https://www.royalmail.experianintact.com/documents/Demographics/MosaicUK.pdf (accessed on 26/02/2008).

One of the greatest challenges to global marketers is not only to identify and describe segments but also to define the product—what it is and how it will work and be used. Brechin (2002) describes how this can be addressed by combining market segmentation and personas in the mini-case illustration.

This, and other research, forms an evolving body of evidence showing that in order to describe, access, and take advantage of market segments, a deeper understanding of the needs of the potential segment is needed rather than generalized descriptors such as demographics, economics, and political factors. These may be 'fine-grained' 'course-grained' screening but are far too blunt to use as the basis to devise effective and efficient global segmentation strategies. Market research is one tool to elicit the 'true' characteristics and opportunities of a potential or latent segment, but this is only if the tools of market research methodology evolve to keep pace with the change associated with today's global segments.

THE RELATIONSHIP PERSPECTIVE The world travel and tourism industry

The world travel and tourism industry is huge, worth US$685 billion in 2005, accounting for 28.4% of the world's exports of commercial services. Of the top 15 exporters in 2005, number one was the USA with US$430 billion, number two was Spain with US$47.76 billion, and in fifth place was the UK with US$30.36 billion. The leading importers were (1) the USA with US$73.6 billion, (2) Germany, with US$73 billion and (3) the UK with US$59.5 billion. These three were by far and away the biggest. (www.wto.org 2008). It is also one of the most highly segmented industries and has one important feature—it is connected by an intricate network of providers, including hotels, carriers (e.g. airlines), travel agents, internet portals, insurance agencies, etc. Yet there are, around the world, those strategic equivalent segments (SES) that make the varied tourist destinations lucrative.

The tourist industry is segmented by every possible means—socio-demographic, psychographic, lifestyle, etc. For example, holidays for the over 50s (socio-demographic or grey segment) provided by Saga; for the family (the theme park or young family segments) provided by Disney and Universal Studios; for the adventurous (the young or 'adrenaline junkies' segment) provided by Sobek or Overland; for the pleasure seekers (the 'hedonistic' segment), provided by Sandals. There are specialist holidays for those who like art or beer festivals, lifestyle holidays for those who like farming or ranching, and 'cause related' holidays for those who are wilderness lovers.

These destinations are linked by a series of 'providers' which are themselves segmented. Qantas (www.qantas.com) and Lufthansa (www.lufthansa.com) are air carrier providers offering seats for the economy class, the business class, and first-class tourist, segmented on the basis of income, type of holiday, etc. Other air carrier providers are for the charter market, e.g. Monarch (www.monarch-airlines.com). Travel agents provide facilitation services, such as agenting for tour operators, and may offer a total package deal, e.g. Thomas Cook (www.thomascook.

com), or may be providers of information, with a brochure and an advice facility. Other providers offer health insurance, e.g. Legal and General (www.legalandgeneral.com), baggage handling services and airport facilities, e.g. British Airports Authority (www.baa.com), and other vital yet invisible services such as computer systems and ticketing facilities, e.g. Galileo (www.galileo.com), and market research facilities for the improvement of service offerings. Every destination transaction leaves a footprint of data which can be captured, stored, and interrogated to segment the market further, and, when combined, enable the discovery and description of global market segments such as the 'health tourist' or 'adventure seeker'. Currently, the cruise segment is one of the fastest-growing, enabling 'providers' like Cunard (www.cunard.co.uk), P&O (www.pocruises.com), and Star Lines (www.seastarline .com) to invest in bigger, more luxurious ships.

The market linked to networks and technology has spawned new global strategies. easyJet (www.easyjet.com), Ryanair (www.ryanair.com), and BMI Baby (www.bmibaby.com), and others like them, spotted a gap in the market for a 'no frills', low-cost, reliable service and, in the last ten years, carved out a niche internationally. This enables the likes of Ryanair and easyJet to boast that they are among the largest airlines in Europe. The full-price service carriers, such as British Airways (www.ba.com), Lufthansa (www.lufthansa.com), American Airlines (www.american-air.com), and Cathay Pacific (www.cathaypacific.com), have adopted other strategies, forming their ovwn global alliances. For example, One World (www.oneworldalliance.com) and Star Alliance (www. staralliance.com) offer the tourist and business person alike a seamless ticketing and flight availability service.

The challenge is to find new and undiscovered holiday products to match a seemingly endless appetite for new and exciting things to do and see.

MINI-CASE ILLUSTRATION Market segmentation and personas

Market segmentation and personas are techniques that are not conflicting but complementary. Segmentation, whether by demographics, lifestyles, or other more refined classificatory methods, such as VALS and PRIZM, has been the subject of much research and practical application, and has become a powerful tool in marketing. (PRIZM NE is a market segmentation system developed by Claritas Inc. (www.claritas.com), a part of the AC Nielson organization (www.acnielson.com) under its My Best Segment Suite. As such, it is one of many commercially produced market segmentation systems.) These consumer-modelling techniques are not just useful for forecasting marketplace acceptance of goods and services, but they can help executives make decisions on building products and services and calculate potential return on investment.

However, understanding why somebody wants to buy something is not the same as defining the product—what it is, how it will work, and how it will be used. While segmentation is an excellent tool for helping to solve product definition products, it can be too blunt an instrument. For example, market segmentation information may suggest that a particular car may appeal to the needs of consumers on a tight budget. But how do you design the car to meet the needs of those consumers?

What is required is a more refined instrument to show what motivates people to use a product so that the decisions on product features and how to communicate them are informed. The tool must be every bit as effective in determining the definition of a product as market segmentation is at forecasting market acceptance. The Cooper consulting company (www.cooper.com) has found success in defining products by creating user models called 'personas'. According to the company, personas are a set of fictional, representative user archetypes based on the behaviours, attitudes, and goals of the people. They have names, personalities, pictures, personal backgrounds, families, and, most importantly, goals; they are not average users but specific characters. A persona is a stand-in for a group of people who share common goals. At the same time persona characteristics encompass those people in widely different demographic groups who may have similar goals.

At the beginning of every design project, designers conduct qualitative research that includes reviewing the client's market segmentation and demographic data. Designers also interview stakeholders, customers, and users in order to gain insight into the product domain and user population. This information feeds directly into the characteristics of the personas. Personas and market segments provide different information. Market segmentation provides a quantitative breakdown of the market while personas provide a qualitative analysis of user behaviour. These techniques also serve different purposes. Market segmentation identifies attitudes and potential buying habits. For example, Cooper found that in a survey of rear-seat entertainment (RSE) systems, respondents believed it was a lifestyle purchase for parents trying to entertain their children while driving, and was suitable for children between the ages of 4 and 15, as children needed to be old enough to use headsets as well as some form of remote control. Personas, on the other hand, reveal motivations and potential usage patterns. Consumers' motivation is what gets them interested in using a product. For example, a stay-at-home mother with children she drives to school in her car is thinking about buying a rear-seat entertainment system to keep the children entertained on the forthcoming trip to see family. She does not want to be distracted by noise from the back seat. She would also like to ensure that her children are watching appropriate programmes and so would like to have a channel control. The designers are challenged to design a system where the children do not need to wear the headphones for the entire journey as the mother would like to talk to them but also retain the ability for the children to have control of the system from the rear seat.

Both market segmentation and personas provide useful information; one informs the other. Using the appropriate tool for the task without bending, adding, or removing can provide a rich complementary set of user and consumer models that can ultimately create a useful and more successful product definition than either could in isolation.

Sources: Brechin (2002); www.cooper.com.

Chapter Summary

1. Analysing global market opportunities and subsequent market selection are key global strategic decisions. In order to conduct this activity in an effective way, a market selection process is needed. Hollensen's (2007) model is one such process.

2. However sophisticated, a marketing information system (MKIS) should be developed by an organization for systematic data collection, data analysis, and dissemination of information to key decision-makers on those market opportunities to prospect. Market research plays a vital role in the establishment and population of the MKIS. Data are collected either on a continuous and/or *ad hoc* basis, from secondary and primary data sources. The information gathered is general marketing environmental data such as

demographics, socio-economic and political data, and country-specific data like lifestyle and product usage. Data gathered can be used to screen markets for potential as a basis for segmenting markets and for identifying specific segments.

3. Marketers face the dilemma of whether to segment the market based on a country-by-country basis or global segment basis. The key is to find a variable(s) that describes the global segment. Recent research suggests that convenience (for shopping) and membership of trading blocs, for example, may form the basis for global segments.

4. General market data, such as demographics and political and economic data, have proved poor predictors of actual behaviour. Psychographics have proved better, as have global descriptors like the grey market for the over-50 age group, but these have not yet been fully validated as useful alternatives.

END-OF-CHAPTER CASE STUDY The challenge of retailing British wine

FROM THE VINEYARD TO YOUR DOOR

British wine drinkers are consuming more than ever; the UK is the biggest wine-importing nation by value in the world. Wine consumption has increased 40% over the last ten years. Yet the increase is among established, not new, drinkers. By far the biggest purchasers of wine are the 35–50 year-olds. Wine in the UK is sold either 'off trade' or retail, or 'on trade', i.e. in the same place where it is purchased, for example public houses and wine bars. The former is by far the largest sector, accounting for 80% of sales. During 2002 the off-trade sector increased by 5.9% in volume and 6% in value. In 1995, the Old World producers (France, Germany, Italy, and Spain) accounted for two-thirds of UK wine consumption, but this has fallen to 35% and is still falling. Due to huge promotional programmes, wines from the New World surged in the same period, Australia (a 23.4% increase), the USA (17%), and South Africa (26.5%). France remains the largest source of wine with 30% market share. Bulgaria, Chile, Argentina, and Hungary add to the list of wine-exporting countries.

White wine sales have decreased due to the demand in red wines. These are popular with 18–24 year-olds. Different regions of the UK have different patterns of consumption. This is accounted for by different tastes and sub-cultures existing within the market segments (see Case Study Table 1).

The reasons for the pre-eminence of wine drinking in the UK appear to be many and varied. They can be grouped as internal and external variables.

Case Study Table 1 Wine drinking by region

Region	All users %	Heavy users %	Medium users %	Light users %
South East/East Anglia	73.0	28.4	28.1	11.5
South West	72.3	31.3	24.4	11.1
Greater London	64.9	30.0	21.1	9.5
East and West Midlands	64.8	23.0	26.5	10.7
North West	63.3	23.2	24.9	10.3
North	62.0	22.9	22.1	11.4
Yorkshire and Humberside	61.7	24.4	22.5	10.8
Wales	60.6	21.9	21.4	12.0
Scotland	57.5	23.5	22.3	8.1

Source: Based on data sourced at Mintel International Group Ltd. 2003.

Internal factors

- Culture—a willingness to accept a wide choice of wines from around the world. However, in the UK wine consumption is not homogeneous. Women generally prefer white and men prefer red. Younger people prefer smooth wines and older people stronger ones.

- Social—individuals seek opinions and share values and beliefs about wine from other people before purchase, particularly from friends and then family. Wealthier groups are inclined to buy more expensive wines and less wealthy groups, cheaper ones. Wine drinking is linked with food consumed, i.e. white wine and fish.

- Age—the highest consumers of wine are the 35–64 year-old category while the 18–34 age group shows little interest in wine consumption.

- Psychological—the motivation to purchase wine is dependent on the perception of the buying situation, e.g. a more expensive wine for special celebrations and expensive wines if out to impress. Wealthier groups will be willing to buy more expensive wines to transfer their status. Heavy users prefer to drink wines from the New World and medium and light users from the Old World.

External factors

- Product—taste is a key factor in the purchase of wines. Packaging is relatively important but only from a preservation of the product and information point of view. Country and region of origin, the colour, and brand are important determinants, rather than a brand *per se*. The 'regular' bottle shape is preferred.

- Place—supermarkets and grocery stores are seen as the main outlets.

- Price—price is a critical factor. Consumers do the 'price/quality' relationship in wine purchase, the more expensive wines being associated with higher quality.

- Promotion—many promotional means are used to communicate about wines in the UK, including retailer promotions, television, and the press. Specialist mail retailers Laithwaites (www.laithwaites.co.uk) often team up with other companies, such as the Sunday Times Wine Club (www.sundaytimewineclub.co.uk) and Nectar (www.nectar.com) in the UK for cross-promotional activities. Word-of-mouth and peer communication/recommendation are two of the most effective methods. Wine journalism does not have much effect.

The factors affecting UK wine consumption are depicted in Case Study Figure 1.

As can be seen from this case, the factors affecting wine consumption in the UK are many and varied. Importers and sellers of wine from non-domestic countries face a challenge if they are to find a niche in this segmented and crowded market.

Source: Perez (2004).

Case Study Figure 1 Factors affecting British wine consumption

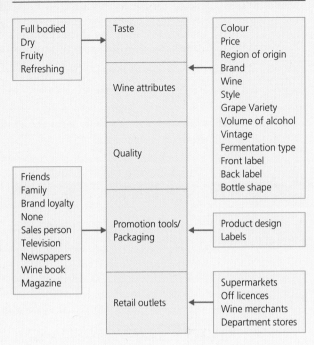

Case discussion questions

1 Identify and classify the variables affecting wine purchasing in the UK into bases for segmenting the UK wine market.

2 As a potential new wine entrant in the UK market, describe the market research needed in order to come to a decision on whether to enter. How would the data be used to 'fine' and 'coarse screen' the potential market?

3 What alternative means could be used to classify the wine consuming segments in the UK other than those described in the case? How would you go about identifying and classifying such alternative segments?

END-OF-CHAPTER EXERCISES

1 Why is it important to the success of global marketing operations that marketers segment global markets?

2 Describe the role market research plays in identifying and describing potential global marketing opportunities.

3 Discuss the argument that it is better to segment markets on a global market segment basis than a country-by-country basis.

4 Critically appraise the recent attempts to describe global market segments on the basis of single descriptors, e.g. 'convenience' for consumer shopping.

DISCUSSION AND EXAMINATION QUESTIONS

1 Critically discuss the role of marketing research and the marketing information system in the identification and description of potential market opportunities and market segments.

2 Examine the arguments for and against the use of country-by-country versus global market segment descriptors as bases for market segmentation. Provide evidence to support your arguments.

3 Critically assess the criteria, both internally and externally, for selecting potential market opportunities/segments.

FURTHER READING

Bryman, A. and Bell, E. (2006), *Business Research Methods,* Oxford: Oxford University Press.

Doole, I. and Lowe, R. (2008), *International Marketing Strategy: Analysis, Development and Implementation,* 5th edn., London: Thomson Learning, Chapter 4.

Hollensen, S. (2007), *Global Marketing: A Market Responsive Approach,* 4th edn., London: Pearson Education, Chapters 5 and 8.

Jeannet, J. P. and Hussey, H. D. (2004), *Global Marketing Strategies,* 6th edn., Boston, MA: Houghton Mifflin, Chapters 5 and 6.

Saunders, M., Lewis, P., and Thornhill, A. (2006), *Research Methods for Business Students,* 4th edn., Harlow: FT/Prentice Hall.

REFERENCES

Aaker, J. (1997), 'Brand Personality Dimensions Framework', www.valuebasedmanagement.net/methods_aaker_brands_persoanlity_framework.htm (accessed on 03/03/2004).

Aurifeille, J.-M., Quester, P. G., Lockshin, L., and Spawton, T. (2002), 'Global vs. international involvement-based segmentation: a cross-national exploratory study', *International Marketing Review,* 19(4), 369–86.

Brechin, E. (2002), 'Reconciling market segments and personas', *The Cooper Journal,* www.cooper.com/journal/2002/03/reconciling_market_segments_and_personas.html (accessed on 20/10/2008).

Burt, S. and Gabbott, M. (1995), 'The elderly consumer and non-food purchase behaviour', *European Journal of Marketing,* 29(2), 43–57.

Buxel, H. and Walsh, G. (2003), 'Customer-specific marketing on the internet on the basis of customer profiles', *Yearbook of Marketing and Consumer Research,* 1, pp. 68–88.

Carrigan, M. (1998), 'Segmenting the grey market: the case for fifty-plus "lifegroups"; *Journal of Marketing Practice: Applied Marketing Science,* 4(2), 43–56.

Churchill, G. A. (2002), *Marketing Research—Methodological Foundations,* 8th edn., Fort Worth, TX: Dryden Press.

Doole, I. and Lowe, R. (2004), *International Marketing Strategy: Analysis, Development and Implementation,* 4th edn., London: Thomson Learning.

Fuat Firat, A. and Shultz II, C. J. (1997), 'From segmentation to fragmentation: markets and marketing strategy in the postmodern era', *European Journal of Marketing,* 31(3\4), 183–207.

Gilligan, C. and Hird, M. (1985), *International Marketing,* London: Routledge.

Gonzalez, A. N. and Bello, L. (2002), 'The construct "lifestyle" in market segmentation', *European Journal of Marketing,* 36(1/2), 51–85.

Harrel G. D. and Keifer, R. D. (1993), 'Multinational market portfolio in global strategy development', *International Marketing Review,* 10(1), 60–72.

Hasan, S. and Katsanis, L. (1994), 'Global market segmentation strategies and trends', in Kayak, E. and Hasan, S. (eds.), *Globalization of Consumer Markets: Structures and Strategies,* New York: International Business Press, pp. 47–63.

Hofstede, F. Steenkamp, J. B. E. M., and Wedel, M. (1999), 'International market segmentation based on consumer–product relations', *Journal of Market Research,* 31(1), 1–17.

Hollensen, S. (2007), *Global Marketing: A Market Responsive Approach,* 4th edn., London: Pearson Education.

Janetzko, D. (1999), 'Statistical Applications in the internet', quoted in Buxel, H. and Walsh, G. (2004), 'Customer-specific marketing on the internet on the basis of customer profiles', *Yearbook of Marketing and Consumer Research,* 1, 68–88.

Johanson, J. and Vahlne, J. E. (1990), 'The mechanism of internationalisation', *International Marketing Review,* 7(4), 11–24.

Kale, S. H. and Sudharshan, D. A. (1987), 'A strategic approach to international segmentation', *International Marketing Review,* Summer, 60–70.

Keegan, W. J. (1989), *Marketing Management,* London: Prentice Hall.

Kashani, K. (1989), 'Beware the pitfalls of global marketing', *Harvard Business Review,* Sept.–Oct., 91–8.

Lesser, J. A. and Hughes, M. A. (1986), 'The generalizability of psychographic market segments across geographic locations', *Journal of Marketing,* 50 (January), 18–27.

Lindridge, A. and Dibb, S. (2002), 'Is "culture" a justifiable variable for market segmentation: a cross-cultural example', *Journal of Consumer Behaviour,* 2(3), 269–86.

Luqmani, M., Yavas, U., and Quraeshi, Z. (1994), 'A convenience-orientated approach to country segmentation: implications for global marketing strategies', *Journal of Consumer Marketing,* 11(4), 29–41.

Malhotra, N., Agarwal, J., and Baalbaki, I. (1998), 'Heterogenity of regional trading blocs and global marketing strategies: a multicultural approach', *International Marketing Review,* 15(6), 476–506.

Perez, R. (2004), 'A Study of the British Wine Consumer Behaviour in the Retail Sector', unpublished MBA dissertation, University of Derby, UK.

Rundh, B. (2003), 'Rethinking the international marketing strategy: new dimensions in a competitive world', *Marketing Intelligence and Planning,* 21(4), 249–57.

Saunders, M., Lewis, P., and Thornhill, A. (2006), *Research Methods for Business Students,* 4th edn., Harlow: FT/Prentice Hall.

Scheuing, S. and Carter, S. (1998), 'An On-line Real-time Approach to the Strategic Marketing Planning Process', Proceedings of the 3rd International Conference on the Dynamics of Strategy, University of Surrey, 23–24 April.

Schiffman, L. and Kanuk, L. (2004), *Consumer Behaviour,* 8th edn., Englewood Cliffs, NJ: Prentice-Hall.

Valentine, C. F. (1989), 'Blunders abroad', *Nations Business,* March, 54, 56.

Woolley, L. (2004), *'Chasing the Consumer: The Evolution of Coffee Culture to the Changing Consumer Lifestyle and Society',* unpublished independent studies, Derbyshire Business School, University of Derby, UK.

online resource centre

Visit the companion website to this book for lots of interesting additional material, including self-assessment questions, internet exercises, and links for each chapter:

http://www.oxfordtextbooks.co/uk/orc/lee_carter2e/

PART ONE CASE STUDY Daimler AG (Mercedes-Benz)—The Place of an Icon in Global Marketing

Daimler AG (formerly DaimlerChrysler AG), known globally by its world famous marque, Mercedes-Benz, is a German-based (Stuttgart) manufacturer of luxury cars, trucks, and coaches. It also provides financial services through its Daimler Financial Services arm. It is the world's oldest automobile company. Its origins lie with the invention of the world's first car by Karl Benz in January 1886. A few months after Benz's achievement, Gottlieb Daimler (the parent company is named Daimler AG after him) and engineer, Wilhelm Maybach (today the Maybach marque is Mercedes' most expensive production car) also produced an automobile, and in 1901 the first Mercedes vehicle was produced. In 1926, the merging of Karl Benz's and Gottlieb Daimler's companies resulted in the Daimler-Benz company, which produced the first Mercedes-Benz vehicles. Mercedes-Benz has, over the years, introduced many technological and safety features that have become common in modern vehicles, including 'radar-assisted' front hazard warning, which applies the vehicle's brakes automatically. Today, Mercedes is one of the largest (thirteenth largest manufacturer) and most respected vehicle manufacturers in the world (with its distinctive three star badge) and is consistently appearing in the world's top ten brand tables. The company also holds major stakes in aerospace group EADS, auto engineers McLaren Group, Japanese truckmaker Mitsubishi Fuso Truck and Bus Corporation, and US car maker Chrysler Holding, LLC.

There are 13 major players in the European automobile industry. These are BMW, DaimlerChrysler, FIAT, Ford of Europe, General Motors Europe, MAN Nutzfahrzeuge (mainly commercial vehicles), Porsche, PSA Peugeot Citroïn, Renault, Scania, Volkswagen (VW), and Volvo. While these are European-based, outside Europe giants such as Toyota and Nissan have manufacturing plants in Britain. SEAT, Audi, and Skoda all are part of the Volkswagen Group. The UK has virtually lost its car manufacturing capacity, while Germany, with Mercedes, VW, and Porsche, remain strong. Most of the European manufacturers are global in operation, with subsidiary manufacturing and component parts being located throughout the world. For example, Mercedes has a manufacturing plant in South Africa. Nearly one-third of all passenger cars are manufactured in the EU, with manufacturers producing 18.6 million passenger cars, trucks, and buses per annum, representing 27% of world wide vehicle production (2006 figures). The industry has a technological edge with €20 billion (in 2006) being spent on Rand D, i.e. 4% of turnover.

Motor manufacturing in Europe is a source of worker mobility, and social and cultural activity. More than 12 million families depend on automobile employment, with 2.3 million direct jobs and 10 million being employed in related sectors, e.g. electrics, panel suppliers, tyres, etc. Vehicle taxes delivered €41.6 billion in government revenues annually in 2006, 3.5% of GDP.

Today Mercedes-Benz has a full range of passenger, light commercial, and heavy commercial vehicles. Production is on a

global basis. The Smart brand of city cars has also been part of the Mercedes-Benz Group since 1994. The brand came out of a cooperation with Swatch watches and Mercedes-Benz. Today the city car is all that remains of a range that included a five-door saloon and a roadster. Traditionally, Mercedes-Benz has operated in the luxury car market segment, and though this is still true of its bigger range of passenger cars, the Maybach, R and S Class, it has made considerable inroads into the 'small', 'economy', and 'sports utility' markets. The 'A' Class saloon (known more famously for failing the so-called 'Moose Test' when it first came out) is a much better car now and is competing, along with the 'B' Class saloon in the MPV/small car market, with the likes of VW and its 'Golf' range. The new 'C' Class saloon is giving BMW and the Ford Mondeo a run for its money. The 'E' Class saloon, in many ways the epitome of the Mercedes-Benz marque, is a smooth and highly competent performer, pitched against the bigger BMWs, Jaguars, and Volvos. With a huge range of engines, both diesel and petrol, and a host of extras to meet any customer demand, the car range is very impressive. Service and back-up is essential to any car manufacturer and Mercedes-Benz has that in its dealership network. Today's Mercedes come equipped with a host of extras, which, in the past, had to be purchased separately, considerably adding to the cost.

Daimler's product range includes:

(a) Mercedes-Benz cars—Mercedes-Benz (A, B, C, G, GL, CLK, CLS E, ML, R, S, SL, SLK, SLR models), Mercedes-Benz-AMG, Maybach, and Smart. Passenger car sales in 2007 were 1,293,200 units. Mercedes-Benz easily leads car sales in the luxury car market. Sales to the USA were relatively static but strong in Eastern Europe (+37%), China (+64%), and South Africa (+14%). The Mercedes-Benz cars division, with the brands Mercedes-Benz, AMG, Smart, and Maybach, sold a total of 111,100 vehicles in May 2008, a decrease of 4% from the 116,000 units sold in May 2007. However, unit sales over the first five months of the year rose 10% at the division, reaching the new record level of 548,800 vehicles (January–May 2007: 500,500). In May, the Mercedes-Benz brand delivered 98,100 new passenger cars, or 5% fewer than the 103,400 units recorded for the same month last year. At the beginning of 2008, there was a total of 493,200 customers worldwide.

(b) Commercial vehicles, trucks, buses, and components— Freightliner, Mercedes-Benz truck group, Mitsubishi Fuso, Thomas Built Buses, Sterling Trucks, Western Star, Detroit Diesel, Mercedes-Benz, Daimler Buses, Orion Bus Industries, Setra, Mercedes-Benz vans. Daimler sold 467,000 heavy, medium, and light trucks in 2007. There was a drop in demand from the USA, Canada, and Japan due to stricter emission regulations. Sales to Europe and Latin America rose 13% and Trucks Asia-Mitsubishi Fuso in particular rose on the back of strong exports to Indonesia. In 2007, Daimler sold 39,000 complete Mercedes-Benz, Setra, and Orion buses and chassis worldwide.

(c) Daimler Financial Services—Mercedes-Benz, Mercedes-Benz Financial, Daimler Truck Financial. Business for financial services in 2007 stood at €27.6 billion. Growth stimulus came mainly from Europe, Africa, and Asia.

The two companies which were merged to form the Mercedes-Benz brand in 1926 had both already enjoyed success in the new sport of motor racing throughout their separate histories—both had entries in the very first automobile race from Paris to Rouen in 1894. Mercedes has continued to take part in sports car racing. On several occasions Mercedes-Benz has withdrawn completely from motorsport for a significant period, notably in the late 1930s and in 1955 after a spectator was killed in the Le Mans 24-hour race. It was not until the late 1980s that Mercedes-Benz returned to frontline competition, returning to Le Mans and sports car racing with Sauber.

Mercedes-Benz is currently active in three forms of motorsport: Formula One, Formula Three, and DTM. In Formula One, the company part owns Team McLaren, and has supplied the team with engines since 1995. Its current drivers include Lewis Hamilton of the UK, who made a stunning Formula One debut in 2007, finishing second in the Championship in his rookie season. The Team McLaren has brought success in world championships. The collaboration with McLaren has been extended into the production of road-going cars, such as the Mercedes-Benz SLR McLaren.

At the 2007 Frankfurt motor show, Mercedes-Benz showed seven hybrid models, including the F700 concept car which combined hybrid drive with the innovative DiesOtto engine.

Since its inception, Mercedes-Benz has had a reputation for quality and durability. Objective measures, such as J.D. Power (www.jdpower.com) passenger car surveys, demonstrated a downturn in reputation in this area in the late 1990s and early 2000s. By 2005, Mercedes temporarily returned to the industry average for initial quality, according to J.D. Power. In J.D. Power's Initial Quality Study for the first quarter of 2007, Mercedes showed a dramatic improvement by climbing to fourth place, surpassing quality leader Toyota and earning several awards for its models. One reason for this was bringing 'in-house' the manufacture of several hundred components, e.g. some 2,000 components for the E Class saloon.

Mercedes-Benz automobiles are available at dealerships in over 130 countries and their work fleet (trucks and commercial vehicles) are available from a group of dealers worldwide as well as from the factory direct. Purchasers of passenger cars have a delivery option whereby instead of picking the car up from a dealer, they can visit the factory in Germany and can pick up their car personally. As with several European brand automobiles, Mercedes has offered a European delivery option for American customers purchasing of a Mercedes-Benz automobile. The dealership network underwent a considerable change in the early 2000s, responding, in part, to a change in European legislation, which envisaged the end of 'tied and exclusive' dealer networks.

A feature of the UK car industry over the last 20 years has been the importation of cars direct from the continent by customers at a cheaper price than the cars could be sourced in the UK through the authorized dealers. One way to combat this was for UK dealers, allegedly, not to honour the full warranty because the cars were slightly different from the UK spec. Other means of distribution has been by specialist car importers and web-based dealers (e.g. www.jamjar.com), which again offer a price dividend.

Car manufacturers spend billions of pounds on every form of advertising and promotion annually. 'Above the line' expenditure includes, TV, bill board, radio, and online advertising to name a few, and 'below the line' expenditure includes dealer trade-in and manufacturer's 'cash backs'. Sponsorship (e.g. Mercedes Formula One), and other public relations exercises also form part of the integrated communications mix. Personal selling is also key, as few buyers will purchase such a relatively high value and 'emotional' item as a car solely by 'above the line' exposure. The purchase can often be family-oriented, so an opportunity to test drive, see the car, and talk to a salesperson is an essential part of the process. For company purchases and fleet operators such as car hire firms, reliability, price, and economy are essential, so 'negotiation' and 'relationship building' are key.

Manufacturers pay attention to the need to continuously monitor the market for trends and customer satisfaction. Mercedes is no exception, paying close attention to customer feedback, especially when it is a new sale, via an after-sales questionnaire, dealer call backs, newsletters, etc.

Key data for the group for the period 2005–07 can be found in Table 1.

Table 1 Key figures Daimler, 2005–07 (£ millions)

	2005	**2006**	**2007**
Revenue	95,209	99,222	99,399
Operating profit (loss)/EBIT	2,873	4,992	8,710
Operating margin	3.0%	5.0%	8.8%
Dividend per share	1.50	1.50	2.0
Total assets	228,012	217,634	135,094
Equity ratio	15.1%	16.5%	26.8%
Net assets (annual average)	48,313	48,585	39,187
Number of employees (annual average)	296,109	277,771	271,704

Note: EBIT stands for earnings before interest.
Source: Daimler AG (2007).

The sale of the Chrysler, with whom Daimler merged in 1998, may well have had an effect on the figures, along with other factors (see section on Selected Markets 'The United Kingdom', 'Emergent markets', and 'other' below). DaimlerChrysler was founded in 1998 when Daimler-Benz (1926–98) merged with the US-based Chrysler Corporation. The deal created a new, and what seemed at the time a synergistic, entity, DaimlerChrysler. However, the buyout failed to produce the transatlantic automotive powerhouse deal-makers had hoped for, and on 14 May 2007 DaimlerChrysler announced that it would sell Chrysler to Cerebrus Capital Management of New York, a private equity firm that specializes in restructuring troubled companies. DaimlerChrysler had reportedly approached other carmakers and investment groups as potential buyers of Chrysler in early 2007. General Motors was reported to be a suitor, while VW, the Renault–Nissan auto alliance, and Hyundai Motor Company had said that they were not interested in buying the company. The terms saw Daimler pay Cerebrus US$650 million to take Chrysler and associated liabilities off its hands. This represented a huge difference between the US$36 billion paid to acquire Chrysler in 1998. Of the US$7.4 billion purchase price, Cerebrus Capital Management will invest US$5 billion in Chrysler Holdings and US$1.05 billion in Chrysler's financial unit. The de-merged Daimler AG received US$1.35 billion directly from Cerebrus but directly invested US$2 billion in Chrysler itself.

On 4 October, 2007 a DaimlerChrysler Extraordinary Shareholders' Meeting approved the renaming of the company. From 5 October, 2007, the company has been titled Daimler AG. The US company adopted the name Chrysler LLC when the sale completed on 2 August 2007. The original agreement stated that Cerebrus would take an 80.1% stake in the new company, Chrysler Holding LLC. DaimlerChrysler changed its name to Daimler AG and retained the remaining 19.9% stake in the separated Chrysler.

Throughout most of its history, Chrysler has been the third largest of the 'Big 3' US auto makers, but in January 2007, DaimlerChrysler, excluding its luxury Mercedes and Maybach lines, also outsold traditionally second place Ford, though it was still behind General Motors and Toyota. Lee Iacocca of Chrysler was once one of the 'icons' of the 'academic' literature, renowned for trans-

forming Chrysler. Chrysler reported losses of US$1.5 billion in 2006. It then announced plans to lay off 13,000 employees in mid-February 2007, close a major assembly plant, and reduce production at other plants in order to restore profitability by 2008.

The merger was contentious, with investors launching lawsuits over whether the transaction was the 'merger of equals' that senior management claimed or actually amounted to a Daimler-Benz takeover of Chrysler. The merger was also the subject of a book *Taken for a Ride: How Daimler-Benz Drove Off with Chrysler* (2000) by Bill Vlasic and Bradley A. Stertz.

Another issue of contention is whether the merger delivered promised synergies and successfully integrated the two businesses. As late as 2002, DaimlerChrysler appeared to run two independent product lines. Later that year, the company launched products that appear to integrate elements from both sides of the company, including the Chrysler Crossfire, which extensivly used Mercedes parts.

The average age of a European car fleet is eight years, and about 70% of cars on the EU roads are less than 10 years old. The average annual distance travelled by a car in the EU is 15,000 km, 30% of which is diesel powered. Car density per 1,000 inhabitants in Western Europe is 508, and in new member states it is 186 (2005 figures).

The following details give a selection of three car markets: one 'mature' market (the UK), the other where some 'emergent' markets are doing well, and finally, 'other' world markets which are a mixture of 'emergent' and 'mature' markets.

(a) The United Kingdom

The UK new car market has eased in recent years, after a peak of 2.579 million units in 2003. The market is now contested by many marques. Fuel-efficiency is a big issue. The new commercial vehicle market is strong and stable, due to a robust demand for vans, but with some major distortions. The UK vehicle output has declined, but will recover over the next 18 months.

In 2006 the UK new car market eased to 2.345 million units, its lowest level since 2001. The market was expected to be flat in 2007. The CV market almost matched the 2004 peak of just under 390,000 units in 2006. The LCV market accounts for almost 85% of all CV registrations and remains robust. HCV registration growth has stalled on the downside of major regulatory changes in 2006.

(b) Emergent markets

Global markets are very positive, largely driven by Asian demand, in particular in China and India.

Table 2 Market size and growth—New car registrations (in 000s)

Market	**2001**	**2006**	**% Change**
ASEAN	1,167	1,893	62%
India	818	1,750	114%
Ukraine	75	371	395%
Russia (light vehicles)	1,272	2,129	67%
MERCOSUR	1,778	2,389	34%

Source: VDA, *Global Insight,* ACEA (2007/8).

(c) Other markets

Table 3 Market size and growth—New car registrations (in 000s) in other selected world countries

Market	2004	2005	2006	% Change
Europe	19,680	20,928	21,446	2.5
USA	17,298	17,445	17,048	−2.3
Brazil	1,581	1,715	1,928	12.4
Japan	5,853	5,852	5,740	−1.9
South Korea	1,131	1,184	1,218	2.9
China	4,574	5,314	6,560	23.4
Rest of the World	1,503	1,557	1,709	3.1

Source: ACEA, VDA (2007/8).

The next ten years holds a somewhat uncertain future for the world's vehicle manufacturers. The leading industry giants, such as US car maker General Motors, has been posting annual loses of billions of dollars for a few years now. Despite computer-assisted design and manufacture (CAD and CAM), outsourcing, and the use of new materials, keeping the costs of manufacture down is a struggle. To say, 'things could be better' would probably be an accurate description in the short term.

In traditional and mature markets, such as Europe and the USA, certain forces are at work, making life uneasy for the large manufacturers. The USA has its own product specification and safety laws, requiring product changes for exports there. For Europe, cutting CO_2 emissions and recycling is a priority for the EU bureaucrats and legislation. The current financial credit crisis is making consumers think twice about their new car purchases and so used cars are becoming an increasing attraction. There is simply too much 'metal' about in the markets. Added to this is the rapidly increasing cost of fuel, which is now becoming a major factor for car buyers. Competition from the Eastern manufacturers, such as Toyota, Nissan, Mazda, and the

Table 4 Daimler AG market share

Vehicle	2007	2006
Mercedes-Benz cars		
Europe	4.6	4.6
USA	1.6	1.5
Daimler Trucks		
Med Heavy—Europe	21.7	22.0
Heavy—NAFTA	32.7	33.2
Med-Heavy—Brazil	30.7	31.9
Mercedes-Benz Vans—Europe	16.4	16.0
Buses—Western Europe	26.0	25.4

Source: Daimler AG (2007).

Koreans (e.g. Kia and Hyundai), offering unbelievable five and seven year warranties as well as 'fully loaded' vehicles, are a constant threat. Coupled with this is the eco argument, especially the one on the need to find quickly an alternative to fossil fuels, hence the development of hybrid cars, like the Toyota Prius. These forces, among others, are a headache for car makers planning new models, for, in spite of the many advantageous computers have brought in shortening the 'concept to market' time, a new model can still take up to two years or more to see the light of day.

New markets, like the burgeoning demand from China and India, should, in theory, provide some respite for the industry. But even here, there are problems. China, for example, has not yet fully implemented its WTO commitments across a wide range of areas, causing real concern. China is also creating non-tariff barriers. On top of such restrictions, the eco lobby is busy targeting countries like China and India to cut their carbon dioxide emissions and pollution. Of course, in all markets, the 'anti-globalization lobby' is omnipresent.

Daimler AG, with its diverse product line, is facing these future challenges, on all fronts.

Sources:
Daimler AG (2007), *Annual Report*, www.access.daimler.com (accessed on 14/06/2008)
European Automobile Manufacturers' Association (2007/08), Industry Report 2007/8,(ACEA), www.acea.be (accessed on 18/06/08)
German Association of the Automotive Industry (VDA), www.vda.de. *Global Insight*, www.globalinsight.com.
Vlasic, B. and Stertz, B. A. (2000), *Taken for a Ride: How Daimler-Benz Drove off with Chrysler*, New York: HarperCollins.

Discussion questions

1 Identify the global marketing 'environmentals' in this case. Show, with reference to Daimler's product markets, how it might monitor and meet these environmental challenges in the next three years.

2 Using appropriate concepts and techniques:

(a) Describe the basis on which Daimler segments its current markets and suggest alternative bases, fully justifying your answer.

(b) Conduct a new market opportunity analysis for Daimler's range of products over the next three years.

3 With reference to the information available in the case and your observations, identify the social and ethical issues which are impacting on Daimler's global market operations currently and in the future. How should the company respond to these issues?

PART TWO
The Development of Global Marketing Strategies

The focus of Part Two is on the development of global marketing strategies which would enable organizations to successfully pursue opportunities and compete in today's global marketplace. There are eight chapters in this part dealing with the important areas that confront global marketers when developing and planning for global marketing.

The first chapter of this part considers the decisions associated with the development of a market entry strategy. In doing so, this chapter examines the theories of internationalization, market entry strategies, modes of market entry, the market entry process and the factors which dictate the decisions in organizations. Subsequent chapters address the issues, challenges, and methods of operationalizing the marketing mix decisions globally. Chapter 8 discusses the important issue of creating, developing, and maintaining competitive advantage in global operations, focusing on contemporary issues such as 'cooperating to compete' and the effect of the World Wide Web. Other chapters address issues of product and brand management, global services marketing, management of global communications, marketing channel management, pricing decisions, and managing global relationships. Cross-cultural services marketing is a highly contemporary, important issue for organizations, especially in competing in post-industrial society. Developing and maintaining a competitive knowledge asset in this sector is a vital priority it companies are to deliver value-added, unique customer experiences. Chapter 13 is dedicated to the increasingly important issue of relationship management. Forging long-term and profitable relationships with all stakeholders is just as important in global operations as it is in domestic operations, with the added complications of distance and culture.

In each of these chapters, the concepts and basics of implementing these mix elements are covered but, more importantly, the current changes and challenges affecting the international marketing mix, in a global context, are addressed. To facilitate effective learning, all chapters are illustrated with contemporary research, examples, and case studies to reinforce the theory and issues highlighted.

CHAPTER SEVEN
Market Entry Strategies

Chapter overview

Chapter Introduction 210

The International Marketing Environment and its Effect on Market Entry Strategies 211

The Process of Internationalization 213
 The Uppsala or incremental approach (stage model) 214
 The industrial network approach (network model) 219
 The bargaining power approach 221
 Born global 223

Other Theories of Internationalization 224
 Transactional cost analysis theory 224
 Eclectic theory or contingency theory 224
 The agency approach 225
 The business strategy approach 225

International Business Models 226
 Subscription business model 226
 Razor and blades business model 226
 Multi-level marketing 226
 Network effect 226
 Monopoly 227
 Cutting out the middleman 227
 Auction 228
 Online auction 228

Clicks and mortar 228
Loyalty business model 228
The service quality model 228
Collective business system 229
Industrialization of services business model 229
Low-cost carriers (LCCs) 229
The transformational model 229

Market Entry Modes 230
 Export mode entry 232
 Agents and distributors 232
 Intermediate modes of entry 232
 Contract manufacturing 232
 Licensing 233
 Franchising 233
 Joint ventures/strategic alliances 233
 Management contracting 233
 Hierarchical modes of entry 233
 Foreign divestment: exit from a foreign market 234

The Electronic Marketplace 235

Marketing Strategy and Mode of Entry 235

Chapter Summary 238

Learning objectives

After studying this chapter, the reader will be able to:

- consider the different theories of internationalization and their effect on market entry strategies;
- examine the factors to be considered in the choice of market entry strategies;
- describe and discuss the different types of market entry mode;
- examine some of the critical strategic considerations in market entry.

Management issues

The management issues that arise from this chapter include:

- With reference to the different forms of internationalization, what are the implications for the management and marketing of your business?

- What factors affect the choice of different market entry methods? Which method gives your organization maximum strategic advantage?

- What are the strategic considerations in considering different forms of internationalization and their effect on market entry?

Chapter Introduction

Internationalization and market entry are inextricably linked (Whitelock, 2002). As we shall see, the form of internationalization and its impact on market entry is a key strategic decision in globalization. Consider the following quote by Liu and Cheng (2000: 227):

> It has been argued that pioneer marketers gain competitive advantage by building brand loyalty faster, attaining distribution and customer awareness more easily, and, in turn, achieving higher market shares in the long run (Gultinan and Paul, 1994; Marthi et al., 1996). Some scholars, on the other hand, have expressed reservations on the absolute superiority of pioneer strategy over the follower strategy in terms of its high initial market costs and questionable effectiveness (Golder and Tellis, 1993; Lilien and Yoon, 1990; Sullivan, 1991). Kerin et al. (1992) attribute these contradictory findings to a number of contingency factors, such as demand uncertainty, entry scale, advertising intensity, entry time of followers, and the scope of the economy.

This encapsulates the difficulty of the international market entry decision. There are so many unknowns to contend with that the task is not only to maximize the returns but, in so doing, assess, choose, and put in place a strategy which minimizes the risks. Alternatively, with the advent of IT, particularly the deployment of advanced information and communication technologies (ICTs), the task of entering the international market has been made much easier, in theory at least. In 2000, the Group of Eight (G8 countries) announced that 'IT empowers, benefits and links people the world over'. The United Nations (2000) High Level Panel on Information and Communication Technologies endorsed the view that when firms in developing countries connect to global networks, they should be able to compete on a more even footing.

The expectation, therefore, is that the expansion of global communications and the internet must provide a new means for small and medium-sized enterprises (SMEs) and developing countries, for example, to benefit from participation in the global economy. But as Mansell (2001) points out, this all depends on whether the technology merely replicates the distribution of market power, and the ability of developing countries to evolve the appropriate institutions to support electronic commerce. This includes not only physical institutions like order fulfilment, but a trained workforce and management.

The International Marketing Environment and its Effect on Market Entry Strategies

The effect of the international 'environment' on the international market entry decision and operation is critical. This is illustrated in Fig. 7.1.

When considering market entry strategy and mode, the effect of the marketing 'uncontrollables' in the environment must be carefully considered. While the organization may have carefully considered its own well-developed market objectives and means to achieve them, these may have to be tempered after consideration of socio-economic, political, legal, competitive, technological, and ethical factors. While tools like Porter's (1985) five forces analysis may be useful in this regard, an environmental audit would be desirable (see Chapter 16). At the very least, a risk analysis should be carried out. After this, and similar analyses, the effect may be considered minor, neutral, or major, and the appropriate adjustments to strategy and entry mode made. This is exemplified later in the chapter, particularly in the cases described by Liu and Cheng (2000) and Colla (2003). Monitoring the effects of the environment must not be purely a 'one-off' event conducted before entering a market. It should be an ongoing activity as changes in the environment are often sudden and unexpected. For example, while the use of agents or distributors may be the most effective mode of market entry initially into a developing country, as the country adopts a more widespread usage of the internet (change in the technological environment), a switch to the internet may be more economic and controllable from the firm's, and more convenient from the customer's, point of view. Changes in the environment may be picked up in a number of ways, including a relatively sophisticated marketing information system to sales force feedback. The environmental factors to be considered are shown in Table 7.1. They will vary by product type, consumer or business-to-business, and service type.

Fig. 7.1 The effects of the international market environment on the market entry decision

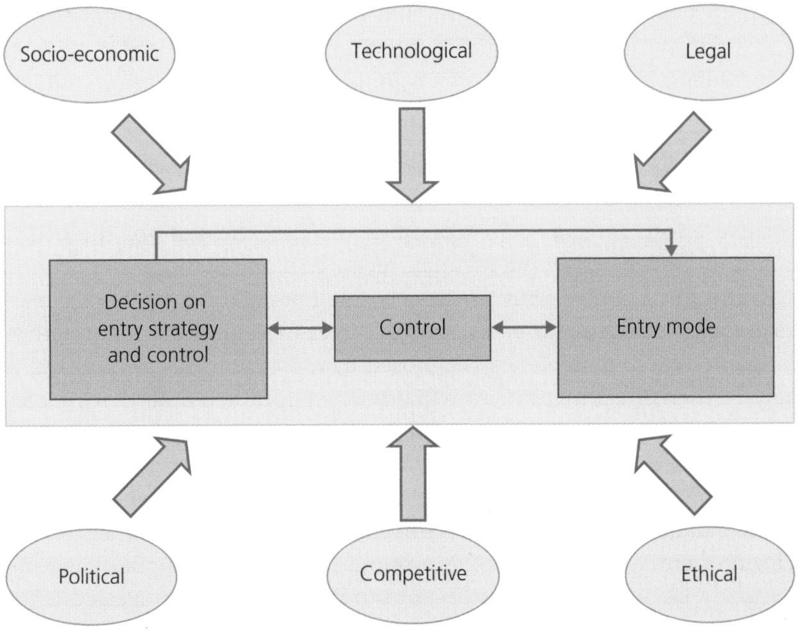

Socio-economic · Technological · Legal · Decision on entry strategy and control · Control · Entry mode · Political · Competitive · Ethical

Table 7.1 International marketing environmental factors to be considered in international market entry decisions

Marketing Environmental Factors	Description
Socio-economic	State of market development
	Population size, growth, density, concentration, disposable income, age distribution, urbanization and economic activity, inflation rates, economic activity, and state of infrastructural development, including communications
	Geographical dispersion of consumers
	State of distribution system development and structure
	Social organization
	Climate
	Ethics
Political	Terms of entry and doing business
	Political leaning of government
	Climate for investment
	Stability of government
	Attitudes to international investment
Legal	Local business laws
	Intending entrants' domestic laws
	International laws
Competition	Industrial and commercial structures, size, and concentrations
	Leader or follower
	Level and type of domestic and international investment
	Transaction costs and margins
Currency	Exchange fluctuations and conversion rates
	Exchange transfers
	Exchangeability of currency
	Inflation and deflation

The factors described in Table 7.1 will have a considerable effect on the international strategy decision and entry mode. As the examples show, these factors can have a negative or positive effect. After a socio-economic analysis, the state of the infrastructural and distribution system development may mean that population is concentrated into urban areas, and this, coupled with a relatively small population, may make market entry by in-country agents and distributors, and/or direct exporting, more attractive than direct investment. Where markets are diagnosed as risky, after, say, a 'political' and 'currency' analysis, then direct investment will not be an option. Similarly with a technology analysis. If a market has a relatively undeveloped or limited internet connectivity, this form of direct selling as an entry mode will not be an option immediately but may become one later on as the network coverage widens. A competitive analysis is important. Again, as the examples will show, the concentration of direct competitors may mean that one form of entry strategy is not an option, but another may be. The Korean automobile company Daewoo (www.daewoo-auto.com) entered the congested UK market in

Fig. 7.2 Market entry strategy

Theoretical Approach	Process of Internationalization			
	Stages models	Networks	Bargaining power	Born global

Corporate Level	International Business Model		
	Subscription	Multi-level marketing	Network effect
	Razor and blade	Monopoly	Auction
	Disintermediation	Clicks and mortar	Loyalty business

Country or Market Level	Market Entry Modes		
	Direct or indirect exporting	Joint venture	Franchise
	Strategic alliance	Acquisition or merger	Foreign direct investment

the 1990s using a unique entry strategy. It did not use franchised dealers, but an 'open' showroom distribution network linked to Halfords (www.ukshops.co.uk), the bicycle and car accessory retailers.

International market entry methods are predicated on a chosen business model. However, before a business model and a specific entry mode are chosen, it is necessary to understand the underlying theories in the internationalization process. The following sections, therefore, discuss the different processes of internationalization, the various business models, and the impact of both on modes of market entry. Fig. 7.2 illustrates the three levels in the development of a market entry strategy, i.e. process of internationalization, business model, and market entry modes.

The Process of Internationalization

There are a number of theories to the process on internationalization. The most popular four theories—i.e. stage models, networks, bargaining power, and born global—are discussd in detail below and reference is made to the others. These approaches are often classified as either 'stage' or 'network' models of internationalization. The principle stage models are those known as the 'Uppsala School' and the 'network' models.

The Uppsala or incremental approach (stage model)

The stage models of internationalization originated from the Nordic School in Sweden. It has 'its theoretical base in the behavioural theory of the organization (Cyert and

March, 1963; Aharoni, 1966) and Penrose's (1959) theory of the growth of the organization, and is seen as a *process* in which the enterprise gradually increases its international involvement' (Johanson and Vahlne, 1990: 11). The Nordic School has looked for solutions not to problems of why organizations go overseas but rather to problems of how foreign direct investment takes place in terms of the underlying forces of a process and the overall behavioural pattern. Internationalization is considered a learning process based upon a gradual accumulation of experiential knowledge in foreign markets, and it acknowledges the lack of complete information and the importance of risk or uncertainty in managerial decision-making. It is hence frequently termed the *gradualist* or *incrementalist* approach.

The Uppsala model of internationalization, which centred on a longitudinal case study of four Swedish companies involved in international operations with over two-thirds of their turnover coming from overseas, is perhaps the most significant contribution within the Nordic School. It conforms to the Nordic School of thought that interprets the internationalization phenomenon as a process of gradual development over time and emphasizes the sequential nature of the experiential learning obtained by means of a series of steps which reflect a growing commitment to foreign markets. According to Johanson and Valhne (1990: 11), 'a distinction is made between *state* and *change* aspects of internationalization' (added emphasis). The state aspects of internationalization are *market commitment* and *market knowledge*; the change aspects are *current business activities* and *commitment decisions*. Market knowledge and market commitment are assumed to affect decisions regarding commitment of resources to foreign markets and the way current activities are performed. Market knowledge and market commitment are, in turn, affected by current activities and commitment decisions (see Fig. 7.3).

The Uppsala model explains two patterns in the internationalization of an organization. One is that an organization's engagement in a specific foreign market develops according

Fig. 7.3 Internationalization process of organizations

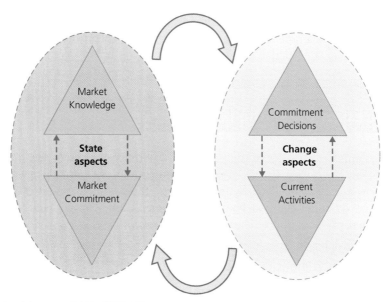

Source: Based on Johanson and Vahlne (1990: 12).

to an establishment chain, i.e. at the start no export activities are performed in the market, then export takes place via independent representatives, later through a sales subsidiary, and eventually overseas production may follow.

Stage 1: No regular export activities.

Stage 2: Export via independent representatives (agents).

Stage 3: Establishment of an overseas sales subsidiary.

Stage 4: Overseas production/manufacturing units.

The second pattern is that organizations enter new markets with successively greater psychic distance in terms of cultural, economic, and political differences and also in relation to their geographical proximity (Johanson and Wiedersheim-Paul, 1975).

The work of Johanson and Wiedersheim-Paul was further developed and refined by Johanson and Vahlne (1990, 1997), who confirmed the establishment chain proposition, that a strong link could be traced along a chain of internationalization stages from export activity through agents and sales representatives to the formation of a manufacturing subsidiary in the overseas market.

Other behavioural models in later empirical studies have reported findings that are consistent with those of the Uppsala School (Bilkey and Tesar, 1977; Cavusgil, 1980; Reid, 1981; Czinkota, 1982). As summarized by Rialp and Rialp (2001: 59):

'while they conform to the notion that SME (small and medium-sized enterprises) internationalization is an incremental process, they argue that organizations would progress through a series of specific *stages* reflecting changes in the attitudinal and behavioural commitment of managers and the organization resulting in international orientation. These models argue that the perceptions and beliefs of managers both influence and are shaped by incremental involvement in foreign markets. As a consequence, their organizations gradually pursue active expansion into more unknown markets and become increasingly committed to international growth'.

This pattern explains the internationalization decision as an innovation-adoption for the organization.

The difference between these innovation-related internationalization models is the number of stages and the description of each stage provided. Typically, an organization begins with no or little exporting and then progresses through a specific number of stages before becoming a committed international organization. The works of Bilkey and Tesar (1977), Cavusgil (1980), Czinkota (1982) and Reid (1981) represent some of the most prominent studies explaining the internationalization process from an innovation-related perspective.

All the models present an incremental stepwise or stage approach to internationalization and generally confirm the relevance of cultural and psychological distance. They see that the incremental pattern of the organization's internationalization process is attributed to two reasons: (1) the lack of knowledge, especially experiential knowledge; and (2) the uncertainty associated with the decision to internationalize. This pattern is perceived here to help explain the internationalization process of SMEs with rather limited experience abroad, where an increase of commitment of resources abroad is adopted only after the uncertainty is reduced as a result of gaining experiential knowledge.

Rialp and Rialp (2001) summarize the stepwise approach as a pattern of slow and evolutionary development in time rather than a rational and/or deliberately planned sequence, where the incremental nature of learning becomes a key factor through the course (apparently predetermined) of a sequence of successive stages. The central feature of this approach lies, therefore, in assuming that a large part of the capabilities required by organizations for internationalizing their activities are acquired through a process of sequential and accumulative learning, in the form of a series of phases that reflect a higher commitment to foreign markets (Melin, 1992).

The Uppsala or incremental approach is characterized by organizations developing their activities abroad in an incremental fashion as their knowledge develops. This development is based on the concept of 'psychic' knowledge where organizations expand first into markets that are physically close and then into more distant markets as their knowledge develops. Knowledge, in this case, is 'experiential' knowledge rather than objective knowledge gained through the objective study of international marketing. This concept is evidenced by German, US, and Japanese organizations (see Johanson and Vahlne, 1990, 1997). However, Buckley et al. (1987) have questioned the 'familiar' export through sales subsidiary mode, citing that many organizations use a mixed entry mode strategy. This has been more recently substantiated by Quinn and Alexander (2002) who studied the international expansion strategies of companies such as Marks and Spencer (www.marksandspencer.co.uk) and British Home Stores (UK) (www.bhs.co.uk) and hypermarkets like Casino (France), which used a variety of entry modes. Root (1987) suggests that companies manufacturing high technology products may use licensing as the first mode of market entry, e.g. pharmaceutical products. Johanson and Vahlne (1990) give three exceptions to their incremental approach in response to increased market knowledge. One is where resources are large, e.g. car manufacturers such as Toyota (www.toyota.com) and Nissan (www.nissanmotors.com), which built plants directly in the UK. Another is where market conditions are stable and homogeneous market knowledge can be gained in ways other than by experience, e.g. European grocery discounters Aldi (www.aldi.com) and Netto (www.netto-supermarket.de). One exception is where conditions are similar and allow generalization across markets. South African Breweries' expansion into neighbouring Botswana, Namibia, Zambia, Malawi, and Zimbabwe is a good example of this.

For SMEs the incrementalist approach based on initial cautious exporting may be a wise move, although e-commerce possibilities may allow a more ambitious approach, e.g. Amazon (www.amazon.com) books. Coviello and McCauley (1996), Lindqvist (1998, in Rundh, 2001), and Bell (1995) have written on the internationalization process by small companies. Lindqvist (in Rundh, 2001) suggested that the pace and pattern of international market growth and choice of entry mode are influenced by close relationships with customers. Bell (1995) suggested that relationships with clients and suppliers, for example, appear influential in both market selection and mode of entry for small companies. Johanson and Mattson (1988) suggest that a company's success in entering new international markets is more dependent on position in the network and relationships within current markets than on market and cultural factors. Rundh (2001) attempted to describe and analyse factors that influence the international market development in SMEs and to analyse factors of importance in the companies' international market behaviour. He found that the most important reason for starting an international development by exporting different products was management judgement that it was possible to reach growth and profit possibilities outside the domestic market. A small home market within a specific product area was another reason for building relations with customers outside the domestic confines. Other reasons were the management's genuine interest for export business, unique products or technology, and the possibility of spreading risks. The SMEs in Rundh's research chose to start their international activities by different market entry modes in different markets. This was affected by the market structure, the competitive situation, and the product itself.

Contrary to expectations, the SMEs in Rundh's study used a variety of entry modes, including direct export, established agents, and even setting up their own production facilities. The size of the market and proximity to the customer were important factors in this decision. Where the product was complex and where the risk of competitors getting an insight into the production process was high, the SMEs chose a direct export method. Rundh also found that the obstacles of entering the international markets were both internal, such as risk aversion behaviour by top management, but also external, such as economic distance, language, and culture. The difficulty of finding suitable channels of distribution and the service levels demanded by the customers were also barriers. The ability to build international networks was a significant factor in exporting. Good contacts within the industry were important but lack of experience sometimes forced the necessity of depending on networks.

Czinkota and Johnston (1981) showed that the decision to start internationalization could be a step-by-step development; others, such as Young et al., (1989, in Rundh, 2001), that other factors were important *vis-à-vis* their business or competitive strategy. According to Rundh (2001), this process can be threefold: to research and analyse markets to work up in a certain product area; to evaluate alternative market entry mode; and to choose a possible/available entry mode. The choice of entry mode can depend on the company's resources, product characteristics, number of presumptive customers, and market structure. In order to build up different local export markets, SMEs may have to adapt their marketing strategy to the requirements of local customers. To be competitive, the SME has to meet demand from the local market in relation to technology and product quality. To be able to customize the product, long-term relationships need to be built with local customers. This requires commitment from top management and, often difficult to acquire, resources. Rundh concludes that incrementalism is one way for SMEs to internationalize, but a company's knowledge of international business is dependent on employees' experience within the company and experience from other companies as well as the transfer of knowledge from previous international excursions. While incremental entry may be possible, Rundh's research showed that SMEs chose their entry mode based on the individual situation. Top management's total engagement is also necessary, as is the flexibility to adapt the product to local conditions and choose other entry modes as determined by the product/market. Chapter 9 provides further discussion on standardization and adaptation global product strategies. Establishing long-term relationships (although demanding and complex) is essential in an ever-changing international environment. Knowledge of the competitive changes in the marketplace is an essential, but not an easy, task.

The sceptical view of the stage models

The overwhelming support for the stage models of an organization's internationalization is perhaps self-explanatory. However, the models have also attracted a considerable amount of criticism and a number of empirical studies have challenged their basic proposition.

Firstly, the stage models of internationalization seem to ignore the market- and organization-specific characteristics that account for the organization's export development process and behaviour (Reid, 1981, 1984). Intra- and inter-organizational variability in resource endowments, market opportunities, and managerial philosophies could have an impact on an organization's internationalization. For example, in a study of 24 UK companies operating in three different industrial sectors (i.e. large marine diesel engines, motor vehicle components, and telecommunications equipment), Turnbull (1987) found that the stage theory of internationalization inaccurately portrayed the expansion of these companies, as companies tended to show significant differences in their patterns of expansion according to the industrial sectors they were in. His study concludes that a company's stage of internationalization is largely determined by the operating environment, industry structure, and its own marketing strategies.

THE DIGITAL IMPACT Trading on eBay

eBay (www.ebay.com) is one of the world's most successful internet auction sites and the largest e-commerce site. Its reach is global, and is an example of the new ways of selling and distributing products and services. Founded ten years ago by a French-born systems developer, Pierre Omidyar, it now has a value of some £30 billion. Omidyar advertised on the internet for plastic spring-loaded Pez sweet dispensers for his collector girlfriend and obtained a huge response. Now the site receives 121,500 hits a minute, 175 million searches and 10 million bids every day. Set up in the UK in 1999, the site has 6 million users and accounts for one-third of all UK internet traffic. There are some 21 million items on sale with 3 million new ones offered each day. Goods are traded in more than 45,000 categories and include clothes (worth over £1 billion in 2004), alcohol, credit cards, snails, mailing lists, firearms, and items of celebrity and novelty value such as the Mercedes once owned by the Manchester United football icon, Sir Bobby Charlton and a Margaret Thatcher handbag sold for £103,000. eBay employs 300 people to minimize fraud but the traders also self-regulate. In 2001, 10,000 people in the USA gave up their jobs to become eBay traders, in 2004 the number had risen to 150,000.

Secondly, the underlying assumption of the stepwise progression and forward motion of the stage models does not always hold true as many organizations accommodate both forward and backward movements without obvious problem (Cannon and Willis, 1981). Furthermore, organizations may miss out particular stages to accelerate the process. Depending on how favourable the global investment climate is at a given time, an organization may choose to deepen its involvement in or temporarily withdraw from international business activities as it sees fit.

Lastly, many organizations may not necessarily follow the incremental stepwise but prefer a 'shorter route' strategy for internationalizing their business activities. For instance, in a study undertaken by Hedlund and Kverneland (1985) on strategies of Swedish organizations in Japan, almost half of the 18 organizations investigated went directly from a sales agent to a manufacturing subsidiary, omitting the intermediate step of a sales subsidiary. The internationalization process of these organizations seems to suggest that the establishment and growth strategies on foreign markets are changing towards more direct and rapid entry modes than those implied by theories of gradual and slow internationalization process.

These findings are supported by Millington and Bayliss's (1990) study of 50 UK manufacturing companies operating in the EU designed to test the stage models of the internationalization process. They found that over half of the samples in their study had 'made a jump' from low stages of internationalization process, e.g. licensing and direct exporting, to becoming a fully established overseas manufacturing operation. The results did not support a narrowly incremental view of the internationalization process, with a stepwise process being the exception rather than the rule. Rather, they appeared to support a life-cycle model based on the international development of the organization. In the early stages of international development the organization relies on market experience and incremental adjustment. As the degree of international experience increases, this process is superseded by formal planning and systematic search for international opportunities. In the final stages of development, international experience may be transferred across markets and between products, thereby enabling organizations to leapfrog the incremental process within markets.

The industrial network approach (network model)

The network perspective of internationalization represents some of the more recent and significant research efforts to conceptualize the phenomenon of internationalization. Of particular concern to this perspective is how organizations make use of business networks as a mechanism to internationalize their activities. It proposes that organizations in industrial markets establish, develop, and maintain lasting business relationships with other business parties in the market. These relationships are connected by a network which develops as a consequence of the interaction between organizations. The specific organization is engaged in a network of business relationships comprising a number of different parties—e.g. customers, customers' customers, competitors, supplementary suppliers, suppliers, distributors, agents, and consultants as well as regulatory and other public agencies (Johanson and Vahlne, 1990). Fig. 7.4 is an example of this so-called 'network effect' of business relationships, which begins within the domestic markets. Organizations eventually are able to internationalize their activities by leveraging these networks of suppliers, customers, distributors, and so on.

Most organizations are initially engaged in a network of business relationships which is primarily domestic. Through the domestic network, the organization eventually develops business relationships in networks in other countries, which can be achieved: (1) through the establishment of positions in relation to counterparts in national nets that are new to the firm, i.e. international extension; (2) by developing the positions and increasing resource commitments in those nets abroad in which the organization already has positions,

Fig. 7.4 The network effect

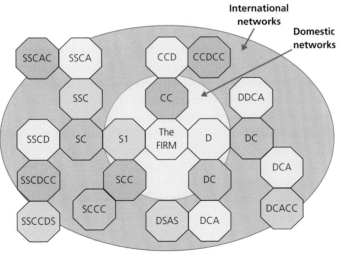

Key:
S = supplier
D = distributor
C = customer
A = agent

i.e. penetration; and (3) by increasing cooperation between positions in different national nets, i.e. international integration (Johanson and Mattsson, 1988). The emphasis of this approach is on the organization's relative position in the network. At each point the organization has certain positions which characterize its relations with other organizations. They are the results of cumulative activities by the organizations and its counterparts in the network, and define the base for development possibilities as well as constraints of the organizations in present and future activities. An organization's position changes over time (through marketing activities) as relationships are established, maintained, developed, and broken in order to secure profits, growth, and long-term survival. Such relationships give the organization access to important resources for the sale of its products and services (Barrett and Naidu, 1986).

Blankenburg's (1992) study on foreign market entry is regarded as one of the major attempts to conceptualize internationalization from a network perspective. She points out that the network approach to foreign market entry assumes activities and processes in the network are multilateral as a consequence of interactions between network actors. Moreover, the resources of the organization within the network are to a large extent seen as an inter-organizational matter. Organizations' resources are subject to adaptation, making them dependent on each other, which simultaneously reduces the control over their own resources and gives them some control over the resources of other network actors. Since no organization exists in a vacuum, one can presume that every organization is more or less connected to its surrounding actors, who are in turn connected to others. If these connected relationships consist of international actors, they would serve as a mechanism or middleman that brings the organization into new foreign markets.

It is perhaps important to note that the network approach to internationalization does not necessarily refute the existing views concerning the incremental nature of the stage models of internationalization. Indeed, it aims to rectify some of the deficiencies of stage models by widening the traditional concept of internationalization and tries to provide new ways of thinking about the complex nature of organizations' internationalization.

As summarized by Johanson and Mattsson (1988: 310), 'both the network approach and the stage models stress the cumulative nature of the organization's activities. While the stage models focus on the internal development of the organization's knowledge and other resources, the network approach offers a model of the market and the organization's relations to that market'. From a network perspective, internationalization is a process of forming relationships in new international markets which may involve building on existing relationships in the home and/or host country. It provides an alternative view to the traditional stage models and empowered it to generate explanations for the emergence of new, more flexible, and innovative market entry strategies, and the acceleration of the international involvement of organizations.

The industrial network approach (Whitelock, 2002), addresses the major weakness of both the Uppsala and the eclectic paradigm in that both see the international decision as one taken by an individual(s) within an organization. According to Johanson and Mattsson (1988) the characteristics of the firm and the market are important in the internationalization process. According to the International Marketing and Purchasing Group (IMP) (quoted in Whitelock, 2002) 'the industrial system is a network of firms engaged in the production, distribution and use of goods and services through which lasting business relationships are established, developed and maintained'. Four variables are seen as important in the interaction process: the elements and processes of interaction; the characteristics of the parties involved (buyers/suppliers); the atmosphere surrounding the interaction; and the environment in which the interaction takes place (Whitelock, 2002).

Hence, in the industrial network approach, the organization will need to evaluate its position in relation to customers as well as the environment of the target market in relation to competition. However, this model need not be solely applicable to business-to-business products. As we see in Chapter 14, horticultural produce exporters use a complex network of growers and numerous agents to get their produce from the growing site to the market. This is illustrated in the Relationship Perspective.

The bargaining power approach

The bargaining power (BP) approach sees the choice of entry mode as the outcome of negotiations between the organization and the government of the host country. Other than a few pieces of research (see Gomes-Casseres, 1990), BP has not been as well developed from a theoretical standpoint compared to the stage and network models. The assumptions certainly fit the Far Eastern perspective on international expansion. Taylor et al. (2000)

THE RELATIONSHIP PERSPECTIVE Zambian high-value horticultural exports

Any perishable produce export relies on smooth cooperation between growers, cool-chain logistical support providers, transport (particularly air), and government. A breakdown in any of these partners in the network means a loss of crop and, potentially, large amounts of money. This is not just in lost crop sales but possibly damaging law suits for breach of contract. As the network theory of internationalization suggests, these players rely on each other to fulfil their individual roles precisely. Moreover, the relationships between the principals in the process (buyers and sellers) are affected by the environment in which they operate, and this is largely under the control of governments. It is government which must provide the infrastructurals (roads) and business environmentals (exchange and tax facilities) which facilitate the transaction.

In Zambia, while there may be some large-scale producers of high-value horticultural products (babycorn, mangetout, etc.), a proportion of produce is provided by small outgrowers. These rely on the government and donors to provide extension services and credit (although the latter is now mainly privatized) in order to obtain seed, fertilizer, tractor power, and growing know-how. Before any produce is shipped, the seller must obtain a contract from a supermarket like Tesco or Asda. Armed with this contract, the seller must either grow or have grown (by outgrowers) produce to meet the contract in terms of quantity, quality, and hygiene requirements (known as phytosanitary requirements, which are covered by strict EU regulations which govern packaging, labelling, endorseable pesticides, and herbicides, etc.). These requirements are usually enforced by government officials or a government agency. Once the produce is harvested, it must be transported to a packhouse for quality checks, weighing, grading, and packing. From the packhouse, produce is carried to the airport where it will await uplift in refrigerated conditions. This

facility may be provided by the growers' association, like the Zambian Export Growers Association (ZEGA), or contractors. Air uplift facilities must be available, chartered, and booked in advance. Produce is then packed for air transport, uploaded, freighted to the UK, unloaded into the UK logistical system, warehoused, and delivered to the retailer. All this must take about 24 hours in order for the product to stay fresh. There is also an army of support services facilitating the process—insurance agents, freight forwarders, contract agents, banks, accountants, clerks to check the statutory paperwork for the EU and Zambian government, currency exchange facilities, credit facilities, farm workers, input providers (seed, fertilizers), market researchers, etc. After the deductions for facilitation, the producer, on average, receives about 10–15% of the final selling price, but with this industry providing vital employment and foreign exchange, it is worth the risk.

Source: Carter (1991).

found that BP fitted the context of Japanese multinational development. They found that it was more aligned to Japanese business practice in that the theory assumes both parties are looking to negotiate an outcome in their long-term interests (Yip, 1996). The focus of bargaining power theory involving negotiation is also consistent with the competitive declaration that has often been ascribed to Japanese firms. Taylor et al. state that BP starts from the premise that an organization has a natural preference for a high-control mode of entry since this is the most desirable outcome in terms of the organization's longer-term ability to dominate a foreign market. However, the organization may be forced to settle for a lower control mode of entry if it has low bargaining power. They identified eight factors which played a role in the foreign market entry mode decisions by Japanese companies, and some of these have echoes in the business strategy approach. The factors are:

1. The stake of the company.
2. The stake of the host country.
3. The need for local contribution to the venture.
4. The riskiness of the investment.
5. The intensity of the competition for the investment.
6. The level of resource commitment by the company to the foreign market.
7. Host government restrictions.
8. The size of the company.

The authors found that five of the above factors were important in the investment decision. First, when the host country perceives a significant stake in attracting investment, Japanese companies are likely to negotiate a full ownership arrangement, e.g. Toyota and Nissan car plants in the UK. Secondly, Japanese Multinational Corporations (MNCs) tend to opt for high control methods when the risk of doing business in the host country is high. Western MNCs are likely to use low control modes such as licensing and franchising. The third factor is resource commitment. When resource commitment is high, Japanese companies are less likely to negotiate for a high control mode of entry, so they go for joint ventures or licensing. Government restrictions are the fourth factor which plays a significant part in the entry mode of Japanese businesses. When restrictions are high, such as local content, foreign exchange control, or ownership level, Japanese companies are unlikely to negotiate for a high control entry, thus resorting to joint ventures, etc. This is certainly true of Japanese investment in Malaysia, where the Malaysian government insisted on a high local involvement and financial stake, an example being Mitsubishi's (www.mitsubishicars.com) involvement in Proton (www.proton.com) car manufacture. Finally, the need for local contribution is a significant factor in Japanese investment. Surprisingly, when Japanese MNCs have more need for local contribution they seek a high control mode to enter the host country. One explanation for this finding is that Japanese MNCs may attach greater importance to overseeing production, marketing, and distribution operations when a local contribution is needed. Fear of becoming too dependent on local firms or loss of proprietary knowledge may contribute to the desire for greater control. Another explanation may be Japanese long-term thinking. One of the most fascinating findings is that a tenet of BP, suggesting that the need for greater involvement by local parties decreases the bargaining power of the MNC which, in turn, leads to negotiation of a low control of entry mode, may have to take account of different power perceptions that exist across cultures. It may be the case that the need for a local contribution increases the bargaining power of Japanese MNCs by allowing the host country to perceive a greater locus of control than is the reality, thus perceptually limiting the power of the MNC in the foreign country.

Born global

In recent years, a number of authors (e.g. Jolly et al., 1992; Knight and Cavusgil, 1996; McAuley, 1999) have begun to examine the phenomenon of 'instant international' or 'born global' organizations in a number of sectors (Fillis, 2001) that do not conform to the traditional incremental patterns of internationalization. Instead, these organizations often have a global outlook and adopt a global approach to doing business from the beginning. In contrast to a typical domestic-based organization which usually starts exporting after they have achieved a foothold in their home markets, a 'born global' would begin exporting, collaborate with foreign partners and/or sourcing internationally, and derive a great proportion of their revenues from international sales within a short period of its inception (i.e. within two years).

The reasons behind this global pattern of growth in the number of born globals lie in the dynamic interrelationships between consumer preferences, changing manufacturing and information technology, and changing competitive conditions (Rennie, 1993: 48):

- Consumer preferences have shifted radically in the past two decades. Standard products have had their day; consumers are demanding specialized and customized products. As a result, niche markets have become an important source of opportunities for small organizations, which are usually quicker than their larger counterparts to adapt product offerings to meet emerging market needs.

- Until the 1960s, process innovations usually favoured large-scale operations that created economies of scale in production. With the advent of electronic process technology, SMEs are now able to compete with larger organizations on cost and quality—often with more flexibility.

- Developments in communications are affecting the boundaries between organizations. Large, vertically integrated organizations had a competitive advantage when information flows were expensive and slow. Using the latest telecommunications and computer technology, however, enables organizations of any size to manage business systems that extend beyond their own boundaries. The Japanese—whose car industry is a leading example—were among the first to adopt this approach.

- In a world where product life cycles are shrinking and consumer tastes change quickly, smaller organizations are often more adaptable and cost-effective, as they are not burdened with bureaucracy and high fixed costs.

Examples of born global are not confined to the high-tech sectors. In a study of 102 small Scottish arts and crafts businesses, McAuley (1999) found that these businesses have an international vision, an innovative product or service that is marketed through a strong network and tightly managed organization focused on international sales growth. Many 'have internationalized rapidly by developing international networks, offering adapted and customised products and generally being much more flexible and faster in their approach to business than their larger competitors' (Fillis, 2001: 777). Their patterns of internationalization once again defied the logics of the traditional stage models as 'they do not concentrate on the domestic market first, nor do they develop markets in psychologically close countries, nor is the process characterised by a steady, logical, controlled sequential progression' (McAuley, 1999: 80).

Growth in the number of born globals worldwide provides important implications for business practice as well as academic research. As the case studies show, the emergence of these organizations is not about particular technologies or sectors of the economy. Organizations which are born global or 'instantly international' are set up to exploit international market opportunities in almost any sector. In addition, SMEs, which are traditionally regarded as disadvantaged in internationalization due to limited size and resources, are playing an important role in this type of internationalization. While it is not possible to isolate a particular mechanism which these organizations use to globalize their activities, it is suggested that the forces of globalization—in particular, technological advances in communications and transportation; market convergence due to regionalism and harmonization of technical standards; and globalization of competition as a result of liberalization, deregulation, and privatization—may be promoting their development.

Other Theories of Internationalization

Transactional cost analysis theory

Transactional cost analysis theory (TCA) is based on the theory that an organization will internationalize if it can perform at a lower transaction cost than if it exported or entered into a contractual arrangement with a local partner. The underlying assumption is that markets are competitive and, therefore, that low control entry methods, like vertical integration, are favoured. When there are few suppliers, the costs associated with low control methods are increased, through the need for stringent negotiation and maintenance of contractural relationships, hence entry methods giving higher control are more favoured. The benefits of integration must be compared to the costs of integration. According to Whitelock (2002), TCA predicts that firms integrate when asset specificity is high, so as to retain control over the specific advantages they offer. Research has shown that TCA may not be applicable to non-Western economies like Japan. Transactional cost analysis theory asserts that the way in which institutions are structured within a country effects transaction costs and many East Asian economies have different institutional structures from those in the West (see North, 1981). Hill (1995) questioned the applicability of TCA to Japan because Japan's culture differs markedly from that of the West, particularly in respect of collectivism, group identification, loyalty, harmony, and reciprocal obligation, all of which reduce the cost of partnering. Taylor et al. (2000) also consider that the eclectic theory (or OLI—ownership, location, internationalization) of entry choice, advocated by Dunning (1988), is equally unacceptable. Taylor, et al. (2000) found in their study of Japanese foreign entry strategies that the Japanese tend not to adhere to the TCA model, instead favouring the bargaining power (BP) approach discussed above.

Eclectic theory or contingency theory

Eclectic theory, or contingency theory (Dunning, 1988), integrates many strands of international business theories. The theory is built on three factors: ownership specific, location, and internationalization. Researchers such as Li (1994) have confirmed a positive relationship between ownership-specific factors and internationalization. Dunning emphasizes the importance of location-specific factors as having a significant impact on non-production costs, i.e. transaction costs. These are now important as location-specific costs are rising faster than production costs. Ownership-specific factors include technology, marketing skills, financial and size variables. The ownership of a unique approach to car marketing partly explains the successful launch of Daewoo cars into the UK in the 1990s. Without owning a dealer franchise, Daewoo outsold its longer established rivals such as Malaysia's Proton by having a showroom where sales-people acted as consultants to the customer, without the commission-driven pressure to sell.

The agency approach

The agency approach to entry mode selection (Carney and Gedajlovic, 1991) is based on the principle of a contract where one party delegates to another. Franchises, licensing, joint venture, and alliances are examples. The decision is twofold—which mode to use to target a specific market and how to evaluate the performance of the agent. The first decision is informed via collection of relevant information and the second by writing a performance contract. Cross-cultural uncertainty may make both tasks difficult, especially aspects of gathering information and monitoring performance. This approach to the basis of entry mode selection has been subject to critical debate (see Senbet and Taylor, 1986) as most agency theory propositions have been based on the relative efficiency of only two modes of entry: licensing and direct investment. Agency theory and TCA are complementary approaches as both look at how functional relationships are organized efficiently and assume that both parties in the relationship are motivated by economic self-interest. Both explicitly incorporate different exogenous variables, i.e. asset specificity in the case of TCA and risk preferences in the case of agency theory. They differ in approach in that TCA concentrates on the transaction as the unit of analysis and agency theory on the individual agent. Agency theory has been used to describe the international expansion of banks (see Dunning, 1988)

The business strategy approach

The business strategy approach to internationalization is based on pragmatism, with the organization making trade-offs between the number of variables in its internationalization decision and the methods it adopts to do so. Reid (1984) contends that expansion strategies are based on contingency, i.e. an analysis of market opportunity, organizational resources, and managerial philosophy. Root (1987) and Turnbull and Ellwood (1996) believe that the market factors to be considered include market attractiveness, psychic distance, accessibility, and informal barriers, whereas the choice of organizational structure to serve the market includes an evaluation of international trading history, size, export orientation, and commitment.

The choice of entry strategy is a key decision because the choice of strategy will determine the entry method. An incorrect decision could result in a sub-optimal choice of entry mode and cause the organization to lose market opportunity and/or incur a financial penalty. Many companies are rushing to join the exodus from doing business in China, however there are many strategic factors to be considered. Liu and Cheng (2000), in a study on entering China's pharmaceutical market, identified that the health insurance system, distribution system, legislative system, and China's advertising policies were key factors to be added to the product- and firm-specific factors. Product-specific factors, such as product maturity, product technology, brand loyalty, and product demand, and organization-specific factors, such as company directives, company policy, marketing spending, and marketing channels, had an indirect effect on market entry. External environmental factors, such as government policies, the socio-economic situation, and the competitive situation, had a direct effect. Added to these factors were whether the pharmaceutical company was a 'pioneer' or 'follower'.

International Business Models

The sections above have discussed the necessary underlying theories of internationalization. This section discusses the second part of the market entry strategy, that of the choice of International Business Model. This is a strategic decision and the third step—the choice of specific mode—is an operational decision, flowing out of the choice of business model. The company has to combine and manage its physical and non-physical (e.g. management skills) capabilities to match the needs of the target market and achieve its objectives. It does this through the choice of a business model, which may change over time. It may, for example, choose an 'export' mode, which, as the organization grows in confidence in operating internationally, may change into a 'direct' mode. This change requires a different business model, organizational structure, and management style.

According to Osterwalder et al. (2005), a business model is a conceptual tool that describes the value that a company offers to one or several segments of customers and of the architecture of the firm and its network of partners for creating, marketing, and delivering this value and relationship capital, to generate profitable and sustainable revenue streams. It is the mechanism by which a business intends to generate revenue and profits, and involves selecting a core strategy and implementation. The literature suggests there are 15 established business models.

Subscription business model

The subscription model applies to companies that charge subscribers a fee, normally to view text or graphical information. A subscription model also applies to companies that provide services rather than information (Doherty, 2000). The subscription business model is a model that has long been used by magazines, book clubs, and record clubs, e.g. telephone companies, pay TV channels such as Sky (www.sky.com), and tow/rescue service companies such as the AA (www.theaa.com) or RAC (www.rac.co.uk).

Razor and blades business model

The razor and blades business model was introduced in the early 1990s by selling a 'master' product at a lower price. This business model originated from King C. Gillette (Adams, 1978), who used this business model for the sales of razor handles and disposable razor blades. Other businesses, such as cell phones, printers, and ink cartridges, are also running this particular business model.

Multi-level marketing

Multi-level marketing (MLM) refers to a marketing strategy where products are sold through a distributor structure that has many levels. The idea behind MLM is to grow a business through word of mouth. People are encouraged to introduce others to the business. In return, they get a commission on the sales made (Bloch, 1996). US direct selling company Nu Skin (www.nuskin.com) is a typical successful case for this model (see mini case illustration).

Network effect

The term 'network effect' was coined by Robert Metcalfe, the founder of the Ethernet. The value of the network was proportional to the square of the number of users. The concept allowed customers to share access to expensive resources, such as disk drives and printers,

MINI-CASE ILLUSTRATION Nu Skin Enterprises

Nu Skin (www.nuskin.com), originally founded in the USA by Blake Rooney in 1984, has extended its business model, products, and services to some 30 countries globally, including the USA, the UK, Norway, Malaysia, and China, and had a turnover in 2002 of around US$1 billion. The company uses the internet as a selling medium to sell directly, using individuals, to customers in three business areas: cosmetics, multivitamin supplements, and communications technology. Its internationalization strategy could, therefore, be agency-theory based, and its entry mode, direct. It also provides a fascinating example of how a large 'mother' corporation can support the development of numerous individual and small enterprises.

Nu Skin's mission statement is 'to be a force for good throughout the world by empowering people to improve lives with rewarding business applications, innovative products and an enriching and uplifting culture'. This mission is discharged 'by selling exceptional products, direct sales and by supporting distributors, stockholders, consumers and employees in ways that improve the quality of life'. It sets product and selling industry standards.

The company has three core businesses: Nu Skin, Pharmanex, and BigPlanet. Nu Skin has over 100 products in its range, covering body care, haircare, oral care, and aromatics. Some 100 million orders have been fulfilled and over 250 million products sold. In 1998, the Nu Skin Center for Dermatological Research was founded at Stanford University School of Medicine. The institute funds research into well-being and personal image. Pharmanex deals with multivitamin/mineral supplement lines, standardized herbal and general nutrition specialities, plus weight management, botanicals, and sports nutrition specialities. It has 50 staff scientists in its research and development team who work with 150 scientists around the world at universities such as Harvard, Stanford, Purdue, and Shanghai. BigPlanet is an innovative communications product and services for individuals and small businesses, making 'lives better' by getting people connected to the internet using industry- leading communications tools. This 'high tech', 'high touch' approach enables the power of person-to-person marketing and makes the internet work for the distributors/member accounts. In many ways, Nu Skin has created a powerful global network of consumers, distributors, and suppliers.

The company is also very socially aware. The Nu Skin Force for Good Foundation, for example, helps preserve indigenous culture, protect fragile environments, finance medical research into serious diseases, and provides humanitarian assistance. It provides funds for these works by donating a percentage of a product's sales to the cause.

Nu Skin uses individuals who wish to run their own business as their distributors as well as individual customers. The Nu Skin website provides details of how 'to become your own boss', or order products via the internet. This web-based enterprise creates distributor/member web accounts, of which there are some 600,000 independent distributors around the world, supporting their own personalized business. Nu Skin boasts that there are a number of advantages to becoming a Nu Skin Enterprise Distributor, including being provided with cutting-edge products and innovations, business tools, no inventory needs, virtually no bookkeeping, no overheads, and the backing of a sound US corporation. It also boasts one of the most generous compensation plans in the business.

Source: www.nuskin.com.

send e-mail, and access to the internet. The network effect causes a good or service to have a value to a potential customer dependent on the number of customers already owning that good or using that service. Telephones, fax machines, and computer operating systems are good examples to this business model.

Monopoly

Monopoly is characterized by an absence of competition, which often results in high prices and inferior products. This would happen in the case where there is a barrier to enrtry in an industry that allows the single company to operate without competition. In a monopoly, the market is controlled by one seller and the seller also manages the logistic and the price of the commodity or service. With virtually no competitors, profit is maximized. It allows only one company to benefit and ignores competition. While, in theory, monopolies do not exist, in practice, they are defined as companies with more than the combined market share of their rivals. De Beers in diamonds is an example.

Cutting out the middleman

In economics, disintermediation is the removal of intermediaries in a supply chain, known as 'cutting out the middleman'. Instead of going through traditional distribution channels, which have some type of intermediate (such as a distributor, wholesaler, broker, or agent), companies may now deal with every customer directly, e.g. via the internet. One of the end results of 'cutting out the middleman' is the drop in the cost of servicing customers directly. This model reduces transaction costs and processing time, and brings the producer or manufacturer of the product/service closer to the customer. Tesco is the typical example of this model as there is no barrier between Tesco and its customers.

Auction

An auction is an event in which goods or properties are sold by offering them up for a bid, taking bids, and then selling the items to the highest bidder. Being open to the public ensures a wide range of bids and this can sometimes lead to items fetching surprisingly high prices. In economic theory, an auction is a method for determining the value of a commodity that has an undetermined or variable price. Examples include Sotheby's.

Online auction

The online auction business model is one in which participants bid for products and service over the internet. The functionality of buying and selling in an online auction format is made possible through an auction software which regulates the various processes involved. For example, eBay, the world's largest online auction site, does not sell goods that it owns or produces. It merely lists and displays goods from individual sellers and facilitates the bidding and payment methods.

Clicks and mortar

The clicks and mortar business model started in the 1990s. The rise of the internet opened up opportunities for online trading. The businesses are not limited to either traditional stores or online trading, but make use of both. It is a business model in e-commerce by which a company attempts to integrate both online and physical presences. For example, an electronics store may allow the user to order online and immediately pick up their order at a local store.

Loyalty business model

The loyalty business model is used in strategic management. Company resources are employed so as to increase the loyalty of customers and other stakeholders in the expectation that corporate objectives will be met or surpassed. A typical example of this type of model is that the quality of a product or service leads to customer satisfaction, which leads to customer loyalty, which leads to profitability. Examples include car sales, education, air miles, and beauty and cosmetic products. In actuality, any other business model can become a loyalty business when their brand gains great success and is widely recognized by the public.

The service quality model

The service quality model emphasizes customer satisfaction. This assessment depends on prior expectations of overall quality compared to the actual performance received. If the recent experience exceeds prior expectations, customer satisfaction is likely to be high.

Customer satisfaction can also be high even with mediocre performance quality if the customer has low expectations. This occurs when a quality service is priced very high and the transaction provides little value for money. (Storbacka et al., 1994). The model then examines the link between relationship strength and customer loyalty. If customer satisfaction is high, it will increase the level of customer loyalty. Examples include cars and travel companies.

Collective business system

The collective business system is a business organization or association typically comprising relatively large numbers of businesses, tradespersons, or professionals in the same or related fields of endeavour, which share resources and information or provide other benefits for their members. Basically, there are two kinds of traditional collective business systems: the association and the cooperative. Both are non-profit organizations in which the members are companies in a common business pursuit. In contrast, a franchise is a for-profit collective business system. Examples include chartered accountancy firms, the Co-operative Society, and Spar supermarkets.

Industrialization of services business model

The industrialization of services business model is a business model used in strategic management and services marketing that treats service provision as an industrial process, subject to industrial optimization procedures. For example, IBM considers its business as a service business. Although it still manufactures computers, it sees the physical goods as a small part of its 'business solutions' industry.

Low-cost carriers (LCCs)

The low-cost carrier is an airline that offers low fares but eliminates most traditional passenger services (Whinston and Collins, 1992). With the advent of aviation deregulation the model spread to Europe in 1970s. The most notable successes are Ireland's Ryanair, which began low-fares operations in 1991, and easyJet which was established in 1995. As of 2004, low-cost carriers are now edging into Australasia, led by operators such as Malaysia's Air Asia (www.airasia.com) and Australia's Virgin Blue (www.virginblue.com.au) (Dresner et al., 1996).

The transformational model

The transformational business model is a new addition (Jiang, 2008). It is a dynamic model incorporating changes to management style, organizational structure, and the resultant changes to the business model, in response to internal and external forces over time. An example is retailing, where companies like McDonald's (www.mcdonalds.com) and Tesco have changed their business model as a result of experience in operating in different countries.

In looking at how Nu Skin, McDonald's, and Tesco developed internationally, Jiang (2008) proposes this more 'dynamic', model, which takes into account the changes in internal and external factors and the consequent change in management style, organizational structure, and business model. So, for example, Tesco, over time, has evolved its business model from one of 'franchise' to 'joint venture' in a single market and changed its management style and organizational structure accordingly.

Market Entry Modes

This section gives an overview of the third step in the market entry strategy, that of the choice of specific market entry mode. This section highlights some of the principal modes adopted by today's global marketers. The choice and importance of the market entry mode depends on a number of factors (see Fig. 7.5) (Tallman and Shenkar, 1994).

This analysis assumes a more incremental approach to the entry decision. As we shall see, incrementalism is not the only decision analysis method. Often, it may be necessary to take high risks for long-term gain and to adjust the entry mode for different markets. The factors influencing the choice and importance of entry mode are:

- What are the organization's corporate and market objectives, i.e. what does the organization wish to achieve in the market?

- How large is the organization and what are its financial, physical, and human resources?

- What does it already know about marketing in other countries and what is the extent of its expertise?

- What is the workforce attitude to marketing overseas and does it have the right skills or can it obtain them?

- What is the nature of the market, competition, product, consumer, and market coverage?

- What unique skills and competitive advantage does it possess?

- What is the organization's competitive advantage and can it be exploited?

Fig. 7.5 Factors influencing the choice and importance of market entry mode

Corporate and market objectives	Financial, physical and human resources	Previous experience and existing expertise	Workforce attitude
Nature of market	Unique skills	Competitive advantage	Timing—international life cycle
Level of involvement	Investment and market costs	Administrative requirements	Entry mode flexibility
Time horizon of payback	Levels of risk and control	Terms of entry	Ease of exit

- When is the right time to enter the market? At what stage is the market in the international life cycle?

- What is the level of involvement? The greater the involvement, the greater the likelihood of a choice of shared or wholly owned and controlled mode of entry.

- What are the investment and marketing costs? Higher marketing and investment costs will favour more contractual and marketing modes.

- What are the administrative requirements? Are they large or small? What type of administration? What functions should it provide?

- Is there any flexibility in the mode of entry, e.g. with agents, distributors, and retailers?

- What is the time horizon for payback? Japanese firms tend to take a longer-term view on this than Western firms (see Taylor et al., 2000).

- What are the levels of risk and control? The greater the political, financial, contractual, distributive, and cultural risk, the greater the likelihood of a marketing oriented or contractual mode of entry.

- Are there any tariff or non-tariff barriers, or other requirements affecting the mode of entry?

- Can contingencies be developed if things go wrong? Is there an easy exit?

The principal modes of market entry modes are given in Table 7.2.

Taylor et al. (2000) provide some definitions for the major types of entry mode. Exporting ('making it here and selling it there') is where a company sells its physical products, which are manufactured outside the target country, to the target country.

Table 7.2 Principal market entry modes, involvement, risk, and control

Marketing oriented	Contractual	Shared owned and controlled	Wholly owned and fully controlled
Direct exporting	Licensing	Joint ventures	Subsidiaries
• Agents	Franchising	Partial mergers and acquisitions	Representatives Assembly
• Distributors	Contract manufacture		
• E-commerce	Alliances		
• E-business	Management service contracts		
• Interactive TV			
Indirect exporting			
• Via domestic organizations			
• Trading companies			
• Export houses			
• Piggy backing			

Level of involvement

Low   High

Low   High

Level of risk and control

Licensing and franchising arrangements are non-equity associations between international companies and a party in a host country, involving the transfer of technology or total management systems (including the name) to that party, with a result that the party can operate a business to exactly the same standards and formats as the franchisor. Normally the franchisee pays a fee for the acquisition of the franchise and continuation. The USA has traditionally been the home of franchising. A joint venture is an arrangement where a firm is required to share equity and control of a venture with a partner from the host country. Full ownership of a facility in a host country is another entry alternative, where the parent company takes a full stake in the operation in the foreign country. Full ownership ('making it there and selling it there or elsewhere') may come about by taking over an existing business or investing in a new business in the host country. During the 'great fire sale' of Far Eastern companies (especially in Malaysia and Thailand), following the currency collapse of 1997–98 in the region, it was British and American firms that were the major buyers. Such a 'cheap' opportunity for market entry comes along rarely. (See Zhan and Ozawa (2001) for a full discussion of the financial crisis in Asia and subsequent foreign direct investment (FDI).)

The following provide some detail of the different entry modes, based on the work of Hollensen (2007). For further detail on entry modes, and the advantages and disadvantages of each mode, see Carter (2003) and Doole and Lowe (2008).

Export mode entry

Exporting is the most common mode for initial entry into international markets. Sometimes an order is received from a foreign country, or a domestic customer expands internationally and places an order for its international operations. Exporting may be the initial entry but it would gradually evolve towards more foreign-based operations. Export channels may take many different forms, such as agents, distributors, brokers, and piggyback, where one product is sold on the 'back' of another, e.g. computer installation and service.

Agents and distributors

Agents and distributors are direct export modes, in which the manufacturer or exporter sells directly to an overseas importer. Using existing business contacts and employing foreign nationals, they sell through either commission or profit margin. Brokers and piggyback are indirect export modes, in which the exporting manufacturer uses independent organizations located in the producer's country. The firm is not really engaging in global marketing because its products are carried abroad by others.

Intermediate modes of entry

These are different from the hierarchical entry modes in that there is no full ownership (by the parent firm) involved, but ownership and control are shared. In addition, it is different from exporting, because this model does not deal directly with businesses in foreign market. For example, contract manufacturing, joint venture, licensing, franchising all belong to this mode.

Contract manufacturing

Contract manufacturing enables the firm to have foreign sourcing (production) without having to make a full and final commitment. Management may lack resources or be unwilling to invest equity to establish a complete manufacturing and selling operation. For example, Benetton (www.benetton.com) and IKEA (www.ikea.com) rely heavily on the contractual network of small overseas manufactures.

Licensing

Licensing is distinguished from contract manufacturing in that licensing is a long-term agreement. In the process of licensing, a good proportion of the licensor's functions is transferred to the licensee. The licensee needs to pay a loyalty fee to the licensor. Coca-Cola (www.coke.com) and Pepsi (www.pepsi.com) are typical examples.

Franchising

Franchising is a method of selling a business service, often to small independent investors who have working capital but little or no prior business experience or knowledge (Saleh and Kleiner, 2005).

There are two major types of franchising: one is the product and trade name franchising, where suppliers make contracts with dealers to buy or sell products or product lines. The other method is business-format franchising, where the franchisee establishes a business and runs it profitably in the host country. In return, the franchisor receives a loyalty fee from the franchisee's turnover. The best-known global franchise companies are McDonald's, Burger King (www.burgerking.com), and Pizza Hut (www.pizzahut.com).

Joint ventures/strategic alliances

A joint venture or a strategic alliance is a partnership between two or more parties. In international joint ventures these parties will be based in different countries (Yang and Lee, 2002). The formal difference between a joint venture and a strategic alliance is that a strategic alliance is typically non-equity cooperation, meaning the partners do not commit equity into or invest in the alliance (Das and Kumar, 2007). The joint venture can be either a contractual non-equity joint ventures or an equity joint venture.

Management contracting

Management contracting emphasizes the growing importance of service and management know-how. Normally, the contracts undertaken are concerned with management operating/control systems and training local staff to take over when the contracts are completed. It is usually not the intention of the contractor to continue operating after the contract expires (Burstow, 1994).

Hierarchical modes of entry

With hierarchical modes of entry the firm completely owns and controls the foreign company. The degree of control that the head office can exert on the subsidiary will depend on how many and which value chain functions can be transferred to the market. It also relies on the responsibility and competence of the local subsidiaries. Companies may transfer or deliver some functions, such as marketing, sales, research, investment, and service to local subsidiaries, and then decentralize its structure.

Table 7.3 Comparison of the various entry modes

	Up-front Investment	Speed of entry	Penetration of market	Market control	Political risk	Competitive exposure	Managerial complexity	Potential ROI
Wholly owned	High	Slow	Medium	High	High	Low	High	High
Agent/ Distributor	Low	Possibly quick	Medium/ Low	Low/Nil	Low	Low	Low	Potentially High/Low
Representative	Low/ Medium	Low	Low	Low	Low	Low	Medium	Potentially high/Low
Acquisition	High	Quick	High	High	High	Low	High	High
Joint Venture	Medium	Quick	Medium/ High	Medium	Medium	High/ Medium	High	Medium
Licensing	Low	Medium	Medium/ Low	Nil	Low	High	Low	Low/High
Greenfield	High	Slow	Potentially high	High	Medium	Low	Medium	Low/High
Internet	Medium	Quick	Quick	High	Low	High	Low	High

Source: After Lasserre (2003).

There are two main methods: acquisition and greenfield (Root, 1987). Acquisition enables rapid market entry and often provides access to distribution channels. In saturated markets or those with substantial entry barriers, there is little room for a new entrant. In such circumstance, acquisition may be the only feasible way of establishing a base globally. A greenfield investment often has an objective of integrating operations across countries and as a base for further expansion. It takes longer to build plants than to acquire them. It is costly but after the operation at least full ownership is assured.

Table 7.3 summarizes the characteristics of the different entry modes.

Foreign divestment: exit from a foreign market

Many literatures have examined modes to enter to a foreign market, while few consider the exit strategy. There are various reasons for leaving a market, such as sustained losses, ethical issues, and resource relocation. Exiting a foreign market is not easy, but it is an option for companies that are rethinking and evaluating both the organization itself and the business environment. Tesco is a good example in that it withdrew from the Irish market as a result of an unsuccessful acquisition.

The Electronic Marketplace

As of 12 April 2008, there were 1,319,872,109 internet users worldwide (source: www
.internetworldstats.com). Despite the large number of dot.com collapses, some of which
were high profile, e-commerce and other forms of interactive media, such as television
shopping, are a growing market entry phenomenon. Electronic marketing or 'viral marketing'
as it is now called, is all-pervasisve. It is difficult to obtain accurate figures, but in 2006,
internet sales rose by 29% in the UK, to £130.4 billion compared to £101 billion in 2005.
Internet sales accounted for 6.5% of the value of all non-financial sector business sales in
2006 and accounted for 36.5% of the value of sales over all kinds of ICT, up from 33.1%
in 2005 (source: www.statistics.gov.uk). In e-commerce, books (www.Amazon.com), air
tickets (www.easyJet.com.), food (www.Asda.com), holidays (www.firstchoice.com), auction
sites (www.ebay.com), insurance (www.saga.co.uk), and cars (www.jamjar.co.uk) can all
be purchased from the internet, provided they can be paid for and delivered. Covisint
(www.covisint.com) for cars and e-Steel (www.esteel.com) are example of e-business sites.
Mansell (2001) believes that the growth of telecentres offer a platform for SMEs especially
in developing countries, to sell to the developed world. They also provide business support services for SMEs, e.g. micro-credit entrepreneurs. For more detail of the electronic
marketplace, see Chapter 2, 'The Technological Environment'. The mini-case illustration
of Nu Skin Enterprises above offers an excellent example of harnessing the technology of
the internet to a direct mode of distribution.

Marketing Strategy and Mode of Entry

Matching strategy and the appropriate form of entry mode is a challenge. Take the example of global services. The General Agreement of Trade in Services (GATS) has had
an interesting effect on entry strategies adopted by global providers of services such
as banking. Abdel-Maquid Lotayif (2003) reports on the reaction of Egyptian banks to
potential foreign direct investment (FDI) by foreign banks. In particular, he attempted
to tie up 'defensive marketing strategies' (Griffin et al., 1995) to be adopted by Egyptian
banks with the market entry mode deployed by potential entrants. There is a widely
held belief that customer loyalty is the engine of profitability in services industries and
this has led to a recommendation away from offensive marketing strategies to more
defensive marketing strategies. Offensive strategies aim to gain new customers, whereas
defensive strategies aim to satisfy and retain current customers (Tax and Brown, 1998).
Customers thus become the 'shield' against competition. According to Abdel-Maquid
Lotayif (2003), many authors have contributed to the identification of the elements
which can be deployed in a defensive strategy. These are business intelligence strategy
(BI), customer service strategy (CI), customer complaint management strategy (CCM),
Aikido strategy (AIKO), free telephone line strategy (FTL), focus strategy (FOC), differentiation strategy (DIFF), or market diversification and cost leadership strategy (CL).
At the end of his study of Egyptian banks, Abdel-Maquid Lotayif (2003) suggested a
framework which matched the appropriate defensive strategy to be adopted by Egyptian banks for different possible entry modes by incoming investors into the banking
sector (see Table 7.4).

These results, while relevant to the Egyptian banking sector, are fascinating. The
answer to FDI seems to be in business intelligence and getting closer to the customer.

Table 7.4 Entry modes and different marketing strategies

Defensive strategy	Wholly owned, i.e. branches and subsidiaries	Shared owned, i.e. mergers & acquisitions & joint ventures	Contractual, i.e. licensing, franchising, and alliances	Marketing oriented, i.e. direct or indirect exporting
Business intelligence	X			
Customer services	X			
Customer complaints management		X		
Aikido		X		
Free telephone lines			X	
Differentiation			X	
Focus				X
Cost leadership				X

Source: Abdel-Maquid Lotayif (2003: 371).

This makes sense in that the aim to direct and adjacent competitive pressure is to build up competitive intelligence and loyal customers, the potential to act faster than competitors being the only real sustainable competitive advantage. Again, logically and intuitively, a focus or cost leadership strategy would seem appropriate for an onslaught of direct or indirect exporting. However, as manufacturers in the UK are experiencing, many low-cost manufactured goods are succumbing to the unreachable low production costs of China, e.g. torches, calculators, and toys. Of all the entry modes, franchising is fast becoming a driving force, especially in the service industries (see Quinn and Alexander, 2002). Likewise, international retailing has also become a feature of global distribution systems. According to Quinn and Alexander (2002), when retailers consider international expansion they have the choice of market entry through acquisitions, organic growth, franchising, and in-store concessions. While franchising is well known in fast food, e.g. McDonald's and Burger King, retailers like Yves Rocher

WHOSE RESPONSIBILITY IS IT? Euro 2004 and China

One of the features of the Euro 2004 football competition was the sudden appearance of the flag of St George (England's flag) adorning windows, flagpoles, and thousands of cars. However, behind the scenes, migrant workers in Shaoxing, China, were working long hours to produce the flags for a pay packet of £40 per month. One factory claimed it could make 100,000 car flags a week given sufficient notice. In fact, in one week, it exported 10,000 flags to Manchester. Flags produced in the factory at 13 pence each were being sold in the UK high street for £2.99. The migrant workers in China, meanwhile, were sending most of the little they were being paid back to their families.

This is by no means the first time that sweatshop accusations have appeared. Many famous names have been accused of such practice. Who, if anyone, is to blame? The consumer, the distributor, the factory bosses, government, the World Trade Organization (WTO, www.wto.org), or a combination? The distributors would say that the price escalation is mainly due to supply chain costs (Chapter 12 explores this issue further) and that what sounds like a poor wage to Westerners is in fact the going rate in China. Whatever the truth, while there is business to be had and the practice is legal, it will go on.

(www.yves-rocher.co.uk), Benetton and the Body Shop (www.thebodyshop.com) have increasingly adopted the mode. Franchising offers a cost-effective mode of globalization (Treadgold, 1988). Against this trend, retailers like Marks and Spencer and BHS have used a variety of entry methods. Increasingly, franchising has become a strategy for growth in both developed and developing countries alike.

Fast foods, car hire, retailing, and hotels all utilize franchising as a growth strategy. By the mid-1990s, according to Central Intelligence Group (CIG, 1996), out of 92 UK companies with overseas interests, 35 employed franchising. The major forms of franchising are master/area, joint venture, direct investment, and direct franchising. The first of these is a firm favourite given its 'exclusive rights' pedigree, 7-Eleven (www.7-eleven.com) being a good example. The literature suggests that international franchising should take a form similar to international marketing expansion (i.e. the incrementalist view, where international ventures are based on domestic experience), but this is not always the case. In practice, retailers may make strategic decisions to franchise in domestic markets but when it comes to international expansion may prefer another form of entry, e.g. Marks and Spencer use franchising in their domestic operations but not in their international operations. The same is true of chocolate makers. Thornton's (www.thorntons.co.uk) use franchising in the UK but in expansion into France acquired a retail operation. The same was true of the then Rowntrees, now Nestlé (www.nestle.co.uk) confectionary company in the 1980s, which used retailers in the UK but in the USA purchased a vending machine operator. Their research findings, led Quinn and Alexander (2002) to posit two retailer paths to the franchise entry method: one where domestic franchise experience led to franchise entry ('pull' factors like unsolicited enquiries from would-be franchisees played a dominant role); and the second path where acquisitions, franchising, or organic growth was utilized ('push' factors like proactivity on behalf of the firm played a significant role). Jaeger (www.jaeger.co.uk), Next (www.next,co.uk), and Mothercare (www.mothercare.com) are all examples of UK companies which have little international experience but used franchising from a non-franchise UK base to enter new markets like the Middle East and Asia Pacific. These, and other retailers, have therefore skipped stages in McIntyre and Huszagh's (1995) theory of 'culturally adjacent market' international development and used a variety of modes which fit their strategic assessment of the international expansion possibilities. This research by Quinn and Alexander (2002) shows the complexity of the entry mode decision and that there is no one easy entry strategy solution to international expansion.

At the beginning of this chapter, we discussed the difficulty in both the strategy and mode of entry in international marketing, compounded by the ever-changing marketing environment. This complexity is making marketers, other than perhaps first-timers, adopt a mixed entry strategy, matched to product, market, and financial and competitive conditions. This complexity is exemplified by Colla (2003) in describing research on the international expansion and strategies of discount retailers in Europe. In 2000, discount retailing in Europe accounted for 14.9% of food sales. Market shares ranged from 4.2% in Greece to 42.9% in Norway (Colla, 2003). Along with franchising it is one of the key internationalization driving forces, witness the US-based Wal-Mart take-over of UK-based food retailer, Asda (www.asda.com) in 2002. Colla defined three strategic groups of retailers in international discount: (1) hard discount specialists e.g. Aldi, Lidl, Netto, and Norma; (2) soft discount groups specializing abroad, e.g. Plus, Penny, Rema 1000; and (3) soft discount diversified groups, e.g. Dia, and Leader Price.

Aldi (www.aldi.com), Lidl (www.lidl.co.uk) and Norma (www.norma-online.de) are German-based, Netto (www.netto.co.uk) is Denmark-based, Penny and Plus are German-based, and Rema 1000 (www.rema1000.dk) is Norway-based. Dia (www.dia.es) and Leader Price (www.leader-price-int.com) are both based in France. The German hard discount retailers are leaders in discount retailing in their domestic markets, having substantial market share. They are aggressive internationalists, present in many countries with large market shares, and their rate of international expansion has been higher in terms of stores opened rather than penetration into new countries. They have penetrated countries with large purchasing power where retailing is modern and large supermarkets or hypermarkets exist, brands are strong, and customer service is high. The German soft discount retailers belong to large diversified groups, mainly operating domestically, and benefit from advantages derived from large purchasing power and price differentials. They benefit less from synergies abroad than discount retailers in the next category. They use cautious internationalization strategies in countries that are geographically and culturally adjacent. The synergies available within multiple format groups favour the international expansion of soft retailers like Dia and Leader Price in countries where the groups in which these brand names operate (Carrefour, www.carrefour.fr and Casino, www.groupe-casino.fr) are present in force. They may reduce the risk of market entry for their particular discount format into new developing countries due to the synergies with other formats.

Colla (2003) concludes that the winners in the race for international expansion are the leaders in the first group, i.e. hard discount specialized retailers, but important niches in several foreign markets can facilitate growth, at least in the short term, for retailers in the second and third strategic groups.

Chapter Summary

1. The choice of market entry strategy, business model, and entry mode is a complex decision due to differing objectives of management, product/service markets, and cultural and competitive factors, coupled with the degree of risk and ability to exercise control over the entry mode.

2. There are seven approaches to international strategy development which affect the entry mode adopted. These are the Uppsala or incremental approach, the industrial network approach, the bargaining power approach, born global, the transactional cost analysis (TCA) approach, the eclectic or contingency approach, the agency approach, and the business strategy approach. Each is based on the strategic stance of the firm and a different assessment of risk, control, cultural knowledge, relationships between the players in the system, costs incurred in the transaction, and management's perception of its bargaining power.

3. There are 15 established models of business. Most models present a 'static' picture and are independent. However, the transformational model presents a 'dynamic' picture which takes account of internal and external changes in the international marketing environment and the associated adjustments in organizational structure, management style, and business model to account for these changes.

4. There are numerous types of entry mode based on the perceived degree of risk, market involvement, and degree of control. These are marketing-oriented, indirect, or direct methods; contractual methods such as licensing, franchising alliances, and management services; shared owned and controlled methods such as joint ventures and partial acquisitions and mergers; and wholly owned and fully controlled methods such as subsidiaries, representatives, and assembly.

5. International franchising and retailing are two of the most important drivers to internationalization and exemplify the complexity of matching a successful market entry strategy and mode.

 END-OF-CHAPTER CASE STUDY The Samsung Group

Samsung (www.samsung.com) is one of the world's biggest multi-nationals. Founded in 1938 in South Korea, it is currently chaired by Kun-Hee Lee, who also acts as its CEO. The group has multiple affiliated companies, each acting independently, covering electronics, engineering, hotels, communications, and a host of other activities. Samsung also has academic and educational interests, including Samsung Human Resources and Samsung Fashion Industries. It has over 200 overseas operations in over 60 countries, split into three core businesses: electronics, finance, and trade and services. Its essential financial details are given in Table 1.

Table 1 The Samsung Group figures (US$ billion)

Figure	1997	2006
Net sales	96.1	158.9
Total assets	111.8	280.8
Total liabilities	96.5	181.7
Stockholder equity	15.3	99.1
Net income	0.29	12.9
Employees (000s)	175,000	254,000

Two of its largest affiliate companies are Samsung Corporation and Samsung Electronics.

Samsung Corporation
Founded in 1938 as Samsung Trading, its main business is in trading, construction, housing development, and the internet. It is one of Korea's leading overseas businesses and was designated by government as the first trading company (GTC) in 1975. In 2006 it had a turnover of US$158.9 billion and employed 254,000 people worldwide. In 1996, Samsung Corporation merged with Samsung Engineering and Construction and added retailing to its existing business portfolio of trading and clothing manufacturing. After spinning off its hypermarket stores in a joint venture with Tesco UK, it now has three major business groupings: trading,

construction, and housing development. With the advent of the internet, Samsung became the largest online shopping market in Korea (www.samsungmall.co.kr) and industry specific e-marketplaces for chemicals and seafood products. It also operates an award-winning online catalogue trading system and a market intelligence system for the export of industrial and commodity goods.

Operating from overseas production, sales, and branch offices (see Table 2), the trading group is involved in a wide range of business projects worldwide. The company's main exports include semiconductors, plants, chemicals, and textiles. Another part of the group exports energy, chemicals, and machinery. In addition to international trade, the division carries out project engineering, organizing business, natural resources development, and investment in privatization projects for developing countries as well as promising start-ups.

The Construction Group carries out various construction, civil engineering, industrial plant, and land development projects as well as nuclear process plant construction. One of its most notable

Table 2 Location of production, sales, and branch offices

Production	Sales	Branch office
North America	North America	Middle and South America
Europe	Europe	CIS
China	China	China
South East Asia	South East Asia	Middle East, Asia, and Africa
Middle and South America	Middle and South America	
South West Asia	Japan	
	CIS	
	Middle East, Asia, and Africa	

achievements was the construction of the world's tallest building, the Petronas Towers in Kuala Lumpur, Malaysia.

Samsung Electronics

Samsung Electronics has more than 54,000 staff operating in some 50 countries. Samsung Electronics and its affiliates manufacture a vast range of electrical and allied products, including television and audio equipment, video, CCTV, home appliances, phones, electrical parts and components, next generation memory chips, colour TV picture tubes, and glass bulbs as well as developing computer systems. Samsung's affiliates are independent companies but work together to produce Samsung products.

Samsung Electronics emerged as a global enterprise through projects with leading overseas companies, along with technology transfer arrangements and joint investments. Based on open management and the desire to bring the world together, Samsung Electronics, together with overseas companies which are leading electronics world businesses in their own right, make products which 'will help people have rich and more abundant lives'. Some of the more recent strategic alliances are outlined in Table 3.

The Samsung Group is a major world player, including in its portfolio many consumer and business-to-business products and services at the cutting-edge of technology.

Case discussion questions

1 Identify and describe what you think are the reasons for Samsung's different market entry strategies.

2 Samsung has utilized numerous market entry modes in its global expansion. Identify the product/market groupings under each entry mode and what you think are the reasons for this.

3 Identify what evolution is likely to take place in Samsung's market entry strategies in the future, and give reasons for your answer.

Table 3 Samsung strategic alliances since February 2005

Partners	Date	Areas of cooperation
Nokia	April 2007	Co-develop technology for handsets and DVB-H standardization solutions
Limo	January 2007	Establish a joint venture for developing a Linux platform (SAMSUNG Electronics, Vodafone, DoCoMo, Motorola, and NEC)
Alcatel	October 2006	Cooperate on satellite DVB-H
Sony (S-LCD)	July 2006	Jointly invest in 8th-generation LCD line (2200 mm × 2500 mm motherglass)
IBM	March 2006	Co-develop and market technologies for industrial printer solutions
Intel & Microsoft	March 2006	Co-develop UMPCs
Discovery	September 2005	Cooperate on high-definition contents
Salvarani	July 2005	Co-develop new built-in products combining household electronics and furniture
Sun Microsystems	July 2005	Cooperation in solution business and next-generation business computing systems
Covad	July 2005	Supply access gateways
Lowe's	July 2005	Supply household electronics to 1,100 Lowe's stores
VDL	February 2005	Cooperate in commercialization of terrestrial DMB

Source: www.samsung.com.uk (accessed 12/04/2008).

END-OF-CHAPTER EXERCISES

1 Identify and describe the factors which have given rise to different theories of internationalization.

2 Critically discuss the different theories of market entry strategies.

3 Identify and describe the factors which determine the mode of market entry.

4 Describe the most appropriate market entry mode for:

- cars
- aero engines

- retail insurance services

- horticultural products and give reasons for your answers.

5 How does a market entry strategy inform a market entry mode? Illustrate with an example of your choice.

DISCUSSION AND EXAMINATION QUESTIONS

1 Discuss the importance of the market entry strategy decision in terms of a global expansion policy.

2 Critically discuss the factors that determine the choice of market entry mode. Are the factors mutually exclusive?

3 Market entry strategy and mode decisions are interlinked. Identify the factors that give rise to this complexity, illustrating your answers with examples.

4 Critically discuss how an organization's marketing strategy will influence the international market entry strategy.

FURTHER READING

Doole, I. and Lowe, R. (2008) *International Marketing Strategy: Analysis, Development and Implementation*, 4th edn., London: Thomson Learning, Chapter 7.

Hollensen, S. (2007), *Global Marketing*, 4th edn., Harlow: FT/Prentice Hall, Chapters 9–12.

REFERENCES

Abdel-Maquid Lotayif, M. S. M. (2003), GATS Impacts on Entry Modes and Defensive Strategies in the Egyptian Banking Sector, unpublished PhD thesis, University of Plymouth, UK.

Adams, R. B., Jr (1978) *King C. Gillette: The Man and His Wonderful Shaving Device*, Boston and Toronto: Little Brown & Co.

Aharoni, Y. (1966), *The Foreign Investment Decision Process,* Boston, MA: Harvard Business School.

Barrett, N. J. and Naidu, G. M. (1986), The Study of the Internationalization of Australian Firms, unpublished dissertation, University of New South Wales, Australia.

Bell, J. (1995), 'The internationalization of small computer software forms: a further challenge to stage theories', *European Journal of Marketing*, 29(8), 60–75.

Bilkey, W. J. and Tesar, G. (1977), 'The export behaviour of smaller-sized wisconsin manufacturing firms', *Journal of International Business Studies,* 8, 93–8.

Blankenberg, D. (1992), 'The Foreign Market Entry Process: a Network Perspective', in Moller, K. E. and Wilson, D. T. (eds.), *Business Marketing: Relationships and Networks*, Belmont, CA: PWS Kent.

Bloch, B. (1996), 'Multilevel marketing: what's the catch?' *Journal of Consumer Marketing*, 13, 18–24.

Buckley, P. J., Mirza, H., and Sparkes, J. R. (1987), 'Direct foreign investment in Japan as a means of market entry: the case of European firms', *Journal of Marketing Management*, 2(3), 241–58.

Burstow, A. (1994), 'A client's guide to deciding the duration of a facilities management contract', *Facilities*, 12(13), 14–18.

Cannon, T. and Willis, M. (1981), 'The smaller firm in international trade', *European Small Business Journal*, 1(3), 45–55.

Carney, M. and Gedajlovic, E. (1991), 'Vertical integration in franchise systems: agency theory and resource explanations', *Strategic Management Journal,* 12 (Nov.), 607–28.

Carter, S. (ed.) (1991), *Proceedings of the Marketing Management in the Horticulture Industry Workshop,* Harare: FAO.

Carter, S. (2003), *International Marketing Strategy 2003–2004*, Oxford: Butterworth Heinemann.

Cavusgil, S. T. (1980), 'On the internationalization process of firms', *European Research*, 8(6), 273–81.

Central Intelligence Group (CIG) (1996) *Retailing in Eastern Europe*, London: Corporate Intelligence Group.

Colla, E. (2003), 'International expansion and strategies of discount grocery retailers: the winning models', *International Journal of Retail and Distribution Management*, 1(1), 55–66.

Coviello, N. and McAuley, N. A. (1996), 'Internationalization processes and the smaller firm: a review of contemporary research', Working Paper, Faculty of Management, University of Calgary, Calgary.

Cyert, R. M. and March, J. G. (1963), *The Behavioural Theory of the Firm*, Englewood Cliffs, NJ: Prentice-Hall.

Czinkota, M. R. (1982), *Export Development Strategies: US Promotion Policy*, New York: Praeger.

Czinkota, M. R. and Johnston, W. J. (1981), 'Segmenting US firms for export development', *Journal of Business Research*, 9, 353–65.

Das, T. K. and Kumar, R. (2007), 'Interpartner legitimacy in the alliance development process', *Journal of Management Studies,* 44 (8).

Doherty, A. M. (2000), 'Factors influencing international retailers' market entry mode strategy: qualitative evidence from the UK fashion sector', *Journal of Marketing Management*, 16(1–3), 223–45.

Doole, I. and Lowe, R. (2008), *International Marketing Strategy*: *Analysis, Development and Implementation*, 5th edn., London: South Western Cengage Learning, Chapter 7.

Dresner., M. E. Lin, J. S., and Windle, R. (1996), 'The impacts of low-cost carriers on airport and route competition, *Journal of Transport Economics and Policy*, 30 (3), (September), 309–28.

Dunning, J. H. (1988), 'The eclectic paradigm of international production: a restatement of some possible extensions', *Journal of International Business Studies*, 19, 1–31.

Fillis, I. (2001), 'Small firm internationalization: an investigative survey and future research directions', *Management Decision,* 39(9), 767–83.

G8 Countries (2000), 'G8 Communiqué, Okinawa 2000', Preamble and Annex 2, Okinawa, G8 Countries, 23 July.

Gomes-Casseres, B. (1990), 'Firm ownership preferences and host government restrictions: an integrated approach', *Journal of International Business Studies*, 21(1), 1–22.

Griffin, A., Gleason, G., Preiss, R., and Shevenaugh, D. (1995), 'Best practices for customer satisfaction in manufacturing firms', *Sloan Management Review*, 36 (Winter), 87–98.

Hedlund, G. and Kverneland, A. (1985), 'Are strategies for foreign markets changing? The case of Swedich Investment in Japan', *International Studies of Management and Organisation*, XV(2), 41–59.

Hill, C. W. J. (1995), National Institutional Structures, transaction cost economizing and competitive advantage: the case of Japan, *Organization Science*, 1, 119–30.

Hollensen, S. (2007), *Global Marketing: A Market Response Approach*, 4th edn., Harlow: FT/Prentice Hall.

Jiang, N. (2008), Franchising as a Method of Internationalization: Time-related Changes (1990–2006) in Business Strategy, Management Style and Organizational Structure, Unpublished PhD thesis, University of Derby, Derby, UK.

Johanson, J. and Mattson, L. G. (1988), 'Internationalization in industrial systems—a network approach', in Hood, N. and Vahlne, J.-E. (eds.), *Strategies in Global Competition*, Beckenham: Croom Helm.

Johanson, J. and Vahlne, J. E. (1990), 'The mechanism of internationalization', *International Marketing Review*, 7(4), 11–24.

—— —— (1997), 'The internationalization process of the firm: a model of knowledge development and increasing foreign market commitment', *Journal of International Business Studies*, 8(1), Spring/ Summer, 23–32.

—— and Wiedersheim-Paul, F. (1975), 'The internationalisation of the firm—four Swedish case studies', *Journal of Management Studies*, 12, 305–22.

Jolly, V. K., Alahuhta, M., and Jeannet, J.-P. (1992), 'Challenging the incumbents: how high technology start-ups compete globally', *Journal of Strategic Change*, 1, 71–82.

Knight, G. and Cavusgil, S. T. (1996), 'The born global firm: a challenge to traditional internationalization theory', in Cavusgil, S. T. and Madsen, T. K. (eds.), *Advances in International Marketing*, Vol. 8, London: JAI Press, pp. 11–26.

Lasserre, P. (2003), *Global Strategic Management,* New York: Palgrave Macmillan.

Li, J. (1994), 'Experience effects and international expansion: strategies of service MNC's in the Asia Pacific region', *Management International Review*, 34(3), 217–34.

Liu, S. S. and Cheng, M. (2000), 'Toward a framework for entering China's pharmaceutical market', *Marketing Intelligence and Planning*, 18(5), 227–35.

Mansell, R. (2001), 'Digital opportunities and the missing link for developing countries', *Oxford Review of Economic Policy*, 17(2), 282–329.

McAuley, A. (1999), 'Entrepreneurial instant exporters in the Scottish arts and crafts sector', *Journal of International Marketing*, 17(4), 62–82.

McIntyre, F. S. and Huszagh, S. M. (1995), 'Retail franchising in Britain and Italy', in McGoldrick, P. J. and Davies, G. (eds.), *International Retailing: Trends and Strategies*, London: Pitman, 151–67.

Melin, L. (1992), 'Internationalization as a strategy process', *Strategic Management Review*, 13, 99–118.

Millington, A. I. and Bayliss, B. T. (1990) 'The process of internationalization: UK companies in the EC', *Management International Review*, 30, 151–61.

North, D. C. (1981), *Institutions, Institutional Change and Economic Performance*, Cambridge: Cambridge University Press.

Osterwalder, A., Pigneur, Y., and Tucci, C. L., (2005), 'Clarifying business models: origins, present, and future of the concept', *Communications of the Association for Information Systems*, 16, 1–25.

Penrose, E. (1959), *The Theory of the Growth of the Firm*, London: Basil Blackwell.

Porter, E. M. (1985), *The Competitive Advantage: Creating and Sustaining Superior Performance*, New York: Macmillan.

Quinn, B. and Alexander, N. (2002), 'International retail franchising: a conceptual framework', *International Journal of Retail and Distribution Management*, 30(5), 264–76.

Reid, S. D. (1981), 'The decision-maker, export entry and expansion', *Journal of International Business Studies*, Fall, 101–12.

—— (1984), 'Market Expansion and Firm Internationalization', in Kaynak et al. (eds.), *International Marketing Management*, New York: Praeger, pp. 197–206.

Rennie, M. W. (1993), 'Born global', *The McKinsey Quarterly*, 4, 45–52.

Rialp, A. and Rialp, J. (2001), 'Conceptual Frameworks on SMEs' Internationalization: Past, Present and Future Trends of Research', in Axinn, C. N. and Matthyssens, p. (eds.), *Reassessing the Internationalization of the Firm*: *Advances in International Marketing*, Vol. 11, Stanford, CT: JAI Press.

Root, F. R. (1987), *Entry Strategies for International Markets*, Lexington, MA: D. C. Health.

Rundh, B. (2001), 'International market development: new patterns in SME's international market behaviour', *Marketing Intelligence and Planning*, 19(5), 319–29.

Saleh, S. and Kleiner, B. H. (2005), 'Effective franchise management', *Management Research News*, 28(2/3), 56–62.

Senbet, L. W. and Taylor, W. (1986), 'Direct Foreign Investment with Imperfect Information', Working Paper, Madison, WI: University of Wisconsin–Madison.

Storbacka, K., Strandvik, T., and Grönroos, C. (1994), 'Managing customer relationships for profit: the dynamic of relationship quality', *International Journal of Service Industry Management*, 5 (5), 21–38.

Tallman, S. B. and Shenkar, O. (1994), 'A managerial decision model of international cooperative venture formation', *Journal of International Business Studies*, 25(1), 91–113.

Tax, S. S. and Brown, S. W. (1998), 'Recovering and learning from service failures', *Sloan Management Review*, 40(1), Fall, 75–80.

Taylor, C. R., Zou, S., and Osland, G. E. (2000), 'Foreign market entry strategies of Japanese MNCs', *International Marketing Review*, 17(2), 146–63.

Treadgold, A. (1988), 'Retailing without frontiers', *Retail and Distribution Management*, 16(8), 8–12.

Turnbull, P. W. (1987), 'A Challenge to the Stages Theory of the Internationalization Process', in Rosson, P. J. and Reid, S. D. (eds.), *Managing Export Entry and Expansion*, New York: Praeger, pp. 21–40.

—— and Ellwood, S. (1996), 'Internationalization in the Information Technology Industry', in Turnbull, P. W. and Paliwoda, S. J. (eds.), *Research in International Marketing*, London: Croom Helm.

United Nations (2000), *Report of the High Level Panel on Information and Communication Technology*, 17–20 April, New York: United Nations.

Whinston, M. D. and Collins, S.C. (1992), 'Entry and competitive structure in deregulated airline markets: an event study analysis of people express', *The Rand Journal of Economics,* 23(4), 445–62.

Whitelock, J. (2002), 'Theories of internationalization and their effect on market entry', *International Marketing Review*, 19 (4), 342–7.

Yang, J. and Lee, H. (2002), 'Identifying key factors for successful joint venture in China', *Industrial Management and Data Systems*, 102(2), 98–109.

Yip, G. S. (1996), 'Global strategy as a factor in Japanese success', *International Executive*, 38(1), 145–67.

Zhan, J. X. and Ozawa, T. (2001), *Business Restructuring in Asia: Cross-border M and As in the Crisis Period*, Copenhagen: Copenhagen Business School.

online resource centre

Visit the companion website to this book for lots of interesting additional material, including self-assessment questions, internet exercises, and links for each chapter:

http://www.oxfordtextbooks.co.uk/orc/lee_carter2e/

CHAPTER EIGHT

Creating, Developing, and Maintaining Competitive Advantage

Chapter overview

Chapter Introduction 246

National Competitiveness and
Global Competition 246

Factors Affecting the Growth
of Global Competition 248

    Changing nature of the microeconomic
    business environment 249

    Increasing sophistication of business
    operations and strategy 252

Strategy and Competitive Advantage 254

The Anatomy of Competitive Advantage 255

    S—substance of competitive advantage 256

    E—expression of competitive advantage 257

    L—locale of competitive advantage 258

    E—effect of competitive advantage 258

    C—cause of competitive advantage 259

    T—time-span of competitive advantage 260

Creating Competitive Advantage through
Generic Strategies 260

    Cost leadership 260

    Differentiation 262

    Focus 262

    'Stuck in the middle' 263

The Resource-based Theory of
Competitive Advantage 263

    Capability leverage 265

    Capability building 265

New Sources of Competitive Advantage 266

    Doing well by doing good 266

    Knowledge as a transformation agent 268

    Information technology as the driver of change 269

    Harnessing relationships for advantage 271

Chapter Summary 272

Learning objectives

After studying this chapter, the reader will be able to:

- understand the nature of national competitiveness and global competition;
- examine the environmental factors driving increased global competition;
- investigate the multiple facets of a firm's competitive advantage;
- discuss the various approaches to creating and developing sustainable competitive advantage in the global marketplace;
- consider the new sources from which organizations can seek to develop differential advantage.

Management issues

The management issues that arise from this chapter include:

- To what extent does the microeconomic environment and industry conditions impact on the organization's global competitiveness?
- What are the market and organizational influences that impact on the growth of international/global competition?

- What are the multiple facets of a firm's competitive advantage and how do they affect the organization's strategic resource planning and commitment?
- What are the approaches to creating and developing a competitive edge that would enable the organization to consistently outperform the competition? How sustainable is it?

Chapter Introduction

The globalization of business has changed the way in which manufacturers and service providers make and deliver their wares. During the 1980s and 1990s, European and US businesses saw their manufacturing base move to less costly emergent/developing countries, making them all too aware that they must consider the world as their marketplace to remain competitive. An industry is only competitive if the price, quality, and performance of its products is at least equal to that of its competitors and provides the combination demanded by customers (Hunt, 1995). According to Hunt, an extended period of US domination in manufacturing innovation, process engineering, productivity, and market share ended in the 1980s, and other countries, like Japan, became leaders in certain industries, e.g. consumer electronics. This was often associated with huge government support, e.g. the Chaebols, which, as privately owned companies, used to be the favoured trading companies of the South Korean government. Hunt argued that the USA had failed to adapt sufficiently to the new environment compared to foreign producers. He suggested that breakthroughs in electronics, communications, and automation had to be employed to keep lower costs of labour, materials, overheads, and inventory. He further suggested that it was not sufficient to do the same thing better, but would require new management techniques, organizational structures, and operation procedures to strengthen competitiveness. The challenge to global marketers is twofold: the identification of the best way to sustain competitive advantage globally; and the management problem of how best to implement the process once identified.

In this chapter, we consider the implications of several competitive principles that underpin the success of global organizations and seek to understand the relationship between national competitiveness and global competition. We then examine the key environmental factors driving increased global competition. An effective response to competitive change requires a clear understanding of the current and future business environment. Having looked at the drivers of competitive change and their subsequent challenges, we examine the specific strategies, processes, and techniques which global marketers employ to seek and retain competitive advantage.

National Competitiveness and Global Competition

What makes an organization consistently outperform its rivals in the global marketplace remains an elusive concept despite widespread academic and industrial interests. The work of Michael Porter (1985, 1990), the distinguished professor of competitive strategy at Harvard University, in understanding the notion of competitiveness is undoubtedly the most significant and influential contribution in this area. It sets out to provide an insight into the reasons why particular industries in particular nations obtain and sustain a competitive advantage against competitors. It should be recognized, as O'Shaughnessy (1996: 12) cautions, 'that answering this question would not explain directly the competitive advantage of nations or the wealth of nations except in the trivial sense that if sufficient industries in a country were world leaders, the nation probably has something that gives it a general advantage'.

Porter considers that the starting point to understanding competitiveness must be the sources of a nation's prosperity. A nation's standard of living is determined by the productivity of its economy, which is measured by the value of goods and services produced per unit of the nation's human, capital, and natural resources. Productivity depends both on the value of a nation's products and services, measured by the prices they command in open markets, and the efficiency with which they can be produced. Stable political, legal, and social institutions, and sound macroeconomic policies create potential for improving national prosperity, which provides a positive climate for businesses to thrive. The competitiveness of an industry is, however, determined at the microeconomic level which rests on two interrelated areas:

(a) the sophistication of business operations and strategy; and

(b) the quality of the microeconomic business environment.

The competitiveness of an industry is ultimately conditioned by the competitiveness of the organizations within it. An industry cannot be competitive unless the businesses that operate within it are competitive, whether they are domestic companies or foreign subsidiaries. The level of sophistication in company operations is inextricably linked to the quality of the national business environment. More sophisticated company strategies require more highly skilled people, better information, improved infrastructure, better suppliers, more advanced research institutions and strong competitive pressure.

In contrast, the microeconomic business environment is generally shaped by four interrelated elements:

1. Factors conditions—the efficiency, quality, and specialization of underlying factors/inputs that organizations draw on in competing.
2. Demand conditions—the sophistication of home demand and the pressure from local buyers to upgrade products and services.
3. Related and supporting Industries—the availability and quality of local suppliers and related industries, and the state of development of clusters.
4. Context for firm strategy and rivalry—the context shaping the extent of corporate investment, the types of strategies employed, and the intensity of local rivalry.

The 'diamond' factors essentially form a system which represents a set of interdependent parts that together form a unitary whole so that weaknesses in one part of the system can undermine the whole.

Government plays an important role in economic development because its policies affect many aspects of the business environment. For example, government shapes conditions through its training and infrastructure policies. The sophistication of home demand derives in part from regulatory standards, consumer protection laws, public sector purchasing practices, and openness to foreign investors.

The element of 'chance' also plays a role in shaping the competitive environment. It concerns events beyond the control of governments, industries, or organizations, such as natural disasters, global economic downturns, and scientific breakthroughs. Chance events can cause disruption to an existing thriving business environment (e.g. civil unrest) or create new opportunities for industries (e.g. discovery of oil in many Middle East nations has brought about a prosperous business climate for consumer retailing and tourism).

MINI-CASE ILLUSTRATION **The changing fortunes of Royal Selangor**

Malaysia-based Royal Selangor (www.royalselangor.com) is probably the most well-known pewter manufacturer in the world. It produces over 1,000 types of tableware and gift items, ranging from traditional tankards and elegant tea sets to photo frames and desk accessories. The company has more than 40 shops worldwide, including in London, Toronto, Melbourne, Tokyo, and Singapore.

Since the company was set up in Kuala Lumpur in 1885 by an immigrant Chinese-born pewter apprentice, the company has evolved in tandem with that of the nation—against the background of a colony ruled by the British Empire. The story of the company presents a perfect example reflecting how a private enterprise is subject to the changing political and social fortunes of a country. In the early days, for instance, items were mainly incense burners and candleholders for the oriental market. Under British rule, products expanded to tankards, ashtrays, and even tea services. The brand was then known as Selangor Pewter. During the Japanese occupation between 1942 and 1945, its business began to crumble when European expatriates who had been the company's core clientele fled or were interned. The business barely survived after the Japanese declared tin a

controlled commodity and restricted its production to making cups for sake.

After the war, the business began to grow again as the Malaysian economy improved. Fuelled by an ambition to take the business into a new era, the company introduced technology that would change the consumer perception of pewter products. As the company became firmly entrenched in the Malaysian market and gained international recognition of its innovations, the then Selangor state's Sultan appointed it the royal pewterer in 1979. The company changed its name to become Royal Selangor as we know it today.

Source: www.royalselangor.com; Chen (2004).

Factors Affecting the Growth of Global Competition

Over the past two decades there have been many reasons why competition has become increasingly fierce. Domestic and global competition has threatened the growth, profitability, and survival of organizations. Consider the global car industry. Over-capacity in the manufacturing sector, especially in the early twenty-first century, forced a spate of mergers and acquisitions as manufacturers felt the effects of competition. Examples include Volvo (www.volvo.com), Nissan (www.nissan.com), Renault (www.renault.com), Ford (www.ford.com), and Jaguar (www.jaguar.com). The giant Fiat group of Italy (www.fiat.com) claims Ferrari among its family. Most other manufacturers, such as Proton (www.proton.com), Toyota (www.toyota.com), and Honda (www.honda.com) share development activities with other organizations. Organizational and environmental factors like technology are combining to create a customer-focused, highly competitive environment. These factors have changed so quickly that the degree of uncertainty and market unpredictability, have made it difficult for organizations to plan for the long term (Turban et al., 2002). Many new products will enter the market with shorter development cycles and, possibly, shorter life cycles. Some industries may have smaller production volumes with more product customization and variety, e.g. TVR (www.tvr.com), the specialist sports car producer based in the UK, whereas others, e.g. drug companies such as Glaxo-Smith Kline (www.gsk.com), may have larger production volumes based on technology-driven optimal production processes and improvements in product quality. Dyson (www.dyson.co.uk), the revolutionary vacuum cyclone cleaner company, developed by British inventor James Dyson, relocated production from the UK to the Far East due to the competitive pressure on high production costs of the UK.

Fig. 8.1 Factors driving increased global competition

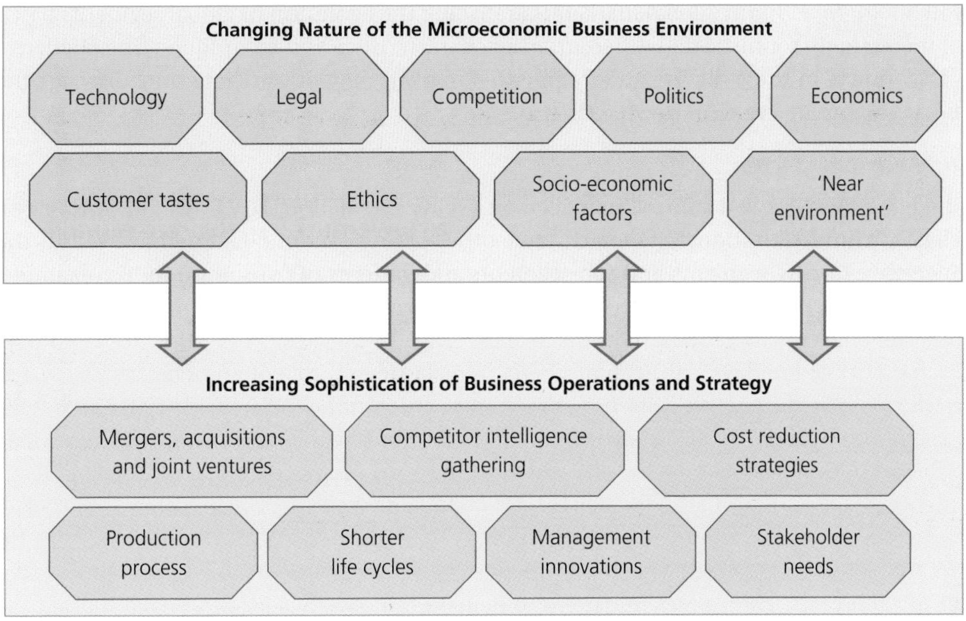

In short, the increasing globalization of markets has posed challenges for many businesses while offering growth opportunities to others capable of achieving global reach (Taylor, 1991). No organization, large or small, public or private, can afford to ignore these changes. Fig. 8.1 shows the environmental and organizational factors which have driven increased competition in the last two decades.

Changing nature of the microeconomic business environment

Technology

The rate of change and incidence of technology has rapidly accelerated over the last decade. For example, the car industry had 'innovatively stalled' until the early 1990s, then a whole spate of innovations occurred, including electronic stability programmes, halogen lights, paddle gear shifts, rain sensor wipers, kerb tracking headlights, and side safety bags. Most of these were driven by innovations in the motor racing industry, sponsored by the major car manufacturers, e.g. Mercedes-Benz (www.mercedes-benz.com). Similar innovation can be seen in other areas, including mobile phones, computing, space exploration, the financial services industry, the World Wide Web, and organic foods. The challenge to global marketers is to monitor, match or, better still, anticipate changes in technology. Failure to do so will result in falling behind or extinction from the market because innovation has the effect of shrinking markets. The answer to the challenge lies in keeping close to the customer and competitor, through a sensitive intelligence system.

Customer tastes

'Fashion, fads and throwaways' are the currency of twenty-first-century consumers. With most electrical appliances, such as radios, personal stereos, and televisions, it is often cheaper to replace the item rather than repair it. Customers are also becoming more knowledgeable due to the internet and the proliferation of specialist magazines, organizations, and television programmes, such as consumer watchdogs (e.g. www.bbc.co.uk/watchdog). In addition, global marketers are facing the evolution of global segments based on increasingly sophisticated differentiating characteristics and techniques. The challenge is to compete in these diverse and fragmented markets and, at the same time, manage the shortening of life cycles in new products.

Socio-economic factors

Changing lifestyles and cultural practices, an ageing population, HIV/AIDS infection rates, religion, rising educational standards, and other socio-economic factors have led to the emergence of new segments and sub-segments and patterns of consumption. For example, although the grey and ethnic markets have long been in existence, it is only recently that marketers have turned their attention to these. Saga (www.saga.co.uk), the UK-based over 50s provider of holidays, car insurance, etc., is a classic example of an organization geared to the over 50s age segment. But how many companies in the UK are 'ethnically oriented'? S and A Asian Foods (www.sa-foods.co.uk) in the UK may be one rare example, while others include housing associations, travel, and clothing firms. As an example of new emergent patterns of consumption, the incidence of HIV/AIDS infection has been a contributory factor to changes in consumption patterns, for instance, the increase of condom use in southern Africa where this form of prophylactic was not widespread until the heavy AIDS toll of the last ten years. The rising standards and demand for quality education have spurred the growth of an international market for higher education. Higher education is now one of the UK's, the USA's, and Australia's most lucrative exports. Universities and colleges alike have found niches for their degrees and diplomas in many countries, including China, Malaysia, South America, Africa, and India. Much of this has been based on the ability to 'culturally empathize' and to offer courses to suit both the potential student and, as in Malaysia, their fee-paying parents.

Responding appropriately to cultural changes is one of the great challenges facing global marketers and yet, at the same time, can become a potentially fruitful source of competitive advantage.

Politics

Politics can affect the nature of competition. The recent wars in Iraq have led to contractors from the coalition forces' nations being favoured over non-coalition nations, e.g. Bechtel (www.bechtel.com)

Most consumer products today experience a much shorter product life cycle due to fast changing consumer tastes.

from the USA and Mowlem (www.mowlem.com) from the UK. Embargoes on countries, e.g. Zimbabwe under its current dictatorial president Mr Mugabe, can remove competition overnight. Changes in government also affect who is favoured when it comes to countries to do business with. Political actions cause great concern to organizations operating within the global arena as the changes can be both unpredictable and large. India recently forced Coca-Cola (www.coke.com) out of the country, driven by a need to protect local manufacturing.

Economics

As one country progresses from one stage of development to another, so the nature of competition changes. In the last 20 years, the UK economy has changed from one of manufacturing to a service economy. The percentage of GDP accounted for by manufacturing has fallen to 19%, whereas services has risen to almost 60% in 2004. This shift means that manufacturers have to look elsewhere to compete and service providers are facing an increasingly competitive environment. The UK's water and train services have been the target of French service providers, as have its other utilities. Malaysia and Singapore's determination to become 'knowledge-based' economies has opened up opportunities for high-tech manufacturers, many competing on the same technology. The emergence of new trading blocs and the recent WTO round has given a tremendous boost to competition. Many organizations are now competing in the Chinese market after its entry into WTO. Companies like Tesco (www.tesco.co.uk), in food marketing, are opening up in cities and in southern Africa companies like Shoprite (www.shoprite.com) are opening up in neighbouring countries, often competing for a share of the market with local rivals, such as PTC supermarkets in Malawi.

Legal

When the law intervenes, competition can be immediately affected. The legal system may prohibit the entry of certain goods and services into a country, e.g. sexually explicit literature into Middle Eastern countries and many sub-Saharan countries. The increasing number of lawsuits and litigations can also affect the scope and type of competition.

Ethics

Companies which embrace a social and ethical approach towards business can find the investment rewarding. Often the law requires such an approach, for example in the selling of financial services and in chemical production. For those organizations which adopt a voluntary approach, the rewards can be both oral (e.g. a positive, word-of-mouth reputation) and fiscal. By adopting a 'cause-related marketing approach', Tesco supermarkets successfully projected a positive image as a socially responsible employer in the community. This was achieved through active participation and contribution to local charities and community-based activities such as the 'free computers for schools' campaign. See mini-case illustration for another example.

Competition

With the advent of the new internet and communications technologies, competition has become unpredictable both in form and timing of entry. New approaches to branding, e.g. co-branding (Blackett and Boad, 1999), distribution (e.g. using the internet to manage the international supply chain), product differentiation (e.g. lifestyle and personality segmentation), substitutes (i.e. the so-called 'lookalikes'), and cost advantages (e.g. by manufacturing in developing countries) can all alter the rules of the competitive game. No longer does a classic 'competitive analysis' included in an 'environmental analysis' suffice. The internet has spawned customer personalization and, these days, it is not in the marketer's

MINI-CASE ILLUSTRATION **Ariel's Clean Water Campaign**

Water is an essential element of life, but over 1 billion people don't have access to safe, clean drinking water. Each year, lack of safe water and proper sanitation result in 2 million child deaths globally and 443 million missed school days. Half of all hospital beds in many poor developing countries are filled with people sick from waterborne diseases. More people die of diarrhoea from unsafe water and poor sanitation than from armed conflict (source: www.psi.org). Treating drinking water costs less than one penny per family per day, and could save one million children's lives each year.

Ariel, the washing detergent manufacturer, is one of a growing number of companies which embrace a social and ethical approach by linking its products with a good community-based charity programme. It has launched a cause-related marketing campaign to encourage its customers to get involved by helping to provide safe drinking water to those who need it most. Working in partnership with the Children's Safe Drinking Water Programme and Five and

Alive programme of Population Services International (www.psi.org), Ariel aims to donate and distribute ten litres of safe drinking water to those in the developing world when customers make a purchase of every special pack of Ariel. At the end of the campaign, Ariel would provide a total of 80 million litres of safe drinking water to children in developing countries.

Sources: www.Ariel.co.uk; www.psi.org.

interest to try to satisfy every customer. Some customers are simply 'too expensive' to 'satisfy', e.g. the mobile phone operators have recently found that prepaid customers are less profitable than contract customers. Trying to lose customers, an anathema to the old school of marketing, is now the norm as companies find the concepts of loyalty and 'zero defections' merely 'rainbow' concepts (Carnelsen, 2003: 28).

The 'near environment'

Suppliers, distributors, facilitators (e.g. banks), and stakeholders can all provide competitive challenges. Suppliers and distributors can become so powerful that they become a source of competition. Steve Jobs, once a star of the Microsoft (www.microsoft.com) phenomenon, has now successfully created a digital computer animated company, Pixar (www.pixar.com), yet he was once an animation program supplier. There are many examples where employees have left organizations to create their own companies which have then rivalled the organization they once worked for.

The changing nature of the microeconomic business environment provides the 'fuel' for competitive change. Often, due to the nature of these changes, they are unpredictable and volatile. Only a sensitive external intelligence orientation will suffice to capture them and only intelligent, and often intuitive, interpretation will provide the strategy to meet them.

Increasing sophistication of business operations and strategy

Production processes

As organizations strive to introduce lower cost production processes and quality improvements, new techniques in production are sought and introduced. The early 1990s saw the introduction of robots into car production plants as an early manifestation of this, but this has now been extended to service quality agreements in service industries, nano-technologies (www.nano.gov), total quality management (TQM), and business process re-engineering (BPR) to name but a few. Outsourcing has become a major source of process re-engineering with its resultant cost reduction.

Shorter life cycles

Not only are life cycles being shortened by changes in consumer taste but also by manufacturers seeking sources of competitive advantage. The ever-increasing rate of new car model introductions and obsolescence of computer hardware and software are examples of this phenomenon.

Cost reduction strategies

Manufacturers may seek new locations for production (e.g. Nissan (www.nissaneurope.com) going to Europe rather than the UK), new marketing strategies (e.g. insurance companies that deliver their services entirely on the internet), and new sources of human and financial capital (e.g. British Airways (www.british-airways.com) moving their booking capacity to India) in the quest for lower costs of production in order to compete more effectively on cost.

Management innovations

Structural and organizational changes (downsizing), value chain management, customer relationship management, best practice, and benchmarking are some of the techniques that have recently been employed to make organizations more competitive. In the late 1990s, the UK's leading financial institutions, among them Halifax Bank (www.halifax.co.uk) and National Westminster Bank (www.natwest.co.uk), undertook a joint benchmarking exercise to effect efficiencies in the banking sector. Such activity left those not taking part at a competitive disadvantage. Investments in the 'knowledge management' era, e.g. IBM (www.ibm.com) and Skandia (www.skandia.com) finance, linked to the intranet, have given these companies a competitive edge in levering their knowledge assets around the globe. Adoption of these smarter paradigms of production, marketing, and administration are a source of potential competitive advantage which need to be first identified and then exploited.

Mergers, acquisitions, and joint ventures

Such activities can alter the competitive playing field overnight. The spate of bank mergers in the UK in the late 1990s and more recently mergers among the drug manufacturers altered the competitive landscape. A few years ago, Prudential (www.prudential.com) in the UK launched its internet banking service, Egg (www.egg.com). Who would have envisaged its potential sale to US-based credit card company MBNA (www.mbna.com) for £1.4 billion just four years later? Mergers can also bring economies of scale in order for the nascent company to remain competitive. In 2004, Interbrew (www.inbev.com), which has the Stella Artois (www.stella-artois.com) brand in its portfolio, announced impending closure of some of its breweries after merging with Brazilian firm AmBev (www.ambev.com.br). The Chief Executive said it would not need 75 breweries and that the group needed a more integrated business that would be far more cost-effective.

Competitor intelligence gathering

Smarter database systems and their integration have led to better intelligence gathering, especially about the customer. 'Personalization' and 'adding customer value' have been afforded by the internet in particular. Customer foot-printing and profiling have enabled internet marketers to tailor their products and services to individual customers via astute marrying of databases and internet technology. This has led to new forms of competition of which eBay (www.ebay.com), the online auction house, is a classic example.

Stakeholder needs

Today's global marketers face a host of stakeholders: employees, shareholders, government interests, environmentalists, community, to name but a few. All these are seeking monetary/non-monetary gain from the operations of business. This behoves organizations to identify their exploitable competences and use them to satisfy all stakeholders. For example, oil producers need to turn their expertise not only to making profits for shareholders but also to satisfying environmentalists, interested governments, and communities while maintaining an edge against the competition.

An effective response to competitive change, be it changes in production or service processes, methods of marketing and managing, requires a clear understanding of the current and future business environment, the market and customer, and the speedy and effective management of organizational capabilities to respond. Organizations need to be 'agile and learning-oriented' (De Gues, 1999; Ranchod, 2004). A key element of this is to keep close to the customer, who, even in global terms, is becoming increasingly knowledgeable and more sophisticated, with higher expectations and demanding more products and services at a higher quality and lower price. Organizations will be under increasing pressure to produce more with fewer resources (Turban et al., 2002).

Strategy and Competitive Advantage

A strategy is essentially a master plan setting out how the organization will achieve its mission and objectives. In undertaking a strategy, companies look to maximize competitive advantage and minimize competitive disadvantage. A successful strategy, as Keegan (2002) argues, requires an understanding of the unique value that will be the source of the organization's competitive advantage. Organizations ultimately succeed because of their ability to carry out specific activities or groups of activities better than their competitors. These activities enable the organization to create unique value for their customers, and it is this value that is central to achieving and sustaining competitive advantage. Indeed, value is the customers' overall assessment of the utility of a product or service based on perceptions of what is received and what is given (Kandampully and Duddy, 1999). Therefore, competitive advantage is fundamentally about the value customers put on the product assessed by how much they are willing to pay, and the organization that better serves the customer has the differential attribute or dimension to create better customer value (Ma, 1999).

Christopher (1996) suggests that customer value is created when the perception of benefits received from a transaction exceeds the costs of ownership. An organization needs to continuously and consistently invest in transactions (Kandampully and Duddy, 1999) and understand its own needs as well as the needs of the customer as service loyalty can encourage the development of a long-term relationship with the customer, and emphasize the creation or enhancement of customer value. Highly perceived values of an organization's product can be considered as customer-based assets (strengths existing in the minds of customers), which can be expressed as:

Customer value = Perceptions of benefits – total cost of ownership

The value a customer puts on a product can be determined by its cost, performance and uniqueness, and these factors can determine the competitiveness of the organization within its industry. The organization can deliver significantly superior performance through communicating a value proposition, which is recognized by the target market as a better proposition than that presented by competitors. By focusing on the cost and value

Fig. 8.2 Superior vs. inferior perceived values

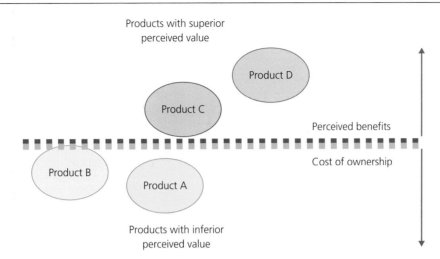

Products with superior
perceived value

Product D

Product C

Perceived benefits

Cost of ownership

Product B

Product A

Products with inferior
perceived value

of the product, the organization can manipulate the value proposition of 'what you give' and 'what you get' (Kandampully and Duddy, 1999), as illustrated in Fig. 8.2.

Competitive advantage has also been attributed to the organization's ability to think beyond the present (anticipation of changing customer needs), to think for the customer (continuous product and service innovations), and to think beyond the parameters of the organization (leverage added values from external as well as internal relationships). One of the traits managers of leading organizations possess is the ability to forecast, far in advance of the reality, the progressive nature of customer needs. Effective management can be achieved through strategies that embrace and interpret customers' concerns and dreams for the future. Organizations are thus required to think both as a customer and on behalf of the customer, developing the products and services that tomorrow's customers want before they become a reality (Kandampully and Duddy, 1999: 54).

The term 'competitive advantage' remains a concept that is not well understood, despite widespread acceptance of its importance. The term can be defined as the skills, expertise, exclusive relationships, core competences, and/or ownership of unique resources that enable the organization to outperform others within its competitive environment. Where does a competitive advantage come from? What are its contents and effects? Does it reside inside or outside the organization? How sustainable is it? To answer these questions, we examine the multiple facets of competitive advantage.

The Anatomy of Competitive Advantage

A competitive advantage that enables an organization to excel and sustain its market dominance is unique to the organization. In developing competitive advantage, it is important to first understand the multiple facets of competitive advantage and the ways in which they influence the organization and its chances of succeeding in the marketplace.

Ma's (1999) work[1] on conceptualizing the multiple facets of competitive advantage is significant. It advances an integrative framework that, for the first time, enables managers

[1] This section here draws heavily from Ma (1999: 710–15).

Fig. 8.3 The anatomy of competitive advantage

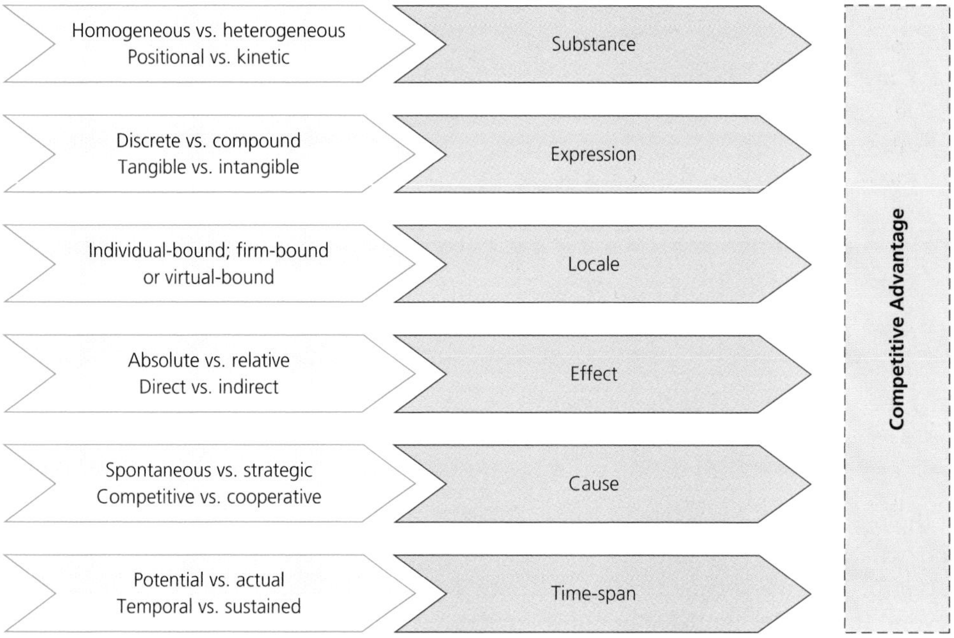

Source: Based on Ma (1999: 710).

to systematically analyse the 'anatomy' of competitive advantage. The framework can help organizations to make the ultimate choice of matching resource commitment with changing opportunities for gaining and sustaining competitive advantages. As such, he argues, it is only fitting that the framework should be termed in acronym as SELECT, a tool designed to help an organization to choose the right configuration of its competitive advantages. An illustration of the SELECT framework based on Ma's work is given in Fig. 8.3.

S—substance of competitive advantage

Two basic schemes can be used to categorize the substance of competitive advantage:

(a) Positioning vs. kinetic advantages

Organizations with a *positional* advantage generate competitiveness from their superior attributes or endowments, which are often static and primarily ownership- or access-based. Examples include managerial talents and/or dedicated skilled employees (e.g. Electrolux (www.electrolux.com)—see mini-case illustration on p. 269); size-based advantages such as economies of scale (e.g. Carrefour (www.carrefour.fr), with its 'hypermarkets' chain in France); good relationship with collaborator (e.g. the collaboration between Sony (www.sony.com) and Ericsson (www.ericsson.com) in third-generation mobile communications technology); dominant position in the supply chain (e.g. British Telecommunication (www.bt.com) in the UK home telephone market due to its ownership of access infrastructure); and ownership of technological standards (e.g. Microsoft in PC operating systems).

Kinetic advantages are often knowledge- and capability-based which allows an organization to perform its operations more effectively or efficiently than others. Examples include entrepreneurial capabilities such as creative exploitation of market opportunities (e.g. Stelio Haji-Ioannou, the creative entrepreneur behind the success of Easy Group (www.easy.com); and technical expertise that results in superior business processes and systems (e.g. Oracle (www.oracle.com), the global leader in internet-based business systems). Kinetic advantage can also be sourced from the strategic capabilities that enable creation and deployment of knowledge and competences to changing market opportunities. For instance, the current success of the South Korea-based Samsung Group (www.samsung.com) in mobile communications and home entertainment is the result of strategic deployment of resources and technical competences within the group.

(b) Homogeneous vs. heterogeneous advantages

An organization which outperforms its rivals, competing on a similar basis, can be described as having *homogeneous* advantage (e.g. Dreamworks (www.dreamworks.com) and Walt Disney (www.disney.com) in animation film production). Alternatively, an organization can enjoy *heterogeneous* advantages over its rivals by competing on a different basis. For instance, the internet bank First Direct (www.firstdirect.com), unlike the high street banks, delivers all its financial services online.

E—expression of competitive advantage

The expression or form of competitive advantage can be captured using two categories:

(a) Tangible vs. intangible advantages

Tangible advantages are presented in physical forms which can be readily observed, such as ownership of strategic tangible assets. For instance, Avis (www.avis.com), the world's second largest general-use car rental business, has more than 1,700 locations strategically located in popular airports and holiday destinations in the USA, Canada, Australia, New Zealand, and the Latin American/Caribbean region. This helps to deter potential entrants and sustain superior competitive advantage.

In contrast, *intangible* advantages are not easily recognized as they are hidden in human and/or other factors. They are more difficult to replicate as they are likely to be derived from organization traits, characteristics, and culture which are socially complex. For example, the KPMG Group (www.kpmg.com), the world's well-known general consultancy firm, enjoys a tremendous reputation advantage all over the world due to its wealth of cross-cultural business experience and knowledge in developing corporate excellence.

(b) Discrete vs. compound advantages

A *discrete* advantage is one that functions in stand-alone, discrete fashion. Typical examples include superior property locations, unique physical assets, patent and other intellectual properties, exclusive contract, import or export licence, or cash reserves. For example, the success of Bluetooth (www.bluetooth.com) derives almost entirely from its patented wireless technologies.

A *compound* advantage, on the other hand, consists of multiple individual advantages that work together as an integrative whole. For instance, Canon's (www.canon.com) capability to harness multiple competences in image processing and to leverage its manufacturing and marketing strengths has enabled it to introduce a wide range of innovative products of high quality at lower costs.

L—locale of competitive advantage

The locale of competitive advantage can exist on three levels:

(a) Individual-bound advantages

These come from particular *individual* or certain mobile assets. The success of many small companies relies on the motivation and personal contacts of the business owners. For example, Ennovation (www.ennovation.co.uk), a micro-business in the UK which specializes in customer management software, derives approximately 90% of its revenues from the business networks of its two founders.

(b) Firm-bound advantages

Firm-bound advantages are either stored in or shared by many people in the organization, and hence are less mobile and more difficult to duplicate. A corporate culture such as Nike (www.nike.com), which values innovation and creativity, for instance, can provide an advantage over its rivals.

(c) Virtual-bound advantages

Virtual-bound advantages reside outside the organizations. These include strategic networks (e.g. international airlines which operate within a global operational network such as the Star Alliance (www.star-alliance.com)—see The Digital Impact), exclusive relationships (e.g. Microsoft, and Intel (www.intel.com), the computer chip manufacturer), or other entities to which the organization has access.

E—effect of competitive advantage

To justify investment in the pursuit of competitive advantage, it is necessary to ensure that the efforts deliver desirable effects for the organization, e.g. the existence of a competitive advantage leads to measurable perceived customer value. The strengths of an advantage's effect could be observed as being either:

(a) Absolute or relative

An organization has an *absolute* advantage when it competes with magnitude that appears insurmountable to its rivals. For instance, the Sultan of Brunei and his oil production company has an absolute advantage over the oil processing and exports in the country. If, however, the organization's advantage is merely in small differentials, the advantage is *relative*. Most small guesthouses for holiday makers in popular holiday destinations in the UK have only relative advantage over one another due to the small differentials in the services provided.

(b) Direct or indirect

A *direct* advantage, as the term suggests, is one that directly creates and adds values to the business operations. A direct advantage is typically more tangible in nature. For instance, Honda's excellence in making quality engines which adds direct values to its competitiveness in the global car markets. However, an *indirect* advantage indirectly contributes to such a practice. Within a university, an established learning culture that stimulates scholarly excellence is an advantage that adds indirect value to its overall reputation.

THE DIGITAL IMPACT Managing the flow of information around the globe

The Star Alliance network was launched by Air Canada, Lufthansa, Scandinavian Airlines, Thai Airways International, and United in May 1997. Today, the Star Alliance network is a global airline network which comprises 21 airlines and 975 airports in 162 countries with over 18,000 daily departures. The objective of forming this Alliance was to offer passengers a seamless, worldwide service. Since its network includes diverse companies with multiple nationalities and global geographical distribution, it faces a daunting challenge in creating a harmonized network of processes and systems in order to operate as one unified entity. Serving its customers effectively requires access to accurate and secure information. For its member airlines' 416,845 employees worldwide, accessing accurate information at any location and time zone for all these employees is critical to its smooth operation globally. Seeking to enhance and improve its common infrastructure, the Star Alliance network turned to Novell (www.novell.com), the US-based specialist in computer and information networking.

Developing an information and communications infrastructure of this scale was not going to happen overnight. In the initial phase, the Alliance created the Star Alliance Global Directory, which centrally stores and administers key user and resource information contributed by member airlines and the Star Alliance organization. This phase also included establishing an authentication framework to ensure control of access to the network as well as encryption of key data. In the second phase, the Global Directory expanded to include and manage the access of all its users and resources on the Star Alliance network. The new system enables the synchronization of new information across the network, making the updating of information in real time a reality. In its final phase, the new system will support cross-airline application process, enabling employees of one member airline to use applications hosted at and controlled by another member airline using a defined role or profile.

With the help of Novell, Star Alliance Services GmbH has developed an IT network that represents the next generation of airline IT technology, which has contributed to substantial cost saving by increasing standardization and efficiency among its members. More importantly, it has fostered the exchange and integration of the best expertise, ideas, corporate cultures, and technologies of its members in order to create a more seamless and intelligent service for its customers.

Sources: www.staralliance.com; and www.novell.com.

C—cause of competitive advantage

The cause of competitive advantage answers the questions of 'where does it come from?' and 'through what means?' The causes can be categorized as:

(a) Spontaneous advantages

Organizations can enjoy a competitive advantage over their rivals simply by 'luck' due to certain historical accidents. These historical accidents might have enabled certain organizations to acquire valuable resources denied to others. The phenomenal rise of the Chaebols in South Korea, including Hyundai (www.hyundai.com), Daewoo (www.daewoo.com), and Samsung in the past benefited enormously from government support and protection.

(b) Strategic advantages

Competitive advantage can be acquired through purposeful strategizing. Porter (1990) suggests that the combination of intense competition and demanding customers that exist in a small domestic market such as Japan has kept the Japanese car makers at the cutting-edge of competitiveness. Such hostile competitive environments can help hone their skills and leads to competitive advantage as they expand in the international market.

Advantage can also be gained through strategic cooperations. The increasing research and development costs and shortening of the product life cycles make cooperation on expensive projects an attractive choice for many organizations. Airbus (www.airbus.com), the European commercial aircraft manufacturer, is a consortium of British, German, Spanish, and French companies which collaborate to compete with their US rivals.

T—time-span of competitive advantage

It is important to understand the life cycle of competitive advantage to determine: (i) when a potential advantage will materialize; (ii) the sustainability of such an advantage. Accordingly, the time-span can be either:

(a) Potential or actual

An *actual* advantage is one that is currently in effect, while a *potential* advantage can be one that is in reserve, yet untapped, under-utilized, or misplaced. Managing the life-span of competitive advantage is similar to managing the life cycle of a product. This can be achieved through effective portfolio management. Actual competitive advantages generate extraordinary values to the organizations that can be ploughed back to identifying and nurturing potential competitive advantages that will eventually replace the 'ageing' ones.

(b) Temporal or sustainable

A *temporal* advantage is one that is short term, transient, and unsustained. This is most commonly observed in competition based on price. On the other hand, a *sustainable* advantage refers to an advantage that is long-lasting and not easily surpassed or duplicated by competitors. Developing competitive advantage with high sustainability requires the organization to commit to long-term and consistent investments.

Creating Competitive Advantage through Generic Strategies

According to Porter (1985), there are three generic routes to competitive advantage that an organization can adopt to create distinguished customer value: (1) cost leadership; (2) differentiation; and (3) focus (see Fig. 8.4). He suggests that any attempt to create firms' competitive advantage should emphasize the need to identify a clear and meaningful selling proposition for the organization. In other words, what is the organization's competitive stance? What does it stand for in the eyes of the customers? Any failure on the part of the organization to identify and communicate the selling proposition and strategy is likely to lead to a dilution of the offer and to the company being stuck in the middle.

Cost leadership

An organization which sets out to become the low-cost producer in its industry is one which pursues the cost leadership advantage. Low-cost producers exploit the experience curve effects to achieve market penetration, where the key is to develop a low-cost structure to allow high returns even when competition is intense.

Fig. 8.4 Generic competitive strategies

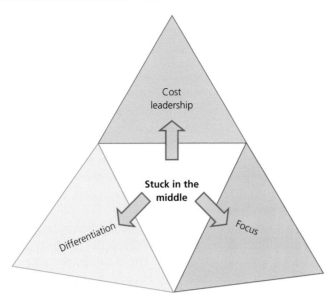

Source: Based on Porter (1990) and Wilson and Gilligan (1999).

By pursuing a strategy of cost leadership, the organization concentrates on achieving the lowest costs of production and/or distribution so that it has the capability of setting its prices at the lowest level. Whether it chooses to do this depends on its objectives and its perception of the market. For example, IBM (www.ibm.com) and Boeing (www.boeing. com) are cost leaders who have chosen to use their lower costs not to reduce prices but to generate higher returns which have subsequently been invested in marketing, R&D and manufacturing as a means of maintaining and strengthening their position. In tackling costs, the organization needs to recognize in advance the potential complexity of the task, since the evidence suggests that true cost leaders generally achieve this by tight and consistent control across all areas of the business, including engineering, purchasing, manufacturing, distribution, and marketing. An important element is the scale of operations and the scope that exists for economies of scale. Basis for costs reduction include (Wilson and Gilligan, 1999: 329–30):

- speeding up the learning curve;
- the globalization of operations;
- concentrating the manufacturing effort in one or two very large plants in countries such as South Korea and Taiwan with a lower cost base;
- modifying designs to simplify the manufacturing process and make use of new materials;
- achieving greater labour effectiveness by investing in new processes.

Many organizations find it very difficult to pursue a long-term cost leadership strategy. For example, Japan based much of its success in the 1960s on aggressive cost management but then found that because of a combination of increasing domestic costs and the emergence of new and lower cost competitors/countries (e.g. Taiwan and South Korea), the position was unsustainable in the longer term (Wilson and Gilligan, 1999).

Differentiation

Differentiation involves organizations developing a product or service that is unique or superior in some way which often commands higher than average prices. According to Porter (1990), differentiation leads to superior performance if the price premium achieved exceeds any added costs of being unique. An organization can only outperform rivals by establishing a difference that it can preserve. Therefore, it must focus on a unique set of activities. For instance, the organization can seek to sustain an advantage on a particular element of the marketing mix that is seen by customers as important and as a result provides a meaningful basis for competitive advantage. The organization may therefore attempt to be the 'quality leader' (e.g. Mercedes-Benz with cars, Bang and Olufsen (www.bang-olufsen.com) with hi-fi systems, 'service leader' (e.g. Singapore Airlines, www.singaporeair.com), 'marketing leader' (e.g. Coca-Cola), or with 'technological leader' (e.g. Sun Microsystems, www.sun.com in computer networking) (Wilson and Gilligan, 1999).

Differentiation can also be achieved by means of the brand image and packaging, a position particularly suited to mature markets in which the products are often physically indistinguishable (Wilson and Gilligan, 1999). For example, the cola drinks with Pepsi Cola (www.pepsi.com) and supermarkets' own brands and the fashion clothing industry with Gap (www.gap.com) and Banana Republic (www.bananarepublic.com), which design casual clothes aimed primarily at the same customer demographics.

It is clear that sellers of highly differentiated products are able to charge a premium in their prices. Given higher margins, the organization following a differentiation strategy is able to reinvest the premium into maintaining the perception of differentiation through a policy of new product development, promotional activity, customer service, etc., and thereby strengthen the barriers to entry for would-be competitors.

Focus

Organizations that adopt the focus posture concentrate their efforts on particular segments of the market, allowing them to service particular sub-groups of customers.

The focus strategy relies on the selection of a target segment or group, and tailors its strategy to serving them to the exclusion of others. The organization can achieve this by choosing to be cost-focused or differentiation-focused. Cost-focused organizations exploit differences in cost behaviour in some segments, while differentiation-focused ones exploit the special needs of buyers in certain segments. With either strategy, the organization will want to determine its ability to acquire customer loyalty by fulfilling customers' present needs, accurately anticipating their prospective needs, and consistently enhancing the ongoing relationship.

These strategies only work well if the organization's target segment has distinguished buying needs or the production and delivery system that best serves the target segment differs from that of other target segments. If the organization's focus is on a target segment that is the same as other segments, then the focus strategy will be unlikely to succeed.

A number of high-street fashion clothing brands design casual clothes aimed primarily at the same consumer demographics. Establishing a clear brand differentiation is crucial to market success.

'Stuck in the middle'

Underlying the concept of generic strategies are the premises that competitive advantage is at the heart of any strategy, and achieving competitive advantage requires an organization to make a choice. According to Porter (1990), these choices are the type of competitive advantage an organization looks to attain and the scope within which the organization will attain it. Failing to adopt any clear generic strategic posture will result in the organization being unable to deliver a superior value proposition to its customers, hence it becomes 'stuck in the middle'. An organization that is stuck in the middle has no competitive advantage. The organization competes at a disadvantage because the cost leaders, differentiators, or focusers would be better positioned to compete in any customer segment. To avoid this (im)position, the organization must create an advantage by consistent long-term efforts and investment.

To achieve any advantage in business, an organization has to look systematically at what it has, what it knows, and what it can get. An advantage can come from the differential in any of the organization's attributes, whether it is ownership of valuable resources, exclusive access to market, or proficiency in organizational learning. Any factor that contributes to the existence and/or enlargement of such a differential could serve as a source of advantage.

The Resource-based Theory of Competitive Advantage

Strategy has been defined as 'the match an organization makes between its internal resources and skills . . . and the opportunities and risks created by its external environment' (Hofer and Schendel, 1978: 12). The resource-based theory emphasizes the role of the organization's resources and capabilities as the foundation for developing competitive advantage.

According to Grant (1991: 118):

> there is a key distinction between resources and capabilities. Resources are inputs into the production process—they are the basic units of analysis. The individual resources of the firm include items of capital equipment, skills of individual employees, patents, brand names, finance, and so on. But on their own, few resources are productive. Productive activity requires the cooperation and coordination of teams of resources. A capability is the capacity for a team of resources to perform some task or activity. While resources are the source of a firm's capabilities, capabilities are the main source of its competitive advantages.

For example, McDonald's (www.mcdonalds.com) possesses distinctive capabilities within product development, market research, human resource management, financial control, and operations management. Critical to its competitive advantage, however, is the integration of these functional capabilities to create McDonald's remarkable consistency of products and services in thousands of restaurants around the world.

Any resource-based approach to competitive advantage and strategy formulation should begin with developing a framework which systematically integrates the identification, analysis, and evaluation of the organization's resources and capabilities in terms of their potential for sustainable competitive advantage and financial returns. The framework presented in Fig. 8.5 shows the process of how an organization can gain sustainable competitive advantage in the global marketplace by basing its strategy on building and leveraging the unique internal capabilities. It is built on the work of Prahalad and Hamel (1990) and

Fig. 8.5 Creating and leveraging capabilities

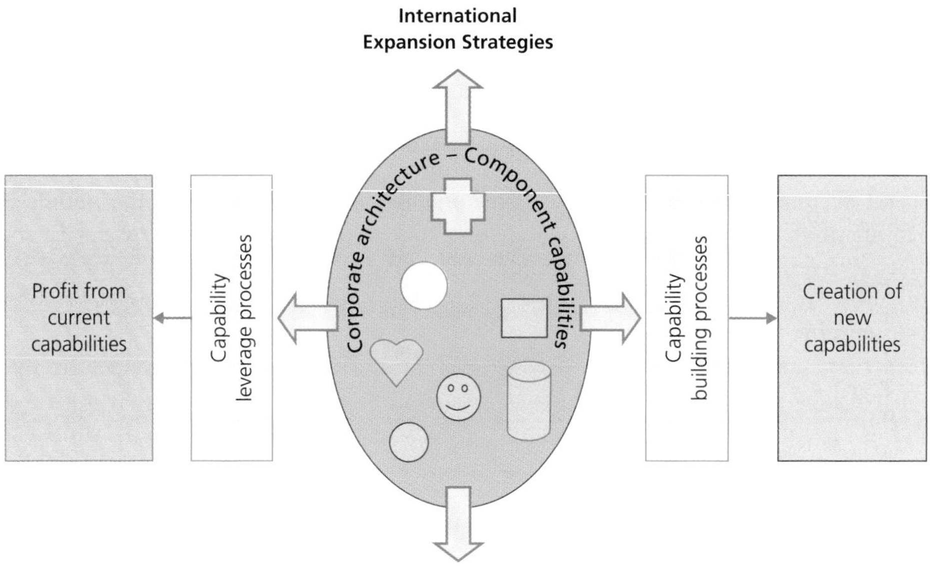

Source: Based on Tallman and Fladmoe-Lindquist (2002: 119).

adopts the view that competitive advantage is the consequence of holding and combining unique resources and capabilities and creating a *strategic architecture* to apply the resulting core capabilities across product and business units. It considers the organization's attempt to build, protect, and exploit a set of unique capabilities and resources as key factors to determine performance levels and the key forces that drive organizations into international and global strategies. These organization-specific complex capabilities and resources are built and leveraged for long-term success in worldwide markets through strategies of international expansion and global integration.

According to Tallman and Fladmoe-Lindquist (2002), there are two types of resource-related capabilities in organizations that are, in general, relevant to international and global operations:[2]

(a) Business-level component capabilities

These relate to the competitive advantage of the organization in its business area(s) and include its ability to produce better products, devise superior processes, and generate more effective marketing. These capabilities are essentially the unique bundles of strategic resources and capabilities needed to operate the business. They are normally embedded in the knowledge base of the organization. At the functional level, this may also involve the broader set of actions and structures critical to competitive advantage and the corporate strategy.

(b) Corporate-level architectural capabilities

These are defined as organization-wide routines for integrating the components of the organization for productive purposes, and are the sources of the organizational synergies at the core of the business. Architectural capabilities are developed in the organization-

[2] This draws heavily on Tallman and Fladmoe-Lindquist (2002).

specific process of operating the business and are tied closely to its administrative history. They relate to the ability and knowledge of the organization to organize so as to function competitively in different contexts and apply its component capabilities in ways that are truly newly effective—that is, truly adding value not simply preventing its erosion.

The two key processes of 'capability leverage' and 'capability building' provide the essential mechanisms to drive a capability-based strategy.

Capability leverage

Capability leverage involves the efforts the organization makes to gain competitive advantage from the exploitation of its existing capabilities in the marketplace. All organizations rely on their existing capabilities to gain the profits needed to provide returns to investors, to pay for further expansion and to finance new assets and capabilities. Multinationals simply apply these leverage processes across global markets.

Competitive advantage can be leveraged from the business-level components and corporate-level architectural capabilities. In terms of business-level component capabilities, return on investments in the combinations of resources (i.e. physical, financial, and intellectual assets) and skills (i.e. know-how and unique expertise) involved in business capabilities improve if the cost base established for the domestic market can be exploited in the broader international marketplace. For instance, products and processes, brand names, advertising programmes, and other business-related resources and skills can often be leveraged across borders without radical modifications. Coca-Cola is a classic example and has enjoyed enormous success in the leverage of its business-level component capabilities in its 'one-world approach' to global marketing.

Leveraging corporate-level capabilities involves raising managerial capabilities for organizing component knowledge into profit-generating bundles as drivers of organizational expansion. For instance, the wealth of experience and knowledge acquired from managing international business operations can be used to enhance the process of new market development in untapped markets.

Capability building

New capabilities must be created to replace existing ones as they erode over time and to ensure leveraging capabilities in the marketplace continue to generate competitive advantage for the organization. Both business-level and corporate-level capabilities need continuous improvement, re-invention, or innovation through global learning. No region or country has a monopoly of business-level component capabilities and forward-looking organizations are continually searching for the latest resources and skills around the world. The decision of Hewlett-Packard (www.hp.com) to upgrade its then Singaporean manufacturing facilities to one of its strategic global research and development centres provides a good example of capability building through global integration of resources and business knowledge.

At the corporate level, building new component capabilities requires highly sophisticated internal systems and a managerial structure that can thrive in the changing characteristics of global businesses. For example, ABB (www.abb.com), a world leader in power and automation technologies, transformed its corporate architectural capabilities by developing entirely new internal processes for coordinating its global businesses, including strategic human resource policies, accounting systems, and the creation of a new organizational culture.

The resource-based view strives to identify and nurture those resources and capabilities that enable organizations to develop competitive advantage. However, it is important for an organization to take account of the unrelenting dynamic environment that calls for a new generation of resources and capabilities as the context continues to shift. The organization has to develop a new generation of resources and capabilities in order to retain its competitiveness. There is a need to balance 'living' and 'unborn' resources, which is achieved when the organization succeeds in marrying sustainability and competitive advantage (Chaharbaghi and Lynch, 1999).

New Sources of Competitive Advantage

The debate on competitive advantage has been dominated by the work of Porter (1985), which encourages organizations to seek out market-based sources of advantage through differentiation or cost efficiency, and by the work of Prahalad and Hamel (1990), which seeks to find advantage through an internal analysis of the organization's key resources and capabilities (Sanderson, 1998). Both approaches, in essence, seek to improve operational effectiveness as a reflexive response to hyper-competition and the increasing customer demand for better products and quality services at lower prices. As Lang (2001) rightly argues, this no longer enables businesses to create a competitive advantage that is truly sustainable. The quality movement that saw the diffusion of best practices which improved national competitiveness (especially in the emerging economies) significantly shortened the time frame in which competitive advantage could be extracted from any given improvement in operational effectiveness. By learning how to learn, international competitors can now match almost any improvement rooted in a new technological or managerial innovation. This means that product innovation and quality can no longer provide a lasting competitive edge. In addition, the search for decisive economies of size and scale in the 1990s, which led to 'asset-stripping' in many organizations, has now deprived them of the essential resources, people, and assets which could have been crucial to the building of new capabilities and competences.

The basis on which organizations compete in today's market environment needs to be broadened beyond operational effectiveness. The pressures to outperform competition and satisfy customers have propelled many forward-looking organizations to seek out new sources of differential advantage, which in the long term not only enable them to maintain a competitive edge but also provide global leadership.

Doing well by doing good

Corporate social responsibility (CSR) and the ways in which organizations discharge their moral and ethical responsibilities is a vital feature in any contemporary debate concerning the management of the business organization. As multinational organizations have grown in size, so have their power and influence on the lives of global citizens and the physical environments. This has resulted in greater external enquiry into their behaviour in terms of the use, or abuse, of this power and its impact on a range of stakeholders. The development of the new economy, increased globalization, and issues such as knowledge management are some of the factors which require the organization to consider ethical impacts as well as commercial opportunities.

CSR has come to represent more to stakeholders than ever before. Indeed, 'few remember a time when the impact of business on society has been scrutinized more critically' (Armitstead, 2004: 3). Evidence suggests that people like to work for ethical organizations and avoid employment with an unethical 'feel' (Clutterbuck et al., 1990). Research in the

UK suggests that 73% of people would be more loyal to an employer that supports the local community, while 81% of consumers agree that when price and quality are equal they are more likely to buy products associated with a good cause (societyandbusiness. gov.uk). According to the 2002 MORI-Annual CSR Study, 80% of UK shareholders expect to see a copy of the organization's social report. For many forward-looking organizations, the ethical decision-making and the strategic and practical ways in which they choose to manage their corporate responsibilities are increasingly seen as a potential source of competitive advantage.

Many business organizations are taking positive steps towards a more constructive attitude to ethical corporate responsibilities. For instance, more than three-quarters of FTSE-100 companies now produce CSR reports, although few carry CSR through to a meaningful programme of management activities (Bartram, 2003). This suggests that today's organizations are eager to give the impression that CSR is at the core of their business (see Whose Responsibility Is It?). The business case for CSR rests on protecting corporate reputations among consumers, clients, and suppliers; motivating and retaining key staff; wasting fewer resources; and building long-term relationships with stakeholders as part of the so-called 'licence to operate' (Macbean, 2003).

The phenomenal worldwide success of the Body Shop (www.bodyshop.com) is a classic example of how a business organization can seek to create lasting differentiation and competitive advantage by consistently promoting its 'ethical business' global image. The unambiguous stance against animal testing, human rights abuses, and unfair trading practices in the developing world have earned the company an enviable reputation and a competitive advantage that few businesses can emulate.

WHOSE RESPONSIBILITY IS IT? Promoting decent working conditions

Many food and clothing companies in the UK are under increasing pressure from consumers, trade unions, and non-governmental organizations (NGOs) to ensure decent working conditions for the people (in poor developing nations) who produce the goods they sell. The typical responses from companies tend to go little beyond setting out minimum labour standards with which they expect their suppliers to comply. But little is normally done to enforce compliance in the host countries.

The Ethical Trading Initiative (ETI) is an alliance of companies, NGOs, and trade union organizations set up 1998 to promote and improve the implementation of corporate codes of practice which cover supply chain working conditions. Its objective is to ensure that the working conditions of workers producing for the UK market meet or exceed international labour standards. It brings the combined knowledge and influence of relevant NGOs and the international trade union movement to work alongside these companies in identifying and promoting good practice in code implementation.

A number of experimental projects have been launched to establish how a decent corporate code of practice can be applied, implemented, and monitored. For instance, the Smallholders Project was set up in Kenya in 2003 to improve conditions for small agricultural producers (smallholder farmers and their workers), who are frequently marginalized and vulnerable. These farmers are at the bottom of the supply chain and may lack access to market information,

training, credit, and agricultural inputs. Since then, a local Project Officer has been appointed, and draft Guidelines established after consulting with the smallholders, exporters, government, unions, and NGOs. The project will continue to develop through working and consulting with stakeholders in tea and fresh produce in Kenya to ensure that working conditions continue to improve.

Source: www.ethicaltrade.org.

The sustainability of the Body Shop's competitiveness lies in the company's conviction (rather than compliance) to balance the commercial interests of the business with its social responsibilities and obligations. It comes from taking additional voluntary measures that go beyond the legislation that already sets minimum standards to regulate the impact of business on society and the environment. Compliance CSR rarely creates any lasting effects as the approach adopted to 'doing good' is seldom well defined. For instance, Walkers Crisps' (www.walkers.co.uk) 'Free Books for Schools' campaign, which invited schoolchildren to eat more crisps in return for free books for their schools, received widespread criticism from the general public. In an extreme example, pupils at one primary school consumed, over a four-month period, 14,000 bags of crisps (i.e. an average 636 bags per pupil), a total of 115,116 calories, 2.8kg of salt, 160kg of fat, and 9.8kg of sugar. Cadbury's 'Get Active' campaign, which invited schoolchildren to eat the equivalent of 5,440 bars of chocolate for a free volleyball was also singled out for similar criticism.

From initial passive reactions to pressure from stakeholders, non-governmental organizations, and the general public, many organizations now adopt a proactive stance towards CSR based on their experience of such practice providing positive impacts on business financial performance. Seeing CSR and ethical practice as a source of competitive advantage is a far cry from the long-held view of CSR as a business cost, a matter of compliance with legislation, or a means to circumvent negative publicity. For these organizations, socially responsible practice and ethical behaviour become not just better business but smarter business.

Chapter 5 provides a detailed discussion of the issues that organizations operating in today's global marketplace need to address if they are to be considered socially responsible business practitioners. It also seeks to demonstrate how businesses can use corporate social responsibility and ethical practices not only to increase trade but also as a source of global competitive advantage.

Knowledge as a transformation agent

The greater interest in resource-based strategies has increasingly focused attention not on what organizations own in the form of physical assets, but on what they know in the form of intellectual assets. Key to strategic advantage as a basis of competitive success will be the ability of organizations to manage knowledge (Sanderson, 1998).

In the new fast-changing global market environment, if an organization is to thrive, it must organize and coordinate information and knowledge sources in a way that is very different from the past. The case for more strategic management of knowledge embedded in the organization, as Neef (1999: 76–7) maintains, is indeed compelling. Organizations today need not only to focus on innovative products and services which complement the high-tech marketplace, but also to re-think their global strategy, reassessing the cost effectiveness of plant and labour location, organizing themselves in a way that helps them to benefit from the opportunities provided by newly-emerging markets and lower cost labour regimes. To leverage and share ideas and techniques that bring efficiency and innovation to the company globally, organizations need to create new patterns of communication that will help break down cultural barriers and promote closer working relationships among groups of employees and partners with similar skills and duties. The effective management of knowledge, supported by intelligent internet technologies, will enable organizations to capture leading practices electronically and communicate them worldwide, and to mobilize knowledge to encourage sharing of lessons learned to prevent the recurrence of costly mistakes. This means promoting policies and providing the infrastructure to help employees at all levels to recognize and respond to constantly changing trends and markets. This encourages creativity and innovation, and enables the knowledge workers continuously to learn and improve productivity.

Understanding, creating, and managing knowledge in a way that enhances competitiveness is difficult for many organizations. In theory, effective knowledge management involves developing a strategic orientation that enables knowledge to be systematically created and integrated not only to improve the intellectual capital of the organization, but to aid decision-making and generate new responses to innovative thinking. In practice, however, it means providing answers to the question of how knowledge adds value and creates sustainable advantage. For instance, how intellectual capital will be transformed into intellectual assets such as new technologies and innovation which have strategic value. How, if at all, does it impact on the communication systems and organizational designs? Organizations need to develop methodologies to link knowledge to objectives, critical success factors which involve both the organization and the customers. Many organizations, including Hewlett Packard (www.hp.com) and Rolls-Royce (www.rolls-royce.com), are already making efforts to map the relationship between value-adding activities and knowledge. The continuing interest in knowledge management ensures that it will have radical impacts on the way organizations are managed in the future (Sanderson, 1998).

Information technology as the driver of change

Much rhetoric has been dedicated to the explosion in new information and communications technologies (ICTs) and the ways in which they can revolutionize businesses and organizations. Central to the development of these technologies is the advent of the

MINI-CASE ILLUSTRATION **Electrolux develops its people to their full potential**

The management of talents has long been recognized as fundamental to the success of organizations. For a global company like Electrolux, with over 57,000 employees, getting the right people to the right positions, and retaining them within the company, is an ongoing challenge.

In 2001, Electrolux launched 'Talent Management', a programme designed specifically to facilitate all sectors within the company to fill efficiently the managerial positions of its many successful businesses. An important objective of the programme is to ensure that the valued employees feel that the company can offer them a rewarding career and opportunity to fulfil their full potential.

A cornerstone of the programme is the talent review process, which involves middle and senior managers. It provides a structured environment, such as talent review meetings and appraisal talks, for both the company and the employees to review the status of an individual's development. Based on the changing needs of individual managers, the company then provides training and coaching programmes to help managers to realize their full potential. To encourage mobility across sectors within the company, employees can utilize Open Labour Market (OLM), an interactive job-posting database, to find challenging new positions within the Group.

For Electrolux, there is a great business case to be made for properly managing talent. First, the retention of top performers is a clear indication that the company is outperforming its competition.

© Electrolux. Reproduced with permission.

The benefits of Talent Management can be fully measured and benchmarked against best practice. Secondly, the mobility and cross-fertilization between sectors, functions, and geographical areas can be prioritized according to the changing needs of the company.

Source: www.electrolux.com (accessed 10/07/2004).

internet and the World Wide Web. The internet, as Harris and Cohen (2003) report, has reduced the distance between buyers and sellers, allowing dis-intermediation and in some cases the elimination of the need for an expensive sales force, distributor, or other intermediary. It offers a number of opportunities arising from its potential as a powerful distribution channel, a medium for marketing communications, and a market in and of itself. These opportunities are associated with the technology and the interactive nature of the medium. Understanding, interpreting, and using these technologies may enable a possible competitive advantage to be identified and obtained.

One of the prime benefits of using the new electronic media comes from giving customers and other stakeholders options on how and when information will be made available to them, to be accessed at a time and place most convenient to them, with a highly customized message or offer relevant to their circumstances. Targeted and timely communications can potentially help organizations to avoid a huge quantity of unwanted, wasteful, and costly communications associated with unselective mass media advertising. It is more effective and efficient to align limited corporate resources to target prioritized customers based on their idiosyncratic information needs, projected potential returns based on previous spend, and, perhaps, brand loyalty.

The advances in new electronic media have provided organizations with the ability to 'close the feedback loop' in the communication process—'the ability to actually measure the behaviour of customers and prospects in the real world and in some cases, in real time rather than simply measuring changes in awareness or attitudes' (Schultz, 1996: 142). New technologies that enable the capture, storage, and analysis of information on customers, consumers, and prospects have fuelled an explosion of database applications among organizations of all sizes and industries. The use of data-driven marketing has provided the framework for creating closed-loop evaluation systems, which increasingly underpin the delivery of any forms of marketing communications (Schultz and Schultz, 1998).

The combined effects of tailored interactive communications and closed-loop evaluation systems would facilitate the building of long-term satisfying relations with key parties—customers, suppliers, distributors—in order not just to retain their long-term preference and business (Falk and Schmidt, 1997), but to allow them to become intimately involved in the design and production process (Harris and Cohen, 2003). A growing trend towards online community relationships and exchange is demonstrated by the technical support function at Cisco (www.cisco.com), which allows customers to help other customers solve their problems by setting up an online community self-help system (Chaffey et al., 2000). Customers are given open online access to Cisco's knowledge base and user community, its resources and systems.

The internet provides instantaneous information and facilitates the processing and communication of that information which in turn enables the rapid diffusion of ideas and technologies. The development of the internet as the global communications and business infrastructure is altering the very nature of how and where work can be done, by allowing organizations to base different parts of their business in different locations and connect them by computer networks. Market trends can be sensed and responded to with greater accuracy and speed (Neef, 1999). The entire supply chain—from in-bound and out-bound transportation, new containerization techniques, electronic scheduling to advanced port management—is now accomplished globally without boundaries due to these technological advances. Organizations need to take advantage of the new computing and telecommunications technologies available to develop a technical infrastructure capable of capturing and transferring information and knowledge in a way that delivers real competitive advantage.

Harnessing relationships for advantage

The management of relationships has never been more important in the newly evolved hyper-competitive marketing environment. This sentiment was well articulated by Doyle (1995: 32):

> The objective of business is to create relationships with customers which support future profits and growth. Customers no longer need to accept shoddy quality products or high prices in most markets. Strong customer satisfaction and loyalty depends on the value they receive from suppliers. Marketing managers need to appreciate that such value is not under the control of the marketing department. It is a function of the relationships between people within the firm and across the organizations with which the firm deals.

The constant search for sources of competitive advantage has inevitably forced organizations to recognize that competing as a single entity carries with it the risk that other greater advantages owned by competitors will outweigh their performance in the marketplace. This has given rise to the growth of cooperation as a strategy through joint ventures and strategic alliances (Sanderson, 1998). It became clear that collaborating with suppliers, customers, and even competitors was an essential characteristic of successful businesses in the increasingly volatile environment. Organizations move from a confrontational to a partnership culture because they understand that while confrontational tactics may reduce component costs, the impact on total system costs is small. A bigger and more sustainable impact would be to redesign the whole process to lower total manufacturing or marketing costs. The only sustainable route to achieving higher value-added is by being the first to bring new, higher-value products to the market through strategic collaboration.

After the corporate restructuring and consolidation of the 1990s, many 'streamlined' organizations have outsourced processes they perceive as non-essential to their core competences. 'Going alone' is not an option for these organizations as they no longer possess the internal capabilities to conduct closed core processes. The ability to build and sustain external and internal relationships has become a crucial management skill as relationship management has effectively become the engine for developing and sustaining core capabilities and, therefore, the value-generating processes of the organization.

Intelligent and forward-looking organizations have begun to form industry-wide collaborative networks with their partners throughout the supply chain. This collaboration is based on internet technologies in order that suppliers, distributors, retailers, and customers are linked horizontally and vertically to resolve business process problems important to the customer. It looks at the entire value chain, where all enterprises—retailers, distributors, manufacturers, raw materials, and component suppliers—are linked and viewed as one entity competing as a chain, to focus on satisfying the customer (Lang, 2001).

In short, pressures to cut costs, improve core processes, acquire new skills, and adapt rapidly to changing market opportunities are shifting organizations from confrontational transactions to partnerships with external and internal partners. Improving competitiveness requires careful management of strategic relationships. The discussion in Chapter 13 reflects this trend and examines processes of global marketing within this context. It demonstrates how an understanding of the principles of relationship marketing (RM) can offer organizations the potential to achieve sustainable competitive advantage.

THE RELATIONSHIP PERSPECTIVE Mixing business with pleasure

Oxfam (www.oxfam.org.uk) is a UK-based development, relief, and campaigning organization that works with others to find lasting solutions to poverty and suffering around the world. To realize its ambitious mission, which requires substantial and consistent funding, Oxfam recently turned to more innovative ways to encourage donations from the general public. It has achieved this by:

• launching the world's first charity music download website; and

• opening its own high street fair trade coffee shops.

In collaboration with OnDemand Distribution (OD2), Europe's leading digital distributor of music, Oxfam launched its charity music download website in May 2004. It offers music lovers a facility to download from a choice of 300,000 tracks while donating money to help Oxfam raise much-needed funds for its work, through the Big Noise Music website (www.bignoisemusic.com). With songs costing as little as 75p, every pound spent on the website will generate a 10p donation to Oxfam. Site visitors are also able to sign up to Oxfam's global petition called 'Big Noise', calling for governments and politicians to make trade fairer for the world's poorest people. An estimated 5 million people, including the Dalai Lama and Coldplay's lead singer Chris Martin, have already signed the petition.

With the help of Matthew Algie, the UK's largest supplier of fair trade coffee to the food industry, Oxfam recently announced that it is to open a chain of high street fair trade coffee shops which will be part-owned by growers' cooperatives from some of the world's most impoverished nations, including Indonesia, Ethiopia, and Honduras. The coffee chain is to be branded as The Progreso, and will be set up to help poor coffee growers to sell their products at fair trade prices, share directly in the profits and showcase their high-quality produce to UK consumers.

From a charity organization's perspective, these business ventures at Oxfam offer an alternative business model to conventional charity fundraising—mixing charity fundraising with consumers' pleasure. To help capture a larger share of consumers' disposable income, both commercial and charity organizations realize that they can create a win-win situation if they work together. For the commercial partner, it may be a platform on which to discharge its social responsibility. For the charity partner, it has the opportunity to tap into the social conscience of the customers of its commercial partner.

Sources: www.oxfam.org.uk; and www.guardianunlimited.co.uk.

Chapter Summary

1. The competitiveness of an industry is determined by the competitiveness of the organizations within it. An industry cannot be competitive unless the businesses within it are competitive, whether they are domestic companies or foreign subsidiaries. The level of sophistication in company operations is inextricably linked to the quality of the national microeconomic business environment, which rests on two interrelated areas: (a) the sophistication of business operations and strategy; and (b) the quality of the microeconomic business environment.

2. There have been many reasons, over the past two decades, for competition becoming increasingly fierce. The changing nature of the microeconomic business environment and the increasing sophistication of business operations and strategy have intensified domestic and global competition which increasingly threaten the growth, profitability, and survival of organizations.

3. In undertaking a strategy, companies aim to maximize competitive advantage and minimize competitive disadvantage. Organizations succeed because of their ability to carry out specific activities or groups of activities better than their competitors.

4. Competitive advantage can be defined as the skills, expertise, exclusive relationships, core competences, and/or ownership of unique resources which enable the organization to outperform others within its competitive environment.

5. A competitive advantage that enables an organization to excel and sustain its market dominance is (and should be) unique to the organization. It comes in different shapes and sizes. In developing competitive advantage, it is therefore important, first, to understand the multiple facets of competitive advantage and the ways in which they influence the organization and its chances of succeeding in the marketplace. The SELECT framework is a tool designed to help an organization choose the right configuration of its competitive advantages.

6. According to Porter (1985), there are three generic routes to competitive advantage that an organization can adopt to create distinguished customer value: (1) cost leadership; (2) differentiation; and (3) focus. Any attempt to create a firm's competitive advantage should emphasize the need to identify a clear and meaningful selling proposition for the organization. Any failure on the part of the organization to identify and communicate the selling proposition and strategy is, he suggests, likely to lead to a dilution of the offer and to the company ending up 'stuck in the middle'.

7. The resource-based theory emphasizes the role of the organization's resources and capabilities as the foundation for developing competitive advantage. Any resource-based approach to competitive advantage and strategy formulation should begin with a developing framework that systematically integrates the identification, analysis, and evaluation of the organization's resources and capabilities in terms of their potential for sustainable competitive advantage and financial returns.

8. An organization can gain sustainable competitive advantage in the global marketplace by basing its strategy on building and leveraging unique internal capabilities. Competitive advantage is the consequence of holding and combining unique resources and capabilities, and creating a *strategic architecture* to apply the resulting core capabilities across product and business units.

9. Corporate social responsibility (CSR) and the ways in which organizations discharge their moral and ethical responsibilities is a vital feature in any contemporary debate concerning the management of the business organization. Many forward-looking businesses use CSR and ethical practices not only to increase trade, but also as a source of global competitive advantage.

10. The increased interest in resource-based strategies has focused attention not on what organizations own in the form of physical assets but on what they know in the form of intellectual assets. Effective knowledge management involves developing a strategic orientation to enable knowledge to be systematically created and integrated not only to improve the intellectual capital of the organization but to aid decision-making and generate new responses to innovative thinking.

11. The internet has reduced the distance between buyers and sellers, allowing dis-intermediation and in some cases the elimination of the need for an expensive salesforce, distributor, or other intermediary. It offers a number of opportunities arising from a

potential as a powerful distribution channel, a medium for marketing communications, and a market in and of itself. Understanding, interpreting, and using these technologies may enable a competitive advantage to be identified and obtained.

12. The management of relationships has never been more important in the newly evolved hyper-competitive marketing environment. Pressures to cut costs, improve core processes, acquire new skills, and adapt rapidly to changing market opportunities is moving organizations from confrontational transactions to partnerships with external and internal partners. Improving competitiveness requires careful management of strategic relationships.

 END-OF-CHAPTER CASE STUDY Proton: The challenge to survive in the global market

Proton, the Malaysian national car producer Perusahaan Otomobil Nasional Bhd (www.proton.com), is a symbol of national pride for Malaysians. When the company was first established in 1983 by the previous Prime Minister, Tun Mahathir Mohamad, the goal of this national car project was not so much to take pride in the end product but to spearhead Malaysia's industrialization. The first model, Saga, was launched in September 1985 using Mitsubishi technology and parts. The launch of Proton Waja in the early 2000s, which boasts 95% local content minus the Powertrain, is an achievement Malaysians are proud of. According to management at Proton, the Waja marks a significant milestone in Proton's technological achievement. By leveraging on the design and engineering expertise of Lotus, its British subsidiary, the car has reduced its dependence on its strategic partners—Mitsubishi and Citroën—for technology. The indigenous design means that Proton now owns the intellectual property rights to the platform on which the Waja is built, thereby saving on royalty payment to others. The first fully Malaysian-developed car, from chassis and engine, was introduced into the market on 8 February 2004. It was appropriately named 'Gen2' to symbolize Proton's success in propelling itself into a new generation of its evolution. The first-year sales revenue of Gen2 reached almost RM1.4 billion (US$413 million), which made up of 22.98% of the total sales.

It is hard for any Malaysians to imagine Proton as anything but a stunning success. It is nonetheless important to note that the Malaysian government played a major role in the success of Proton. Since its inception in 1983, the government sheltered Proton from local and foreign competitors by imposing duties ranging from 40% to 300% on imported cars and car parts. Due to protection from foreign competition, Proton was able to grow and established itself firmly in the Malaysian car market. Within a decade, it owned almost 60% of a protected home car market that was growing at a rate of 20% year-on-year due to the booming Malaysian economy.

However, Proton's unchallenged position in the Malaysian car market was about to change. Under the South East Asian free-trade pact (instigated by the ASEAN Free Trade Area (AFTA) agreement), proposed by the ten-member Association of Southeast Asian Nations, tariffs on manufactured goods—including cars and car parts manufactured in the region—were to be reduced to no more than 5% by 2003. In response, the then Chief Executive of Proton requested the government for a prolonged tariff protection. The request was a

public admission that Proton, despite the optimism, was not ready to compete with other global car producers on an equal footing. Under the rules governing the free trade area, the Malaysian government, while agreeing to the overall AFTA pact, had once again given in to Proton's request for special treatment by delaying tariff cuts on cars and components until 1 January 2005, when duties were to be reduced to no more than 20%, instead of the 5% mandated by AFTA.

The AFTA agreement has today opened up the 530,000 unit-a-year Malaysian vehicle market, which is South East Asia's largest, to increased international competition. AFTA guidelines state that any car manufacturer which sources at least 40% of its components from ASEAN countries is considered 'local' and therefore qualifies for a member country's minimum import duties. This means major international car manufacturers which have set up plants in Thailand, for example, are now able to challenge Proton's long-standing dominance of the Malaysian market. Proton's rivals are now able to price their products very competitively, something which was previously not possible due to the exorbitant import duties. Sales of all Proton models fell to around 40% from around two-thirds of the market in the 1990s. Meanwhile, locally assembled foreign cars—led by Toyota and Honda—saw sales rise 62% in the same period. Without government subsidies, Proton would make a loss on every unit sold abroad. Faced with stiff competition from low-priced Japanese and South Korean imports, Proton has been struggling to recoup domestic market share.

The global landscape of the automotive industry is rapidly changing. Mergers and acquisitions are commonplace as the industry continues to rationalize and consolidate. With global car production standing at over 75 million vehicles per year, 23 million (or 30%) of these vehicles remain unsold. Domestically, Proton still has the advantage in terms of dominant market share and a well-established distribution and service network. This situation will remain while the Malaysian government delays its 'full' international commitment to free trade.

Proton needs to strengthen its export markets if it is to become a global player. Its disappointing performance in the export markets is indicative of its lack of vision. Since the early 1990s it has exported 20,000–30,000 units per year—a modest figure in comparison to Thailand's truck exports of around 250,000–300,000 in 2008. Thailand began exporting in 1998; Malaysia in the late 1980s.

It is becoming clear that trade and market liberalization will have significant implications on how business is conducted in a globalized world. Many industries have been directly affected and the automotive sector is no exception. The market forces of liberalization will expose the weaker and more inefficient market players in favour of the stronger ones. To meet the challenges of liberalization, it is imperative that Proton accelerates its organizational learning, develop sustainable competitive advantage, and, more importantly, transform its business to become a global organization efficient in production and effective in delivering customer values.

This will not be an easy task. First, Proton's brand image continues to be perceived as 'inferior' to other car producers, even among current Malaysian Proton owners. Despite the improvement in quality and design, it is still widely perceived as 'lacking excitement' although relatively good value compared to Japanese or South Korean makes. Given a 'real' choice, most Malaysian car buyers would swap their Protons for a 'superior' foreign marque, especially among younger and more affluent consumers. Secondly, productivity levels are not increasing fast enough to keep up with other car manufacturers. It has limited funds for research and development. The bulk of its exports is mostly confined to less mature markets, including China, the ASEAN countries and the Gulf

states. Thirdly, the company needs more desirable models, which are critical to revive sales. Proton's Campro engine, which is the main staple of its product line, is hardly cutting-edge given today's technology. It also lacks an engine or platform to expand into the SUV and MPV markets, or the 2.0-litre and above segments. In the longer term, many of the green engine technologies that are emerging as a result of rising fuel prices and global warming would dictate the direction of automotive development, and these are beyond Proton's capabilities. Most importantly, the management at Proton seems to have difficulty in devising a strategy for developing competitive advantage that will be sustainable on a global level.

The ultimate test will be when all protectionist measures are removed. The latest spate of achievements has undoubtedly placed the car in a better position to compete with its more established counterparts. The commitment to fully honour the AFTA agreement and beyond, are irreversible. In 2004 Malaysian officials agreed with neighbouring countries a delay on tariff cuts for the automotive sector. It is unlikely that there will be more lifelines. Malaysia's car industry will face immense competitive pressure in the immediate future.

Sources: Data used in the case study are sourced from the Malaysian National News Agency: Bernama (www.bernama.com); and Chacko (2006).

Case discussion questions

1 What are the internal and external challenges confronting the management at Proton? Explain how these challenges present a threat to Proton's long-term survival.

2 Discuss how, in your opinion, Proton should respond to each of these challenges?

3 The ability to create and sustain a competitive advantage is vital to success in the global car market. Explore and evaluate the sources from which you think a small global player such as Proton should seek to build sustainable global competitive advantage.

END-OF-CHAPTER EXERCISES

1 Briefly describe the two interrelated areas that determine the competitiveness of an industry at the microeconomic level.

2 What are the major environmental factors driving increased global competition?

3 What is competitive advantage? Why is it important for organizations to develop and maintain a competitive advantage in the marketplace?

4 Briefly discuss how to use the SELECT framework to analyse the competitive advantage of an organization.

5 Explain how an organization can adopt the generic strategies of cost leadership, differentiation, and focus to create a posture to outperform its rivals.

6   What is the so-called resource-based theory of competitive advantage? In what ways does it enable an organization to acquire a competitive advantage?

7   Why do you think there is a need for today's organizations to seek new sources of competitive advantage?

DISCUSSION AND EXAMINATION QUESTIONS

1   An effective response to competitive change requires a clear understanding of the current and future business environment. Examine, with examples, the factors driving the increased global competition and their implications on global marketing.

2   The term 'competitive advantage' is not a concept which is easily understood. How would you define the term? How would you analyse it in order to help organizations to develop and manage it?

3   Discuss, with examples, how competitive advantage can be achieved through Porter's generic strategies.

4   The resource-based theory emphasizes the role of the organization's resources and capabilities as the foundation for developing competitive advantage. Discuss, with examples, how an organization can leverage and build new resources and capabilities for competitive advantage.

5   The basis on which organizations compete in today's marketplace needs to be broadened beyond operational effectiveness. Discuss some of the new sources from which organizations can develop differential advantage.

FURTHER READING

Porter, M.E. (1985), *Competitive Advantage: Creating and Sustaining Competitive Performance*, New York: Free Press.

—— (1990), *The Competitive Advantage of Nations*, New York: Palgrave.

Prahalad, C. K. and Hamel, G. (1990), 'The core competence of the corporation', *Harvard Business Review*, May/June, 79–91.

Ranchod, A. (2004), *Marketing Strategies: A Twenty-first Century Approach*, Harlow: Prentice Hall, pp. 151–70.

REFERENCES

Armitstead, L. (2004), 'Counting on reponsibility', *Companies that Count: The Sunday Times Supplement*, 14 March.

Bartram, P. (2003), 'Special report: keeping promises', *Marketing Week*, October.

Blackett, T. and Boad, B. (1999), *Co-Branding: The Science of Alliances*, Basingstoke: Macmillan Business.

Carnelsen, J. (2003), 'What is the Customer Worth? Customer Value Analyses in Relationship Marketing on the Basis of Car Buyers', *Yearbook of Marketing and Consumer Research*, Vol. 1, 27–46.

Chacko, G. K. (2006), 'Proton transitioning to Malaysian engine', *Management Research News*, 29(3), 139–51.

Chaffey, D., Mayer, R., Johnston, K., and Ellis-Chadwick, F. (2000), *Internet Marketing*, London: Prentice Hall.

Chaharbaghi, K. and Lynch, R. (1999), 'Sustainable competitive advantage: towards a dynamic resource-based strategy', *Management Decision*, 37(1), 45–50.

Chen, M. Y. (2004), *The Royal Selangor Story: Born and Bred in Pewter Dust*, Singapore: Butterworth-Heinemann.

Christopher, M. (1996), 'Applied marketing science: from brand values to customer value', *Journal of Marketing Practice*, 2(1), 55–6.

Clutterbuck, D., Dearlove, D., and Snow, D. (1990), *Actions Speak Louder: A Management Guide to Corporate Social Responsibility*, London: Kogan Page.

De Gues, A. (1999), *The Living Company: Growth, Learning and Longevity in Business*, London: Nicholas Brearley Publishing.

Doyle, P. (1995), 'Marketing in the new millennium', *European Journal of Marketing*, 29(13), 23–41.

Falk, H. and Schmidt, A. (1997), 'The impact of new media on the communication process: using the internet as a marketing communication tool', in *Fit for the Global Future*, ESOMAR, ARF, JMA, Conference, Lisbon (Portugal), 13–16 July.

Grant, R. M. (1991), 'The Resource-based theory of competitive advantage: implications for strategy formulation', *California Management Review*, Spring, 114–35.

Harris, L. and Cohen, G. (2003), 'Marketing in the internet age: what can we learn from the past?', *Management Decision*, 41(9), 944–56.

Hofer, C. W. and Schendel, D. (1978), *Strategy Formulation: Analytic Concepts*, St Paul, MN: West.

Hunt, V. D. (1995), *Reengineering: Leveraging the Power of Integrated Product Development*, New York: Wiley.

Kandampully, J. and Duddy, R. (1999), 'Competitive advantage through anticipation, innovation and relationships', *Management Decision*, 37(1), 51–6.

Keegan, W. J. (2002), *Global Marketing Management, 7th International Edition*, Englewood Cliffs, NJ: Prentice-Hall International.

Lang, J. C. (2001), 'Managing in knowledge-based competition', *Journal of Organizational Change Management*, 14(6), 539–53.

Ma, H. (1999), 'Anatomy of competitive advantage, "a SELECT Framework'", *Management Decision*, 37(9), 709–18.

Macbean, N. (2003), 'Corporate social responsibility in China: is it any of your business', *China-Britain Trade Review*, March, 16–17.

Neef, D. (1999), 'Making the case for knowledge management: the bigger picture', *Management Decision*, 37(1), 72–8.

O'Shaughnessey, N. J. (1996), 'Michael Porter's *Competitive Advantage* Revisited', *Management Decision*, 34(6), 12–20.

Porter, M. E. (1985), *Competitive Advantage: Creating and Sustaining Competitive Performance*, New York: Free Press.

—— (1990), *The Competitive Advantage of Nations*, New York: Palgrave.

Prahalad, C. K. and Hamel, G. (1990), 'The core competence of the corporation', *Harvard Business Review*, May/June, 79–91.

Ranchod, A. (2004), *Marketing Strategies: A Twenty-first Century Approach*, Harlow: Prentice Hall.

Sanderson, S. M. (1998), 'New approaches to strategy: new ways of thinking for the millennium', *Management Decision*, 36(1), 9–13.

Schultz, D. E. (1996), 'The inevitability of integrated communications', *Journal of Business Research*, 37, 139–46.

—— and Schultz, H. F. (1998), 'Transitioning marketing communication into the twenty-first century', *Journal of Marketing Communications*, 4, 9–26.

Tallman, S. and Fladmoe-Lindquist, K. (2002), 'Internationalization, globalization and capability-based strategy', *California Management Review*, Fall, 116–35.

Taylor, C. R. (1991), *Global Presence and Competitiveness of US Manufacturers*, The Conference Board, Report No. 977, New York: Conference Board.

Turban, E., McLean, E., and Wetherebe, J. C. (2002), *Information Technology for Management Transforming Business in the Digital Economy*, 3rd edn., New York: J. Wiley & Sons Inc.

Wilson, R. M. S. and Gilligan, C. (1999), *Strategic Marketing Management: Planning, Implementation and Control*, Oxford: Butterworth-Heinemann.

**online
resource
centre**

Visit the companion website to this book for lots of interesting additional material, including self-assessment questions, internet exercises, and links for each chapter:

http://www.oxfordtextbooks.co.uk/orc/lee_carter2e/

CHAPTER NINE

Product and
Brand Management

Chapter overview

Chapter Introduction	280	Strategic International Branding	293
The Components of the International Product	280	Local vs. global brands	297
International Product Management	282	The architecture of an international brand	298
Product Strategy	288	New Product Development	302
The product trade cycle	288	Chapter Summary	306
The product life cycle	289		
Matrices to portfolio management	290		
The Ansoff matrix: product growth strategies	292		

Learning objectives

After studying this chapter, the reader will be able to:

- consider the significance of product management in the global economy;
- examine the necessity for adaptation of product strategies in global marketing;
- understand the elements of product strategies in a global context;
- examine how added value can be achieved and maintained by an active product portfolio strategy.

Management issues

The management issues that arise from this chapter include:

- With reference to your business, why is it important to have an active product in international operations?
- How can we add (or develop new) value in international markets through a proactive product strategy?

Chapter Introduction

We live in a shrinking world, aided by advances in transport, communications, converging lifestyles, product availability, and price competition. Markets around the globe are maturing and it is becoming increasingly difficult to compete on the core product or service offering alone. Packaging, warranties, image, etc. are playing an important part. Consider the global car industry, for example, and the small car market in particular. What differentiates a VW Polo (www.vw.com) from a Ford Fiesta (www.ford.com), a Nissan Micra (www.nissanmotors.com) from a Fiat Punto (www.fiat.com)? Is it real product differences or 'extended' (attribute) differences like the image of the company, extended warranties, 'made in', or interest-free easy purchase schemes? In essence, is being different, extended product-wise, being 'original' or is being 'original' different? Is the car argument described here applicable to a Rolls-Royce (www.rolls-roycemotorcars.com) or Bentley (www.bentley-motors.com), or are they original enough without the extensions, and therefore different?

A successful global product and brand strategy needs to assess which products, current or future, in the portfolio, need to be promoted, deleted, or developed to match the market segments currently served, evolving, or planned. To achieve this requires an understanding of customer and market needs and when to provide a product or service to satisfy transnational segments or to adapt the product or service needs to local requirements. International markets often provide product opportunities, existing or new, which may be an incentive to enter international markets. These opportunities may be the result of analysing customer purchase motives globally and the benefits which the product or service can supply. For instance, how many global customers purchase the Manchester United Football Club 'brand' (e.g. replica shirts), even though they might not be able to 'buy' the core product, i.e. watch a Manchester United football match at Old Trafford, England, just because they want to be part of the United culture? The replica shirts are fulfilling the 'aspirational' wants of the customers.

In this chapter we use the term 'product' in its widest sense to include services and not-for-profit marketing. Service marketing will be covered in Chapter 10. Services are usually differentiated from physical products in terms of their intangibility, perishability, heterogeneity, and inseparability, with special emphasis on people, process, and physical aspects. These concepts will be explored in that chapter. In this chapter, the emphasis will be on the strategic rather than the operational issues of product management. This raises the question of the influence of the international marketing environmental factors on product management, which lead to decisions on whether to standardize or adapt the product or service to different market conditions.

The Components of the International Product

To decide on what to offer internationally product-wise, it is essential to know: (a) what makes a 'product'; and (b) what needs to be done to make it acceptable to the international market. There are different descriptions of what constitutes a product (Kotler, 1997). Fig. 9.1 shows a description of the 'product' components.

Kotler (1997) describes the product benefits as the elements the consumers see as meeting their needs and providing satisfaction through product performance and image. He views the product attributes as the elements most closely associated with the core product, such

Fig. 9.1 Components of a product or service offer

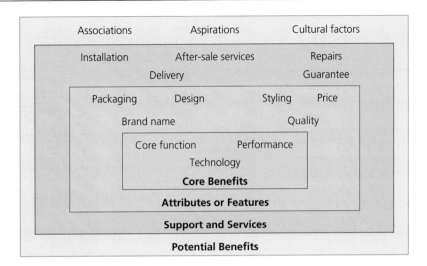

as specifications and quality (see mini-case illustration on ISO 9000), and the marketing support services as additional elements contributing to satisfaction, including delivery and warranties. Kotler (2003: 408) offers a slightly different version of 'basic product', 'expected product', 'augmented product', and 'potential product'.

The status of a brand has been defined as three essential assets, the 'economical asset', which is the brand equity, the 'cultural asset', which is the 'brand intelligence', and the 'social asset', which is the brand relationship. The higher the score on the three parameters, the higher the perceived status of the brand and, therefore, its value in the market. This is an important concept in global marketing as, coupled with the 'country of origin' effect, it has a far-reaching effect on how consumers perceive and accept global brands. For example, how would perfume made in Chile be perceived or accepted in the global market? Yet Japan has shown how this effect can be overcome through time, by astute product innovation and marketing.

After choosing the product components, the global marketer has to decide which will appeal most to all or different market segments. What to offer to the market(s), how to position the product, and how the product will be used have to be decided. While the core product may be suitable for the domestic market, the question is what may have to be done to the product to make it acceptable to overseas markets. Costs may dictate how far the organization is prepared to adapt its product offering to overseas markets, as will the amount of change needed to adapt its strategy and possible competitive advantage to enable it to compete effectively in overseas markets. As we saw in Chapter 7, the UK retailer Marks and Spencer (www.marksandspencer.com) had to adopt a different entry mode (franchising) to enter non-domestic markets. This may mean that its competitive advantage in marketing skills domestically is not directly transferable to the franchisee when it comes to international marketing. Similarly, while it may be exercising a strategy based on contingency theory in the UK, the overseas franchise arrangement may mean a switch to a more agency-based strategy, with an accompanying loss of control.

Changes in product strategy, especially the standardization versus adaptation strategy, may be forced on the organization by a number of variables, including market-based ones, cultural and legal, shortening international product life cycles, different market entry modes, product/market accessibility, and changes in marketing management.

MINI-CASE ILLUSTRATION **Product Attributes: the case of ISO 9000**

The 1990s saw 'quality' emerge as a strategic competitive tool. Previously, a quality product was seen as one with few allowable defects, now it is seen as meeting customer requirements and expectations. It has become one of the most important and sought-after product attributes and is a major reason for repeat purchase and customer satisfaction. The International Organization for Standardization defines quality as all 'features and characteristics of a product or service that (influence) its ability to meet stated or implied needs'. ISO 9000 is probably the most prevalent global quality initiative. It provides the basis for third-party certification of a company's quality system by establishing the standards which must be met. There are many articles on ISO 9000, including the steps to obtain certification, benefits, and costs (DeAngelis, 1991 for example).

ISO 9000 certification is neither risk-free nor cost-free. The cost can be between US$10,000 and $250,000 per company and the first-time failure rate is high. But such are the potential international benefits from certification that many firms are prepared to incur the risks and costs involved. Withers and Ebrahimpour (2001) reported on the experiences of registration in a study they conducted on 11 ISO 9000 certified firms operating in Europe, covering industries such as chemicals and electronics appliances. Their main conclusion was that ISO 9000 serves as an *entrée* into the global marketplace. Specifically, the conclusions were:

- **Obstacles.** Top management involvement was the most frequently cited obstacle for ISO 9000 implementation, with implementation time and system change cited next. The difficulty in interpreting the standards was another obstacle, but not poor existing documentation, as one might expect.

- **Effort.** Activities incurring the greatest time and effort, and therefore costs, were internal quality audits, document and data control, process control, quality systems, and corrective and preventative action.

- **Benefits.** The broadly based benefits found in the study were product quality, service quality, communications, public image, and competitiveness.

The study concluded that 'quality' is a culturally independent system with universal applicability. More research is needed on how big the benefits are universally but there is little doubt that it is one of the most sought-after brand attributes.

Yang (2001) recounts a similar experience within the global software industry. It has grown into a globally complex business where sourcing and software production and operations sharing have become the industry standard. At the same time, the marketplace is less tolerant of poor quality products and hidden maintenance costs. Yang reports on the huge effort going into developing international quality standards based on ISO 9000 registration. However, he warns that registration is only the first step to achieving consistent software quality. Other factors must also be in place, including efforts to prevent software piracy and the often inferior quality which accompanies that activity.

Source: Withers and Ebrahimpour (2001).

International Product Management

Standardization versus adaptation is a standard argument in international marketing. According to Vignali (2001), one of McDonald's (www.mcdonalds.com) aims is to create a standardized set of items that taste the same in Singapore, Spain, or South Africa. However, recent trends towards more healthy eating, and cultural changes, have led McDonald's, to maintain the 'standardized business formula', but make some product adjustments to the market demands. It is difficult to find a completely standardized product or service, although the more technical the product or service, e.g. aero engines and life insurance, the more likely is the standardization. He states that, although substantial cost savings can be obtained through standardization, being able to adapt to an environment ensures success. Therefore, the concept 'think global, act local' (Ohmae, 1989)

Fig. 9.2 Standardization vs. adaptation in international markets

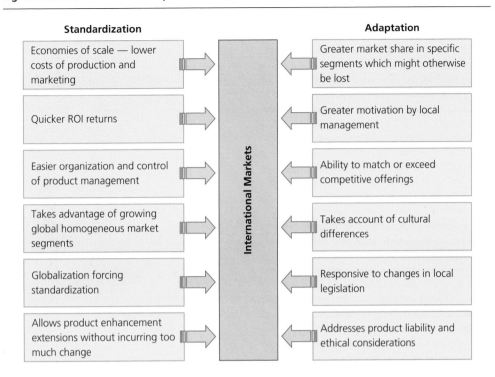

Standardization	International Markets	Adaptation
Economies of scale — lower costs of production and marketing		Greater market share in specific segments which might otherwise be lost
Quicker ROI returns		Greater motivation by local management
Easier organization and control of product management		Ability to match or exceed competitive offerings
Takes advantage of growing global homogeneous market segments		Takes account of cultural differences
Globalization forcing standardization		Responsive to changes in local legislation
Allows product enhancement extensions without incurring too much change		Addresses product liability and ethical considerations

has clearly been adopted by McDonald's (see mini-case illustration). Toyota (www.toyota.com) 'tropicalize' their cars according to the climatic conditions. The key issue is how organizations can use the components of the product or service to differentiate their product or service against international competitors. Fig. 9.2 summarizes the arguments for standardization versus adaptation.

Vignali (2001) concluded that, after analysing the marketing mix of McDonald's, it is clear that the company is 'glocal', i.e. combining elements of globalization and internationalization. McDonald's have achieved this through applying the maxim, 'think global, act local' to all elements of the marketing mix and, until recently, have seen this as such a successful formula that their global expansion has been predicated on it. They can also be said to have utilized the concept of the Boston Consulting Group (www.bcg.com) matrix as they have regarded the USA, their domestic market, as a 'cash cow' with a lower market share than in the global market. Globally,

Food is relatively 'culture bound' so local knowledge is vital to market success. Nonetheless, a number of cuisines have become increasingly 'international', such as Chinese food which is enjoyed in many parts of the world.

MINI-CASE ILLUSTRATION McDonald's—a case of global product adaptation

McDonald's has over 25,000 restaurants in over 100 countries and about 80% are franchises. Richard and Maurice McDonald founded McDonald's as a drive-in restaurant in Pasadena, California, in 1937. In 1954, Ray Kroc, a milkshake salesman, negotiated a franchise deal with exclusive rights to McDonald's in the USA. Kroc offered franchises at US$950 a time, whereas other franchises for ice cream and other restaurants were offered at US$50,000 a time. In 1961 the McDonald's company was sold to Kroc for US$2.7 million. McDonald's first international venture was in Canada in 1967. The rest is history. McDonald's key success drivers have been the use of franchising to local people and delivering what might be seen as quintessential US culture in terms of product and service.

McDonald's have used a 'standardized' strategy based on a standardized set of items, which taste the same globally. However, despite the cost savings, adaptation to the environment has been crucial. Adaptation may be required because of consumer tastes, laws, or customs. McDonald's has responded to them all. In India it serves vegetable nuggets, because Hindus do not eat beef. In Malaysia and Singapore the food was rigorously inspected by Muslim clerics to make sure it was 'clean', i.e. free from pork products. In Germany it serves beer with the products; in Thailand, the samurai pork burger with sweet sauce; and in Uruguay the McHuevo, a poached egg hamburger. The formula is the same, main course (hamburger, cheeseburger, chicken burger, etc.), fries and drink (often Coca-Cola but also tea, coffee, and orange juice). Now included are children's menus—the same formula but cheaper and with a promotional tie-in to the latest film or gadget. The standardized success—not the burger or the drink, but the potato fries. This is the only non-culture-bound element and is the item McDonald's concentrates on to maintain its success. McDonald's is proof of Ohmae's (1989) maxim 'think global, act local'.

In the early 2000s, McDonald's made its only one year quarter loss. The 'health' culture finally caught up. But with McDonald's resilience,

it was only be a matter of time before McDonald's hit back. By January 2005, through selling porridge and salads, among other things, McDonald's was rapidly shedding its 'junk' food image and returning to a healthy sales position. This was reinforced by McDonald's commitment to sponsoring 'sport', sport being a healthy associative activity. This culminated in McDonald's being a prime sponsor of the International Olympic Committee, although not without courting controversy from those who thought the idea of McDonalds sponsoring a healthy activity was pushing the bounds of credibility.

Source: Based on Vignali (2001) and selected extracts from www.McDonalds.com.

they are seen as a 'star' brand and have the ability to gain large market growth and, hence, profitability.

Rundh (2001), in addressing the problem of small and medium enterprises (SMEs) in the internationalization process, acknowledged the fact that the standardization versus adaptation argument was equally applicable to small as well as large enterprises, especially SMEs in developing countries. Developing networks for export purposes is one suggestion but, in order to work up local export markets it is necessary to adjust the marketing strategy to the local requirements of different customers. The need to adapt the product may vary between industries and product areas and these have an influence on other variables in the marketing mix. Rundh argues that to be competitive in the international marketplace it is necessary to meet the local market in relation to technology and product quality.

THE RELATIONSHIP PERSPECTIVE Hollywood and branding

Hollywood is arguably the biggest advertising agency in the world. For years, it made films shown in their thousands all over the world. Blockbusters like the *Star Wars*, *Indiana Jones*, and *Spiderman* originals, sequels, and prequels have earned billions in revenue. Yet it was not until the 1980s that the 'co-branding' possibilities of 'marrying' film and products or services used in the film, or 'brand developments' used in film production, were fully realized. It is now commonplace. The James Bond films saw car makers BMW (www.bmw.com) and Aston Martin (www.astonmartins.com), and Omega watches (www.Omega.com) capitalize on the association, in global branding and communications terms. A number of brands have been created from film production facilities. George Lucas's Lucas Light and Film organization saw its origins in *Star Wars*, and Steve Job's Pixar digital animation organization was key in the Walt Disney film, *Finding Nemo*. Sony is another brand that has benefited from association with films and television.

The need for local customization is of great importance. Rundh sees the key to this as the ability to build up long-term relationships with customers in the local markets. This requires a high degree of commitment from top management and different resources for different markets—which SMEs may not be able to afford. For SMEs, standardization may be the best initial entry strategy of adaptation for a few markets only, unless they can network with other SMEs and obtain resources to enter more markets with more adapted products or services.

MINI-CASE ILLUSTRATION The melting pot: holiday homes in the sun

In recent years, there has been an explosion of British families buying either holiday homes or permanent homes overseas or in mainland Europe. Spain, France, Cyprus, and Florida are popular destinations. The reasons for this interest in overseas property are a desire for a different lifestyle, cheap house purchase finance, cheap air travel through the low-cost air travel operators, and an increased advertising and promotion campaign in the media by property builders and agents. Such is the boom that in one Spanish town, Torrevieja on the Costa Blanca, nearly half the population is from other countries. According to *Euro Weekly News*, 3–9 June 2004, between January 2003 and June 2004 the population increased by 12% from 81,000 to 90,843. Of these, 41,986 were foreigners, from 138 different countries. The British account for 26% of the population (10,943), Germans 11.5% (4,818), Russians 5.65% (2,372), and Columbians 5.5%. Other sizeable communities include Ukrainians, Norwegians, Ecuadorians, Moroccans, Belgians, Finns, and Argentines. A total of 14,830 residents are aged between 61 and 70, representing 16.32% of the population. The town has an approximate 50/50 split of males and females. In 2008, the influx of foreigners had swelled the population of the town to 103,154 and rising. Of this, 53.6% (55,284) were foreigners, outnumbering the locals. By far the largest numbers were the British (12,675 of the foreign population), followed by the Germans (3,750), then the Moroccans (3,116), Russians (2,985), the Swedes (2,720), and the Colombians (2,563). Now the foreigners have overtaken the locals as the major inhabitants of the town.

Source: Based on *Euro Weekly News* (3–9 June 2004) and www.kyero.com.

Gray et al. (2003) suggest an alternative to that depicted in Fig. 9.2. By combining the Medina and Duffy (1998) brand typology with that of the White and Griffith (1997) marketing strategy typology, they suggest a number of possible customer-oriented international business strategies:

- A combined cost-effectiveness and standardization strategy to target price-sensitive customers, and appealing primarily to frugality and simplicity values, e.g. Lidl supermarkets (www.lidl.de) of Germany.

- A combined customer-based and adaptation strategy to target markets with similar core product needs but differing augmented product features because of legal or other market constraints, and appealing primarily to reliability and longevity values, e.g. VW cars.

- A combined customer-based and customization strategy to target markets with culturally sensitive consumer values and differing core and augmented product needs, and appealing primarily to leisure and aesthetic values, e.g. specialist holidays.

- An innovation and globalization strategy to target sophisticated global segments, and appealing to reliability, longevity, leisure, and aesthetic values, e.g. second homes abroad (see mini-case illustration).

Increasingly, organizations are finding that standardization of the core benefits based on a technological breakthrough (e.g. the plasma television screen by LG, www.lg.com)

WHOSE RESPONSIBILITY IS IT? Obesity—the new sword of Damocles

In June 2004, British people were shocked to hear that a 3 year-old had died of obesity and that this was not an isolated incident. It was revealed (*Daily Mail*, 27 May 2004) that England had the fastest-growing obesity problem in Europe; it had increased by 400% in 25 years and was costing £7.4 billion a year in treatment and lost employment. Nearly 75% of the adult population was overweight, with 22% classed as clinically obese. One in ten 6 year-olds were classed as obese and almost one in five by the age of 15. Current death rates through weight-related problems were put at 1,000 per week. In 2008, Britons topped the female European obesity league, with Scotland (59.7%) leading, followed by England (58%), then Cyprus (58%), and with Latvia (45.6%) at the bottom. The males did little better, with Cyprus (72.6%) at the top, England (69.5%) second, and Scotland in tenth place (65.4%). Latvian males (44.6%) were again at the bottom of the league tables. In the USA, it is estimated that there are 2 million super-morbidly obese people, and this is blamed mainly on the abundance of fast food and constant advertising (the US fast-food industry in 2007 was worth US$101 billion). The reasons for the increase in obesity rates are the attitudes of parents, the demise of healthy school dinners (replaced by snacks), and the role global advertisers in the food and drinks industry. Global 'heroes' were being paid millions to promote brands, alleged by some to be unhealthy, and this is cited as a major contributor to the problem. David Beckham and Brittany Spears have promoted Pepsi and Lawrence Dallaglio has promoted McDonald's. Members of Parliament (MPs) in the UK are so concerned about the promotion of alleged 'junk food' that a

ban on advertising during children's television programmes is being considered. MPs are also calling on the food industry and advertisers to implement a voluntary withdrawal for advertisements for foods with high fat, sugar, and salt content. Almost 1,500 alleged 'junk' food commercials are shown during children's television programmes every day and many of these are well-known global brands. Something has to be done by those concerned: parents, advertisers, individuals, manufacturers, and governments.

Source: Based on articles in the *Daily Mail* (27 May 2004 and 15 May 2008).

are being replaced by standardization of non-core elements as competition invades the original core differentiation. There is now so little perceived product difference between the major car manufacturers that some are now competing on image—Renault with 'Createur d'automobiles' and Toyota with 'Today, Tomorrow, Toyota'. The slogans mean little but convey 'Frenchness, style and flair' and 'reliability', respectively. Culture has played an important part in the adaptation argument. Food is notoriously culture-bound, witness McDonald's change of ingredients when sold in different religious cultures. Product usage may also mean adaptation is the best option, as do legal standards, product liability issues, product acceptability, and ethical issues. To sell 4×4 vehicles to Africa, Toyota 'tropicalize' them. Certain pharmaceutical companies find that it is not possible to sell their products universally due to differences in health legislation. For instance, the pharmaceutical manufacturer CAPS of Zimbabwe (www.caps.co.zw) may find it difficult to sell its anti-malaria tablets in the UK. European car manufacturers have to change their specifications to sell to the USA and manufacturers of other products need to be aware of the culture of 'litigation' in the USA and the UK. Consumers globally are becoming knowledgeable and it is increasingly difficult to sell a standardized product which is 'past its sell-by cycle' into less developed countries (LDCs) in particular. These and other considerations inform the decision on whether to standardize or adapt the product offering.

Growing attention to ethical and social responsibility issues are a common feature of product management in multinational enterprises (MNEs). For instance, fast-food manufacturers are increasingly being confronted with the social impact of their products on their customers, as illustrated in the mini-case on obesity below. Consumers are increasingly worried about degradation of the environment and are quick to boycott the products of global brands which are shown to be socially or ethically unsound. Companies such as the Body Shop (www.thebodyshop.com) have made a virtue of their concern for the environment and Ford has adopted the world environmental standard ISO 4001. Markedly, it is the USA, not underdeveloped countries, which is behind in adopting the principles of the Kyoto Agreement on greenhouse gas emissions. And organizations like Greenpeace (www.greenpeace.org) and Friends of the Earth (www.foe.co.uk) have consistently been at the forefront of green and environmental issues.

Increasing globalization has led to a concentration of suppliers anxious to match competitive offerings with huge investments in research and development. These investments require quick returns to satisfy shareholders and other stakeholders. Much of this money is invested in product improvement, thus hastening the decline of the product life cycle. Product managers are having to cope with these changes as well as being instigators of the process. Managing a product 'out', and trying to knowingly manage another one 'in' often exercises creative ingenuity. Employing different market entry modes may enable the international product manager to exploit the necessities of product developments. In order to achieve the resources to develop products and market them in the fastest and most cost-effective way to maximize returns, MNEs may resort to a planned campaign of joint venture and strategic appliance as well as franchising to maximize market exposure rapidly. One such example is that of General Electric (www.ge.com), which has teamed up with French manufacturer SNECMA (www.snecma.com) to become the sole supplier of aero engines for the Boeing 737.

Changes in life cycles, methods of market entry, and product adaptation strategies have spawned a new type of marketing management. Improvements in gathering market intelligence, performance (such as world-class manufacturing, WCM), and networking mean product management is becoming more sophisticated and demanding, and product development is constantly necessary to find and satisfy international market segments.

Product Strategy

An organization may decide to embark on an international product strategy based on a number of factors:

- the company's overall market objectives;
- its decision on the resources to be committed to international development;
- market and customer expectations;
- the products and services themselves;
- marketing mix support;
- environmental constraints;
- risk and control.

As far back as 1989, Keegan identified five international strategies as being a combination of standardization and adaptation of the product/market mix (see Table 9.1). The chosen strategy will be informed by international trade and product life cycles (see Kotler, 2003: 328–40 for a full discussion on the product life cycle concept). Other management tools, such as the Boston Consulting Group's growth–share matrix (BCG), the General Electric Grid, and the Ansoff product/market matrix will also inform the process (see Kotler et al., 2001: 86–9 for a full description of these concepts).

The product trade cycle

The product trade cycle or product life cycle (Vernon, 1966; Wells, 1968) suggests that many products go through a cycle during which high-income, mass-consumption countries, which are initial exporters, lose their markets and finally become importers of the product. At the same time, other countries, primarily developing countries move from being importers to exporters.

For a high-income country, phase 1 involves exporting based on domestic product strength and surplus; phase 2 is when foreign production begins, phase 3 when production in the foreign country becomes competitive; and phase 4 when import competition begins. The assumption is that new products are usually launched in high-income markets because (a) there is greater potential, and (b) the product can best be tested domestically near the source of production. Thus, new products usually emanate from

---

Table 9.1 International strategies

Strategy	Basis	Example
One product, one message globally	Global reliability	Pratt and Whitney aero engines
Product extension, promotion adaptation	Local customers	University degrees
Product adaptation, promotion extension	Local market conditions	IBM computing solutions
Dual adaptation	Total differentiation	Insurance
Product invention	Tailored, new to market	Limited editions

Source: Based on Keegan (1989).

high-income countries and then orders are solicited from lower income countries, so a thriving export market develops. Entrepreneurs realize that the markets to which they are selling have lower production costs, therefore production for the new products is relocated, and so starts the second stage. Foreign and high-income-country production begins to supply the same export market. When foreign producers expand and gain experience, their competition displaces the high-income production source. At this point high-income production countries begin to invest in foreign markets to protect their share. As foreign producers expand, their economies of scale make them a source for third-country markets where they compete with high-income exporters. The final stages of the cycle occur when the foreign producer achieves such a scale that it starts exporting to the original high-income producer at a production cost lower than its original high-income supplier. High-income producers then face competition at home. The cycle continues as the production capability extends from other advanced countries to less developed countries at home, then in international trade, and finally, in other advanced countries' home markets.

The underlying principle behind the product trade cycle is that it begins with the export of new product ideas from high-income countries to low-income countries and the low-income countries begin production of the product. Sometimes an exporter puts a product into a high/low income country that is simply unable to respond. The trade cycle then ceases to be the underpinning concept. This may be due to a number of factors, such as lack of access to capital to build facilities, lack of skills, or that the cost of local production cannot get down to the level of costs of the imported product. In the latter case, product substitution may occur between the exporter and importer. An example of the trade cycle is that of Sunsplash. Sunsplash, based in Masvingo in Zimbabwe, produced a variety of fruit juices for the local market. When Zimbabwe began its economic structural adjustment programme in 1990, it moved from a command to a market economy, part of which allowed the free import of foreign products. The market share of Sunsplash fell from 1 million litres annually to 400,000 litres, primarily through imports from neighbouring South Africa. On this reduced volume, coupled with higher transport costs, the company could not compete and closed down in January 1995. Other problems included expenditure on imported machinery which was hit by rising interest rates and the transition to aseptic packaging which would have alleviated the need for chemical preservations and enhanced unrefrigerated shelf life. However, cash flow constraints within the holding company (AFDIS) made the US$5.8 million investment unviable.

The product life cycle

The product life cycle, is also used as the theoretical basis for new or even existing product expansion. In domestic marketing, the product life cycle has been cited as a useful planning concept which can also be used in international marketing (see Fig. 9.3).

The traditional five-stage life cycle—conception and pre-launch, introduction, growth, maturity, and decline—is well documented. Attempts are usually made in the maturity stage to extend the life cycle either by introducing new products or extensions of existing products. Extension may be made by introducing the product into other markets. Not all markets are in the same stage of the life cycle. Therefore, what may be an old product in one market may be a new one in another market. An example of this is the iphone (www.apple.com), extant in Asia but relatively new to Europe and virtually unknown in sub-Saharan Africa.

Fig. 9.3 Product life cycle

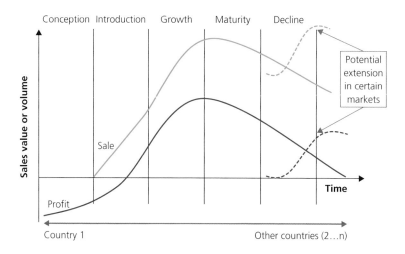

Matrices to portfolio management

There are a number of matrix approaches developed to aid product strategy, including the Boston Consulting Group (BCG growth–share matrix) and the General Electric Market Attractiveness–Competitive position Matrix (developed by McKinsey and Co., (www .mckinsey.com) (Day and Wensley, 1983). As an example, we shall look at the BCG.

The BCG is a matrix of market growth and market share. This is illustrated in Fig. 9.4.

Market growth rate, in Fig. 9.4, indicates an annual growth rate of between 0% and 15% in which each product operates. Market share indicates the product's share relative to its largest competitor. The division between high and low market share is 1, the line being a proxy dividing high share (1–10) and low share (1–6). The box also shows that cash flow, not profit, is dependent on the box in which the product falls. 'Cash cows' are likely to have a large market share in a mature market and thus generate cash, which should fund the 'question marks' to become stars. 'Stars' still use cash but generate

Fig. 9.4 The BCG matrix

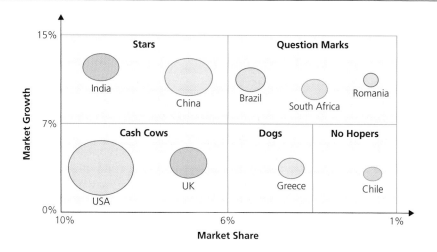

more than they use, whereas as 'dogs', with low share and low market growth, use cash more than they generate. They might become 'question marks' or 'stars', but if they continue to drain cash and still continue to achieve low market share, then they become 'dogs', or worse, the 'no hopers', and should be eliminated. Similarly, if 'question marks' do not become stars but continue to lose more cash than they generate, then they should be deleted.

The portfolio is a useful tool to help set objectives for products and in maintaining a balanced portfolio. As for the former, objectives for star products would include building share or sales, investing to maintain leadership, and beating off competitors, typical of market-leading car manufacturers. Cash cows' objectives would include maintaining sales, defending the position, and using excess cash generated to fund new product development or question marks, typical of companies like Guinness (www.guinness.com). Dogs would be harvested, divested, or have objectives that find a defensible niche—Anglo divesting themselves of gold might be an example. Question marks might have objectives which would see selective building, harvesting, divesting, or niche building.

As for maintaining a balanced portfolio, the matrix shows how vital this is to organizations. Too many dogs will put the business at risk, as will too many question marks. Equally, too many cash cows, although an enviable position to be in, would mean that there are no new products coming through for the future. A balanced portfolio, made up of a number of stars, supported by a few cash cows, with as few dogs and question marks as possible would be ideal, but difficult often to achieve.

The Boston Consulting Group's matrix of market growth against market share is particularly complex when applied to global markets. If competition is fierce, relative market share by country and product may be hard to assess, making it difficult to choose a retention, growth, or elimination strategy. A matrix analysis is useful in attempting to balance the portfolio of international market involvement with the allocation of investment funds. Many firms are currently investing in China to take advantage of expected market growth, but they are investing more slowly in the Middle East, where expected growth is lower. A company's market objectives stage in the product life cycle, and manufacturing and marketing capacity, will all influence the decision to add to, eliminate, grow, or consolidate the products in different markets.

An analytical tool, such as the BCG matrix, will also enable organizations to assess the focus of their business. Companies such as British Gypsum (www.britishgypsum.com), one of the world's leading manufacturers of plaster and plasterboard products, has been divesting its paper-making capacity and concentrating on its core business, purchasing companies which make similar products throughout the world.

The product life cycle and matrix approaches have been subjected to critical review (Kotler, 2003). Some products do not go through the 'S' shaped product life cycle, e.g. bricks, which show more of an undulating cycle corresponding to surges and troughs in building cycles. The matrix approaches have suffered from the 'snapshot in time' syndrome and some of the major problems are in predicting market growth rates, competitive share, the assumption that cash flow is dependent on the product's position in the box, and predicting investment accurately. Other problems include the assumption that products are self-funding, ignoring interdependencies between products and the problem of product placement precision. What if products are on the boundaries? How well and accurately can data be gathered to both construct and plot the products in the matrix? When is the right time to introduce a product to the market, or delete one? Nonetheless, these concepts have survived the criticisms and evolved to meet many of them, and still remain the often-quoted and used global strategy conceptual building blocks. Its particular role in product strategy is the recognition that different products should have different roles in the product portfolio and so different types of manager and resultant reward systems should be in place.

The Ansoff matrix: product growth strategies

Matrix approaches look at managing existing products whereas the Ansoff (1957) matrix looks at future opportunities. Fig. 9.5 illustrates the possibilities.

Market penetration involves taking an existing product in an existing market and trying to improve share by encouraging customers to take more of the product: two for the price of one, discounts, loyalty schemes, etc. This is typical of consumer goods.

Product development involves increasing sales by improving existing products or developing new ones for current markets. Car manufacturers adopt this practice regularly.

Market development is typical where current products are sold into new markets via exporting or other means. This can be expensive and the product trade cycle and life cycle concepts can be useful for this strategy. This is a common form for many global marketers, although the whole issue of standardization versus adaption is important here.

Diversification occurs when new products are developed for new markets and is the most costly and risky strategy of them all. Heinz (www.heinz.com), with its successful 'weight watchers' products in the UK and USA, is a typical example. Where product synergy is present, the strategy is more likely to work. The Digital Impact below illustrates how the emerging digital technologies have enabled some companies to deliver new types of service.

With the growth of globalization and the 'convergent consumer' global products are becoming more of a reality, aided and abetted by shared CAD/CAM (computer aided development/manufacture). Unilever (www.unilever.com), Volkswagen (www.volkswagen.com), John Deere (www.deere.com), and Black and Decker (www.blackanddecker.co.uk) are all 'global product' manufacturers taking a 'platform/modular' approach, based on shared product features, to reduce costs of production, marketing, and spares. For example, the Volkswagen Group uses the same chassis and other components for the VW Golf, Seat Leon, Skoda Octavia, and the Audi A3.

No matter how a manufacturer wishes to prolong a product's life, eventually most products will need to be replaced. This can be a 'deliberate' strategy on the manufacturer's part as technology and competition dictate the speed of change, e.g. television sets, hi-fi, digital cameras, cars, and airplanes. It may also be a necessity simply to survive. Some products have seemingly incredible 'longevity', e.g. HP sauce (www.hp.com), now part of Heinz, was first marketed in 1903 and has become an 'icon' in the UK and many countries.

Fig. 9.5 Product growth strategies

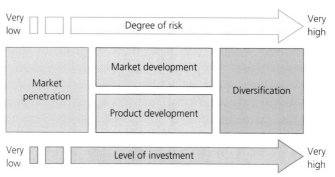

Source: Based on Ansoff (1957).

THE DIGITAL IMPACT New (and old) products for all

One of the many advantages of the internet is its ability to be a 'world' marketplace for products and services, both new and old. In 2007, almost £5 billion was spent on internet-sourced Christmas presents. Customers searching for new cars can easily interrogate global and local car companies to find any model. There are even virtual car dealerships where customers can 'browse' at leisure. The internet has product applications in various businesses. Plans for new buildings, tunnels, airports, or other structures can be moved digitally all over the world, to experts and/or customers for comment. Virtual ideas or concepts for new product development can be sent to panels of consumers to ascertain reactions. But perhaps one of the most interesting developments is the ability to conduct a new product or service development *process* online. A company based in the north of England has developed a system (Sarcophagus) where the process of 'new build' is monitored on the intranet. Many people and processes are involved in a new building, including the client, the main builder, the sub-contractors, material suppliers, architects, and project managers.

For international projects, the logistics can be daunting as suppliers and sub-contractors may be sourced globally. Sarcophagus is a system designed so that all the players can 'talk to each other' digitally. Building plans, build sequences, and critical dates are logged in the system which can 'remind', or track electron-

ically, who should have done what and when. This way the project can be kept on time without the need for meetings to pinpoint the delay. The system also acts as an archive (hence the name) to store plans, the location of pipes and ducts, etc. This is an invaluable service for future maintenance.

Strategic International Branding

Brands play a crucial role in establishing an organization's position and visibility in the global marketplace. The image and value associated with a brand are perhaps the most important intangible assets for all globally recognized organizations today. According to the global brand consultancy Interbrand Report (www.interbrand.com)—a well-known global brand study conducted annually—there is a compelling case that those which place high importance on managing the economic value of their intangible assets, and primarily their brands, consistently outperform basic economic measures. Table 9.2 shows the top ten international brands and their market value in 2007. Tangible asset growth is often a slow process that requires deep and resource-intensive long-term planning. Intangible asset growth, on the other hand, involves getting the best out of something that the company already owns. It is a case of managing these assets more effectively, and it's an efficient method of adding very real value to business.

Different markets attribute different values to brands. Consumer acceptance depends on their assessment of the brand's intrinsic features (e.g. design, emotions, etc.) and extrinsic features (e.g. name, logo, country of origin, etc.). Lack of knowledge of the range of product features leads to generalizations of the brand based on country of origin. For instance, goods made in China can be viewed negatively whereas Swiss products conjure up a positive image. Overcoming these stereotypes can be a challenge to marketers. Nike (www.nike.com), Puma (www.puma.com), and Reebok (www.reebok.com) sports shoes are synonymous with quality and style, but what about Power sports shoes from Bata (www.bata.com)? The reality is that these brand giants manufacture and design in different countries but the location of their headquarters overrides any prejudice. This is true of Nike, headquartered in the USA but manufacturing in Indonesia and Thailand (see Thakor and Kohli, 1996, for research into this effect).

Table 9.2 The top ten global brands, 2007

Rank	Brand	Country of origin	Sector	Value ($ million)
1	Coca-Cola	USA	Drinks	65,324
2	Microsoft	USA	Software	58,709
3	IBM	USA	Computing	57,091
4	GE	USA	Diversified	51.569
5	Nokia	Sweden	Computer electronics	39,696
6	Toyota	Japan	Automobile	32,070
7	Intel	USA	Computer hardware	30,954
8	McDonald's	USA	Restaurants	29,398
9	Disney	USA	Media	29,210
10	Mercedes	Germany	Automobile	23,568

Source: Interbrand (www.interbrand.com).

Company image has a considerable effect on consumers' brand perceptions. There-fore, a great deal of effort is spent cultivating the company image. British Airways (www.ba.com), Lufthansa (www.lufthansa.com), and Singapore Airlines (www.singaporeair.com) spend millions creating an upmarket image, whereas easyJet (www.easyJet.com) and Rya-nair (www.ryanair.com), low-cost operators in the same business, spend millions cultivat-ing a 'no frills' approach. Perversely, in the case of popular music and clothes, the 'rebel' image unintentionally creates the opposite effect and achieves classic or style status, such as designer 'torn jeans' and 'punk' music. International reputation can create an image competitors find difficult to challenge, e.g. Porsche (www.porsche.com), Harrods (www.harrods.com), Microsoft (www.microsoft.com), KFC (www.kfc.com), and NASA (www.nasa.com). Compare Table 9.2 with Table 9.3 as a further example. Table 9.3 shows the results

Table 9.3 Most admired international brands

Rank	Brand	Country of origin	Sector
1	GE	USA	Diversified
2	Microsoft	USA	Software
3	Toyota	Japan	Automobile
4	IBM	USA	Computing
5	Wal-Mart	USA	Retail
6	Coca-Cola	USA	Drinks
7	Dell	USA	Computer hardware
8	Berkshire Hathaway	USA	Executive jet
9	Daimler Chrysler	Germany	Automobile
10	Sony	Japan	Computer electronics

Source: Metro, 21 January 2004.

Fig. 9.6 The themes of a brand as differentiators

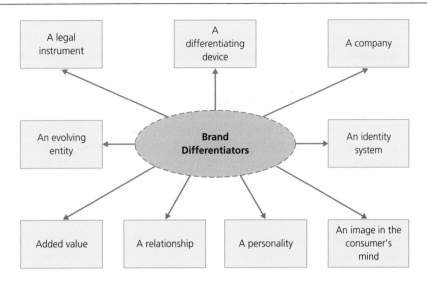

of a survey of 1,000 business executives (*source*: *Metro*, 21 January 2004) and their admiration of companies based on power, integrity, and sense of social responsibility. Bill Gates of Microsoft was the most respected leader. This, besides showing that 70% of the companies are US owned, is an example of perceptions of both the brand's intrinsic and extrinsic features.

Brands are the means customers use to differentiate products and services based on extrinsic and intrinsic features and are a source of an organization's differential advantage. De Chernatony (1989) suggests nine themes which differentiate a brand, as illustrated in Fig. 9.6. These themes suggest that brands convey intangible and tangible benefits and appeal to a range of feelings (e.g. status). An example is young people buying a pair of Nike sports shoes to emulate the sporting heroes who are often displayed in the advertising, e.g. Michael Jordan the basketball player. A powerful brand or co-brand, such as James Bond films and BMW cars (www.bmw.com) (which appeared in James Bond films), can give an organization entry to international markets. The brand value can be a combination of intrinsic and extrinsic features, not necessarily in the same quantity, which add value in international markets. The meaning attached to the brand is not necessarily the same in all cultures and countries. Long-lasting brands carry a core value to customers by name association. The 'great brands' use large investment in advertising, brand-building, and consistent management to achieve their status. Brand valuation can be both subjective and objective. Accountants have devised a way to put a balance sheet figure on brands as an example of objective measurement (see Ambler and Styles, 2000 for discussion on brand valuation). Brands may decline due to poor management, strong competition, and brand stretching. Classic examples include Amstrad (www.amstrad.com) in desktop computers, TWA airlines, which went out of business, and Marks and Spencer, which lost ground in the clothing sector.

Five recognized branding strategies are depicted in Fig. 9.7. Each strategy has implications for international markets. Identification of the core product may be a strategic consideration, and its extension via extrinsic valuation an operational decision. Nissan and Toyota, for example, produce 'basic' core (family name) products like 4 × 4 vehicles. Yet in

Fig. 9.7 Branding strategies

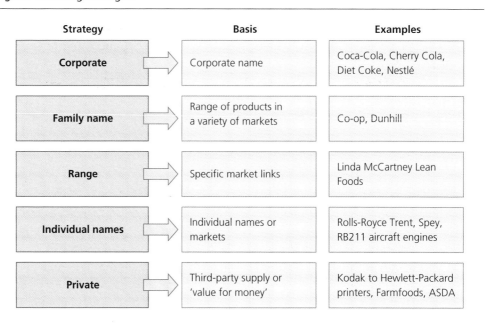

different markets they may 'add' the extrinsic characteristics, created by an advertising image for example, to gain market share. In South Africa, the 4 × 4 may be sold on the image of a rugged off-roader, capable of carrying loads on less developed roads. This image would not succeed in the UK, where the 4 × 4 serves other images, such as the 'sports utility' or 'school run' vehicle. In both cases, the core product remains basically unchanged but the extended product has changed to meet market expectations. Companies can charge a different price due to the extrinsic product features, e. g. in South Africa the 4 × 4 would cost less than in the UK.

Globally recognized international brands are often regarded by consumers as leaders across the world. Although their customers may come from different countries and cultures, they are driven by a desire to 'own' a single-minded global brand experience. To create a 'unified' perception and desire in the minds of the customers, organizations must develop in their brands a very clear brand position that is consistent across diverse geographies, cultures, and market segments. Organizations seeking to establish or reinforce the position can use: (a) 'objective' product characteristics such as size, shape, etc.; and/or (b) 'subjective' elements such as image, packaging, and using market conditions such as stage of development and occasion of use. For instance, a Mercedes-Benz (www.mercedes-benz.com) is perceived as a luxury in sub-Saharan Africa and the UK, but in Germany it can also be perceived as serving a utilitarian purpose, e.g. a taxi. Ever-growing consumer sophistication and demand mean that organizations must resort to creative positioning strategies based on factors other than price differentiation. Successful positioning comes from the perception of customers and their estimation of the degree of difference and/or similarity *vis-à-vis* competitive offerings. Marketing research becomes a necessity as a basis for successful positioning to elicit the price/quality dimensions, product attributes, and competitive comparisons, as seen by the consumer. This will differentiate the organization's offering from that of its rivals. To face up this challenge, organizations must commit to and implement focused and realistic brand strategies in multiple geographical and cultural settings. This demands that brands transform the information and input they receive along the way into activities that build a global reputation. It requires constant measurement to ensure that actions complement, and holistically push, the brand towards its strategic goals.

Local vs. global brands

There appears to be an emerging trend that many multinational organizations are moving from a multi-domestic marketing approach to a global marketing approach. These organizations have concentrated their efforts on the development of international brands. Unilever (www.unilever.com), for instance, has removed over 1,000 (mostly local) brands from its brand portfolio to concentrate on 400 international brands. L'Oréal (www.loreal.com) focuses its marketing strategy on just 16 brands worldwide. Within this market context, international marketers are confronted with difficult decisions when developing the ideal international brand portfolio. They must decide not only how to build their international brands but also which local brands to build, which to eliminate, which to sell, and which to assimilate under a more globally recognized international brand name. There are important decisions that significantly determine global market success (Schuiling and Kapferer, 2004). In making these decisions, it would be useful to develop an understanding of the real differences between 'local' brands and 'global' brands and the strategic advantages with each of these approaches to international branding.

Local brands normally exist in one country or a geographical region. Multinational organizations such as Nestlé (www.nestle.com) have successfully used local brands for specific markets to create local product or service identity that often reflects the more authentic consumer preferences. The sales volumes of strong local brands do not benefit from the global economies of scale associated with global brands. Nevertheless, local brands, as Schuiling and Kapferer (2004) observe, represent many years of investment, are well known in their markets, and often have strong relationships with local consumers over the years. There are many strategic advantages associated with local brands that must be considered in making international branding decisions:

1. **Better response to local needs.** A local brand can be designed to respond to needs which are specific to the market. It has the flexibility to produce a unique product or service and brand positioning to reflect the local cultural insights, language, and preferences.

2. **Flexibility of pricing strategy.** Pricing strategies of local brands are more flexible as they do not have to be linked to the regional pricing strategy of an international or global brand. Such flexibility can lead to higher profitability because prices can be fixed at higher levels.

3. **Possibility of responding to local or international competition.** A local brand may respond to competition with greater ease as all marketing mix decisions can be adapted quickly. The marketing strategy for an international or global brand, however, must follow a predefined, highly centralized global strategy.

4. **Possibility of balancing a portfolio of brands.** An international portfolio that mostly comprises a small number of international and global brands presents significant risks for organizations. A problem that arises with one global brand in a particular country or region can create a 'ripple effect' to other parts of the world.

5. **Possibility of responding to needs not covered by international brands.** Profitable segments of the markets that are unique to certain countries may represent attractive opportunities for local brands. A transnational organization can reach these segments by acquiring a existing local brand as a way to enter this market directly without further large investment.

The strategic advantages of building global or international brands are substantial and follow an inexorable logic. They include:

1. **Strong economies of scale.** A standardized brand can generate substantial cost reductions in all areas of the business systems and processes, e.g. research and development, manufacturing, logistics, packaging, and communications costs.

2. **Development of a unique brand image across countries.** The simplicity of the 'one vision, one logo' branding concept can be applied to all products within selected categories, which can be used to target segments of consumers worldwide.

3. **Speed to market for new product initiatives.** Due to the strong economies of scale, organizations can often invest heavily in research and development to speed up new product launches. The new product development cycles would otherwise take much longer when the brand strategies are not globalized.

4. **Supporting branding with large budgets for global communications.** Global brands are normally supported by large budgets for global communications as the return of investment for global products or services are very attractive for organizations to do so. With large budgets, global brands can take advantage of employing the best advertising agencies and global media to reach a substantial number of potential customers.

The development of international or global brands can bring significant strategic advantages to multinational organizations. Because of their global market reach, these brands generate very attractive financial returns for shareholders, create high barriers of entry, and benefit from a unique global image visibility. Adopting a strong multi-domestic approach to branding by creating local brands can nevertheless bring with it strategic advantages and opportunities which would otherwise not been possible with a global approach. There is a strong argument for an organization's brand portfolio to maintain a balance of both good local and global brands.

The architecture of an international brand

An organization's international branding strategy is usually formed through an evolutionary process that results from decisions to enter new country markets or expand product offerings within an existing country. Decisions are often made on a country-by-country or product-by-product basis without considering the overall balance or coherence of branding in international markets from a strategic, global perspective. As the international markets become more interconnected and globalized, organizations need to place greater emphasis on the coherence of branding decisions across national markets and build an effective international brand architecture that underpins the development of a sound global branding strategy. In particular, organizations must decide how to manage brands that span different geographic markets and product lines. They must establish a rationale for harmonizing branding decisions at different levels of the organization and across different geographic locations. These decisions would provide strategic direction and indicate which brands should be emphasized at what levels in the organization, how brands are used and extended across product line and countries, and the extent of brand coordination across national boundaries. (Douglas et al., 2001).

Developing the architecture of a globally recognized international brand fit for the twenty-first century is no easy task. Since the late 1990s, a number of transnational companies, including Coca-Cola, McDonald's, Nike, and Gap, have come to the attention of non-governmental organizations (NGOs) and have become the targets of anti-globalization protestors. The angry demonstrations at the meetings of the World Trade Organization (WTO, www.wto.org) and G8 in recent years, as portrayed in the international media, are often directed at transnational companies whose brands have become the most visible symbols of economic globalization. Due to their global visibility, they are often used as the symbol of social ills associated with globalization, such as global poverty, exploitative wages, environmental degradation, and cultural imperialism. It is hard for any global brands to escape notice. Indeed, most multinational corporations (MNCs) need to realize that people view them differently from other organizations. Many consumers are awed by economic and political power of MNCs that produce revenues which exceed the GDPs of small nations and, consequently, their impact on the welfare of communities, nations, and the planet itself (Holt et al., 2004). Because of their pervasive nature, global brands are perceived as powerful institutions capable of doing great good and causing considerable harm.

In their research, which involved 3,300 consumers in 41 countries, Holt et al. (2004) found that most people choose one global brand over another because of differences in the brands' global qualities. They found that there are three significant dimensions to a global brand that affect consumer preference: (a) quality signal; (b) global myth; and (c) social responsibility (see Fig. 9.8). Despite the fact that 62 of the world's 100 most valuable global

Fig. 9.8 Dimensions of global brand

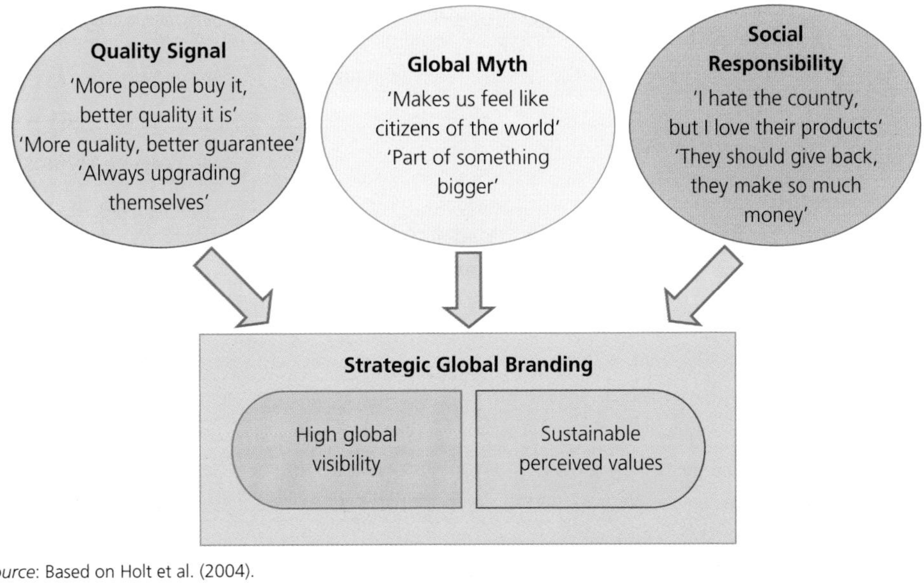

Source: Based on Holt et al. (2004).

brands are American in origin (*source*: Interbrand), the so-called 'American values' (or 'culture of origin') play an insignificant role in influencing consumer preference.

(a) **Quality signal.** In the eyes of the consumers, a global brand signifies an exceptional high level of quality. The fact that it is globally desirable to consumers and successfully outperforms its competitive rivals impress consumers. These perceptions on quality create a strong rationale for MNCs to charge a high premium on their products or services. Globally recognized brands are perceived as delivering greater value for money, frequent technological breakthroughs, and consistent product and service quality.

(b) **Global myth.** Global brands are regarded by consumers as symbols of cultural ideals, not just in terms of lifestyle but also in beliefs, values, and citizenship. Brands can be perceived as being part of a powerful, imagined global identity, which can be shared with other like-minded people globally. Through purchasing certain brands, consumers can feel that they are a part of something 'bigger' or that they have a 'sense of belonging' to a large group.

(c) **Social responsibility.** Increasingly, consumers are expecting transnational corporations, due to their vast resources, to demonstrate a social responsibility by addressing social problems linked to what they sell and how they conduct business. The availability of global media is making the business activities of transnational corporations increasingly transparent to consumers. Reports of Nestlé's infant formula sales in Africa since the 1980s and Union Carbide's Bhopal gas tragedy in 1984 have convinced global consumers that global brands have a special duty to tackle social issues.

Research by Holt et al. (2004) shows that these global dimensions, taken together, can, offer powerful insights into why and how consumers behave towards global brands, and these can become the building blocks of a global brand's architecture (Fig. 9.9). To compete

Fig. 9.9 Architecture of a global brand

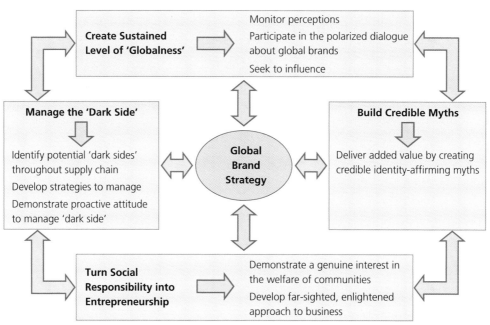

Source: Based on Halt et al. (2004).

successfully, global brands must develop an architecture with the superior ability to do the following:

1. **Create a sustained level of 'globalness'.** Global brands are global symbols because consumers perceive them to be so. However, people around the world attach different values and emotions to brands, ranging from the very positive to the extremely adversarial. Consumer understandings of global brands are framed by the mass media and various discourses that spread over the internet. Organizations must therefore learn to create a sustained level of 'globalness' by monitoring these perceptions, participating in these polarized conversations about global brands, and seeking to influence them.

2. **Manage the 'dark side'.** Global brands often have a 'dark side' that needs to be managed. For instance, the direct (and often indirect) involvement of many high street clothing retailers in exploitative cheap labour in developing countries has been recently portrayed as the 'dark side' of these companies. To avoid negative publicity, most clothing retailers invest heavily to demonstrate to customers their 'changed' behaviour towards ethical and social responsibility issues within their supply chain.

3. **Build credible myths.** Globally successful brands can deliver added value to consumers by creating identify-affirming myths. Microsoft has been particularly successful in achieving this with an advertising campaign built around the strap-line 'Where do you want to go today?' The campaign unfolded stories about common people, such as university students and small business owners, using technology to unleash personal passions. The message was described as 'philosophical', not 'technological': 'Anybody who says that one person can't make a difference is wrong. Try to push, don't give up, don't give up, don't give up. Where do you want to go today?' The company was selling the dream of personal empowerment, which is very different from its competitive rivals' focus on 'the technology'.

4. **Turn social responsibility into entrepreneurship.** Rather than turning social responsibility initiatives into a new form of public relations and repackaging philanthropic efforts using the new 'ethical' language, transnational organizations need to develop a more far-sighted, enlightened approach to their business by turning social responsibility into entrepreneurship. For instance, Procter & Gamble identified safe drinking water as a critical social problem that fell within its scope of expertise. It leverages its knowledge of household sanitation to develop a water purification system that would be effective in poor countries. The potential global social impact could be hugely beneficial as well as profitable.

It is indisputable that international and global brands bring many benefits to consumers as well as to the multinational corporations which own them. Within the current context of market globalization, it is rational for organizations to accelerate the development of powerful, globally recognizable brands. Global brands bring long-term attractive financial returns, create global economies of scale, and create barriers to entry. However, the application of a strong global marketing approach to branding can create risks that global marketers must consider. As globally visible symbols, global brands can quickly come under attack from NGOs and sceptical consumer groups, and be portrayed as opportunistic and exploitative in their business activities. To become truly global, brands must adopt a more enlightened and intelligent approach by demonstrating that they have harnessed their ample resources to benefit society.

They must overcome their short-sighted, shareholders-driven instinct by shouldering greater social responsibility towards the communities and the physical environment in which they operate.

New Product Development

New products are a necessity in global product management strategies. Not only are they a source of competitive advantage, but they are also essential when market segments tire of product offerings, when products have come to the end of their life cycle, or when competitors produce better ones. In general, there are few new products. James Dyson's (www.dyson.com) revolutionary cyclone vacuum cleaner (now manufactured in the Far East due to escalating costs in the UK), the Stealth bomber and the Apple iPod digital music player are examples in this category. Most new products are revisions or improvements to existing ones, e.g. the many versions of the Ford Fiesta. They may also be additions to product lines (e.g. BMW 4 × 4) or cost reductions (e.g. personal computers). Others are new product lines (e.g. versions of soft drinks in different packaging, such as Robinson's 'Shoot' drinks (www.britvic.com)) or repositionings (e.g. British Airways' ill-fated attempt at a no frills airline, 'Go'). Truly new products are expensive to develop and joint developments are often used. This is particularly true in the business-to-business (B2B) market. Market diffusion, often by different modes of entry, is one way of introducing products to new markets, just as new product lines may be 'more new' to companies than mere process or other cost-reduction new products. The new product development process is illustrated in Fig. 9.10.

New product ideas come from within the firm, customers, competitors, a deliberate search, brainstorming, or other similar sources. The ideas are screened for suitability against company objectives and 'fit' criteria before a thorough market and business analysis. This will include financial return on investment and market and product acceptability. Ideas are then put into market test and those which survive will be fully developed and an appropriate marketing mix chosen. In global marketing this can be a long, costly, and difficult process, especially when 'world brands' are being developed.

Fig. 9.10 Process of new product development

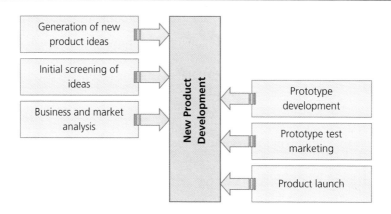

Often specialist divisions are created to help meet the challenges of the global market environment.

The process for developing new products for global markets is similar to that of domestic development except that the antecedents to the process are, probably, more critical. Once products are developed, the company may wish to protect its competitive advantage by patent or licensing agreement and, most certainly, the entry strategy will play its part. 'Time to market' is crucial in this regard. The quicker the organization can go to market, the better. This has led companies like Mazda (www.mazda.com) to adopt a 'velocity strategy'. The idea is to put the product into the market as quickly as possible and allow the market to 'iron out' the faults. Wong (2002), in addressing new product rollout time, refers to the fact that the introduction of new products and speed to market have a positive impact on success. This has led to many normative suggestions on how to accelerate the new product of development (NPD) process, for example, but it does not always follow that because the organization has reduced the NPD process it will get the product into the target market on time. For instance, Mercedes-Benz' launch of the new A-class into key European markets was delayed by instability problems (i.e. it failed the infamous 'moose test') and had to be revised at considerable cost.

Technology is increasingly used in the NPD process. Computer-aided design (CAD) and virtual reality are widely used in product generation and 'customer' feedback. Rapid prototyping enables once long developmental processes to be considerably shortened. Once the 'concept to market' process in aircraft and cars was about 12 and three years, respectively, but now have been cut to six and two years due to CAD and rapid prototyping. However, these techniques are not always fail-safe. Airbus's (www.airbus.com) double-deck A380 and Boeing's (www.boeing.com) Dreamliner aircraft both experienced teething problems although the prototypes have already flown, having been designed and made in relative quick time. The Airbus A380 is now in operation. Flexible manufacturing processes such as 'just in time' (JIT) and electronic purchase order systems (EPOS) have all helped reduce the manufacturing time.

Successful and timely product launch into multiple countries depends on the coordination and integration of NPD project tasks. NPD researchers have classified the drivers of new product success into four broad categories: (1) the external environment; (2) the firm's internal environment; (3) the new product development process; and (4) the product's competitive advantage. Wong (2002) offers a comprehensive review of the principal authors and researchers of these categories. For the external environment, competition can be a threat to the timeliness of rollout, in that management's response to the competitive threat, rather than competitive intensity *per se*, affects the firm's commitment of resources to the project. This has the additional effect of raising management's emphasis on effective coordination of HQ subsidiaries/agents' activities to achieve market launch on time. The technological and customer/market environment are also important. The rate of technological change could affect the NPD process as fears of developing outdated products or services are omnipresent. Similarly, the less homogeneous the market is perceived to be, the less it will stimulate the commitment of larger resources than a more homogeneous market—unless the market is very lucrative, e.g. nuclear material reprocessing. Internally, resource allocation plays an important part in delaying or delivering the NPD project, as does the amount of time and effort needed to coordinate HQ subsidiaries/agents. Material shortages, mis-scheduling materials and activities and operational problems all delay the process. The more superior advantage the product has in the marketplace, the more it is likely to stimulate subsidiaries/agents' efforts in delivering it to market on time. The greater the advantage, the more likely top management will devote resources to, and reduce delays in, the NPD process. 'Best practice' needs to be evolved. Wong (2002) concludes by offering a conceptual model of antecedents of international new product rollout timeliness. It reinforces the need to take a 'holistic' approach to the process, but also emphasizes the need to have a market intelligence system which captures the 'right' information and is capable of interpreting and informing implementation to ensure, as far as possible, NPD process and rollout success.

Shortening life cycles, risks, costs, and the time involved in product development have led to many companies abandoning the heuristic or sequential approach in favour of approaches such as 'risk and revenue'. This involves a number of partners, manufacturers, component makers, and sometimes universities, being prepared to carry the risks and costs of new development for a share in future revenues. The famous University of Warwick Manufacturing Group (www.wmg.warwick.ac.uk) and Jaguar (www.jaguar.com) are a good example of this form of cooperation, as is the US company Nu Skin (www.nuskin.com), which cooperates with a number of universities and research institutes around the world to develop new skincare products. This enhances workers' specialist skills, shortens development time, and enables a greater concentration on core activities.

The nature and location of research and development activities is another key decision. Smaller companies will usually concentrate on R&D in, and to benefit, the domestic market. As they grow, they may have to make decisions on the location, whether to buy it in wholly or in part, license the technology, or enter into strategic alliances. Many large corporations still adopt a 'home country' approach. Examples are pharmaceutical companies where 'secrecy' is the key given the high potential revenue from products in 'breakthrough' drugs. A company which develops a cure for AIDS is an example of this category. Nike (www.nike.com) has a central US-based R&D facility. However, like global car manufacturers, there is often sufficient volume in regional markets to make the home country concept meaningless, and therefore to warrant an R&D facility in numerous locations. The arguments for centralization include the possibility of economies of scale, better coordination, communications and control, and synergy gains, with pressure from subsidiaries, local governments, proximity to market, and access to technology being powerful arguments against.

The costs of new product failure can be enormous, e.g. hundreds of millions of dollars for the nicotine-free New Smoking Material (NSM). Another example is Coca-Cola's attempt at launching Dasani, a bottled spring water in the UK, which was unsuccessful when it was discovered that the water came from a tap, causing the company eventually to withdraw the brand. Sources of failure include ill-defined market needs, poor planning and timing, cultural insensitivity, local competition, tariff and non-tariff barriers, and over optimism from top management:

- **Cultural insensitivity**—trying to sell products in countries which have cultural objections to them.

- **Lack of a unique selling proposition**—the product has no distinctive demonstrable or 'image' features.

- **Product deficiencies**—the product 'in service' fails quickly or has the same common fault (e.g. De Laurean cars).

- **Tariff and non-tariff barriers**—'deliberate'/legal barriers imposed by governments to keep a product out in order to protect local industry (e.g. Coca-Cola in India).

- **Subsidies to local producers**—home governments help to protect home producers (e.g., farm produce).

- **Poor planning**—misguided or insufficient new product planning, such as failing to assess or misinterpreting product/market needs or cost escalation (e.g. the UK government and the TSR.2 fighter aircraft).

- **Top management enthusiasm**—misguided or over-optimistic enthusiasm.

Ways to minimize the risk include a customer-focused superior product, a planned and carefully executed NPD process, research into product/market needs, and an exhaustive risk assessment. The conventional NPD process is one source of competitive advantage and can provide a sustained position in global markets. However, there are less conventional sources, especially those spawned out of cost reduction or process developments. Business process re-engineering, 'reverse engineering', or pursuit of business excellence may also result in new products. In recent years, much has been made of benchmarking as a competitive technology, particularly for improving quality and, therefore, as a means of improving competitive position. A benchmark is the value of parameters used as a reference point within one organization to compare it with similar reference points within another. Chen (2002) stated that recent industry practices have evolved their strategic and operational decisions, taking customer-orientation into consideration. His research attempted to build benchmarking from the 'voice' of the customer. He proposed a quality benchmarking deployment (QBD) technique and used CKS International Airport as a case study. After incorporating the 'voice' of the consumer, Chen found that the 'convenience of transport facilities connecting to the outside', the 'interior design and layout', and the 'information service of the airport' should be priorities for benchmarking activities. He argued that airport benchmarking could provide the CKS International Airport Authority with a long-term vision and a valuable strategic planning tool.

Recent developments in nano-technology promise a rich, profitable, and sustained source of new products. Developments in virtual reality, computer-aided design and manufacturing (CAD and CAM) and communications, particularly internet-based design sources, provide relatively cheap and innovative sources. These advances include the development of remote access medical operations where, using equipment, robotics, software, and communications, a US-based surgeon is able to carry out complex medical operations in the UK without leaving US soil.

Advances in computer-aidded design (CAD) and computer-aided manufacturing (CAM) technologies have enabled organizations to develop and manufacture new products at low costs and within a much shorter time period.

Chapter Summary

1. A product/service is made up of a bundle of benefits including the core benefits, attributes, support and service, and potential. It is essential to understand how the existing/ potential customer perceives these benefits, which may differ from country to country.

2. A key international product strategy decision is whether to offer a standardized or adapted product based on a number of criteria, including resources, degree of local versus central control, product/market similarities and differences, and costs.

3. There are five global product strategies: one global product and message; product extension and promotion adaptation; product adaptation and promotion extension; dual adaptation; and product adaptation. Which one to implement depends on factors such as the company's marketing objectives, resources to be committed, market and customer expectations, the products and services themselves, the marketing mix support, environmental constraints, and risk and control.

4. Concepts such as the international product trade cycle, the product life cycle, matrices, and market/product matrices are useful in planning product strategies.

5. Building a company image, brand, and competitive position are essential to a successful strategy. There are five recognized global branding strategies: corporate, family name, range, individual names, and private brands.

6. Global brands are often regarded by consumers as leaders across the world. Consumers may come from different countries and cultures, but they are driven by a desire to 'own' a single-minded global brand experience. To create a 'unified' perception and desire in the minds of the customers, organizations must develop in their brands a very clear brand position that is consistent across diverse geographies, cultures, and market segments.

7. The development of global brands can bring significant strategic advantages to multinational organizations. Because of their global market reach, these brands generate very attractive financial returns for shareholders, create high barriers of entry, and benefit from a unique global image visibility. However, adopting a strong multi-domestic approach to branding by creating local brands can bring with it strategic advantages and opportunities which would otherwise not been possible with a global approach.

8. A new product development process and/or process development are sources of new products. New products are essential to sustain product/market growth and increase market share. New products can be either new product lines, revision improvements, cost reductions, repositionings, additions to product lines, or new to the world.

  END-OF-CHAPTER CASE STUDY **Formula One and Bernie Ecclestone**

Formula One (F1, www. formula1.com) racing is one of the world's most recognized brands. Ask many young boys around the world what they would like to be when they grow up, and a F1 racing driver is high on the list. Crowds of half a million attend race days are millions more watch on television around the world. Teams like Ferrari (www.ferrari.com), McLaren (www.mclaren.co.uk), and Jordan (www.f1jordan.com) are household names, as are the drivers Michael Schumacher, David Coulthard, and Lewis Hamilton. Drivers come from all nationalities—British, German, Italian, Japanese, Brazilian, Malaysian, and French to name but a few. Sometimes drivers 'come with the sponsor', e.g. the Malaysian driver with Petronas (www.petronas.com.my), the Malaysian state oil company which sponsors the Sauber (www.sauber.ch)

team, and a Japanese driver with the Toyota team. The cars cost £1 million each, with engines generating over 700 bhp (the average family car manages about 118 bhp) and capable of speeds in excess of 200 mph. The cost of running a Formula One team is such that team owners seek sponsorship from many sources. Every square centimetre of the driver's overall is covered with advertising, cashing in on the massive worldwide audience and publicity. Mercedes-Benz supplies engines to McLaren, Hewlett-Packard sponsor the BMW Williams team and, until recently, world tobacco giants, such as Marlboro, poured millions of dollars into the sport. The cars compete on Good Year or Bridgestone tyres and are powered by Shell or Texaco fuel. Not a single sponsorship opportunity is lost, be it banking (HSBC, www.hsbc.com), clothes (Boss, www.hugo.com) or watches (Tag Heuer, www.tagheuer.com).

Formula one's annual calendar is global and takes in 18 (in 2004) races covering Asia (Australia, Malaysia, and Japan), the Middle East (Bahrain), Europe (the mainstay of F1), and North and South America (Canada, the USA, and Brazil). Merchandizing is through specialist F1 outlets worldwide, selling replica model cars, baseball caps, jackets and other memorabilia, all custom-made and packaged with the F1 logo. Even in David Coulthard's hometown of Twynholm, Scotland, you can purchase souvenirs in the David Coulthard museum. The technological innovations of the track are translated into innovations in the ordinary family car. Formula one gave us paddle gear changes, low-profile tyres, engine management systems, and aerodynamic technology for sleeker and more wind-resistant body shapes.

Formula One and Bernie Ecclestone are synonymous. He is the most important component of Formula One and one of the highest-salaried executives in the world. He owns Formula One Holdings, which controls almost every part of the sport. He was paid £54 million in 1995–96 and was expected to become even richer if the company floated on the Stock Exchange, which had been scheduled for summer 2004. Reports suggested the delay was caused by divisions between Ecclestone and some Formula One teams over revenue-sharing and whether they should get a stake in the floated business. One of the company's main assets is its 25-year contract with the sport's governing body, the Federation Internationale de l'Automobile (FIA), to sell television rights. There is speculation that the lengthy contract might be challenged in the courts. When interviewed, Ecclestone said his determination to proceed with the sale of the company was driven by fear that the business could fail when he retired. He said: 'I would hate to see it go down the drain because it was badly managed. If all the teams owned it, they'd destroy it. They can't agree on anything, not even on how to share their money out. They think they can run the business—I know they can't.'

Ecclestone, the son of a trawler captain, left school at 16 to work at the gasworks. His passion was motorcycle scrambling and he began competing after World War II. Machinery was scarce and he began buying and selling motorcycle parts during his lunch break. He went on to form the Compton & Ecclestone motorcycle dealership, and later bought out Compton and built the business into one of the UK's biggest motorcycle dealers. He tried Formula

3 racing but, after an accident, decided to concentrate on his business which grew to include the Weekend Car Auctions firm (which he eventually sold to British Car Auctions), loan financing, and property. In 1957 Ecclestone returned to racing as a manager and later bought the F1 Connaught team. After a spell away from the sport, he bought the Brabham team in 1972. He was one of the founders of the F1 Constructors' Association (FOCA) and in 1978 became Chief Executive of FOCA and began a battle with the FIA's new affiliate, FISA (Fédération International edes d'Aviron). The battle for the commercial control of the sport continued until March 1981 when the Concorde Agreement gave FOCA the right to negotiate TV contracts. At the end of the first Concorde Agreement, in 1987, Ecclestone became the FIA Vice-President in charge of Promotional Affairs and began to spend less time on Brabham. He sold the team to Alfa Romeo (www.alfaromeo.com).

In the early days the F1 television rights business was risky and not very profitable. Ecclestone distanced himself from the other team owners and eventually established Formula One Promotions and Administration (FOPA) to manage the rights for them. Revenues were split, with 47% going to the teams, 30% to the FIA, and 23% to FOPA. FOPA received all the fees paid by promoters in exchange for paying prize money to the teams. In 1995 the FIA granted the F1 commercial rights to Formula One Management for a period of 14 years, in exchange for an annual payment from Ecclestone. The F1 teams realized that they had lost the rights, and McLaren, Williams, and Tyrrell refused to sign the new 1997 Concorde Agreement. An agreement was eventually reached for a ten-year deal with the teams and a 15-year deal with the FIA. Ecclestone began to plan for flotation of his company. The European Commission began an investigation into Formula One and this led to the flotation being cancelled.

In 1999 Ecclestone issued a US$1.4 billion Eurobond, secured on the future profits of the company. Later that year he sold 12.5% of the business to the venture capitalist company, Morgan Grenfell Private Equity, for US$325 million. In 2000 he sold another 37.5% to the San Francisco investment company, Hellman & Friedman, for US$725.5 million. The two then combined their shares and sold them to Thomas Haffa of EM.TV in exchange for US$1.65 billion in cash and shares. When EM.TV ran into trouble the shares passed to Leo Kirch, who acquired another 25% of the business, leaving the Ecclestone family only 25% of the business but Ecclestone remains firmly in charge. His fortune is estimated at £2.2 billion in 2006 and he has spent £70 million and 30 years of his life building up Formula One—much of the company is now owned by his wife. Ecclestone is now co-owner of Queen's Park Rangers football team, which he bought with fellow Formula One mogul, Flavio Briatore, in September 2007. Lakshmi Mittal, the fourth richest man in the world, joined them, purchasing a 24% stake in December 2007.

Sources: www.formula1.com; www.grandprix.com/gps/cref-eccber.htm/; http://news.bbc.co.uk/2/hi/uk_news/29426/stm.

Case discussion questions

1 Identify what you think are the attributes that made Formula One into a global brand.

2 Is Formula One a standardized or adaptation strategy? Give reasons to support your answer.

3 Describe the role of Ecclestone as Formula One's 'product champion', particularly his product globalization strategy.

4 What lessons can be learned by global marketers from the Formula One ingredients of unique product, global media exposure, and financial acumen.

END-OF-CHAPTER EXERCISES

1 Identify and describe the elements of the product. Why is it important to identify the different elements of the product in a global context?

2 List the factors that determine a standardized or adaptation global strategy. Illustrate your answer with relevant examples.

3 With examples, describe the different types of international product strategy.

4 What are the themes which can be used to differentiate a brand?

5 In what ways does a global or international brand differ from a local brand?

6 What are the dimensions of a global brand?

7 What are the different forms of new product? Outline the steps in the new product development process, stating the possible problems and their solution.

8 What are the antecedents to the new product development process? Why is it important to identify and take them into account in the new product development process?

DISCUSSION AND EXAMINATION EXERCISES

1 Critically evaluate the notion that the product 'attributes', rather than the core benefits, sell competitive products or services.

2 Identify and evaluate the role of customers' perceptions in the success of a global brand. Illustrate your answer with examples.

3 Explain the role and importance of the product life cycle concept and product/market matrices in global product planning.

4 Illustrating your answer with examples, discuss the various dimensions of a global brand and the ways in which an organization can build a brand to achieve global success.

5 Critically discuss the notion that it is the cost, market, market environment, and 'time to market' considerations which determine the form and extent of new product development and introduction.

FURTHER READING

Ambler, T. and Styles, C. (2000), *The Silk Road to International Marketing*, London: FT/Prentice Hall.

Anholt, S. (2004), *Proceedings of the Academy of Marketing Annual Conference*, July 2004, University of Gloucestershire.

Day, G. S. and Wensley, R. (1983), 'Marketing theory with a strategic orientation', *Journal of Marketing*, Fall, 79–89.

Holt, D. B., Quelch, J. A., and Taylor, E. L. (2004), 'How global brands compete', *Harvard Business Review*, September, 68–75.

Schuiling, I. and Kapferer, J.-N. (2004), 'Executive insights: real differences between local and international brands: strategic implications for international marketers', *Journal of International Marketing*, 12(4), 97–112.

REFERENCES

Ambler, T. and Styles, C. (2000), *The Silk Road to International Marketing*, London: FT/Prentice Hall.

Ansoff, H. I. (1957), 'Strategies for diversification', *Harvard Business Review*, Sept.–Oct., 114.

Chen, H.-L. (2002), 'Benchmarking and quality improvement: a quality benchmarking deployment approach', *International Journal of Quality and Reliability Management*, 19(6), 757–73.

Day, G.S. and Wensley, R. (1983), 'Marketing theory with a strategic orientation', *Journal of Marketing*, 47(4), 79–89.

DeAngelis, C. A. (1991), 'ICI advanced materials implement ISO 9000 program', Quality Progress, 49–51.

De Chernatony, L. (1989), 'Understanding consumer perceptions of competitive tiers – can perceived risk help?', *Journal of Marketing Management*, 4(3), 288–99.

Douglas S. P., Craig, C. S., and Nijssen, E. J. (2001), 'Executive insights: integrating branding strategy across markets: building international brand architecture', *Journal of International Marketing*, 9(2), 97–114.

Holt, D. B., Quelch, J. A., and Taylor, E. L. (2004), 'How global brands compete', *Harvard Business Review*, September, 68–75.

Gray, B. J., Fam, K. S., and Llanes V. A. (2003), 'Branding universities in Asian markets', *Journal of Product and Brand Management*, 12(2), 108–20.

Keegan, W. (1989), *Multinational Marketing Management*, Harlow: Prentice Hall.

Kotler, P. (1997), *Marketing Management: Analysis, Planning, Implementation and Control*, 9th edn., Harlow: Prentice Hall.

—— (2003), *Marketing Management: Analysis, Planning, Implementation and Control*, 11th edn., Harlow: Prentice Hall.

—— Armstrong, G., Saunders, J., and Wong, V. (2001), *Principles of Marketing*, Harlow: Pearson Education.

Medina, J. F. and Duffy, M. F. (1998), 'Standardization vs. globalization: a new perspective of brand strategies', *Journal of Product and Brand Management*, 7(3), 223–43.

Ohmae, K. (1989), 'Managing in a borderless world', *Harvard Business Review*, May–June, 152–61.

Rundh, B. (2001), 'International market development: new patterns in SMEs, international market behaviour?', *Marketing Intelligence and Planning*, 19(3), 319–29.

Schuiling, I. and Kapferer, J.-N. (2004), 'Executive insights: real differences between local and international brands: strategic implications for international marketers', *Journal of International Marketing*, 12(4), 97–112.

Thakor, M. V. and Kohli, C. S. (1996), 'Aspects of consumer reaction', *Journal of Consumer Marketing*, 13(3), 27–42.

Vernon, R. (1966), 'International investment and international trade in the product life cycle', *Quarterly Journal of Economics*, May, 190–207.

Vignali, C. (2001), 'McDonald's: "think global, act local" the marketing mix', *British Food Journal*, 103(2), 97–111.

Wells, L. T. (1968), 'A product life cycle for international trade?', *Journal of Marketing,* 33(July), 1–6.

White, D. S. and Griffith, D. A. (1997), 'Combining corporate and marketing strategy for global competitiveness', *Marketing Intelligence and Planning*, 15(4), 173–8.

Withers, B. E. and Ebrahimpour, M. (2001), 'Impacts of ISO 9000 registration on European firms: a case analysis', *Integrated Manufacturing Systems* 12(2), 139–51.

Wong, V. (2002), 'Antecedents of international new product rollout timeliness', *International Marketing Review*, 19(2), 120–32.

Yang, Y. H. (2001), 'Software quality management and ISO 9000 implementation', *Industrial Management and Data Systems*, 101(7), 329–38.

online resource centre

Visit the companion website to this book for lots of interesting additional material, including self-assessment questions, internet exercises, and links for each chapter:

http://www.oxfordtextbooks.co.uk/orc/lee_carter2e/

CHAPTER TEN

Global Services Marketing

Chapter overview

Chapter Introduction	312	
The Significance of Services in the Global Economy	312	
The Drivers for Growth in Cross-border Services	314	
Deregulation and liberalization of trade in services	314	
Quality service as a business imperative	315	
Homogenization of global consumers	316	
Global economies of scale	317	
Enabling technologies	317	
Following the clients	318	
Defining Cross-border Services	319	
Definition by degree of intangibility	319	
Definition by degree of consumer–producer interaction	320	
Definition by using multi-variant classification systems	321	
The Challenges of Marketing Services Internationally	324	
Intangibility	324	

Heterogeneity	325
Inseparability	327
Perishability	327
International Retail Franchising	328
The Strategic Considerations for Marketing Services Globally	330
Knowledge as the fundamental source of competitive advantage	330
Standardization vs. customization	332
Managing the process of service delivery	334
Using physical evidence to communicate service quality	335
Socio-cultural differences	335
The role of technology	336
Ensuring service quality and standards	336
Chapter Summary	338

Learning objectives

After studying this chapter, the reader will be able to:

- consider the increasing significance of services in today's global economy;
- examine the drivers that fuel the growth of global services;
- understand the characteristics of services and their implications on marketing and managing services;
- discuss the complexity and approaches to defining and categorizing services;
- examine some of the critical strategic considerations for marketing services globally.

Management issues

The management issues that arise from this chapter include:

- With reference to the increasing importance of services in the current global business environment, what are the implications for marketing and the management of your business?

- How is the marketing of services different from the marketing of tangible goods? How can we add (new) values to existing products/services by understanding the components of a service encounter?

- What are the strategic considerations for marketing services internationally or globally?

Chapter Introduction

Marketing and managing services globally is a challenge for marketing academics and practitioners alike. Unlike the global trade in physical goods, which is an exchange of tangibles across borders where market access can be assessed in terms of the incidence of border measures and other explicit trade restrictions, the trade in services is a great deal more complex due to the nature of services. For instance, it is difficult (for most services) to separate the production of services from their consumption, which means that the producer or the consumer must be mobilized across national borders in order for the 'exchange' or transaction to take place. The World Trade Organization's Economic Research and Analysis Division (www.wto.org) points out that the production and consumption of services are additionally subject to a range of interventions by governmental policies which have usually been developed without regard for their trade effects because they serve other political, economic, or social objectives. Many markets, including rail transport, basic telecommunications, and healthcare, have traditionally been reserved for monopoly suppliers or are subject to strict regulation and entry control, often for political reasons such as security of supply and protection of the public interest. For example, in light of the influx of overseas non-British nationals taking advantage of the free facilities of the National Health Service (NHS) for medical treatment, the UK government is finding ways to impose policies and erect barriers to prevent the so-called 'health tourists'.

This chapter will consider the rising significance of services in today's global economy, followed by an evaluation of the drivers that have fuelled the growth of services in recent years. We will then discuss the characteristics of services and how they are presenting challenges to service marketers, the problems relating to marketing services in foreign countries, and the strategic considerations for successful global service marketing.

The Significance of Services in the Global Economy

Services production is a dominant economic activity in most countries irrespective of their level of development. The World Bank (www.worldbank.org) estimates that the services sector represents over 60% of world gross domestic product although there are variations across country groupings. Available data suggest that the size of the sector is closely related to income. For example, services are estimated to account for 38% of GDP in low-income economies; 56% in middle-income countries; and 65% in high-income economies. Tourism, according to the World Travel and Tourism Council (www.wttc.org), is the world's largest employer, accounting for one in ten workers worldwide. The International Monetary Fund (IMF, www.imf.org) claims that tourism accounts for 33% of global services exports and 6.5% of total world exports.

Table 10.1 World trade in commercial services by category, 2006

	Value (US$ billion)		Share (%)	
	2006	2004	2005	2006
Exports				
All commercial services	2,755	100	100	100
Transportation services	630	23	23.4	22.9
Travel	745	28.8	27.9	27.1
Other commercial services	1,380	48.2	48.7	50
Imports				
All commercial services	2,650	100	100	100
Transportation services	750	27.7	28.4	28.4
Travel	695	27.9	27.1	26.2
Other commercial services	1,205	44.4	44.5	45.4

Source: Based on data published by WTO (www.wto.org).

The value of cross-border trade in services is estimated to be in excess of US$2.7 trillion, or about 20% of total cross-border trade. The largest commercial services by category in export and import are transportation services and travel (see Table 10.1), which are services that facilitate businesses that take place globally. The WTO claims that this understates the true size of global trade in services, much of which takes place through establishment in the export market, and is not recorded in the balance-of-payment statistics. Market research, marketing, transportation, labelling and packaging, legal advice, export guidance, and other services that take place in the domestic market are not normally taken into account and, hence, are invisible in the statistics.

The visible trade in services has been the fastest-growing sector in global trade for the past two decades, with an annual world growth rate averaging 15–20% in real terms compared with 6% for merchandise trade. Most developed countries have an interest in the increasing globalization of services as their economies are now largely made up of trade in services. For example, 77% of US GDP is generated from the services sectors which employ 80% of its workforce. The UK economy shares a similar pattern with 70% of GDP generated from services and only 18% from manufacturing. In Hong Kong, the services industries now account for 89% of GDP and 80% of employment. The world's leading exporters and importers of commercial services are some of the world's most developed and largest economies, i.e. the USA, the UK, Germany, Japan, and France.

It is important to acknowledge that the growth of services has also been buoyant in developing countries. Between 1980 and 1998, the services share of world GDP reportedly rose by 5%, but the corresponding increase for low- and middle-income countries was estimated at 9%. The cumulative export services growth in recent years in the emerging market economies such as India, Estonia, Romania, and China has been particularly spectacular, as illustrated in Fig. 10.1. The liberalization of services in developing countries could provide as much as US$6 trillion in additional income for these countries by 2015, four times the gains coming from trade in goods liberalization (World Bank, 2001). Brown

Fig. 10.1 Cumulative services export growth, 1994–2003 (%)

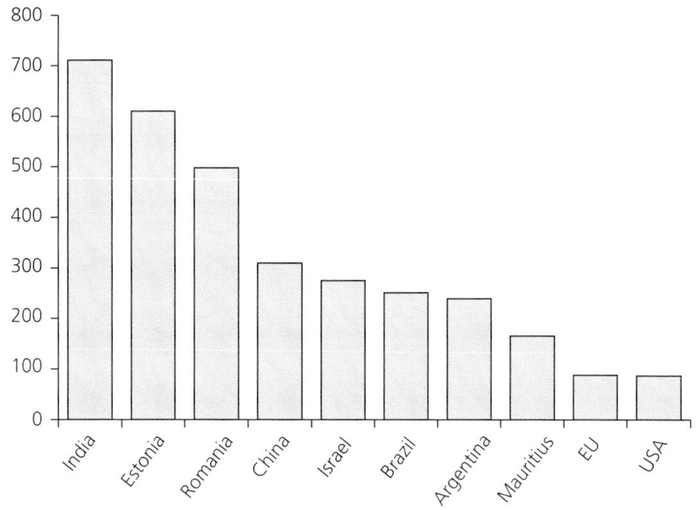

Source: World Bank Economic Prospect 2007 (www.worldbank.org).

et al. (2001) estimate that gains from a cut of 33% in barriers to services trade could raise global economic welfare by US$389.6 billion, which exceeds their estimated gains from manufactures liberalization of US$210.7 billion.

In summary, services today occupy a vital and growing role in the global marketplace. While some countries suffered a setback due to financial and economic turmoil in the late 1990s and the early years of the twenty-first century, global trade in services over the past two decades has been growing on average at a higher rate than trade in merchandise and is set to accelerate in the immediate future due to the removal of more trade barriers in services. The increased global trade offers significant economic benefits to countries at all levels of development as well as businesses which operate internationally.

The Drivers for Growth in Cross-border Services

The spectacular growth in cross-border services has been facilitated by a number of developments in the political, economic, technological, and competitive environments. This is illustrated in Fig. 10.2.

Deregulation and liberalization of trade in services

It is difficult for any nation to prosper under an inefficient and expensive services infrastructure in today's world market environment. Without adequate access to banking, insurance, accountancy, telecommunications, and transportation, producers and exporters of primary goods, including agricultural produce and industrial commodities, would face difficulty in trading internationally and competing effectively. The inability of developing countries such as Ethiopia and Bangladesh to provide sufficient services to exporters, such as market intelligence, working capital, and a reliable means of communication, is inhibiting their economic growth.

In the pursuit of creating a more efficient services infrastructure, the governments of many developed as well as developing countries have sought to deregulate and liberalize

Fig. 10.2 Drivers for growth in cross-border services

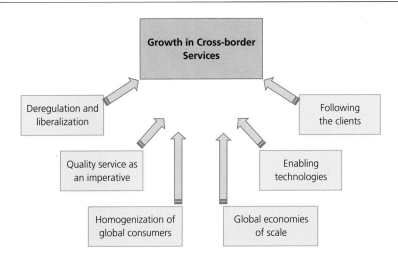

previously nationalized service industries. At the national level, the past two decades have witnessed some of the most progressive deregulation of many large nationalized service industries, including airlines, financial services, telecommunications, rail transport, and the postal service. These deregulatory moves represent the determination of governments to transform previously inefficient national services in order to create an efficient, cost-effective, and competitive infrastructure to promote economic prosperity by accelerating growth. At the same time, these transformations are beginning to be reflected at the global level. The enactment of the General Agreement on Trade in Services (GATS), which came into force in January 1995, and the new round of GATS negotiations in 2000 are proof to the commitment of over 140 WTO member governments to improve competitiveness in services and promote liberalization of trade in services.

The deregulation coupled with the liberalization have provided great impetus for services as a sector to emerge as a vital entity of the global market environment. In order to compete effectively and to ensure the efficient delivery of quality services, providers now demand new approaches and strategies for better understanding their customers, exploiting emerging opportunities, and strengthening their positioning.

Quality service as a business imperative

Providing a 'good' level of service is no longer simply an option for most businesses that operate globally today. As observed by Zeithaml and Bitner (2003: 7):

> the quick pace of developing technologies and increasing competition make it difficult to gain strategic competitive advantage through physical product alone. Customers are becoming more demanding. They not only expect excellent, high-quality goods; they also expect high levels of service along with them.

Customers no longer buy a car simply as a product; their decision-making and selection are increasingly based on the level of after-sale customer care (e.g. maintenance, breakdown recovery) as well as affiliated service-based features (e.g. financial packages, insurance, warranty, trade-in, and owner's club) being offered by the supplier. To compete, traditional manufacturing giants such as IBM (www.ibm.com), General Electric (www.ge.com), Microsoft (www.microsoft.com), and Hewlett-Packard (www.hp.com) are now aggressively positioning themselves as the service leaders or solution providers for other businesses. They understand that quality service is a business imperative, as competitive advantage is increasingly being gained through a differentiation in the provision of a distinctive and consistent service in addition to a quality physical product.

Homogenization of global consumers

It is a generalization to claim that all consumers globally are becoming homogeneous in their consumption of goods and services. The differences in political, economic, socio-cultural, and technological contexts still influence the availability of goods and services and consumer preference and tastes. However, the increasing invasiveness of global media broadcasting channels (e.g. CNN, www.cnn.com, MTV, www.mtv.com, Sky, www.sky.com, QVC, www.qvc. com, and TNT, www.tnt.com), coupled with the reduction in costs in communications, air travel, and information transfer, are contributing to growth of the so-called 'global consumers', who often share a degree of similarity in tastes and interests. This opens up opportunities for companies to develop and market services targeted to these consumers. It is most evident in the emergence of global brands such as American Express (www.amex.com) in travel and financial services, Marriott Hotels (www.marriott.com) in hospitality, McDonald's (www. mcdonalds.com) in restaurants, KPMG (www.kpmg.com) in corporate services, IBM in computers and software, and Federal Express (www.fedex.com) in courier and shipping services.

There seems to be some truth in the globalization of global consumers, as suggested by authors such as Levitt (1983) and Ohmae (1990). This is an important driver for growth: there is increasing demand for products and services globally which leads to a proliferation of services such as international travel, credit cards, insurance, banking, and entertainment.

MINI-CASE ILLUSTRATION Competing for the best talents

Hiring the best employees to perform the service is a key characteristic in successful services marketing. A major cause of poor service quality is the failure of service organizations successfully to recruit and retain their most valuable assets, the employees. Competing for talent market share requires organizations to aim high, use multiple recruiting methods, cast wide, and segment the market. Given the intense competition for capable employees, it is tempting to lower recruitment standards to fill positions. Intelligent and forward-looking organizations resist this and instead work harder than their competitors to find the right people.

According to a survey by the William Olsten Center (www. olsten.com), as many as three-quarters of companies in the USA and Canada have problems finding qualified employees. To attract the most talented workers, some employers have developed interesting solutions. The following are examples:

- Dinner and flowers-to-go. Amgen (www.amgen.com), the California-based biotechnology company, tempts workers with an onsite childcare centre that parents can visit during breaks, an inhouse florist, a photo developer, and a cafeteria which prepares take-away family-sized meals.

- Perks for new parents. Patagonia Inc. (www.patagonia.com), the US-based sports product manufacturer, offers new mums and dads eight weeks' paid leave and a 'work-family' programme that reintroduces parents to the workplace slowly.

- A company home? Sprint (www.sprint.com), the US telecommunications giant, provides employees with a programme to finance continued education and matches employee contributions to educational institutes. Sprint also buys homes that are later made available for employee purchase. If an employee buys a Sprint home, the company gives back 2% of the sale price.

Sources: Berry and Parasuraman (1992); www.employmentspot.com.

To cater for demand, companies need to offer more services to support and facilitate the development, marketing, and delivery of these products and services to the consumers, e.g. services that help consumers to find out 'what they want to buy, how to use products and what to do when things go wrong' (Vandermerwe and Chadwick, 1989: 79). It is important to note that these 'support services' also play a role in the overall growth in the global trade of services and products.

Global economies of scale

Economies of scale is a term normally used in a production situation, which occurs when greater levels of production result in lower costs per unit, which then increases profitability. Similar to many manufacturing organizations, leveraging economies of scale through geographical expansion of operations to identify markets for existing products/services in other countries is a key driver for growth for many service organizations. This is usually triggered by a number of factors, including excess capacity due to saturation and/or declining domestic markets, management aspiration to pursue organizational growth, and perceived potential for high profitability in overseas markets. In order to maintain and/or increase the gains in economies of scale in production, service organizations seek to exploit market potential by internationalizing their business operations.

Successful services internationalization and the realization of economies of scale in production are usually underpinned by the organization's core capabilities and distinctive competences, such as superior quality, technological expertise, cost efficiency, and a strong corporate or brand image. The lack of core capabilities and distinctive competences make it difficult for a service organization to gain scale economies due to the high costs of market entry and training, which are usually significantly higher than exporting a tangible merchandise.

The effect of global scale economies varies according to the level of fixed costs required to enter an industry, and the degree to which the service can be standardized. It is usually less favourable for services that are primarily people-based and face lesser-scale economies (e.g. hairdressing) since it is difficult and/or prohibitively expensive to bring together the supplier in one country and the consumer in another for the transaction to take place. One common solution for the would-be global company is that used by McDonald's (i.e. substitute equipment for labour) in order to achieve lower costs and better performance than local companies using traditional business systems. However, the need for 'customer involvement in production' and 'people as part of the service experience' work against being able to concentrate production to achieve scale. So, service providers typically have to find global-scale economies by standardizing production processes rather than through physical concentration, as well as by concentrating the upstream, rather than the downstream, stages of the value chain (Lovelock and Yip, 1996).

Enabling technologies

The fact that services internationalization has lagged behind merchandise internationalization is, to a great extent, due to the nature of services, i.e. the need for simultaneous presence of producers and users, and the impossibility of disconnecting production from consumption and supplying customers at a distance. Dramatic changes and technical innovations in the new communication technologies are rapidly changing the situation in a number of sectors. The delivery of health services (e.g. tele-health), education (e.g. tele-education and e-learning), and banking (e.g. tele-banking and internet banking) are prime examples of the dramatic impact of these technologies on the marketing and delivery of a service. In a similar vein, technological advancement in air travel has helped to reduce the costs of long-distance travel to a point where global consumer mobility makes it possible, in certain services such as health and tourism, to replace domestic supply by consumption abroad. The advancement of these 'enabling' or 'facilitating' technologies is 'enabling firms to transport existing and new services anytime and anywhere where regulation and the infrastructure permit' (Vandermerwe and Chadwick, 1989: 80). More importantly, new technologies are dramatically influencing services internationalization due to:

- the increased use of information technology in service offerings, which is influencing not only which services are being internationalized, but also how companies are spreading their services across the world, e.g. database marketing technology;

- the ease of modern telecommunication infrastructures which are facilitating different forms of service delivery on a global scale, e.g. global wireless technology; and

- the changing nature of services due to advanced technologies which are radically altering the methods by which some firms can globalize their services. Rather than purely or mostly labour-intensive activities, many services are now triggered and delivered through goods and, increasingly, are embodied in goods (Vandermerwe and Chadwick, 1989), e.g. software developments for internet-based shopping activities.

In short, the availability of new enabling technologies is making services more 'tradable' internationally and differently. This is an important driver for growth in global services trade as organizations are increasingly able to overcome the barriers for services internationalization (i.e. simultaneous production and consumption) by using new technologies to reach and service their customers (almost) unconstrained by distance and time. 'This does not obliterate the interactive aspects of services. Customization, traditionally achieved through interaction with people, can now be achieved remotely, via machines' (Vandermerwe and Chadwick, 1989: 80).

Following the clients

In order to cater for their needs and simplify the array of services they consume, many large companies require their service providers to follow when they internationalize their operations. To facilitate cross-border financial transactions (e.g. foreign exchange, payment arrangement, cheque clearance, etc.), a company usually engages a bank that is able to provide these services for its overseas subsidiaries. The bank needs to 'follow its client' and establish a base of operation or set up formal arrangements with a local financial institution to cater for the client's financial needs. What begins as 'following the clients' will eventually help these service providers to internationalize and eventually globalize their operations as their clientele grows. Accountancy, management consultancy, and business logistics are other good examples of this type of services globalization.

Hospitality businesses such as a restaurant are primarily people-based services. They tend to face less scale economies and a flatter experience curve.

This mode of services globalization also applies to companies which cater for general consumers when they purchase goods and services abroad. Consumers are more likely to purchase a brand of goods or services that they trust and are familiar with. Many UK travel-related service providers, such as banking (e.g. Barclays, www.barclays.com), mobile communications (e.g. Vodafone, www.vodafone.com), car rental (e.g. Europcar, www.europcar.com), and emergency support (e.g. AA, www.theaa.co.uk), have exploited this opportunity, e.g. by setting up operational bases in popular European tourist resorts to provide for UK travellers.

Defining Cross-border Services

It is difficult to define cross-border or international services because the service industry comprises a broad range of services which can be inferred as performances (e.g. healthcare services) or experiences (e.g. theme parks), which may be equipment-based (e.g. air travel) or people-based (e.g. management consultancy). Defining or categorizing such a vast spectrum with a precision that reflects the varied nature of services seems impossible. But far from being a pure academic exercise, as Lovelock (1981) argues, it is crucial in helping any service provider to understand the nature of the service act, the type of relationship it has with its customers, the amount of room there is for customization and judgements, the nature of demand and supply for the service, and how the service is to be delivered.

Definition by degree of intangibility

Defining a service by its degree of intangibility provides one of the simplest means to understanding services. A service can be described or positioned along a continuum according to the degree of intangibility, as illustrated in Fig. 10.3. In this instance, 'this ranges from intangible dominant or pure services', such as consulting and teaching, via semi-tangible services, such as telecommunication and healthcare, 'to services that are embedded in goods', such as software, music CDs, films, and restaurants (Patterson and Cicic, 1995: 60).

Services that resides towards the 'pure' services end (i.e. to the left) of the continuum are often performances, and hence it is not possible for the customer to experience, try, or inspect them prior to purchase. Services more embedded in physical goods, such as entertainment stored on a CD or DVD, are more tangible and easier for the customer to 'sample' before purchase.

Understanding a service and its degree of intangibility can be useful in identifying the marketing implications. In general, it is harder for pure services to achieve meaningful product differentiation than services embedded in goods, which can more easily rely on tangible cues

Fig. 10.3 The services and intangibility continuum

A theme park is a service provider which provides entertainment and 'fun' experiences for its customers. Its services are embedded in goods as it relies on equipment built specifically for experiences like Nemesis for thrill-seeking customers.

or representation to communicate their benefits and attributes. In addition, pure services are more likely to be constrained by the problem of inseparability, as the production and consumption take place simultaneously, than, say, a piece of software which can be produced, stored in a medium (e.g. music CDs), and exported for consumption at a convenient time and location. To enable a transaction for a pure service, the service providers need to either 'follow their clients' by setting up a physical presence in the international markets in which their clients operate or persuade foreign customers to come to them (e.g. a theme park). Finally, service providers supplying services embedded in goods tend to be more experienced and rely more on sales from international markets, in part because market entry is considered less risky, and more entry options are available.

Definition by degree of consumer–producer interaction

A service can be defined by the degree of interaction between the producer and consumer when it is being delivered. Some services (such as management consulting, hospitality and tourism, and software and systems training and support) require a high degree of service provider/client contact and interaction during the service delivery (Patterson and Cicic, 1995). However, services such as banking, insurance and finance, medical diagnosis, and telecommunications services can be delivered by technology and do not require a high degree of consumer–producer interaction (see Fig. 10.4).

The degree of consumer–producer interaction of a service has implications for how it may be marketed internationally. In general, services which require a high degree of consumer–producer interaction require the service producer to set up a physical presence. For example, RCI (www.rci.com), the luxury time-share resorts company, sets up local subsidiaries in foreign markets in which it operates. This type of service usually requires a high level of customization as the needs and expectations of the consumer are specific. The intensity of contact and interaction with the consumer, coupled with the need for a high level of customization, make it a difficult task to standardize the service offering because the service delivery is heterogeneous and has low transferability. It is consequently more costly and risky for this type of service provider to internationalize its service provision

Fig. 10.4 The consumer–producer interaction

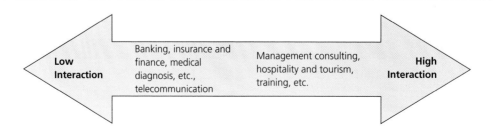

Low Interaction | Banking, insurance and finance, medical diagnosis, etc., telecommunication | Management consulting, hospitality and tourism, training, etc. | High Interaction

into a foreign market because it cannot rely on indirect methods such as export via an agent or piggyback on another organization.

At the other end of the spectrum are services requiring little (if any) producer–consumer interaction during service delivery (e.g. telecommunications, software development, development of distance education courses, standard off-the-shelf market research surveys) (Patterson and Cicic, 1995). The interaction of the service provider with the consumer has not disappeared but is instead aided or replaced by advanced technologies. University Alliance (www.universityalliance.com), a consortium of US universities, deliver its higher education programmes entirely via the internet. These services are also more readily standardized and less sensitive to social and cultural differences than services requiring a high level of interaction.

Definition by using multi-variant classification systems

The tangibility and level of producer–consumer interaction of a service can be described as the 'cornerstone' variables to understanding and defining services. A number of other variables have been put forward in an attempt to improve the defining and classification of the somewhat diverse range of services. These include the level of customization and consumer judgement, the nature of demand and supply for the service, the degree of labour intensity, and the mode of service being delivered.

Clark et al. (1996: 12) argue that these variables 'are developed to suit divergent purposes; however, they have in common the concern, or in what form, services cross national boundaries. They all address this issue because the crossing of national boundaries for intangible services is not straightforward.' It is believed that these definitions, which based their explanatory supremacy on one single variable, are incapable of explaining and triangulating the diversity and variety of services. It would be better to use classification systems which simultaneously incorporate two or more variables to define a service. The following are examples of these systems:

Vandermerwe and Chadwick (1989)

Vandermerwe and Chadwick developed a multi-variant classification system for internationalizing services based on the 'relative involvement of goods' (i.e. pure services/low on goods, services with some goods, or delivered through goods, and services embodied in goods) and the 'degree of customer–producer interaction' (from lower to higher). The result of this two-variant classification is a general six-sector taxonomy illustrated in Fig. 10.5.

Sector 1—Low interaction: Pure service

Goods in this sector do not feature to any extent and the degree of interaction is minimal. Provided anywhere, and with ease, these services are limited in international potential in their present form.

Sector 2—Low interaction: Some tangible

Interaction is low, but goods take on a more significant role. This sector has high internationalization potential because goods that facilitate the service are easily taken to foreign markets.

Sector 3—Low interaction: Highly tangible

Services in this sector are primarily embedded in goods with a low level of interaction. They are more readily exportable and can be globalized easily and quickly.

Fig. 10.5 Six-sector service taxonomy

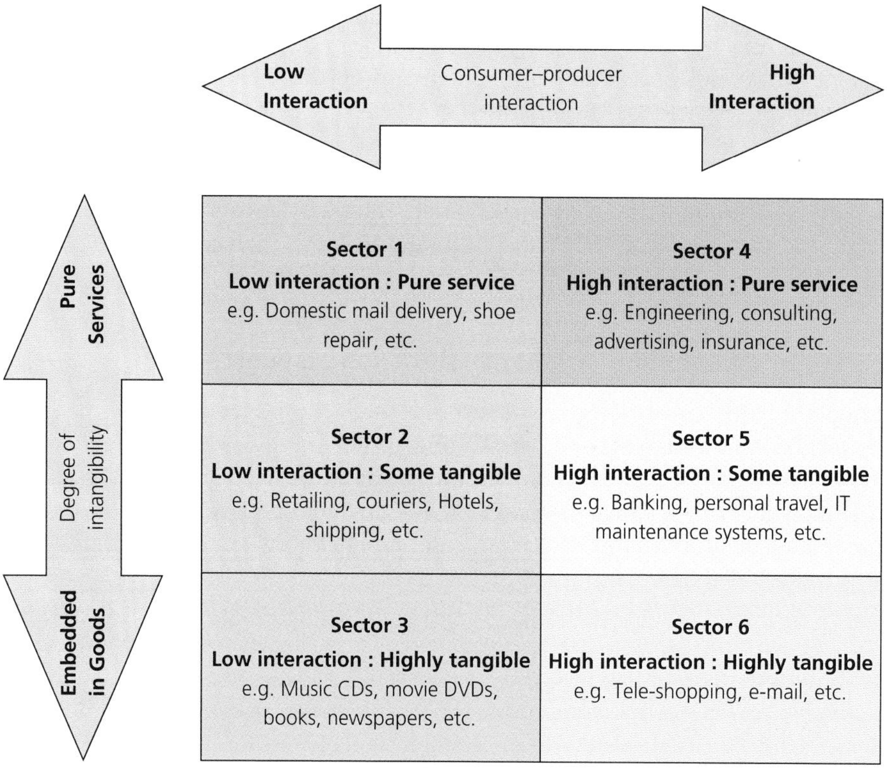

Source: Based on Vandermerwe and Chadwick (1989: 82).

Sector 4—High interaction: Pure service

These are so-called *traditional services* characterized by high interaction between producer and consumer during delivery and low use of goods as inputs to production. The role and interface of customers and staff being so vital, internationalization is more difficult because it principally involves people.

Sector 5—High interaction: Some tangible

Interaction in this sector is high and goods feature to a larger extent. In other words, service providers and consumers interact and the use of goods is also reasonably high. Internationalization involves both people and goods and a balance between the two.

Sector 6—High interaction: Highly tangible

Both the use of goods and interaction are high in this sector. Interaction is two-way but takes place through machines rather than people. With the continued development of new technologies to house and customize services, this sector is likely to become more significant in the future.

Lovelock and Yip (1996)

Lovelock and Yip (1996) argue that the most useful and relevant classification system of services is one which concerns the differences and commonalities in the operation processes, since the way in which inputs are transformed into outputs has a significant effect on strategy. By looking at the differences and commonality of the core element of

Fig. 10.6 Lovelock and Yip (1996): categories of service

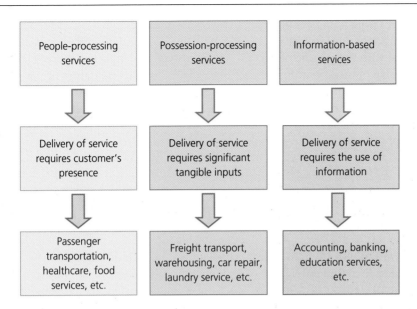

a service in the operation process, we can assign it to one of three broad categories depending on the nature of the process (whether it is primarily tangible or intangible) and the extent to which customers need to be physically present during service production (see Fig. 10.6).

People-processing services

These services involve tangible actions to customers in person. Customers themselves become part of the production process, which tends to be simultaneous with consumption. Examples are passenger transportation, healthcare, food service, and lodging services, where the customer needs to enter the 'service factory' and remain there during service delivery. Either the customer must travel to the factory, or service providers and equipment must come to the customer. In both instances, the service provider needs to maintain a local geographic presence, stationing the necessary personnel, buildings, equipment, vehicles, and suppliers within reach of target customers.

Possession-processing services

Possession-processing services involve tangible actions to physical objects to improve their value to customers. Examples include freight transport, warehousing, equipment installation and maintenance, car repair, laundry, and disposal. The object needs to be involved in the production process, but the customer does not, since consumption of the output tends to follow production. A local geographic presence is usually required when the supplier needs to provide service to physical objects in a specific location on a repeat basis. Modern technologies now allow some service processes to be administered from a distance, using electronic diagnostics to pinpoint and/or rectify the problem.

Information-based services

This is perhaps the most interesting category from the standpoint of global strategy development because the services depend on collecting, manipulating, interpreting, and transmitting data to create value. Examples include accounting, banking, consulting, education, insurance, and legal services. Customer involvement in production of such services is minimal. The advent of global telecommunications, linking intelligent machines to powerful databases, makes it possible to use electronic channels to deliver information-based services from a single 'hub' to almost any location.

Many definitions and classification systems have emerged and often they have been developed to deal with the specific needs of a service. As yet, no single variable or classification system capable of incorporating and conceptualizing the diverse nature of the service industries has been established. This is compounded by the fast-changing nature of services due to the pace of technological changes that are capable of revolutionizing the service industries. New variables and classification systems will (and will continue to) emerge as new ways of defining and understanding services are required.

The Challenges of Marketing Services Internationally

Services have a number of fundamental characteristics which distinguish them from physical goods and therefore pose different challenges for marketers in the way in which they should be marketed globally. In examining these characteristics, which define the nature of services, we shall discuss how the nature of services could create unique challenges for service providers in the marketing and management of services globally.

Intangibility

Services are usually something that cannot be experienced or tested by the customer prior to making the purchase, therefore making the purchasing decision more difficult as the perceived risks associated with the purchase are higher. There are differences in the degree of tangibility (or intangibility) from one type of service to another. The services a customer receives in a restaurant are more tangible than healthcare services received by a patient in a hospital. This is because the customer can see and taste the components of a restaurant's services, but a patient may not be able to do so in the services (e.g. consultation, diagnosis, nursing care, etc.) performed by a hospital. Closely related to the degree of tangibility of a service is the degree of environmental sensitivity. A service with a high degree of environmental sensitivity is dependent on the environment, location, or atmosphere in which it is performed and experienced, and vice versa. A customer's experience of staying in a hotel is sensitive to the environment and holiday destination in which the services are provided. Apart from the quality of the accommodation, a customer also assesses the location, friendliness of staff, food and drinks, and overall impression of the hotel building and cleanliness. Similarly, a customer who goes on a holiday evaluates their experience based on the location in which the services (such as sightseeing, weather, number of tourist attractions, etc.) are consumed. In both examples, there is a high degree of environmental sensitivity for the services experienced by the customer. It is impossible to separate the services from the environment or location in which they take place.

The intangibility of services creates a number of challenges to international marketing. Service providers face difficulty in communicating a service to customers as it is not easy to provide physical evidence to display or demonstrate its benefits before purchase. Customers therefore need to rely more on tangible cues—past experience, personal selling, and word-of-month—to a greater extent than with tangible products (Nicoulaud, 1988). This is particularly acute in international marketing of services as communication

Fig. 10.7 Intangibility vs. environmental sensitivity

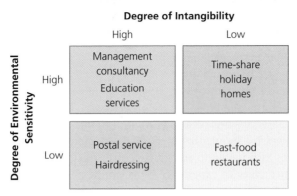

Source: Based on Nicoulaud (1988: 59).

across national borders is made more difficult by physical, cultural, and language barriers. The use of tangible cues or representations in marketing communications takes on a new dimension. 'Tangible objects, animals or other characters that service marketers associate with their products to convey their benefits and reinforce their image, need to transmit the intended message to the foreign audience they are targeted at. The use of international advertising of services must be sensitive to the meaning his/her potential overseas customers give to whatever metaphors, similes, or symbols he/she might wish to use' (Nicoulaud, 1988: 58).

The conclusion to be drawn is that global marketing problems, and strategies to accommodate them, will vary among service organizations and not just between service organizations and merchandise organizations. It is suggested that a useful way of looking at services, and other products, globally is to place them on an intangibility-environmental sensitivity map, illustrated in Fig. 10.7. By plotting the indicative position of a service, it gives an idea about its degree of tangibility and how sensitive it is to the environment in which it takes place. The position a service occupies has implications on how it is to be managed and marketed.

Heterogeneity

In the consumption of a service, the customer is an active participant and essential 'ingredient' in the production process. Without the customer, the service often cannot be produced, performed, or delivered. In most cases, services are designed around the specific requirements of an individual customer, and the delivery or performance of a service depends on (Nicoulaud, 1988: 62):

- The provider—services being more people-based than machine-based are more susceptible to variation than tangible products, because employees may differ in terms of their individual performance and the way in which they deal with each customer, an example being 'consultancy' services.

- The buyer—perception of the whole production process may vary from customer to customer, as each customer is different in their demands, preferences, and/or the way in which they experience the service, an example being different experiences of customers participating in the same service, e.g. business versus economy class airline customers.

- The situation—service performance from the same individual may differ from day to day, so may all the situational factors affecting customers' perception of what they are getting for their money, e.g. regular commuter train passengers versus irregular users.

Unlike the production of tangible products, it is more difficult to standardize the production of services due to their heterogeneous or variable nature. It is also more challenging for a global service provider to ensure a predetermined standard of quality and level of customer satisfaction across all countries in which it operates and this in turn brings greater uncertainty and risk in the global marketing of services.

Many international service organizations attempt to minimize heterogeneity in the provision of their services by standardizing as many elements (e.g. procedures, communication, systems, etc.) as possible to maximize consistency in the delivery and therefore improve the customer's service experience. This can be achieved through rigorous training programmes for employees, standardizing the core processes, and/or replacing people with machines to reduce the impact of people and environment on service quality.

However, it would be unwise for any service organization to assume that by undertaking a combination of these measures to minimize heterogeneity they would necessarily contribute to an increased level of perceived quality and customer satisfaction. Many banks in the UK have turned to interactive technologies, such as automated telephone banking and internet banking, to standardize the day-to-day banking provision for customers. The interaction between banking staff and customers has been kept to a minimum. These banks later discovered that, contrary to their assumption, the perceived quality and customer satisfaction levels had not gone up and, in some instances, had gone down. Attempting to minimize heterogeneity by standardizing the ways in which customers are dealt with caused these banks to treat their customers as a homogeneous group who shared the same demands, preferences, and expectations. British Airways (www.ba.com) standardized its check-in procedures at many UK airports (partly) to minimize the variable waiting time and the need for passengers to queue at check-in counters by introducing the automated check-in facilities. It found that these facilities were not only under-utilized by passengers but caused more irritation for customers than having to wait in a queue. This was because most passengers prefer to deal with people (rather than machines) who can provide a personal service and help with requests. 'All this means that the work of a service provider is quite complicated. The moods of the customer which may change per situation and lead to different preferences are partly due to this. This calls for a proper understanding of consumer behaviour with respect to services and how satisfaction can be created. It also shows that the degree of heterogeneity in the quality of service is affected by many variables and depends on many situational factors' (Kasper et al., 1999: 19).

MINI-CASE ILLUSTRATION Upholding the world-class service standards

Classic examples of the 'heterogeneity' problem are Xerox (www. xerox.com) and Toyota (www.toyota.com). In the 1990s, in African countries where access to foreign currency was restricted, both companies found it more difficult to uphold their world-class service philosophy. In the case of Xerox, local agents often did not have the currency to source component parts, hence customers had to provide this themselves, leading to delays in obtaining components and customer dissatisfaction. Similarly, when ordering Toyota vehicles, customers need to order those spares which would most likely be needed: exhausts, oil filters, etc. This added to the cost of initial purchase. Failure to buy the spares could involve costly delays as the agent attempt to source the foreign currency to buy the parts, with the knock-on effect of customer exasperation and subsequent damage to Toyota's perceived reputation in the minds of the customers.

Inseparability

The customer is an active participant and 'essential ingredient' in the production process. In contrast to a tangible good, which can be produced and consumed in two different places at different times, a service provider cannot manufacture its services at a time and/or location to suit and then deliver them to its customers to be consumed at a time and/or location convenient to them. The service provider and customer 'must interact in order for the benefits of the services to be realised—both must normally meet at a time and a place which is mutually convenient in order that the producer can directly pass on service benefits' (Palmer, 2001: 16).

The 'degree of simultaneous production and consumption' varies from one type of service to another according to its degree of tangibility. Educational services have a high degree of simultaneous production and consumption and very low tangibility. Students, both domestic and international, have to turn up to the learning sessions in an educational institution (e.g. school, college, or university) and interact with the service deliverer (i.e. tutors) and other consumers (i.e. other students) in order for the service benefits to be realized (i.e. the learning). Even when the delivery of an education programme can be achieved by the use of machines, say distance learning via interactive internet programming, the consumer needs to interact with the educational institution, via an internet-linked computer, to benefit from the service. For a service with a low degree of simultaneous production and consumption and very high tangibility, such as a Chinese takeaway meal, the separation of the production (i.e. the preparation and cooking of the food) and consumption (i.e. enjoying the meal later in a different location) is possible.

The issue brings unique challenges to a service provider which operates across national borders. It may, for instance, create difficulties in applying segmentation strategies and accurately matching the company's offerings to intended targets. Each market is conditioned by an idiosyncratic blend of politico-economic and socio-cultural influences, which moulds the needs, wants, expectations, and consumption patterns of the consumers making up that market. Transferring a segmentation strategy from one country to another can therefore be problematic because no two segments in two separate markets are identical. The marketing mix of a service specially formulated for a segment in one country cannot be used to match the requirements of another market. Such difficulties are more likely to be intensified in a multinational/multicultural situation. To ensure successful cross-border services marketing, marketers should study social institutions in the countries they wish to enter, and develop a knowledge and understanding of such concepts as social positions (status), social acceptance, roles, and group identification. For example, while Dubai may exhibit all the trappings of 'Western society', there are local customs and cultural mores beyond which it would be unwise to go, codes of banking practice being one of them.

Perishability

The degree of tangibility of a product or service is related to the degree of perishability. The lower the level of tangibility of a product or service, the higher the degree of perishability. Services are often intangible, and therefore perishable, making them difficult, if not impossible, to be kept in inventory when not consumed. For most service providers, there is no need to tie up capital to keep and manage an inventory of stocks and invest in warehousing. However, the perishable nature of services which cannot be stored if not consumed also means that any unsold services represent missed sales opportunities and lost profits for the service provider. A hotel with empty rooms or an airline company with excess capacity would lose the sales opportunities if there are no customers to purchase them at that time.

If a service is perishable it cannot be 'packed up and exported', e.g. telephone services are globally available but not 'physically packageable'. This has implications for how a service provider internationalizes its business activities, in particular its choice of markets and the method of market entry. Communication and language barriers usually limit a service provider to enter markets which are geographically and/or culturally closer to its country of origin. For market entry method, the physical presence of most service providers is crucial to the delivery of the service. Unlike an exporter of physical goods, it is also more risky to pursue international expansion because the low risk market entry methods, such as indirect exporting or via an export agency, are denied to a service provider.

Perishability may be further complicated by fluctuations in the pattern of demand and supply. Most services have variation in their patterns of demand, for instance demand for hotel accommodation is higher during the week than weekends due to business travellers, and is more heavily subscribed during the summer than the winter. Similarly, there are more people who use public transport during day-time peak hours than off-peak hours. This makes projection of sales and planning for staff requirements a difficult task. If the projection of sales is high, more staff members need to be engaged to deliver the service and materialize the sales. If the projection of sales is low, less staff members are needed to avoid incurring unnecessary costs. Any mistake in the projection of demand within a particular timeframe may result in lost profits. Despite the projection and forward planning, when a service provider is stretched to its full capacity during periods of high demand it has to turn customers away because there is no more capacity to perform the service. This, again, results in lost profits because the (extra) sales opportunities cannot be materialized and are lost.

International Retail Franchising

Franchising is a valuable means by which retailers expand their business operations. Retail franchising has enjoyed substantial growth in both the UK and USA, and is estimated to account for between 30% and 40% of all retail sales. The importance of international franchising as a strategy for retailers to achieve further growth and profitability is evident.

While franchising has been traditionally associated with the service sector and, in particular, the fast-food restaurant business, it has been increasingly adopted across a range of other retail sectors. For niche retailers such as the Body Shop (www.thebodyshop.com), Yves Rocher (www.yves-rocher.com), and Benetton (www.benetton.com), as Quinn and Alexander observe (2002), it has become the major international expansion tool, providing them with the opportunity to rapidly build a global operation on a relatively low-cost basis. Franchising is also being used by retailers without the asset of a strong global concept found in niche retailers. These retailers, which include the supermarket and hypermarket operators Groupe Casino (www.groupe-casino.fr) and GIB (www.gib.be), have used franchising as part of a portfolio of entry strategies rather than as a sole means of international expansion.

There are a number of reasons why franchising is increasing in popularity. It is, arguably, a more economic means of internationalization, and is especially suitable for organizations with limited resources and knowledge to manage a more 'hands-on' international operation. Potential franchisees normally pay an initial fee and invest a substantial stake in the required fixed assets, such as equipment and premises. Because of this, the business risk for the franchiser is significantly reduced.

Successful franchising operations generate a higher level of business activities for the franchiser, especially in the provision of central services such as marketing, research and development, and training. Increased levels of demand in these central provisions are

? **WHOSE RESPONSIBILITY IS IT?** **Codes of ethics and international franchising**

Courtesy of the International Franchise Association

International franchising activities are evident in all corners of the globe. Most franchisers, either formally or informally, adopt a set of minimum standards to ensure ethical business conduct in the countries in which they operate. The older and best known is the Code of Ethics adopted by the International Franchise Association (IFA, www .franchise.org). Within the EU, the Code adopted by the European Franchise Federation (www .eff-franchise.com) applies to all franchises that operate within the member countries. Because of differences among member countries, notably in consumer protection laws, some of the national associations have adopted additional provisions applicable to their own members. Similarly, the IFA Code of Ethics cannot be implemented in complete accord with the principles and practice within the Code, but need to be applied flexibly in order to take account of the range of structures, forms of agreement, and business practices.

Source: Based on Zeidman (2004: 32).

likely to produce economies of scale savings. The requirements for continuous marketing, training, and other support services invariably help the franchiser to continue investing in its human capital, which eventually raises standards in its own operations.

The advent of 'retailing without stores', i.e. on the internet, has revolutionized retailing. The recent emergence and growth of internet-based retailers such as Amazon.com, Interflora (www.interflora.com), and Richer Sounds (www.richersounds.com) are proof that there is growing consumer acceptance of the technology. See the Digital Impact for the development of e-tailing.

@ **THE DIGITAL IMPACT** **The development of e-tailing**

The retail sector is currently experiencing enormous changes owing to the emergence of electronic business. According to Kalakota and Whinston (1997), the impact of e-business in retail franchising is particularly evident in three types of application:

(a) Intra-organizational applications—the use of electronic technologies to enable better flows of information and products within an organization. Kall Kwik UK (www.kallkwik.co.uk), the print franchise company, was one of the first companies to develop a comprehensive intranet system. The system, called InSite, enables every participating franchisee to gain fast access to the wide range of technology that help online tracking of queries and manage information flows within the franchise system.

(b) Inter-organizational applications—the use of electronic technologies to enable better flows of information and products between organizations. Any increase in efficiency in the supply chain due to greater information flows can directly benefit retailers in sourcing and replenishing supplies. The international success of Benetton relies, to a great extent, upon its superior electronic point of sale (EPOS) and electronic data interchange (EDI) systems.

(c) Business-to-consumer applications—the use of electronic business to sell and market goods online. While total retail sales on the internet are small (e.g. 5% in the UK) in comparison with sales on the high street, the number of internet

shoppers is increasing. The trend is particularly prominent in the retail of software, music, and books.

Source: Based on Watson et al. (2002: 234).

The Strategic Considerations for Marketing Services Globally

Knowledge as the fundamental source of competitive advantage

With the world economy set to rely heavily on the services sector and a higher level of information and intelligence, it follows that organizations of all sizes increasingly need to strategically manage their knowledge base—in order to compete. Service organizations which strive for high standards of service delivery often go to great length to set standards to improve the quality of services provided by their employees and monitor their performances. In 'high-contact' services, people become the most important component, which determines the success or failure of the service in the eyes of the customer. The provision of regular training and empowerment of employees are fundamental to achieving this. Employees must understand the appropriate behaviour, service procedures and systems, and are empowered to deal with customers in a way which is consistent with the values of the company. It is primarily through the effective management of people and its knowledge base that the service organization takes control of the 'service factory' in the production and minimizes variable service quality. Effective management of knowledge can, therefore, provide the basis for developing the ability to thrive through creating a source for competitive advantage.

A large number of service-driven or people-based organizations have put knowledge management—i.e. the management of knowledge asset—at the top of the organizational agenda but have concerns about where they should start, what might be the benefits, how it should be organized, and what the system should involve. And also whether it will be similar to their current strategic planning models but with a knowledge rather than business focus, whether it should be part of the overall strategic plan, should the emphasis be on pull or push, and what is best practice.

Effective knowledge management is about smart ways of managing people. Effective knowledge management requires conditions for employees under which they are able to develop and apply their knowledge in an optimal way. Any 'smart' knowledge management should enable (Van der Spek and Kingma, 1999: 20–1):

- sharing of knowledge across 'borders' (functional, divisional, regional, and cultural) in order to improve business performance;
- learning before, during, and after activities to increase efficiency and effectiveness; and
- learning from colleagues, customers, and other parties continuously to improve ways of working, infrastructure, systems, and processes.

The common outcomes of effective knowledge management include (ibid.):

- processes and tools for connecting knowledgeable people dispersed over several units, locations, and different time regions;
- processes and tools for corporate-wide accessibility of information about best practices, guidelines, experiences, ideas, results of teams, and projects;
- learning tools for teams and individuals in order to improve the performance of projects and team activities and to bring the learning perspective into 'ways of working'; and
- inventories of knowledge areas to answer questions such as: What are the relationships between processes and key knowledge areas? Which parties/individuals own this knowledge?

Fig. 10.8 The development of effective knowledge management

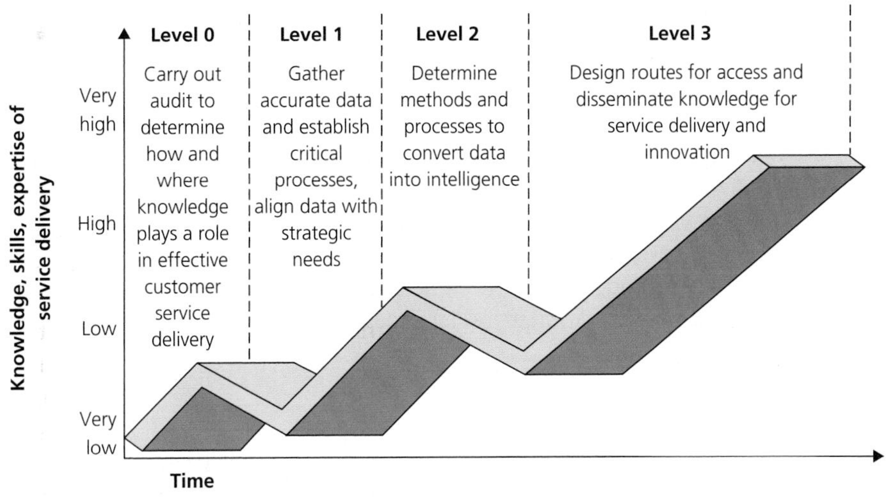

In the delivery of cross-border services, effective knowledge management can help overcome cultural and other market barriers in the host-country environments. The development of a system for the management of knowledge must be capable of adapting to local requirements as well as acquiring new strategic capabilities. This development will not occur quickly and requires taking a long-term approach to planning and implementation.

The evolution of an effective knowledge management system will, typically, go through four levels, as illustrated in Fig. 10.8.

Level 0: Carry out audit to determine how and where knowledge plays a role in effective customer service delivery

Each organization competes in the marketplace in its own way. The knowledge needs therefore vary from one organization to another. The development of a knowledge management system should reflect the knowledge needs of the organization. In identifying its knowledge needs, organizations can perform a *knowledge-base SWOT analysis*, mapping knowledge resources and capabilities against their strategic opportunities and threats to better understand their points of strength and weakness. They can use this analysis to strategically guide their knowledge management efforts, bolstering their knowledge advantages and reducing their knowledge weaknesses, and identifying which knowledge-based resources and capabilities are valuable and unique as well as how those resources and capabilities support the organization's product and market positions.

Level 1: Gather accurate data and establish critical processes, align data with strategic needs

Knowledge building is dependent upon the development of capabilities for organizing and disseminating data in vital business areas. Organizations need to capitalize on the advances in systems and communications technologies to bring greater opportunities for organizations to delivery services with more efficiency and effectiveness. Such a system will embed a process and infrastructure aimed at supporting the creation, harvesting, assimilation, and leverage of knowledge to achieve strategic objectives.

Level 2: Determine methods and processes to convert data into intelligence

The nature of the information that provides the input for knowledge management is not determined only by the interplay of various sources (i.e. internal, external, and research)

but the appropriateness of the methods/processes used to codify information, and managing people and culture.

Knowledge may be explicit and implicit. Explicit knowledge is that which has been formally codified. It is therefore suitable for communication in various forms, including through online databases. Tacit knowledge is that which is not explicit; it is represented in understandings and in actions and may not have been expressed in verbal form. In an organizational context, tacit knowledge held by individuals becomes explicit when it is embedded in products and processes.

People and culture are the most important organization assets. Successful knowledge management will therefore revolve around strong leadership commitment, creating the right culture and environment, and having the right organization conditions. To achieve this, organizations need to embed appropriate social and cultural values, trust, and behaviours.

Level 3: Design routes for access and disseminate knowledge for service delivery and innovation

To ensure optimum success, organizations need to establish well-designed routes for access and disseminate knowledge for service delivery and innovation. They need to invest in education and training programmes, and seek to attract premium workers to enrich their knowledge base. The higher the investment in high-quality inputs (i.e. people, knowledge, experience, training, education, etc.), the higher and better quality it is for the outputs (i.e. more innovations, higher growth, and external competitive advantage). To incentivize participation in knowledge creation and sharing, organizations should also consider restructuring their payment and reward systems to align more closely to the key knowledge management objectives, with recognition of individual contributions and successful outcomes to team projects.

In conclusion, the arguments for being proactive in knowledge management are strong and compelling. Some organizations have recognized this and started to implement long-term programmes. This, in part, may be due to enforced environmental circumstances as information flows, technological improvements, or competitive pressures continue to move rapidly. Many others are still toying with ideas, focusing on *ad hoc* projects or simply dismissing knowledge management as the latest management fad. Whatever approach is taken, there are serious implications for organizations, people, and the nature of work in the future. Adopting a strategic knowledge management strategy is likely to provide a significant opportunity for attaining a position of sustainable competitive advantage.

Standardization vs. customization

Standardization versus customization is a contentious issue in global services marketing. Service organizations are 'caught in a squeeze between customization ("tailor-made"), which service management and marketing theory emphasizes, and standardization (or industrialization), which classic economic theory emphasizes' (Sundbo, 2002: 93). Put simply, standardization is the approach that aims to achieve uniformity in service delivery whenever or wherever the service is consumed (e.g. McDonald's restaurants in London and Moscow share the same marketing elements); whereas customization is the approach in which the service offering is developed and delivered as a tailor-made solution to the customer's specific needs (e.g. a management consultant employed to solve a specific management problem).

The emphasis of the notion of standardization for a service provider is on achieving maximum productivity through standardization of service design and delivery, economies of scales, and reduction of costs. It follows that only prices and quantities exist and consumers assess the quality of a (service) product and compare the price with the price of similar products. Individual customer care is unnecessary because the customer has the knowledge to classify the product according to type and quality, and when he has done so, only price counts (Sundbo, 2002). Service providers are arguably able to benefit from a number of advantages, including: (1) an increased level of customer satisfaction—due to higher reliability in the standard of service delivery and possible cost savings passed on; and (2) an increased level of efficiency gains—due to increased productivity through the 'mass production' of standardized service packages.

However, the notion of customization stresses the customer encounter and the customer's participation in service production, thus it becomes a natural core of the interpretation of the service production. Customization means that the single customer receives individual service (Sundbo, 2002). In contrast to the standardization logic, the customization logic cares little about productivity and economies of scale but emphasizes personal contact with customers and the ability to undertake personal marketing to customize the service offering. Service providers could derive competitive advantage from: (1) exceeding customer expectations—as customers pay only for service solutions that are specifically designed and delivered for their problems; (2) premium pricing—as customers are more willing to pay a premium for custom-designed services; and (3) an in-depth understanding of customers—due to the increased intimate contact and interaction with customers during the service process.

The degree of standardization or customization of a service internationally depends largely on its degree of intangibility and the degree of producer–consumer contact during service delivery. By combining these variables, Patterson and Cicic (1995: 67) developed a typology of four strategic options for cross-border services marketing which can be used to profile the level of customization or standardization needed for each type of service. In general, standardization can be more readily achieved for services which are 'more tangible' (i.e. embedded in goods) and have a lower requirement for face-to-face producer–consumer contact during service delivery (see Fig. 10.9).

Fig. 10.9 Strategic options for cross-border services marketing

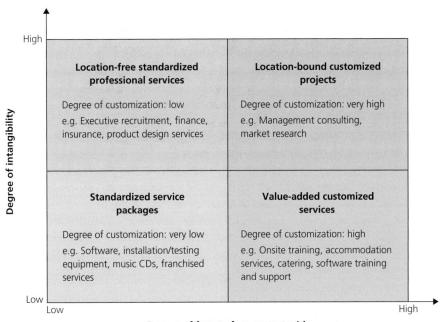

Source: Based on Patterson and Cicic (1995: 67).

- **Location-free standardized professional services**

  These are essentially low-contact services which can be partially or entirely standardized. The presence of the customer is not required during service delivery and the service provider is not location-bound in the sense that employees need only to travel to the foreign country for a relatively short period to meet the client but need not stay to deliver the service.

- **Location-bound customized projects**

  These services require considerably more contact with the client for successful service delivery. They require a great deal of customization as the service provider needs to exercise more executional latitude and situational adaptation. In serving an international market, this often requires some form of local presence close to the clients.

- **Standardized service packages**

  Services that can be bundled with goods tend to be more readily standardized and are often marketed as a 'service package' with off-the-shelf standardized service components. They lend themselves to being exported in a more traditional manner, thus reducing accompanying costs and risks.

- **Value-added customized services**

  These services require a high degree of supplier–client interaction for successful service delivery. A high level of customization is needed because they are viewed as more value-adding and designed to meet specific client's needs.

Managing the process of service delivery

The production and delivery of a service is essentially a process rather than a tangible object. This process not only consists of 'a front office and a back office but also of inter-action in actions, episodes and relationships' (Kasper et al., 1999: 458) and a set of procedures, systems, mechanisms, and/or a flow of activities that make up the entire service product. The composition and execution of the process would most certainly influence the way in which the service is experienced by the customer. For example, a customer who chooses to shop online via the internet for his groceries is different from another customer who prefers to shop in the local supermarket. It is therefore crucial to manage the delivery of the service, especially at the interface between the service deliverer and the customer. Shostack (1985) has defined this interface during which a consumer directly interacts with a service as the 'service encounter'.

The production and delivery of some services are more complex than others. Complex services are usually characterized by 'multiple-service encounters' which require a constructive approach to designing and managing the intricacy of the processes involved. 'Blueprinting', developed by Shostack (1987), is a useful tool for structural process design, which provides a comprehensive visual model of a service process in the form of a blueprint. It is an effective management tool for any service providers to readily 'identify strong and weak links in the process, and evaluate the effects of potential structural changes such as greater customization or an expanded range of services' (Baron and Harris, 2003: 96).

There is probably no such thing as the perfect 'blueprint' for a service design. Due to the variable nature of services, which involve the participation of the service deliverer and the customer, it is inevitable that either party may on occasion make a mistake. If, however, 'these occasions can be anticipated, and the mistake prevented from turning into a service defect hence a service failure, then the effort spent in service design may be justified' (Baron and Harris, 2003: 104).

In the absence of a physical product, service providers use 'tangible cues' such as pleasant atmosphere which customers use to make a judgement on the service quality.

Using physical evidence to communicate service quality

Physical evidence refers to the 'build environment', location, or atmosphere in which the service is delivered and any tangible goods that facilitate the performance and communication of the service (Jobber, 2001). In the absence of a physical product, service deliverers need to consider the 'tangible cues' that the customers use to make a judgement on the service quality. It occurs where the customer experiences the interpersonal interactions with the service deliverers that take place within the confines of a given service environment. For example, a travel agent uses colourful brochures of holiday destinations, the ambiance, the staff uniform, computer equipment, and so on as physical evidence to convey the type and quality of holiday services that it has to offer.

Socio-cultural differences

Different cultures have varying effects on the marketing of services internationally. Cultural elements such as religion, materialism, language, education, family structure, gender role, customers, and time orientation are intertwined with national culture. These elements have a significant impact on the acceptability and adoption patterns of services (Javalgi and White, 2002). There is considerable variance in the interactions of people with different cultures as each culture assigns its own meaning and expression to gestures such as body movement, eye contact, body touch, etc. The development of trusting relationships with customers, especially for those service providers directly involved with customer contact, is particularly challenging as cultural and language barriers need to be overcome (ibid.).

Tai and Chan (2001), in their cross-cultural studies on advertising content, found that there is a strong association between information content and socio-cultural values. In a

MINI-CASE ILLUSTRATION **The Louis Organization**

The Louis Organization (www.louistravel.com) of Cyprus is an example of an organization which displays many of the elements of service discussed, included that of added value, extended marketing mix, and customer product interaction. The organization is involved, along with other activities, in the tourist trade, having a chain of hotels in Mediterranean destinations such as Cyprus, Crete, and Greece. Recognizing that there are opportunities both to add value and also create separate market segments, the group owns and operates cruise liners and is involved in airport handling services. This not only enables it to offer these services in their own right, to potential tourists, but

enables Louis to provide these services to airline operators and other tour operators, such as First Choice (www.firstchoice.co.uk), enabling it to cross-market these services at different price and promotional regimes. For example, a tourist could buy a Louis Cruise package from the Louis brochure or take a Louis Hotel package. The tourist will know they are dealing with the Louis Organization. Alternatively, the tourist may buy a First Choice Cyprus holiday, but in a Louis Hotel, have their baggage handled by Louis ground staff at Paphos Airport and buy a two-day excursion on a Louis cruise liner from the First Choice resort representative but not necessarily know about the Louis Organization.

high-context culture, such as India or China, consumers prefer image-based or symbolic appeals that express the positive social consequences of a particular service purchase, e.g. membership of a health club. The country of origin (COO) effects on the evaluation of services are particularly evident in these cultures. Consumers from these cultures are more likely to prefer service providers from economically progressed countries, as their brand names bring high perceived status and service.

In a low-context culture, such as Denmark or the USA, consumers rely more on rational thinking and are likely to seek independent sources in making purchase decisions. This means that the content of the information and the credibility of the source are critical to them as they influence the decision-making processes.

The role of technology

It is hard to find an example of service that does not involve the use of technology in aiding the design, development, and/or delivery of it. For example, a domestic servant hired to provide cleaning, cooking, and other domestic services in a family home would not be able to provide those services without the help of modern technology, e.g. vacuum cleaner, washing machine.

In today's society, it is a widely accepted view that technology will increasingly dominate the future of services. Indeed, new technologies have already brought a number of benefits to service businesses, including:

• Increased productivity—through economies of scale by making cost savings in the rationalization and automation of business processes and servicing more customers at the same time.

• Enhancing decision-making—especially at front-line and middle-management levels where decisions are routinized and standardized. Sophisticated computerized systems are often utilized for problem analysis to help decision-making on strategic issues.

• The delivery of services—through the use of internet technologies. Last-minute.com, the UK online travel and leisure services agent, processes the entire 'service encounter' for each customer online using a combination of sophisticated interactive website interfaces, search engine facilities, credit card payment processing, and electronic mailing.

• Customer targeting and relationship management—which can be achieved with the help of advanced database technologies to channel accurate marketing information to the right customer targets, and manage the relationships with existing customers with greater effectiveness.

It is certain that technology will play an important and integrative role in service organizations as mastering new technologies could help to create sustainable competitive advantage. Technologies that accelerate new product (service) development, design of service encounters (both face-to-face and electronic), integrated marketing communication, interactive sales and support functions, and delivery of service components are already used to promote greater efficiency and effectiveness.

Ensuring service quality and standards

The delivery of services internationally is influenced by the nature of the service, customer preferences, and the degree of control sought by the organization. The decision of market entry mode, for instance, depends upon the degree of tangibility/intangibility of the offering and the degree of consumer–producer interaction. Services which are 'separable' (i.e. high degree of tangibility) can be 'produced' and then 'exported' for consumption later. Providers of these services, such as music producers and artists, can rely on export and import agents to manage the international service delivery without getting directly involved in the process. For 'inseparable services', such as hotels and air travel, where the production and consumption of the service take place simultaneously, setting up foreign subsidiaries where the service is delivered is likely to be the preferred mode of market entry (Javalgi and White, 2002). The internationalization of these service providers may not go through a sequential pattern that begins with exporting, involving low 'hands on' management; they are more likely to require a direct market entry mode in order to operate internationally.

Service providers recognize the importance of attaining service quality superiority in securing greater customer loyalty and building a competitive advantage. Much effort is made to identify the important dimensions of service quality. SERVQUAL, developed by Parasuraman et al. (1985, 1988), is perhaps the most widely cited framework used to evaluate service quality. The dimensions vital to ensuring a superior service quality are reliability, access, responsiveness, competence, courtesy, communication, credibility, security, understanding of the customer, and tangible considerations. Due to socio-cultural differences,

 THE RELATIONSHIP PERSPECTIVE Strategic outsourcing—the new collaborative structure

How many employees must an organization have to support a US$160 million business? For Nokia Display Products, a US subsidiary of the Finnish electronics giant, the answer was five. Everything else, (including sales, customer service, logistics, advertising, and manufacturing) was outsourced to companies specializing in those business functions.

In the knowledge economy, outsourcing offers strategic advantages allowing for greater flexibility and letting companies concentrate on absolute core competences, such as product development and marketing, rather than dissipating resources to build, learn, and support systems better left to outside experts. IT service providers have pioneered this new collaborative structure.

While outsourcing used to be a tactical solution for temporarily bolstering a workforce, the new outsourcing relationship relies on service providers to develop, expand, or maintain a company's critical but non-core operations in the long term.

Outsourcing experts suggest that any process that does not appear on an accounts receivable invoice is a process that can be outsourced. For example, moving IT support and customer support outside the enterprise allows in-house MIS (marketing information system) personnel to specialize in maintaining and upgrading the core information systems rather than spending their time answering users' simple and often redundant queries.

Most companies choose to outsource their technical support to leverage the outsource provider's specialized tools, processes, and IT infrastructure. They want to tap the expertise and knowledge possessed by the outsourcer's staff without incurring the costs in-house.

Outsourcing the help desk has some additional benefits. The customer support business is already clear on the fact that knowledge management technology can enhance problem resolution. But the data gained through a carefully crafted and expertly maintained support desk knowledge base can and should go much further than problem-solving. The information can be utilized in employee training, in product planning and configuration, and in sales and marketing materials.

Source: Extracts from Delio (1999).

the dimensions of service quality should be emphasized differently in different markets to reflect the idiosyncratic needs of consumers in the host country.

Rather than providing the global consumer with a higher level of service, there is in fact a growing body of evidence which suggests that the opposite is true (Ritzer, 2007). For examples, a local restaurant can really provide a high level of service in that the waiter serves fewer customers and the chef can provide the menu nuances that customers demand. However, with a global company such as McDonald's, the global business model can mean that in fact the global customer receives less service. This is evidenced by the fact that the customer has to queue in the outlet, has less menu choices and is served by counter staff who may have little or no knowledge of the product being offered or any training in how to deal with customer complaints or requests outside the 'formula' offered. The same argument could be applied to cruise ships and airlines, the latter where the customers are increasingly being asked to do the services which were normally provided in the price of the air ticket, e.g. online check-in and payment for hold check-in baggage. Ritzer refers to this as the 'globalization of nothing'.

Chapter Summary

1. The characteristics that distinguish services from tangible goods are intangibility, heterogeneity, inseparability, and perishability.

2. Services production is a dominant economic activity in virtually all countries irrespective of their level of development. The visible trade in services has been the fastest-growing sector in international trade for the past two decades, with an annual world growth rate averaging 15–20% in real terms compared with 6% for merchandise trade.

3. A number of factors have contributed to the phenomenal growth of services globally. These include the deregulation and liberalization of trade in services; the provision of quality service, which has become a business imperative; the emergence of global consumers; the benefits of global economies of scale; the availability of enabling technologies: and opportunities to follow the clients when they internationalize their business activities.

4. The task of defining international or global services is one laden with difficulty due to the complex and diverse nature of services. Many definitions and classification systems have emerged and are often developed to deal with the specific needs of a service.

5. Franchising is a valuable means by which retailers expand their business operations internationally. In recent years, retail franchising has enjoyed substantial growth in both the UK and the USA, and is estimated to account for 30–40% of all retail sales. Expansion into new markets by a growing number of retail operations will continue into the twenty-first century.

6. Service organizations which operate internationally or globally need to consider a number of strategic issues. Different cultures have varying effects on the marketing of services. Cultural elements such as religion, materialism, language, education, family structure, gender role, customers, and time orientation are intertwined with national culture. These elements have a significant impact on the acceptability and adoption patterns of services. Considerations also need to be given to the level of customization and standardization; the extended marketing mix of people, process, and physical evidence; managing international delivery; and the role of technology.

The ambition to design, market, and deliver a world-class consumer air transport service is becoming increasingly difficult to achieve. First, rapid technological innovation has led to a significant increase in the complexity of service delivery, influencing the design and production processes, and the customer interface of services. Secondly, customer expectations are much higher today as they become more experienced through more regular consumption of services. Provision of highly reliable and customized services is taken for granted, making it increasingly difficult for service providers to create meaningful and sustainable differentiation in the global marketplace.

It was in May 1995 in a ballroom at a hotel airport that arguments began about whether Heathrow Airport should build a new terminal which would be the new home of British Airways' (www.ba.com) operations. It was to become Britain's longest planning inquiry, but finally in 2001 the British government gave permission to build Terminal 5 (T5).

The construction of the new airport building fit for a twenty-first-century air travel service was an enormous challenge, but it was a challenge that was not confined to the construction of the building itself. An estimated 60,000 workers had worked a total of 100 million hours over six years to build T5. Built on the site of a former sewage works at the western end of the existing airport, T5 is designed by 2006 Stirling Prize winners Roger Stirk at Harbour and Partners architect firm (www.rsh-p.com). To enable the long runways and transport infrastructure to be built, two rivers had to be diverted and extensions dug to connect the airport to the London Underground and Heathrow Express rail lines. A new road tunnel was bored, and a taller Control Tower erected to give better oversight of the bigger airfield.

Despite all the engineering challenges, the so-called '21st century's gateway to the world' was completed on time as it opened its door on 27 March 2008; and on budget at £4.3 billion. It now stands huge at the far end of the Heathrow Airport, its size can only be truly appreciated when you arrive at its doors. British Airways, which has exclusive use of the place, believes that T5 will transform its passengers' experience of air travel and banish its previous poor reputation as the 'Heathrow Hell' for good. In the new airport, it is anticipated that 80% of passengers will check-in online or at computer stations in the vast departure area, making the handling of baggage easier. A state-of-the-art system of conveyor belts, computerized baggage trucks, and a new reclaim area will help improve the airline's reputation for losing its passengers' luggage. No passengers will walk more than five minutes to board their flights as the aircraft can pull up at air bridges connected to the main building itself. The extra number of departure gates is designed to make aircraft operations easier, especially when things go wrong.

As soon as T5 opened its door to the world for business, disaster hit the airport in a way that the management failed to anticipate! The state-of-the-art baggage-handling operation began to malfunction. Within a matter of hours, passenger bags had piled up by their thousands in the basement of T5, forcing British Airways to begin delaying or canceling its flights. This meant passengers

already at the airport had the choice of either flying with just hand luggage, getting an alternative flight, or claiming a refund. By the end of T5's first traumatic day, a total of 34 flights had been cancelled and hundreds of passengers had been left stranded, either for a flight or their bags.

The first warning signs came as early as 4.00am on the first day when passengers began to arrive, only to be confronted with the problems of trying to find somewhere to park. The road signs were not clear outside the terminal building, creating further confusion. Passengers arrived at the airport lounge to find that all the check-in desks were closed as many staff members were late due to their unfamiliarity with their new environment and security clearance procedures. Passengers were left with no option other than to form a long queue to wait for check-in. As the day wore on, most passengers had to endure a wait of up to two-and-a-half hours to check-in their bags as well as collect their suitcases from baggage reclaim.

A few days later, T5 saw nearly 30,000 bags separated from their owners, causing the cancellation of more than 500 flights. BA shares fell following a number of damaging comments from the media. It has been estimated that the opening disaster at T5 has cost BA between £20 million and £50 million in lost revenue and passenger compensation. Willie Walsh, the British Airways Chief Executive, stood before the media and accepted personal blame for the shambles. Gareth Kirkwood, Director of Operations at BA, and David Noyes, Head of Customer Relations, were fired as Walsh took personal charge of running the terminal. Both executives were considered rising stars at the airline but a week of chaos at Heathrow's flagship terminal brought their BA careers to an abrupt end. Analysts said the move increased the pressure on the Chief Executive, who has no one else to blame if there are further problems at T5 under his watch.

So, what seemed to be the problem that caused such a disaster for the airport that calls itself 'The 21st Century Gateway to Britain'? The problem appeared to be due to a combination of factors. Some were technical, involving glitches with the sophisticated new baggage handling system, which is designed to handle 12,000 bags an hour. Some were human resource-related as many staff members were believed to be so poorly trained that they were unable to find their way to the staff car park on the first day, let alone handle the system. The 'initial teething problems' with car parking had caused delays in getting staff through security screening and the lack of staff familiarization with the new system had resulted in a backlog of baggage which meant severe delays and flight cancellations over the days that followed.

A key challenge in managing a highly complex package of services, such as that of T5, is to understand, manage and control all service elements of the entire operation. In its attempt to deliver 'a new era for air travel', British Airways and T5's owner, BAA (www.baa.com), set out to re-engineer the entire customer experience cycle by reformulating human-intensive activities and technology-based processes (e.g. providing self-help check-in computer stations to encourage customers to help themselves and, in doing so, reduce the need to queue). To create a more comfortable 'feel' for passengers, T5 was also designed with different floor plans to make the place more spacious and accessible. All the key processes of customer service delivery were re-sequenced to produce a new, unique 'service blueprint', with the aim to win over customers who have long been disenfranchised by their poor experiences at Heathrow Airport.

There are many lessons to be learnt from the chaos at T5. Company performance is highly dependent on its ability not just to harness the best that new technologies have to offer but to manage the practical applications of service delivery. However much a company spends trying to be innovative in the service design and production, it will not compensate for the lack of diligent planning to ensure that the fundamental mechanisms of delivery are in place to meet customer expectations.

Sources: *The Guardian* (www.guardianunlimited.co.uk); BBC News (www.bbc.co.uk).

Case discussion questions

1 Using the information from the case study and your own knowledge, conduct a SWOT analysis to identify the issues confronting British Airways in today's global airlines industry.

2 What was the problem that the management at Heathrow Terminal 5 failed to anticipate at the opening of the new terminal building? What were the contributing factors that created the problem?

3 In the planning and delivery of Terminal 5's highly complex services, what do you think are the strategic considerations which should have been taken into account in order prevent the mistake made by its management?

END-OF-CHAPTER EXERCISES

1 What is the evidence that shows the increasing importance of the role that services play in the global economy today?

2 Identify and discuss the drivers for growth in global services.

3 What are the differences between tangible goods and intangible services?

4 Think of five services and position them on to the services and intangibility continuum.

5 What are the benefits of standardizing and customizing services respectively?

6 What role does technology play in the marketing of services internationally?

DISCUSSION AND EXAMINATION QUESTIONS

1 Discuss the role that services play in the current global economy and the reasons why it is becoming a business imperative for all businesses.

2 Examine the characteristics that define the nature of services and evaluate how they present unique challenges for service providers in marketing and managing services internationally or globally.

3 Why do you think the task of defining services is so complex? Identify and discuss some of the approaches which can be used for this purpose.

4 For service organizations that operate in today's global environment, discuss the strategic considerations which need to be taken into account to ensure success in cross-border services marketing.

FURTHER READING

Chourides, P., Longbottom, D., and Murphy, W. (2003), 'Excellence in knowledge management: an empirical study to identify critical success factors and performance measures', *Journal of Measuring Business Excellence,* 7(2), 29–45.

Parasuramam, A., Zeithaml, V. A., and Berry, L. L. (1988), 'SERVQUAL: a multiple item scale for measuring consumer perceptions of service quality', *Journal of Marketing*, 64(1), 12–40.

Ritzer, G. (2007), *The Globalization of Nothing,* Thousand Oaks, CA: Pine Forge Press.

Zeithaml, V. A. and Bitner, M. J. (2005), *Services Marketing: Integrating Customer Focus Across the Firm,* 3rd international edn., Singapore: McGraw-Hill/Irwin.

REFERENCES

Baron, S. and Harris, K. (2003), *Services Marketing: Texts and Cases,* New York: Palgrave.

Berry, L. L. and Parasuraman, A. (1992), 'Services marketing starts from within', *Marketing Management,* Winter, 5–15.

Brown, D., Deardorff, A., and Stern, R. (2001), 'CGE Modelling and Analysis of Multilateral and Regional Negotiating Options', in Stern, R. (ed.), *Issues and Options for US–Japan Trade Policies,* Ann Arbor, MI: University of Michigan Press.

Clark, T., Rajaratnam, D., and Smith, T. (1996), 'Toward a theory of international services: marketing intangibles in a world of nations', *Journal of International Marketing,* 4(2), 9–28.

Delio, M. (1999), 'Strategic outsourcing', *Knowledge Management Magazine,* July (www .kmmagazine.com).

Javalgi, R. G. and White, D. S. (2002), 'Strategic challenges for the marketing of services internationally', *International Marketing Review,* 19(6), 563–81.

Jobber, D. (2001), *Principles and Practice of Marketing,* 3rd edn., Maidenhead: McGraw-Hill.

Kalakota, R. and Whinston, A. B. (1997), *Electronic Commerce,* Reading, MA: Addison-Wesley.

Kasper, H., Helsdingen, P. V., and de Vries, W. (1999), *Services Marketing Management: An International Perspective,* Chichester: Wiley.

Levitt, T. (1983), 'The globalization of markets', *Harvard Business Review,* May–June, 92–102.

Lovelock, C. H. (1981), 'Why Marketing Management Needs to be Different for Services', in Donnolly, J. H. and George, W. R. (eds.), *Marketing of Services,* Chicago: American Marketing Association, 5–9.

—— and Yip, G. S. (1996), 'Developing global strategies for service businesses', *California Management Review,* 38(2), Winter, 64–86.

Nicoulaud, B. (1988), 'Problems and strategies in the international marketing of services', *European Journal of Marketing,* 23(6), 55–66.

Ohmae, K. (1990), *The Borderless World,* New York: Citicorp.

Palmer, A. (2001), *Principles of Services Marketing,* 3rd edn., London: McGraw-Hill.

Parasuramam, A., Zeithaml, V. A., and Berry, L. L. (1985), 'A conceptual model of service quality and its implications for future research', *Journal of Marketing,* 49(4), 41–50.

——, —— and, —— (1988), 'SERVQUAL: a multiple item scale for measuring consumer perceptions of service quality', *Journal of Marketing,* 64(1), 12–40.

Patterson, P. G. and Cicic, M. (1995), 'A typology of services firms in international markets: an empirical investigation', *Journal of International Marketing,* 3(4), 57–83.

Quinn, B. and Alexander, N. (2002), 'International retail franchising: a conceptual framework', *International Retail and Retail Management,* 30(5), 264–76.

Ritzer, G. (2007), *The Globalization of Nothing,* Thousand Oaks, CA: Pine Forge Press.

Shostack, L. G. (1985), 'Planning the service encounter', in Czepiel et al. (eds.), *The Service Encounter,* Lexington, MA: Lexington Books, 243–53.

—— (1987), 'Services positioning through structural change', *Journal of Marketing,* 51(Jan.), 34–43.

Sundbo, J. (2002), 'The service economy: standardization or customization?', *The Service Industry Journal,* 22(4), October, 93–106.

Tai, H. C. S. and Chan, Y. K. R. (2001), 'Cross-cultural studies on information content of service advertising', *Journal of Services of Marketing,* 15(7), 547–64.

Vandermerwe, S. and Chadwick, M. (1989), 'The internationalization of services', *Services Industries Journal,* 9(1), 79–93.

van der Spek, K. and Kingma, J. (1999), 'Achieving Successful Knowledge Management Initiatives', in J. Reeves (ed.), *Liberating Knowledge: Business Guide,* London: Caspian Publishing.

Watson, A., Kirby, D. A., and Egan, J. (2002), 'Franchising, retailing and the development of e-commerce', *International Journal of Retail and Distribution Management,* 30(5), 228–37.

World Bank (2001), *Global Economic Prospects for Developing Countries,* Washington, DC: World Bank.

Zeidman, P. (2004), 'Codes of ethics and international franchising: who cares?', *Franchising World,* April, 32–3.

Zeithaml, V. A. and Bitner, M. J. (2003), *Services Marketing: Integrating Customer Focus across the Firm,* 3rd international edn., Singapore: McGraw-Hill/Irwin.

online resource centre

Visit the companion website to this book for lots of interesting additional material, including self-assessment questions, internet exercises, and links for each chapter:

http://www.oxfordtextbooks.co.uk/orc/lee_carter2e/

CHAPTER ELEVEN

Management of Global Communications

Chapter overview

Chapter Introduction	344	Sponsorship	366
Changes and Issues in Marketing Communications	344	Planning of sponsorship campaign	367
Moving beyond the 'Standardize or Localize' Debate	344	Exhibitions and Trade Fairs	368
		Planning exhibitions and trade fairs	370
The Drive towards Integration	347	Planning for Online Communications	371
Advertising	350	Advertising	371
The creative plan	350	Sales promotion	373
Global marketing communications in action: the Bertolli spread	357	Publicity	374
		Personal selling	374
Public Relations	359	Chapter Summary	375
Direct-response Marketing	362		
Planning a direct-response campaign	364		

Learning objectives

After studying this chapter, the reader will be able to:

- present an overview of the changes and emerging issues that impact on the planning of international/global marketing communications;

- appreciate the differences between the standardization and the adaptation approaches to developing cross-cultural marketing communications;

- understand the importance and concept of integrated marketing communications;

- examine the important communication tools for global marketing communications, including advertising, public relations, direct-response marketing, sponsorship, exhibitions, and online communications.

Management issues

The management issues that arise from this chapter include:

- In what ways do the changes and emerging issues in marketing communications impact on the organization's existing international/global marketing communications strategy?

- If greater integration in the planning of marketing communications is inevitable, what are the immediate and longer-term challenges of implementing it?

- How do we benchmark the organization's existing marketing communications strategy against the best practices of other organizations?

Chapter Introduction

Marketing communications can be defined as 'the process whereby organizations seek to create commonness of thought and meaning between themselves and/or individuals and/or intermediaries in the distribution chain, or more likely with publics or audiences who could impact on organizational success' (Kitchen, 1997: 156). While the process of communications may be relatively similar to that in the domestic context, the contextual application of international/global communications is likely to vary due to prevailing environmental circumstances (ibid.).

This chapter will explore the complex issues and changes impacting on the planning of international marketing communications in today's global marketplace. First, we examine ways in which marketing communications have developed and the consequent implications on its practice. Within an increasingly crowded global market, marketing communications are increasingly being charged with not merely moving products and services forward but with creating a distinctive competitive edge. We shall then examine the promotional tools for global marketing communications, including advertising, public relations, direct-response marketing, sponsorship, and exhibitions. This chapter also discusses the planning of online communications for marketing.

Changes and Issues in Marketing Communications

The planning and deployment of marketing communications strategies that effectively 'communicate a range of messages about value, quality, reliability and brand image to a whole variety of global audiences' (Monye, 2000: 4) is perhaps one of the most perplexing challenges facing international/global marketers. Accelerating pace of change in technologies, deepening integration of regional trading blocs, changing consumer demographics, fragmentation of media, intensive competition, and the proclaimed emergence of 'global consumers' are just some of the market developments which exacerbate the complexity of managing domestic and multinational marketing communications. Organizations increasingly 'need to break through smudge and clutter and deliver pertinent timely messages to clearly targeted markets' (Kitchen, 1997: 158). Consumers are no longer passive recipients of marketing messages; they have become more sophisticated, knowledgeable, and resistant to direct approaches (ibid.). To understand the new challenges that confront marketing and marketing communications managers, it is necessary to examine the changes and issues in marketing and marketing communications which have developed and evolved over recent years. These will be discussed under the headings 'Moving beyond the "standardize or localize" debate' and 'The drive towards integration'.

Moving beyond the 'Standardize or Localize' Debate

In today's global business environment, the development and execution of marketing communication campaigns that 'travel well' across cultures can be an especially challenging task for those organizations that market their products or services globally. This difficulty arises because these organizations are confronted with the decision of whether to standardize their advertising campaigns across countries or to adapt/localize their programmes in every country (Cutler and Javalgi, 1992). The standardization/adaptation debate continues to attract diametrically opposing views and remains a fiercely divisive issue among academics and practitioners alike. In the standardization purists' camp the banners read, 'One Sight, One Sound, One Sell' and the talk is of cultural 'common denominators' that will allow advertisements to 'travel' well worldwide. The faithful in the localization camp hold that marketing campaigns tailored to individual cultures are more effective and will more than pay for the additional creative and production costs (Rutigliano, 1986).

Advocates of the standardization approach, such as Elinder (1965), Fatt (1967), and Levitt (1983), argue that consumers everywhere have the same basic needs and desires and can therefore be persuaded by universal appeals. There are four major benefits of standardization: (1) cost reductions or greater efficiency in planning and control; (2) the building of international brand and company image; (3) the simplification of coordination and control; and (4) the exploitation of good ideas (Rutigliano, 1986). There appears to be ample evidence that organizations have successfully transferred their advertising campaigns and that standardized themes have provided unified brand images. Consumers around the world smoke Marlboro (www.marlboro.com) cigarettes and use Parker pens (www.parkerpen.co.uk), McDonald's (www.mcdonalds.com) and Wendy's (www.wendys.com) serve up hamburgers in Paris, and German consumers make their purchases with American Express (www.Amex.com) cards (Mueller, 1992).

Proponents of the adaptation/localization approach (e.g. Ricks et al., 1974; Mueller, 1987; Synodinos et al., 1989) assert that consumers differ from country to country and accordingly must be reached by communications tailored to their respective countries. In its purest sense, global advertising is rarely practised even for companies like Coca-Cola (www.coke.com), a shining example of a truly global brand. The company had a considerable difficulty calling its leading soft drink Coca-Cola in China since the calligraphy producing those sounds translates as 'bite the wax tadpole' or 'beat the mare with wax'. Also, Coke's celebrated Mean Joe Green television spot, which was initially used worldwide, means nothing to most children outside the USA, and Coke had to resort to using local sports stars in otherwise identical TV spots shown in 14 countries (Mueller, 1987).

Most blunders in international/global communications occur because marketers fail to understand foreign cultures and adapt accordingly (Kanso, 1992). Too often, marketing communications are implemented across countries for the wrong reasons. Short-term pressures on budgets make it tempting to re-use or modify material that has proved successful in one country for rollout to others. Due to competitive pressures, this may also be a timing issue ('let's use this ad until we have time to develop a better one'), which can be particularly damaging since it often leaves insufficient time to research the creative material locally, and to a high enough standard. The result can be wasted media-spend supporting ineffective copy, or worse still, directly damaging the brand. The existence of 'global tribes' or the single European market may be more of a concept than a reality. What are the factors that force us to look beyond globally harmonized marketing communications? We have grouped these into 'market differences' and 'consumer differences' (Wilkins, 2002), illustrated in Fig. 11.1:

Market differences. The importance of these factors varies according to the specific brand, sector, and country:

1. Economic factors: the stage of development and state of the economy play a fundamental role. What is affordable to most consumers in one country may be a luxury in other less wealthy markets, affecting the tone and positioning of brand communications.

Fig. 11.1 Factors preventing standardization of marketing communications

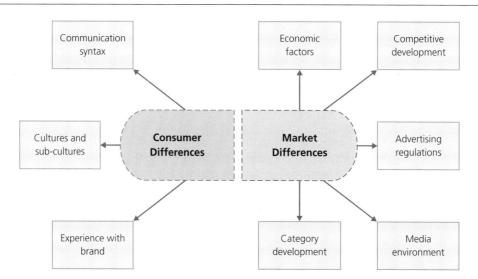

2. Media environment: although global media exist, all markets have local media landscapes. This affects which media people encounter and how people consume advertising.

3. Advertising regulations/restriction: sometimes these may prohibit advertising to certain target groups or products, e.g. to children in Sweden, or cigarettes in many countries. They can also restrict the content permitted.

4. Category development: this is one of the most common variables and is a popular means of segmenting markets into less-developed and better-developed groupings, e.g. mobile telecommunications markets in Western Europe compared to the Middle East.

5. Competitive development: though a brand may be international, the competitive set can vary widely between countries, both in number and positioning. Contrast the competitive context for Stella Artois in the UK (where lager consumption is proportionally higher) and France (where wine consumption is proportionally higher). Equally, the order of entry into the market may play a key role, even if the main brands are the same.

Consumer differences. Some market differences are intertwined with consumer differences partly reflecting the market's characteristics:

1. Cultural differences: the cultural heritage, values, and habits of a country (and different sub-cultures within it) influence perceptions and reactions to creative styles, driving the use of humour, settings, casting, and tonality. This attitude towards the consumption of snacks, such as crisps in the UK, is entirely different from, say, France, where consumers generally follow regular meal patterns.

2. Communication syntax: each country has social habits or values that influence the expression of emotions, gestures, facial expressions, body language, and even verbal communications.

3. Experience with the brand: how consumers use, consume, and interact with the brand may differ, as may their level of experience of the brand.

Global communications has evolved from a centrally mandated message handed down to the regions—where it often has little resonance—to a highly decentralized local message that varies widely around the world. Many companies are following 'the third option'—a combination of both strategies. Global media provides an important platform for promoting the brand on a global basis and channelling valuable support for local marketing activities (Scott, 2001). It is recognized that global marketers need to develop communications that speak to their audiences at a local level, leading to a more decentralized approach to the brand, while maintaining a high level of *global visibility*. This is particularly true for mass consumer products or services. For business or high-end consumer products local adaptation is less important. In these cases, it is possible to identify common audience characteristics that transcend the cultural identities of the consumer, whether they are business travellers or purchasing a technology product for themselves or their company. Agilent (www.agilent.com), a spin-off company of Hewlett-Packard (www.hp.com), which specializes in innovative technologies and solutions to a wide range of customers in communications, electronics, life sciences, and chemical analysis, needed to get its message to the world with six weeks' lead time. It was imperative that they hit 80% of their revenue in 27 countries. To create effective brand-building, a tiered approach was used in all the markets. This was achieved by maximizing prime exposure during CNN's (www.cnn.com) 24 hours of the millennium, and Agilent's worldwide launch at Telecom '99 with sponsorship of the multimedia CMMI,[1] Time (www.time.com), and Fortune Telecom (www.fortunetele.com) '99 platform. The campaign was supported by local activities. Within the first month, awareness increased from 0% to 26%; four months later, awareness levels were at nearly 60% (Scott, 2001).

The Drive towards Integration

Few topics have received more attention and publicity in contemporary marketing literature than that of integrated marketing communications (IMC). IMC has been defined as a concept of marketing communications planning that recognizes the added value of a comprehensive plan that evaluates the strategic roles of a variety of communications disciplines (e.g., general advertising, direct response, sales promotion, and public relations) and combines these disciplines to provide clarity, consistency, and maximum communications impact.

A further breakdown of how IMC is defined may include: (1) the creation of one voice (i.e. a single 'theme' and 'image'); (2) the integration of both product image and relevant aspects of consumer behaviour in promotion management, as opposed to a focus on only one; and (3) the coordinated management of promotion-mix disciplines (Gould et al., 1999).

Grein and Gould (1996: 143) propose the concept of globally integrated marketing communications (GIMC), which extends IMC by adding the 'international' dimension:

> [A] system of active promotional management which strategically coordinates global communications in all of its component parts both horizontally in terms of countries and organizations and vertically in terms of promotional discipline. It contingently takes into account the full range of standardized versus adaptive market options, synergies, variations among target populations and other marketplace and business conditions.

This would entail making strategic decisions through the integrated *tracking, comparison,* and *coordination* of marketing communications across all relevant global markets, units, or

[1] CMMI is a model for improving and appraising the performance of development organizations. It stands for Capability Maturity Model Integration. It helps organizations gain visibility into their projects and processes.

offices in order to maximize both organizational learning and the efficient allocation of resources. The potential benefits of GIMC (Gould et al., 1999: 144) include:

- coordination of marketing communications across disciplines and countries;
- standardization of communications to reduce costs;
- taking advantage of cross-border spill-over of communications (e.g. television broadcasts spill over in neighbouring countries);
- developing a consistent brand name and image; and
- exploitation of knowledge from different country operations for the benefit of all company operations.

Some of the most forceful supporters for the integration of communications have argued that the question 'integration or not' is, in fact, futile as the drive towards IMC is inevitable due to:

- **The ICTs revolution.** The revolution in internet and communications technologies (ICTs) has provided new possibilities in the delivery of cost-effective and targeted marketing communications. These developments are reflected in 'the boom in direct database marketing, new ways to automate salesforce management, and the sudden blossoming of the World Wide Web [which] all suggest that the discipline is under pressure to reshape' (Falk and Schmidt, 1997: 240). Utilization of sophisticated computerized mailing systems to create personalized messages and customized offers is an example of this, as is the development of smart card loyalty programmes, information distribution through the internet or proprietary intranets, and the use of in-house satellite television to communicate with employees and suppliers (Schultz and Schultz, 1998). The range of applications in marketing communications appears to be endless: from data capture, storage, and analysis to automated and interactive customer services and, to delivery mechanisms such as postal, internet, telephone, mobile telephone, and portable computers.

  As a result of the advent of these new communication technologies, the flow of information, data capture, storage, and analysis are increasingly shifting away from the manufacturer or retailer of the distribution channel towards the consumer or end user. Fig. 11.2 demonstrates how consumers now have a much greater control and influence of information flow in the marketing communications process. Inherent in this power shift (of the control of information flow), as argued by Schultz and Kitchen (2000), is the equalization of manufacturers and channels. The strategic decisions made by both are no longer driven by their dominant positions but by the needs of consumers and end users. They must now collectively develop the skills and expertise to respond and manage the interactive and multimedia communications with their customers, and do so with synergy and greater effectiveness. This is a major transition for most organizations as they have been accustomed to finding potential benefits for the product or service and then developing forms and methods of sending messages about those benefits to prospective customers or users. In the new reality, efficient delivery

Sophisticated computerized mailing systems are easily available today for organizations to create personalized messages and/or customized offers.

Fig. 11.2 Consumer-driven communication process

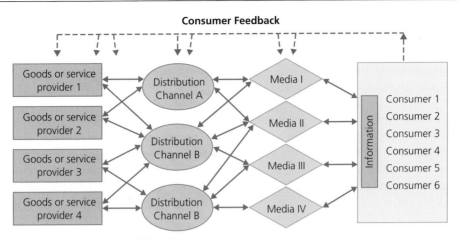

Source: Based on Schultz and Schultz (1998: 10).

of messages or incentives will no longer be the driving force in marketing communications. Instead, the challenge is how quickly and completely the organization can respond to consumer requests or needs. The goal of communication instead becomes a question of how to engage meaningfully with the customer or prospect to obtain a behavioural response that will lead to an action or affirmative response.

Due to the vast economic and infrastructural differences that exist between different trading regions, multinational organizations may find themselves operating simultaneously in a range of marketplaces at varying stages of ICT development. The challenge is therefore to plan, execute, and integrate their increasingly complex programme of marketing communications with cultural sensitivity, precision, and effectiveness.

- **An enlightened understanding of the nature of communications.** There have been numerous challenges to the traditional concepts of how marketing communications work and how consumers respond to these marketing efforts. The processes of marketing, communications, promotion, and advertising were assumed to be linear, i.e. products move from producer to wholesaler to retailer to consumer; advertising moves from marketer to agency to media to consumer. To understand the relationship, for example, between advertising and purchase behaviour, it is assumed that we can study it as a piece or a part of the brand's communications in isolation, rather than as part of the whole process. In today's ever more complex, interconnected world of communications and promotion, it does not appear to be possible (or practical) to do so. It is very difficult to create a clean, clear, uncontaminated environment where advertising or other communication elements can be studied in isolation. It would be more practical and valuable to understand the process of communications in its totality. Further, consumers integrate and synthesize communication messages by instinct, regardless of whether these messages have been integrated. It is therefore a futile exercise for the marketers to argue over 'whether to integrate or not', as integration already occurs as a natural process at the consumer or receiver level. The best marketers and advertisers can do is to understand the integration process and modify their approaches and concepts to maximize the return on the integration which occur naturally (Schultz and Kitchen, 2000).

The majority of IMC thinking and discussions originated in the early 1990s. While there has been considerable debate and discussion of the subject—who does it, how it is done, etc.—the formal presentation of research, theory development, and other materials by either practitioners or academics has been slow (Kitchen and Schultz, 1997). It is hard not to have been confronted with and influenced by the writings on IMC (e.g. Schultz, 1996; Kitchen, 1997; Kitchen and Schultz, 1999;). In reflecting on the 'potentialities' associated with IMC, or the seemingly simple solutions that it offers for the complexity of managing marketing communications across organizations (Conrelissen and Lock, 2000), it is perhaps not surprising that the concept and practice of IMC have been adopted by many. Despite increased attention and widespread discussion, there is not yet 'any consistent or mutually agreed definition, description, or process to identify what IMC is and what it is not' (Kitchen and Schultz, 1999: 22). Those opposed to the concept, as commonly defined in the media, have challenged the principles presented as being nothing more than traditional marketing and advertising dressed up in fancy words and a new language (Miller and Rose, 1994; Sloan, 1994). Although the subject is generally accepted in the marketing literature, there are still many areas in need of greater exposition and clarification.

Advertising

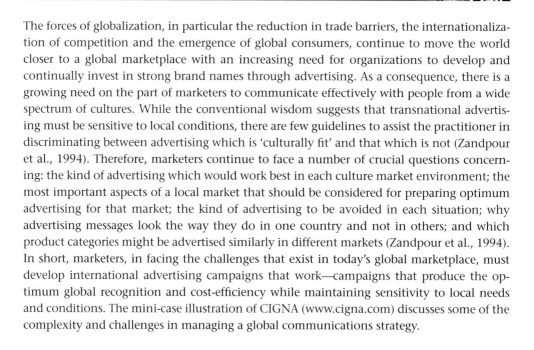

The forces of globalization, in particular the reduction in trade barriers, the internationalization of competition and the emergence of global consumers, continue to move the world closer to a global marketplace with an increasing need for organizations to develop and continually invest in strong brand names through advertising. As a consequence, there is a growing need on the part of marketers to communicate effectively with people from a wide spectrum of cultures. While the conventional wisdom suggests that transnational advertising must be sensitive to local conditions, there are few guidelines to assist the practitioner in discriminating between advertising which is 'culturally fit' and that which is not (Zandpour et al., 1994). Therefore, marketers continue to face a number of crucial questions concerning: the kind of advertising which would work best in each culture market environment; the most important aspects of a local market that should be considered for preparing optimum advertising for that market; the kind of advertising to be avoided in each situation; why advertising messages look the way they do in one country and not in others; and which product categories might be advertised similarly in different markets (Zandpour et al., 1994). In short, marketers, in facing the challenges that exist in today's global marketplace, must develop international advertising campaigns that work—campaigns that produce the optimum global recognition and cost-efficiency while maintaining sensitivity to local needs and conditions. The mini-case illustration of CIGNA (www.cigna.com) discusses some of the complexity and challenges in managing a global communications strategy.

The creative plan

To market brands that will be noticed and trusted by the consumer, the advertisement will first have to stand out. Advertising will therefore have to catch the consumer's attention and deliver the message in an original way that will enable the consumer to remember and identify with both the message and the brand. Advertising in general, and international advertising in particular, must enable organizations to compete successfully in the marketplace while delivering optimum rationalization of investment in executing international advertising campaigns. As most organizations competing in specific markets have at their disposal the same financial and human resources, and similar marketing and production know-how, they have few options at their disposal but to *outsmart* (rather than *outspend*)

The mantra for every experienced global marketer is 'never under-estimate the power of local cultures in driving sales'.

CIGNA understands and respects the subtleties of local cultures, and that understanding drives their global marketing communications approach: build a framework of guidelines that reinforce a consistent corporate brand, yet support local marketing efforts. The company has offices in 24 countries in Asia and the Pacific Rim, Europe and the Americas. It is one of the few organizations that offer insurance and financial services on an international scale. Its portfolio includes healthcare, life, accident and supplemental health insurance, pensions, and expatriate benefits programmes.

Due to the breadth of its portfolio, CIGNA's global marketing challenge is not simply related to country-specific distinctions, but also to its varied business activities within each country. For instance, within its 24 global businesses there are seven healthcare operations, principally located in Latin America and Europe; specialized expatriate insurance programmes, which provide global healthcare to employees working outside their country of citizenship; life insurance companies selling life, accident, and supplemental health products in 12 countries and throughout the European Union; and pension operations in Brazil and Japan.

In addition to distinct cultures and customer needs, each country has a unique mix of business lines. Each business line has distinct marketing strategies, different local competitors and diverse regulatory requirements that are subject to change. In Japan and Brazil, changes in government regulations have only recently paved the way for starting up its pension operations, which offer employer-sponsored pension programmes similar to 401(k) plans in the USA. On the healthcare side, systems around the world are diverse due to cultural attitudes, political environments, and economic conditions. For those countries in which it operates, it develops services appropriate to the level of need. Countries with less comprehensive public healthcare systems, such as Brazil, require more extensive insurance, whereas those with stronger systems, such as the UK, generally need supplemental health products to fill in the gaps. Its marketing and sales approaches include employer and affinity group-sponsored sales, direct mail, telemarketing, internet, dedicated sales representatives, and insurance agents.

As a result, CIGNA International takes a unique approach to each business, leveraging its global expertise to tailor insurance and financial services to meet local business conditions and customer needs. And the global marketing strategy has always been in line with its overall business approach—build a consistent brand presence around the world by leveraging corporate marketing guidelines and standards. The company accomplishes this by disseminating standards to its local offices, where country managers and marketing representatives are responsible for developing and implementing local marketing plans. Aware of CIGNA's global strategy of a unified brand, key local management are given the flexibility to adapt the corporate standards, within reason and when necessary, to address unique environments.

Source: Based on Woodington (2001).

competitors in building distinctive brands and images that are salient to the consumer's needs (Appelbaum and Halliburton, 1993). To do so, these brands will have to be communicated through a creative plan that is not only original and effective, but also has the flexibility to accommodate local adaptations so that they can be rolled out internationally.

The development of a successful creative plan—'what is said', and 'how it is said'—for an international advertising campaign needs to consider the following (see Fig. 11.3):

Positioning

Positioning is the very difficult answer to the very simple question: 'what does the product do, for whom, and in place of what?'. In this sense, it can be defined as what the product represents in the eyes of consumers in reference to the competition (Appelbaum and Halliburton, 1993). It can be classified according to two elements: a *functional* element (what the product does), and an *emotional* element. The relationship between the functional and emotional elements of the position will depend on two issues which relate to the *information* needs of the consumer: (a) the consumer's awareness of a need; and (b) the consumer's knowledge of the available products. As illustrated in Fig. 11.4, the creative positioning can therefore be (Kroeber-Riel, 1990 in Appelbaum and Halliburton, 1993):

(a) the 100% information positioning (100 info)—the advertisement includes only information about the product or its use.

Fig. 11.3 Development of a creative plan

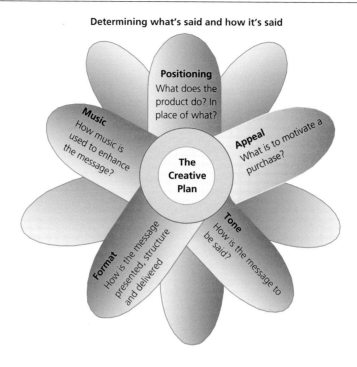

Fig. 11.4 Development of a creative plan: determining creative 'positioning'

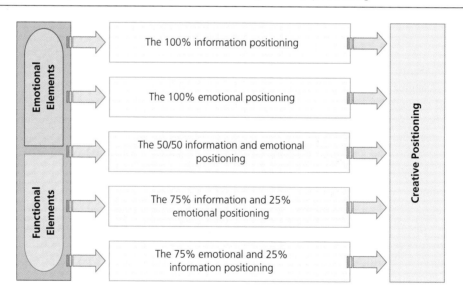

(b) the 100% emotional positioning (100 emo)—the advertisement aims to associate (only) emotions to the product.

(c) the information and emotional positioning (50/50)—this kind of advertisement includes information as well as emotions. It is important to note that it is not possible to identify exactly the proportion of information and emotion in any advertisement.

(d) the 75% information and 25% emotional positioning (75/25 info)—the advertisement provides mainly information but is supported by strong emotions. The purpose of the advertiser seems to be the provision of information 'wrapped up' in an emotional content.

(e) the 75% emotional and 25% information positioning (75/25 emo)—the advertisement is used to convey mainly emotions, but some information is included. The purpose of the advertiser seems to link emotions to the product.

The creative positioning selected in each international market may be adapted according to the life-cycle stage of the product or service. The positioning tends to be informative in the introduction stage and become increasingly emotional in the growth stage. In the maturity stage it becomes mainly emotional as the consumer's need and information requirements become trivial, i.e. the consumer is aware of the need and knows all about the products that can satisfy their need.

The power of the MasterCard[2] brand (www.mastercard.com), with its award-winning 'Priceless' campaign and which transforming the effects on the MasterCard franchise, is an excellent case study of emotionally salient, targeted advertising coordinated and integrated on a global scale. Before the Priceless campaign, the brand lacked a distinct and consistent *positioning* that would capture the minds of consumers. While its member banks determine the fees, rates, rewards, and benefits, MasterCard defines and communicates the brand. How the brand performs is largely due to its positioning and marketing.

Development of the campaign was based on research which revealed that what consumers considered important were the values of family and relationships, as they 'seek refuge' from the materialistic environment. With that in mind, the Priceless theme, 'the best way to pay for everything that matters', was launched in 1997.

The Priceless campaign continues to cross cultures and geography, providing a transcendent platform for all MasterCard's payment programmes and marketing activities. It reinforces the message that MasterCard knows 'what is truly important in life'. Research on the brand equity reveals positive consumer perceptions of the MasterCard as *everyday* (to displace cash and cheques), *practical* (the card that is an enabler for what matters in life), and *unpretentious* (standing for core values universal to all cultures). By the end of 2002, the campaign had been used in over 90 countries in over 45 languages. MasterCard, quite rightly, prides its campaign as the only payments brand advertising that is consistent on a global scale. The campaign has helped MasterCard realize a 64% gain in gross dollar volume since 1997 as well as increase the number of MasterCard-branded cards in circulation by more than 52% over the same period.

Appeal

A creative appeal may be defined as any message designed to motivate the consumer to purchase. It seeks to provide the consumer with 'the reason why' they should make a selection of one brand over another. The appeal can vary considerably in different countries. For instance, it makes little sense to use the 'social reward' appeal for a food product in a country where individuality is a highly cherished cultural value.

Creating the right appeal is crucial to the success of BMW (www.bmw.com),[3] the premium car manufacturer. While the BMW brand has always been carefully promoted and its advertising campaign immaculately executed worldwide to position its cars as the 'ultimate

---

[2] The Mastercard example is based on Coughlin, D. M. (2002), 'The power of the brand: a best case look at a brand transformation: MasterCard's "Priceless" campaign', *The Advertiser,* October.

[3] The BMW example is based on McDowell, J. (2002), 'The art of global marketing: finding the right balance between global strategy and local execution', The Advertiser, June.

driving machines', the company recognizes that each market is unique in culture, competitive set, regulatory environment and, of course, advertising regulations. The company accepts that to emulate some of the brilliant, award-winning advertising that transcends cultures is difficult and often risks becoming the lowest-common-denominator 'global' solution. It prefers to execute its global strategic brief by the best possible local team in touch with every nuance of its own language and culture. This is especially true for products and brands in the highly emotional and engaging categories such as premium cars.

To achieve effective market penetration, the company needs to adopt a different appeal in its creative strategy in each market. In Europe, where traffic density is high, the appeal of high-tech navigation systems that identify traffic jams on the Autobahn and automatically suggest alternative routes is projected to be much higher than they will be in the USA. Due to greater consumer concern for environmental pollution, the interest in hydrogen-powered cars—one of BMW's primary technological pushes—is also much higher in Europe than it is in the USA and Asia. While the US customers may find cars with larger and more powerful engines more appealing, Europeans may find less energy-efficient cars less appealing and are more willing to accept lower performance in exchange for reduced carbon-dioxide emissions. In Germany, where drivers are enthusiasts of fine engineering and design, the appeal of the BMW brand emphasizes both the car's performance and accomplished German manufacturing. In Japan, status plays a larger role in the company's creative strategy.

Tone

In order to communicate the creative positioning, the advertiser has to decide on the tone and format of the creative—how it is said?' The tone and format, which are sometimes referred to as the advertising concept, are an integral part of the advertising plan. They are important to attain credibility and create the desired image around the product. The tone of a creative can take several forms (Appelbaum and Halliburton, 1993):

(a) **The use of humour.** The use of humour is notoriously difficult in international advertising as humour is often embedded in language and culture. It is only effective when the communication objective is to attract attention and create awareness, but may be distractive if the communication aims to achieve comprehension.

The food giant Unilever has used 'humour' to appeal to UK consumers in marketing its Pot Noodles. For example, one of the television adverts begins with a couple eating sandwiches. The man is seen making a secret phone call and then visiting the 'red light' district in search of Pot Noodles. He approaches a number of women and, in each case, is slapped on the face when he asks for the product. He then enters a shop and is told by the female assistant to meet her 'round the back', where both are then seen enjoying Pot Noodles.

(b) **Argumentative vs. narrative.** An argumentative advertisement is one in which viewers are directly addressed. They are passive recipients of the message that they are expected to process. It attempts to address viewers at the rational level (Olsen, 1989). In a narrative advertisement, viewers are not directly addressed. They are more of a witness to a 'story' being presented and interpret the content of the advertisement. The aim is to build a relationship between the consumer and the product, and generate an emotional response.

(c) **Competitive vs. non-competitive.** This refers to the level of comparison of the product to competition. Advertisements in the USA tend to be more competitive than those in Europe in making direct product-to-product comparison to demonstrate superiority.

(d) **Hard-sell vs. soft-sell.** Soft-sell appeal implies that mood and atmosphere are conveyed through a beautiful scene or the development of an emotional story or verse. Human emotional

WHOSE RESPONSIBILITY IS IT? Climate change? Or is it just bad weather?

For more than a century, people have relied on fossil fuels such as oil, coal, and gas for their energy needs. Now, worldwide, people and the environment are experiencing the consequences. Global warming, caused by burning fossil fuels, is the worst environmental problem we face.

People are changing the climate that made life possible and the results are disastrous—extreme weather events, such as droughts and floods, disruption of water supplies, melting polar regions, rising sea levels, the loss of coral reefs, and more. Scientists and governments worldwide agree on the latest and starkest evidence of human-induced climate change, its impacts, and the predictions of what is to come.

By burning fossil fuels humans pump billions of tonnes of carbon dioxide (CO_2—the most important greenhouse gas emitted by human activities) and other greenhouse gases into the atmosphere. These gases create a 'greenhouse effect', thickening the natural canopy of gases in the atmosphere and causing more heat to become trapped. As a result, the global temperature is increasing, throwing the world's climate out of its natural balance and into chaos.

The main source of these human-produced greenhouse gases is burning large amounts of fossil fuels for energy production and transport. Changes in land use and deforestation also release CO_2 into the environment. Trees, for example, are natural 'carbon sinks'—they absorb CO_2—and when they are destroyed, CO_2 is released into the atmosphere.

While many greenhouse gases occur naturally, the rate humans are adding them to the atmosphere is far from natural. It is estimated that concentrations of CO_2 are 30% higher than before the industrial revolution, when the wide-scale burning of fossil fuels started. Humans are also creating new greenhouse gases such as hydrofluorocarbons (HFCs) from industrial activities. Even if all greenhouse gas emissions were stopped, the effects from past activities would persist for centuries, due to the life of greenhouse gases in the atmosphere and the time required for transfer of heat from the atmosphere to the oceans.

The latest report from the International Panel on Climate Change (IPCC) says that hundreds of technologies are already available, at very low cost, to reduce climate-damaging emissions, and that government policies need to remove the barriers to these technologies. Implementing these solutions will not require humans to make sacrifices or otherwise impede their quality of life. Instead, they will enable people to usher in a new era of energy, one that will bring

© fStop

economic growth, new jobs, technological innovation and, most importantly, environmental protection. However, for green solutions to global warming to find a foothold in the market, governments and corporations need to lead the shift away from polluting technology.

Wind power is already a significant source of energy in many parts of the world. It can supply 10% of the world's electricity within two decades. Solar power has been growing in a global capacity by 33% annually. Greenpeace and industry research show that with government support, the solar industry could supply electricity to over 2 billion people in the next 20 years. By 2040 solar photovoltaics could supply nearly 25% of global electricity demand.

A report conducted by global financial analysts KPMG (www. kpmg.com) shows that solar power would become cost competitive with traditional fossil fuels if the production of photovoltaic panels was increased to 500 megawatts a year. A renewable power plant in Asia could have the same costs and provide the same jobs as a coal-fired plant, but with significant environmental advantages.

Source: Greenpeace (www.greenpeace.org).

sentiments are emphasized over clear-cut product-related appeals. Hard-sell appeal, however, implies sales orientation is emphasized, stressing brand name and product recommendations. Explicit mention may be made of competitive products, sometimes by name, and the product's advantage depends on performance (Mueller, 1987).

(e) **Direct vs. indirect.** In the direct approach, information about the product is conveyed through *words*, whereas in the indirect approach, it is conveyed through *images*. To minimize problems with language translation, there is increasing usage of images

The food giant Unilever has used 'humour' to appeal to UK consumers in marketing its Pot Noodles.

Reproduced with kind permission of Unilever.

(rather than words) in international advertisements which may be broadcast with minimum adaptation in multiple countries. Conveying the information through images, however, carries the risk that the message may be misunderstood by the consumer.

The *tone* adopted in advertising seems to be highly contingent on the communication style of a culture. Communication styles in high-context cultures emphasize interpersonal relationships, non-verbal expression, physical setting, and social circumstances. In low-context cultures, however, communication styles stress clearly articulated and spoken messages.

In Japan, the use of soft-sell approach is more common in advertising. The tone adopted in successful campaigns tends to be subtle, and the primary emphasis is on creating a mood or an atmosphere rather than on highlighting the product and its features. The communication style tends to be more suggestive than direct. The hard-sell approach tends to be more prevalent in US advertising. The primary emphasis is on distinguishing the product from the competition. Comparisons, either of a particular criterion or the product in general, are common. The tone is high key and the communication style is aggressive and direct (Mueller, 1992). Advertisements that adopt the hard-sell and direct approach tend to have a greater emphasis on the product, rather than the context. This could mean that the product is displayed more often and/or in a larger size in the advertisements. In addition, it is expected these advertisements would emphasize: (1) greater use of colour; (2) greater use of photographs; (3) larger product portrayal; and (4) more frequent mention of price (Cutler and Javalgi, 1992).

Format

The format of a creative plan is the way an advertisement is presented, structured, and delivered. It helps build the brand but also attempts to solve the credibility problem that the advertiser has to face. The format of an advertising creative may take several forms (Appelbaum and Halliburton, 1993):

(a) slice of life;

(b) little story around the product;

(c) testimonials by experts or a famous personality;

(d) talking heads;

(e) characters or animals associated with the products;

(f) demonstration;

(g) product in action;

(h) cartoon;

(i) international vs. national.

The format of a creative plays an important role in capturing the attention of the targeted audience. The Japanese consumers, as Burton observes (1983), are said to have a marked preference for foreign-sounding brand names because they lend prestige to the product. English is especially favoured because it is regarded as the universal language. There is strong evidence that English words within headlines and body copy of advertisements are also commonplace, making consumers feel like members of a cosmopolitan society (Haarmann, 1986). The experience of Japanese manufacturers suggests that an effective way to transmit the Western style of life is to use testimonials by famous foreign personalities, characters, or 'talking heads'.

Use of music

Music is an important tool that often transmits and evokes emotions better than words in international advertising. Much of today's music is international in character, be it classical or popular. The use of music enables the advertiser to avoid problems in language translation while uniting consumers in different countries by stimulating the desired emotions.

Global marketing communications in action: the Bertolli spread[4]

Bertolli (www.bertolli.com), which was previously Olivio—the first bread spread to contain olive oil—was created in the UK by Unilever Bestfoods with a view to possible rollout in other markets. The power of this brand has taken Bertolli from a €40 million brand in 1997 to a €100 million brand in 2001, growing 150% in just four years. Bertolli provides an excellent case study of how a successful advertising campaign can be developed to work across countries in the same way in all markets.

Positioning

Conventional wisdom states that food advertising does not work on a global level. Cultural sensitivities make it immensely difficult to find a globally relevant solution. However, the experience of Bertolli shows that one campaign can work in many countries if it is rooted in relevant *positioning* that provides the right emotional associations. The company had a clear conceptual model for how the advertising worked in the UK, borne out by statistical analysis. The campaign drove awareness and built engagement with the brand benefit. This then drove trial, and the depth of its emotional connection, and would prompt triallists to talk about the brand, recruiting friends and family to Bertolli. Building genuine emotional engagement in its creative strategy was the single most important factor in driving success. At its international marketing communications rollout, the company was unsure whether it could make the same emotional connection in other countries with different attitudes to food.

In examining other markets, the company discovered that although differences in specific eating habits were manifold, common trends emerged at a higher level. For instance, while attitudes to food remained diverse, attitudes to life were converging. Bertolli's focus on higher-order benefits offered the key to extending the brand into other markets.

Appeal

The key to successful international rollout lay in the breakthrough thinking behind the UK strategy. In reaction to the punitive health regimes of the 1980s, people were increasingly adopting more holistic and natural attitudes, the so-called 'positive health'. The Mediterranean was seen as the cradle of 'positive health', conjuring up images of happy, relaxed individuals enjoying life. More importantly for Bertolli, olive oil was seen as

---

[4] The Bertolli example is based on Holmes, M., McDonald, P., and Firth, H. (2002), 'Divided we dined, united we dream: how the UK campaign for Bertolli spread crossed borders against all odds', Advertising Effectiveness Awards at the Institute of Practitioners in Advertising, London, WARC, www.warc.com (accessed on 15/11/2003).

the epitome of this Mediterranean lifestyle. By emphasizing olive oil as the symbol of the whole Mediterranean approach to life, Bertolli created a whole brand world based on the Mediterranean idyll of enjoying a longer and fuller life. By harnessing an idea about how people want to live rather than how they want to eat, this appeal could transcend everyday attitudes to food and health to connect with consumers at a higher level. Just as the Mediterranean dream could bypass everyday attitudes to food in the UK, it appeared to unite consumers across countries.

Extensive research into eating habits and attitudes across Europe revealed that consumers increasingly regarded health as the key to active enjoyment of life. There were more consumers aware of the need for a holistic approach, recognizing the link between a healthy mind and a healthy body, eschewing stress and punitive action in favour of balance. Food might be local, but the Bertolli vision seemed universal.

The tone and format

Although convinced that the same campaign would work across markets, the company nevertheless needed to be aware of local sensitivities. When considering executional rollout, it consulted creative teams in the local markets which aided understanding of local relevance, building awareness of linguistic and cultural differences. The tone and format are important to attain credibility and create the desired image around the product. To achieve this, the company developed a series of advertisements which usually evolved around the happy and healthy existence of elderly Italians surrounded by friends and family enjoying a longer and more fulfilling life. All the advertisements adopted a slightly humorous tone designed to create emotional engagement with their target audience. Unlike its main competitor Benecol (www.benecol.com), which addressed the audience at the rational level (e.g. the 'clinically proven to reduce cholesterol' campaign), Bertolli adopted a non-competitive tone to avoid direct comparison with competitive products by presenting 'stories' of happy living that deepened the emotional relationship with the brand.

Belgium was the first new market to roll out its communications strategy. The spread was launched as Bertolli in 1997. As in the UK, Bertolli created an olive oil spreads sector, and the brand has been supported consistently ever since, beginning with the 'Football' advertisement in 1997, followed by 'Tug' in 1998–99.

For the narrative of the 'story', a consistent local voice-over artist was used across all executions, building warmth and familiarity towards the brand and becoming the 'voice' of Bertolli in Belgium. While the Bertolli world remained constant, it made subtle changes to voice-over and titling to accommodate local market dynamics. As the spreading margarine sector is less developed in Belgium, it needed to spell out the usage occasion and differentiate between cooking products, with the end-line 'All the goodness of olive oil on your bread'. Given Bertolli's olive oil presence, the advertisement emphasized Italian authenticity by referencing the brand's origins in 1865.

Success in Belgium accelerated the rollout plans in other countries. Bertolli spread was launched in Holland in 1998, followed by Germany in 2000, with supporting advertising campaigns that featured the 'Football' and 'Tug' advertisements. Minor creative tweaks were required to accommodate local tastes—for instance, the Mediterranean fantasy was compelling, too strong an olive oil taste was not. In Germany, its end-line was revised to 'The new spread with *mild* olive oil'. In Holland, it is 'Bertolli for your bread with *mild* olive oil'. Again in each market a consistent voice-over artist with local appeal became the brand 'voice'.

The main objective of Bertolli's advertising campaign was not just to retain its market share but to draw in younger consumers, who found the brand world inspirational but had not tried the product, by increasing relevance and 'youthfulness'. The creative idea evolved around 'Club 18–130' by featuring advertisements that showed its familiar elderly Mediterranean characters on holiday, getting up to antics that were even cheekier than before. Four executions were developed in 1999: two 30-second advertisements, 'Holiday' and 'Exposure'; two 10-second advertisements, 'Lilo' and 'Banana'; along with two print executions for 6-sheet and for women's magazines.

The entire campaign played on the Club 18–130 pun and introduced a youthfulness and zest for life into the brand world. It successfully evolved Bertolli's creative vehicle, deepening consumers' emotional relationship with the brand. It also drove a significant increase in volume gained from its younger target. Under 35s accounted for 10.3% of total volume in 1998, rising to 16.2% in 2001. Penetration among this group in the UK rose by 5% year-on-year in the first year of Club 18–130.

The Bertolli model offers an unconventional way of thinking about global advertising, as it did not start out as an international campaign. There was an eye to long-term rollout, but the immediate focus was the UK. The secret of the campaign's success is that it thought big from the beginning; becoming brand leader in the UK required an emotional connection that would transcend the rational nuances of price and product differentiation. Success in the rest of the world required an emotional connection that would transcend local attitudes to food. The secret is not necessarily to 'think global', but to 'think big'. Consumers do not know whether an advertisement is global—only whether it is good.

Public Relations

The British Institute of Public Relations has defined public relations (hereafter abbreviated to PR) as the planned and sustained effort to establish and maintain goodwill and mutual understanding between an organization and its publics. The publics concerned by PR can be internal, such as employees, or external, such as the general public, customers, suppliers, distributors, or the media. PR 'consists of a set of coordinated communication programmes between an organization and its publics, designed to improve, maintain or protect a company product or image' (Usunier, 2000: 521). When PR is applied internationally, it aims to promote 'mutual understanding and good relations where it is necessary to bridge cultural, geographical or linguistic gaps' (Black, 2000: 103).

The accelerating process of global integration and the consequent growth of international relations are fuelling interest in international PR. In the global marketplace, where trade barriers are fast disappearing and information flows effortlessly, it is no longer possible for organizations simply to operate within the limits of the law and assume that they have met their international responsibilities.

As an organization's international business operations increase in size and coverage, the organization's survival and prosperity become increasingly dependent upon its ability to inform and involve its publics of its actions and policies in order to maintain good relationships with the various interest groups. 'When large-scale negative company-related incidents occur they can be very important because they have the potential of directly and indirectly affecting large number of people' (Jorgensen, 1994: 348). The BSE crisis, which affected the beef industry in the UK and its consequent collapse of international exports into the EU and other countries, attests to the high level of publicity that these incidents generate. From a marketing perspective, company-related disasters and crises can be particularly damaging when a company's products bear the company name. Brand equity and customer loyalty may drop rapidly if a company is blamed for a serious negative incident (Jorgensen, 1994).

There are various developments in the business environment that are creating opportunities and challenges to the practice of international PR (Dibb et al., 1996). Each of these factors serves to create the need for good communications:

- The growing need for effective employee communications, which is especially recognized during periods of corporate change. The implementation of IT programmes, the need for corporate downsizing which often necessitates redundancies, and the actions taken during business process re-engineering—all current issues in many businesses—present unstable conditions for labour relations and raise the potential for management/labour tension. Executives are now realizing the importance of good internal and external communications in maintaining good relations with the workforce during these periods.

- Increasing importance is placed on both corporate branding and product branding. PR is seen as a means to increase this brand awareness, building favourable attitudes among customers and, in turn, increasing sales. It is no longer sufficient for a company to simply brand its products, as consumers are increasingly curious about the practices of the company behind the brand name and demand accountability for its actions.

- The Brent Spar incident is an example in which the actions of an environmental special interest group—i.e. Greenpeace (www.greenpeace.org)—succeeded in turning an isolated incident into a symbol of careless corporate attitudes towards environmental pollution. The facts of this incident were perhaps not as important as the image of Shell (www.shell.com), the oil company involved, and the interpretation of its actions. PR was used effectively by Greenpeace. It transmitted dramatic television images worldwide via satellite—showing a Greenpeace helicopter landing on the deck of the Brent Spar while water cannons tried to repel it—and sent a clear and consistent message that Shell would dump a huge oil rig at the bottom of the ocean (Grein and Gould, 1996). This is unlikely to be the last high-profile case, due to growing consumer awareness of green issues.

- Political and economic changes in today's global business environment, such as the growing regional integration in the form of trading blocs (e.g. the EU, ASEAN, and NAFTA) and the opening up of new markets (e.g. Eastern Europe, the former Soviet Union, and China), are creating significant impacts on organizations and their industries. As a consequence, there is an increasing need for organizations to lobby for legislation and regulations which promote their respective interests.

The functions of PR are twofold. First, PR must seek to create and enhance a favourable corporate image with various publics, with the view that a foreign organization is particularly susceptible to nationalistic criticism. Secondly, in crisis situations such as boycotts, accidents, strikes, product recalls, etc., PR must serve to maintain goodwill by responding to criticism, explaining remedial action that is taken to overcome the problem, and anticipating and countering messages that may damage the corporate image (Usunier, 2000). Since PR is conditioned by reputation, credibility, confidence, harmony, and mutual understanding, it is essential to take into account the subtle relationships which result from national feelings (Black, 2000) and cultural traits of countries in which an organization operates. For instance, it is necessary to avoid ambiguity. Even using the services of a national speaker may not avoid problems unless they are familiar with the subject of the message. In one country, a car did not sell because its name, when translated, meant 'coffin'. An airline produced an advertisement publicizing its 'rendezvous lounges' only to find out that in the local language it meant 'a place to have sex' (Black, 2000).

According to Usunier (2000: 522–3), cultural variance may occur in the following aspects of the PR process:

(a) The recommendations for making contact concern promoting and/or enhancing mutual understanding (it is not about selling), which may make the contact both easier (there being no money involved) and less efficient (PR may be considered purposeless). The lack of understanding of the functions of PR in some cultures may lead to a suspicion of the organization's intentions to reach out to its interest groups.

(b) Managing relationships of all stakeholders. The concept of different groups influencing an organization, and in turn being influenced, is an important element in the development of integrated marketing communications. It enables an organization to identify those parties and individuals who can be or are influenced by the strategies and policies of the organization. When companies form a partnership (see The Relationship Perspective), they need to consider how their internal decisions are going to affect their partner. Effective management of all stakeholders' relationships facilitates the development of strategies to consider the power and interests of those who have a stake in the organization.

(c) Disclosing information, especially in the case of private, secret or sensitive information. This reflects the prevailing sense of responsibility in relation to the community but also the company's sense of secrecy and its view of what is culturally appropriate for dealing with these events: adopting a low profile and waiting for the tempest to calm down, or adopting a high profile, pleading either guilty or not guilty.

(d) Developing arguments/statements for a PR campaign, some of which cannot be understood locally because their basic logic clashes with the host country culture. For instance, in the USA (and to a lesser degree, the UK), companies argue that they need to reward their chief executives with massive pay packages (often disregarding the company's performance) in order to maintain competitiveness. This is viewed as totally unacceptable in countries where social and income equalities are highly valued.

(e) Dealing with nationalistic feelings. The emphasis on local citizenship is always necessary. It must be done with unambiguous commitment to the local community. Bata (www.bata.com), the shoe manufacturer, used this approach to emphasize its importance as a local employer which creates jobs directly and indirectly within the community.

 THE RELATIONSHIP PERSPECTIVE Collaborate to innovate

Napster (www.napster.com), the now legal online music download provider, teamed up with the then UK's largest broadband Internet Service Provider (ISP)—NTL (www.ntl.com)—to bundle its service with the company's fat pipe subscriptions. The tie-up between Napster and NTL officially started in July 2004. The timing of the launch was crucial as iTunes (www.itunes.com), its largest potential competitor, was to be officially launched in France, Germany, and the UK shortly thereafter. The US iTunes service has sold over 85 million downloads to date and holds a 70% global market share.

There was a clear synergy between NTL and Napster. For Napster, the deal provided direct access to the customer base of the biggest provider of broadband services in the UK. NTL had over a million UK broadband subscribers and, according to the company, three-quarters of those with high-speed web access already downloaded music.

For NTL, Napster's download service was an ideal application to promote its broadband internet connectivity. Under the partnership, NTL would bundle the Napster subscription service with its Broadband Plus package—giving its 1 million-plus broadband customers access to the world's largest online music catalogue. Napster has now sold in excess of 10 million downloads across its US, UK, and Canadian services.

To create a unique environment for their customers, both companies needed to work together not just to overcome the technological barriers but to maintain a high level of synergy to maximize product and service innovations.

Sources: www.theregister.co.uk; and news.zdnet.co.uk.

Fig. 11.5 Considerations of public relations planning in a cross-cultural context

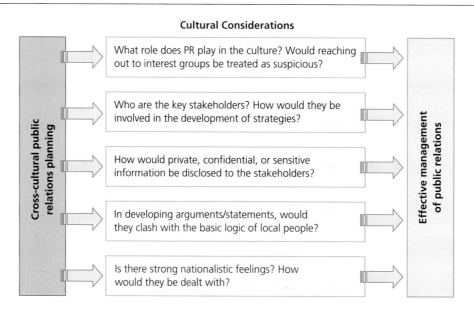

Cultural Considerations

Cross-cultural public relations planning

- What role does PR play in the culture? Would reaching out to interest groups be treated as suspicious?
- Who are the key stakeholders? How would they be involved in the development of strategies?
- How would private, confidential, or sensitive information be disclosed to the stakeholders?
- In developing arguments/statements, would they clash with the basic logic of local people?
- Is there strong nationalistic feelings? How would they be dealt with?

Effective management of public relations

In the planning of a cross-cultural PR campaign, these aspects must be taken into consideration in order to ensure that the role of the organization and its activities in the local community are viewed by its stakeholders as positive, beneficial and, more importantly, culturally sensitive. This process is illustrated in Fig. 11.5.

The BT (www.bt.com) Global Challenge illustrated in the mini-case illustration below is an excellent example of an effective utilization of PR in a global campaign.

Direct-response Marketing

The Direct Marketing Association (DMA, www.dma.org.uk), has defined direct-response marketing as:

> Communications where data is used systematically to achieve quantifiable marketing objectives and where direct contact is made, or invited, between a company and its existing and prospective customers . . . where the distinguishing feature is the gathering and use of individual customer data and measurement as the foundation of all activity.

Unlike conventional media tools (e.g. mass media advertising), direct-response marketing is essentially interactive 'because there is two-way communication between the company and customer, either can initiate the dialogue. Direct-response offers are designed to generate an immediate behavioural response, as opposed to many advertising messages whose primary objective is to create awareness, offer information, or reinforce or change customer attitudes' (Duncan, 2002: 600). It challenges the established processes of advertising as it changes the emphasis of advertising and channels it into a series of 'precise procedures'. The process of direct-response marketing is linked to a database, which triggers off a number of activities to engage the target audiences, such as the handling of response, fulfilment of orders, response evaluation, and follow-up customer communications.

MINI-CASE ILLUSTRATION **The BT Global Challenge**

Often referred to as the world's toughest yacht race, the BT Global Challenge is an extensive ten-month PR programme that sees 12 identical ocean-going yachts and over 200 international crew volunteers circumnavigate the globe. Text 100 (www.text100.com) was the company charged with the challenge of PR to maximize publicity for British Telecommunications (BT). In managing the programme in the 2000–01 race, Text 100 had to contend with several major issues.

BT has invested heavily in third-generation (3G) licences and is committed to making these profitable. At the time of the Global Challenge, Text 100 needed to emphasize BT's continuous commitment to invest in business and technology which will make 3G a success in all its international business interests.

One of the biggest challenges which faced Text 100 was to devise a plan that would not only attract the target audiences' attention, but also maintain interest for a ten-month period. The race would start in September 2000, reaching Cape Town in April 2001. As the second to last stopover, creative tactics would have to be deployed to ensure that the level of interest did not wane by the time the yachts arrived in South Africa. It decided to launch a three-part campaign that would focus activity on the months prior to the yachts' arrival and the stopover period. This would maximize the impact and awareness of the race and avoid media boredom, while still maintaining a continuous level of interest over the length of the race.

Phase One: July 2000–September 2000

Broadening the journalist network: Due to a limited budget, which restricted the use of expensive outreach PR programmes and events, Text 100 focused on maximizing its media relationships to ensure high exposure by feeding regular news stories about progress of the race preparation to the media.

Building awareness: Before the race began, Text 100 developed low-cost, creative, information packs tailored to different media audiences, and made suggestions on possible media angles for the duration of the race.

The race start: The media was alerted when the race started in Southampton. Video footage was arranged for the local news stations to use in their coverage.

Phase Two: October 2000–May 2001

Maintain ongoing awareness: As the yachts made their way around the world, the momentum and media interest were kept up by localizing international releases on the race.

Pre-arrival live radio link-up: Seven live radio link-ups were arranged to increase anticipation of the yachts' arrivals in Cape Town and to demonstrate the advanced BT communication technology onboard.

Creative tactics: As rugby is South Africa's sport of choice, Text 100 leveraged the country's national obsession with anything rugby-related by arranging for a rugby ball, signed by a number of international rugby captains, to travel from port to port aboard one of the yachts. The ball was auctioned off for charity at the end of the race, resulting in further coverage opportunity.

Stopover period: PR activity focused primarily on the four-week stopover period, including the management of media during all yacht arrivals, departures, and the activity in between, including VIP involvement (BT's VIPs visiting local charities), working with dignitaries (Minister of Sport for South Africa), maximizing sponsor value (in receiving exposure by association with the race), and interviews and press releases.

Phase Three: June 2001–July 2001

Wrapping up: PR activity focused on the arrival of the yachts at La Rochelle, France and Southampton, UK, its last destination.

Campaign evaluation: Evaluation of the success of the campaign used a range of measures, including awareness, media coverage, market positioning of BT, yacht sponsor value, and feedback.

Source: Based on Text100 case study (www.text100.com/case studies), 'British Telecom: The World's Toughest Yacht Race' (accessed 10/10/2003).

Advances in ICTs and new media are good news for the growing direct marketing industry. There is a vast, and growing, overlap between the two areas of activity as both the conventional direct-response techniques (e.g. direct mail) and new media (e.g. SMS marketing) are applied in line with the basic principles of direct marketing to generate measurable and cost-effective results for businesses. The marriage between direct-response marketing and interactive media is considered in the Digital Impact illustration.

THE DIGITAL IMPACT **The marriage of direct marketing and interactive media**

The nature of direct marketing has been transformed by the interactive media of telephone and internet. The annual DMA press monitor has found that internet/e-mail addresses now appear in over 80% of press advertisements, 64% of magazine advertisements, and 62% of regional press. The annual Department of Trade and Industry (DTI) Benchmarking Study shows that the UK is one of the leading nations in terms of the deployment of interactive technology in marketing activity.

In addition, DTI research shows that a quarter of the UK businesses surveyed are now able to take orders online and twice as many (50%) place orders online with other companies, confirming the strength and growth of the business-to-business online market. This trend is consistent across all other OECD countries.

The much-vaunted arrival of 3G in 2003 should be of interest to direct marketers, especially whether Hutchison's '3' will lead the way to sufficient critical mass to see if this platform takes off.

Broadband, similarly, holds great potential for a richer interface between company and customer which direct marketers will doubtless be quick to exploit once critical mass is reached. Again, despite the enthusiasm with which both BT and the government are promoting the concept of Broadband Britain, this reality, too,

is some way off, although its effects should not be underestimated in the longer term.

Source: Based on DMA Census of the direct marketing industry 2002–03.

Planning a direct-response campaign

The planning and execution of a cross-border direct-response campaign can be complex. Issues have to be dealt with at the earliest possible stage. Organizations often underestimate the difficulties and complexities. This is particularly true of US-based companies entering the European markets, often with little concept of the cultural sensitivities and regulatory differences between individual countries. These factors have to be considered, for instance, in finding the best international direct-mail solution. The key areas most often overlooked are covered below.[5]

Data and data processing

When gathering and processing 'foreign' data, it is important to ensure that the computer systems are able to allow the use of characters such as accents, diphthongs, and cedillas. If the full character representation is to be retained throughout the data-processing stream, each processing element must be able to process the appropriate character correctly. For example, the letter 'é' (with an acute accent) will have a different internal value on the computer to the letter 'e' (with no accent). These characters can also vary from a computer in one country to a computer in another so attention is needed to check source character sets and the character sets on all data processing elements to ensure data accuracy and integrity.

The format of addresses can vary from country to country. In Hungary, the street name is in the third line of the address, whereas in others, it would be the second line with the postal code and town name in the third line. Some postal authorities, such as Deutsche

[5] This section draws heavily on Brown (2003).

Post in Germany, have strict rules about using the correct address format. Pre-sorted mail with a wrongly presented postal format can result in the addressees being charged a penalty. The amount involved can be very considerable. The alternative, when offered, of taking the mail back to the point of origin and resorting it can mean considerable delays. When sending a large amount of direct mails to international customers, it is important to check these out for each country to avoid costly mistakes.

Data protection

There are considerable differences in data legislation between countries. For instance, the Data Protection Directive of 1995 applies to the European Economic Area (EEA), which includes all members of the EU plus Norway, Liechtenstein, and Iceland. Data can be transferred freely between all member nations of the EEA and also to Hungary and Switzerland, whose laws are deemed to provide 'adequate protection' for personal data. Transfers of data to the USA must be covered by either registration of the US organization which is receiving the data with the American Department of Commerce's Safe Harbor scheme or contractually between the organizations in both countries to ensure adequate protection. This is the responsibility of the 'data controller'.

The data controller is the person or organization responsible for determining how personal data will be used. When a company accesses lists of European prospects and analyses or addresses mail in the USA, the list owner remains the data controller unless the data is sold to the company. When data is merely being processed (e.g. address correction) by a third party, that party is not a data controller but only a data processor. It can be highly complex to determine who has direct responsibility as it may not be the person or organization holding or processing the data. However, no processing must take place without the data controller's specific instructions. The data must:

- be processed fairly;
- be accurate;
- be relevant;
- not be excessive; and
- be used for a specific purpose only.

In the UK, as in other countries in Europe, the data controller is legally responsible for ensuring that there are appropriate security and technical processes in place for adequate protection of the individual's data. If the data controller uses a third-party data processor, the data controller is required to ensure that the data processor meets the legal requirements. They must also ensure that a written contract is in place between the data controller and the data processor, which places an obligation on the data processor to ensure that there is adequate security.

Creative guidelines

For a multi-country direct mailing campaign, it is critical to develop a creative concept that will work across a number of countries, be cost-effective, stand out from the crowd, and conform to the guidelines of the various postal authorities. Translating headlines is often problematic. A heading rarely translates itself easily across several languages. Copy has to be appropriate to the language of the consumer. A badly translated colloquialism can alienate target customers and should be avoided at all costs.

Copy count can vary from language to language. For instance, a German text occupies about 30% more space than its English translation. In all issues of translation, it is highly recommended that only agencies with native-tongue speakers who are experienced in the translation and regionalization of marketing copy are commissioned to carry out the translation work. Knowledge of local consumer law is also important—an offer of a discount in one country might not be legally acceptable in another.

If used, images needs to be selected with similar sensitivity and, if necessary, substituted to make them 'culturally appropriate' for a particular country. For instance, a shot of a woman dancing in a sleeveless evening dress would be perfectly acceptable in Europe but could cause offence in an Arab country. Similarly, the use of feet in Asian countries is equally taboo.

Production and distribution

The production and distribution costs of international mailings will have an impact on the decisions on the choice of format, appearance, and materials. Specifications for pre-sorted postal tariffs vary from country to country and are determined by weight and by size. In the UK, for instance, there is a flat rate charge on pre-sorted, standard-sized services up to 60gms. Deutsche Post in Germany has a flat charge up to 20gms and Le Poste in France has a flat rate up to 35gms with straight line increments thereafter. Each of these countries operates format-based pricing, so for a pan-European direct mailing campaign it is prudent to use a format that complies with the postal regulations of each country to minimize the overall costs and paper wastage.

The campaign strategy will also impact postage cost. For instance, does the company want its mailing to appear as though it were mailed locally? If so, then it will need to carry the postal *indicia* of that country and the mail must be entered directly with the appropriate postal authority. However, if the company is looking for the cheapest postal solution, this may not necessarily be through a direct entry service but by mailing direct from its country of origin. In some countries, direct mails that carry an overseas post mark may have a negative impact on customer response. A mailing received in France carrying British Post *indicia* might not be well received by everyone there. In some cases, however, mailing from overseas can generate a highly positive response. Charities have inspired givers to respond by mailing from the country to which they are trying attract funds in a disaster appeal.

Sponsorship

Sponsorship can be defined as 'a mutually acceptable commercial relationship between two or more parties in which one party (i.e. the sponsor) acting in the course of business, trade, profession or calling, seeks to promote or enhance an image, product or service in association with an individual, event, happening, property or object (i.e. the sponsored)' (Owusu-Frimpong, 2000: 158). As consumers are increasingly besieged by marketing and advertising at all levels, cynicism and immunity to traditional forms of marketing are increasing. Sponsorship has become a means for brands to communicate with their target audience by attaching themselves to a brand or trusted property—giving brands an excuse to talk to an audience happy to listen (Earl, 2002). In the case of events sponsorship, such as sports or music festivals, companies may find it an effective communication tool to project their brands as 'the facilitator of good times' (Bagnall, 2002).

Sponsorship as a marketing communication tool is quickly gaining ground in a race for a share of companies' marketing spending. According to SponsorClick (www.sponsorclick. com), the growth in the sponsorship market has been buoyant since the late 1990s and reached a total estimated worth of £43 billion worldwide in 2005.

The dramatic growth of commercial sponsorship is due to a number of factors (Owusu-Frimpong, 2000: 160–1):

- New opportunities due to increased leisure activity. Increasingly, leisure-conscious societies provide opportunities for sponsorship involvement. This is clear from the wide range of activities currently pursued in both sports and arts compared with earlier decades.

- Greater global media coverage of sponsorship events. Media coverage, particularly on television, is being directed towards sports and cultural activities, thereby creating opportunities for broadcast sponsorship.

- Escalating cost of advertising media. Sponsorship provides a cost-effective marketing communication tool compared with traditional advertising.

- Government policies on tobacco and alcohol. Changing government policies on advertising for alcohol and cigarettes caused these manufacturers to seek alternative promotional media.

Successful marketing requires careful integration of the promotional and non-promotional elements. Sponsorship offers the potential to support the broader PR strategy, both directly and indirectly. Directly, it can provide a venue for meeting key customers or suppliers in an informal setting or, more generally, improve awareness and attitudes towards the sponsorship company. Indirectly, it can support employees, government, and community relations, emphasizing the sponsor's enlightened sense of social responsibility and good corporate citizenship (Owusu-Frimpong, 2000).

As part of an integrated marketing communications effort, sponsorship provides marketers with 'an additional platform' from which to shape consumer attitudes and provide perks for clients. The advantages of a sponsorship marketing platform are numerous (Colin, 2003):

- Media visibility: measurement of brand exposure obtained through the sponsorship.

- Corporate hospitality: valuation of benefits associated with the operation.

- Direct marketing: generation of leads from sponsored partners' contacts.

- E-marketing: valuation of generated web traffic and content.

- Awareness: improvement in brand/product perception of relevant target audiences.

- Commercial impact: measurement of sales increase.

- Other benefits: offered entry tickets, value of naming rights, discount on other operations.

Planning of sponsorship campaign

Sponsorship marketing is a complex marketing platform which needs to be used in conjunction with many other components of the promotional mix to achieve maximum impact. The typical organizational models used for advertising, direct-response marketing, or PR may be inefficient and ineffective when used for sponsorship marketing. For certain brands or products, using a regional communications agency to implement a local PR, direct marketing, or advertising campaign is often the best choice. For sponsorship, however, the regional model is inappropriate (Colin, 2003):

Fig. 11.6 Types of sponsorship and associated values

Sports events	Create association with being...	Healthy, youthful, energetic, vibrant, sporty and/or masculine
Exclusive events	Create association with being...	Elitist, sophisticated, exclusive, up-market and/or desirable
Popular events	Create association with being...	Contemporary, accessible, innovative and/or commercial
Events for charities or social causes	Create association with being...	Caring, charitable, concerned, generous and/or community-oriented
Environmental programmes	Create association with being...	Eco-friendly, admirable, caring, intelligent and/or forward-thinking

Source: Based on Jobber (2007: 654).

- Sponsorship marketing is inextricably linked to the brand essence. This type of involvement requires continual monitoring to prevent confusion of values in the minds of customers and clients—see Fig. 11.6 for the various types of sponsorship and their associated values for a brand. Great care must be taken to avoid investing in territories not validated by central marketing.

- Sponsorship marketing investments have to be managed according to the 'portfolio' requirements and needs, given the risks of, for example, an athlete's performance or the changing success of a music festival. This type of management requires a global vision.

- The best return on investment (ROI) of sponsorship is attained when a global partnership is skilfully activated at subsidiary/business unit level.

While sponsorship may bring a unique opportunity to capture the imagination of a targeted audience—the kind of people who are hard to reach and often cynical about traditional forms of advertising—there is a danger of being perceived as 'intrusive', thus exacerbating consumer cynicism. In the case of events sponsorship, as Bagnall (2002) observes, people are looking for a place of entertainment as well as a place to escape from 'brand overload', where they are free to do as they wish without being targeted for commercial interests. The presence of brands may take away this sense of 'escapism'. It is therefore important for organizations not to enter into sponsorship without careful thought about how 'naturally' their brands would fit with the event or object, how the brand should get involved, and to what extent, without repulsing the targeted audience.

Exhibitions and Trade Fairs

Exhibitions and trade fairs are an effective marketing communication tool to enable organizations to interact face to face with a tightly focused and interested audience. These events 'offer the best opportunity to interact directly, in a very short span of time, with a large number of people—customers (existing and potential), competitors, suppliers, decision-maker/influencers, service provides—all important to the company' (Boukersi, 2000: 124). If used in conjunction with other communication tools, trade fairs and exhibitions can bring significant benefits to an organization's market exposure.

The benefits are many and powerful (Boukersi, 2000 124–7):

Selling benefits

Participating in trade fairs and exhibitions allows the participating organizations to maintain contact with regular customers as well as to meet potential ones. The former consolidates existing relationships and ensures customer satisfaction. The latter is a method of developing new customer links and building a prospective list. Indeed, as Shipley and Wong (1993) observe, high proportions of exhibition attendees consist not only of buyers but engineers, quality controllers, accountants, marketers, etc., who occupy crucial specifying, influencing, or deciding roles in customer decision-making units. Further, they can also be used as an opportunity to recruit high-quality sales representatives, dealers, and franchising agents.

International trade fairs or exhibitions can be an effective channel through which small and medium-sized companies acquire sales leads and/or develop relationships with foreign buyers/agencies. For instance, Orthopaedic Innovation (www.o-i.co.uk), a small medical implants manufacturer based in the UK, regularly attends specialist exhibitions, including the international annual MEDICA exhibition (www.medica.com) in Munich, Germany, and the ArabHealth exhibition (www.arabonline.com) in Dubai, UAE, to establish new contacts with potential foreign agents and generate direct sales.

Promotional benefits

Exhibitions and trade fairs should not be viewed as merely a selling tool but one that serves a much broader marketing function, since they have profound implications for the overall marketing mix. These events bring into play all the organization's policies on product, pricing, distribution, and communications. An exhibition or trade fair may be used as a platform for the organization's 'marketing package' to be in direct contact with prospective customers who can experiment with the desired products and acquire technical information. The face-to-face contact also shortens the communication process between exhibitors and visitors. Thus, the major instruments of this process can be integrated to form an effective promotional programme.

Research benefits

Trade fairs and exhibitions provide a golden opportunity for low-cost but highly effective market research as they attract a tightly focused and targeted audience. They offer exhibitors valuable first-hand information and in-depth feedback as well as an environment in which to conduct pre-launch market and product testing. To promote the benefits of exhibitions as an effective communication tool to potential exhibitors, most event organizers conduct in-depth research and/or profiling on the visitors at individual events. The findings help exhibitors decide which events offer the best ROI based on measurable outcomes.

Strategic benefits

Attending exhibitions and trade shows is one of the most effective ways of understanding international competition and keeping abreast of technologies and new trends. Most specialist fairs, especially in specialized product areas, are considered as corporate summit meetings attended by 'opinion leaders' in the sector. Large companies adopt the 'we cannot afford not to be there' attitude with the sole objective of entertaining existing customers.

For smaller or less-established companies, especially those from foreign countries, specialist trade fairs or exhibitions can be a cost-effective marketing tool to meet buyers and representatives, display their products alongside competitors, and determine the potential of succeeding in international markets.

Planning exhibitions and trade fairs

The planning and implementation of an exhibition or trade fair is both costly and time-consuming as it involves a vast and disproportional amount of management time and resources. To take a small team of staff away from their normal work to prepare and attend an international event can incur substantial direct costs as well as indirect opportunity costs. To exploit fully the benefits of an event, accurate and detailed advanced planning is imperative (see Fig. 11.7).

First, organizations intending to participate at an event need to determine the role that the exhibition is to play in the broader marketing communications strategy. The exhibition's objectives may relate to both *selling* and *non-selling* achievements. *Selling* objectives may be directly concerned with sales and revenue generation and can be short-term (e.g. product demonstrations, sales presentation, and order-taking) or longer-term (e.g. new product launch, publicity, or leads generation). *Non-selling* objectives are either qualitative (e.g. customer relationship-building, competitor intelligence-gathering, and image-building) or quantitative (e.g. cost control, new contacts established, brochures issued). Prudent companies recognize the mix of potential benefits of exhibiting and set a mixed range of these objectives (Shipley and Wong, 1993).

Secondly, the number of visitors to a particular stand or booth is largely a function of location, frontage space, attractiveness, and pre-event publicity. The consideration of event tactics is paramount: exhibitors need to determine in advance the stand design and floor location, personnel selection and behaviour, entertainment activities and customer interaction, and intelligence-gathering (Shipley and Wong, 1993). In a large-scale international exhibition or trade fair, it may be difficult for visitors to navigate to the exhibition stand.

Fig. 11.7 Planning for a promotional event

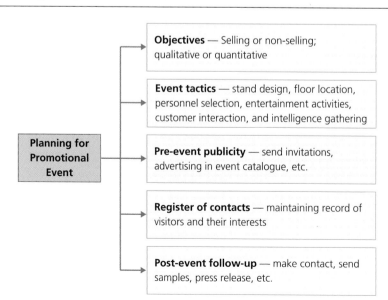

Thirdly, pre-event publicity, e.g. sending show invitations with a clear map of the show-ground and/or advertising in the show catalogue or handbook, is widely used to 'generate traffic'. Fourthly, maintaining a register of addresses of contacts established needs to be carefully managed for post-event follow-up.

Finally, planning post-event follow-up tactics is important to maximize opportunities at the exhibition. Sales leads should be chased quickly, before interest erodes, with the use of brochures and, where relevant, samples. Other promotional opportunities should also be exploited, for example, a press release concerning dramatic sales, the use of a guest celebrity, or contact established with a famous visitor.

Planning for Online Communications

The new world of communications has much to offer marketers in the communication mix of advertising, sales promotion, publicity, personal selling, and direct marketing.

Advertising

Due to the unique nature of the technology, advertising on the internet is different from advertising in other media. The audience, in general, chooses where to go and what to look at. Despite the fact that there is a potential to reach tens of million of users, it is impossible, and perhaps pointless, to target every one of them. The advertiser must be clear about exactly who to target.

There are a number of online advertising channels which can be used as sources of interactive communications for marketing purposes:

- **Direct e-mails.** During the early development of the internet, it was common practice among online marketers to use untargeted e-mails (also known as 'spam') to raise brand awareness and generate leads. Consumer hostility quickly developed due to the intrusion of this type of personal communication.

  Subscription e-mail is now a popular and acceptable form of direct e-mail. Organizations collect personal data from competitions, news groups, sponsorship subscriptions, or website registration, and send materials to consumers relevant to the original source of personal data. Subscription e-mail is a key part of an online loyalty reinforcing campaign, as it maintains a brand's position in the mind of the consumer and encourages them to interact with the brand. Not unlike direct mail, which is at the heart of relationship marketing offline, direct e-mail is at the heart of relationship marketing online. While the relationship is justified, subscription e-mail is effective at involving consumers with the brand and reinforcing continued loyalty.

  The use of e-mail evolves as the capacity and functionality of internet technology advances. The newly introduced 'enriched e-mail' includes streaming audio, video capabilities, and order options. With improved tracking capabilities, marketers can assess if a message has been opened, what time of day it was opened, how long the message was viewed for, and whether it was forwarded on. According to Forrester Research (www. forrester.com), enriched e-mails enjoy a response rate of 12.5% compared with the 10% response rate of traditional text-based e-mails. There is a positive relationship between the level of personalization and the corresponding response rate.

- **Banner advertising.** Banners occupy designed space for rent on web pages and are similar to the print advertising model used by magazines and newspapers. Most

MINI-CASE ILLUSTRATION Monster.com

The success of the online recruitment site Monster.com (www .monster.com) is dependent on its effectiveness in tailoring the offer to its customers' specific preferences and needs. Monster .com acts as an originator by creating useful original content in its 'career centre', where visitors find information ranging from career advice to articles as well as discussions on career development and job issues. It also acts as an integrator by packaging and combining thousands of job postings and CVs into a single working database. As a distributor, it replicates these two outputs but tailors them to a specific geographic audience. Therefore the German website will have a different focus and

expression from the UK website. In an industry where technology plays a critical role in the delivery of its offer, the company achieves its success by delivering the experience in the most straightforward way.

banners are *hyperlinked* to the advertiser's or brand's website and designed to increase 'web traffic' to the designated content. Many banner advertisements feature animation which captures greater attention on an otherwise static page. The animation can be continuous or loop through a fixed number of times, stopping on the final frame.

The use of interactive banner advertisements is also on the increase. Interactive banners enable the user or browser to interact through the provision of a service or function, which may include (Chaffey et al., 2002):

- entering the amount of loan required to give an indication of its cost;
- entering the destination of a flight to show the cheapest fare available;
- buying a product; or
- filling in an e-mail address for further information on an offer.

The sale of banner advertising space constitutes the bulk of current advertising revenues for major internet service providers and until recently has been the preferred form of online advertising for many companies. Companies that have relied heavily on banners may need to diversify by adopting more creative approaches to communicating with consumers online.

- **Interactive TV advertising.** Although still in its early stage of development, interactive TV (iTV) has finally made a legitimate entrance into many homes around the world. While the broadcasters and iTV companies are positioning their brands in the pay-TV market and announcing their programme schedules, iTV advertising has taken a number of different formats, with vastly differing results and levels of functionality.

For the first time, consumers are able to record, live-pause, fast forward, participate in online polls, tag advertisements, and even customize their own programme schedules. For example, TiVo (www.tivo.com) and Replay (www.digitalnetworksna.com), both personal video recorders, allow viewers to record, live-pause, and fast-forwarding programming. Worldgate (www.worldgate.com), Microsoft's WebTV (www.webtv.net), and AOLTV (www.aoltv.com) allow viewers to surf the internet via their remote controls and televisions; whereas the Wink (www.wink.com) and Watchpoint (www.aggroup.com) networks layer programming and advertising with interactive elements such as icons that can be clicked to bring up the information overlay on screen (Schumann et al., 2001). This is similar to Freeview (www.freeview.co.uk), a free digital iTV service with a network of broadcasters, including the BBC (www.bbc.co.uk) and ITV (www.itv.com) in the UK.

iTV advertising is said to combine the exchange opportunities available on the internet, with the brand presentation capabilities of television advertising. While this might appear to be a panacea for advertisers, a number of problems need to be resolved as a result of this merger of technologies. First, the success of iTV advertising hinges on the willingness of consumers to take a more active role in what is traditionally regarded as a passive activity. The lesson learned from the massive failure of dot.coms in the late 1990s proves how slowly consumers change their behaviours. Secondly, television in its present form does not lend itself to the information-rich PC presentations. To receive comparable information via television takes considerably more effort and investment on the part of the consumer, for instance in new multimedia-enabled TV sets, digital set-top boxes, or broadband or cable subscription.

- **Wireless devices.** The advent of wireless technologies, such as mobile broadband, in the form of a series of hand-held mobile devices (e.g. laptops or personal digital assistants (PDA) has taken the electronic communication revolution to a new level. Consumers can access information that previously was available only through wired internet connections. Many companies have already pioneered their interactive advertising campaigns using the Short Message Service (SMS) or 'text messaging' to gain insights into the effectiveness of such campaigns. According to a study conducted by Ovum (www.ovum.com), a London-based technology consulting firm, advertising expenditures via a wireless device had reached more than US$16 billion worldwide. The study also anticipates that wireless advertising will generate response rates two or three times higher than that of the standard internet banner advert.

  The future of wireless electronic media seems to offer promising opportunities in broadening the global reach of consumers, enabling customized communications, and facilitating 24/7 transactions. With the use of global positioning satellite (GPS) technology, which is likely to become mandatory worldwide on all wireless devices for emergency purposes (as in the USA), marketers will be able to track wireless users' locations to within 100 feet and make recommendations regarding local retailers, services, etc.

- **DVD technology.** The use of Digital Versatile Discs (DVD) technology is increasingly widespread due to its versatility in providing online and offline interactivity. A DVD can be used to store digital catalogues, interactive menus, full-motion digital video as well as provide internet connection and order options. It is a very cost-effective tool as it costs less than US$1 to manufacture and can be effective for targeting consumers who do not have reliable access to the internet. Customers can take as long as they like to view the content, and then make connection to the internet when they are ready to make a purchase via the pre-designed web connectivity.

Sales promotion

Sales promotion can be defined as the marketing activities that stimulate consumer purchases, such as displays, shows and exhibitions, demonstrations, and various non-recurrent selling efforts not in the ordinary routine. The main objectives of sales promotion are: (1) to encourage customers to product trials; and (2) to encourage repeat purchases.

Customer awareness of a product may not be sufficient to encourage customers to make a purchase. New products especially need a high level of sales promotion to support the advertising campaign to encourage product trials and eventually make a purchase.

Encouraging product trials is the most popular sales promotion technique used on the internet. It is believed that the easier it is for internet shoppers to sample products from the comfort of their homes, the more likely they are to make a purchase and return regularly. Good examples are downloadable music CD tracks, movie clips, and selected chapters of books.

Encouraging repeat purchases is not difficult once the customers have made their first purchase and left their details. The customers' personal details can be used for effective electronic mail-shots to encourage them to try a similar book or music CD, and offer them an incentive (e.g. a small discount or a '3 for the price of 2') to make a second purchase. Since companies are making savings on cutting out the middleman or wholesaler, these savings can be used to reduce prices and/or offer more discount schemes to entice customers.

Publicity

Publicity is crucial to the success of a website. A website is similar to an interactive brochure floating on the internet and no one will visit unless the visitors can find it and are invited to visit.

First, companies must ensure that their domain names are listed in all the relevant search engines. These search engines will then index the domain name and specified keywords in their database. Due to high traffic, many search engines require companies to re-register every few weeks to remain on their list. A good internet service provider should be able to provide this service as part of their website maintenance service.

Organizations must also remember that the best publicity is to print their internet access details on their conventional promotional materials, including catalogues, flyers, business cards, letterheads, and compliment slips. This practice will enhance the corporate image as forward-thinking and add value to conventional promotional materials.

Finally, organizations can also write personally to the relevant internet magazines and newspapers for a review. Many industry-specific publications will write an impressive review if an organization spends a certain amount on advertising.

Personal selling

In conventional marketing, personal selling is defined as an oral presentation in conversation with one or more prospective purchasers for the purpose of making sales. During the early stages of development of the internet, it was anticipated that personal selling for consumer goods and services would be made redundant if the so-called interactive electronic storefronts were to replace or minimize sales personnel. The internet had the potential to revolutionize the process of selling by eliminating the sales personnel while interacting with millions of customers at the same time.

The 'revolution' in personal selling did not (or has yet to) come through. According to what Marriot (2002) terms the 'Law of Unintended Consequences', the history of technology is overlaid with examples of the saying, 'the more things change, the more they stay the same'. Marriot gives the example of the introduction of ATM machines in the late 1970s. Banks assumed that their investment in these machines would lower costs over time as the need for bank cashiers diminished. They offered the added benefit of making it easier for the customer to do business with the bank. The cost savings never materialized. With the ability to get money whenever they chose, people no longer limited their bank visits to a once or twice weekly cash withdrawal. They demanded wider access to these machines. Over time, the cost of servicing each account increased. Surprisingly, the banks learned this lesson a second time after they offered online banking. Customers using online banking did not give up using ATMs or cashier services and banks were left supporting yet another channel.

With the emergence of multiple new electronic media, marketers face complicated choices about how to engage most effectively with customers. Personal selling no longer nvolves face-to-face oral conversation with customers. However, the interactivity of personal selling can be (partially) moved to the internet with the use of e-mail communications, engaging potential customers in a conversation in forum or chatroom and/or instant messaging facilities.

This mode of promotion is unlikely to change the buying behaviour for bulky industrial products which normally involves sophisticated selling and negotiations, and highly specialized knowledge. For industrial product companies, the internet can perhaps increase their speed of reaction to the changing global market and enhance their conventional marketing activities.

Chapter Summary

1. There is a growing need on the part of marketers to communicate effectively with people from a wide spectrum of cultures. While conventional wisdom suggests that transnational advertising must be sensitive to local conditions, there are few guidelines to assist the practitioner in discriminating between advertising which is 'culturally fit' and that which is not. Marketers must develop international advertising campaigns that work—campaigns that produce the optimum global recognition and cost-efficiency while maintaining sensitivity to local needs and conditions.

2. Advocates of the standardization approach to global marketing communications argue that consumers everywhere have the same basic needs and can therefore be persuaded by universal appeals. The consumer may be satisfied with similar products or advertising messages. The proponents of the adaptation/localization approach assert that consumers differ from country to country and must accordingly be reached by communications tailored to their respective countries.

3. The concept of globally integrated marketing communications (GIMC) is defined as 'a system of active promotional management which strategically coordinates global communications in all of its component parts both horizontally in terms of countries and organizations and vertically in terms of promotional discipline. It contingently takes into account the full range of standardized versus adaptive market options, synergies, variations among target populations and other marketplace and business conditions'.

4. International advertising must enable organizations to compete successfully in the marketplace while delivering optimum rationalization of investment in executing international advertising campaigns. As most organizations competing in specific markets have at their disposal the same financial and human resources, and similar marketing and production know-how, they have few options at their disposal but to *outsmart* (rather than *outspend*) competitors in building distinctive brands and images salient to the consumer's needs.

5. The accelerating process of global integration and the consequent growth of international relations are fuelling an interest in international public relations. As an organization's international business operations increase in size and coverage, the organization's survival and prosperity become increasingly dependent upon its ability to inform and involve its publics of its actions and policies in order to maintain good relationships with the various interest groups.

6. Direct-response marketing has been the fastest-growing sector of marketing communications for the past 15 years. The nature of direct marketing has been transformed by the interactive media of the telephone and internet. A quarter of UK businesses are now able to take orders online and twice as many (50%) place orders online with other companies, confirming the strength and growth of the business-to-business online marketplace. This trend is consistent across all other OECD countries.

7. Sponsorship offers the potential to support the broader PR strategy, both directly and indirectly. Directly, it can provide a venue for meeting key customers or suppliers in an informal setting or, more generally, improve awareness and attitudes towards the sponsorship company. Indirectly, it can support employees, government, and community relations, emphasizing the sponsor's enlightened sense of social responsibility and good corporate citizenship.

8. Exhibitions and trade fairs are some of the most exciting and effective marketing communication tools, which enable organizations to interact face to face with a tightly focused and interested audience. These events offer the best opportunity to interact directly, in a very short span of time, with a large number of people—customers (existing and potential), competitors, suppliers, decision-maker/influencers, service providers.

9. Online communication is becoming more popular than ever as companies spend aggressively to gain an online presence. There are a number of online communication tools which can be used as sources of interactive communications for marketing purposes, including advertising, sales promotion, publicity, and personal selling.

END-OF-CHAPTER CASE STUDY Think globally, act locally—the case of Jack Daniel's

Billions of people are now exposed to a growing number of international brands, such as MTV (www.mtv.com), McDonald's, Coke, BMW, Sony (www.sony.com), or Levi's (www.levi.com). What do these phenomenally successful worldwide brands have in common? They all appear to have the same recognizable identity and the ability to translate its value across cultures.

To build or create a successful global brand, the positioning of the brand should be flexible enough to take on local flavour in the communication and execution process without changing the core values, equity, identity, or imagery. Jack Daniel's Tennessee Whiskey (www.jackdaniels.com) is an excellent example of this philosophy. It is a well-known brand in more than 135 countries, in which seven million cases of Jack Daniel's branded whiskeys are consumed every year.

Jack Daniels was named after its founder, who took pride and care in making his product. In the distilling process, the spirit drips through ten feet of charcoal for 11 days before being sealed in barrels of American oak and transported to a warehouse, where it is allowed to mellow for a number of years.

The evolution of Jack Daniel's print campaign illustrates the importance of a flexible global communications strategy. Since 1954, every advertising campaign for Jack Daniel's has been crafted to reflect its founder's pride for his whiskey and the brand's core value of authenticity. The role of advertising since the beginning was not to 'sell whiskey' as much as it has been to communicate the story of the brand. Over the years, the well-known black-and-white Jack

Daniel's print campaign, known as 'Postcards from Lynchburg', has been extended to television, cinema, and radio ads. Regardless of the medium, each advertisement delivers the Jack Daniel's message of a premium, authentic, and masculine brand. While the advertising communicates the brand's universal qualities, how the message is translated into each specific market is based on local factors. Adaptations of the traditional US black-and-white print ads are currently running with great success in the UK, Australia, Japan, Canada, Germany, and South Africa.

In some markets, Jack Daniel's marketing takes on a different look to accommodate a local market custom. When Jack Daniel's was first marketed in Asia, it used the 'Postcard from Lynchburg's' advertising. These ads featured the Jack Daniel's distillery and the craftsmen who make the whiskey in their working attire of denim overalls. For Americans, this campaign calls up nostalgic images of a simpler life when there was time to do things well. But in Asia's booming, dynamic economies, wearing overalls, working at a slow pace and leading a 'simple life' was not something to which most Asians aspired. As a result, the Jack Daniel's campaign in Asia was modified to focus less on the craftsmen and the location (Lynchburg, Tennessee, population 361), and more on the craftsmanship, special ingredients, and time-honoured production process. By redirecting attention to different parts of the Jack Daniel's story, the company is able to change the idea to meet the needs of the market, thus practising flexibility without affecting the brand's core equity.

An obvious ingredient of any successful global communications strategy is a clear understanding of consumers. On a global basis, it is important to understand consumer behaviour overall; and on a local basis, it is important to understand the dynamics that make the market unique. For instance, in the USA the majority of the population are considered middle-class. Nearly every family has some disposable income and, therefore, the majority of products on the market are accessible to most consumers. In this market, Jack Daniel's is an affordable product and one that most people can buy on a regular basis. In many other countries, the income scale is different. Although consumers may be in the middle-income range, they probably cannot afford regularly to buy a bottle of Jack Daniel's. For these consumers, Jack Daniel's is likely to be considered a special occasion brand. Consumption and entertaining patterns are also widely different. The USA has a strong tradition of entertaining and consuming alcohol at home. But in many areas of the world, socializing and alcohol consumption are more frequently done in restaurants and bars.

Even in the 'global village', customs and traditions remain entrenched. Holidays, rites of passage, and other cultural traditions are not universally celebrated and communications strategy or advertising may need to be changed to adapt to the local environment and taste. This happened with the celebration of Jack Daniel's birthday. The company saw this as an opportunity for a global promotion to emphasize that Jack, who was by then deceased, had been a real person and to tell how he came to make the world's best whiskey. A global campaign was introduced. In the process, the company learned that it is a cultural taboo for Asians to celebrate the birthday of a dead person. The challenge was then to find a way to use the birthday theme to promote Jack Daniel's in a way that did not offend Asian local custom. The solution was simple. Instead of celebrating Jack's birthday, the programme invited consumers to celebrate their September birthdays with Jack Daniel's. Parties, birthday cakes, and celebrations were targeted at consumers who were born in the month of September, like Jack. This approach has enabled the promotion to run successfully on a global level for three years and has kept the brand's core equity intact.

Jack Daniel's global marketing communications continue to evolve through major creative phases to recognizes changes in the media. For instance, the advertising has evolved from exclusively black-and-white postcards to include colour adverts to create a 'contemporary feel' to the brand while preserving its contextual relevance, iconography, and authenticity.

Sources: Based on Dunlap (2004) and Sarfin (2001).

Case discussion questions

1 What is Jack Daniel's global communications strategy?

2 What are the cultural and market factors which may have an impact on Jack Daniel's global communication strategy? How do these factors affect the ways in which the company communicates with its customers and market its products in different countries?

3 Jack Daniel's is a successful brand that has managed to communicate a consistent and recognizable identity globally. If you were to be asked to develop a creative plan which seeks to modernize its brand image, how would you go about doing it and what would it be?

END-OF-CHAPTER EXERCISES

1 In what ways does international marketing communications differ from domestic marketing communications?

2 What does it mean when an organization adopts a standardization approach to international marketing communications? Under what circumstances might a standardization approach not work?

3 The forces of globalization have continued to propel organizations to invest in strong brand names through advertising. Why do you think this is the case?

4 What is a 'creative plan'? Briefly discuss the process of developing a creative plan.

5 What is the purpose of using international public relations? What does it aim to achieve?

6 What is direct-response marketing? Why do you think it is becoming an important promotional tool for global marketing?

7 Outline the functions of international sponsorship and exhibitions.

8 What are the different types of electronic advertising channel that can be used to create an interactive marketing communication campaign?

9 Briefly discuss how sales promotion, publicity, and personal selling can be applied to the online marketplace.

DISCUSSION AND EXAMINATION QUESTIONS

1 With relevant examples, discuss the pros and cons of using a standardization approach to the planning of cross-cultural marketing communications. Under what circumstances might a standardization approach be problematic?

2 What is 'integrated marketing communications'? What are the reasons why organizations increasingly feel the need to become more integrated in their marketing communications strategy?

3 'The revolution in internet and communications technologies (ICT) has provided new possibilities in the delivery of cost-effective and targeted marketing communications.' Discuss.

4 With the use of relevant examples, discuss how you might develop and manage a cross-cultural advertising campaign?

5 Why do you think international public relations is becoming an increasingly important marketing communications tool in global marketing management? What are the barriers to developing an effective international public relations strategy?

6 With appropriate examples, compare and contrast the different types of online advertising channel.

FURTHER READING

Guirdham, M. (2005), *Communicating across Cultures at Work*, Basingstoke: Palgrave Macmillan.

Rugimbana, R. and Nwankwo, S. (2003), *Cross-Cultural Marketing*, London: Thomson Learning.

Usunier, J.-D. and Lee, J. A. (2005), *Marketing across Cultures*, Harlow: FT/Prentice Hall.

REFERENCES

Appelbaum, U. and Halliburton, C. (1993), 'How to develop international advertising campaigns that work', *International Journal of Advertising*, 11(3), 223–41.

Bagnall, M. (2002), 'Event sponsorship: "is the worst yet to come?"', *Admap, April*, World Advertising Research Centre (WARC), www.warc.com (accessed on 15/11/2003).

Black, S. (2000), 'International Public Relations Management', in Monye, S. O. (ed.), *The Handbook of International Marketing Communications,* Oxford: Blackwell.

Boukersi, L. (2000), 'The Role of Trade Fairs and Exhibitions in International Marketing Communications', in Monye, S. O. (ed.), *The Handbook of International Marketing Communications*, Oxford: Blackwell.

Brown, J. (2003), 'Taking the stress out of international direct marketing', www.the-dma.org (accessed on 13/11/03).

Burton, J. (1983), 'Buy any other name? Not in Japanese', *Advertising Age*, 25 February.

Chaffey, D., Mayer, K., Johnston, K., and Ellis-Chadwick, F. (2002). *Internet Marketing*, 2nd edn., London: FT/Prentice Hall.

Colin, P. (2003), 'Sponsorship marketing goes global: the importance of integrating a sponsorship marketing programme into your overall marketing plans', *The Advertiser*, June, Association of National Advertisers Inc.

Conrelissen, J. P. and Lock, A. R. (2000), 'Theoretical concept or management fashion? Examining the significance of IMC', *Journal of Advertising Research*, 40(5), 7–16.

Coughlin, D. M. (2002), 'The power of the brand: a best case look at a brand transformation—MasterCard's "Priceless" campaign', *The Advertiser*, October.

Cutler, B. D. and Javalgi, R. G. (1992), 'A cross-cultural analysis of the visual components of print advertising', *Journal of Advertising Research*, 32(Feb./Mar.), 71–80.

Dibb, S., Simkin, L. and Vancini, A. (1996), 'Competition, strategy, technology and people: the challenges facing PR', *International Journal of Advertising*, 15(2), 116–27.

Duncan, T. (2002), *IMC: Using Advertising and Promotion to Build Brands*, international edn., New York: McGraw-Hill/Irwin.

Dunlap, J. (2004), 'Jack Daniel's Tennessee Whiskey celebrates 50 years of advertising success', *The Advertiser*, December, WARC, www.warc.com (accessed on 1/6/2008).

Earl, K. (2002), 'How sports sponsorship can always win', *Admap*, 432(October), WARC, www.warc.com (accessed on 15/11/2003).

Elinder, E. (1965), 'How international can european advertising be?', *Journal of Marketing*, 29(2), 7–11.

Falk, H. and Schmidt, A. (1997), 'The impact of new media on the communication process: using the internet as a marketing communication tool', in *Fit for the Global Future*, ESOMAR Conference, Lisbon (Portugal), 13–16 July.

Fatt, A. C. (1967), 'The danger of "local" international advertising', *Journal of Marketing*, 31(1), 60–2.

Gould, S. J., Lerman, D. B., and Grain, A. F. (1999), 'Agency perceptions and practices on global IMC', *Journal of Advertising Research*, 39(1), 7–20.

Grein, A. F. and Gould, S. J. (1996), 'Globally integrated marketing communications', *Journal of Marketing Communications*, 2, 141–58.

Haarmann, H. (1986), 'Verbal strategies in Japanese fashion magazines—a study in impersonal bilingualism and ethnosymbolism', *International Journal of the Sociology of Language*, 58, 107–21.

Holmes, M., McDonald, P., and Firth, H. (2002), 'Divided we dine, united we dream', Advertising Effectiveness Awards at the Institute of Practitioners in Advertising, WARC, www.warc.com (accessed on 15/11/2003).

Jobber, D. (2007), *Principles and Practice of Marketing*, 5th edn., Maidenhead: McGraw-Hill.

Jorgensen, B. K. (1994), 'Consumer reaction to company-related disasters: the effect of multiple versus single explanations', *Advances in Consumer Research*, 21, 348–52.

Kanso, A. (1992), 'International advertising strategies: global commitment to local vision', *Journal of Advertising Research*, Jan./Feb., 10–14.

Kitchen, P. J. (1997), 'For now we see through a glass darkly: light on global marketing communications' in *Fit for the Global Future*, ESOMAR Conference, Lisbon (Portugal), 13–16 July.

—— and Schultz, D. E. (1997), 'Integrated marketing communications: what is it and why are companies working that way', in *New Ways for Optimising Integrated Communications*, Amsterdam: ESOMAR, 1–24.

—— —— (1999), 'A multi-country comparison of the drive for IMC', *Journal of Advertising Research*, Jan./Feb., 21–38.

Levitt, T. (1983), 'Globalisation of markets', *Harvard Business Review*, 61(3), 92–102.

Marriot, C. (2002), 'New devices, old rules: the impact of new internet appliances on your marketing strategies', *The Advertiser*, January, Associated of National Advertisers, Inc.

McDowell, J. (2002), 'The art of global marketing: finding the right balance between global strategy and local execution', *Advertiser*, June.

Miller, D. A. and Rose, P. B. (1994), 'Integrated communications: a look at reality instead of theory', *Public Relations Quarterly* 39(1), Spring, 13–16.

Monye, S. O. (ed.) (2000), *The Handbook of International Marketing*, Oxford: Blackwell.

Mueller, B. (1987), 'Reflections of culture in analysis of Japanese and American advertising appeals', *Journal of Advertising Research*, 27(3), 51–9.

_____ (1992), 'Standardisation vs. specialisation: an examination of westernisation in Japanese advertising', *Journal of Advertising Research*, Jan./Feb., 15–24.

Olsen, B. C. (1989), 'Wie Werburg Wirkt: narrative and argumentative Werburg in Vergleich', *Werbeforschung und Praxis*, 4, 135–6.

Owusu-Frimpong, N. (2000), 'The Theory and Practice of Sponsorship in International Marketing Communications', in Monye, S. O. (ed.), *The Handbook of International Marketing Communications*, Oxford: Blackwell.

Ricks, D., Jeffery, A., and Fu, M. (1974) 'Pitfalls in advertising overseas', *Journal of Advertising Research*, 14(6), 47–51.

Rutigliano, A. J. (1986), 'Global vs. local advertising', *Management Review*, June, 27–31.

Sarfin, S. (2001), 'So you want to go global: building a strong global marketing strategy', *The Advertiser*, May, Association of National Advertisers Inc.

Schultz, D. E. (1996), 'The inevitability of integrated communications', *Journal of Business Research*, 37, 139–46.

—— and Kitchen, P. J. (2000), *Communicating Globally: An Integrated Marketing Approach*, London: Macmillan.

—— and Schultz, H. F. (1998), 'Transitioning marketing communication into the twenty-first century', *Journal of Marketing Communications*, 4, 9–26.

Schumann, D. W., Artis, A., and Rivera R. (2001), 'The future of interactive advertising viewed through an IMC lens', *The Journal of Interactive Advertising*, 1(2), http://jiad.com

Scott, P. (2001), 'The role of global media in the global marketing mix', *The Advertiser*, May, Association of National Advertisers, Inc.

Shipley, D. and Wong, W. S. (1993), 'Exhibiting strategy and implementation', *International Journal of Advertising*, 11(2), 117–30.

Sloan, J. (1994), 'Ad agencies should learn the facts of life', *Marketing News*, 28 February, 4.

Synodinos, N., Keown, C., and Jacobs, L. (1989) 'Transitional advertising practices: a survey of leading brand advertising', *Journal of Advertising Research*, 29(2), 43–50.

Usunier, J.-C. (2000), *Marketing Across Cultures*, 3rd edn., Harlow: FT/Prentice Hall.

Wilkins, J. (2002), 'Why is global advertising still the exception, not the rule?', *Admap*, February, WARC, www.warc.com (accessed on 15/11/2003).

Woodlington, L. J. (2001), 'Global guidelines drive local marketing', *The Advertiser*, May.

Zandpour, F., Campos, V., Catalano, J., Chang, C., Cho, Y. D., Hoobyar, R., Jiang, S.-F., Lin, M.-C., Madrid, S., Scheideler, H., and Osborn, S. T. (1994), 'Global reach and local touch: achieving cultural fitness in TV advertising', *Journal of Advertising Research*, Sept./Oct., 35–63.

online resource centre

Visit the companion website to this book for lots of interesting additional material, including self-assessment questions, internet exercises, and links for each chapter:

http://www.oxfordtextbooks.co.uk/orc/lee_carter2e/

CHAPTER TWELVE

Managing Supply Chain and Distribution

Chapter overview

Chapter Introduction   382

A New Approach to Managing Supply
Chains and Distribution   383
    Effective management of risk   384
    Effective management of trade-offs   384
    Effective management of strategic relationships 385

Factors Affecting Global Supply
Chain Decisions   386
    Country characteristics   386
    Industry characteristics   388
    International supply chain strategy   389

Collaboration in the Supply Chain   391
    Types of buyer–supplier relationship   392
    The scope of collaboration   393

Developing Market-responsive Supply
Chain Strategies   397
    Global sourcing   398
    Market responsive manufacturing   401
    Integrated policies and processes   403
    Information-sharing   404
    Performance measurement   406

Chapter Summary   407

Learning objectives

After studying this chapter, the reader will be able to:

- discuss the challenges and complexity of developing and managing supply chains that create sustainable advantage in the global marketplace;
- examine the factors affecting global supply chain decisions;
- consider the rationale for collaboration and the types of relationship that exist in the supply chain;
- discuss the important processes and considerations in developing modern and intelligent supply chain strategies.

Management issues

The management issues that arise from this chapter include:

- In view of the changing nature of global business environment and competition, what are the most immediate impacts on the supply chain and its management?
- What are the market and organizational influences that impact on international/global supply chain decisions?
- What are the rationale and quantifiable benefits of supply chain collaborations?
- What are the important considerations in the development of a modern and intelligent supply chain fit for the twenty-first century?

Chapter Introduction

Radical changes are reshaping the global economy as we enter into the twenty-first century. The marketplace is becoming increasingly global. The fragmentation of markets is widely witnessed in many sectors. Customers want smaller quantities of more customized products, and they demand to be treated individually. Most organizations now have wider product ranges, are introducing new products more quickly, and are focusing their marketing efforts on more thinly segmented niche markets. We are on the cusp of the information age and these changes are ushering in new and exciting challenges.

The changing global competitive and technological environments are transforming the way products are produced and moved around the world. For instance, retailers and wholesalers who specialize in distribution and commerce are looking to globalize their activities as part of their growth strategy. This requires global coordination between distribution and manufacturing activities. Globalization of retailers and wholesalers drives globalization of manufacturing companies that sell through them. When a retailer co-ordinates its purchasing and assortment across markets, the manufacturers/suppliers of goods to those retailers will be influenced in terms of either the conditions to supply those markets where it is already present and the opportunities to supply new markets, or the threat of being replaced by alternative suppliers (Mattsson, 2003). More organizations are globalizing their manufacturing and procurement to spatially dispersed locations in order to gain competitive advantage in the specialization of production resources and activities to leverage greater values from their upstream and downstream supply chains. This will require substantial reorganization of distribution activities and their links to complementary distribution specialists, such as freight forwarders, and wholesalers/agents. Wholesalers, retailers, freight forwarders, and other service providers involved in physical distribution will aim to globalize in order to fulfil the needs of their customers.

Gaining a competitive advantage in international supply chains requires matching the value-adding activities of a chain with the unique comparative advantages offered by nations that make up the chain. Organizations must identify and control the factors that influence the performance of the chain in *procurement*, *processing*, and *distribution* (Prasad and Sounderpandian, 2003). The value-adding activities of a supply chain can be strategically dispersed between various countries and coordinated to produce a high (and quantifiable) level of sustainable competitive advantage.

This chapter considers the changes, new challenges, and strategic issues in developing and managing global supply chains. We begin with a discussion on the challenges and complexity of supply chain management in the fast-changing global marketplace. This

Technological advances in freight forwardinig and shipping have made it possible for the physical distribution of goods to all corners of the globe.

includes consideration of the fundamental aspects of an international/global supply chain. This is followed by an examination of the factors or influences that affect global supply chain decisions. We then cover the business rationale for supply chain collaborations, the scope for collaboration, and the types of relationship that exist in the supply chain, followed by important considerations in developing modern and intelligent supply chain strategies.

A New Approach to Managing Supply Chains and Distribution

The management of an effective supply chain requires the coordination of a range of activities and 'flows' that extend across functional and organizational boundaries. These activities include: (a) inbound logistics (e.g. purchasing and material releasing, inbound transportation, receiving, materials handling); (b) operations (e.g. inventory control and management, demand and supply planning, production planning); (c) outbound logistics (e.g. warehousing and distribution, outbound transportation); (d) marketing and sales (e.g. order receiving order processing and scheduling); (e) customer service (e.g. after-sales support and maintenance). This is illustrated in Fig. 12.1.

Supply chains should be viewed as a set of interrelated processes/activities that need to be aligned, coordinated, and synchronized, rather than a series of discrete, non-aligned activities. These processes are designed to achieve a specific objective or outcome. A well-defined, well-communicated process provides every function in the organization with a

Fig. 12.1 An international supply chain

Country A Supplier S1 Supplier S2 Supplier S3	⇒	**Inbound Logistics** e.g. purchasing and material releasing, inbound transportation, receiving, materials handling	**Outbound Logistics** e.g. warehousing and distribution, outbound transportation	⇒	**Country I** Customer segment SC1 Customer segment SC2

| **Country B**
Supplier S1
Supplier S2
Supplier S3
Supplier S4
Supplier S5
Supplier S6 | ⇒ | **Operations**
e.g. inventory control and management, demand and supply planning, production planning | **Marketing and Sales**
e.g. order receiving, order processing and scheduling | ⇒ | **Country II**
Customer segment SC1
Customer segment SC2
Customer segment SC3

Country III
Customer segment SC1 |

| **Country C**
Supplier S1
Supplier S2 | ⇒ | | **Customer Service**
e.g. after-sales support and maintenance | ⇒ | **Country IV**
Customer segment SC1
Customer segment SC2
Customer segment SC3 |

Upstream supply chain: materials/services supply management — **Downstream supply chain: logistic and channel management**

Source: Based on Trent (2004: 54).

Fig. 12.2 Fundamentals of effective supply chain management

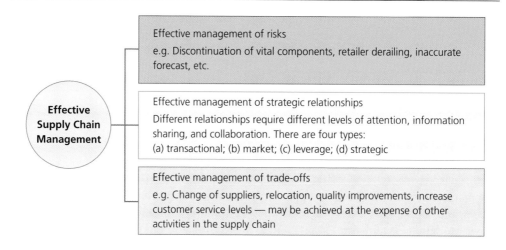

standardized workflow and eliminates the need to reinvent procedures every time the organization develops a product, fulfils an order, or evaluates a supplier. Further, having a systematic process makes it easier to incorporate best practices and knowledge which enhance the likelihood of success. More importantly, if an organization has formally defined processes, it can document and measure them, which facilitate supply chain improvements. Viewing supply chain activities within the context of globally aligned processes makes it possible to implement consistency across geographic units (Trent, 2004).

Developing modern and intelligent supply chains that create sustainable advantage in the marketplace is a highly complex endeavour. What is the best approach to formulate a supply chain strategy that leverages maximum values from the chain? It begins with an understanding of the fundamental principles that underpin today's management of supply chains: managing risks, supply chain relationships, and trade-offs (see Fig. 12.2). These three key supply chain management principles are discussed below (Trent, 2004: 55–7).

Effective management of risk

Risk or uncertainty that exists in the supply chain can stem from a number of scenarios, such as the discontinuation of a vital component or material, a retailer derailing, or an inaccurate forecast which may result in costly bottlenecks and lost sales opportunities.

Similar to other forms of business planning, a certain amount of risk is always present. It is, however, possible to develop cost-effective ways to prevent risk and, if a risk materializes, minimize its effect. Practices such as quality certification, supplier development, information sharing, improved forecasting, and effective contracting can prevent risk.

Effective management of trade-offs

Although trade-offs are not exclusive to supply chain management, the scope of activities involved in managing the entire chain makes trade-offs common in practice. Increasing customer service levels usually require higher inventory levels and faster delivery, which increase supply chain costs. Increased variety and features create new part numbers, which affect forecasting complexity, product placement across the chain, and inventory costs. Any attempts to reduce transportation frequency, hence costs, will inevitably increase lead times. The effective management of these trade-offs can not only ensure optimum levels of cost efficiency but directly impact on long-term competitiveness.

Effective management of strategic relationships

The increasing sophistication in products and services means that few organizations have the means and/or expertise to supply a 'complete' competitive offering. There may be up to 40 or 50 specialist skills needed to run a modern hospital, each member in the supply chain with its own rules, regulations, and budgets. For illustration purposes, we will assume that there is a 'stable demand' for its services. When the supply of specialized surgical instruments, equipment, and drugs is running low, the regional warehouse of a large medical company is alerted by the hospital procurement department so that it can replenish surgical supplies to maintain agreed levels of supply availability. To replenish its own stock, the regional warehouse contacts its company headquarters, which then sources its products from a number of manufacturers.

In a market with stable demand, the supply chain operates smoothly but this may not occur in a hospital environment (not least due to the volatile nature of demand in medical services) because each member in the chain seldom takes the effect of its actions on the other. Often it is because the entire process operates sequentially and has not been sufficiently well analysed in relation to its overall objective of consumer service. For example, the regional warehouse may not want to hold high levels of stock and is selective in stocking only those types of surgical product which are in high demand, as doing either will directly increase the costs. To reduce the risk of theft, the hospital may prefer to rely heavily on regular 'smaller' orders to maintain its surgical supplies. These 'self-centred' behaviours have been documented in numerous supply chains. The result is a combination of less than ideal customer service, excess capacities at various stages, excess inventory, waste and, therefore, a higher than necessary total cost of supply. Value chain management aims systematically to reduce these 'inefficiencies' through the active cooperation of key players in the chain.

Creating and maintaining effective supply chain relationships are critical to success in the supply chain. However, not all supply chain relationships are unique or special. Different relationships require different levels of attention, information sharing, and collaboration.

Supply chain relationships can be broadly categorized into four types: (a) transactional; (b) market; (c) leverage; and (d) strategic (see Fig. 12.3):

(a) **Transactional**—transactional relationships are widely adopted when the cost of searching for and comparing sources outweighs the value resulting from this effort.

Fig. 12.3 Supply chain relationships and approaches

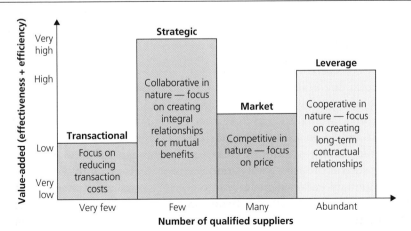

Source: Based on Trent (2004: 56).

Values are created by reducing the transaction cost of the purchase. This approach is common when the goods and services being sourced are of low value and/or highly commoditized in nature.

(b) **Market**—market relationships are adopted when the items being sourced are of lower-to-medium values, and characterized by many suppliers and low supplier switching costs. The organization may rely on competitive bidding, shorter-term contracting, reverse internet auctions, and blanket purchase orders when obtaining market items. Pursuing a higher-level relationship here would be unproductive because the cost of doing so would probably outweigh the resulting benefits.

(c) **Leverage**—these relationships feature goods and services that benefit from consolidating volumes with fewer supply chain members. Longer-term contracts are used, and negotiations tend to focus on factors such as cost, quality, delivery, packaging, logistics, inventory management, and service.

(d) **Strategic**—forming strategic relationships are crucial when the items being sourced consume a large portion of total purchase cost, and are essential to a product's function or help differentiate the product in a way valued by the end customer. These items often involve customization rather than standardization. The benefits of close collaboration outweigh the costs of pursuing these relationships.

Factors Affecting Global Supply Chain Decisions

To develop an effective global supply chain, an organization needs to examine its value-adding activities in relation to the comparative advantages offered by markets in which it operates. Matching these activities and the sourcing decisions with appropriate country conditions can lead to strategic benefits in cost, quality, lead times and, perhaps, innovation. Prasad and Sounderpandian (2003: 242–6) have identified the importance of *country*, *industry type*, and *international supply chain strategy* in shaping the location of operations, procurement networks, and distribution depots. They argue that the ways in which country, industry, and international supply chain strategy variables work through the supply chain areas of procurement, processing, and distribution can positively influence the competitive strengths in cost, quality, lead times, and innovation. This is illustrated in Fig. 12.4.

Country characteristics

Endowment factors

Countries vary considerably in their endowment factors. A country can be an attractive sourcing platform due to its primary, secondary, or tertiary endowment factors. Primary factors include access to low-cost labour or raw materials. There is no shortage of examples of branded sports clothing, such as Nike and Reebok locating manufacturing operations in the Far East and South East Asia to take advantage of low-cost labour. Secondary endowment factors include availability of specialist skills/expertise and the quality of the infrastructure, such as the accessibility and reliability of telecommunications, ports, roads, and airports. Tertiary endowment factors consist of the country's demand and operating conditions. Many multinationals have located part of their value chain activities in certain countries to gain entry into the local markets. For example, many Japanese car manufacturers, such as Toyota (www.toyota.com) and Honda (www.honda.com), establish

Fig. 12.4 Influential factors in international supply chain

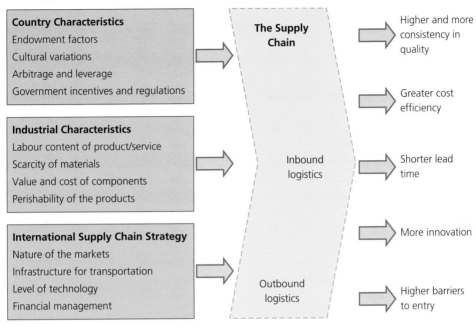

Source: Based on Prasad and Sounderpandian (2003: 242).

a manufacturing facility in the UK in order to serve huge existing markets as well as gaining access to the wider EU markets.

Cultural variations

Organizations may find that variations in social patterns, cultural mores, and working practices can make setting up an effective supply chain a difficult task. Variations in cultural practices can cause errors in the communications between partners, who may speak different languages and operate in different time zones. For instance, the supply chain of a typical computer electronics company can involve no less than 8–10 key external partners in five countries and six time zones. To keep every partner working in parallel to deliver optimum results can prove a real challenge.

Arbitrage and leverage

Due to the international nature of the supply chains, multinationals can use their information systems to rapidly leverage and arbitrage the movement of material and location of activities, not only to minimize some of these difficulties, but to gain a competitive advantage. For instance, a purchasing manager can leverage varying exchange rates to the company's advantage by sourcing from countries with weakening currencies and limiting production in countries exhibiting strengthening currencies. The absence of standardized tax structures among countries provides opportunities to arbitrage tax regimes via transfer pricing and multi-channel remittances.

Government incentives and regulations

The governments of many nations have realized the importance of their country serving as part of the multinationals' supply chains or distributional channels. Such activities can provide much needed employment, additional tax revenues, and, in some cases, local industrial development. As a result, these governments provide an array of incentives such as low import/export tariffs, tax refunds, land, and/or low-cost infrastructure to become a sourcing platform, processing location, and/or distributional depot. Multinational organizations can benefit from these incentives by strategically locating their sourcing, processing, and distributional activities in these countries.

Industry characteristics

The type of industry influences the structure and management of the supply chains. Factors affecting supply chain include the following.

Labour content of the products/services

The greater the labour content, the more difficult it is to manage the process of manufacturing and quality control, hence higher costs are involved. Organizations with high labour content products may locate their processing facilities in countries where there is an abundance of low-cost but highly skilled labour.

Scarcity of materials

The greater the scarcity of raw materials, the more organizations normally locate their sourcing and processing platforms near the source of raw materials to minimize transportation cost and complexity.

Value and cost of components

High-value components need to be carefully managed, processed, and/or transported as mistakes or damage in the handling of components can be costly. In planning supply chains, organizations have the tendency to locate their sourcing, processing, and storage activities so that movements of high-value components are minimized, while low-value components can be transported from other parts of the world.

Perishability of the products

Highly perishable products, such as meats and fresh flowers, need to have a much shorter shelf life than non-perishable products such as textiles and printing paper. The lead time needed for processing, packaging, and distribution of these products is distinctly shorter than that for non-perishable goods.

Aablo Inc. (www.aablo.nl) is a medium-sized international supplier of cut flowers and potted plants based in the Netherlands. In order to fulfil the orders of its customers (which include wholesale dealers, garden centres, supermarkets, shops, and hotels), it has developed highly sophisticated systems of order-processing, international procurement, storage, packaging, and delivery.

© Courtesy of Aablo Inc.

International supply chain strategy

A successful global marketing strategy is dependent on effective supply chains that: (a) deliver products of high quality to customers; (b) price competitively through careful cost management; (c) operate within short lead times; and (d) provide excellent after-market supporting services. Synchronizing these dimensions requires organizations to manage their supply chain with greater strategic planning and to work more closely with suppliers, transport agencies, and potential customers.

The development of an effective supply chain strategy needs to consider the following (see Fig. 12.5).

Nature of the markets

This includes understanding the rate of change, rate of growth, and the relative size of the markets. For instance, a country with a substantial market size or potential for growth may demand local production or assembling facilities in order effectively to meet its domestic demand. On a global scale, organizations will need to decide upon the degree to which the supply networks can be rationalized. Organizations entering individual countries will face unique market conditions—such as ability to pay, competition, level of customer expectations, order size, and product life cycles—which may pose varying degrees of operational challenges in their supply chain management.

Infrastructure for transportation

The inadequacy or lack of effective transportation infrastructure can inhibit the success of a global supply chain. A number of key issues need to be carefully examined, including the cost, accessibility, shipping patterns, reliability, service level, storage capacity and locations, routing constraints, ratio of intra- to inter-company traffic, types of transportation mode, carrier qualifications, and inter-modal systems. In addition, supply chain managers may find a number of difficulties in the transportation area operating in an international environment. For instance, regulations and bureaucratic barriers in some countries can

Fig. 12.5 Considerations in developing an international supply chain

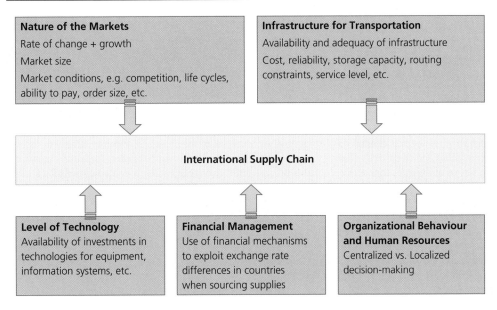

be time-consuming. In China, many foreign companies rely on the services of third-party freight forwarders to expedite materials through customs of provincial authorities.

Level of technology

Technological investments in the supply chain can be in terms of machines and equipment, work methods, or information systems. Through the use of e-commerce, multinational organizations can gain enormous economies of scale in R&D, sourcing, processing, and distribution as technologies developed from these investments can be spread through their operations globally (see The Digital Impact).

Financial management

A global supply chain can provide a financial hedge in turbulent international conditions. By having a number of suppliers across various regions of the world, for instance, a multinational organization could take advantage of the exchange rate volatility and vary the flow from one country to another as the currency values fluctuate. Through rationalization

THE DIGITAL IMPACT Supply chain management and e-commerce

One of the biggest opportunities and challenges facing businesses today is the deployment of web-enabled technologies. As a new channel for commercial transactions, the use of e-commerce opens up fresh sources of revenue and opportunities for organizations that have carefully structured strategies. The outcome of the cost/benefit calculus of e-commerce solutions depends on a number of factors that can be analysed by use of a theoretical framework. At the core of the attractiveness of e-commerce is the ability to gain four possible sources of competitive advantage:

(a) reduction in intermediation costs associated with wholesale and retail activities;

(b) the ability to lower costs associated with purchasing by curbing the time and effort involved in supply and logistics operations;

(c) improved information-gathering and processing that permit improved management of the supply chain; and

(d) the prospect of expanding market share and/or developing new markets by lowering the cost of gathering and processing information on the wants of existing and potential customers.

In the UK many companies have developed strategies and are gaining valuable experience of deploying web-based solutions in their supply chains. For example, the Co-operative Bank (www.co-operativebank.co.uk) is the first clearing bank to offer all its personal current account and credit-card holders a full online internet banking service at no extra cost. RS Components (www.rs-components.com), through its internet e-commerce interface, provides its customers with online selection and purchasing from 100,000 industrial products held in stock. It allows fast search, online ordering and retrieval, and differentiates the company from its competitors. Mitsubishi (www.mitsubishi.com), the consumer electronics giant, uses a dealer extranet to give its dealers access not only to product updates and technical bulletins, but also to the Modcomp's ViewMax 2000 Electronic Commerce module for online ordering and order tracking. The dealer has full control of the process, allowing Mitsubishi to focus resources on manufacturing and fulfilment. For a truly global brand like the BBC (www.bbc.co.uk), the internet provides a unique opportunity to address new markets, and reinforcing and securing the brand via the website is very important. 'Beeb@BBC' is an alliance forged between ICL and the Corporation's commercial arm, BBC Worldwide, to create and promote an information-packed website that is both functional and consumer friendly.

Source: Based on Fraser et al. (2000).

of the supply chain, multinationals can reduce costs by carefully managing the transfer prices for products emanating from overseas and hedging against currency fluctuations.

Organizational behaviour and human resources

The management of complex systems demands an international organizational structure staffed with trained personnel. Organizational culture of management plays a significant role in determining the decision-making process throughout the supply chain. An organization with a highly centralized decision-making culture tends to centralize decision-making on sourcing, processing, and distribution at headquarters or regional centres, and vice versa. The organization would have to evaluate the human resources and training needs, and tailor them to the international environment.

Collaboration in the Supply Chain

Many organizations, especially those that operate in the international retailing and construction sectors, have long recognized the major economic benefits of strategic supply chain management. Market pressure for increased product complexity and variety, based on a wide range of technologies, and response at higher levels of quality and reliability but declining cost, have demonstrated that few, if any, organizations can do it all themselves. Consequently, they need to supplement their core competences by joining with other providers of complementary competences to satisfy their customers. Real productivity, design, and quality improvements are not obtainable unless both partners innovate to the best of their abilities. Many organizations recognize that their ability to become world-class competitors is based to a large degree on their ability to establish high levels of trust and cooperation with their suppliers (Humphreys et al., 2001). The mini-case illustrates the challenges facing electronic manufacturers and the rationale for collaboration.

An effective management of supply chain can provide substantial inventory-driven cost savings in procurement, inventory management, and order fulfilment. According to IBM's Business Consulting Analysis report (IBM Global Services, 2002), typical companies which operate in the electronics industry spend 65–85% of their revenues on procured materials—that is, activities that depend on partners outside the traditional 'four walls' perspective. It would be a mistake, as Horvath (2001) argues, for businesses to think of supply chain management as limited to these functions alone. Enhanced supply chain capabilities can create efficiencies and cost savings across a wide range of business processes, from marketing and product design through to the accounts receivable department. The most immediate benefits that businesses can expect from strategically managing supply chains are lowered inventory risks and costs, along with reductions in warehousing, distribution, and transportation costs.

Over time, businesses will also experience sustainable cost savings through increased productivity and streamlined business processes in procurement and purchasing, order fulfilment, accounts receivable and payable, and exception management. More subtle benefits can include accelerated product delivery times, more efficient product development efforts, and lower product manufacturing costs. In the long run, businesses can expect dramatic improvement of customer responsiveness, increased flexibility for changing market conditions, improved customer service and satisfaction, increased customer retention, and more effective marketing.

MINI-CASE ILLUSTRATION Factors driving increased partnerships in Toys 'R' Us

For any fast-moving-consumer-goods (FMCG) manufacturers that operate globally, the operational challenges of running a successful business are enormous. Rapid and continual declines in selling prices for products make inventory ownership extraordinarily costly. At the same time, continually improving products requires the introduction of new components, many of which face ramp-up complexities and low yields in the early phases. Further, FMCG products today no longer enjoy a period of stable demand between introduction and end-of-life, as promotions and competitive pressures can lead to dramatic short-run changes in end-customer demand. The combination of strategic industry change with the operational challenges of keeping inventories low but not disrupting the continuous cycle of new product introductions has given new importance to an old problem: how to work effectively with business partners.

Toys 'R' Us (www.toysrus.com) is a model company with proven business systems, extensive product and service offers, deep strategic partnerships, major market share, and wide business experience.

When it launched its web-retailing site, it applied the same business practices of its bricks-and-mortar operations, thereby ensuring that business milestones were met and profits made. It achieved this by leveraging its existing bases of competitive advantage in at least three ways. First, it uses offline operations to support its online efforts. Customers are encouraged to return items bought online to their shops, saving them the expense and bother of posting returns back to the warehouse. Letting the customers choose the channel they prefer to shop in, return an item or gather information creates a stress-free shopping experience. Secondly, the company applies its in-store expertise in handling millions of small orders to its online retailing business. The retailer's offline track record in customer service presents a tangible advantage in reassuring online customers of its commitment to customer satisfaction. Finally, the Toys 'R' Us brand name, with over 50 years of experience in toy retailing and an established reputation as the 'worldwide authority on toys and fun', is fully exploited.

Types of buyer–supplier relationship

There are two main types of relationship between buyer and suppliers: (1) traditional 'transactional' and (2) 'collaborative partnership' (Humphreys et al., 2001: 153–4). The primary goal of the traditional transactional approach is to minimize the price of purchased goods and services, and is dependent upon three activities:

(1) The buyer relies on a large number of suppliers who can play off against each other to gain price concessions and ensure continuity of supply.

(2) The buyer allocates amounts to suppliers to keep them in line.

(3) The buyer assumes an arm's length posture and uses only short-term contracts.

When such relationships are engaged, the buyer relies on a large number of suppliers and uses only short-term contracts in order to obtain a higher bargaining position compared to that of other suppliers. It assumes no differences in suppliers' abilities to provide value-added services, technology gains, process innovations, and other methods of gaining competitive advantage and therefore does little to foster long-term coordination or cooperation between buyer and supplier.

Collaborative partnership requires trust and commitment for long-term cooperation along with a willingness to share risks. In contrast to the adversarial competitive approach, the primary goal of the collaborative partnership approach is to focus on long-term strategic gains by establishing reliable and highly value-added relationships. Collaborative partnerships depend on the following:

(1) The buyer relies on a small number of strategic partners who can work closely together to gain price stability and ensure continuity of supply.

(2) The buyer and suppliers make joint decisions on research and development, total quality management, and continuous improvements.

(3) The buyer and suppliers integrate their operational processes to leverage greater efficiency and better responses to changing market environments.

Table 12.1 Comparison of transactional and collaborative relationships

Relationship factor	Transactional in nature	Collaborative in nature
1. Nature of competition in supply market	Price/cost based; competitive	Collaborative; relationship-based
2. Basis for sourcing decision	Competitive bidding	Oriented towards long-term performance
3. Management of information flow	One-way; closed	Two-way; high transparency
4. Approach to capacity planning	Independent	Joined-up planning
5. Logistic practices	Laden with uncertainties	Integrative—use of JIT or similar practices
6. Pressure on quality improvement	Low—purchaser will go elsewhere if dissatisfied	High—continuous improvement to identify better methods and materials leading to lower costs

Source: Based on Lamming (1993), in Humphreys et al. (2001: 154).

The comparison of transactional and collaborative relationships is outlined in Table 12.1.

Cultural perceptions of quality, service and price have significant influence on the partner selection criteria for multinational companies sourcing globally. The performance of an organization is often influenced by the source country's economic conditions, level of technological development, business customers, and political situation. In general, suppliers in highly industrialized countries, such as Germany and Japan, are chosen for quality products, but when companies want to purchase low-price products, Chinese suppliers might be chosen rather than their Japanese counterparts. Japanese suppliers often emerge as the preferred partner in terms of financial stability and trust. They are perceived as strong technological competitors due to increased R&D investment strategies coupled with innovative new product development programmes.

The scope of collaboration

There are a variety of forms of potential supply chain collaboration, which can be divided into three categories (Simatupang and Sridharan, 2002): vertical, horizontal, and lateral. *Vertical collaboration* occurs when two or more organizations, such as manufacturer, distributor, carrier, and retailer, share their responsibilities, resources, and performance information to serve relatively similar end customers. This can include collaboration with suppliers (upstream) and internally (across functions), and even with specific customers (downstream), which is common when the transactions are frequent and substantial in volume and/or value. An example of a business which has faced challenges in managing its vertical collaboration in a volatile market is Marks and Spencer (M&S, www.marksandspencer.com), a well-known UK retailer. The company had had a century of unbridled success prior to their fall from grace in the 1990s. In the 1920s, the business adopted the then revolutionary policy of buying direct from manufacturers instead of through wholesalers. These supplier relationships gave the business an advantage few of its rivals could match. M&S designed most of its clothes in-house before putting the designs forward to favoured manufacturers with notoriously strict specifications regarding the finished product. These manufacturers provided dedicated facilities for M&S, who required suppliers to refrain from working for other clients. These relationships relieved

THE RELATIONSHIP PERSPECTIVE Managing supplier relationships in China

There are an increasing number of joint ventures between foreign and Chinese companies. For instance, the investments of Canadian companies in China increased by 700% between 1991 and 1995. In establishing these collaborations, it is important to have an appreciation of the criteria viewed as important by each partner. If both parties place the same importance on the collaborative criteria, the implementation process should be made easier and cultural conflicts reduced. However, if differences arise, the collaborating partners can focus attention on these areas in order to minimize any negative effect.

It has long been acknowledged that 'quanxi relationships' is a key element in business practice in China. Quanxi relationships are characterized by mutual trust and willingness to engage in a process that produces benefits for both parties in the business relationship. It is also important to appreciate that face (or 'mianzi') is an important component in the quanxi relationships. Mianzi is an intangible form of social currency and status. The Chinese believe that once they have established quanxi relationships, they should trust their partners and that they are committed to one another for mutual benefit. Consequently, if they request to examine, say, their supplier partner's cost information, the implication is that they do not trust their supplier and this may lead to both parties losing mianzi.

Source: Based on Humphreys et al. (2001).

M&S of the need to allocate resources to technological research and development activities. Servicing such a demanding client invoked a culture of continuous improvement within the suppliers' organizations and loyalty to M&S (Christopher and Towill, 2002).

Horizontal collaboration occurs when two or more unrelated or competing organizations cooperate to share information or resources, such as joint distribution centres. This can include collaboration with competitors, internally, and with non-competitors, e.g. sharing manufacturing capacity. This form of collaboration may be a prerequisite to successful market entry into certain lucrative markets, in particular China.

More and more companies are entering China to leverage the country's cheap labour costs and establish long-term competitive advantage in, potentially, the world's largest market. To be successful in the long term, foreign companies need to establish, maintain, and strengthen their supply chains in the country. As observed by Jiang (2002: 185–6), foreign firms face many supply chain-related difficulties, including the country's overburdened, underdeveloped physical infrastructure; inexpert, under-funded, state-owned distribution companies; an enormous, fragmented distribution and logistics sector; and regional protectionism. In addition, foreign companies face bureaucratic restrictions that prohibit them from legally importing, selling, and servicing products in a straightforward manner.

McDonald's (www.mcdonalds.com) successfully entered China in 1992. Its need for high-tech logistics meant it did not have the option of outsourcing to local underdeveloped logistics companies. So McDonald's convinced its long-term logistics provider, HAVI Group LP (www.haviphils.com), to come with it. HAVI is responsible for ensuring that hundreds of McDonald's around China receive their frozen food at the right temperature and their napkins and packages on time. The only way to ensure high levels of accuracy and precision in delivery was to own and manage a fleet of trucks operating out of distribution centres dotted strategically around the country.

Not every company has the power or resources to convince their suppliers to follow them. Some companies try to outsource their logistics to non-Chinese third-party logistics (3PL) providers. Royal Dutch Shell (www.shell.com) has sold industrial lubricants in

China since the early 1990s. In 1998 the company decided to pursue a nationwide marketing strategy and outsourced the work to EAC Logistics. This northern European company had been in China for a short time and had only 125 employees. However, this allowed it to be flexible in dealing with local provincial regulations. Some provinces and municipalities make it so onerous for outside haulage companies to secure licences that shipments must be offloaded at each border and reloaded on to the next jurisdiction's trucks; average freight distance by road in China is only 58 km. Most small, dedicated logistics companies have managed to obtain a patchwork of local haulage licences and thus attained a degree of national coverage. In this way, EAC established 11 logistics centres around China. Other foreign companies lured by the huge Chinese market hesitate to invest heavily and are now following Shell's logistics strategy in China.

Finally, a *lateral collaboration* aims to gain more flexibility by combining and sharing capabilities in both a vertical and horizontal manner. An example of this can be seen at Matsushita (www.panasonic.com), a Japanese-based industry leader in consumer electrical brands, including Technics and JVC, who has had to fight to remain competitive in the face of low-cost Chinese competitors. Faced with declining sales and profits due to cost deficiencies in its supply chain, Matsushita realized that its long-term success was contingent on supply chain realignment. As summarized by Jiang and Hansen (2003: 185–8), this alignment included the transfer of many tasks to China.

The first step was taken in 1994 when Matsushita opened a microwave oven manufacturing facility in Shanghai with an annual capacity of 500,000 units. The plant imported most parts and materials from Japan. Matsushita believed this strategy would allow the company to maintain its traditional advantage of high-quality Japanese components while still benefiting from the economies associated with China's low-cost labour and land. This initiative was effective in reducing costs; a microwave produced in the company's Shanghai facility was 30% less expensive than one produced in the Japanese manufacturing facility.

Unfortunately, this shift in production provided only a temporary respite from the cost problems facing Matsushita. The company's Chinese competitors were not only reaping the benefits of China's lower land and labour costs, but also capitalizing on less expensive Chinese components and technical expertise. The company embarked on a more radical supply-chain realignment project that would:

(a) move all manufacturing activities to China—while Matsushita still produce heavily in Germany, the USA, and Japan, it is already making constructive plans to transfer manufacturing activities to China;

(b) establish R&D in China—in 2001, Matsushita announced that it would be moving much of its R&D to China with the opening of the Matsushita Electric R&D centre in Beijing. The Beijing centre would be the second largest of the company's 16 R&D centres through-out the world. Through this centre, Matsushita hopes to develop a closer link to the Chinese consumer;

Away from the big cities, the transport infrastructure in rural China is not well established, making it difficult and expensive to achieve effective market penetration.

© Courtesy of Hania Arentsen-Berdys

(c) procure most supplies in China—aided by the Chinese government, Matsushita is gaining access to many

WHOSE RESPONSIBILITY IS IT? Corporate social responsibility—is it any of your business?

Corporate social responsibility (CSR) has risen up the agenda as politicians and business leaders respond to criticism—from consumer groups, non-governmental organizations (NGOs), and trade unions—that big business is exploiting the vulnerable in its global search for profit. Foreign companies operating in poor developing countries are most likely to face human rights challenges in the abuse of minimum labour standards and use of forced labour; complicity in restrictions to freedom of association and expression; corruption; and the expropriation of rights to land and other resources.

Western multinationals that directly employ factory workers in developing countries, such as Indonesia and China, are normally operating in a technologically advanced industry and their staff benefit from above-average wages and conditions. Many of these companies, however, are implicated in the exploitation of labour through companies operating in their supply chain. Consumer and NGO activity has brought discredit to many household names by highlighting the sweatshop conditions in which their branded products are made.

Unravelling the supply chain can be a complex process and many companies are unaware of who their suppliers are. Labour-intensive factories producing for the international textile, shoe, and toy markets may well defy the host country's law and international labour standards. For instance, many Chinese factories are accused of demanding excessive overtime with no overtime rates of pay; physical and psychological intimidation of workers; deposits required to secure jobs; and workers subject to lock-ins, invasive body searches, and sometimes appalling health and safety conditions.

Supporting CSR principles as part of the strategy and day-to-day operations of a company can be complex where activities span different countries, working cultures, and regulatory environments. Codes of conduct do not translate easily into local practices and languages. In Chinese, the word 'stakeholder' (*liyixiang-guanzhe*), a central concept in CSR, is a new term and few outside the social sciences recognize the word, let alone the meaning. Threatening to withdraw business from licensees who fail to comply with codes of conduct may still not placate NGO

critics, as Disney (www.disney.com) found after Chinese workers lost their jobs as a result of the entertainment giant cancelling production contracts with individual Guangdong suppliers.

Implementing CSR requires total supply chain management and working in partnership with government, suppliers, and workers to improve standards and address the problems posed by poor performers. Corporate initiatives focused on partnerships have sought to improve human rights in the workplace through training. A ground-breaking project funded by the Macarthur Foundation (www.macfound.org) recently brought together Hong Kong-based NGOs, multinational companies, including Adidas (www.adidas.com) and Reebok (www.reebok.com), and their Chinese suppliers for factory-based training on occupational health and safety committees with worker representation. Although the project encountered obstacles in fully implementing worker participation following training, all participants agreed that worker participation was beneficial in improving working conditions. The project provides a benchmark of what can be achieved in bringing key stakeholders together.

Source: Based on Macbean (2003).

low-cost suppliers. Due to China's undeveloped infrastructure and regionally fragmented distribution, the government has devised a system through which suppliers and customers are brought together. This has helped to establish greater price transparency, hence reduce costs; and

(d) establish more effective channels of distributions in China—due to logistical difficulties most foreign companies operate in the coastal markets while neglecting the inland markets, which represent 70% of the population. Powerful Chinese companies, such as Galanz (www.galanz.com), Matsushita's chief rival, have successfully increased sales in these inland markets, which has gained greater economies of scale and further reduced costs.

Due to the intricacies associated with reaching inland markets, Matsushita chose to enter into a strategic alliance with TCL Holdings (www.tclcom.com), the largest producer of televisions in China. Both companies had something the other wanted. Matsushita coveted TCL's rural logistics networks, which included 32 regional distributional subsidiaries, 174 distribution centres, and 4,000 sales agents. Through this system, TCL has the ability to reach nearly 20,000 retailers in the Chinese markets. In turn, TCL coveted Matsushita's technological prowess. The alliance granted Matsushita rights to TCL's established distribution network in rural China, while TCL was granted access to Matsushita's latest patents on DVD players, digital televisions, and air conditioners.

The case of Matsushita shows that the company's improved supply chain has paid substantial dividends to its global market position and profitability. The company's success demonstrates that supply chain excellence can serve as a source of differentiation, as gaining a competitive advantage by product alone becomes more difficult. As it seeks to maintain its leadership position, Matsushita has come to realize that complete process reorganization is necessary in order to take advantage of the manufacturing and production economies available in China.

Developing Market-responsive Supply Chain Strategies

Many marketplaces are now volatile and demand is difficult to predict. The acceleration of technological and fashion changes has resulted in shorter product life cycles. In this environment, failure within the supply chains to match demand with supply, and to enable the seamless flows of supplies and replenishment can make the difference between profit and loss.

The development of intelligent and competitive supply chains is complex due, in part, to outsourcing and the globalization of procurement and manufacture. Process change involves multiple organizations that both compete and collaborate as well as multiple technology standards and business processes. A modern supply chain should enable the organization to compete successfully in today's global market environment where (Maskell, 2001: 6):

- everything is changing quickly and unpredictably;
- low volume, high quality, customer and specific products are required;
- products have very short life cycles and very short development and production lead times; and
- customers want to be treated as individuals.

Supply chain management has become a people-intensive, relationship-driven operation. Perfect quality and highly customized service are required. This trend shift towards a multiplicity of finished products with short development and production lead times has led many organizations into problems with inventories, overheads, and efficiencies. Applying the traditional mass-production approach without realizing the whole environment has changed can result in costly losses. Mass production does not apply to products where the customers require small quantities of highly customized, design-to-order products, and where additional services and value-added benefits, such as product upgrades and future reconfigurations, are as important as the product itself (Maskell, 2001). These challenges will grow as organizations deal with numerous collaboration possibilities, each of which may run on a different schedule and use different formats or technical standards.

Designing a market responsive supply chain that involves different collaborative activities working together is far simpler on the drawing board than it is in reality. Success means continually improving trust, speed, and efficiency, where customers provide accurate forecasts and planners use that information along with reliable supply data to generate feasible and accurate plans. Poor forecasts and infeasible plans, however, lead to a destructive cycle of manipulation and dishonesty in the network.

Global sourcing

Global sourcing is becoming a prerequisite to competing in today's marketplace. It has become a competitive weapon to maintain or gain market share and requires the procurement manager to view the world as a potential source for raw materials, components, services, and finished goods. Organizations pursue international sourcing as a reaction to increased worldwide competition or a proactive strategy to gain competition advantage.

Traditionally, the most widely recognized benefit of global sourcing is to lower costs. Manufacturing companies are typically confronted with up to 70% of the average manufacture's total costs in sourcing materials, so it behoves management to consider strategies to minimize these costs. Global sourcing is also often seen as an opportunity for multinationals to acquire potential tax advantages. For instance, many countries use tax incentives (e.g. free-trade zones, reduction tariffs) to lure foreign companies' process and/or assembly products and then re-export them. This helps multinationals that operate in these countries to eliminate inventory-holding taxes and import/export duties. Some organizations source globally to strengthen the reliability of their supply, supplement their domestic sources, or meet increases in product demand. Technical specifications or capabilities of products manufactured elsewhere may exceed those which can be found domestically (Herbig and O'Hara, 1995).

As an organization develops international sourcing experience (Monczka and Trent, 1991: 3–4), it typically progresses through four phases of the internationalization of procurement process (Fig. 12.6).

Phase 1: domestic sourcing

In Phase 1, the organization does not engage in any direct foreign buying activities, as it does not perceive a need or have the expertise to pursue international sourcing. However, the organization may purchase from other domestic suppliers which source or produce goods internationally.

Fig. 12.6 Internationalization of the procurement process

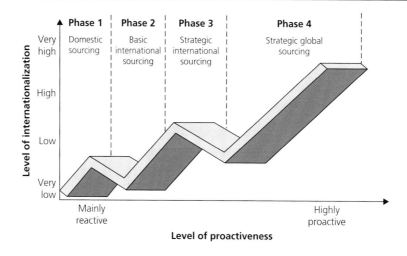

Phase 2: basic international sourcing

In Phase 2, the organization progresses to basic international sourcing because it is confronted with a requirement for which no suitable domestic supplier exists, or because competitors are gaining an advantage due to international sourcing. This may be a reactive strategy due to inadequacy of the domestic supply base to satisfy customer requirements. Further, the increase in foreign competition in the domestic market can push the organization to initiate international sourcing in order to remain cost competitive and/or to provide performance and quality improvements.

Phase 3: Strategic international sourcing

In Phase 3, the organization realizes that a focused international sourcing strategy results in significant performance gains. As a result, the organization is likely to pursue an aggressive international sourcing strategy that views the world as one potential market for sourcing. There is likely to be concentration of sourcing activities at carefully selected strategic locations in order to exploit cost and quality advantages, and satisfaction of customer requirements.

Phase 4: Strategic global sourcing

The final phase occurs when the organization realizes greater benefit through the integration and coordination of procurement requirements on a global basis. Phase 4 represents the most sophisticated development of the global sourcing strategy. In order to maximize the benefit of global sourcing, the organizations must possess worldwide information systems, sophisticated personnel capabilities, coordination mechanisms, an effective organizational structure, and the highest level of management support. Operations at this level also require procurement, manufacturing, and technology groups to work together to establish the best worldwide design network and develop optimal supplier capabilities.

Mohan and Berkowitz (1988) provide a successful example of global sourcing in the Japanese steel industry. Japanese trading companies coordinate the procurement of raw materials for the steel industry by acting as a single customer in international markets. This strategy involves extensive use of long-term contracts, rather than relying on short-term spot-market transactions to fulfil the material requirements. The accumulation of large demand requirements coupled with the use of longer-term contracts has induced Japanese suppliers to invest in more productive equipment, expand facilities, and develop techniques that increase productivity and reduce costs. This strategy can provide the same benefits to an individual buying organization. By bringing the accumulated procurement requirements of the organization to the fore, it can expect greater benefit in the areas of price, delivery, security of supply, and access to supplier technology (Monczka and Trent, 1991).

The mini-case of Green Isle Foods is an example of the way in which a pizza manufacturing company undertook a major restructuring of its procurement and manufacturing processes to deliver substantial process improvements that enable the business to survive.

Developing relationships with foreign suppliers demands a significant commitment of time and resources. In the formation of buyer–seller relationships, buyers are subservient to a host of personal, cultural, and organizational influences in connection with their purchasing decisions. For instance, the procurement manager's preferences, perceptions, and personal motivations can have a profound impact on how buying decisions are analysed and subsequently determined. Individual characteristics, such as age, income, education, personality, attitudes towards risk, and job position can also have a strong influence on a participant's overall philosophy towards the buying process. A successful purchasing style for doing business with a vendor in Germany, for example, may not be appropriate for interacting with a supplier from Japan (Herbig and O'Hara, 1995).

MINI-CASE ILLUSTRATION Green Isle Foods

Green Isle Foods is a subsidiary of Northern Foods plc. (www. northern-foods.co.uk) one of the UK's largest food manufacturers. Based in the Republic of Ireland, Green Isle produces frozen convenience foods (pizza, pastry, and breaded-fish products) for the Irish and UK retail markets. The company has a broad product portfolio comprising its own branded products, including the UK brand leader in frozen pizzas (Goodfellas), supermarket own-label products, and contract manufacturing of other branded products. The company has invested in state-of-the-art manufacturing technology in its six plants and describes itself as a specialist in food conversion/assembly, with manufacturing capability as its core competence. The frozen convenience foods category within the UK retail market is fiercely competitive and in recent years Green Isle has been facing growing pressure on three fronts:

1 The rapidly rising demand for chilled convenience foods is eating into the market share and growth of frozen products.

2 Retail strategies designed to increase the share of own-label products (from which they generally take a larger margin than on branded lines) is placing pressure on branded lines.

3 The excessive use of price discounts and promotions to stimulate demand in a category that is growing slowly is placing further margin pressure across the whole range of products, and retailers are increasingly putting this business out to tender, generating significant uncertainty among incumbent suppliers.

In response to this competitive pressure, Green Isle is striving to maintain its status of preferred supplier through improved customer service, stronger support for its branded products, and improved management of its supply base to deliver process efficiencies that will enable Green Isle to remain competitive. Its supply chain mission statement is: 'To make Green Isle the most efficient, reliable and hassle-free supplier to the retail trade in the UK and Ireland.'

With three diverse business units (pizza, pastry, fish) operating out of six plants, one of Green Isle's challenges was to gain leverage in its purchasing activities, a problem not helped by the fact that until the mid-1990s they had no single person responsible for (or with specialist experience/knowledge in) purchasing. This changed in 1996, with the hiring of a purchasing manager who had experience from the electronics industry. The purchasing manager immediately set about developing an integrated materials management model for the business, covering all three business units. Green Isle's purchasing strategy is based on six principles:

(1) local sourcing wherever competitive and possible;

(2) long-term relationships;

(3) shared information and technical expertise;

(4) no more than two potential sources of supply for all major raw materials;

(5) positive release;

(6) value for money.

Historically, the company took the view that local sourcing was an important way of securing supplies and achieving consistency, while maintaining a degree of loyalty among the supply base. This was consistent with the underlying philosophy of developing long-term, sustainable relationships with their suppliers, many of whom have been supplying the business for over ten years. The importance of flexibility and consistent quality, coupled with substantial switching costs, means that it is in Green Isle's interests to develop and maintain strong and lasting supplier relationships. Rationalization of the supply base continues and this leads to greater dependency on suppliers, so Green Isle has to gain commercial benefits from reducing its supply base. It does this by passing the quality control function upstream (positive release), enabling ingredients to be delivered direct on a just-in-time basis which, in turn, can only be achieved if adequate information is shared with suppliers. Green Isle is continually looking for cost savings in their raw materials, but this is done collaboratively with suppliers.

With cheese by far the most significant ingredient, in terms of cost, Green Isle presented a proposal to its largest cheese supplier—all cheese to be blended, cubed, and delivered through the lead supplier. There was no contract and all necessary capital investment was to be undertaken by the supplier. For the latter, the incentive was the development of a relationship that would secure preferred status and volume growth in a food ingredient market that is commodity-oriented and in which long-term planning is difficult and market risk a significant problem. In addition, Green Isle agreed to pay a price premium to cover the additional costs. The project was complete 18 months later and Green Isle was able to mothball its cubing plant and refocus on its core competence.

The packaging project was different from the cheese project in several ways. Inventories were excessive and in-bound logistics were inefficient but there were no sub-processes to be removed, so there were no manufacturing issues to be dealt with. This made the internal buy-in easier as there was little, if any, internal vested interest in the existing packaging arrangements. However, external buy-in would be more difficult, with 42 disparate suppliers, none of whom were as dependent on Green Isle for business as the cheese suppliers were.

The lead packaging supplier took longer to accept the clustering principle. Indeed, it required the intervention of senior management to convince the packaging supplier of the benefits of a long-term contract with a price premium to cover the additional costs of warehousing and logistics, based once again on open-book accounting. The lead supplier managed the risk by setting up a consulting business to manage the process, to allow the packaging operations to continue while the warehousing and inbound logistics problems were resolved externally. The task was completed 12 months later.

Green Isle recognizes that it has a long way to go from buy–make–sell to sell–source–ship, but the outsourcing of non-core activities and the creation and continued development of supplier clusters has been a critical element in its strategy for sustainable competitive advantage.

Source: Based on Ryder and Fearne (2003: 12–16).

However, organizational dimensions also play a key role in the development of buyer–seller relationships. The behaviour of organizational buyers can be moderated by their company's specific corporate objectives, policies and procedures, organizational structure, and internal systems. The dominant policies and procedures established within the organization may induce different tactics with regard to how the purchasing department operates. For example, corporate policies may allow the use of intermediaries in foreign markets. Thus, if the organization relies on middlemen's part of the purchasing process, what types are to be employed? Can the *sogo-shoshas* used in dealing with the Japanese in their market, for example, be used when Japanese companies deal with foreign suppliers (Herbig and O'Hara, 1995: 13)?

Despite the benefits of global sourcing, there are drawbacks to this approach. High costs of travel and communications are common among organizations that pursue this strategy. In addition, increased costs associated with physical distribution—the extra logistics involved can add as much as 10–15% to the per unit cost of the product and the need for additional inventory buffers can add as much as 5–10% to the per unit cost—cash flow issues and paperwork concerns are considerations for the procurement manager to take into account (Herbig and O'Hara, 1995). The mini-case on Griffin Manufacturing illustrates the hidden costs in the pursuit of this strategy. A more detailed discussion on how supply chain costs affect international pricing, is covered in Chapter 14.

Market responsive manufacturing

Intelligent and highly competitive supply chains are characterized by a unique set of relations that typify the interconnections in a network which enables the achievement of competitive advantage through lower costs and/or greater differentiation. Christopher and Towill (2002) suggest the focus on supply chain strategies must shift from the idea of *cost* as the 'order winner' to *responsiveness* as the 'market winner'. The implication is that the emphasis in manufacturing in the future must be on *agility*.

The so-called 'agile' approach to manufacturing means that organizations must serve customers with small quantities of custom-designed parts with perfect quality, 100% on-time delivery, and at very low cost. Maskell (2001: 6–10) posits that the most important aspects of agile manufacturing include customer prosperity, people and information, and fitness for change, discussed below.

Customer prosperity

Agile manufacturers place a greater emphasis on being close to the customer and the value-added to the customer through the provision of products and services. This requires an intimate understanding of customers' needs, in the short-, medium-, and long-term.

To address the customer's real needs the organization must sell 'solutions' rather than 'products'. It needs to design or develop solutions focused specifically on an individual customer's requirements. Product design will need to be closely integrated with the production

MINI-CASE ILLUSTRATION The 'real' costs of offshore manufacturing

Griffin Manufacturing, Inc. (www.fashiondex.com) is a US sports-wear manufacturer. Established in 1990, Griffin has enjoyed a period of steady growth of approximately 20% per year. Within the first three years of operation, it was producing 20,000 garments per week.

The company went through a period of dramatic change in 1993 when it began to move the manufacturing to Honduras, while gradually eliminating domestic manufacturing. At first, the sewing that moved offshore was of basic styles. 'Basics' are the ongoing styles in a few colours that sell all year round. It made sense to move these offshore because the training required for machinery was minimum. The relative low labour and manufacturing costs in Honduras represented a significant efficiency saving. For example, a typical low-end sport bra at Griffin has six minutes of sewing labour, the average New England labour is US$7.50 per hour, resulting in a direct labour cost of US$0.75. Labour rates in Honduras are around US$0.29 per hour, for an assembly cost of US$0.03. Since overhead costs are at least twice the labour costs, reasonable estimates for the total labour costs are: Griffin, US$1.50, Honduras, US$0.06. Transportation and logistics costs are to be added, which amount to less than a penny a garment. From this perspective, the 'business case' is overwhelming: if you can sew the garment in Honduras for less than five cents, why bother making it in the USA for US$1.50?

Griffin quickly learned that there were a number of 'hidden costs' which did not appear in the direct (financial) costing:

(1) The Honduras cost of US$0.06 is not the real cost. Operator efficiency is significantly lower than in the USA. The efficiency slowly improves over time as operators learn and companies invest in new machines. Labour turnover in Caribbean factories can be very high, and rates of 40% a year are not unknown. This dramatically affects the quality and costs in training.

Logistics problems arise continually, and additional expensive staffs are required to manage the import and export of fabric and garments, e.g. garment labels that show the country of manufacture as well as style information, bar codes, washing instructions, etc. These labels are frequently late because they require detailed information from several departments and coordination is notoriously difficult. As a result, these labels are frequently express-mailed around the world at great expense.

There are also overheads that not always correctly attributed to the manufacturing budget. A US manufacturer that takes on a relationship with a factory in the Caribbean incurs significant overhead expenses as staff members travel abroad to correct problems.

(2) Fluctuations in consumer buying patterns and retailers demanding instant response stress the long production cycle times associated with offshore production. There is a trend in the retailing industry towards instant delivery, which the following example illustrates. Griffin received an emergency order for 500 white shorts with a 48-hour delivery schedule. The company had the right fabric on hand and was able to fulfil the order, which was part of a sales order worth US$950,000 for the customer, and it had been possible for this customer to generate almost a million dollars in sales only because Griffin was able to make the shorts—the extra cost of one dollar per garment was inconsequential compared to the opportunity to help the customer generate sales. For the first time, Griffin had found a cost justification to help move away from its goal of manufacturing everything offshore.

(3) The costs of unsold inventory can exceed the savings from offshore manufacturing. It is not unusual for both retailers and manufacturers to make a 25% error in the sales forecast of a significant percentage of styles. The forecasts for basic ongoing styles are usually rather better.

If the forecast for a mid-range jogging bra is 1,000 units, the current trend of manufacturing offshore means that an order must be placed some six to nine months in advance. It is only when the season begins that true customer demand is realized. If demand is high, the store will not have the inventory to satisfy their customers. Not only will the store lose sales, it also runs the risk of losing the customers. If demand is low, the store will be left with excess inventory. Some excess is acceptable because the store can draw in customers with sales and discounts. However, the overall result is costly. For example, the store purchased 250 extra garments at US$10, therefore accumulating US$2,500 of excess in inventory. Using the benchmark of US$1 per garment in labour savings (offshore manufacturing), the manufacture of all 1,000 garments offshore saved US$1,000, significantly less than the US$2,500 excess inventory.

If the store offered a 2-for-1 sale, it might argue that it would at least recover its wholesale cost. However, the overall margin for that style declines. There is also a hidden cost associated with selling the excess inventory at a discount. A customer who buys two items does not need to come in next season to buy another. The conclusion is that forecast errors can be much more costly than the savings from manufacturing offshore.

Source: Based on Warburton and Stratton (2002: 101–8).

process. This means the traditional approach of having all new products routed through a design area must be eliminated as this frequently causes delay and misunderstanding between product designers and the production floor. Products can be modularized to allow configuration rather than using separate designs for each product, thus simplifying the process.

People and information (i.e. the knowledge base)

The emphasis on customization of solutions and long-term relationships means that the organization increasingly needs to rely on the skills and knowledge of its people to manage the production and service delivery processes. This includes product knowledge and experience of customers' needs, anxieties, and service requirements. The relationships that develop between the organization and the customer become a part of the product.

This level of customer enrichment can only be achieved through the use of knowledge-based systems—linking the customers' information systems into the organization's systems. Orders can be placed automatically from customer and scheduled within the plant, yielding accurate delivery promises. The design requirements can be automatically picked up in the customers' information systems without drawings or specifications being printed and passed. This enables the organization to address customer needs with great agility.

Fitness for change

Change and customer focus require the people closest to the customer to have authority to change the organization's methods to address the customers' needs. For local decision-making to be effective, an organization must have a highly educated and trained workforce. They must be people who know and understand the organization's vision and principles, the customers' requirements, and the customization of products and services to fulfil those requirements. They must also know how to create cooperative alliances, how to reconfigure products, when to 'go the extra mile', and how to combine expertise towards a common goal. An agile organization often has smaller production and service centres geographically dispersed to enable customers to be served locally.

Integrated policies and processes

Most organizations have developed ways of doing things for historical reasons. They have made such processes difficult to change by computerizing them but have failed to attain the full benefits because they have not simplified, standardized, or integrated them into their supply chains. An order to deliver is the same transaction as an order to move something, or to process a metal, or to treat a patient, provided that the detail is handled via master data and not in the transaction, i.e. all supply chain orders are in essence performing the same function (McGuffog and Wadsley, 1999). How can cooperation be fostered without one endangering the other and losing the overall benefit to the final consumer of the product or service?

Since the functions of members are interdependent, integration of policies must be achieved. The supply chain members can jointly identify outdated policies, and assess how to compensate for making the changes. At the strategic level, senior management is responsible for broad policy-making, long-range planning, and resource allocation. They can jointly resolve conflicting issues which may arise from the creation of the competitive advantage that guides collaborative activities. For example, if a particular product mix is decided for a market segment, then the quality, price, and stock quantity must fit the predetermined policy. At the tactical level, procedural guidelines, such as collaborative plans, can be developed to reconcile conflicting decision criteria or individual objectives. Irrespective of their forms, all policies serve the primary purpose of aligning supply chain member behaviour with overall profitability (Simatupang and Sridharan, 2002).

In addition, alignment of internal process capability with the process requirement resulting from the collaboration initiative is crucial to enabling effective information exchange. In a study of supply chain collaboration in the electronics supply chain, IBM (2002: 11) found that the need to improve internal process capability might not be initially apparent to many companies. For example, at a communication original equipment manufacturer (OEM), the business consequences of a lack of forecast accuracy became obvious only when this company outsourced part of its manufacturing process and had to collaborate with the contract manufacturing company, which, in turn, had to make purchasing decisions based on that forecast. When the forecasting and procurement functions were reporting to the same organization, process inaccuracies could be masked with inventory. This was not possible with business partners contractually committed to target inventory levels based on the agreed forecast. In order to transition successfully to an outsourced model, this company had to upgrade its forecasting capabilities. The study concluded that process change is an opportunity to leverage emerging industries standards such as RosettaNet (www.rosettanet.org) for the electronics industry, and, by doing so, converge on process definitions with which business partners can easily integrate. The benefit of process standardization and integration is twofold. First, it will increase business partners' acceptance of collaboration as the proposed process will be more likely to fit their own processes. Secondly, it will facilitate the ongoing maintenance of the collaboration solution because only one unique process instance needs to be maintained and upgraded.

Information-sharing

Information, in particular the transparency and quality of information flows, plays an important role in many parts of strategic supply chain management. Supply chain members share the information in both forward and backward flows that provide adequate visibility across both internal functions and organizations. The data which are often shared, as Simatupang and Sridharan (2002) summarize, include the availability of resources (e.g. capacity, inventory, funds, and capability), the status of performance (e.g. time, quality, costs, and flexibility), the status of processes (e.g. forecasting, ordering, delivering, replenishing, and servicing), and the status of contract. Based on accurate data, the supply chain members can consider both external and internal factors to make informed decisions that directly relate to sales generation to end customers. A retailer, for instance, should be able to place an order on time with optimum quantity to meet unexpected demand by considering inventory data at the upstream sites, transportation costs, and delivery lead times.

Information-sharing provides substantial benefits to participating members. At the strategic level, information-sharing of business objectives enables individual managers to achieve mutual understanding of competitive advantage and cost efficiency throughout the chain. At the tactical level, the information integration helps the chain members to mitigate demand uncertainty and cope with decision-making complexity at different levels of planning in different organizations.

Developing a market responsive supply chain demands collaboration among all participants in the value chain, whatever their size, function, or relative position. It is the ability to respond to the changing needs of customers far down the demand chain that produces such strategic benefits as improved project design and more effective marketing. The order of magnitude increase in levels of collaboration and information-sharing will demand a new form of collaborative technology infrastructure. While there is no exact specification for an effective information-sharing infrastructure, certain fundamental attributes of a strategic supply chain network are crucial, including (Horvath, 2001: 206–7):

- Open, low-cost connectivity—smaller players must be able to access a collaborative infrastructure without major investments in proprietary technology. The role of application service providers, who host specific applications for use by others, will be critical in enabling smaller players to tap into a variety of collaborative systems in the collaborative process.

- Very large, flexible, multimedia data storage capabilities—the infrastructure for the value chain must be able to store and relate large quantities of data from many sources, in many media. These could include images, engineering drawings, and program codes as well as conventional data files and text documents.

- Systems and channel integration—participants must be able to integrate and access information regardless of the applications used (i.e. from sales to account payable to order management) or channels (e.g. websites, online marketplaces, intranets, call centres, etc.).

- Higher level self-service capabilities—to assure prompt and widespread customer adoption, these new capabilities must be easy to use, requiring little training. They should not only include access to order tracking, logistics, and billing information, but also 'intelligence' capabilities for automated product configuration, payment, and dispute resolution.

- Intelligence gathering and analysis—business intelligence capabilities need to be built in to analyse the ongoing flow of information that higher level self-service capabilities will generate. By analysing information drawn from the entire value chain, organizations can make improvements in internal operations and collaborative capabilities an ongoing process.

- Supply chain collaboration exchanges—advanced intelligent supply chain systems will offer exchanges that allow members of the value chain to collaborate in the design and development of products, manufacturing processes, logistic and distribution strategies, and all related forms of supply chain and demand chain planning.

- Sophisticated security capabilities—strategic collaboration makes more sensitive information available to larger constituencies. Infrastructure components, such as supply chain management exchanges, will need to enable fast and accurate decisions about access to sensitive engineering, financial, and customer data.

- New electronic commerce capabilities—to reduce costs and speedy settlements, the collaborative infrastructure will need to incorporate innovative financial arrangements, such as electronic billing and payment, automatic progress payments on expensive engineered products, and settlement netting among parties.

The use of information technology to share data between all actors is, in effect, creating a virtual supply chain. Virtual supply chains are information-based, rather than inventory-based. Shared information between supply chain partners can only be fully leveraged through process integration—collaborative working between buyers and suppliers, joint product development, common systems, and shared intelligence. As Christopher and Towill (2002) argue, this form of collaboration in the supply chain is becoming more prevalent as organizations focus on managing their core competences and outsource all other 'non-core' activities.

Performance measurement

The establishment of clear measures and measurement systems is fundamental to supporting collaborative supply chain excellence for a number of reasons. First, objective measurement facilitates fact-based decision-making, which is an important criteria of effective collaborative supply chain management. Secondly, measurement is an ideal way to communicate requirements to other members of the supply chain and to promote continuous improvement and change. Thirdly, measurement conveys to employees what is important by linking critical measures to desired business outcomes. Lastly, the measurement process helps companies identify whether new initiatives are producing the desired results. Measurement may be the single best tool to control a diverse set of supply chain activities and process (Trent, 2004) which, in the case of a multinational corporation, may be scattered across the globe.

There is no definitive or prescriptive set of supply chain measures, nor is there one best way to measure supply chain performance. However, the broad process of a performance measurement system requires the supply chain member to carry out four steps: design performance, facilitate performance, encourage performance, and intensify performance (Simatupang and Sridharan (2002: 21–3).

- Design performance means to develop a performance system that enables the chain members to monitor and improve chain performance. There are three components of a performance system, i.e. performance model, metrics, and measurement method. A performance model is a framework that links the overall performance with different levels of decision hierarchy among the individual members in meeting the objectives of the supply chain. For example, the balanced scorecard approach can be adopted as an initial performance model that provides a framework for looking at a strategy from four perspectives: financial, customer, internal business processes, and learning and growth.

  Performance metrics refer to measures that indicate the extent to which the mutual objectives have been accomplished. These may include level of customer satisfaction, supply chain response time, supply chain total costs, total inventory, and asset utilization. These measures can be translated into secondary measures for each of the members in the chain. They may then regularly collect, display, transfer, and analyse to determine how well their individual performance compares with desired global standards.

- Facilitating performance means developing an adequate performance information-sharing system and resource allocation. A performance information-sharing system provides dynamic communication to monitor and control the actual performance, and hence facilitates resource allocation.

- To encourage consistent performance, supply chain members need to provide a sufficient number of incentives that participating members value. Since members in the chain may have different needs for enforcement, incentives should be tailored so that members can choose from a menu of equitable-valued options.

- To intensify a performance system means regularly to compare and modify performance measures to suit emerging competitive imperatives. For example, the members may appoint external auditors to conduct customer satisfaction surveys or evaluate sales performance. The analysis can then be used to benchmark against the best practices of other competitive supply chains within (or even outside) the industry.

Chapter Summary

1. Gaining a competitive advantage in international supply chains requires matching the value-adding activities of a chain with the unique comparative advantages offered by diverse nations that make up the chain. The management of an effective supply chain requires the coordination of a wide range of activities and flows that extend across functional and organizational boundaries. These activities include: (a) inbound logistics; (b) operations; (c) outbound logistics; (d) marketing and sales; and (e) customer service.

2. Supply chains should be viewed as a set of interrelated processes/activities that need to be aligned, coordinated, and synchronized, rather than a series of discrete, non-aligned activities. These processes are designed to achieve a specific objective or outcome. Matching these activities and the sourcing decisions with appropriate country conditions can lead to strategic benefits in cost, quality, lead times, and perhaps innovation.

3. Market pressures for increased product complexity and variety based on a wide range of technologies and response at higher levels of quality and reliability but declining cost have demonstrated that few, if any, organizations can do it by themselves. Consequently, they need to supplement their core competences by joining with other providers of complementary competences to satisfy their customers.

4. There are two major types of relationship between buyer and suppliers: traditional 'adversarial competitive' and 'collaborative partnership'. The primary goal of the traditional adversarial approach is to minimize the price of purchased goods and services. The primary goal of the collaborative partnership approach is to focus on long-term strategic gains by establishing reliable and highly value-added relationships.

5. There are a variety of forms of potential supply chain collaboration, which can be divided into three main categories. Vertical collaboration occurs when two or more organizations, such as the manufacturers, the distributor, the carrier, and the retailer, share their responsibilities, resources, and performance information to serve similar end customers. Horizontal collaboration occurs when two or more unrelated or competing organizations cooperate to share information or resources, such as a joint distribution centre. A lateral collaboration aims to gain more flexibility by combining and sharing capabilities in both a vertical and horizontal manner.

6. Global sourcing is rapidly becoming a prerequisite to competing in today's marketplace. It has become a competitive weapon to maintain or gain market share. It requires the procurement manager to view the world as a potential source for raw materials, components, services, and finished goods. Organizations pursue international sourcing as a reaction to increased worldwide competition or a proactive strategy to gain competition advantage.

7. Intelligent and highly competitive supply chains are characterized by a unique set of relations that typify the interconnections between organizations in a network which enables the achievement of competitive advantage through lower costs and/or greater differentiation. The focus on supply chain strategies must shift from the idea of *cost* as the 'order winner' to *responsiveness* as the 'market winner'. The implication is that the emphasis in manufacturing in the future must be on *agility*. The agile approach to manufacturing means that organizations must serve customers with small quantities of custom-designed parts with perfect quality, 100% on-time delivery, and at very low cost.

8. Information, in particular the transparency and quality of information flows, plays an important role in many parts of strategic supply chain management. Supply chain members share information in both forward and backward flows that provide adequate visibility across both internal functions and organizations. It is the ability to respond to the changing needs of customers far down the demand chain that produces such strategic benefits as improved project design and more effective marketing.

9. The establishment of clear measures and measurement systems is fundamental to supporting supply chain excellence. There is no definitive or prescriptive set of supply chain measures, nor is there one best way to measure supply chain performance. However, the broad process of a performance measurement system requires the supply chain member to carry out four steps: design performance, facilitate performance, encourage performance, and intensify performance.

 END-OF-CHAPTER CASE STUDY **Re-engineering supply chain to achieve global competitive advantage**

Founded in Taiwan in 1988, Yue Yuen (www.yueyuen.com) is today's largest branded athletic and casual footwear manufacturer in the world, with production facilities in China, Vietnam, and Indonesia. The company is an original equipment manufacturer (OEM) as well as an original design manufacturer (ODM) for a number of high street brands, including Nike (www.nike.com), Adidas (www.adidas.com), Asics (www.asics.com), New Balance (www.newbalance.com), Puma (www.puma.com), Timberland (www.timberland.com), and Rockport (www.rockport.com).

Yue Yuen achieved good financial results in 2005 despite a challenging and increasingly demanding market environment. Sales rose 16% year-on-year to US$3.155 billion, making it the thirteenth consecutive year in which it achieved an increase in sales since listing on the Hong Kong Stock Exchange. Underpinning the rise was a sustained increase in orders from existing customers and the addition of new accounts. However, the surge in the contribution from Chinese retail operations was the driver behind its phenomenal growth. The company now accounts for approximately 17% of the combined wholesale value of the world's athletic and casual shoes market.

Nonetheless, the market environment is getting more difficult due to the surge in oil and petrochemical prices, increases in labour costs, higher utility costs, and the appreciation in the Chinese yuan. Production costs cannot be contained without drastically re-engineering its global supply chain. To achieve this, the company needs to establish much closer working relationships with its all its partners. Cooperative planning, real-time exchange of information, and commitment to high service levels are essential for each partner. The company needs to constantly re-evaluates its operational partnerships, including raw material suppliers, manufacturers, and logistics providers. It also needs to enhance its partnerships with key retailers to ensure that the supply chain is optimized from end to end, from the raw material supplier to the retailer.

To achieve this, the company has set the following strategic goals:

• to eliminate 10 weeks from product development and four weeks from the procurement cycle (20% lead-time reduction versus the 2000 cycle); and

• to reduce the time from product concept to retail delivery from the current 18 months to less than nine months over the next three years (50% lead-time reduction versus the 2000 cycle).

The company realizes that only when the so-called 'upstream' and 'downstream' activities within its supply chains are completely integrated would it be possible to ensure its production reaches the right quality at the right cost. **Design and development** is at the beginning of the supply chain. In this process, customer concepts of demand are transformed into shoe samples. The quality of design and development has a strong effect on sales and market share. Within this process, the company has developed an information system that feeds into the computer-aided design (CAD), communication, and work-flow control, event-tracking, inventory-management, etc. The entire design and development function is centralized in a purpose-built Development Centre supported by over a 1,000 employees, which is twice the size of a typical Chinese shoe factory. The Development Centre makes it possible to convert product concepts into shoe prototypes for customer evaluation, and then quickly into production. The R&D efforts are focused on the development of new raw materials and the streamlining of production processes, with the aim of developing well-designed footwear and shorter production cycles.

After the product is designed, the company set about **planning production and scheduling**. This planning has two levels: (a) macro planning, which forecasts production and turnover rates for periods up to a year ahead; and (b) micro planning, which involves planning the production process for each product line. Inputs to this process include semi-manufactured goods such as leather, sole, and other component materials, and output is the finished shoes. In this process, semi-manufactured goods are fed to production lines according to production plans that are based on customer orders. All aspects of this particular production process, including raw material purchasing, semi-manufactured goods manufacturing, manufacturing of finished goods, etc., are planned to the last detail.

This is then followed by the last aspect of the supply chain—**outbound logistics**. It consists of: (a) physical distribution and transportation; (b) invoice and payment management; and (c) inventory control and information flows. Wholesaling and retailing are two processes that push finished goods to the consumption process from the production process; they are bridges between production and consumption, and relate to sales. Operations in these two processes include packing, display, etc., and finished goods are moved from racks to boxes and then on to the retailers. Transportation is a critical process in wholesale and retailing. The factory receives transportation data in electronic form, and finished goods are moved from the manufacturer's warehouse to customer warehouses by land (or by air if finished goods are delayed or there is a special customer request).

To implement its re-engineered supply chain management strategy, Yue Yuen needs the most important ingredient—its people. From administrative employees to management executives, everyone in the company has to embrace a new corporate culture which orientes towards long-term stable and continuous development. This means that they no longer care only about the development itself, but endeavour towards a win–win process for all the 'chains' in the supply chain, requiring a focus on the connections among and cooperation with all their partners. They no longer regard themselves as one independent Group, but as a supply chain partner.

Source: Based on Du (2007: 527–43).

Case discussion questions

1 Using information in the case study and your own knowledge of the footwear industry, conduct a brief analysis of the opportunities and threats confronting Yue Yuen in the future. In what ways do the results of your analysis provide a rationale for the company to re-engineer its global supply chain?

2 Discuss how the re-engineering of Yue Yeun's supply chain may benefit its business. What do you think may be the potential, hidden problems?

3 In developing a 'new' corporate culture' for the re-engineered supply chain management strategy, what do you think would be the problems that the company might encounter?

END-OF-CHAPTER EXERCISES

1 What is a supply chain? What activities does a supply chain consist of?

2 Briefly explain the fundamentals of effective supply chain management.

3 Discuss the factors that affect global supply chain decisions.

4 Why do organizations collaborate in the supply chain?

5 What are the two main types of buyer–seller relationship?

6 Briefly describe the three categories of supply chain collaboration.

7 What is global sourcing? What can organizations gain from such a practice?

8 What is the so-called 'agile' approach to manufacturing? Why is agility so important in today's manufacturing?

9 When organizations collaborate, why is it important to consider integrated policies and processes, and information-sharing?

10 Briefly discuss the main reasons for establishing clear measures and measurement systems in supporting supply chain collaborations.

DISCUSSION AND EXAMINATION QUESTIONS

1 Why should supply chains be viewed as a set of interrelated processes and activities that need to be aligned, coordinated, and synchronized, rather than a series of discrete, non-aligned activities? What are the fundamentals of effective supply chain management?

2 With examples, discuss the influential factors which affect a global supply chain and their implications on organizations within the chain.

3 The ability to become a world-class competitor in today's global marketplace is based to a great degree on the ability to establish high levels of trust and cooperation with partners in the supply chain. Taking an example of a supply chain of your choice, show how the establishment of trust and cooperation with partners in the supply has made the organization world-class.

4 Global sourcing is rapidly becoming a prerequisite for competing in today's marketplace. Why do you think this is? Discuss how an organization may seek to develop its international sourcing experience.

5 The establishment of clear measures and measurement systems are fundamental to supporting collaborative supply chain excellence. Examine the validity of this statement to an organization with which you are familiar.

6 Why do you think information-sharing and establishing integrated policies and processes are critical to supply chain collaborations? Discuss with examples.

FURTHER READING

Barratt, M. (2004), 'Understanding the meaning of collaboration in the supply chain', *Supply Chain Management: An International Journal*, 9(1), 30–42.

Du, L. (2007), 'Acquiring competitive advantage in industry through supply chain integration: a case study of Yue Yuen Industrial Holdings Ltd.', *Journal of Enterprise Information Management*, 20(5), 527–43.

Ryder, R. and Fearne, A. (2003), 'Procurement best practice in the food industry: supplier clustering as a source of strategic competitive advantage', *Supply Chain Management: An International Journal*, 8(1), 12–16.

Warburton, R. D. H. and Stratton, R. (2002), 'Questioning the relentless shift to offshore manufacturing', *Supply Chain Management: An International Journal*, 7(2), 101–8.

REFERENCES

Christopher, M. and Towill, D. R. (2002), 'Developing market-specific supply chain strategies', *The International Journal of Logistics Management*, 12(1), 1–14.

Du, L. (2007), 'Acquiring competitive advantage in industry through supply chain integration: a case study of Yue Yuen Industrial Holdings Ltd.', *Journal of Enterprise Information Management*, 20(5), 527–43.

Fraser, J., Fraser, N., and McDonald, F. (2000), 'The strategic challenge of electronic commerce', *Supply Chain Management: An International Journal*, 5(1), 7–14.

Herbig, P. and O'Hara, B. S. (1995), 'Broadening horizons: the practice of global relationships in procurement', *Management Decisions*, 33(9), 12–16.

Horvath, L. (2001), 'Collaboration: the key to value creation in supply chain management', *Supply Chain Management: An International Journal*, 6(5), 205–7.

Humphreys, P. K., Shiu, W. K., and Chan, F. T. S. (2001), 'Collaborative buyer–supplier relationships in Hong Kong manufacturing firms', *Supply Chain Management: An International Journal*, 6(4), 152–62.

IBM Global Services (2002), 'All together now: supply chain collaboration in the electronics value chain', www.ibm.com.

Jiang, B. (2002), 'How international firms are coping with supply chain issues in China', *Supply Chain Management: An International Journal*, 7(4), 184–8.

—— and Hansen, J. D. (2003), 'Matsushita realigns its supply chain in China', *Supply Chain Management: An International Journal*, 8(3), 185–9.

Macbean, N. (2003), 'Corporate social responsibility in China: is it any of your business?', *China–Britain Trade Review*, March.

Maskell, B. (2001), 'The age of agile manufacturing', *Supply Chain Management: An International Journal*, 6(1), 5–11.

Mattsson, L.-G. (2003), 'Reorganisation of distribution in globalisation of markets: the dynamic context of supply chain management', *Supply Chain Management: An International Journal*, 8(5), 416–26.

McGuffog, T. and Wadsley, N. (1999), 'The general principles of value chain management', *Supply Chain Management: An International Journal*, 4(5), 218–25.

Mohan, K. and Berkowitz, M. (1988), 'Raw material procurement strategy: the differential advantage in the success of japanese steel', *Journal of Purchasing and Materials Management*, 24(1), Spring.

Monczka, R. M. and Trent, R. J. (1991), 'Global sourcing: a development approach', *International Journal of Purchasing and Materials Management*, Spring, 2–8.

Prasad, S. and Sounderpandian, F. (2003), 'Factors influencing global supply chain efficiency: implications for information systems', *Supply Chain Management: An International Journal*, 8(3), 241–50.

Ryder, R. and Fearne, A. (2003), 'Procurement best practice in the food industry: supplier clustering as a source of strategic competitive advantage', *Supply Chain Management: An International Journal*, 8(1), 12–16.

Simatupang, T. M. and Sridharan, R. (2002), 'The Collaborative Supply Chain', *International Journal of Logistics Management*, 12(1), 15–30.

Trent, R. J. (2004), 'What everyone needs to know about SCM', *Supply Chain Management Review*, March, 52–60.

Warburton, R. D. H. and Stratton, R. (2002), 'Questioning the relentless shift to offshore manufacturing', *Supply Chain Management: An International Journal*, 7(2), 101–8.

online resource centre

Visit the companion website to this book for lots of interesting additional material, including self-assessment questions, internet exercises, and links for each chapter:

http://www.oxfordtextbooks.co.uk/orc/lee_carter2e/

CHAPTER THIRTEEN

Managing Global Marketing Relationships

Chapter overview

Chapter Introduction — 413

What is a Marketing Relationship? — 413

    The importance of managing relationships — 413

    Key drivers in the growth of relational perspectives — 414

    From transactional marketing to relationship marketing? — 416

Managing Marketing Relationships — 419

    Some key characteristics of RM — 419

    Managerial implications — 421

Relationships and Networks — 424

    A network perspective — 424

    Classifying relationships and stakeholders — 424

Customer (Vertical Downstream) Relationships — 425

    B2C relations — 425

    B2B relations — 427

Supplier (Vertical Upstream) Relationships — 428

    Relations with goods suppliers — 428

    Relations with service suppliers — 428

Lateral (Horizontal) Partnerships — 430

    Competitor and other alliances — 430

    NGOs and NFP organizations — 433

    National governments — 434

Internal Partnerships — 434

    Employees — 434

    Functional departments — 435

Strategic Challenges in Managing Relationships — 436

    E-commerce relationships — 436

    Measuring relationship success — 437

    Potential complexity in management — 439

Chapter Summary — 441

Learning objectives

After studying this chapter, the reader will be able to:

- understand how relationship management can contribute to an organization's success;
- recognize the various global partners or stakeholders with which an organization may form relationships;
- adopt a network perspective to global marketing strategy formulation.

Management issues

The management issues that arise from this chapter include:

- In what ways does relationship management add value to the success of a business?
- Does a 'one-size-fits-all' approach do justice to the complexities of relationship management in a global context?
- How should an organization best manage its global relationships, particularly with regard to corporate social responsibility?

Chapter Introduction

Relationship management has become an important element of strategic thinking. Organizations worldwide (or more accurately, the managers who represent them) realize the need to build and sustain relationships with their customers and with other key stakeholders. It has been argued that the goal of marketing activity has now shifted from a transactional, short-term focus towards a need to seek and forge long-term (typically profitable) relationships with targeted customers (or stakeholders). This chapter reflects this trend and examines processes of global marketing within this challenging context. It demonstrates how an understanding of the principles of relationship marketing can offer organizations the potential to achieve sustainable competitive advantage.

The chapter begins by explaining why relationship marketing has become such a significant issue in today's global marketplace. The managerial implications of a relational approach are outlined. We then extend the notion of relationships to one of global networks and outline the various stakeholder 'markets' with which it may be necessary for an organization trading globally to maintain good relationships. Managing relations with each key stakeholder group is explored in detail and examples of good and bad practice are provided. These examples will reflect consumer and business markets (including not-for-profit organizations), and examine relationships in goods and service sectors. The impact of new technologies on relationship management practices will also be addressed.

What is a Marketing Relationship?

The importance of managing relationships

The poet John Donne (1572–1631) pronounced that 'no man is an island', and it is becoming clear to managers in forward-looking organizations that 'no business is an island'. Every organization needs to interact with other organizations—and every manager with other managers—in order for successful market exchanges to take place. This is especially important in business-to-business (B2B) markets within typical supply chains, but extends to organizations operating in business-to-customer (B2C) markets as well.

Evidence abounds of the importance of relationships, especially those termed 'alliances', i.e. where organizations cooperate closely with other organizations, sometimes even with their apparent competitors. Such relationships have a significant impact on commercial performance, with one recent survey showing that the most 'alliance-intensive' fast-moving consumer goods (FMCG) manufacturers typically delivered returns to their shareholders four times greater than average (Cook et al., 2003). These are examples of global corporations who have committed over 20% of their assets to alliances:

- Pepsi's (www.pepsi.com) joint venture with Starbucks (www.starbucks.com) has created innovative new products such as 'ready-to-drink' coffees like Frappucino.
- General Mills (www.generalmills.com) has formed a partnership with Nestlé (www.nestle.com) in order to market breakfast cereals outside North America.
- Hewlett-Packard (www.hp.com) has 70 engineers working closely with designers from its Taiwanese suppliers, enabling HP to introduce 40% more new laptop models every year.

- Coca-Cola (www.coke.com) collaborates with Danone (www.danonegroup.com) in bottled water distribution, allowing the two companies to reach new market segments.
- Mobile phone company '3' (www.three.co.uk/index.omp) has teamed up with MTV Europe (www.mtveurope.com) to offer music video downloads to its subscribers.

It is not only businesses that gain from these partnerships; customers benefit too. In the airline sector, the combination of code-sharing and anti-trust (monopoly) immunity currently held by some members of the Star Alliance means that customers saved US$100 million in 1999. Airlines working together in this alliance include Air Canada (www.aircanada.ca), Lufthansa (www.lufthansa.com), Singapore Airlines (www.singaporeair.com), and United Airlines (www.ual.com). The relationships forged between these companies have allowed customers access to routes worldwide via a travel experience that is as seamless as flying on just one airline. In addition to the convenience gains, passengers also benefit from lower fares (Egan, 2001).

'Relationship marketing' (RM) has brought 'relationships' back into mainstream marketing theory and practice (Sheth and Parvatiyar, 1995), at least in Western corporate markets. Relationships have always been a fundamental part of exchange in many Eastern cultures. Even in Western cultures, relationship management has been used, especially in the marketing activities of small and medium-sized enterprises (SMEs). Nevertheless, RM is now high profile and we shall explore some of the reasons for its development, especially on the global stage.

Key drivers in the growth of relational perspectives

A number of factors have led to the prominence of relational thinking in modern corporate strategy. Relationships, particularly at the inter-organizational level, present organizations with value-enhancing opportunities. They can be used to leverage competences in order to offer superior customer value. Within manufacturing, relationships allow organizations to achieve modularity in product and process design, whereby component parts can be designed separately yet function as a whole. Value can be enhanced 'upstream' in a marketing channel through cooperation on research and development and prototypes, and 'downstream' in more effective distribution and promotion (Samie and Walters, 2003).

Ever-increasing levels of macro environmental turbulence and market diversity have also lead to the growth of relationships. Organizations need to be able to respond quickly to changing customer needs. They frequently seek partnerships with other organizations in order to serve fragmented markets, particularly those involving complex technologies. In most sectors, R&D costs have escalated and the 'window of opportunity' for getting products and services to market has shortened, pushing organizations to work together in joint new product development (NPD) programmes (Sheth and Parvatiyar, 1995). Here, collaboration can reduce risks by minimizing ownership and investment in production, distribution, and human resources.

A good example of this is the group of manufacturers collaborating with Mercedes-Benz (www.mercedes-benz.com) to produce the 'Smart Car' (www.smart.com). This was started as a collaborative venture between Daimler Benz (www.daimlerchrysler.com) and the Swiss watch company behind 'Swatch' (www.swatch.com). The car is assembled at a factory in France from modules provided by seven strategic partners which operate their own facilities alongside the main assembly line. For instance, ThyssenKrupp (www.thyssenkrupp.de) makes the engine mounting while Bosch (www.bosch.com) manufactures the front module. All the partners are responsible for running their own area of the operation and paying their own workforce. The companies get financial rewards only when the cars are built.

MINI-CASE ILLUSTRATION Cutting it in the world of fashion

An organization that manages its relationships with great success is Benetton (www.benetton.com), the manufacturer and marketer of fashion knitwear, based in northern Italy. This company has grown in 30 years from a 'cottage industry' to become Italy's largest clothing company. Its downstream retail network, many of which are franchises, are able to re-order stock with confidence due to the company's excellent EDI (electronic data exchange) system. Careful planning of production upstream enables Benetton to call on the relationships it has developed with local sub-contractors. Thus, only operations such as design and packing, which enhance cost-efficiency through economies of scale, are performed in-house. All other manufacturing, including labour-intensive finishing, are completed by a local network of 200 suppliers and 850 sub-contractors, most of which are small family businesses. These companies are closely linked to Benetton's information systems. The company's investment in managing relationships has been repaid with the fastest cycle times in the industry and near-perfect customer service (Christopher, 1997). As long as these factors are valued sufficiently highly by customers, they allow companies like Benetton to maintain high margins in their selling prices.

In economic terms, there has been widespread recognition of the profitability impact of customer retention. Research suggests a number of reasons for this (e.g. Reicheld and Sasser, 1990). The cost of acquiring new customers can be substantial. Established customers tend to buy more and place more consistent orders, thus becoming less costly to serve. Satisfied customers may be willing to pay premium prices to a supplier they know and trust, and often refer new customers through positive word of mouth (WOM). Finally, the ability to retain customers can be a significant barrier to entry to competitors.

Maximizing the 'lifetime value' of a customer is thus a fundamental goal of relationship management. This can be defined as the future flow of net profit, discounted back to the present, that can be attributed to a particular customer (Christopher et al., 2002). In taking this approach, companies are forced to recognize that not all customers are equally profitable, so they must customize their strategies to enhance the profitability of the customers they wish to target. The so-called 'Pareto rule' suggests that 80% of the total sales volume of a company is generated by just 20% of its customers. Furthermore, 80% of the total costs of servicing a company's customers will probably be incurred by only 20% of the customers (unfortunately not the same 20%). Organizations must be careful not to invest in unselective customer acquisition only to find they have attracted a customer base that is unprofitable. This happened in the mobile phone market, where many low-usage consumers were gained by organizations which had not considered the long-term impact of maintaining relationships with these individuals.

In B2C markets most attempts at building customer loyalty have focused on creating strong brands, typically involving mass-media communications. Today, however, evidence points to a gradual decline in brand loyalty. Instead, we find an increased willingness by consumers to choose from a portfolio of brands. One explanation for this is that customers do not perceive much difference in product quality between competing brands. Another factor is that consumers see their relationship as being more with the retailer than with the brand. Thus, store loyalty must also be considered by manufacturers (Christopher et al., 2002). This means maintaining good relations with intermediaries, something which can be difficult. But how can companies regain the loyalty of their end users? Some organizations have found ways of developing a dialogue with consumers that complements existing indirect channels. This can be achieved by the internet, e.g. in the case of car manufacturers Ford (www.ford.com), General Motors (www.gm.com), and Daimler-Chrysler (www.daimlerchrysler.com), which have established the parts-buying website Covisint. This enables them to offer end customers a huge assortment of products plus lower prices through greater buying power over global suppliers. The parts suppliers' catalogues have had to be integrated in order to cope with language and currency differences (Karpinski, 2002).

A relational approach can build on partnerships to reduce uncertainty of foreign markets by bridging the knowledge gap, a gap that can be especially challenging when the exporting company and its products are not well known. The gathering and exchange of market information has been facilitated by changes in technology, but the value of that information can be greatly enhanced if relationships are built on knowledge (Peppers and Rogers, 2000). When a customer gives an organization information, then it is the responsibility of the company to customize its offering to that customer. From that point, the relationship can be said to have begun and should get 'smarter' with every interaction.

Organizations in 'smart' relationships are clearly in a strong position to challenge globally. Hence, we find FMCG manufacturers happy to trade information on their best-performing brands with retailers in exchange for their knowledge of local sales patterns. This provides both organizations with better information on burgeoning consumer markets, such as Poland where supermarket retailing is set to expand rapidly. The UK retailer Sainsbury's (www.sainsbury.co.uk) has opened stores throughout Eastern Europe and is able to provide manufacturers with comprehensive insight into trading conditions and customer needs. In theory, all members of the supply chain, from supplier to end user, should benefit from these relationships, in what has become known as efficient consumer response (ECR).

A significant trend in B2B relations is the decision by many large manufacturers to reduce the number of suppliers with whom they deal. The buying organization gains in a number of ways: costs of switching between suppliers are eliminated, decision-making is simplified, suppliers organize themselves in a more buyer-focused manner, and quantity discounts may be negotiated. Car giants such as Ford and General Motors have been ruthless in cutting their supplier numbers by over 50% in the last decade. This means that purchasing managers look to place a much greater share of their spend with a smaller set of trusted suppliers. Moreover, due to the increased globalization of manufacturing, a supplier who wishes to gain US business typically has to be able to supply parts to factories in Germany or Brazil. Unless a component supplier can offer Ford (as a company) an extremely reliable service and a high amount of information exchange over production schedules, and offer the purchasing manager (as an individual) a suitable degree of respect and cooperation, then the supplier will not be regarded as a 'preferred supplier'. Without careful relationship management, a supplier could clearly lose business.

These changes have begun to shape managerial perspectives of what 'marketing' means.

From transactional marketing to relationship marketing?

The marketing discipline was initially dominated by US-based consumer goods mass-marketing approaches. However, the so-called '4Ps' (or marketing mix) model of transactional marketing (TM) was to become too restrictive for modern business practice. After the 1960s the market conditions that had favoured TM began to change. Many consumer markets became saturated, population growth was declining, and customers were becoming more demanding. However, much marketing practice did not reflect these changes and continued to be based on short-term economic transactions. Managers appeared to be guilty of viewing their customers in two ways: (a) as virtually passive recipients of promotional messages from marketers, and/or (b) as one half of adversarial relationships. This left TM as nothing more than 'hit and run' marketing (Buttle, 1996), without any consideration of future contact. Expenditure was usually directed at acquiring more customers instead of looking after existing ones.

During the 1980s and 1990s relationship marketing (RM) emerged as an alternative approach to TM. Rather than basing its principles on consumer goods markets, RM developed from relationship issues surfacing in industrial and service marketing. Instead of manipulating the marketing mix, RM attempted to manage the relationships that are the context for trading. Relationships are founded on the creation and delivery of superior customer value on a sustained basis. For relationships to succeed, both parties must receive a degree of 'value'.

For instance, the value proposition of Dell Computers (www.dell.com) is based on a promise to assemble a disparate set of technical equipment in the way that the individual global customer desires, and to have it working properly at the customer's premises within a few days. In order to achieve this rapid response, Dell has an exclusive deal with Business Post (www.business-post.com), a UK parcel delivery company. Business Post delivers PCs made by Dell, at their European manufacturing plant in Ireland, to UK homes and offices (Thapar, 2004). As long as Dell's target customers continue to value the customization and speed of service that the company offers, Dell should be able to maintain good relations with its customers, who in turn will provide the value that Dell require by continuing to spend money with them and not with their competitors.

Rather than attempting to manage customer awareness and preferences through mass communication, as is often the case with TM, RM seeks to establish individualized, personal links with customers. It tries to create this 'intimacy' via strong personal appeal and continuing commitment, recognizing that at all times customers can be a highly active agents (Varey, 2002), capable of taking their business elsewhere if their needs are ignored.

The ways in which RM differs from the transactional perspective of marketing is illustrated in Fig. 13.1.

RM embodies the following elements (Christopher et al., 2002):

- It involves a managerial shift in perspective from purely economic transactions to the 'fuzzier' boundaries of socio-economic exchange (i.e. recognizing that relationships involve *people*).

- It understands the economics of customer retention, as opposed to merely attracting customers.

- It recognizes the need for quality, customer service, and marketing to be closely integrated.

Fig. 13.1 The shift from 'transactions' to 'relationships'

- It extends the principles of relationship management to a range of market domains.
- It highlights the role of internal marketing in achieving external marketing success and ensures that marketing is considered cross-functionally.

Reflecting the notion of lifetime value in managing relationships, Gordon (1998: 9) describes RM as: 'The process of identifying and creating new value with individual customers and then sharing the benefits of this over the lifetime of association.' Another widely cited definition of RM is that of Grönroos (1994: 9), in which he describes the objectives of RM as to:

> [i]dentify and establish, maintain and enhance and, when necessary, terminate relationships with customers and other stakeholders, at a profit so that the objectives of all parties involved are met; and this is done by mutual exchange and fulfilment of promises.

No definition is ever perfect, but this, with its reference to a series of stakeholders, is sufficient with an added caveat—the achievement of 'profit' is, of course, not necessarily an objective of the not-for-profit (NFP) organizations covered below.

The practice of marketing is never as clear-cut as any textbook definition would suggest. In fact, marketing managers themselves confirm that there may be four types of marketing practised by contemporary organizations, sometimes simultaneously (Brodie et al., 1997). These range from TM to three types of RM:

- database marketing;
- interactive marketing; and
- network marketing.

There is a degree of overlap between the terms and the strategies used (Egan, 2001). These forms of RM can be described more generally as:

- direct marketing;
- relationship marketing (B2C); and
- relationship marketing (B2B).

It is thus too simplistic to see marketing strategy merely as TM versus RM. Generally, it is possible only to have close relations with a limited number of customers, whether they are business customers or consumers. This applies equally to managing relationships with suppliers.

 MINI-CASE ILLUSTRATION Making waves in the swimwear market

The relationship portfolio approach is illustrated by the international maker of swimwear, Speedo (www.speedo.com). The company has three distinct 'interface structures' (Christopher and Juttner, 2000). First, it has a traditional sales force that deals with small independent sports stores. Because these stores are low-volume customers for Speedo but represent channels where the company's brand power might be eroded by competitors, the company places strong emphasis on experienced salespeople and staff retention. Secondly, the segment represented by high street retailers and sports multiples accounts for a growing share of the company's business. Here dedicated account managers in both Speedo and its trade customers work closely, supported by

other functions within the company. Thirdly, the company is developing even closer relationships with two particular customers, one of which is Europe's biggest independent sports retailer. This relationship is crucial for Speedo since, as well as the high economic potential, the retailer stocks only leading brands and no own-label products. A specially selected team, led by the company's operations director, works exclusively on this account. In addition, Speedo forges relationships with its end users (i.e. individual swimmers), for example by sponsoring children's swimming clubs. Finally, the company continues to invest in building its brand profile via conventional (TM-based) advertising campaigns.

A hybrid managerial approach incorporating elements of both RM and TM may be the most appropriate response to prevailing market circumstances. Rather than suggesting that, for example, a highly interactive 'one-to-one' form of RM should take over as an organization's single new marketing strategy, a more viable approach is to develop a portfolio of relationships.

Managing Marketing Relationships

We now turn to consider what a marketer should take into account in attempting to manage relationships.

Some key characteristics of RM

A fundamental tenet of RM is an emphasis on 'loyalty' through strategies that aim to retain customers, and thus improve profitability. This can be seen with Vodafone (www.vodafone.com). Rather than enticing mobile phone users with introductory offers and associated free gifts, the company decided to focus on encouraging its distribution channel to generate long-term customers who will be retained through the company's superior customer service. In an arrangement that affects the management of relations between Vodafone and its distributors, these partners will receive reduced bonuses for winning 'pay as you go' customers. Even though this increases high street starting prices, the company's senior management believe that their move to reward distributors for what they term 'quality customers' rather than the quantity of customers is the right one for the development of the business in Europe, the Middle East, and Africa (Christopher et al., 2002).

In general, we can identify several stages of relationship development. These are shown in Fig. 13.2. The ladder is relevant for all elements of a company's supply chain: company buyers, intermediaries, and end users. The ideal is to move a customer up the ladder, from being merely a 'prospect', through the 'customer' stage, and on to becoming a 'partner', or at least an 'advocate'.

In order for loyalty and a relationship to flourish there should be trust, commitment, and communication between the interested parties. The first two of these elements are

Fig. 13.2 The stages of relationship development

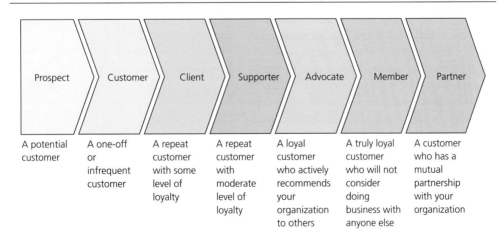

Prospect	Customer	Client	Supporter	Advocate	Member	Partner
A potential customer	A one-off or infrequent customer	A repeat customer with some level of loyalty	A repeat customer with moderate level of loyalty	A loyal customer who actively recommends your organization to others	A truly loyal customer who will not consider doing business with anyone else	A customer who has a mutual partnership with your organization

Source: Based on Christopher et al. (2002).

almost inseparable. Trust within business is a highly complex area, but has been defined by Blois (1997: 58) as: 'An acceptance of vulnerability to another's possible, but not expected, ill will or lack of good will.'

Trust can be viewed as a relationship 'atmosphere' that results from cooperation, based on predictability, dependability, and faith. It appears to reduce risk perception in relationships, i.e. each party believes that the other will not take unfair advantage. Trust that develops through social interaction between individuals can often be more important than legally binding contracts. Thus, if a Caribbean banana producer is confident that a US supermarket's produce buyer will not ruthlessly exploit their powerful position in the marketing channel (perhaps by constantly demanding unreasonable price cuts), a good relationship is possible.

Commitment is defined by Morgan and Hunt (1994: 230) as: 'An exchange partner believing that an ongoing relationship with another is so important as to warrant maximum efforts at maintaining it.' Commitment motivates partners' efforts to preserve a relationship and to resist alternative offers. It is unclear whether commitment is the outcome of growing trust or whether trust develops from the decision to commit to one supplier. Nevertheless, trust and commitment are required for organizations to consider adaptations to meet partner needs, especially in international markets. For instance, Toyota UK (www.toyota.com.uk) may request that a European component supplier radically redesigns its production line in order to fulfil orders for a new car model. Without a belief that Toyota UK will remain a loyal customer, the supplier will be reluctant to invest in adapting its facilities accordingly. Trust and commitment also provide a barrier to a customer leaving the relationship in favour of short-term (possibly cheaper) supply.

It is largely through communication that trust and commitment are developed. Whichever source of communication is employed, consistency is the key, with inconsistency leading to annoyance and antipathy. Customers can easily become disenchanted, for example, if they receive a mail-shot from an international hotel chain telling them about a special offer, and then find, via the hotel's website, that the offer is restricted (e.g. applies only to stays of three nights or more). And then discover, when they phone for a personal explanation, a computerized answering machine. Organization should focus on creating a 'relationship dialogue'. This will enable both the company and the customer to 'reason' together and eventually develop a 'knowledge platform' that will add value to customers as well as help to forge the relationship (Grönroos, 2000).

Customer service is also important in forging relationships. There is, after all, little point encouraging dialogue in a relationship if the feedback from customers is about the poor service. The challenge to the organization is to align marketing, quality, and customer service strategies closely (Christopher et al., 2002). Organizational structures that allow diverse functions, such as production, sales, and logistics, to interact with a common goal of fulfilling customer relationship maintenance are essential (see section on Functional Departments below). In the case of our hotel company, information systems for central bookings, telesales, tourist web pages, and individual hotel reception desks should clearly be linked, something which leading chains such as Holiday

Provision of quality service plays a vital role in forging relationships with customers. Customers who are fed up with poor customer service are unlikely to want to engage in a meaningful dialogue.

Inn (www.holiday-inn.com) and Best Western (www.bestwestern.co.uk) appear to have got right.

Finally, a strong relationship is characterized by shared benefits and a sense of mutuality (Varey, 2002). For most selling organizations, the benefit is revenue. In contrast, what might staff in a non-profit organization, such as a health authority, gain from an 'exchange', perhaps based on educating a target market? The satisfaction of lowering mortality rates from heart disease in the UK or from AIDS in Africa? For customers, benefits are typically those derived from ownership and/or access to a good quality product or service. They also include emotional benefits such as reduced anxiety, recognition, or preferential treatment. Mutuality implies that relationships should be 'win-win' reciprocal situations where each partner provides for the other through exchange. Each exchange interaction will be affected by what has gone before and what may happen in the future. Thus the 'hit and run' mentality of TM has severe limitations in a relationship-building context. For instance, an aggressive, high-pressure salesperson who always achieves his/her monthly sales volume targets, but does so by misleading clients, will be costing a company's long-term income stream. This was certainly the case in the UK's financial services industry. Here, mis-selling errors occurred in the 1990s when some major international institutions, such as HSBC (www.hsbc.com) and Barclays (www.barclays.co.uk), were alleged to have given poor mortgage advice to householders. Their corporate reputations were severely tarnished as result.

Managerial implications

The relational drivers and characteristics outlined above mean that marketers must consider the relationship dynamics of international operations (Donaldson and O'Toole, 2002). For example:

(a) markets may be entry-blocked by existing local relationships and organizations;

(b) entry and location decisions may be driven by customer organizations;

(c) personal contacts may inform companies about which markets they could enter;

(d) relationship failures may force an exit from certain markets; or

(e) close intra-cultural relations may exclude a business from a particular network.

A relational view assumes that organizations are interdependent on other organizations and therefore cannot control the traditional sequential methods of decision-making in international marketing. We therefore need to learn more about relationships in a global context (Axelsson and Johansson, 1992). Managers may need to ask:

• Who are the main players in the target international market?

• What are the relative positions of each of the organizations in the network?

• What are the relations of the manager's organization to actors/stakeholders in the potential international market?

• How can the resources of other actors be mobilized in support of market entry?

There are a number of managerial implications resulting from the growth of an RM approach to global marketing. First is perhaps the realization that managers trained under a competitive and hierarchical management philosophy may require a different set of skills to achieve cooperation among partners. A greater understanding of the mutual needs of the relationship partner, whether at the organizational or the personal level, is essential. This reinforces the basic advice in most marketing textbooks on 'marketing orientation', but true RM demands more interaction than merely basic customer awareness. For instance, it will be important for managers to consult partners before acting in any decision process, such as a global FMCG manufacturer's plans to launch a new brand. It will be necessary to know the plans for the own-label ranges of the organization's main retail customers around the world. Furthermore, negotiated outcomes in relationships should represent compromises that lead to 'win–win' outcomes for all parties. This joint benefit should always underpin relational practice. Can an agreement be reached for the manufacturer to produce certain own-label goods at low cost for the retailers, who then also agree to stock the manufacturer's new brand in prominent in-store locations?

As interaction between individuals is vital to successful RM, the more that the 'social element' of a relationship can be enhanced through, for example, multiple contact points between organizations, the better. This need not necessarily involve a high degree of 'socializing' (dinner parties or golf tournaments), but should give managers in particular functional areas in a selling company (e.g. R&D) the chance to communicate with managers in certain key roles within a buying company (e.g. production). Thus, a move away from simple key account management (KAM) with a single point of contact (i.e. sales manager and buying officer) towards a larger number of 'interfaces' between departments should be encouraged (Hutt and Speh, 1998)—as illustrated in Fig. 13.3. This may be a difficult area for senior managers in international contexts to control, but will provide a bond that is difficult to break (Donaldson and O'Toole, 2002).

Learning in global marketing relationships is often the major form of added value that occurs between organizations. It is harder to achieve across cultures, but to facilitate learning, routines should be built into the relationship, such as formal and informal mechanisms for communicating and sharing new knowledge. This requires an openness on behalf of managers and a willingness to learn (Elg and Johansson, 2001). A helpful model has been put forward

Fig. 13.3 Alternative approaches to inter-organizational interaction

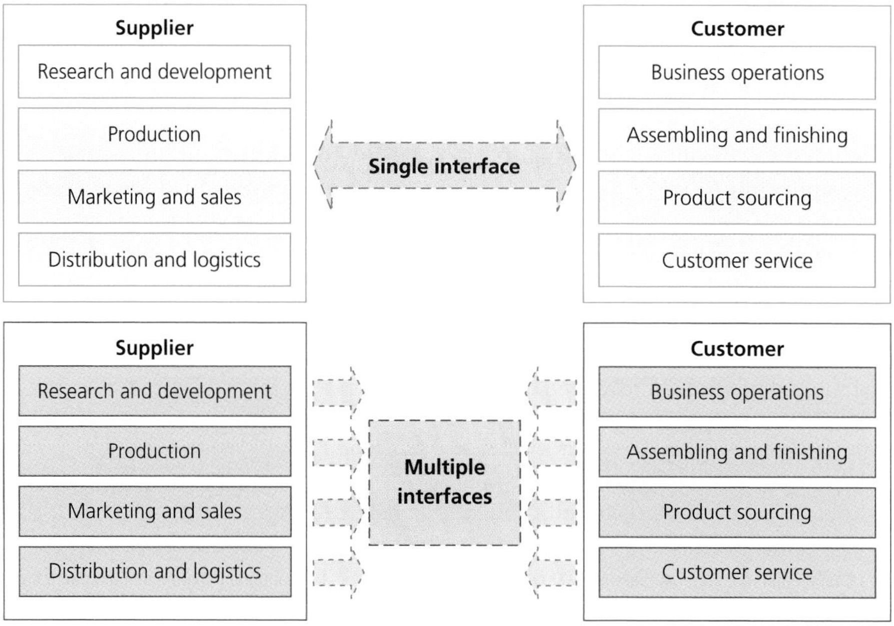

Source: Based on Egan (2001).

by Kanter (1994), which suggests that eight 'I's are needed to facilitate a more collaborative approach to managing relationships:

(1) Individual excellence—both parties should bring strengths and competences to the relationship.

(2) Importance—both parties see the relationship as strategic.

(3) Interdependence—both parties need and complement each other.

(4) Investment—both parties are prepared to commit resources to the relationship.

(5) Information—both parties share information and communicate continuously.

(6) Integration—there are numerous linkages between the parties.

(7) Institutionalization—the relationship becomes formal and company-wide, not just between the two managers who may have instigated it.

(8) Integrity—both parties behave in a way that reinforces mutual trust.

In terms of planning in relationships, managers need to set strategic objectives that represent acceptable targets for all parties and for the relationship itself. These might include increased revenues for two competing organizations in an alliance, or increased data exchange on end-user behaviour for organizations cooperating within a marketing channel. The outcome of the relationship in each case might be a reduction of costs through economies of scale in IT systems, for instance. Flexibility is also essential, both in terms of possible conflict resolution and a willingness to change practices if market conditions alter. Some give and take will inevitably be required, especially when partnerships are formed across cultures.

Marketers, therefore, need to study network cultures in different markets. A good example is that of *quanxi* networks in China. The *quanxi* approach, or business connections, is a widely misunderstood concept, yet it is the foundation of much Chinese commerce (Ambler, 1995). An important feature here is reciprocity. While the West might rely on contract law to ensure that organizations honour their obligations, this is not necessarily required in China. The relationship is built first and then, if it is successful, transactions follow. Another cultural complication is the influence of Taosim in the recognition of the fact that two perspectives can exist together. This is in contrast to Western notions of dualism between contradictory forces. In trying to build a commercially viable relationship, Western managers may fail:

(a) because they have paid insufficient attention to building personal relationships before moving on to complete a transaction, and

(b) because they may assume that two options (e.g. low costs and high quality) are alternatives, while their Chinese counterpart may feel it possible for both to coexist.

Interestingly, it has been suggested that global competition and the move to an urban society, with less emphasis on family connections, is tempering the influence of *guanxi* in China (Donaldson and O'Toole, 2002). Nevertheless, in Asian and other cultures worldwide, a seller should aim to encourage the development of a relationship with a buyer through:

• the way that the customer is treated by the organization (or, effectively, by its staff);

• the location (e.g. physical or 'cyberspace') where the interaction occurs;

• the atmosphere (e.g. cooperative or adversarial) in which it takes place; and

• by any attempts to raise the economic interaction to a socio-emotional level.

With relationships increasingly being seen as core assets for organizations, the development of relationship management capabilities will be central to the success of the globally-oriented organization. Further models and examples are discussed below.

Relationships and Networks

A network perspective

The approach towards RM is a holistic one. Relational thinking has developed away from a strictly 'two-way' dialogue between supplier and customer. It has come to represent the whole series of relationships that an organization (or more strictly, the company's employees) undertakes as part of their commercial dealings. In order to facilitate the supplier–customer relationship (e.g. retailer–consumer, manufacturer–retailer), other parties have to be involved in the RM process.

There is much to be said for managers embracing a stakeholder perspective (Freeman, 1984) towards business strategy. Stakeholders are parties with a stake, or interest, in an organization. They can include customers, suppliers, employees, and shareholders. While it is clear to marketers that the customer is a key stakeholder, it is important to remember other potential partners in a company's relationship portfolio. In service sectors such as hotels, where the quality of customers' experience is dictated by staff performance, the frontline employees are particularly important stakeholders.

By envisaging the organization as embedded in a network of relationships with a series of stakeholders or 'markets' (Ballantyne et al., 2003), it is possible to see that actions in the customer market, for example, will have an impact on the supplier market. The value chain, in effect, can be seen as spanning several organizations that work as partners in creating and bringing products to market. If, in a response to consumer demand, a supermarket intends to promote organic vegetables, then some farmers will inevitably have to be persuaded to change their growing practices. Furthermore, independent consumer agencies may wish to check that any 'organic' claims are true, particularly when ultimate producers are located internationally. In this way, businesses find themselves operating in loose-knit stakeholder networks that may be very hard to define.

The extent to which organizations can influence their global operating context varies, depending on which perspective of marketing is taken (Bridgewater and Egan, 2002). Traditional marketing views the international environment as uncontrollable, whereas RM focuses on building relationships with other stakeholders/markets in these contexts. A network perspective takes a broader view and recognizes the complex patterns of interaction between organizations and stakeholders throughout their international setting. It is therefore possible to say that in TM, international marketing strategy is like a global chess game where organizations seek market share at each other's expense. In contrast, within RM, international marketing revolves around adding value in cross-border relationships. The nature of these relationships forms an atmosphere of conflict or cooperation, which may affect the relationship's success (Hakansson, 1982). In a network approach, organizations are attempting to build positions in global networks of direct and indirect relationships to every other stakeholder.

Classifying relationships and stakeholders

The international marketing manager is clearly faced with an operating environment of considerable complexity. How might we classify these relationships in order to make sense of the possibilities? A common ground between various models of stakeholder relations is that RM should accommodate notions of the core organization and its partnerships. These are known variously as 'six markets' (Christopher et al., 1991), 'four partnerships and ten relationships' (Morgan and Hunt, 1994), or the '30Rs' (Gummesson, 1999).

Comprehensive though the 30Rs classification is, a combination of the other two models offers the most convenient way to structure the discussion of global relationships. This is refined by the notion of *horizontal* relationships, and upstream and downstream versions of *vertical* relationships (Egan, 2001). We shall consider:

- customer (or vertical downstream) partnerships, including B2C and B2B;
- supplier (or vertical upstream) partnerships for goods and services;
- lateral (or horizontal) partnerships, including competitor alliances, non-governmental organizations (NGOs) and NFP organizations, and governments;
- internal partnerships, including employees and functional departments.

Vertical relationships represent those that integrate parts of the supply chain, e.g. through component suppliers, manufacturers, and distribution intermediaries, to the end consumer. Horizontal relationships include those with organizations at the same point in the supply chain (or marketing channel) who may seek to collaborate for mutual benefit.

It can be seen how such a view of partnerships could guide an organization seeking to make market-entry decisions. A strong element of lateral relationship assessment at each stage of the decision process would be advisable. For example, a large company might begin with macro-level assessments of partnerships with governments and state agencies in the countries considered. A smaller company might look vertically to contacts in its current network of buyers and suppliers, or laterally to its competitors (Donaldson and O'Toole, 2002). This often means that it is the company's ability to develop relationships that will determine its success in a foreign market, as illustrated by the Chinese consumer electronics manufacturer TCL which has formed an alliance with the French group Thomson (www.thomson.net). This agreement gives TCL effective control of Thomson's television plants in France, Poland, and Thailand, and provides cover against any possible trade actions from customer nations against China (Chandler, 2004).

The majority of examples of management practice under each partnership heading discussed below are international. However, in some B2C contexts, domestic examples of best practice in RM are given. Here, the reader should: (a) make comparisons with organizations in their own countries; and, more critically, (b) assess whether such practices could be 'exported' across international borders.

Customer (Vertical Downstream) Relationships

B2C relations

In business-to-consumer (B2C) markets, many organizations find that in order to build stronger relationships with end consumers they need to change the emphasis and expenditure of their marketing efforts at different channel levels. For instance, General Electric's (GE, www.ge.com) Appliance Division in the USA has built closer B2C relations through establishing a major call centre. According to GE, this was set up with the aim of 'personalizing GE to the consumer' and vice versa (Wayland and Cole, 1997). The current network of five centres receives several million calls each year from across North America, increasing the value of customer relationships in three ways:

(a) by resolving immediate problems quickly, resulting in a high repurchase rate;

(b) by increasing customers' awareness of the GE appliance line; and

(c) by using the knowledge gained by customer interaction as input into the NPD process.

A high-profile example of RM is provided by the 'loyalty schemes' operated by many B2C organizations. Although these schemes are often seen as recent innovations, the principle of attempting to 'buy' the loyalty of consumers (via what could be viewed as glorified sales promotion) is not new. The UK cooperative movement has run a loyalty scheme for decades, mostly in the form of trading stamps. Petrol retailers have also run these programmes in the form of 'collectable' cards and coins. More recently, of course, supermarket schemes such as Tesco's Club Card and the Nectar scheme (www.nectar.com) were introduced. The latter programme is a fascinating example of RM. Not only does it reward returning consumers with 'points' that may be exchanged for goods or holidays, but it does so by bringing together several partner organizations, including Sainsbury's, Debenhams (www.debenhams.com), and BP (www.bp.com). So far, this scheme has been confined to UK organizations, but there is reason to suppose that it could be expanded across national borders. It will be interesting to see which organizations might become suitable international partners, and in which countries the scheme might work.

Some organizations link their loyalty schemes to the stages of relationship development (Fig. 13.2). Travel businesses are particularly adept at this and have launched clubs where members enjoy privileges that ordinary consumers do not. British Airways (BA, www.ba.com) differentiate between levels of membership depending on the customer's commitment (which, of course, is determined by expenditure). Executive Club members based worldwide receive different levels of privileges, such as access to private departure lounges, depending on their status: blue, silver, or gold cardholders (Egan, 2001). Consider the relative success of BA in managing relationships with their customers, and contrast this with the company's record of employee relations that resulted in losses through strike action in summer 2003. Through not concentrating on their employee stakeholders, BA affected relationships with their hitherto loyal passengers. Loyalty schemes are therefore meaningless if the core service does not live up to expectations. They are also meaningless if consumers are members of more than one similar scheme—many shoppers carry 'loyalty' cards for two or three rival supermarkets.

Particularly skilled organizations have learned to integrate RM with brand loyalty. A good example is the Saturn car, launched in the USA by GM in 1990. In 2002 there were over 400 Saturn dealers in the USA, 15 in Canada, and 22 in Japan. An important part of Saturn's brand identity is its relationship with its customers. A strong connection has been established in the organization's corporate culture between brand personality, interpersonal relationships, and emotions. An archetypal Saturn customer might be characterized as young at heart, honest, friendly, and down to earth. Saturn dealers talk of customer pride in a US car that has beaten Japanese rivals on quality, reliability, and service. They also praise the employees for their commitment and achievement. Because the brand is not built on product attributes, the purchase of a Saturn expresses a customer's values and personality (Varey, 2002). For instance, owners have attended several two-day nationwide 'customer enthusiasm' events, called 'Homecomings', and people featured in Saturn TV advertisements are owners, not actors. Excellent press coverage and WOM has helped to produce record sales for GM.

Within the FMCG sector, Ben & Jerry's (www.benjerry.com) ice-cream business has adopted 'caring capitalism'. While relationships with customers need to be profitable in order to sustain the business, the company claims that a deep respect is maintained for each person, whether employee, customer, supplier, or the communities of which they are a part (Varey, 2002). Customer loyalty is earned by the organization through caring responses to customer issues rather than via formal loyalty programmes. Consumers and employees participate in tours of production plants, roadshows, and charity events. They also take part in NPD contests, resulting in the naming of flavours such as Cherry-Garcia (in the USA) and Cool Britannia (in the UK). A range of websites is provided in several countries to facilitate interaction and the involvement of consumers in the business.

An evocative example from the restaurant sector also shows the positive power of a relationship approach to consumers. Distinctive aspects of Brazilian culture have helped the South American barbecue chain Plataforma to gain a competitive advantage in New York. Although there is undoubtedly a proportion of 'ex-pat' clients, the intimacy between employees and US customers, the casual 'we are family' atmosphere, and the overall tendency of Brazilians to personalize relationships have made this service an international marketing success story (DeFreitas et al., 2003).

B2B relations

A critical point in B2B relations is that individuals are vital in making relationships work. Fig. 13.4 suggests some of the criteria managers might use to evaluate the value of strategic relationships, both for themselves and their organizations.

In achieving these outcomes, personal interaction is inevitable. This increases the role of human differences and similarities. In global contexts this becomes more pronounced as interaction takes place between people with different cultural backgrounds and different expectations of behaviours (Hallen and Sandstrom, 1991). In order to facilitate these relationships it will be necessary to understand the motivations and perceptions of individual managers. Before making generalizations about national cultures, marketing managers need to be cautious to avoid putting important individual relationships in jeopardy (Bridgewater and Egan, 2002).

Fig. 13.4 Criteria for evaluating the value of strategic relationships

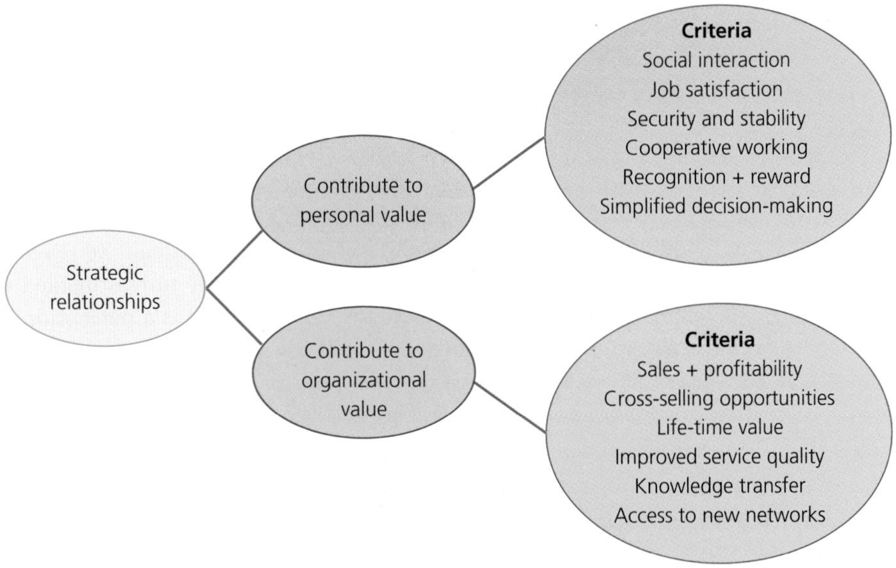

Source: Based on Varey (2002: 76).

THE RELATIONSHIP PERSPECTIVE Fabric of relationships

Networks (or chains) of organizations are now competing, rather than individual companies. The relationships within these networks must be carefully managed, as exemplified by Cisco Systems (www .cisco.com), a world leader in providing equipment for internet communication. Cisco is effectively a 'virtual business', something it has achieved by creating a web of global partners to which it outsources most of its manufacturing. It also bypasses conventional distribution centres by using specialist logistics companies to perform 'merge in transit' operations (Bowman, 2000). It captures most of its orders via the internet and shares that information almost in real time with its network partners. Managers from many of Cisco's key suppliers (e.g. Solectron) participate in the focal organization's daily production meetings and NPD programmes.

An indication of the mutuality within these arrangements is shown by the fact that Cisco shares cost savings with suppliers and even purchases component inventory on their behalf. From the start of its operations, Cisco viewed its supply chain as a 'fabric of relationships' rather than a simple pipeline. The company moved beyond the internal focus of the software systems designed for enterprise resource planning (ERP) to an external view which encompassed its trading partners. All 14 of its global manufacturing sites, plus two distributors, are now linked via an extranet, creating a virtual single enterprise. In this way, contract manufacturers produce components according to a daily 'build plan', derived from a single long-term forecast shared throughout the supply chain, rather than responding to specific one-off orders.

Supplier (Vertical Upstream) Relationships

Relations with goods suppliers

A key factor in supplier relationships is power. Any imbalance in power, where one partner is seen as dominant and the other dependent, creates opportunities for partners to pursue short-term advantage. This can often happen when SMEs are dealing with larger companies, though not, it would appear, with the skilful way in which Benetton handles its supplier relations. In fact, the quality of buyer–seller relationships is thought to be higher among smaller businesses operating in 'closed communities' typically found in less developed economies (Palmer, 2000). Indeed, it could be suggested that it has only been with the growth of mass-market distribution that traditional relationships between members of the distribution chain have become so strained. Despite the positive examples of marketing channel cooperation given above, this strain is especially evident in the changing relationships between brand suppliers and retail intermediaries. Historically, manufacturers attempted to attract consumers 'over the heads' of the retailer, whereas now retail chains have the most power (Egan, 2001). The legacy of these changes has been one of often adversarial, and arguably unethical, relationships within the retail supply chain.

There are claims that supermarket produce buyers are 'laughing at' the latest Code of Practice (CoP) drawn up, supposedly in partnership, by retailers and farmers (Beddall, 2002). Suppliers allege that pressured buyers from the multiples have increased the unreasonable use of their powers, e.g. there are allegations of buyer bullying. In fact, there is a perception that, in some chains, public expressions of support for the CoP by senior executives are not being passed down to the buyers. Yet public expression of support for CoPs is an explicit element in the corporate image of some retailers. Which begs the question: is there a difference between the rhetoric and reality of RM?

Relations with service suppliers

It is often hard to separate service provision from more tangible product offerings. Discussions of global services in this section are therefore drawn from what could be considered as hybrid product/service contexts. For instance, Durr (www.durr.com), the German-based

WHOSE RESPONSIBILITY IS IT? Assuming social responsibility in managing international relationships

The issue of fair trade leads to one particular impact of globalization: its impact on stakeholders in less developed nations. In moving production 'off-shore' to regions with lower wage cost, such as Latin America, clothing retailers arguably have a responsibility to all their suppliers. While most large retailers have CoPs for their suppliers, designed to ensure that civil rights of workers are maintained, these codes do not apply to the retailer. Thus, they do not stop the retailers from 'squeezing' their suppliers at the same time as expecting them to act ethically (Lewthwaite-Page, 1998). Whatever the profit implications of such action, this is not a good example of relationship management by the retailers, since bad practices by their suppliers may reflect on them, damaging their brand names and their reputations.

Even if some equity is achieved between buying and selling organizations, what protection do CoPs offer to the often-neglected stakeholder, the indigenous work force? Many US retailers employ inspectors to monitor working conditions, characterized as 'sweatshops' by some commentators, but because they try to avoid offending factory owners, they do not often probe deeply (Hasty and Reardon, 1997). Retailers claim that they cannot realistically enforce the codes because the number of contractors and factories may be in the thousands. They therefore have to depend on the contractors to police themselves. This self-scrutiny is unfortunately often far from satisfactory. By mid-1999, the 'sweatshop' issue had degenerated, with little evidence of a universal standard of ethical corporate behaviour that could be applied globally (Klein, 2000). Such codes often seem to have been drafted by PR departments following media investigations into supply chain scandals involving organizations in issues such as child and prison labour.

Why might this lack of ethics persist? Perhaps because marketing and purchasing managers are typically not trained to account for corporate social responsibility in their decision-making (Varey, 2002). Tensions clearly exist within the stakeholder concept, particularly at the individual manager level. These happen when managers employed in roles which typically require them to maximize profits for their company's shareholders, also try to reconcile this responsibility with a relational expectation of mutuality. This means acknowledging the counter-claims of non-owner stakeholder groups (Calton and Kurland, 1996), such as a fair price for a supplier's goods and honest treatment of customers. Managers need to show good returns to their bosses, but the RM view is also telling them not to neglect their suppliers or their customers, neither of whom should be exploited. This dilemma seems to challenge what is arguably the basic principle of RM—a promise of reciprocally fair treatment to all stakeholders.

Finally, one radical view of global relationship is worth further thought. A criticism of network-based RM is the promise it seemingly holds for improved conditions for global stakeholders in the so-called 'free market'. However, some observers argue that free market fundamentalism is built on an assumption (i.e. that the market maximizes growth and wealth in the world, and optimizes the distribution of that increased wealth) that is open to dispute (Hobsbawm, 2000). From the perspective of the stakeholders in the supply chain who might collectively be termed 'the peasantry', such as individual Columbian coffee farmers, globalization seems to have offered little in the way of progress. These stakeholders, who make up a significant number of the world's population, have been largely forgotten in the management textbooks (Ghosal and Westney, 1993). This would seem to be a challenge for managers considering their obligations in managing international relationships. Or is it? Management careers might be affected by such issues.

world leader in paint shops for cars, maintains excellent relations with its customers by locating its staff and operations wherever their customers are. Durr's business has evolved from being a systems supplier to car manufacturers to being a service consultant in this process. The company now performs a major international service role and as a result over one-third of its sales are outside Europe (Donaldson and O'Toole, 2002).

Another good example of managing customer service (and costs) in B2B markets is provided by UK-based RS Components (www.rswww.com). This international supplier of electrical components has begun to use the internet alongside its more conventional channels. The company deals with its customers through branches, a call centre and, now, a highly sophisticated and personalized website. It has improved its service levels and hence its profitability, and also gained a significant number of new customers worldwide via its internet-based sales channel (Christopher et al., 2002).

The area of healthcare is a fascinating global case. Health services bought and sold internationally within OECD countries have been estimated as rising to US$4 trillion per annum by 2005. One way to facilitate healthcare worldwide may be the phenomenon of 'e-health', which is an umbrella term for telephone advice as well as more recent internet applications that can be delivered 'live' or via 'store and forward' modes. Global e-health recognizes the interdependence of all nations and the mutual benefit of a networked flow of health information and knowledge among and between countries. Concerns have been raised, however, over the future of e-health initiatives due to the increasing number of stakeholders in the process. Influential organizations now include development banks, multilateral development agencies, NFP organizations such as international foundations, professional bodies, academic institutions and last, but not least, the private sector that produces medical products, services, and IT. Each partner has its own priorities that may not coincide with the interests of communities and countries (Scott and Palacios, 2002). Some of the changes seen in recent years include:

(a) the World Bank's role being affected by resource constraints attributable to cuts in national government contributions to the World Health Organization (www.who.org);

(b) the challenge to the role of NGOs presented by the growth of foundations, often created by private companies (e.g. the Bill and Melinda Gates Foundation); and

(c) multinational businesses' possession of much of the funding and technical expertise for innovation and R&D.

There is a danger that processes of communication and the ability to see common ground will be hampered. The issue of global relationship management thus arises, with governments having to recognize the growing influence of business partners in e-health programmes.

Lateral (Horizontal) Partnerships

As with the previous section, the focus here is almost wholly on the B2B sector. Although there is some growth in lateral consumer networks, particularly via the internet, it is in the B2B market that collaborations are more obvious. One reason for the limited development of consumer networks is that the more widespread the membership, the less collaborators have an opportunity to meet. The internet does have the potential to remove this geographical dependence, as shown by cost-conscious North American consumers trawling the internet to find further potential buyers for new cars. This enables them to present dealerships with multiple orders and thus negotiate lower prices, but this is still a relatively rare practice.

Competitor and other alliances

As we have seen, alliances are a key element of much cross-border trading. If an organization does not possess the skills and resources necessary to meet global challenges, then forming international strategic alliances can be an important way forward. A partner may also provide the organization with access to new channels of distribution and contact with new suppliers. The partner's credibility, brand name, and image are also potentially valuable assets.

Managers should be aware, however, that if the preservation of a strong domestic position remains strategically significant, then consideration of alliances should also evaluate whether such collaboration supports the organization's domestic relationships (Elg and Johansson, 2001). Vertical and horizontal relations will have to be taken into account. For instance, improving the competences and position, of a potential competitor can have a negative influence on an organization's vertical position, whereas horizontal cooperation may improve collective bargaining power in relation to vertical relationships. The focal organization also has the option of assisting a horizontal partner to enter its domestic market, something which could be particularly desirable if the entry of the alliance partner would weaken the position of domestic competitors. Thus, the importance of a network view to managing global marketing relationships can be seen.

The Swedish food retailer ICA (www.ica.se) joined the Associated Marketing Services (AMS, www.ams-marketing.com) group and the result provides a good illustration of the complexity of international B2B relations. AMS, which includes 13 large European retailers, aims to improve efficiency in areas such as purchasing, branding, IT, and new product development. Joining AMS gave ICA an 'inside route' to foreign suppliers since its limited size and historical lack of activity outside Sweden had made it difficult for the company to attract large European producers. Furthermore, exchange of supplier data in areas like product quality and pricing made ICA better informed (Elg and Johansson, 2001). These benefits strengthened ICA's bargaining position in Sweden. For instance, once its membership of AMS made it easier for the retailer to source foreign alternatives for own-label manufacture, the hitherto uncooperative Swedish manufacturers became more willing to work in partnership with ICA. Although some Swedish producers expressed concern over decreasing profits, ICA was also able to use its AMS contacts to help these suppliers win foreign customers.

Collaboration can also involve arrangements between organizations from different market sectors. In these cases, each partner brings different competences and assets to the relationship with the aim of improving a service package, as with British Airways and Hertz car rental (www.hertz.com). This can also result in mutual benefits to partner organizations from co-branding a service. Customers exposed to one element of a service are made aware of the brands of linked businesses, providing opportunities for cross-selling. A good example is that of mytravel.com which represents a global, branded, integrated travel service through which holiday and travel goods can be purchased via multiple channels, such as the internet, telephone, and high street outlets. The service is based on the integration of relationship management and distribution systems founded on partnerships between BT (www.bt.com), Oracle (www.oracle.com), Sun Microsystems (www.sun.com), Lonely Planet (www. lonelyplanet.com), Telewest (www.telewest.com), and Airtours (www. uk.mytravel.com). The distribution structure effectively puts value into the hands of the consumer and also provides them with a loyalty programme that rewards customers with 'points' throughout their holiday experience (Varey, 2002).

It is not unusual to find direct competitors working collaboratively in the supply chain. For instance, multinationals Lever Faberge (www.leverfaberge.co.uk) and Colgate Palmolive (www.colgate.com) share the same distribution centre in the UK, making combined deliveries to common customers. Although the branded products of these two organizations compete head-to-head in the consumer marketplace, managers argue that they do not compete in the warehouse or delivery lorry, and therefore both organizations benefit through collaboration (Christopher et al., 2002). Similarly, the long-established cooperative brand of Californian fruit growers, Sunkist (www.sunkist.com), represents a partnership undertaken in order to organize joint marketing and promotion in foreign markets (Donaldson and O'Toole, 2002).

Collaboration should not be mistaken for altruism or as an end to competition. Indeed, in some sectors the level of competition is more intense as one alliance battles with another for greater market share in, for instance, the airline industry. Some collaborative relationships can, however, have monopoly or anti-trust implications, where the resulting inter-organization network is so powerful that legislators around the world monitor such agreements closely. Accusations of cartel-formation have been levelled in the global steel industry, for example. The world's largest producer, Europe-based Arcelor (www.arcelor.com), has restrained production, thus helping other big producers such as Corus (www.corusgroup.com). As a result, buyers of steel claim that in an industry supposedly faced with over-capacity, steel prices have in fact been rising. In 2001, the three largest companies in the tinplate steel sector announced coordinated price increases of 5.5% (*Economist*, 2003). Raising prices in this way is unlikely to strengthen long-term relationships with their customers.

Sometimes what is acceptable cooperation in some countries may not be so in others. For instance, Japanese *keiretsu* relational business practices might be regarded as anti-competitive in the USA or the EU. It could be considered ironic that while Western companies appear to be seeking closer relationships, many of those same companies have been applying pressure via their governments to have such practices curtailed in Japan (Palmer, 1996). *Keiretsu* represent enterprise groups (e.g. Mitsubishi, www.mitsubishi.com) in such areas as component parts, where relationships are often cemented by cross-ownership of stock between a company and its buyers and non-financial suppliers. Some commentators describe *keiretsu* as essentially cartels that have the government's blessing (Gerlach, 1992). These alliances can block foreign suppliers and sometimes result in higher prices to Japanese consumers. Even though the influence of these social institutions is thought to be waning (e.g. at Nissan, www.nissanmotors.com, a new management team from Renault (www.renault.com), the company's partner in France, recently began to divest some of Nissan's 1,300 *keiretsu* investments), for companies wishing to enter the Japanese market, an understanding of *keiretsu* is essential.

The channel to market is viewed as key to any company's success in countries such as China. A majority of companies use joint ventures since local partners may offer a quick route through local bureaucracy. Yet these relationships between foreign entrants and Chinese partners involve four main elements that conspire to restrain any attempts at a relational approach (Lee, 1999):

(1) high uncertainty due to the transitional economy of China with its weak capital structure;

(2) low interdependence due to the existence of many small distributors;

(3) transactions rather than relationships, with price comparisons dictating switching; and

(4) the risk of conflict due to the use of economic sources of power by Western companies such as performance-related bonuses.

Things are changing, however. The majority of multinationals now believe that their alliances in China perform at least as well as those in other emerging markets (Kenevan and Pei, 2003). For these successful companies, an alliance's profitability depends on the Chinese partner's ability to help find assets such as low-cost workers, distribution networks, or land. Also important is the careful formulation and communication of financial targets by foreign partners. Finally, leading companies seem to give partnerships time to develop, but act quickly to restructure those that are not meeting their targets.

We may also note difficulties in the use of local distributors by businesses wishing to enter African markets. In this era of global brands and global service guarantees, some companies are concerned to protect product and service quality. Several multinationals, such as IBM (www.ibm.com), have their own 'missionary' salespeople (Quelch and Austin, 1993) and service technicians working in association with local distributors whose function is often confined to the physical distribution of products. Nevertheless, the relationship between these partners is important. To what extent should multinationals impose international standards on their local partners or accept cultural differences in business practices?

MINI-CASE ILLUSTRATION **Relationships management in NGOs**

An interesting perspective on relationship management can be found in the collaborative social development work of many NGOs and international donor agencies. A project among five international NGOs based in the USA involved monitoring network development processes in Nicaragua and Malawi. Although much was achieved in education and health by these NGOs working together with local organizations, some partnerships were felt to be ineffective (Ashman, 2003). Typical misunderstandings that possibly could have been addressed with a more sensitive RM approach, included:

(a) centralized planning, which alienated country offices of US and national NGOs;

(b) the use of a highly structured model for governance, which resulted in inefficient meetings and absorbed resources; and

(c) underestimating the way in which sub-funding conditions instilled a hierarchy between donors and NGOs. This last issue created dilemmas for managers over the idea of locally empowered staff versus management control by the 'prime' NGO.

NGOs and NFP organizations

One set of stakeholders who are becoming increasingly vocal on the global stage is consumer pressure groups such as non-governmental organizations (NGOs) and not-for-profit (NFP) organizations. Relationships with these stakeholders can be crucial, as we have seen in our discussion of Codes of Practice in 'Relationships with Goods Suppliers' above. For instance, human rights activists have persuaded Abercrombie & Kent (www.abercrombiekent.com), the upmarket travel group, to stop promoting Burma (now Myanmar) in its 2004 brochures (Macalister, 2003). Because of long-standing concerns over the behaviour of the country's military dictatorship, a number of other companies are being targeted in an attempt to make them withdraw commercial links with Burma. These companies include P&O cruise liners (www.pocruises.com) and British American Tobacco (www.bat.com).

One of the most controversial aspects of globalization is the notion of competing religious faiths. For several years, and well before the atrocities of 11 September 2001, conservative evangelical NFP organizations have been attempting to 'export' the notion of Christianity to the Muslim world. These modern-day missionaries are touched by Muslims' material and (supposed) spiritual needs (Van Biema, 2003). Figures suggest that the number of missionaries travelling to Islamic countries almost doubled between 1982 and 2001. Half of the new arrivals are American. These people frequently mean well (they bring not only the Gospel, but also financial aid and charitable work), but some managers of more liberal Christian groups claim that aggressive tactics used by missionaries, such as lying about their identities and faiths to achieve their goals, could put all religious charities at risk. On a more positive note, some individuals have set up businesses, such as travel agencies in North Africa, and have formed social relationships with locals but put them under no religious pressure. Only when asked about their faith have they discussed their own Christian beliefs. In this way, they could be considered to be practising 'relationship evangelism' (Van Biema, 2003). Do principles of relationship management really extend to the 'export' of religion?

National governments

Organizations can form partnerships for political lobbying. Many of these relationships are not common public knowledge. For example, the European Round Table of Industrialists (ERT) is an association of the chief executives of 46 of the largest companies in Europe. From 1983, their purpose has been to link the EU's economies so that their companies could reach the scale necessary to resist competition from non-European businesses. Apparently, the ERT began to threaten national governments that if they did not lend their approval to the integration scheme, big business would take its operations elsewhere, making much of the European workforce redundant. Thus, in a fascinating illustration of the potential strength of horizontal relationships, the ERT effectively became the Single European Act's 'main driving force', a fact acknowledged by EU president, Jaques Delors (Monbiot, 2000: 322).

In a similar move, but on an even broader scale, around 100 chief executives from the USA and Europe gather under the auspices of the Transatlantic Business Dialogue (TABD). Companies represented include ICI (www.ici.com), Unilever (www.unilever.com), Boeing (www.boeing.com), Ford (www.ford.com) and TimeWarner (www.timewarner.com). The balance of power in the TABD's relationship with governments is shown by the view expressed by its Chair that the role of business is to formulate proposals, then submit them to governments for implementation. This network of organizations clearly has great influence, since the US Under-Secretary of Commerce has admitted that 'virtually every market-opening move undertaken by the US and the EU in the last couple of years has been suggested by the TABD' (Hauser, cited by Monbiot, 2000: 327).

Governments are not always so acquiescent to the cross-border demands of business. Home governments can sometimes intervene and 'move the goalposts' in support of their own companies' self-interest. For instance, the USA blocked the sale of the Anglo-French Concorde aircraft to China in 1972, claiming that the plane's US-manufactured navigation system could be converted for use in ballistic missiles (Day, 2003). Domestic commercial interests were clearly at play in applying this pressure. This can be seen from the fact that US businesses and trade officials were simultaneously offering to sell the same system to China as part of an order for (US-built) Boeing 702s. The Concorde order was lost and with it some £42 million of revenue for the UK.

Regional trade issues in global marketing are often legislated for at governmental level. An example is NAFTA (the North American Free Trade Agreement), which seeks to improve trading relationships between the USA, Canada, and Mexico. Introduced in 1994, this was an attempt to lower trade barriers and import tariffs on items such as textiles, automotive products, and agriculture. Unfortunately, the potential for NAFTA to create winners and losers has led the member states to enter disputes over 'unfair' actions, thus severely undermining the closeness of any relationships. A typical trade dispute is the alleged 'dumping' by US exporters of beef and pork in Mexico. Mexican trade officials suggest that, partly due to high government subsidies, US suppliers are selling at up to 30% below cost, in defiance of the NAFTA rules. The USA retorts that this is a normal free market push by farmers who enjoy greater economies of scale (*Wall Street Journal*, 1998).

Internal Partnerships

Employees

As we have seen, the RM approach recognizes the need to motivate and enthuse business employees, especially in a service marketing context. An example of an organization attaching considerable importance to internal marketing is the Walt Disney Corporation (www.disney.com). Employees are rigorously trained to understand that it is their job to satisfy customers. Staff are reminded that they are part of the 'cast' at Disney and must at all times ensure that visitors (or 'guests') at their theme parks have an enjoyable experience. Strict dress codes and conduct rules are imposed to ensure that the organization's standards are maintained (Christopher et al., 2002). Despite the organization's worldwide success, it is possible to counter that such strict enforcement (e.g. over male facial hair) does little to empower staff, and thereby reduces their feelings of any 'stake' in their relationship with Disney. This has certainly been noticeable in the well-documented difficulties Disney found in retaining staff at their French theme park.

One organization that has made a major commitment to its employees is the drinks group Diageo (www.diageo.com). It announced that it would provide its entire African workforce with access to free drugs to address the growing AIDS pandemic (Finch, 2003). The British company, which makes brands such as Guinness (www.guinness.com) and Smirnoff (www.smirnoff.com), is pledging to give the appropriate drugs to all its HIV-positive staff and their dependants. Moreover, once prescribed, the drugs would be available for life, even if the employee loses their job. This is a significant undertaking as Diageo has 5,000 staff in more than 25 African countries employed in brewing, sales, and marketing. The head of the company's African operations said that he had made the decision on humanitarian and commercial grounds. The latter reflects the fact that these people are the company's workers and their consumers. The continent accounts for some 10% of the group's annual sales.

Functional departments

In some industries, globalization has meant that an organization's value chain has been reconfigured. As noted above, some large organizations have relocated their production to a variety of locations with relatively low labour, raw material, and other costs. When this occurs, the quality of relations within the enterprise may influence the value-adding process. This necessitates the management of international relationships between different subsidiaries and functions of the business (Bridgewater and Egan, 2002).

The structure of multinationals such as Phillips (www.phillips.com), Procter & Gamble (www.pg.com), and Ericsson (www.ericsson.com) can be likened to networks. Attempts to monitor and control such organizations are not simple. In the same way that managing relationships across global supply chains and networks can be difficult, managing intra-organization relationships does not lend itself to a 'one size fits all' solution, especially when the enterprise comprises a large number of international subsidiaries (Nohria and Ghoshal, 1997).

Issues facing managers include:

(a) differential resource flows across subsidiaries;

(b) varied organizational structures within each subsidiary;

(c) power differentials between headquarters and subsidiaries; and

(d) differences in cultural and communication patterns across the companies' units.

Here, skilled practice of relationship management is clearly required internally. Key business processes must be managed across functions. In a variation on the 'direction' of relationships, core processes such as customer relationship management (CRM) can be viewed as 'horizontal' in that they cut across traditional 'vertical' functions within an organization (Christopher et al., 2002), as shown in Fig. 13.5.

Fig. 13.5 How internal relationships add value across conventional functions

Management of Innovation
Collaborations between R&D, sales and production departments to facilitate innovations

Management of Supply Chain
Collaborations between supply chain partners to improve efficiency and reduce costs

Management of Customer Relationships
Collaborations with core customer groups and research agencies to manage customers

Management of Employee Relationships
Collaborations with employees and trade unions to improve effectiveness

Conventional functions

Purchasing

Production

Sales

Distribution

Higher and more consistency in quality

Greater cost-efficiency

Shorter lead time

More innovation

Higher barriers to entry

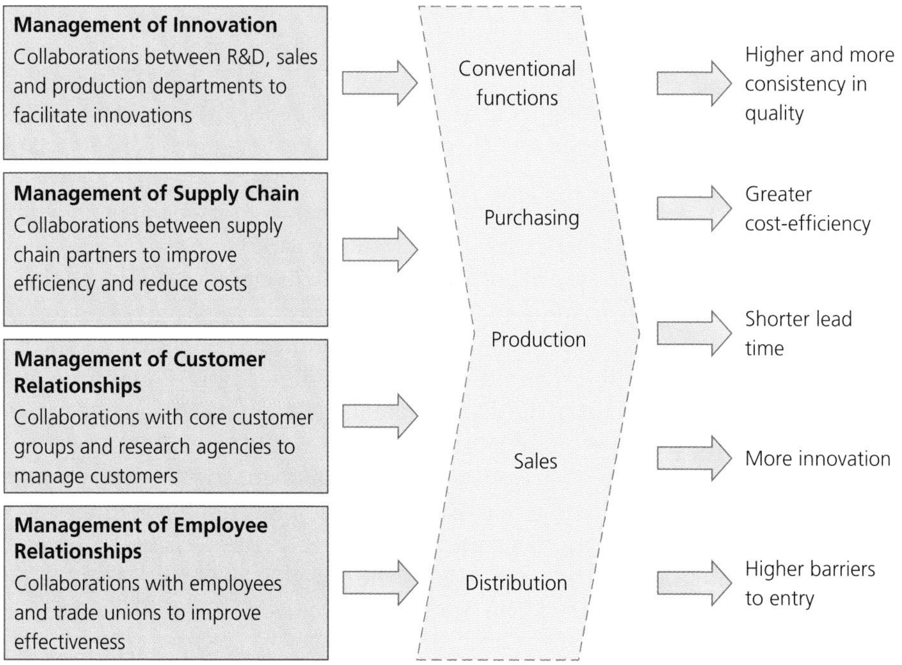

Source: Based on Christopher et al. (2002).

Managers cannot assume that because they have looked after external relationships, then internal relations with stakeholders such as individual employees, trade unions, and functional departments will take care of themselves. As seen in the example of British Airways above, it is necessary to accommodate the needs of all stakeholders that may interact with an organization.

Strategic Challenges in Managing Relationships

There are a number of challenges confronting organizations which seek to build, manage, and maintain their strategic relationships in order to achieve sustainable competitive advantage (Fig. 13.6).

E-commerce relationships

The access to huge numbers of potential customers and the relatively low start-up costs of trading on the internet may meet some company requirements for communication and investment. However, it seems unlikely that a buyer will enter into a B2B relationship with a supplier found on the internet without considerable personal interaction (Melewar et al., 2001). This is particularly so in international relationships where there is often a strong need for cross-cultural understanding. Thus, it is likely that web-based strategies for global relationship management will always require supplementation by human intervention.

Fig. 13.6 Strategic challenges in managing relationships

E-commerce Relationships	**The use of new technologies to enable a high level of accessibility to customers** Do we have the technologies required to reach our customers and enhance relationships?
Measuring Relationship Success	**The determination of return on investment** What is the likely return on investment and timescale of payback? How do we measure success in relationships?
Potential Complexity in Management	**The potential difficulties of building and managing relationships** Loss of control; difficult to predict cross-cultural behaviour in partners; difference in partner expectations

However, if CRM via the internet is done effectively, it can bring an organization significant gains. Tesco.com is an excellent example of an e-commerce success. By 2003, the UK supermarket estimated that over 5% of its annual sales came from its electronic channel, making it the number one online grocery store in Europe, if not the world. Tesco.com appears to be working because its user-friendly website and reliable distribution effectively brings the 'corner shop' to the customer's doorstep (Varey, 2002). This provides consumers with the convenience of an electronic shopping list that 'never forgets' and a delivery driver with a human face. The company seems to have overcome consumer fears that the person who picks the goods will not be as choosy as they are, and that the groceries will be fresh. Tesco.com states that it encourages its pickers to contact customers by phone if there is any doubt over suitability of substitute products if items are out of stock. Furthermore, the addition of the online service to the company's portfolio has increased general awareness of the Tesco brand and actually increased store use. With the retailer's plans to expand internationally firmly in place (Tesco is already the fourth largest company in Thailand, and ninth in Hungary), these 'dot.com' elements of Tesco's business look set to grow (Blackhurst, 2004).

Perhaps the most high-profile international B2C organization to utilize the internet is Amazon.com. Through this technology, the company gives its customers access to a much wider range of books, CDs, etc. than could be stocked by a shop, plus a 24-hour service. The buying process for consumers is convenient as the purchase is done at home and delivery to the door is fast and reliable. Customers are 'recognized' by the computer system and often recommended products via e-mail on the basis of previous purchases and stated preferences (Ritzer and Stillman, 2001). However, books cannot be browsed online and, of course, there is no sales clerk to advise customers. Buyers have to rely on publisher's 'blurb' and cover images, therefore the risk of buying an inappropriate book is considerable.

Measuring relationship success

It is important for organizations to allocate their marketing budget appropriately between acquisition and retention activities, especially if they intend to invest in a CRM system.

THE DIGITAL IMPACT 'E-relationships'

One challenging vision of the future development of B2C relations is where technologies and processes will be integrated in a 'relational marketing system' that is truly (end)user-friendly. In this way, global consumers may become the managers of trading relationships, so that sellers are ready to sell only when buyers are ready to buy. Simply buying in an 'off-the-shelf' electronically-based CRM system is not a viable option. Despite many promises from IT consultants, a system is still awaited which is capable of the following (Varey, 2002):

- to enable responsive and responsible interaction;
- to allow customers to manage their trading relationships;
- to provide an integrated range of modes of contact with a full interaction history;
- to support a degree of human interaction with some sort of 'human feel';
- to instil confidence in users and provide simple processes;
- to register all interactions and support knowledge management accordingly;
- to deliver consistency in treatment of all customers;
- to encourage return to the website or call centre, as appropriate.

The need for careful management of B2C 'e-relationships' can be seen in the banking sector. Increased customer requirements have created a competitive climate whereby the quality of the relationship between the banks and their customers appears to have taken on greater importance than the product *per se*, not least because unlike strong relationships, financial products can easily be copied. The much-vaunted concept of electronically-mediated CRM seems to offer excellent customer service because the banking consumer is somehow freed from queuing at a service counter and the restriction of bank opening hours.

However, the ability for a bank to establish close links with customers may well be compromised when interaction is delegated to technology. Going rather against the mutuality aspect of RM, it is the banking organizations worldwide which have decided to interpret B2C banking interactions as 'relationships', when many consumers simply see banks as places to look after their money. It is also the banks which decide when and how technological advancements and the 'marketspace' (in this case, the internet) add value to customers. Hence the customer's role in the relationship is less empowered than the bank's (Fitchett and McDonagh, 2000). Moreover, the participating parties do not share mutually either the benefits or the conditions of the relationship. For instance,

banks can increase the APR on a loan or introduce an annual fee without negotiating these relational changes with consumers. From the consumers' point of view, they either accept the conditions, try to negotiate, or break off the relationship. In many cases this is difficult and damaging for the consumer. For example, banks and building societies can impose penalties and additional tariffs if customers delay their mortgage or bill payments. Yet in cases where the bank makes an error in billing or records an unauthorized transaction, the consumers do not have the equal power to seek redress.

Marketers must accept that if their CRM strategies are aimed at relationship-building with customers through the use of technological enhancements, then they should also take on board customer requirements, such as a need for some human interaction and more say in how their account is run. Otherwise, banks could be accused of viewing the process of mixing RM and technology as a 'cost-cutting exercise within a relational rhetoric' (O'Malley and Mitussis, 2002: 233). If mutual values traditionally emerge from continuing interaction and dialogue between people, then the idea of blending technology and CRM in order to nourish trust in a relationship can certainly be questioned. Furthermore, the banks are sending negative signals to their existing loyal customers when they offer preferential savings rates to new e-customers in an attempt to woo them away from their existing accounts. This questions the trust and commitment shown by customers.

Does the operating context of your organization offer possibilities for e-commerce? If so, what are the likely hurdles you will have to overcome in ensuring mutually beneficial relationships, especially if they occur with customers in other countries?

If they are to be able to answer awkward questions from company accountants about returns on marketing investment, managers clearly need more than simple market share figures and raw sales data. However, despite the growth of RM, in a recent study senior marketing managers were shown to be slow in switching their marketing metrics towards customer retention criteria (Payne and Frow, 1999): while nearly 70% measured customer acquisition, retention was monitored by only about 50%. In order to address this gap, organizations should follow three steps in enhancing retention and profitability levels:

(1) Measure customer retention.

(2) Identify the main causes of defection and key service issues.

(3) Develop corrective action to improve retention.

At Step 1, managers need to analyse several dimensions in detail. A good CRM system should facilitate this. Marketing metrics should include:

- customer satisfaction ratings;
- retention rates over time;
- measured by market segment;
- broken down by the range of products or services offered by the organization.

If customers buy from several different suppliers, then the 'share of wallet' (i.e. the proportion of a customer's total spend that is received by the manager's organization) should also be identified if possible (Christopher et al., 2002). This combination of information allows managers to understand the current retention picture and the profit potential for each market segment.

Step 2 requires careful marketing research, often needing more than a quickly assembled, mailed questionnaire. A combination of qualitative and quantitative data is usually essential in order to explore the full complexities of relationship dynamics, particularly their social element. In-depth interviews and focus groups with customers can reveal much about why they may be dissatisfied with the service, or indeed, reveal new relationship offerings not previously considered (e.g. a move from a purely information-based website to a trading one). Depending on the degree of any problems identified, Step 3 may involve a fundamental shift in business emphasis towards a more value-driven, relational approach. This is likely to be necessary in organizations where the values of RM have yet to be recognized.

For suppliers and alliance partners, relationship management success might be measured by quality standards, cost reductions, and levels of information exchange. In terms of other lateral relationships, it might be possible to assess the impact of corporate publicity. Finally, for internal markets, staff retention and satisfaction could be measured. Of course, these measures must be decided by managers with a good understanding of the critical success factors for their business. If a high level of technical innovation is crucial to deliver customer value, then any assessment of a competitor-based alliance would have to consider such metrics as time-to-market and R&D costs.

Potential complexity in management

It is necessary, also, to reflect upon some of the limitations of relational strategies. Potential disadvantages of building relationships (Hakansson and Snehota, 1998) include:

- loss of control (managers used to being 'in charge' now have to work with their opposite numbers in partner organizations);
- difficulty in predicting partner behaviour (especially within cross-cultural alliances);

- preclusion from other opportunities (such as trading with a new supplier offering cheaper goods); and

- potentially unexpected demands (perhaps where a partner has different expectations of a firm's ability to respond rapidly to an important order).

Relationships can be seen as assets whose value depends on the relative worth of each customer, or the significance of each supplier. There are, however, considerable costs in developing and maintaining them. In fact, investments such as money, people, time, and procedures can lead to partners becoming 'locked into' the relationship. The issue of time is a particular concern to US managers (e.g. compared to Japanese managers), who frequently see time spent on 'non-business' issues as time wasted (Usunier, 2000). Also, in terms of investment in systems meant to facilitate information exchange, if a partner employs an opportunistic learning strategy and is not prepared to share its knowledge, then the contributions of the relationship will be limited. Moreover, close relationships may not be required for all types of product (Ford, 1990). For example, while it is typically critical from whom a component part is purchased, the sourcing of office stationery is a lot less important. Relationship management with paper suppliers in this context would not normally require significant investment, and as such may suggest that a simple web-based re-ordering system is all that is required.

Interestingly, the many claims made about the economic justifications for RM are beginning to be questioned. Recent research findings indicate that companies will have to re-evaluate the manner in which they manage customer loyalty initiatives and try to find better ways to measure the relationship between loyalty and profitability. This will enable companies to identify more clearly with which customers they should forge relationships and which to 'ignore' (Reinartz and Kumar, 2002). All of which confirms that a firm cannot afford to maintain close relationships with every consumer in a marketplace. Some customers (usually those that are highly demanding and expensive to serve) must be 'let go'. This may be a relatively straightforward decision for the sales manager of a business, but not for the clinical manager of a hospital. Which patients can they ethically 'ignore'? And is the decision different for a private hospital compared to a public one?

Satisfaction does not necessarily lead to loyalty (Varey, 2002). So-called 'loyalty' may sometimes be due to no more than convenience or lethargy on the part of the customer, e.g. most consumers tend not to change the location of their bank accounts. Similarly, dependency is not loyalty. A customer who is 'locked in' may feel that there are too many costs associated with changing suppliers.

This leads to the dilemma of what is meant by 'a relationship'. It is generally thought that two characteristics must be present for an exchange situation to be described as a relationship (Barnes and Howlett, 1998):

(1) The relationship must be mutually perceived to exist.

(2) The relationship goes beyond occasional contact and is recognized as having some special status.

The one-sided nature of most commercial exchanges, particularly for consumer goods, suggests that they have difficulty in fulfilling such criteria. Situations undoubtedly exist where the seller may want to develop 'a relationship' whereas the customer is happier with a transactional approach, as in the discussion of bank marketing above. For many consumers, the organizations, brands, and products with which they interact do not represent objects with which they feel any sense of relational bond, particularly one that might be long-term in nature. As Brown (1998: 177) cynically queries: 'What consumer in their right mind would ever want to establish a relationship with a commercial organization?'

The language of RM (often couched in terms of 'courtship' and 'marriage') can lead managers in some organizations to assume that all customer–supplier contacts are capable of closeness, when many are little more than impersonal exchanges. What these marketers call 'intimacy' some consumers see as 'intrusion'. Nevertheless, in B2B markets, lasting relationships between the personnel of companies are often acknowledged by both sets of managers involved. Perhaps the greatest challenge facing international marketers is whether the relational aspects of inter-organizational exchanges can ever have the same impact in global consumer markets.

Chapter Summary

1. Traditional views of international business have tended to see organizations operating as independent actors making informed choices about foreign markets and the appropriate marketing mix. Under a relational perspective, however, the decisions made by (managers within) an organization are affected by its relationships.

2. Relationships transcend national boundaries and key players in a given supply chain may be located anywhere in the world. Increased emphasis on globalization, cooperative strategies, and intensification of competition has led a growing number of organizations to give RM a central role in marketing strategy.

3. Relationship marketing is predominantly geared towards the management of the customer–supplier relationship. However, in order to facilitate this, other stakeholders in the process have to be involved. These include suppliers, staff, shareholders, competitors, and other lateral partnerships.

4. Managers trained under a traditional management philosophy may require a different set of skills to achieve cooperation among partners. Relationship outcomes should lead to mutual 'win–win' outcomes for all parties. This joint benefit should underpin relational practice.

5. Managing global relationships is far from simple. Issues of trust, commitment, communication, power imbalances, cultural differences, and ethics present significant challenges. All points of engagement between buyer and seller must be embedded in an ongoing dialogue between the parties, a dialogue that is founded upon communicative interaction.

6. The notion of relationships, especially in B2B markets, covers a 'total' interaction between partners—interaction with social content as well as material and economic. The means of handling these interdependencies shape the very existence and development of organizations as well as that of individuals. It may not be too much of an exaggeration to conclude that the approach to managing global relationships has the potential to shape our world(s).

END-OF-CHAPTER CASE STUDY The evolution of customer loyalty schemes

Existing customers are the most important asset of a business. They have chosen one company's product or service over its competitors' offerings. Keeping their custom costs far less than attracting new customers. While good overall service is the best way of retaining customers, sometimes new relationships can be strengthened (or old ones refreshed) by using customer loyalty schemes. These are programmes that use fixed or percentage discounts, extra goods, or prizes to reward customers for behaviour that benefits the business.

In high street retail, customer loyalty schemes have become widespread in recent years. In the UK, there are over 150 of such schemes, resulting in the circulation of more than 40 million cards. Examples of loyalty schemes include: Nectar (www.nectar.com), WH Smiths Clubcard (www.whsmith.co.uk), Homebase Spend and Save (www.homebase.co.uk), Boots Advantage Card (www.boots.com), Argos Premierpoints (www.argos.co.uk), ipoints (www.ipoints.co.uk), and Greasy Palm (www.greasypalm.co.uk). A number of hotel chains and airlines are now operating their own loyalty schemes or frequent flyer programmes: Marriott Rewards (www.marriott.com), Hyatt Gold Passport (goldpassport.hyatt.com), and Virgin Flying Club (www.virgin-atlantic.com).

These loyalty schemes usually involve the customer being issued with a plastic card on which reward points can be collected when the customer makes a purchase. When customers join the loyalty scheme they are asked to provide their personal details which are then entered into a database. Once a customer has an entry in the database, further records of customer purchases can be added, so that ultimately it is possible to build a profile of individual customer purchasing habits. This database of customer purchase profiles can then be used to segment the retailer's customer base, for purposes of direct marketing, and tailoring other marketing communications and special offers to customer requirements.

The rewards are the key mechanism for incentivizing customers to participate in the scheme. Generally, there are two types of reward: (a) cash value (discounts on store purchases or money-off vouchers); and (b) choice of redemption options (a range of products or services are offered as a reward).

The extent to which these loyalty schemes actually create customers who have come to expect a reward as part of the 'normal' shopping experience is increasingly being questioned. Do they actually generate any 'real' value for both the consumer and the scheme's sponsor? Common criticisms include: (a) loyalty schemes are nothing more than a modest discount arrangement; (b) they are an intrusion into customers' privacy; and (c) true loyalty does not exist given the widespread, indiscriminate use of loyal schemes by all major high street retailers.

The Tesco (www.tesco.com) Clubcard loyalty scheme is probably the UK's largest loyalty programme. It is created with the intention of not just acting as a scheme to reward loyal customers but as an extended platform on which it introduces customers and other businesses to each other. Customers earn points through their regular shopping at Tesco and its other retail partners. In return, Tesco rewards customers by offering meals out, glasses and contact lens,

homewares, travel, dry cleaning, and car maintenance. Many of these rewards are carried out in the customer's local Tesco store. The opportunity to earn Clubcard points through partner organizations means that Tesco is able to expand its customer profiles beyond supermarket shopping. For example, customers who earn points through their use of Autocentre provide Tesco with data concerning their type of car. Premium customers are rewarded with an enhanced return when they access Clubcard Deals. In doing so, Tesco encourages its customers, especially the high-spending ones, to engage with other brands. 'Additional' rewards in the form of coupons that are tailored to the customers' habits are sent to them on a regular basis.

The Tesco Clubcard scheme is supported by an online presence (www.tesco.com/clubcard) which provides another gateway to communicate with its members. It is a rich environment for building customer and brand relationships, and for collecting customer data while allowing customers additional access to the Clubcard services.

Clubcard has evolved from being a pure reward scheme to one that offers 'lifestyle options' through its partnership with organizations that can offer a deal for a wide range of life activities. All of these deals are experience-based and they create a perception that Tesco is at the hub of a wide range of relationships—that the Clubcard can open doors to a wide variety of 'good things' in life. At the same time, each of these organizations is gaining exposure through being listed in the Clubcard brochure and in other Tesco channels. Tesco is providing an introduction in the relationship between customers and Tesco's partner businesses. From a branding perspective, they contribute to the creation and delivery of the Tesco promise 'every little helps'.

The concept of the loyalty scheme is evolving and becoming more sophisticated. This new model of loyalty scheme suggests a change in the evolution of loyalty schemes. New models of loyalty schemes are more concerned with developing perceptions of value through brand associations and customized interactions with loyalty scheme members. The focus has shifted from trying to change customer behaviour, to seeking to change customer attitudes. The real opportunity for loyalty schemes is in the conversion of spurious loyalty into sustainable loyalty, and to convert relationships based on convenience to those based on commitment. The quality of service experience through both of these channels (one a distribution channel and the other a communication channel) can have both positive and negative effects on the brand reputation and the brand image.

Source: Based on Rowley (2005).

Case discussion questions

1 In your experience, do loyalty schemes work in (a) retaining your loyalty, and/or (b) increasing your purchases with the retailers?

2 Using examples, briefly discuss the common criticisms associated with customer loyalty schemes.

3 How is the Tesco Clubcard loyalty scheme different from conventional ones? In what ways does the scheme enhance customer loyalty?

END-OF-CHAPTER EXERCISES

1 Discuss the claim that the changing nature of the global marketplace is encouraging organizations to cooperate more closely in international markets.

2 What are the key elements of an RM approach compared with a transactional perspective?

3 Identify the key stakeholders with which a manufacturer of FMCGs seeking to trade in foreign markets may have to build relationships.

4 Why are horizontal partnerships as important as vertical ones in a holistic relationship approach?

DISCUSSION AND EXAMINATION QUESTIONS

1 Discuss the impact of IT on relationship marketing practices in B2C contexts.

2 Using examples, explain what is meant by the term 'partnership' in international supply chain management. Debate whether all such partnerships run smoothly.

3 How can cross-cultural differences affect (a) RM strategies of organizations wishing to enter certain foreign markets, and (b) interpersonal relations between managers working in B2B markets?

4 What advice would you give to (a) a newly appointed marketing manager, and (b) a newly appointed purchasing manager, for an organization sourcing components and selling manufactured goods in global markets?

FURTHER READING

Christopher, M., Payne, A., and Ballantyne, D. (2002), *Relationship Marketing: Creating Stakeholder Value*, Oxford: Butterworth-Heinemann.

Egan, J. (2001), *Relationship Marketing: Exploring Relational Strategies in Marketing*, Harlow: FT/Prentice Hall.

Hingley, M. (2005), 'Power imbalance in UK agri-food supply channels: learning to live with the supermarkets', *Journal of Marketing Management*, 21(1/2), 63–8.

Varey, R. J. (2002), *Relationship Marketing: Dialogue and Networks in the E-commerce Era*, Chichester: John Wiley & Sons.

REFERENCES

Ambler, T. (1995), 'Reflections on China: re-orienting images of marketing', *Marketing Management*, 4(1), 23–30.

Ashman, D. (2003), 'Closing the Gap between Promise and Practice: A Framework for Planning, Monitoring and Evaluating Social Development Networks', in Hibbert, P. (ed.), *Co-creating Emergent Insights: Multi-Organizational Partnerships, Alliances and Networks*, Glasgow: University of Strathclyde Press, 13–19.

Axelsson, B. and Johansson, J. (1992), 'Foreign Market Entry—The Textbook versus the Network View', in Easton, G. and Axelsson, B. (eds.), *Industrial Networks: A New View of Reality*, London: Routledge.

Ballantyne, D., Christopher, M., and Payne, A. (2003), 'Relationship marketing: looking back, looking forward', *Marketing Theory*, 3(1), 159–66.

Barnes, J. G. and Howlett, D. M. (1998), 'Predictors of equity in relationships between service providers and retail customers', *International Journal of Bank Marketing*, 16(1), 5–23.

Beddall, C. (2002), 'The Saturday essay', *The Grocer*, 19 October, 32.

Blackhurst, C. (2004), *TESCO: A Corporate Profile*, Corporate Watch UK, September, www.corporatewatch.org.uk.

Blois, K. J. (1997), 'When is a Relationship a Relationship?', in Gemunden, H. G., Rittert, T., and Walter, A. (eds.), *Relationships and Networks in International Markets*, Oxford: Elsevier, pp. 53–64.

Bowman, R. J. (2000), 'At Cisco Systems, the internet is both business and business model', *Global Logistics and Supply Chain Strategies*, 4(4), 28–38.

Bridgewater, S. and Egan, C. (2002) *International Marketing Relationships*, Basingstoke: Palgrave.

Brodie, R. J., Coviello, N. E., Brookes, R. W., and Little, V. (1997), 'Towards a paradigm shift in marketing: an examination of current marketing practices', *Journal of Marketing Management*, 13(5), 383–406.

Brown, S. (1998), *Postmodern Marketing Two: Telling Tales*, London: International Thompson Business Press.

Buttle, F. (1996), *Relationship Marketing: Theory and Practice*, London: Paul Chapman Publishing.

Calton, J. and Kurland, N. B. (1996), 'A Theory of Stakeholder Enabling', in Boje, D. M., Gephart, R. P., and Thatchenkery, T. J. (eds.), *Postmodern Management and Organizational Theory*, Thousand Oaks, CA: Sage, 154–77.

Chandler, C. (2004), 'TV's Mr Big', *The Business*, 8/9 February, 10.

Christopher, M. (1997), *Marketing Logistics*, Oxford: Butterworth-Heinemann.

—— and Juttner, U. (2000), 'Developing strategic partnerships in the supply chain: practitioner perspective', *European Journal of Purchasing and Supply Management*, 6, 117–27.

——, Payne, A., and Ballantyne, D. (1991) *Relationship Marketing*, Oxford: Butterworth-Heinemann.

——, —— and, —— (2002), *Relationship Marketing: Creating Stakeholder Value*, Oxford: Butterworth-Heinemann.

Cook, J. D., Halevy, T., and Hastie, C. B. (2003), 'Alliances in consumer goods', *The McKinsey Quarterly*, 3 (online journal).

Day, P. (2003), 'USA blocked sales of Concorde to China', *BBC History Magazine*, June, 7.

DeFreitas, H. G., Blundi, M. D., and Casotti, L. (2003), 'Internationalisation of the Churrascaria Platforma: Peculiarities of Brazilian Culture as a Competitive Differential', Academy of Marketing Conference, Aston Business School, Birmingham, 8–10 July.

Donaldson, B. and O'Toole, T. (2002), *Strategic Market Relationships: From Strategy to Implementation*, Chichester: John Wiley & Sons.

Economist (The) (2003), 'European Steel: spot the cartel', 28 June, p. 89.

Egan, J. (2001), *Relationship Marketing: Exploring Relational Strategies in Marketing*, Harlow: FT/Prentice Hall.

Elg, U. and Johansson, U. (2001), 'International alliances: how they contribute to managing the inter-organizational challenges of globalization', *Journal of Strategic Marketing*, 9, 93–110.

Finch, J. (2003), 'Diageo makes HIV pledge to staff', *The Guardian*, 23 September, p. 15.

Fitchett, J. and McDonagh, P. (2000), 'A citizen's critique of relationship marketing in risk society', *Journal of Strategic Marketing*, 8(2), 209–22.

Ford, D. (ed.) (1990), *Understanding Business Markets: Interaction, Relationships and Networks*, London: Academic Press.

Freeman, R. E. (1984), *Strategic Management: A Stakeholder Approach*, Boston, MA: Pitman.

Gerlach, M. L. (1992), 'Twilight of the *keiretsu*? a critical assessment', *Journal of Japanese Studies*, 18(1), 79.

Ghoshal, S. and Westney, E. (1993), *Organization Theory and the Multinational Corporation*, Basingstoke: Macmillan.

Gordon, I. (1998), *Relationship Marketing: New Strategies, Techniques and Technologies to Win the Customers You Want and Keep them Forever*, Ontario: Willey.

Grönroos, C. (1994), 'From marketing mix to relationship marketing: towards a paradigm shift in marketing', *Management Decision*, 32(2), 4–20.

—— (2000), 'Creating a relationship dialogue: communication, interaction and value', *The Marketing Review*, 1(1), 1–13.

Gummesson, E. (1999), *Total Relationship Marketing: Rethinking Marketing Management from 4Ps to 30Rs*, Oxford: Butterworth-Heinemann.

Hakansson, H. (ed.) (1982), *International Marketing and Purchasing of Industrial Goods: An Interaction Approach*, Chichester: John Wiley.

—— and Snehota, I. (1998), 'The Burden of Relationships or Who's Next', in Naude, P. and Turnbull, P. (eds.), *Network Dynamics in International Marketing*, Oxford: Pergamon, pp. 16–25.

Hallen, L. and Sandstrom, M. (1991), 'Relationship Atmosphere in International Business', in Paliwoda, S. (ed.), *New Perspectives in International Marketing*, London: Routledge.

Hasty, R. and Reardon, J. (1997), *Retail Management*, New York: McGraw-Hill.

Hobsbawm, E. (2000), *The New Century*, London: Little, Brown & Co.

Hutt, M. D. and Speh, T. W. (1998), *Business Marketing Management*, Forth Worth, TX: Dryden Press.

Kanter, R. M. (1994), 'Collaborative advantage: the art of alliances', *Harvard Business Review*, July–August, 96–108.

Karpinski, R. (2002), [No title], *Internet Week*, 23 April, http://www.internetweek.com/story/showarticleID=6405995.

Keneven, P. A. and Pei, X. (2003), 'China partners', *The McKinsey Quarterly*, 3 (online journal).

Klein, N. (2000), *No Space, No Choice, No Jobs: No Logo*, London: Flamingo.

Lee, D. Y. (1999), 'Power Sources, Conflict and Satisfaction in a Foreign Joint-Venture Supplier and Chinese Distributor Channel', Fifteenth IMP Conference, University College, Dublin, 2–4 September.

Lewthwaite-Page, A. G. (1998), 'UK clothing retailers squeezing suppliers', *Business Ethics: A European Review*, 7(1), 17–20.

Macalister, T. (2003), 'Burma boycott: activists claim victory over travel links', *The Guardian*, 29 July, p. 13.

Melewar, T. C., Hunt, C., and Bridgewater, S. (2001), 'Business-to-business relationship marketing: an internet and international perspective', *The Marketing Review*, 2, 169–85.

Monbiot, G. (2000), *Captive State: The Corporate Takeover of Britain*, London: Macmillan.

Morgan, R. and Hunt, S. (1994), 'The commitment–trust theory of relationship marketing', *Journal of Marketing*, 58(July), 317–51.

Nohria, N. and Ghoshal, S. (1997), *The Differentiated Network: Organizing Multinational Corporations for Value Creation*, San Francisco: Jossey-Bass.

O'Malley, L. and Mitussis, D. (2002), 'Relationships and technology: strategic implications', *Journal of Strategic Marketing*, 10(3), 225–38.

Palmer, A. (1996), 'Relationship marketing: a universal paradigm or management fad?', *The Learning Organization*, 3(3), 18–25.

—— (2000), 'The evolution of an idea: an environmental explanation of relationship marketing', *Journal of Relationship Marketing*, 1(1), 79–94.

Payne, A. and Frow, P. (1999), 'Developing a segmented service strategy: improving measurement in relationship marketing', *Journal of Marketing Management*, 15(8), 797–818.

Peppers, D. and Rogers, M. (2000), 'Build a one-to-one learning relationship with your customers', *Interactive Marketing*, 1(3), 243–50.

Quelch, J. A. and Austin, J. E. (1993), 'Opinion: should multinationals invest in africa?', *Sloan Management Review*, Spring, 107–19.

Reicheld, F. F. and Sasser, W. E. (1990), 'Zero defections: quality comes to services', *Harvard Business Review*, Sept.–Oct., 106–11.

Reinartz, W. and Kumar, V. (2002), 'The mismanagement of customer loyalty', *Harvard Business Review*, 80(7), 79–86.

Ritzer, G. and Stillman, T. (2001), 'From Person- to System-oriented Service', in Sturdy, A., Grugulis, I., and Willmott, H. (eds.), *Customer Service: Empowerment and Entrapment*, London: Palgrave, pp. 102–16.

Rowley, J. (2005), 'Building brand webs customer relationship management through the Tesco Clubcard loyalty scheme', *International Journal of Retail & Distribution Management*, 33(3), 194–206.

Samie, S. and Walters, P. G. P. (2003), 'Relationship marketing in an international context: a literature review', *International Business Review*, 12, 193–213.

Scott, R. E. and Palacios, M. F. (2002), 'E-health: Challenges of Going Global', in Scott, C. E. and Thurston, W. E. (eds.), *Collaboration in Context*, Calgary: University of Calgary, 45–55.

Sheth, J. N. and Parvatiyar, A. (1995), 'Relationship marketing in consumer markets: antecedents and consequences', *Journal of Academy of Marketing Science*, 23(4), 255–71.

Thapar, N. (2004), 'Benchmark' column, *The Business*, 8/9 February, 30.

Usunier, J.-C. (2000), *Marketing Across Cultures*, 3rd edn., Harlow: FT/Prentice Hall.

Van Biema, D. (2003), 'Missionaries under cover', *Time*, 4 August, 42–9.

Varey, R. J. (2002), *Relationship Marketing: Dialogue and Networks in the E-commerce Era*, Chichester: John Wiley & Sons.

Wall Street Journal (The) (1998), 'Mexican meat producers take on us: dominance of cattle imports prompts cattlemen to act', 5 November, p. A17.

Wayland, R. E. and Cole, P. M. (1997), *Customer Connections: New Strategies for Growth*, Boston, MA: Harvard Business School Press.

online resource centre

Visit the companion website to this book for lots of interesting additional material, including self-assessment questions, internet exercises, and links for each chapter:

http://www.oxfordtextbooks.co.uk/orc/lee_carter2e/

CHAPTER FOURTEEN

Global Pricing and Terms of Access

Chapter overview

Chapter Introduction	448	Devaluation and revaluation	469
Factors Affecting Global Pricing Decisions	449	Inflation	470
		Transfer pricing	470
Pricing Strategy	452	Grey and parallel markets	471
Specific Price Approaches	455	Dumping	472
Cost-oriented pricing	455	Leasing	472
Competitive or flexible cost-plus pricing	456	Counter-trade	473
Market-based pricing	456	Strategies for coordinating prices across subsidiaries	474
Price Adaptation	458	Single European Payments Area	474
Geographical pricing	458	The Export Order Process	475
Price discounts and allowances	459	Terms of Access	475
Promotional pricing	459	Tariffs	475
Market/use pricing	460	Non-tariff barriers	477
Product mix pricing	460	Special Trade Terms in Exporting	477
Price Changes	464		
Special Issues in Global Price Setting	465	Export Documentation	478
Price escalation	465	Export payments	478
Currency fluctuations	466	Export financing	480
Buying forward, options trading, hedging, and spot trading	469	Chapter Summary	481

Learning objectives

After studying this chapter, the reader will be able to:

- consider the importance of the pricing decision in global marketing;
- examine the elements involved in and influencing the pricing of products and services;
- examine the different pricing methods and terms of access and their implications on marketing goods and services globally;
- discuss the interaction between pricing decisions and other marketing mix elements;
- examine some of the critical strategic considerations in pricing goods and services globally.

Management issues

The management issues that arise from this chapter include:

- How can strategic decisions on price affect the global marketing stance of your organization?
- How can the pricing decision affect other elements of your organization's global marketing mix?
- How can price be used, in conjunction with other elements of your global marketing mix, to segment markets for your organization's global markets?

Chapter Introduction

The concept of exchanging money for goods and services received, usually in the form of exchange of bank notes or credit cards or other credit facility, is widely accepted in today's world. Many believe that the price element of the marketing mix is one of the most controllable and immediate in effect. It is the element which generates revenue. Fixing the price, in theory at least, is merely an issue of calculating all direct and indirect costs, adding a margin for profit (maybe adjusting the price to take into account competition or 'what the market can bear'), making sure all the other mix elements are more or less in synergy, and the customers will happily part with their money. However, the pricing decision is not that easy, especially for global marketing. For a comprehensive discussion on the importance of pricing and its associated elements see Lancioni (1989).

Consider the humble Kenya green (fine) bean. To get on to the dinner plate, it has gone through a complex system of logistics, all of which have had to be costed into the final UK supermarket price. First, the exporter has to seek a contract from a UK retailer. Then the product has to be grown, mainly by out-growers, harvested, and transported to the exporter. Strict EU phytosanitary (hygiene) requirements mean that pesticides have to be strictly controlled. The exporter then has to grade and pack the beans to the retailer's strict quality control specifications. He has to transport them to Jomo Kenyatta airport, Nairobi, where they may be cold stored until the flight is ready. Once in the UK, the beans may be further transhipped in refrigerated transport to distribution points then to the supermarket shelf. Each value-adder is receiving a margin. The 'paperwork' behind this transaction is mountainous. The Kenyan exporter needs a certificate of incorporation, a miscellaneous occupational (export) licence, an export licence, a bank account, a contract for supply, a duly completed invoice, a CD (currency declaration) form from the Central Bank, an Appendix HCDA3 form from the Kenyan Horticultural Crops Development Authority, a certificate of origin, and a host of pre-shipment checks by various authorities. This effort and expense has to be costed into the final selling price.

Given the complexity, developing and implementing a pricing strategy for products and services internationally is a real challenge and it is wise to follow a series of steps as indicated in Fig. 14.1.

Fig. 14.1 Steps involved in an international pricing strategy

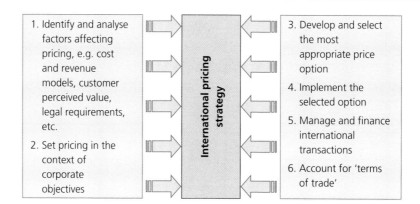

Factors Affecting Global Pricing Decisions

Marsh (2000), examining the factors which must be taken into account when determining international prices, argued that specific country preferences require organizations to adapt pricing. He proposed a framework for examining the micro environment and identified ways in which organizations can use price to gain competitive advantage. He suggested that by examining the crucial micro environmental factors within a country, companies may be able to strategically use price to gain advantage. He cites the examples of Kronenbourg (www.k1664.co.uk) and Stella Artois (www.stella-artois.com) beers, whose owners, by use of astute market sensing, are able strategically to adjust price to the market conditions. Both these products sell in the UK at a premium price, whereas in Belgium and France they are low-priced drinks (for a detailed discussion of this example, see Dawes and Thornes, 1995: 82).

Terpstra and Sarathy (2000) offer a framework for international pricing. Depending on the organization's stance on the 'exporting to global marketing continuum', the pricing decision will escalate from merely a tactical exporting decision based on cost to a strategic decision based on organizational, environmental, and country-specific factors. Take, for example, McDonald's (www.mcdonalds.com), which have been able, through experience and standardization, to charge a more or less equal price for their products throughout the world. Terpstra and Sarathy (2000) provide a comprehensive list of factors to be taken into account when pricing products and services globally, which includes organization level and product-specific, market-specific and environmental factors. Table 14.1 provides an extension to Terpstra and Sarathy (2000) in listing the major factors to be taken into account.

The majority of these elements are self-explanatory, however some are worth expanding from a strategic point of view. Company and marketing objectives are particularly interesting. It has long been accepted that Japanese companies adopt a long-term product perspective as opposed to the short-term approach of the USA, *for example*, where aggressive promotion and selling is important. Recent trends in South East Asia are changing this. Long known for their low cost base, hence the movement of multinationals from one country to another in search of lower-cost operations, these economies are concentrating on enhancing product quality and innovation, e.g. Hyundai (www.hyundai.com) and Kia (www.kia.com) cars give incredible value for money. They achieve this not by moving from one 'low cost of production' economy to another, but by process and product innovation. This trend is in line with the global consumer movement to high quality and low price.

Price standardization is becoming more difficult to achieve (Marsh, 2000). More and more frequently, local conditions are dictating price adaptation. While products and services may appear similar in a physical sense, it is unusual to find any one product or service similarly priced. The frequency of purchase, unit cost, and degree of comparability are important issues, but location is now a major factor. Despite the regulations of the European Union (EU), cars in the UK are still on average 20% more expensive in the UK than the comparable model in Europe. This is explained, in the main, by the cost to European manufacturers of changing the steering from left to right handed, transport costs, and UK taxes.

The Addis Ababa, Ethiopia, Hilton Hotel (www.hilton.com) charges half the price of that charged by the same hotel group in London, despite the fact that it is frequented mainly by international clients as the average Ethiopian cannot afford to stay there. It would, perhaps, be too cynical to suggest that, despite all the plausible reasons for the escalation in prices, geographic isolation is one of the major factors in pricing consumer products. Organizations would claim that they are pursuing classic, flexible cost-plus pricing

Table 14.1 Factors to be considered in pricing products and services globally

Organization-specific	Environmental	Market-specific
Corporate and marketing objectives	Domestic and targeted country(ies) government influences	Consumers expectations, location, ability to pay, market growth potential, frequency of purchase, degree of product comparability and degree of market transience
Cost structures, fixed and variable, experience and scale effects	Currency fluctuations, inflation and deflation	Product/market adaption vs. standardization issues
Product range, life cycle, and substitutes	Business cycle stage	Market structures and market institutions, e.g. command vs. market economies, distribution channels and market support activities, e.g. banks, insurance, credit etc.
Marketing factors—product positioning and segmentation and other marketing mix considerations, e.g. image and differentiation	Terms of trade and access	Competition, objectives and strategies
Transactional activities, e.g. inventory transport, freight, insurance, market research, contracting costs, etc.	Economic and political influences, including interventions from governments and world bodies, e.g. the World Bank	Joint entry/venture strategies and co-marketing possibilities
Desired rates of return and contribution from overseas operations	Risk assessment	Ability to expatriate funds
Access to resources		Degree of cost control
Risk assessment		Risk assessment

Source: Based on Terpstra and Sarathy (2000).

approaches (see later sections). Similarly with services. In South Africa, for example, some banks charge for the privilege of the customer depositing money. There has been research conducted on 'location', and other contributory factors, affecting shopping behaviour. Piron (2002) studied the international outshopping behaviour (a phenomenon rife in the UK, with thousands of Britons crossing the Channel to French shopping complexes everyday) of some 900,000 Singaporean day-trippers per month crossing the Causeway to shop in the Malaysian town of Johor Bahru. The research sought to uncover the influence of demographic and retail characteristics. Additionally, it sought to discover the importance of various types of secondary costs of outshopping and the impact of consumer ethnocentrism on attitudes towards outshopping. The findings revealed that food, beverages, and grocery products were the most frequently outshopped goods. Competitive prices and parking facilities were found to be the major reasons for frequent outshopping and, frequent shoppers perceived secondary costs as less important than infrequent shoppers did. In short, Piron found that outshoppers engage in this form of activity primarily for economic reasons.

Strategic global considerations have led companies to adopt different price strategies. Daewoo (www.daewoo.com) entered the UK market as the car 'you have never heard of', knowing it had no image and no track record. However, its main weapon was its 'value for money' pricing strategy, delivered through its clever 'no dealer' distribution strategy and 'no hassle' salesman-selling strategy. It was targeting other car imports in particular and has established itself well. The low price strategy, giving the perceived image of cheapness was rapidly offset by the in-built quality and additional features of the product. Similarly, Hyundai is now offering a world first—a five-year car warranty. Using price as a differentiating tool in a market or product category can be a key offensive strategy globally.

In today's rapidly changing environment, with corporate scandals and disintegrating or changing economies, such as Zimbabwe, Iraq, and Afghanistan, the global marketer is advised to carry out a risk assessment at all levels: market, potential customer, financial, and internal. The cost of not doing so is, potentially, great. It would not have been possible to envisage the collapse of companies like Enron and Northern Rock, or the total disintegration of a once-rich nation like Zimbabwe, in such a short period of time. The risks of appropriation of profits and blocks on trade, sometimes from unexpected sources, such as consumer product boycotts, can have a disastrous effect, and so risk assessment activities have become commonplace in all global operations.

As equally important as risk is the 'cost' factor, especially as it affects the final price and margins of products and services. With increasing globalization and, specifically, the entry of 'low-cost players' such as China and India, global competition is increasingly dependent on finding a low-cost producing location. However, this has to be tempered by other factors, such as the ability to segment markets, product differentiation, and 'image' benefits which make 'low cost' not always the dominant factor (see the end-of-chapter case study on perfume). In addition, as economies move through the economic development cycle and populations become more affluent (e.g. China), offering the cheapest price is not always the best strategy. In the search for cost reduction, organizations may achieve this through a number of different strategies, including economies of scale, economies of size, the 'learning curve', the introduction of new technologies or processes, and relocation (see Fig. 14.2).

- **Economies of scale** are obtained when the additional cost of one unit of production reduces the per unit cost overall given the same, or only slightly raised, fixed costs. The

Fig. 14.2 Cost reduction strategies

Economies of scale	When additional cost per unit of production reduced overall per unit cost, given similar fixed costs
Economies of size	Achieved from larger scale of operation through greater bargaining power
The learning curve	Cost reduction from greater labour productivity, improved designs, and resource mix
Introduction of new technologies	Improved efficiency gained through new technologies in innovation and processes
Relocation of production	Moving production facilities to countries with substantially lower labour costs

savings achieved by this must offset the cost of investment in additional in-country plants or it is not worth doing. Car manufacturing is a good example.

- **Economies of size** are obtained when the scale of operations is such that costs are reduced overall and so the organization gains through larger bargaining power, e.g. supermarkets expanding overseas.

- **The 'learning curve'**, made famous by the Boston Consulting Group (www. bcg.com), suggests that there is a direct relationship between the cumulative volume of production and the costs in producing the same product benefits. The major sources of savings gained from cumulative experience include greater labour productivity, improved product designs, and changes of the resource mix.

- **The introduction of new technologies, the incidence of innovation or processes** may 'leap frog' the learning curve in that the industry overall costs of production may be lowered or changed or a 'disruptive technology' may destroy the current *modus operandi*. The Toyota (www.toyota.com) hybrid car technology and the Boeing (www. boeing.com) aircraft manufacturer's use of composites rather than aluminum in aircraft bodies are good examples.

- **Relocation of production** is seen by many global producers as key to gaining cost benefits, and therefore greater margins and pricing leeway. Manufacturers such as Coca-Cola (www.coca-cola.com) and IBM (www.ibm.com) and service industries such as British Telecom (www.bt.com) have established call centres in India, for example, to reduce labour costs. Others have set up in China and other parts of South East Asia such as furniture manufacturers in Vietnam. All seek labour and production cost advantages. However, it is not without 'cost'. Recently, many companies have relocated back to the UK, e.g. the financial services industry, as customers have experienced frustrations, especially with call centres located abroad.

Whichever cost reduction strategy is employed, if the costs of so doing outweigh the apparent or non-apparent ('image') cost benefits over time, then the advantageous effect on pricing strategy will be lost.

Pricing Strategy

We now look at the pricing strategies available to the global marketer. These are standardization (ethnocentric) pricing, adaptation (polycentric) pricing, and corridor (geocentric) pricing (for further discussion on corridor pricing strategies, see Keegan and Schlegelmilch, 2001). Table 14.2 shows the key features of these strategies.

Setting a pricing strategy is not easy due to the multiplicity of factors to be taken into account. A standardized approach has much to commend it, not least because it is simple to operate. However, depending on the stage of economic development within a country and the height of the standardized price, not all consumers will be able to afford a global standardized price, so an adaptation pricing policy may be more realistic. This is generally true of less developed economies. A corridor pricing strategy offers the best compromise between the two extremes. Its flexibility allows organizations to charge differential prices, according to market conditions, and may offer the best long-term pricing solution. It depends on what the organization wishes to achieve from its global venture. While financial objectives like sales volume, rate of return, and profits will be essential, it may wish to arrest competitive activity, be in a potential market first, wish strategically to expand, or find an outlet for its saturated home market products and services. The latter is probably the least strategic decision of all.

Table 14.2 Key features of pricing strategy

Feature	Standardization	Adaptation	Corridor/invention
Pricing decision	Central	Local	Central and local
Additions to basic price	Transport and import duties, etc. paid by the customer, hence price variations in country	Final price depends on local transport and other marketing costs Transfer pricing is a corporate decision	Local prices set within the constraints of the long-term objectives of the corporation
Drivers	Decreasing marketing costs Size of market Reduction of trade barriers Increased brand globalization Global sourcing	Customer preferences Cost structures Terms of access, duties, and tariffs Competition	Compromise between unprofitable, low, standardized, and adaptive prices, Market opportunities Changing patterns of demand Long-term considerations
Advantages	Low risk	Responds to local conditions and competition Encourages sales volumes	Responds to local conditions If demand takes off, encourages local investment Encourages long-term profit Discourages grey and parallel markets
Disadvantages	No local conditions are taken into account Does not maximize profits or volumes Encourages parallel and grey market trading	No central control Encourages grey markets	Short-term losses
Example	Commodities	Cars	Holidays

Before considering a specific price in international markets, there are numerous factors to consider at the strategy level. Three factors determine the boundaries of the pricing decision: the floor price (determined by total costs including those of manufacturing and marketing), the price ceiling (determined by the extent and type of competition), and the optimum price (determined by demand and costs). Added to these factors are those of government tax policies, resale prices, dumping, overseas transportation costs, exchange rate fluctuations, and inflation and deflation effects. So-called 'parallel' or grey markets will be considered later in the chapter. These factors determine whether to set a 'skimming' (a high price which aims to recoup product development and market costs quickly), a 'penetration' (low price which aims to gain the maximum sales volume as soon as possible), or a price-market holding price (see Fig. 14.3). There are possibilities for operating a number of pricing policies, as we have seen in the case of flexible cost plus price differentiation, but these are specific approaches which will be discussed below. The floor price, ceiling price, and optimum price lead to three international marketing price-setting approaches: rigid cost plus, competitive or flexible cost plus, where market and competitive factors are taken

WHOSE RESPONSIBILITY IS IT? **The great summer holiday 'rip-off'**

A glance through any holiday brochure will show that, depending on the time of year, the same holiday can cost up to 100% more in summer than in winter. Equally, 'special occasion holidays', such as Easter or Chinese New Year in Asian countries, is the trigger to up the price of hotels. A classic case of corridor pricing or a shameless rip-off? For families it can mean an enormous outlay, in school holidays, for taking a well-deserved break. A two-week holiday in Cyprus, for example, by one of the big tour operators in summer, can cost about £3,000 for a family of three. In winter the same holiday would cost half that amount. The UK government, in July 2004, was so concerned about the difference in prices, often coinciding with school holidays, that it launched an inquiry. Tour operators point to supply and demand, and while there is a good deal of truth in this, it cannot all be explained by sheer economics. Analytical thinkers would suggest that it is profiteering.

Fig. 14.3 Pricing policy options

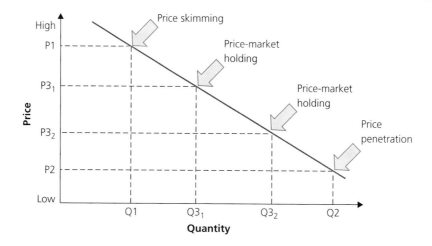

into account, and incremental (penetration) pricing where the desire to make a contribution is paramount.

Economics tell us that there is a relationship between supply, demand sales volumes, and costs. The more a company can produce the more the unit cost falls and, in theory, the higher the demand. This often gives the initial impetus to companies merely to export their surplus without resort to sophisticated pricing policy. It is a question of buyer and seller agreeing a price. This depends on the type of product being sold as some products are price-inelastic whereas others are elastic. Sales volumes can be affected by the price charged. In high-tech, industrial goods (e.g. aircraft, warships, railways, and turnkey projects', demand may be relatively inelastic as other factors, such as after-sales support and quality, are more important. In less high-tech consumer goods, the demand may be very elastic (e.g. beer), where there is a choice of alternatives. Some products can buck the classic price reduction/increased demand syndrome—by reducing the price, demand can fall. Car manufacturers like Porsche (www.porsche.com) and Mercedes-Benz (www.mercedes-benz.com)

maintain their high prices and refuse discounting to protect the used-car market prices. Inelasticity of demand may occur where domestic market saturation has been reached, and so companies may turn to exporting as a solution, basing their prices on the 'absorption costing' model. Providing all fixed costs are covered by domestic sales, the extra overseas sales are seen as providing an additional contribution to overheads.

Specific Price Approaches

There are numerous approaches to fixing a specific price, including cost-oriented, competitive or flexible cost-plus, and market penetration or dynamic incremental pricing (see Brassington and Pettitt, 2006; Jobber, 2006; Doole and Lowe 2008). Each one of these approaches is aimed at achieving a specific pricing objective, illustrated in Table 14.3.

Cost-oriented pricing

Many organizations new to exporting will use a cost-oriented price such as cost-plus pricing. It is based on adding up the costs of production and marketing (direct and indirect costs) and includes shipping and any other charges plus a profit percentage. This has the advantage of easy calculation of costs but ignores market and competitive factors. The manufacturer may also experience too low a price or too high a price, the latter being called price escalation, which will be covered later in the chapter.

Markup pricing is typical of this approach, where a standard markup is added to the cost of the product or service. Lawyers and accountants are typical examples. Markups vary from product to product. Supermarkets may have a small one, maybe 10%, depending on volume to generate profits overall, whereas perfume and branded products may be as much as 100%, depending on the 'name' and quality, e.g. Louis Vuitton (www.louisvuitton.com). High markups can be fatal if competitors are charging a 'penetration' price, but may be very acceptable if the product is new to market. It is a popular method because costs are easy to calculate and where all companies in the industry use this method, prices tend to be similar. It is also seen as a fair method to buyers and sellers.

Target–return pricing is another cost-pricing approach. The company determines a price that yields a target return on investment (ROI). A break-even chart may be used to

Table 14.3 Pricing objectives

Pricing objective	Pricing method
Rate of return on Investment	Cost-oriented, e.g. oil and gas
Competition matching or prevention	Competition-based pricing, e.g. commodities or lower than competition to prevent competitive entry in country
Market share/penetration	Demand-led pricing or geographical pricing: low when product is in plentiful supply, 'least cost sourced', or to get product established, e.g. Chinese-made umbrellas
Market skimming	Demand-led pricing: high when product is in short supply or 'new to market', e.g. Nintendo wii
Product differentiation	Market or 'product in use' pricing, e.g. cars
Early cash recovery	Promotional pricing, price discounting, or allowances where liquidity is an issue, markets are uncertain, or the product is in 'maturity', e.g. 'sales'

determine the volume and prices needed to achieve the target return. Target return pricing tends to ignore price elasticity and competitors reaction.

Competitive or flexible cost-plus pricing

The derivation of this price-setting approach is the same as the one above except that the price is adjusted to take into account local market conditions, nature of the customer, size of order, and competitive conditions. Although this gives the marketer a high degree of flexibility, the aim is still to maintain profit margins. This is the classic market holding price position given at $P3_1/Q3_1$ and $P3_2/Q3_2$ in Fig. 14.3. In single-country operations, this approach often means adjusting prices to local competition, but not always so. In Addis Ababa, Ethiopia, there is plenty of hotel competition but the Hilton keeps its prices relatively low compared with Hilton prices in London. However, in Hangzhou, China, where there is equally strong competition, the Sheraton Hotel prices are at international levels. In both countries, these hotels are mainly patronized by foreigners.

Going-rate pricing is a competitive-based pricing method. The price is fixed on what competitors are charging rather than what the company estimates its costs or demand to be. This is typical of oligopolistic industries such as petrol retailing, where prices are very similar. The price is set on the perceived collective wisdom of the industry and relies less on estimates of costs.

Competitive bid or tendering pricing is a very well known, competitive pricing method and typical where a number of companies are in competition with each other for a contract, e.g. the supply of aero engines or construction projects. The bids are made on the basis of the companies expected profits because, by playing the odds, the likelihood is that the company will make maximum profits in the long run. Companies often go to great lengths to try to estimate the likelihood of winning a contract. Bombardier (www.bombardier.com) and Siemens (www.siemen.com), competitors in the field of railway engineering, are very keen to track their bid failure and success records in order to maximize any future bids.

Market-based pricing

Perceived value pricing is based on the market's view of value and not the sellers view of cost. As such, it brings other elements of the marketing mix in to play, both objective and subjective, such as 'image'. Investment in plant and production is based on whether the company sees a market at the perceived value or not. Caterpillar (www.caterpillar.com) prices its products based on this method. It calculates the price it can command in the market based on its estimate of superior durability, reliability, warranty, and service. The key to perceived value pricing is an accurate estimate of the market's perception of the offer's value, and that is not always easy. Market research is a good way of estimating this.

Psychological pricing is a very well-documented method of pricing. The relationship between price and quality is key in this method, although these days consumers expect high quality but at low prices, or at least, if the price is high, the product is exclusive or has demonstrable superior value. Reference prices are essential in this method. A consumer carries around a reference price in his/her head against which products and services are continuously measured. By starting higher than the manufacturer's price or competitors' prices, retailers may create a favourable reference point. Prices ending with odd or even numbers are other forms of psychological pricing. For example, £3.99 appears to be a bargain compared to £4.00.

EasyJet (www.easyJet.com) and Ryanair (www.ryanair.com) are two of the fastest-growing and most profitable airlines in the UK. Started in the 1990s, both have reached an enviable position in the market, beating, for growth and profitability, mainstream carriers like British Airways (www.ba.com) and Air France (www.airfrance.com) on short-haul European routes. Both started with highly motivated, far-sighted, and entrepreneurial owners, a Greek and Irish national respectively. The business model was simple: fly to little-used airports near major destinations where slots were available and landing prices low, provide no frills on the plane (no drinks, meals, etc. unless the passenger is prepared to pay for them) and be on time, clean, and turn round quickly. The operators gambled that on short-haul flights the luxuries of flying did not matter as long as the price was low. And they were right. The competition believed that the business market would forsake low-cost carriers in favour of the luxuries. They were proved wrong. In the cost-conscious business world, the attraction of a short-haul airline at super low prices was attractive. After 9/11, passengers eschewed long-haul holidays and the scheduled airlines which they believed could be a terrorist target, and holidayed in Europe, further boosting the low-cost operators' growth and profits. Growth and profits in the late 1990s and early 2000s were spectacular, with profits of 10–20% of turnover; most of the major carriers made huge losses in the same period.

But the *pièce de résistance* in the business model lay in the astute use of technology, which cut millions of pounds off operating costs and led the way in the industry. This was the use of online booking with no tickets or boarding cards. By booking online and having a ticketless system not only could passengers book conveniently at home, but they saved money also. For the airlines, they saved huge costs in ticket-issuing operations. But the ingenuity did not stop there. The low-cost operators knew the cost of flying each route. The greater the number of passengers, the lower the operating costs, and the cheaper the price of the tickets. The operators offered a pricing policy based on demand and operating capacity. In order to entice customers, the longer the time the passenger booked in advance, the cheaper the ticket. The dilemma for the customer was how long to wait before booking a ticket and risking a price increase. The formula was spectacularly successful. Major operators such as British Airways ignored the competition, thinking that they could not survive on such a business model. They were then forced by the success of the low-cost operators to try the formula themselves, but failed.

The low-cost operators are now established and Ryanair has become one of the biggest in Europe. Whether they will survive, and even introduce the formula to long-haul flights (as Freddie Laker did in the 1970s), only time will only tell. The danger signs were looming

in mid-2004 as more and more low-cost operators set up in Europe. By that time there were 55 low-cost operators, too few passengers, and soaring fuel costs. EasyJet announced a review of its network after a profit warning, and warned of taking one-sixth of its fleet out of operation, especially on unprofitable routes. However, it still intended to stick to its new jet delivery promise. EasyJet's value had fallen from £2 billion in November 2000 to £629 million in mid-2004. The budget airlines had to respond, in various ways, to the realities of the market environment.

EasyJet did fulfil its promise of new planes delivery and by 2008 had introduced many new Airbus aircraft on to its routes. Ryanair introduced a maximum 14kg baggage allowance, down from the traditional 20kg, and started charging a fee per checked-in bag as well. More routes were added to the low-cost carrier network in a bid to expand the number of passengers carried, but with the major carriers like BA and others offering many incentives to flyers, competition in the airline industry was fierce. With the global financial crisis at the end of 2008, a number of low-cost carriers were facing increasing difficulties, e.g. Ryanair found its profits slashed dramatically. It is becoming more than likely that some low-cost carriers will cease to exist.

The low-cost airlines are an example of charging a competitive, market-based price based on a flexible approach to costs and an astute assessment of market needs. But, as this case shows, profits attract competition and that can spell danger for some.

Market penetration or dynamic incremental pricing is another market-based pricing method. As long as the fixed costs of production are met regardless of international marketing, then the aim is to retrieve the variable and international marketing costs. Overheads are only partially added. In Fig. 14.3, this is price P2/Q2. This approach gives a great deal of freedom. Asian manufacturers, particularly from China, have been selling products into Europe at low prices but, generally, of good quality. The manufacturers are likely to be taking losses and the practice is very close to dumping. New exporters cannot afford such an approach, being unable to sustain losses over long periods. If the product is not patent protected, penetration pricing is a good approach. Again with reference to China, a lot of the merchandise is patent unprotectable, e.g. toys, luggage, and umbrellas. The art is to get as many sales as possible before someone makes it cheaper and better, hence the pricing policy. Having established itself in the market, the price penetrator may either ward off competition by reducing prices further, until its cost base becomes prohibitive, or it may wish to raise the price, especially if this can be done on the back of innovation to the product. The classic case of this was the entry into the UK market of Sony (www.sony.com) and other Japanese manufacturers in the 1960s and 1970s with televisions.

The UK market was dominated by UK-produced mono-colour televisions by companies like Baird and Thorn. These televisions were sold in three sizes only. Spotting a gap in the market for smaller sizes of televisions, the Japanese quickly established themselves and gained volume. By innovation, colour television in particular, they started to encroach on the traditional UK television sizes and mono-colour market. Before UK manufacturers could react, buoyed up by volumes and innovation, the Japanese televisions became cheaper and were in greater demand. Within a decade all UK manufacturers had disappeared.

Dynamic incremental pricing can work in another way. It can be a high price (skimming) strategy (P1/Q1 in Fig. 14.3). The aim is to sell to market segments which value a distinctive price; other product features, both objective and subjective ones, such as 'exclusivity', being more appropriate in adding value for the market. The goal is to maximize revenue on limited volume. This policy is often utilized in the launch stage of a product life cycle, where production and marketing costs are high and market demand is hard to judge. Over time the price could be reduced to match competition. Examples of skimming price approaches are the high-value fashion houses such as Stella McCartney (www.stellamccartney.com) and Giorgio Armani (www.giorgioarmani.com), and first-class air travel.

Price Adaptation

International marketers seldom set a single price for every product and market. Various market locations, costs in reaching the markets, different market segments, perceived value by customers, and purchase timing can all affect the pricing strategy.

Geographical pricing

Organizations price differently in different markets to reflect the costs of reaching them and different demand conditions. For example, cars in the USA are much cheaper than in the UK even though they are the same model, reflecting the differing volumes. There are several forms of geographical pricing, including:

- **Free on board (FOB) origin pricing**, where customers are asked to pay the costs of shipping to different locations. This seems a very fair way to treat different geographical locations.
- **Same (one) delivered pricing**, which is exactly the opposite of FOB pricing and has the advantage of being easy to administer and maintain the nationally advertised delivered price.

- **Zone pricing** falls between FOB pricing and uniform delivered pricing in that the company establishes a number of zones and charges different prices depending on which zone the customer is located in. The problem with this method is that customers just over the border line subsidize the ones just on the other side. Levi jeans (www .levi.com) cost much less in the USA than they do in the UK.

- **Basing point pricing**, where the organization may chose a city or port and charge customers from that point regardless of where they are located. This method has fallen foul of collusive pricing legislation, especially where all competitors use the same point.

- **Freight paid pricing**, which is used for market penetration purposes as the manufacturer absorbs all or part of the freight charges.

Price discounts and allowances

Under this form of pricing, organizations reward customers for early payment, bulk buying, or off-season buying. There are many forms of discounts, including:

- **Cash discounts**: price reductions for prompt payment of bills, aiding liquidity.
- **Quantity discounts**: a price reduction to buyers who buy large quantities. They must be offered to all customers and the savings must exceed the costs. They encourage a customer to buy from one seller rather than multiple sellers.
- **Seasonal discounts**: a price reduction to buyers who buy out of season. This aids the manufacturer by balancing production runs throughout the year.
- **Functional discounts**: trade discounts so that the intermediary will take on certain functions, such as inventory and selling.
- **Invoice discounting**: the buying of one organizations's invoices by another (usually a bank) at a discount, thus aiding cash flow for the selling organization.
- **'Trade in' allowances**: other price deductions from the list price, such as trade-in allowances (e.g. cars) and promotional allowances on certain models.

Promotional pricing

On occasions (e.g. when trying to establish market share), companies may price below list and cost. Such promotional pricing includes:

- **Psychological discounting**: high prices followed by large savings, 'was—now', provided they are lawful.
- **Low interest finance**: typical of car purchase, where 0% finance deals are becoming common. However, there may be catches, such as having to put down a large deposit.
- **Warranties and service contracts**: promote sales via extended warranties or special deals, such as Hyundai's five-year warranty and Mercedes-Benz's service deal.
- **Cash rebates**: stimulate sales without costing the company as much as cutting the price. Again, this strategy is used by car retailers to encourage sales.
- **Loss leader pricing**: typical of supermarkets where the price of one product might be lowered to encourage the sales of other products. The 'buy one get one free' phenomenon has generally overtaken the loss leader because loss leaders can damage the lower-priced brand image.
- **Special event pricing**: special prices for certain seasons, e.g. January 'sales'.

Market/use pricing

Organizations may adjust prices to accommodate differences in customers, locations, and products:

- **Customer segment pricing**: different customers are charged different prices for the same product or service, e.g. flight pricing.
- **Product form pricing**: different forms of the product are priced at different prices, e.g. laptop computers from the same company.
- **Image pricing**: the same product is priced at two different levels based on image differences, e.g. Easter eggs.
- **Location pricing**: different locations are priced differently even though the costs of offering the location are the same, e.g. Disneyland's (disneyland.disney.go.com) fast-pass system.
- **Time pricing**: different pricing for the same product by season, day, or hour, e.g. roses at higher prices on St Valentine's day.

For price discrimination to work, the segments must show different intensities of demand, there must be no between-segment reselling, the costs must not be exceeded by the revenue, customers must not be antagonized, and the price must be legal. However, in international markets this is no easy task. Customers will go to different locations to obtain lower prices, e.g. European shoppers going to New York to shop at Christmas despite the cost of an air fare, and car buyers from the UK going to Europe to purchase the same model because it is cheaper than it is on offer in the UK.

Product mix pricing

Prices may have to be modified when the organization wishes to maximize profits on the total product mix. This is not easy because of competitive factors. The possible product mix pricing methods are:

- **Product line pricing**: carried out on a range of products, price being escalated (premium pricing) when new features are added, related cost increase and the company feels the market will bear the extra price for the perceived benefits. A good example is digital cameras or cars.
- **'Razor and blades' pricing**: a method used when the use of one product requires the use of another. In the car example, often the aftermarket in servicing and parts supply, can generate better profit margins than the original car sale. But care has to be taken in this type of pricing, especially if a 'pirate' market develops selling parts at a cheaper price. In some instances, manufacturers have sough to get round this by invalidating warranties if they see this has happened.
- **Optional feature pricing**: the price is increased as more optional items are added to the basic mode. Again, cars are a classic example, as the basic model is increased in price to account for add on extras.
- **By-product pricing**: some products create by-products and manufacturers or suppliers might sell them off at a price that is less than the cost of disposal e.g. candles as a by product of cattle slaughter.
- **Two-tier pricing**: service companies often charge a fixed fee and a fee based on usage or at certain times e.g. mobile phone providers and electricity supply.

- **Brand bundling pricing**: this is where the brands are bundled together and sold at less than the individual parts like season tickets.

All these approaches depend on the international marketer being able to estimate a number of parameters. These include costs (manufacturing, marketing, and incremental costs), demand, competitors, and environmental factors such as price escalation and inflation. Costs may be difficult to estimate, especially future costs, if demand internationally takes off better than expected. As most activity these days is cost-driven, attempts to reduce costs can only add to the targeted returns. Increased demand may bring economies of scale but these savings have to be looked at in light of the savings in transport and other costs affected by having production based overseas. 'Experience effect' gains may occur through new production processes, more effective marketing, and greater labour efficiency, all of which reduce costs but these gains have to be exploited globally. EasyJet, the low-cost UK air operator, has achieved cost reductions through a combination of experience and economies of scale, for example it has cut marketing costs via the use of an internet booking system. However, it is now facing difficulties because of over-capacity in the industry and lower than expected bookings. Another way of cutting costs is to locate (or relocate production and marketing) to low-cost producing countries. South East Asia used to be a hotbed for low-cost relocation. For example, Sony produced hi-fi components in Malaysia, but as costs began to rise in these economies, it moved into the 'knowledge' industry. China and India have become 'relocation favourites'. Coca-Cola (www.coke.com), IBM, and Motorola (www.motorola.com) are all manufacturing in these countries, and service industries are also relocating there, e.g. British Airways ticketing facilities. In today's knowledge-based economy, relocation need not be physical. Data processing, online consulting, and insurance, for example, can all be done over the internet.

It is far easier for multinationals, with their large resources, to relocate all, or some, of their manufacturing capacity to low-cost economies. Small and medium-sized enterprises (SMEs) often do not have such an abundance of resources. In these cases, the approach may be to find as many economies as possible in the value chain (e.g. use of the internet as a distribution strategy), concentrate on a particular aspect of it (e.g. the computer industry), or network as much as possible. In the latter instance, consulting and advertising industries use networks of individuals with special skills. The mini-case illustration of Solace (www.solace.org.uk) is such an example.

Assessing consumer demand is not easy. Both consumer perceptions and purchasing behaviour have an effect on price. Consumer reaction and sensitivity to price may be affected by the product's physical attributes (price, size, and shape), its objective attributes (image, distinctiveness), and the physical location and spending power of the consumer. Mainstream American cars are not popular in the UK—they are seen as brash and expensive to run. Consumers in many developing countries are enticed by foreign goods—sometimes wearing the designer label on their suit sleeve for all to see. 'Made in' Germany, the UK, Japan, Switzerland, and the USA are usually, but not with all products and services, powerful persuaders—the so-called 'country of origin' effect. This can be transient and it is market transience which can be an incentive to getting the price right. Strategically, price perceptions are an important issue for marketers. Moore et al. (2003) examined the cross-cultural equivalence of price perceptions between US and Polish consumers. As the markets of Eastern Europe continue to liberalize, they are becoming targets for Western retailers. Moore et al. examined and compared consumer perceptions of price as a marketplace cue in Polish and US cultures. They reported a great similarity between the two groups' perceptions of price. Using five constructs of price: price consciousness, sales proneness, price mavenism, price/quality schema, and prestige/sensitivity, the authors found that they were equivalent across the two cultures, indicating that existing price measures are adequate in tapping into the price concepts in both cultures. Only sales proneness was non-significant in the Polish sample, while it was extremely significant in the US sample, indicating a cultural difference in the perception of the sales concept which is not yet well developed in Polish culture. Overall, strategically, the research indicated that US retailers seeking Polish markets had a number of opportunities to standardize domestic price policy. However, the negatives connected with sale mavenism mean that US companies must be cautious in trying to export intensively promotional pricing strategies. Polish consumers use price as a positive cue to signal quality and prestige, but their perception of price as a negative cue does not appear to be well developed. This research confirms the need to be micro-environmentally sensitive to markets in the price decision.

Competitor responses may be hard to predict, depending on their degree of commitment to the market and their product/market range. Assessing competitive reaction should

THE RELATIONSHIP PERSPECTIVE Outsourcing

Outsourcing has become a global phenomenon (see Chapter 16 for discussion of outsourcing). It has become a key element in pricing strategy in that it can be a source of cost reduction in the value chain and thus a means of both providing specialist expertise and, at the same time, a source of overhead and manufacturing cost reduction. All types of businesses can take advantage of the outsourcing: consumer, business-to-business, or service. British Telecom and British Airways have located their call centres and ticketing facilities, respectively, to India. Toyota, Boeing, and Airbus (www.airbus.com) have components manufactured in various parts of the world. Marks and Spencer (www.marksandspencer.com) and Tesco (www.tesco .com) rely on a network of fresh produce and clothing manufacturers to source their needs. Outsourcing can cut up to 30% or more off the costs of manufacture, allowing organizations to be more price competitive in the global economy.

© Tesco. Reproduced with permission.

MINI-CASE ILLUSTRATION Solace

Solace is a UK-based organization providing services in the 'local government arena' both in the UK and internationally. It specializes in providing short-to medium-term consultants/interim management for local government executive positions in the UK and overseas. It has a growing portfolio in overseas election monitoring as well as the provision of short-term staff for assignments in developing economies, e.g. 'governance' assignments in Iraq. To

fulfil its business objectives, it has a small core of permanent staff but a large network of associates, many of whom were once senior local government officers, who are not on the Solace books as full-time employees. In this way, Solace not only keeps its overheads and salary elements low, enabling it to be price competitive, but it can also field an impressive array of highly qualified and specialist staff for other assignments.

THE DIGITAL IMPACT Empowering customers

The internet and interactive television has enabled customers of all types and in all locations, where access is available, to compare prices of competing products and services. Long gone, at least in most consumer goods, are the days when the customer had to call in or phone for written quotes. For example, customers can access the internet and compare airline ticket, car, holiday, and insurance prices. When purchasing a car, organizations such as the Automobile Association (AA, www.theaa.com) and What Car? (www.whatcar.co.uk) enable the prospective buyer to access prices for many vehicles, store them, and compare prices simultaneously. Car manufacturers Nissan (www.nissanmotors.com) and Mercedes-Benz even allow the customer to 'build' a customized vehicle on the web and produce a final price for it. Of course, this may not include negotiated discounts or extras, but it gives an example price to work on. Potential car buyers can access dealers and distributors globally to obtain quotes online. Customers are then empowered to negotiate when purchasing the car and are often able to play one dealer off against another to obtain a discount on the vehicle.

© The AA.com. Reproduced with permission.

Fig. 14.4 The global price-setting decision process

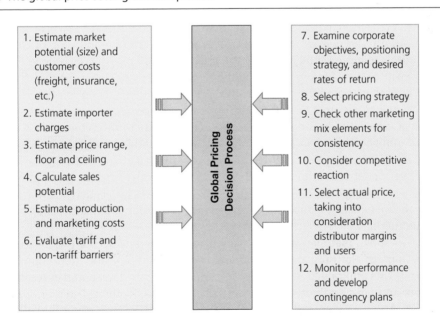

be part of the risk assessment analysis. One aid to this process may be to see what competitors have done in parallel markets. The process of international price setting is shown in Fig. 14.4.

Price Changes

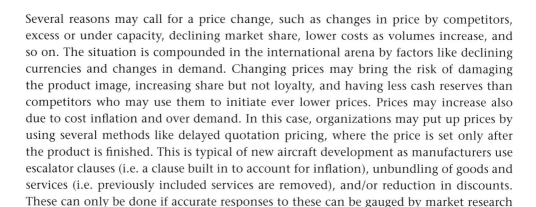

Several reasons may call for a price change, such as changes in price by competitors, excess or under capacity, declining market share, lower costs as volumes increase, and so on. The situation is compounded in the international arena by factors like declining currencies and changes in demand. Changing prices may bring the risk of damaging the product image, increasing share but not loyalty, and having less cash reserves than competitors who may use them to initiate ever lower prices. Prices may increase also due to cost inflation and over demand. In this case, organizations may put up prices by using several methods like delayed quotation pricing, where the price is set only after the product is finished. This is typical of new aircraft development as manufacturers use escalator clauses (i.e. a clause built in to account for inflation), unbundling of goods and services (i.e. previously included services are removed), and/or reduction in discounts. These can only be done if accurate responses to these can be gauged by market research or intelligence.

Companies can also respond to increases in costs or demand without raising prices. These include offering less product for the same money, substituting ingredients for less costly ones, lowering production costs, investing in newer technologies, reducing product or service features, using less expensive packaging, reinforcing other non-price benefits, reducing the number and range of products, or creating new brands or lines. Again, all these can be effected providing the consequences can be reasonably calculated. This is not easy as calculations can involve factors which are difficult to identify. The factors include customers, competitors, distributors, suppliers, and other stakeholders such as government. In government procurement of, say, defence products, often the original price escalates beyond all expectations. For instance, the cost of developing the Eurofighter escalated some £1 billion beyond its original development budget.

Customer's reaction to price changes depends on their perception of the change and product. A reduction in price may signal an imminent discontinuation, whereas an increase could indicate the item is 'hot'. It also depends on the value and type of the product. Competitors might react by following the price reduction or increase. It depends on what the competitor is wishing to achieve and how it interprets the price change. If the market is highly product homogeneous, then the competition has little option but to follow the price change. However, if the market is in a non-homogeneous product market, competitors have more latitude and may decide to reinforce other mix elements such as increasing the number of product features. Market leaders often face aggressive price changes. The market leaders of plasma TV technology based in Japan and South Korea soon found themselves under attack from the other manufacturers, like Philips (www.philips.co.uk), once the technology had disseminated. In this case, these leaders may maintain the price, raise perceived quality, reduce the price, increase both price and quality, and launch a low price fighter line.

Fig. 14.4 shows that there are many factors to be taken into account when setting prices internationally. Not only are there 'internal' elements to consider (e.g. company objectives and costs of production), but also 'external' elements (target market reactions, competition, and tariff and non-tariff barriers). This can make pricing internationally a risky business. Although competitive prices may be a guide if comparable competition exists, it is an extremely difficult task in new product or service pricing. For small- and medium-sized enterprises, getting the price wrong can be fatal. In established multi-product/market enterprises, one pricing failure can often be absorbed without jeopardizing the whole business.

Special Issues in Global Price Setting

There are a number of special issues in global price setting, as illustrated in Fig. 14.5.

Price escalation

Price escalation is a specific feature of global pricing. Tax liabilities, tariffs, insurance, and logistical costs add to the final selling price. But is the importer prepared to pay for these costs over time? Consider the example in Fig. 14.6, where the 9.26 price is less than the domestic price. In this case, the organization may:

- abandon exporting as the costs are too prohibitive;
- consider a marginal pricing policy (see Market penetration or dynamic incremental pricing above);

Fig. 14.5 Special issues in global pricing

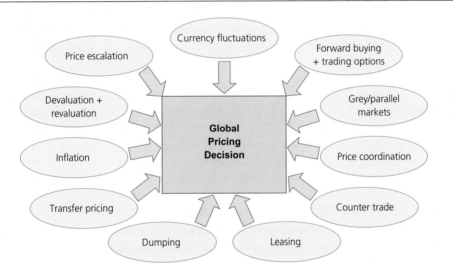

Fig. 14.6 Example of price escalation

Target price in foreign market	25.00
Less 40% retail margin on selling price	10.00
Retailer cost	15.00
Less 15% importer/distributor markup	1.96
Distributor cost	13.04
Less 12% value added tax on landed value and duty	1.40
CIF value plus duty	11.64
Less 9% duty on CIF value	0.96
Landed CIF value	10.68
Less ocean freight and insurance	1.40
Required FOB price to achieve target price	9.26

NB: The final price can even be higher if the importer has to borrow money from a bank or other financial institution to finance the imports. Interest charges will be incurred.

MINI-CASE ILLUSTRATION **The case of fair trading: Oxfam**

Producers, especially in less developed countries, have complained about the fact that high value produce (like horticulture) and goods (like handicrafts), for example, have commanded final selling prices, when sold overseas, out of proportion to the share that the original producers or manufacturers have obtained. In the case of horticultural produce, producers of flowers and mangetout in Thailand, Kenya, Zambia, and Tanzania receive about 10% of the final selling price. This is partly due to price escalation as the goods move through the value-added chain, but it is obviously due to the fact that sellers in developed countries (where most of these goods are sold) can charge a high margin because costs are higher and there is a demand to be satisfied. This is especially true in times of high demand. It is estimated that in the UK demand for roses rises tenfold on St Valentine's day.

Oxfam (www.oxfam.org.uk), the charity relief organization, in the 1990s decided to champion the cause of producers in developing countries. Oxfam has numerous high street charity shops through which it sells pre-owned, quality goods, especially clothing, and goods supplied from less developed countries. It instigated a pricing policy whereby the producers in the less developed countries received a 'fair price', i.e. they received a price for their produce based

on a calculation of the real cost of production. The campaign has been supported by positive publicity. Such has been its success that other organizations, not only charities, have adopted a similar fair price policy, thus making sure that the original producers receive a fair share of the final selling price. Today, it is estimated that about £400 million of business in the UK, mainly in foodstuffs, is done on a 'Fairtrade' basis. This is relatively small in comparison to the total amount spent of foodstuffs in a year. However, it is affecting producers in 100 less developed countries world wide, and the number is growing.

- consider shortening the distribution channel to reduce the added costs, e.g. the distributor margin;
- consider modifying or simplifying the product to make it lighter, smaller, or reallocate its exporting nomenclature or other cost reduction strategies;
- consider finding an alternative source of supply with lower costs;
- consider a different market entry strategy, e.g. local manufacture, with all its implications.

The Fair Trade mini-case illustration of Oxfam examines some of the issues connected with price escalation and attempts to give producers a bigger share of the end price.

Currency fluctuations

In the past, one of the prime reasons for entering international markets was the profit to be made on foreign currency transactions. In the present economic climate it is not so easy. Countries such as Zimbabwe are undergoing severe foreign currency shortages and rampant annual inflation. For instance, Zimbabwe's monthly inflation is now measured in % millions and by the time this book is published, it could be more unless a change occurs. Many countries were severely affected by the East Asian financial crisis and suffered huge currency depreciations, for example, between January 1996 and October 1997, Indonesia (59%), Malaysia (36%), Thailand (58%), Australia (14%), and Japan (21%). Fluctuating exchange rates are caused by a number of economic factors (Table 14.4), such as adverse balance of payments, inappropriate monetary and fiscal policies, and rampant inflation. Escalating rates of inflation, for example, reduce the value of the domestic currency, requiring larger amounts to exchange for a stable foreign currency. A burgeoning economic growth rate can lead to a stronger currency and adversely affect

Table 14.4 Factors affecting currency fluctuations and rates of exchange

Economic factors	Political factors	Psychological factors
Balance of payments	Philosophy of the country's leaders	Expectations
Monetary and fiscal policy	Country's ideological leaning	Forward market prices
Inflation and deflation	Elections	Traders' attitudes
Real and nominal interest rates	State of political parties	
Government controls and incentives	Government	
Rates of economic growth		

exports as prices may be too high for potential buyers who have to pay more of their own currency to buy the currency of the exporter. Political factors like the country's ideological leaning or impending elections can affect exchange rates, positively or negatively. Zimbabwe, for example, has witnessed a rapid decline in its currency since the re-election of President Mugabe. Governments may also intervene and alter exchange rates. Harold Wilson's government devalued the pound in the 1960s to assist exports—the effect was to make UK goods cheaper on the world market. Psychological factors (investor confidence, a nervous market, etc.) can lead to devaluation. The US dollar dipped against the pound and the Euro in early 2004 and continued to do so through 2007/08, losing as much as 30% against the pound from 2004 to 2008, due to a crisis of confidence partly caused by continuing US involvement in Iraq and the collapse of the US sub-prime mortgage market in 2007/08. However, in the second half of 2008 it was the £'s turn to suffer, losing 25% of its value to the US$ and virtually obtaining parity with the Euro. This was due to the financial crisis effecting the UK in particular.

There are two extremes in dealing with currency fluctuations, one is to price in the target market's currency and take the risks involved in any adverse change in exchange rates. The other is to price in home market currency and let the target market find the extra money if there is a slide in target market currency. In practice, it is usually a compromise, except in the case of known and sustained currency depreciation, e.g. Zimbabwe. Companies with a strong competitive position may absorb the losses to maintain market position, but ultimately it depends on the objectives of the organization as to which stance it will take. It is wise to include an exchange rate clause in any contract. This clause may be based on a forecast of exchange rates using the following formulae:

$$S_{t+1} = (S_t) \times \frac{1 + i_n}{1 + i_r}$$

where:

S	=	the spot rate of exchange in the number of units of the home currency equal to one unit of the foreign currency
i_n	=	the inflation rate in the home country
i_r	=	the inflation rate in the foreign country
t	=	the base period or the present time
$t + 1$	=	the future period as defined
1	=	base for comparison

Example:

Assume the exchange rate between Malawi and the UK is Mkw180 = £1.

Assume that the rate of inflation in the UK is 2% per annum and that the rate of inflation in Malawi is 100% per annum. Applying the above formula, the exchange rate after one year in the home country (UK):

St + 1 = (1/180) × (1 + 2%)/(1 + 100%)
St + 1 = 0.0055 × 1.02/2
St + 1 = 0.0028

So, the new exchange rate is UK £0.028 = Mkwl or UK £1 = Mkw 280

Webber (2001) investigated the long-run demand for Australian outbound leisure tourism during the period 1983–97 for nine major tourism destinations. The study used exchange rate volatility as an explanatory variable. Using estimation and hypothesis-testing techniques, Webber found that the variance of the exchange rate was a significant determinant of long-term tourism demand in 50% of estimates. Further, disposable income and substitute prices were found to have inelastic long-term effects on tourism, while the long-run relative price elasticity differed widely across countries. Only Indonesia exhibited an exchange rate that had a more significant impact on tourism than relative price. This further shows the adverse effect of exchange rate fluctuations on demand for goods and services, as evidenced earlier by Marsh (2000). For SMEs in particular, failure to investigate the macro and micro environmental factors before engaging in trade in another country could be catastrophic in terms of the financial implications, particularly if payment terms are lengthy.

Exchange rate fluctuations are a cause of possible discontent between organizations and require early discussion. The introduction of the Euro has, to a great extent, reduced the risk of exchange rate fluctuations in Europe. Until now the UK has refused to join the European Monetary Union and this is causing considerable hardship for UK exporters. The question is what to do with exchange rate appreciation and different countries have different ways of dealing with it. The UK prefers to increase prices more than the rate of appreciation, while Japan tends to absorb the increase in order to maintain market share.

Terpstra and Sarathy (2000) identified three types of risk from exchange rate fluctuations: transaction risk, competitive risk, and market portfolio risk. The first is where currency appreciation may jeopardize trade, e.g. the UK devaluation cited above. The second is where local currency depreciation may disadvantage an overseas manufacturer, e.g. Malaysia. And the third is where a narrowly focused marketer will be more affected than a diversified one, e.g. a car importer. Morgan (2001) suggests that there has been little progress in the attempt to solve the problem of price risk arising from price volatility. Previous attempts at a solution have failed, in particular the demise of the International Commodity Agreements. In 1999, the World Bank set up a task force to look at the price risk in internationally traded goods but even initiatives such as this have not provided a solution.

Various strategies can be employed when currencies are depreciating or appreciating. If the domestic currency is weak, the company could compete on price, insist on cash payments, source in the domestic market, use a full cost approach to pricing, seek various ways to repatriate income (maybe by payment into offshore accounts), and invoice in domestic currency. When the domestic currency is strong, strategies include: invoice in target market currency; invoice in foreign currency having fixed the rate with the bank in advance; borrow foreign currency from the bank; sell in dollars and repay the loan from proceeds of the sale; offset imports in one currency with exports in the same currency (if the currency is available); reduce costs, if possible by the home country; open a foreign currency account; compete on non-price factors; source as much product or service as possible in local currency provided that quality is not compromised; and use counter-trade or borrow in the local money market to expand production (if allowed). Problems associated with currency fluctuations are prevalent in less developed countries. Major problems are the buyer's inability or refusal to pay and the financial restrictions imposed on foreign companies in terms of exportation of money or the scarcity of foreign currency (and its ramifications) to enable the importer to purchase the goods. Many ingenious solutions have been devised, especially in connection with a flourishing parallel currency market. The ultimate solution is to insist on payment in a convertible currency and have payment made in advance, however painful it may be to relationships. For a further example of the effect of exchange rates, and factors such as the effect of trading by dominant multinationals, see Swift (2001).

Buying forward, options trading, hedging, and spot trading

One way to overcome the problems of currency fluctuations is to buy forward, trade in options, or hedge the risk. This can involve both commodities, like or different, and currencies. The trade in 'derivatives', as they are called, is one of the biggest in the world and is worth billions of dollars per annum.

Forward buying is where credit terms have been given and goods have been sold at a price agreed in foreign currency. The risk of changes in the exchange can be covered by taking money 'forward'. An option forward is when an exporter cannot be certain of the exact date when he will receive payment. The 'option' is not whether to proceed but merely an agreement as to the date of delivery of the currency. When the option matures, the exporter could gain, but equally could lose if the currency has depreciated. The option writer is the one who takes the main risk in the event of fluctuations in currency. The client is the one taking out a form of invoice, and the commission charged by the option writer (which can be subtracted) is the premium to cover this. For detailed technical discussion of bond trading, see Nowman and Sorwar (2001).

Spot market is typical of commodities such as oil, but is also applicable to monetary transactions. Spot trading is where goods, services, or money are transferred simultaneously between buyer and seller. Trade takes place on goods already produced and the going price (determined by supply and demand) acts as the source of contracts and incentives. Transactions can take place across several types of market—auctions, private treaty, etc. The advantages of spot trading are numerous: it puts constraints on individuals' budgeting and purchasing; it provides flexibility in that prices are adjusted to market conditions 'on the spot'; market price systems give incentives; the price automatically adjusts to productive effort; and it gives information to economies with market prices summarizing all or most of the information transactions required to conduct trade.

Devaluation and revaluation

Devaluation is the reduction in the value of one currency *vis-à-vis* another country and revaluation is the increase in the value of a currency *vis-à-vis* another country's currency. If a country devalues its currency, then domestically produced goods become cheaper and, in theory, easier to export. Revaluation has the opposite effect. The UK devalued its currency in the 1960s when the pound was strong against other currencies. Many countries, especially South America, sub-Saharan Africa, and the Far East have undertaken World Bank-led economic structural adjustment programmes, one plank of which has been the devaluation of currency, leading to increased exports, higher incomes, and access via higher incomes to a better lifestyle. For a controversial discourse on monetary funds-led structural adjustment programmes, see Belk (2000), who contends that monetary funds ostensibly call for austerity, trimming fat budgets, and material sacrifice within their structural adjustment programmes, but they offer a long-term material promise of a world-class consumer lifestyle. Abundance is the reward that is touted as justifying supposedly short-term hardship. In theory, it was supposed to make it easier for these countries to export, and indeed it did in some cases, but only if the products were of the appropriate quality. In addition, as the countries affected were primarily commodity-oriented exporters, devaluation did little as demand for these commodities, and therefore price, was at the whim of international prices. Tarr (1994), looking at the 'terms of trade effect' on 15 countries in the former Soviet Union after moving to world prices, found that raw material and energy producers, such as Russia, Turkmenistan, and Kazakhstan, were estimated to gain from adopting international prices, whereas countries which concentrated on food and machinery, such as the Baltic, states, Belarus, and Moldovia, were estimated to lose. History has proved right. Marketers facing devaluation or revaluation need to assess the effect this will have on the cost base as devaluation, in particular, can cause a rise in input prices, hence making the product ultimately more expensive to export.

Inflation

Inflation is a fact of life worldwide and can be caused by excess demand or lack of supply, cost escalation, and monetary and fiscal policy, or any combination of these. Businesses have to adjust prices upward to maintain margins and cover the rise in cost of inputs. In times of inflation, the 'first in first out' (FIFO) method of accounting for stock is less appropriate than the 'last in first out' (LIFO) method because the FIFO method would be overstating the stock position. In highly inflationary situations, historical costing methods are less appropriate than replacement costing methods. It is essential to maintain gross and operating profit margins, but this can be done only if government allows this to happen. If there is rampant inflation and currency shortages, governments may act to resist price rises and might even enforce price controls. Government might even require importers to deposit cash in the Central Bank before they import, forcing them to look at cheaper import sources, hence leading to lower future deposits. Government subsidies may exacerbate the situation further. Subsidies make it harder for importers to import or, alternatively, make it easier for exporters to export, e.g. Proton cars from Malaysia. In this case the importer may ask the exporter to source some of the product or labour locally.

Transfer pricing

Transfer pricing has always been a source of controversy as it is seen by many as a device to avoid paying tax. Much has been written on this aspect of international pricing. For examples, see www.wtexec.com for global transfer pricing strategies for China, Japan, the USA, Latin America, the EU, Canada, and Russia; www.tpmba.com for the Transfer Pricing Management Benchmarking Association, and a new OECD initiative on comments on the comparability of transfer pricing, www.oecd.org/deparment/.

Armstrong (1998) provides a discussion on the politics of transfer pricing. Transfer pricing relates to the pricing of goods and services sold within one corporate family and involves the movement of these between subsidiaries, or divisions, in several countries. The objective is to maximize corporate rather than subsidiary objectives, and this is difficult when each division or subsidiary may have the objective of maximizing its own profits. Everything transferred must have a price and if the domestic transfer price is set too high, this will reflect badly on the subsidiary. There are four bases for transfer pricing:

• **Transfer at cost**: Price is set at the level of production cost or cost plus a percentage. In this case the division to which the product is transferred makes all the profit. This method is seldom used.

- **Transfer at cost plus**: Price is set based on direct cost plus overhead and margin. Prices may be set at a level which ignores competition and the market, but many organizations use this method, especially in the UK, Japan, and the USA.

- **Transfer at arm's length**: Price is set at a level at which the subsidiary may buy from any other buyer outside the organization. Problems arise if there are no external buyers or if the subsidiary buys at inferior quality and uncompetitive price. This method is also known as the 'negotiated' transfer method, where there is considerable leeway for corporate and sub-division negotiation.

- **Transfer at market based**: This is based on the price to be market competitive and the only constraint is costs. The decision is whether to base costs on current or planned volumes. In entering a small potential market, outsourcing to a third country may be preferable.

Transfer pricing has its problems. It can create barriers to entry in vertically oriented organizations, such as the oil or car industry. However, if there is any possibility of intervention in the value-added chain, barriers can be overcome. This happened in the computer industry between the 1970s and 1990s. IBM, Hewlett-Packard (www.hp.com), Honeywell (www.honeywell.com), and ICL (www.icl.com) dominated all aspects of the computer world, but the value-added chain was capable of being broken, especially with the advent of the desktop and laptop. When many new manufacturers entered the market—Toshiba (www.Toshiba.com), Sony (www.sony.com), Acer (www.global.acer.com), Siemens (www.siemens.com), Dell (www.dell.com), Gateway (www.gateway.com) etc.—they were rapidly followed by numerous manufacturers of printers, software, palm tops, stationery, and link packages such as BlueTooth (www.bluetooth.com).

Another area where transfer pricing has had its critics is in the payment of tax, both domestic and foreign. Corporations with high domestic tax regimes may be tempted to transfer their products at low transfer prices to subsidiaries with low tax regimes. Similarly, a corporation may transfer to a subsidiary at a low transfer price if there is a hefty import duty on the product. Such practices are reducing as more countries adopt international trade agreement conventions, e.g. the World Trade Organization (WTO, www.wto.org) agreements. The incidence of a high transfer price may also depend on the type of market entry strategy. A company with a licensing or joint venture agreement may wish to sell at a higher price, and thereby avoid sharing too much of the profit. The licensees of the SPSS survey analysis package (www.spss.com) are a good example of this.

Transfer pricing is complicated and requires more than simply the marketer to decide on the best method and practice. The main objective of the marketer should be to ensure that the product or service arrives in the marketplace at a price which guarantees the best deal for all stakeholders. For a discussion on cross-cultural regulatory styles and processes in dealing with transfer pricing, see Sakuri (2002).

Grey and parallel markets

Grey markets consist of the distribution of branded or trade-marked goods through channels of distribution unauthorized by the brand or trademark owner. Grey goods are usually high-priced goods where the cost of transportation, tariffs, etc. may be borne by an unauthorized third party. Unlike counterfeiting, the practice of buying and selling on the grey market is not illegal. The objective is to buy in a low price market and sell in a high price market, where information on international prices may not be widespread. Also, it may be used by those who cannot get foreign currency to purchase a product, but others can and are willing to sell the goods obtained in domestic currency. This is illegal if the buyer who has the foreign currency flaunts government currency exchange controls by buying the product at black market currency exchange rates. Unfortunately, this is widespread in many developing economies experiencing high inflation rates and foreign currency shortages. Grey marketing is also known as parallel importing. Typical products include car imports, tyres, and hi-tech goods. The UK is a classic example. Exasperated by the high UK prices, buyers of certain products and services are prepared to go to Europe and elsewhere to purchase them. Examples include new cars bought and imported from European dealers, and computers and other electronic goods bought and imported from the Far East. There are three types of grey market. First, *parallel importing* is where the product is priced lower in the home market where it is produced than in the market where it is sold. Secondly, *re-importing* is where the product is priced cheaper in an export market than in the home market where it was produced. Thirdly, *lateral exporting*, where there is a price difference between export markets and products are sold from one country to another through unauthorized channels (Doole and Lowe, 2008).

Dumping

If an organization sells a product in a foreign market at a price less than it sells in its domestic market, it is said to be dumping. This is a well-documented subject. For current information, refer to the WTO and World Bank websites at WTO's anti-dumping gateway (www.org/english/tratop), and the World Bank's news and events website (www.worldbank.org/trade). The WTO is divided in its approach to unfair competition. It cannot take action against those suspected of dumping but it defines how governments can or cannot react to it. The key issues are how much lower the export price is than the domestic price and whether it causes injury. Exporting companies found to be in contravention can be asked to raise their prices to an agreed rate.

Governments may use the issue of dumping to protect local businesses, but some marketers are astute at buying in low-cost countries and marketing at what looks like a dumping rate. When is a service sold at a dumped rate internationally? Are cut-price air tickets from an international carrier sold at a dumping rate? What about cut-price insurance?

Over the last few years there has been a spate of anti-dumping legislation and also investigations carried out in the USA, the EU, and Canada. One case in 2002 involved the UK being accused of dumping steel products in the USA. One way of avoiding anti-dumping investigations is to differentiate the product in the marketplace and thus attract a different tariff rating. In 2007, China was accused of dumping ladies undergarments in the UK at less than the price of production and quotas were imposed.

Leasing

Leasing is used when there is not enough money to buy usually high-priced capital goods. The agreement may cover essential maintenance and spares in order that equipment remains operational, and this is particularly important in less developed countries. Leasing is attractive in countries where investment grants and tax breaks are prevalent, allowing the leaser to take advantage. There are many examples of leasing arrangements globally, including aircraft, heavy-duty trucks, railway stock, ships, and oil exploration equipment.

Counter-trade

Counter-trade, such as barter, involves all or part payment in goods and services and the price and financial arrangements are all done in one transaction. Counter-trade accounts for 30% of world trade and provides opportunities for those who cannot pay in cash and gives opportunity for making profits. It is well known in less developed countries, because of currency shortages, as a means to protect local jobs and a way to break into international markets.

There are various forms of counter-trade:

- **Barter**: An exchange of goods with no monetary element. It is not that popular because if exchanges are not done simultaneously, one party is financing the other and also one party may receive unwanted goods. This can be typical in less developed countries. For example, in the 1980s Zimbabwe exchanged tobacco for computers from Eastern Europe. A more recent example was the exchange of oil for food from Iraq to the West in 2003.

- **Buyback**: Part of the cost of equipment purchased may be paid back from the operation of the equipment. This is typical of turnkey projects such as oil exploration. An example is the sale of Iraqi oil to French oil exploration and refining equipment suppliers.

- **Switch deals**: These usually involve a specialist intermediary which deals in barter goods. If a supplier provides goods and receives goods in part payment from the buyer, which it does not want, the intermediary may barter the goods on the supplier's behalf and provide him with more acceptable products.

- **Compensation trading**: This is payment for goods in a combination of cash and goods. A typical example is oil supplied to a less developed country where payment may be in cash and, perhaps, tobacco.

- **Counter-purchase**: This involves two contracts. Simultaneously, the supplier agrees to sell at a price in local currency and the seller agrees to buy goods for an equivalent proportion or whole cash payment, from another local supplier.

- **Offset**: Governments are generally involved. The seller is able to secure more saleable goods from the country in exchange. An example is where deals to purchase Boeing aeroplanes (www.boeing.com) by UK-based airlines included the USA agreeing to purchase UK-included Rolls-Royce (www.rolls-royce.com) aero engines.

Compensation and offset deals are widespread in Japan and South East Asia, counter-trade and barter in less developed countries, and offset in the West. Japan in the 1990s obtained many raw materials from Australia through counter-trade deals involving wool, coal, electronic equipment, and steel, products which both Japan and Australia needed. Hard woods from the forests of Myamar, Thailand, the Philippines, and Indonesia are involved in barter deals between these countries.

Counter-trade deals can be extremely complicated and involve multiple parties. As multinationals begin to build longer-term supply chain relationships, it is likely that mutually advantageous deals will be struck, with the emphasis switching to the buyer, rather than seller, especially where LDCs are involved.

Counter-trade has advantages and disadvantages. Advantages are: multilateral and bilateral counter-trade agreements can strengthen ties between countries; it can be used to enter high-risk areas; it can be a source of profit as government restrictions can be avoided; poorer quality goods can be exchanged and cheaper ones disposed of without arousing dumping suspicions; and it is a way of obtaining technology and exploring new markets.

The disadvantages include: goods taken in exchange may not fit the buyer's needs; dealings can be complicated, especially if governments are involved; it can be an inflexible means of trading as goods may not be available which the seller would like to buy; and it is difficult to evaluate financially.

Strategies for coordinating prices across subsidiaries

Companies face a difficult task in coordinating pricing strategies across the globe and through subsidiaries. They may seek government intervention or hit back to protect themselves. An example is the private importation of marque cars from European suppliers by UK citizens seeking lower than domestic prices, and in so doing circumventing the UK-based dealers. The marque companies have hit back by sometimes honouring the manufacturer's warranty but not the dealer's warranty. The EU removed car dealer exclusivity in 2004.

Companies may deal with the coordination of pricing by imposing a centralized price or a regional price; imposing a formalized price-setting formula; imposing a price through transfer pricing; or having a more informal system whereby global objectives and culture are reinforced. This enables the subsidiaries to have a certain degree of autonomy, but pushes a price strategy akin to the global requirement.

These efforts will not stop the grey market operation. In fact, some giant distributors are forcing the pace. UK supermarket giants such as Asda (www.asda.co.uk) are attempting to sell branded goods at less than recommended prices, incurring the wrath of the branded manufacturers. Levi jeans sell at considerably higher prices in the UK than in the USA and the Far East. This is providing the temptation to source on the grey market. Branded fashion clothing, such as Polo (www.polo.com), is sold more cheaply in Malaysia than in Europe. Visitors to Malaysia get the added bonus of the strong Euro or pound exchange rate. Whatever the company does to try to coordinate a global pricing strategy, there will always be a way to get round it.

Single European Payments Area

European Monetary Union (EMU) is often known as the 'euro zone'. While harmonizing currencies, EMU has hardly harmonized prices. Austria and Finland are seen as 'high priced', France, Belgium, and Germany as 'average priced', and Spain as 'low priced'. Differentials are caused by disparities in taxation, excise duties, wage levels, and production costs. When the EU had different currencies it was not easy to see the differences in benefits to consumers and in buying power as it is now with a common currency. This price transparency has had different effects in different ways. Companies marketing goods direct to the consumer have come under increasing pressure from retailers to reduce margins, and retailers themselves have had to cut prices to meet new price points couched in euros. However, specialized manufacturers are mainly immune from the risk of price transparency. So to compete in the EU, companies have had to develop very sophisticated pricing strategies to coordinate prices across the EU.

The creation of the EMU and euro were supposed to create a market for the free movement of currency as easily as in national markets, and in order to do so the integration of payment facilities into a single financial services market across borders was necessary. In order to achieve this, the Single European Payments Area (SEPA) was created in 2008. SEPA allows companies to conduct any payment within the euro zone as easily and at the same cost as in their domestic market. Cross-border euro payments are treated exactly the same as domestic payments, but it might take three days to transact instead of one, and there could be difficulties for countries outside the euro zone, such as the UK. Common rules for clearance and settlement help reduce costs. The harmonized payment structure will ease e-payment solutions which are destined to grow in the next few years.

The Export Order Process

As seen in the example of Kenya beans, the export order process is complicated and all the activities have to be costed into the price. The export order process may differ from transaction to transaction, but Fig. 14.7 shows a typical example. At each stage of the order process, attention to detail is essential. The process will also aid the decision of which price strategy to adopt. A strategy which minimizes the paperwork would be ideal. An export order process such as this would standardize pricing as much as possible. However, it could lead to a loss of sales and so the employment of specialized contracted-out or in-house facilities should be considered. It is estimated by the UN Conference on Trade and Development (UNCTAD) that paperwork can constitute 10% of world trade flows. The costs could be cut considerably by standardization of procedures and technology, but this is likely to take time.

Terms of Access

Global marketers have to take account of the terms of access and incorporate these into the pricing process. Terms of access refer to the conditions which apply to the importation of goods and are either tariff or non-tariff based. The non-tariff terms can be a way of restricting imports into a country. It is not the intention to cover all the detail of tariff systems here. For an excellent source of reference for tariffs and 'incoterms' (terms used in international marketing for special trade terms), see Branch (2000a, 2000b).

Tariffs

Tariffs are imposed on exporters as government duties in the importing countries and may be 'single' or 'double column', preferential (for essential goods or favoured nations), duties, and other import charges. Tariff classifications originated from the Brussels Nomenclature (BTN) of 1959. As we saw earlier, especially under counter-trade, reclassification can occur and this can distort trade flows. The types of duty which can be imposed include the following:

- *Ad valorem*: expressed as a percentage of the value of the goods.
- **Specific duties**: expressed as a specific amount of currency, for example per weight, volume, or length.
- **Compound of mixed duties**: a mixture of specific and *ad valorem* rates.
- **Anti-dumping duties**: applied if domestic producers are injured.
- **Counter-ruling duties**: additional duties levied to offset subsidies granted in the exporting countries.
- **Harmonized tariff system (HTS)**: convention signed by most WTO members aimed at harmonizing product classification systems and to ease tariff procedures.

Fig. 14.7 The export order process

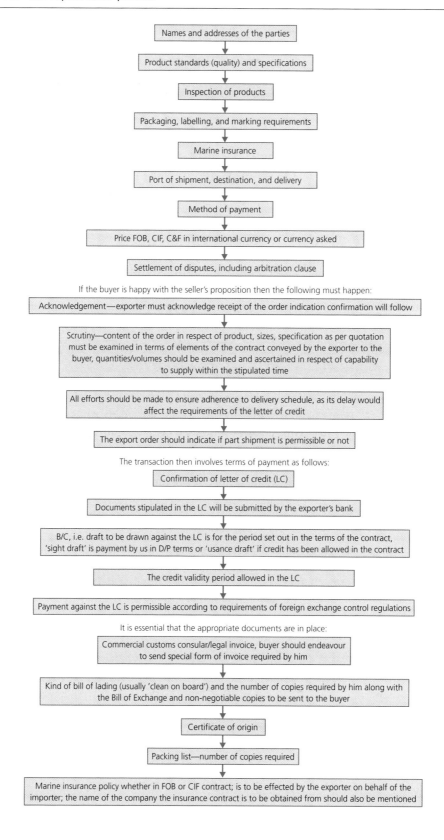

- **Most favoured nation (MFN)**: the most favourable tariff rate is put on imports from a country regarded as 'most favoured'.

Other import charges may include:

- **Variable import charges**: raise the imported price to the domestic level.
- **Temporary import charges**: used as a local industry protection scheme or to make sure a good imported temporarily is exported. This can apply to trade fair exhibits in developing countries to make sure that they are not sold locally but exported after the fair.
- **Compensatory import level**: corresponds to various internal taxes.

The WTO is attempting to effect tariff reductions and abolish some of them on a wide variety of goods and services and also to outlaw a number of prohibitive taxes.

Non-tariff barriers

Non-tariff barriers are measures, public or private, that cause trade goods to be allocated in such a way as to reduce world trade. They are often used by developing countries to prohibit the import of goods which may damage local manufacturers. This is often an admission that the quality of local goods is not good enough and so protects mediocrity. It is ultimately detrimental to their citizens as it deprives them of quality products. Such non-tariff barriers include:

- quotas and trade limits;
- discriminatory government and private procurement policies;
- selective monetary controls and discriminatory exchange rate policies;
- restrictive administrative and technical regulations;
- outright bans, e.g. on pornographic materials or alcohol;
- other: this includes placing customs halls inland from the country's borders with the effect of slowing down the importation process and increasing logistical costs.

While these non-tariff barriers are often difficult to see in advance, they can have an effect on trade and need to be found in advance. Trade missions, embassies, consulates, and chambers of trade and commerce are useful sources of information.

Special Trade Terms in Exporting

For complete and up-to-date information on trade terms in exporting (incoterms), see the *Dictionary of International Trade* (www.worldtradepress.com), the International Chamber of Commerce (ICC) Incoterms 2000 (www.iccwbo.org/index_incoterms), and SITPRO (www.sitpro.org).

Export price quotations set down the legal and cost implications of the buyer and seller. Sellers seek to obtain a quotation in a way which minimizes their costs e.g. FOB (free on board). Buyers prefer one which minimizes their costs also, e.g. CIF (cost, insurance, freight). CIF quotations are more market-oriented pricing approaches than ex-works, which throws the emphasis on the buyer. The possibilities are:

- **Ex-works or ex-warehouse**: the price is set from the works or warehouse. Such prices are most favourable to the seller as the buyer bears the rest of the cost.

- **Free on rail or on truck (FOR/FOT)**: the buyer bears the cost of rail or truck transport which is included in the price. The seller has little to do with the exportation as it is the buyer's responsibility.

- **Free alongside ship (FAS)**: the buyer nominates a ship and the price includes transport to that vessel only.

- **Free on board: named port of shipment (FOB)**: this is a classic approach and enables the seller to provide an additional service to the buyer by including in the price the cost of putting the goods on the vessel.

- **Cost, insurance, freight (CIF)**: the most common and buyer-friendly export clause. There are many variants of CIF, including CIF and C (commission), CIF and E (expenses), CIF and C and I (commission, charges, and interest); date of arrival of ship; C and F (named port of destination); arrival of ex-ship (named ship and named port of arrival).

Export Documentation

Table 14.5 gives a list of the major export documentation which have implications for pricing strategies. We will now examine some of these instruments as they directly affect the pricing decision. The cash flow of an organization is affected by the terms of the financial instrument and the speed at which the goods are delivered to the buyer.

Export payments

Export payments can come from a variety of sources. Each will incur costs, depending on the method and the length of time that the goods and payment are in the 'pipeline'.

- **Bills of exchange**: A bill of exchange is an unconditional order in writing, addressed by one person (drawer) to another (drawee), signed by the drawer, requiring the drawee to pay on demand, or at a fixed or determinable future time, a certain sum of money to, or to the order of, a specified person (payee) or bearer.

- **Letter of credit**: A buyer instructs a bank in his own country (the issuing bank) to obtain a credit with a bank in the seller's country (the advisory bank) in favour of the seller, specifying the documents which the seller has to deliver to the bank in order for the seller to receive payment. There are different types of letter of credit: revocable and unconfirmed, irrevocable and unconfirmed, irrevocable and confirmed (preferable), and transferable.

- **Drafts covering export**: Drawn by the seller on the buyer, who makes it a 'trade acceptance' by inserting the word 'accepted' on the draft.

- **Sales on open account**: Sales terms agreed between buyer and seller without specifying the exact payment period. This is a method built on trust and would it be foolish to conduct when currency is difficult to obtain by the importer.

- **Sale on a consignment basis**: The exporter retains title to the goods until the importer is able to sell them. Payment may be made under a collection agreement, but this method is risky and is usually limited to trade between subsidiaries.

Table 14.5 Export documentation

Commercial documents	Insurance documents	Transport documents	Financial and finance documents
Quotation	Letter of insurance	Air waybill	Bills of exchange
Pro forma invoice	Insurance certificate	Combined transport bill of lading	Promissory note
Commercial invoice	Insurance policy	House bill of lading	Bills of exchange
Certified invoice	Lloyds open cover insurance	Rail consignment note	Open account
Weight note		Road waybill (CMR)	Consignment
Packing list and specification		Bill of lading	Drafts
Manufacturer's analysis certificate		Short form bill of lading	Inspection and sampling order
Third-party certificate of inspection		Bill of lading (liner)	Delivery order
EU documents, EURI, and TZL		Non-negotiable sea waybill	Warehouse receipt
Consular invoice		Mate's receipt	Trust receipt
Legalized invoice		Despatch advice note	
Certificate of origin			
Blacklist certificate			
Health, veterinary, and sanitary certificate			
Exporter's commission advice to agent			
Customs and Excise export entry forms			
Export and import licenses			
Specification sheet			
Dangerous goods declaration			
Certificate of value			

CMR is the Convention for the Contract of the International Carriage of goods by Road, 1956.

- **Promissory note**: Like bills of exchange, but these are made by the person who owes the money, in favour of the beneficiary.
- **Inspection and sampling order**: When banks are protecting stocks for foreign exporters or if they are lending to an importer against a pledge of goods, the goods are usually warehoused in the bank's name pending sale to buyers.
- **Delivery order**: Order on a warehouse instructing it to deliver to a bearer or a party named in the order.

Letters of credit and bills of exchange are the most commonly used form of payment for exports. The credit terms determine the final price to the buyer and may also have a major effect on whether the seller obtains the order. Lengthy credit terms can have an effect on a seller's cash flow, so terms have to be negotiated carefully. When goods are similar, the supplier who gives the best credit terms is likely to be the one who gets the order. In order to obtain payment the seller must tender the documents, which strictly comply with the specification by the buyer, otherwise the correspondent bank may refuse to honour the contract. This is the doctrine of strict compliance. There have been many instances of fraud in letters of credit transactions. In order to make a case, it has to be proven that the shipment of goods was falsified and/or that bills of lading tendered under the credit were falsified or forged. The contract usually stipulates which legal system applies. Several factors are weighed in order to decide which is the correct law of contract e.g. *lex focii*, *lex locii*, and other solutions.

There are many considerations in arriving at the most appropriate selling price. However, there is a further pitfall. If at any time in the transaction something goes wrong, there is always a possibility of litigation which could add considerably to costs.

Export financing

Export financing is important because there can be a lengthy wait to receive payment from a sale. Depending on where the payment comes from, it can add to the cost and hence to the final selling price.

Export finance can be internal or external, as outlined in Table 14.6. Most of these methods are self-explanatory, but some would benefit from expansion. Export credit guarantee schemes can be useful where the payment is risky or over a long period of time. An export credit guarantee scheme, like that operated by the UK government, may consist of a monetary facility, a pre-shipment guarantee, a pre-shipment credit guarantee, and a covered risk. A pre-shipment credit scheme may be provided by a union or government body, e.g. the Malawi Export Guarantee Corporation, which may help exporters obtain certain inputs to complete the growing of crops or provide manufacturers with working capital. A post-shipment credit facility has as its objective the support, through the provision of finance, of the needs of the exporter during the period between shipment of goods and receipt of payment from the buyer. Exporters must be eligible for the credit which comes in the form of advances, packing credit, pre-shipment loans, and post-shipment loans through discounting bills or letters of credit.

Table 14.6 Finance for exports

Internal	External
From subsidiary operations	Host country borrowings
Transfers within the corporation	Export credit schemes/pre- and post-shipment schemes
	Donor agencies and foreign investors
	Government
	Factoring (the selling of letters of credit or the taking over of debt, in cash or kind)
	Confirming houses
	Banks—overdrafts and loans, negotiations of outward collections, letters of credit, acceptance and discount
	International financing markets—foreign currency finance, eurocurrency finance, currency swaps

MINI-CASE ILLUSTRATION Price cooperation in global markets

To compete in global markets, organizations sometimes have to cooperate. This is typical of large turnkey projects such as oil refineries, new airports, dams, and power stations, and large capital equipment purchases like aircraft. No one company can afford to raise the finance and carry the interest burden over the many years it may take to complete the project. Recent examples include the Channel Tunnel, connecting the UK and France, the new Hong Kong International Airport, and the Five Gorges dam project on the Yangtze River in China. Similarly, no one company can provide all the products and services necessary to complete the project. Finance may be provided by government, multilateral agencies such as the World Bank, and private sources, all working together. Capital equipment may come from all over the world, as might services such as project management, engineering consulting services, architecture, insurance, and environmental impact studies. Labour may be sourced domestically and/or overseas.

Building work may been done by a multitude of specialist companies, e.g. experts in tunneling, cement work, steel work, scaffolding, and excavation. In addition, there are a host of government and procurement agencies obtaining work permits, temporary import licences, duty waivers, temporary housing, and other necessary paperwork.

Such projects may be completed by an amalgam of organizations brought together under the umbrella of one organization, the project managers. Such organizations include world-renowned names like Taylor Woodrow (www.taylorwoodrow.com), Bechtel (www.bechtel.com), and Arup and Partners (www.arup.com). These companies have the mammoth task of costing and managing the operation, obtaining and providing competitive quotations, involving hundreds of companies working together to provide a price for the project that is acceptable to all. In other words, they cooperate to compete.

International financial markets may be a source of export finance. This is a form of borrowing money outside national boundaries and it offers a number of advantages:

- interest rates in a specific currency may be lower in some financial markets than in others;
- in some countries rates are too high or sums insufficiently large;
- exchange control barriers may exist.

The latter is particularly relevant in developing countries where commodities may require large and costly volumes of inputs, some not available in country. A good example of this is the Tobacco Association of Zimbabwe, which sources loans offshore to provide tobacco farmers with the money to purchase inputs and other pre-shipment funds until the crop is sold at auction. The money is repaid on sale or by commercial stop orders. Problems arise if governments take on the role as there is no guarantee that the money obtained offshore will go to the intended or needy users.

From a strategic point of view, being able to obtain finance will have a bearing on the pricing strategy. If funds are readily available and can be costed into the pricing decision, the exporter can adopt a more market-oriented pricing policy. If unavailable, then a less market-oriented policy, i.e. a cost-based strategy, will be more appropriate. The organization must be wary. In its effort to be more market-friendly, it may open itself up to risk of default in payment, especially in dealing with less scrupulous developing countries.

International pricing is a challenge and a key strategic decision. It has to be approached carefully, recognizing the relevant internal and external factors. Failure to do so will result in a sub-optimum pricing strategy.

Chapter Summary

1. There are a number of factors affecting the global pricing decision: organization-specific, environmental, and market-specific.

2. Global pricing strategies include the standardization of prices, adaptation or differentiation prices, or corridor/invention prices, according to the global objectives of the organization. Within these the organization may adopt a skimming (high price), penetration price (low price), or market holding price. Whichever strategy is chosen, it should be decided in the context of other elements of the global marketing mix.

3. Specific pricing approaches include cost-oriented, competitive, market, penetrative, adaptive, and promotional or dynamic incremental pricing. A cost-plus approach is likely to be adopted by those new to exporting, a competitive approach takes account of market conditions and a market, penetrative, or dynamic incremental price is based on the principle of absorption costing.

4. In global pricing there are a number of specific issues to take into account when setting the price. These include price escalation, currency fluctuations, buying forward, options trading, hedging and spot trading, devaluation and revaluation, and inflation. These will affect the final selling price of the product and can lead to cost escalation, hence increases in price. Transfer pricing, grey and parallel markets, dumping, leasing, and counter-trade are all specific types of price operation and are applied in specific markets or trading conditions. A particularly difficult task in global marketing is how to coordinate prices across subsidiaries.

5. The export process is complex and has its own nomenclature ('incoterms'). The export process includes obtaining terms of access (tariff and non-tariff) and terms of payment and credit. Documentation has to be in meticulous order.

6. Global marketing could not take place without export financing. Global financing can be obtained internally or externally.

END-OF-CHAPTER CASE STUDY **The (s)cents of the perfume business**

Celebrity endorsement of perfume has rocketed in recent years. Kate Moss, Britney Spears, and Beyonce have created their own, and Jennifer Lopez has not one, but eight lines. Apparently, she has made more than £25 million from them since 2003. It is also a big business, with the industry bringing in £16 billion a year. And it is not just for the women's market. Men's fragrance sales are also rising, with ex-James Bond star Pierce Brosnan busily advocating men's skin care products. Fashion houses are getting in on the act too, like Burberry and Yves St Laurent, sales of which can form a significant percentage of total revenue.

Surely, then, perfume towns like Grasse and Gourdon in France can't go wrong? Well yes, but while highly profitable, it's not all 'smelling of roses' in the industry. Take the price alone. The liquid in the bottle can make up only 3% of the total price, while the other 97% goes into the packaging, advertising, and marketing. The price is such—retailing anywhere in the world at between £14 and £80 per bottle—that it often allows for a 95% profit margin. At such a price you would expect a hefty dose of 'original' liquid (essential oil), like jasmine or rose petal, yet it is more than likely that it is synthetic. Synthetics have been put into scent bottles since 1876, making them linger longer and being capable of 'mass' production. Essential oils are themselves very expensive. Rose petals must be picked by hand at sunrise to make 'rose ab-

solute'. A kilo of the liquid costs £4,000, whereas the equivalent synthetic costs only £400. So why use synthetics? The answer is they cost less and therefore make the product more affordable so more people buy it. Also, perfume can be 'fashionable', so why spend money developing an expensive one if they can be so easily discarded?

Celebrity brand names, while enticing, might not all turn out as expected. This is because perfume dries on the skin and releases odours

in sequence, so what they smelled like in the shop, when the 'head notes' are sampled, might not be what they smell like at home. Marketing also does its bit in the shop. Supported by glossy TV and magazine images, you often buy into a 'lifestyle' or 'image', which may subsequently not turn out to be the real you. This is often referred to as 'ego' purchasing, not 'rational' purchasing. Yet the importance of the purchase cannot be underestimated. Different scents communicate different things to those around you and speak volumes about yourself. Either consciously or subconsciously, it is a reflection of your personality. Smell arouses deep emotions: citrus smells indicate an upbeat personality; sandalwood a more reflective, serious nature.

Such is the size and success of the industry that it has attracted its undesirable elements too. Fake perfumes abound on street corners in some cities, the sellers anxious to cash in on the boom. They are so life-like, down to the last packaging detail, that it is often difficult to tell the real deal apart from the fake. It is only when an allergic reaction sets in or the smell wears off almost immediately that something seems not right.

Source: Based on *Daily Mail*, 31 March 2008.

Case study discussion questions

1 What pricing strategy and pricing method is apparent in the perfume industry, as described in the case?

2 Why can manufacturers charge such a price even though the 'liquid' in the bottle can be only 3% of the selling price?

3 How can branded goods manufacturers deal with the issue of 'fake' goods?

END-OF-CHAPTER EXERCISES

1 Why is 'pricing' one of the key global strategic decisions?

2 What are the key considerations to be taken into account when setting both global pricing strategies and specific pricing approaches?

3 What specific issues affect global pricing and how can these be taken into account when setting prices?

4 Which is the most appropriate pricing strategy for commodities, business-to-business products, and consumer products, and services? Justify your answer with examples.

5 Discuss the different sources of export financing and assess, giving reasons, which ones are the most organization- or market-friendly.

6 What effect does the pricing strategy decision have on other elements of the global marketing mix? Give examples in your answer.

DISCUSSION AND EXAMINATION QUESTIONS

1 'Of all the global marketing mix decisions, the pricing decision is one of the most difficult to make.' Discuss, illustrating your answer with examples.

2 What factors would determine whether the global price strategy was set on a 'standardization', 'adaptation,' or 'invention/corridor' pricing basis? Illustrate your answer with examples.

3 How can the global marketer combat the 'grey or parallel' market through an astute pricing strategy? Give examples in your answer.

4 What are the key factors to be taken into account when setting prices for products and services in countries in different stages of economic development? How do they affect the pricing decision?

FURTHER READING

Brassington, F. and Pettitt, S (2006), *Principles of Marketing*, 4th edn., Maidenhead: Financial Times Press.

Doole, I. and Lowe, R, (2008), *International Marketing Strategy: Analysis, Development and Implementation*, 5th edn., London: Thomson Learning, Chapter 11.

Jobber, D. (2006), *Principles and Practice of Marketing*, 5th edn., Maidenhead: McGraw-Hill.

Sakuri, Y. (2002), 'Comparing cross-cultural regulatory styles and processes in dealing with transfer pricing', *International Journal of the Sociology of Law*, 30, 173–99.

REFERENCES

Armstrong, M. A. (1998), 'The political economy of international transfer pricing, 1945–1994: state, capital and the decomposition of class', *Critical Perspectives on Accounting*, 9(4), August, 391–432.

Belk, R. W. (2000), 'Pimps for paradise: missionaries, monetary funds, and marketers', *Marketing Intelligence and Planning*, 18(6/7), 337–44.

Branch, A. E. (2000a), *Elements of Shipping*, 7th edn., London: Routledge.

—— (2000b), *Export Practice and Management*, London: International Thompson Business Press.

Brassington, F. and Pettitt, S (2006), *Principles of Marketing*, 4th edn., Maidenhead: Financial Times Press.

Dawes, R. and Thornes, S. (1995), *International Business—A European Perspective*, Philadelphia, PA: Transatlantic Publications.

Doole, I. and Lowe, R. (2008), *International Marketing Strategy: Analysis, Development and Implementation*, 5th edn., London: Thomson Learning.

Jobber, D. (2006), *Principles and Practice of Marketing*, 5th edn., Maidenhead: McGraw-Hill.

Keegan, W. J. and Schlegelmilch, B. B. (2001), *Global Marketing Management: A European Perspective*, Harlow: Pearson Education.

Lancioni, R. A. (1989), 'The importance of price in international business development', *European Journal of Marketing*, 23(11), 45–50.

Marsh, G. (2000), 'International pricing—a market perspective', *Marketing Intelligence and Planning*, 18(4), 200–5.

Moore, M., Kennedy, K. McG., and Fairhurst, A. (2003), 'Cross-cultural equivalence of price perceptions between US and Polish consumers', *International Journal of Retail and Distribution Management*, 31(5), 268–79.

Morgan, C. W. (2001), 'Commodity futures markets in LDCs: a review and prospect', *Progress in Development Studies*, 1, 139–50.

Nowman, K. B. and Sorwar, G. (2001), 'An international comparison of pricing callable and puttable bonds in international financial markets', *Managerial Finance*, 27(1/2), 99–110.

Piron, F. (2002), 'International outshopping and ethnocentrism', *European Journal of Marketing*, 36(1), 189–210.

Sakuri, Y. (2002), 'Comparing cross-cultural regulatory styles and processes in dealing with transfer pricing', *International Journal of the Sociology of Law*, 30, 173–99.

Swift, R. (2001), 'Exchange rates and commodity prices: the case of the Australian metal exports', *Applied Economics*, 33, 745–53.

Tarr, D. G. (1994), 'The terms of trade effects of moving to world prices on countries of the former Soviet Union', *Journal of Comparative Economics*, 18, 1–24.

Terpstra, V. and Sarathy, R. (2000), *International Marketing*, Fort Worth, TX: Dryden Press.

Webber, A. G. (2001), 'Exchange rate volatility and cointegration in tourism demand', *Journal of Travel Research*, 39 (May), 398–405.

online resource centre

Visit the companion website to this book for lots of interesting additional material, including self-assessment questions, internet exercises, and links for each chapter:

http://www.oxfordtextbooks.co.uk/orc/lee_carter2e/

From its humble beginnings as a small general retail store in a village situated in the south of Sweden, IKEA has grown into the world's largest furniture retailer with 279 stores in 36 countries today. The name IKEA is formed from the founder's initials I. K. (Ingvar Kamprad) plus the first letters of Elmtaryd (E) and Agunnaryd (A), the farm and village where he grew up. Specializing in furniture and home decoration, IKEA has an annual turnover of £19.8 billion (*source*: IKEA, www.ikea.com, accessed 17/06/2008). The IKEA catalogue is printed in 52 editions in 25 languages, with a global distribution in excess of 160 million copies.

IKEA's success has been nothing short of a global phenomenon. Edvardsson and Edquist (2002) have accounted for the company's rise to global success following a timeline of three development phases. In phase one, IKEA's core concepts were formed as a result of adapting to the market circumstances. The important moments during this period were publishing the first IKEA catalogue in 1951, opening the first furniture showroom in Älmhult in 1953, introducing flat packages in 1956, and finding the key to low-cost production in Poland in the early 1960s. Phase two is characterized by the company's initial expansion into international markets when it reached out to its Scandinavian neighbours in the 1960s. Since the 1970s, the company began to expand farther into other European countries, Australia, and Canada. In 1985, IKEA arrived at the world's largest consumer market—the USA—which proved to be a very different market from those in Europe. Armed with its international experience in Europe and North America, IKEA took the company into the third phase of its development by embarking on a major expansion into the Far East, in particular Japan and China.

IKEA sees the Far Asia as an emerging market still in its infant stage. Its number of retail outlets in Malaysia, Singapore, Taiwan, Beijing, Shanghai, and Hong Kong are very small and comprise a mere 3% of the company's total sales. These stores are expected to be more successful in the near future. IKEA's imminent strategic expansion into this region exemplified its ambitions to dominate this emerging market.

IKEA's entry into mainland China started in 1998 when it opened its first store in Shanghai, followed by Beijing in 1999. IKEA took its time to get to know the Chinese customers. IKEA adopted a prudent approach to market entry and it was five years before it opened its first full-scale standard IKEA store in Shanghai in 2003. The store occupies 33,000 sq m and retails more than 7,000 products. Its signature Småland children's playground is 170 sq m and the free parking area holds 800 cars. A record of 80,000 visitors flocked to the store on the opening day. This new Shanghai store represents an important landmark for IKEA's business development in China. It is the largest of its stores not only in China, but also in Asia. In the same year, the president of IKEA China, Ian Duffy, unveiled a long-term plan to open ten more stores in mid-sized cities, such as Dalian and

© IKEA 2008. Reproduced with permission.

Qingdao, by the end of 2010. This plan would require a US$600 million investment. The expansion plans underscored IKEA's confidence in China considering none of IKEA's retail stores in China has yet turned a profit, making them the only loss-making stores in the entire IKEA group (Wei, 2007). Its expansion in China nonetheless saw its sales revenue increased by 500% from 2000 to 2005.

IKEA brought its distinct organizational culture and retail strategies to China. Its Chinese stores look very similar to its stores in Europe, with its blue and yellow painted logo hung up high outside the building. Customers walk through the showrooms where they can see and try the products before making a decision on which ones to take home. After making up their minds, customers make notes of the design name, aisle, and shelf numbers and then head for the warehouse on the ground floor to collect their purchases. They then find the products in flat-pack by locating the correct aisle and shelf numbers. Once goods are paid for, customers can choose to transport the shopping themselves or have it delivered by IKEA for a surcharge. The so-called IKEA retail experience is no different after being 'transplanted' into another country. The core concept of showrooms, flat-packed products, and do-it-yourself assembly remain intact.

In China, IKEA successfully differentiates itself as an international brand that provides modern furniture with elegant, Western design. Unlike the local furniture brands, IKEA promotes a 'complete solution' to decorating the home. Apart from selling well-designed furniture, it also sells various necessities for the home, including cooking appliances, lighting, and bedding. IKEA was probably the only store in China that offers such a wide range of products for home decoration and a 'do-it-yourself' furnishing concept. It promotes its philosophy of 'how it is not wrong to be different' by offering its customers a range of options to suit the customer's preferences and living requirements. Although this 'individualistic' value is in contrast to the local tradition, Chinese customers seem to gradually appreciate this difference. They start to appreciate the simplicity of the light-coloured, Scandinavian-style of furniture and even consider going to IKEA as experiencing another culture.

Despite the phenomenal growth in the number of visitors and sales volume in recent years, IKEA struggles to break even from its sales revenue. There is a large gap between customers who visit the stores and those who make a purchase. Those who make purchases tend to be small decorative products with low profit margins (which make up 45% of total sales). Continuous losses suggested that the challenges for IKEA in China are complicated and demanding.

To appeal to its Chinese customers, IKEA has made a considerable effort to adapt its products to the local tastes and demands. For instance, IKEA releases a series of products to celebrate the Chinese New Year, which is the most important festival for the Chinese people. In 2006, a red rooster appeared on many IKEA products, greeting the year of the Rooster. This move has won IKEA many customers. It introduced a series of products under the FANBY range that feature red pigs to welcome the 2007 year of the Pig. The colour red suggests good fortune in Chinese culture and is commonly used in decorations to bring good luck. The Swedish kitchen section also provides IKEA with an important element of differentiation from its competitor stores in the Chinese market, but while emphasizing its Swedish origin, IKEA also takes into consideration the Chinese style of cooking and eating. For instance, IKEA Shanghai provides three kinds of meat cleavers and three kinds of chopsticks as well as Western-style knives and forks. Approximately 5% of the products IKEA sells in China are for China only, in contrast to 1% in IKEA's European markets.

While brand new designs for a single market may be very effective in terms of delivering customer value for a specific market, it is an expensive strategy that does not chime well with the IKEA way of being cost-conscientious at every step. It is more cost-effective to produce small adaptations to the features of existing products. For example, the SULTAN HÖGBO series of sprung mattresses are sold in Malmö in the categories of 80 × 200 cm, 90 × 200 cm, 140 × 200 cm, 160 × 200 cm and 180 × 200 cm. In China, different kinds of the SULTAN HÖGBO series are marked as single, double, standard double, and big double. The difference is due to the fact that in Sweden, people are used to putting two single-sized beds together to form a double-sized bed to ensure a good night sleep free from disturbance by the person sharing the bed. This idea does not fit well with the *feng shui* of Chinese culture as sleeping in two separate beds symbolizes a bad relationship between the couple and is believed to bring bad luck.

Product pricing in the Far East, in particular in China, presents a unique challenge for IKEA. IKEA derives its competitive advantage in developed countries from the low-cost production in developing countries supported by aggressive control over the supply chain. Large amounts of raw materials are sourced in the developing countries and production is outsourced to factories in countries with low-cost labour, such as Malaysia, India, and

China. The gap in the raw material and the production costs between developing countries and Western countries is the main source of IKEA's low prices. This cost advantage, however, cannot be maintained in the Chinese market. As a developing country, China's GDP per capita of around US$1,000 is still low even compared with other developing countries in Asia. Prices of furniture provided by local stores are much lower because they often do not invest in original product designs. Most local firms imitate the designs of famous brands (including those of IKEA) and produced furniture at a much lower cost since they are able to access cheap materials and labour locally as well as use less expensive transportation methods. For example, a sofa sold at RMB3,000 in IKEA would be priced at around RMB2,000 at a regular local store such as the OrientHome (www.orienthome.com.cn).

In addition, many Chinese consumers simply do not appreciate IKEA's DIY concept of home furnishing, especially in the light of having to accept the highly priced products without the accompanying personal services, home delivery, and assembly. Although it is making in-roads into the pro-Western 28–35 age group, it is failing to turn the majority of people in more common households into actual buyers. Many young customers, who like the design of IKEA's furniture and decorations, turn to other local stores to buy after wandering around the IKEA store due to the high prices of IKEA's products. There is a perceived incoherence between the consumer groups who understand the IKEA concept and the groups who can afford the product. Chinese consumers with high incomes normally opt for expensive foreign brands, whereas those with a medium or low income tend to shop at local stores. In this regard, IKEA's low-price strategy seems to create confusion among Chinese consumers. Foreign goods are perceived to be more expensive than local brand products. For consumers who are able and willing to pay a high premium for foreign products, foreign brands like IKEA, which prides itself as a low price retailer, make little sense. For those seeking low prices, they find IKEA products more expensive in comparison to the local brands. Therefore, given the 'low price' image with which IKEA associated itself, and the relatively high actual prices, it is difficult for the Chinese consumers to recognize IKEA's value and accept its prices at the same time.

A highly efficient distribution and logistics system plays a fundamental role in enabling IKEA to keep its prices competitive and contributes to every percentage of its profit margins. Under pressure to cut costs and deliver lower prices, IKEA increasingly needs to source its products locally by collaborating with local manufacturers. Its efforts to improve its distribution system are illustrated in its building of two logistics centres in Shanghai. After finishing the first logistics centre in Song Jiang District in December 2005, IKEA is building the second one in Feng Xian. The latter is IKEA's first logistics centre with a quality control centre attached to it. Once it is finished in 2010, both logistics centres can hold 300,000 cubic metres of products. Before these products are distributed to the IKEA shops in the Asia

Pacific region, they will undergo a series of quality control tests (Chen, 2006).

IKEA's efforts to establish an efficient and economic network of logistics and distribution have been met with significant challenges. Distribution systems in China are still relatively underdeveloped. With a large population of 1.3 billion and an inadequate basic road infrastructure, most companies can only access a small part of the population in the most affluent cities. Due to relatively low private car ownership, most IKEA stores in China have to be situated in the city, which is traditionally considered 'non-IKEA' as far as IKEA's retail strategy is concerned. For instance, IKEA Shanghai is built in one of the most expensive districts in downtown Shanghai, Xu Jia Hui District, where there is convenient public transportation. It opens from 10 am to 10 pm daily. Apart from the high retail property costs, transporting thousands of products to city stores inevitably increase distribution costs due to road congestion and logistical complications. Further expansion into the Chinese market cannot be materialized without significant investment in developing its supply chain in China.

Japan has one of the most established consumer markets in the world. Many international companies have tried to establish themselves in Japan without succeess. Although Japan has started to open up its market to foreign competition since the recession in the 1990s, it remains a culturally challenging market for foreign organizations to succeed in.

IKEA first entered into the Japanese home furnishing market in 1974 through a franchise arrangement with a Japanese trading company. It had to withdraw from the Japanese market in 1986 after 12 years of mediocre financial returns. It took IKEA another five years to establish a much deeper understanding of the Japanese consumers before deciding to re-enter the country. During this period, IKEA conducted research on more than 100 Japanese homes in order to understand their way of living and their needs in everyday life, and develop products which would fit well with the Japanese consumer perception.

In 2006, IKEA went into the Japanese market for the second time. Instead of using a franchised arrangement, it opened two IKEA-owned retail outlets—one in Funabashi (Tokyo) and one in Kohoku. It has opened two more stores in 2008, in Kobe and Osaka. All the stores have IKEA's largest store design in the world, occupying 40,000 sq m with an in-store restaurant with over 700 seats. Such a substantial investment signifies IKEA's ambition to dominate the market with one of the world's wealthiest consumers.

On the opening day of IKEA Funabashi, the store attracted 35,000 visitors. Since then, the store generally maintains 30,000–40,000 visitors every weekend. Not unlike other markets, the most important target group for IKEA in Japan is families with children. Their customers tend to be relatively young, with those in their thirties being the largest age segment. The average household size among this group of customers is three people per household, and the annual household income is £40,000–45,000 per year.

For a nation which values simplicity in many aspects of living, the Japanese consumers were expected to appreciate IKEA's well-designed, light-coloured Scandinavian furniture. Compared to other European or Scandinavian furniture manufacturers, IKEA products are priced very competitively, making them very accessible for most Japanese consumers.

IKEA's biggest challenge in Japan is to make the home a more important aspect of Japanese lifestyle. By any measure, Japanese homes are tiny (approximately 50–60 sq m), making it very hard for homeowners to make their homes beautiful while also considering storage space for all of the family's belongings. Most Japanese consumers see their home as a place to sleep and store their personal belongings. Culturally, home furnishings are therefore not regarded as important and little time is spent on decorating the home. It is not in their nature to invite guests to their houses. As Japanese people have a tendency to socialize outside their homes, they spend more time and money on products and accessories, such as Prada (www.prada.com) or Louis Vuitton handbags, mobile phones, and cars, which they can show off in society.

To overcome this cultural apathy towards home furnishings, IKEA needs to find ways to enthuse Japanese consumers and develop the idea of making a home more than just a place to sleep. It needs to make them realize that with home furnishings they can make even small spaces more enjoyable. For instance, IKEA demonstrates this by displaying Japanese-sized apartments in their stores that incorporate a kitchen, a bathroom, a sofa that turns into a bed, and several storage areas. To make it more realistic in relation to Japanese-style homes, IKEA uses the Japanese traditional 'tatami' measures for their display rooms—the only IKEA store in the world where this is practised. Tatami mats are a traditional type of Japanese flooring. They are made of rice straw in individual mats of uniform size and shape bordered by brocade or plain green cloth. All kitchen appliances, such as sinks, taps, dishwashers, fridges, etc., must fulfil Japanese legal requirements, and all cabinets have to be earthquake-safe. While this is a great opportunity for IKEA to be a catalyst of cultural change, this process of change is taking some time as the Japanese view of their homes is deeply rooted in their cutural values.

As in China, the Japanese consumers do not appreciate the DIY concept of self-service, self-delivery, and self-assembly. This aspect has generated some confusion and discussion since a high level of customer service is something that Japanese consumers are culturally accustomed to from every retailer in the country. Although more staff members are now employed in their Japanese stores to adapt to this culture, IKEA limits itself to the amount of service that customers receive. Despite this extra investment, the Japanese customers are still not happy. Customer surveys show that 'staff attitude' to customer service tends to score very poorly.

In conclusion, IKEA's ventures into China and Japan are laden with unique marketing challenges which it has not encountered before in other international markets. Its ambition to conquer the vast Asian markets is reflected in its substantial financial investment and long-term management commitment. Although IKEA strives to implement its own brand of retail strategies, which have been tremendously successful in European markets, it has yet to produce comparable success in Japan and China. Are IKEA's current strategies in these markets going in the right direction? Is the company's retail concept appropriate for the Chinese and Japanese consumers and will it eventually be widely accepted? These are the kinds of questions that IKEA needs to answer if it is to secure a dominant market position in the far East.

Sources

Chen, H. (2006), `IKEA's investing 1.2 billion RMB on another logistics hub of the Asia-Pacific region in Feng Xian District, Shanghai', *National Business Daily.*

Edvardsson, B. and Edquist, B. (2002), '"The IKEA Saga": how service culture derives service strategy', *The Service Industries Journal*, 22(4), 153–86.

Leroux, J., Thamhaksa, D., and Yokoi, H. (2007), 'Home Sweet Home': A Controversial Thought? A Case Study of IKEA in Japan, unpublished Bachelor thesis, Lund University, Lund, Sweden.

Pan, Y. (2005), *Marketing Across Cultures: A Case Study of IKEA Shanghai*, unpublished Masters dissertation, Lund University, Lund, Sweden.

Wei, L.-Q. (2007), 'IKEA in China: facing dilemma in an emerging economy', *Asian Case Research Journal*, 11(1), 1–21.

Discussion Questions

1 Based on your analysis, what are the opportunities and challenges for IKEA in their market operations in (a) China and (b) Japan.

2 With reference to Chapter 7, Fig. 7.2, discuss the market entry strategies that IKEA adopted in China and Japan, respectively.

3 What are IKEA's product, pricing, marketing communication, and distribution decisions in the two Asian markets? To what extent have these marketing mixes been adapted to the preferences and needs of these markets?

4 For each of these markets, discuss and justify what, in your opinion, IKEA's marketing strategy should be in the near future to gain market shares and achieve higher profitability.

PART THREE
Implementing and Coordinating Global Marketing Operations

Part Three addresses the key issues involved in managing and controlling global marketing operations. Efficiency and effectiveness in planning, implementation, and controlling global operations depends on the quality of the marketing management. However, the management of international operations is often neglected.

Part Three contains two chapters addressing the 'people' and management elements of global operations. Chapter 15 looks at sales force management and negotiations. Selling has become an often neglected, unfashionable topic in some quarters, which perceive it (perhaps wrongly) as being replaced with the e-commerce or e-selling. However, in some markets, in particular the business-to-business market, selling remains an important operation. Vital in the process is the ability to conduct sales negotiations across different cultures, which is addressed in this chapter in detail.

Chapter 16 deals with the issue of controlling and monitoring marketing effectiveness. Managing global marketing operations involves the ongoing assessment, monitoring, and alignment of strategies to ensure performance effectiveness. Effective organizational structures are an integral part of this and enable efficient operations and internal communication.

The section covers both traditional and contemporary approaches to the topics and it is illustrated with numerous examples and cases.

CHAPTER FIFTEEN

Sales Force Management and Negotiation

Chapter overview

Chapter Introduction	492
The Changing Nature of Sales Management	493
Behavioural forces	494
Technological forces	494
Managerial forces	494
International Sales Management Decisions	495
Sales force administration	496
Sales force structuring	496
Resource deployment	497
Environmental factors affecting sales force organization decisions	497
Cultural Impact on International Sales Force Management	498
Recruitment and selection	498
Performance, pay, and job satisfaction	501

Developing Customer-oriented Personal Selling	502
Sales Negotiations and the Effect of Culture	503
Preparing for Selling and Negotiating	504
Preparation for Sales Negotiations	505
The Transactional Sales Negotiation Process	507
The Relationship Approach to Sales Negotiation	507
Ethical Considerations in Global Negotiations	510
The Role of Training	512
Chapter Summary	514

Learning objectives

After studying this chapter, the reader will be able to:

- consider the forces that contribute to the changing nature of personal selling and sales management in today's global marketplace;
- examine the challenges of international sales management decision-making and the factors affecting these decisions;
- discuss the cultural impact on international selling and negotiating;
- understand the issues involved in the planning of recruitment and the development of an effective sales force, and methods of motivation and compensation;
- discuss the ethical considerations in international selling and negotiations.

Management issues

The management issues that arise from this chapter include:

- With reference to the changing nature of sales management and personal selling, what will be the challenges of developing and managing an effective international sales force?
- What are the important considerations for the organization in making the international sales management decisions?
- To what extent does culture impact on international selling and sales negotiations?
- What is the organization's policy in dealing with ethical dilemmas in international negotiations?

Chapter Introduction

Personal selling and sales force management have been a neglected area of international marketing. Cavusgil and Nevin (1981) have effectively summed up this apparent lack of academic and managerial attention to the importance of international sales management:

> The entire area of research in international sales management has been virtually neglected in the marketing literature . . . research on a variety of sales management issues would be extremely useful for companies establishing and maintaining their own sales force in countries with different cultural values.

These sentiments are echoed by Mühlbacher et al. (1999: 698–9), who posit that:

> Marketing managers perceived sales simply as part of market communication. There is also a widespread understanding that successful sales activities can be easily transferred from the home country of the company to other country-markets. . . . Marketers also tend to neglect the fact that potential customers in other country-markets often need more information for their buying decision than customers in the home market. Communication problems, such as language barriers or different meanings of verbal and non-verbal language, which become salient in negotiation and buying behaviour, make potential customers feel uncomfortable, not knowing whether they have understood well enough to make the right buying decision . . . Companies doing only some international business tend to consider entering new country-markets as a side issue. Instead of appointing the most capable person to manage sales in a new market, top management tends to have 'somebody' handling that business besides other tasks.

Most of what is known about international sales has been published in anecdotal or case-history form, which tends to concentrate on relatively few industries—general consumer goods, pharmaceutical, industrial, and electronic data processing (EDP) (Hill et al., 1991).

Brooksbank (1995: 61) observes that it is often 'a major oversight on the part of the new breed of marketing protagonists to ignore the importance of personal selling in the marketing process'. There appears to be a tacit (albeit misinformed) understanding that a product or service will 'sell itself' as long as it is well matched to market conditions. The intention of marketing is to make, as far as possible, the role of selling obsolete. In reality, effective personal selling and sales management are an indispensable component of competitive success. As markets are becoming increasingly fragmented, the personalized media of direct selling will become more, rather than less, important. The role of personal selling will continue to be of overwhelming importance in the case of those companies operating in markets characterized by high-value customized goods and services with relatively long and complex decision-making processes.

It is the aim of this chapter to provide insights into this important but neglected area of international marketing. In particular, it examines the specific challenges of developing and managing an effective international sales force that confront international marketing sales managers. It begins with a consideration

Personal selling is often a neglected area of marketing. Potential customers in other countries often need more information for their purchasing decision especially on higher value products.

of the forces that contribute to the changing nature of personal selling and sales management and discusses the various environmental factors affecting international selling and negotiating, and the implications on sales management decision-making. Issues involved in the planning of recruitment, development, and methods of motivation and compensation of an effective sales force are also considered. Finally, we discuss the cultural and ethical considerations in international selling, sales force management, and negotiations.

The Changing Nature of Sales Management

The nature of personal selling and sales management is undergoing dramatic change. Organizations are increasingly looking to new ideas, sales channels, and technologies to sell products, manage buyer–seller relationships, and restructure the sales functions in response to these changes. For instance, as Anderson (1996: 17–21) observes, salespeople are becoming independent of sales managers and moving away from 'selling' towards 'serving' as customer consultants and business partners. At the same time, sales managers are moving away from individual coaching and motivation of field salespeople to developing and managing a hybrid sales force comprising both electronic and field salespeople. New ways are being explored to provide greater value-added service and to develop mutually profitable, ongoing partnerships with customers.

In order to develop and manage an effective international sales force with an accomplished ability to adapt and evolve in the new business landscape, it is important for a marketing/sales manager to understand and account for the forces impacting on personal selling and sales management. These can be categorized into behavioural, technological, and managerial forces (Anderson, 1996: 18–30), as illustrated in Fig. 15.1.

Fig. 15.1 The forces affecting the nature of selling and sales management

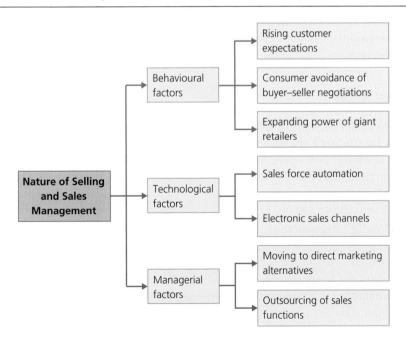

Behavioural forces

- **Rising customer expectations**
  Due to increasing competition in products and services, the expectation for product quality, service, and value for money are rising simultaneously. In order to keep pace, salespeople need constantly to be aware of this through intelligence-gathering, and feed it back to their organizations.

- **Consumer avoidance of buyer–seller negotiations**
  Consumers, frustrated by negative experiences of salespeople, are turning to alternative channels, e.g. the internet and fixed price dealers, especially for high-value items. This explains the popularity of car supermarkets in the UK and Europe.

- **Expanding power of giant retailers**
  Due to their increasing power, dominant retailers are bypassing wholesalers and distributors to buy direct from manufacturers who give them 'key account' status. In the USA, companies such as Wal-Mart (www.walmart.com), Kmart (www.kmart.com), Sears (www.sears.com), and Toys 'R' Us (www.toysrus.com) have grown bigger and more powerful than the manufacturers that supply them and are now dictating the buyer–seller relationship. This change means that managers are required to develop new skills in the negotiating process and inform their sales forces accordingly.

Technological forces

- **Sales force automation**
  New sales and service-oriented computer software is transforming the way salespeople carry out their functions. Time-consuming administrative tasks are being reduced through computer software and developments in hardware, e.g. notebook computers mean that salespeople have a virtual mobile office (see The Digital Impact as an illustration).

- **Electronic sales channels**
  The internet and World Wide Web have enabled organizations to reach a large number of prospective customers. Salespeople have taken advantage of these developments and the technology has also enabled the provision of customer support for basic and self-help services.

Managerial forces

- **Moving to direct marketing alternatives**
  The drive for efficiency is a strong incentive for sales managers to seek alternatives to personal selling, such as telemarketing, direct mail, and teleselling. In business-to-business (B2B) marketing in particular, field sales forces increasingly find themselves as part of a combination of selling personnel, who include telesales representatives, and field sales representatives, for negotiation and relationship-building purposes.

- **Outsourcing of sales functions**
  Outsourcing has become a feature in global organizations wishing to make their operations more efficient. Outsourcing the selling function is no exception. Activities such as complaint handling, scheduling sales calls, and preparing sales presentations are increasingly being outsourced which releases time for the sales force to concentrate on important activities like building relationships.

Companies spend millions of pounds every year supporting brand identity through advertising campaigns, public relations, print marketing, websites, logos, and many other means. These efforts can fail if salespeople then use generic or over-written presentations. Getting it right in the sales presentation is critical because it is often at that point when a prospect becomes a client.

It is a major challenge for an organization to ensure that account representatives accurately and effectively convey brand identity in their sales calls. The question is: 'How do we present the required information in dynamic ways that keep the prospect engaged?' Multimedia presentation technologies can deliver a positive impact by giving sales representatives the ability sell brands as effectively as any advertisements, while informing and educating prospects at the level of a well-written presentation.

With a portable computer, a sales representative can access a number of multimedia tools during meetings. Unlike a sales video, a multimedia presentation can promote discussion by involving the audience more actively in the purchase decision. The combination of onscreen text and images prompt the sales representatives to discuss sales points informally, which can help to develop relationships. In summary, multimedia presentations are a versatile medium that can incorporate video, animation, sound, motion, and graphics to communicate the intended messages.

It is important to note that it is the effectiveness of salespeople, not multimedia screens, which closes sales and builds long-term relationships. The role of the multimedia presentation is to support the sales conversation, not to dominate it. The sales representative

plays the key role in the presentation as guide, brand storyteller, and, in some cases, consultant. The development team should not relegate presenters to the role of lecturer, screen reader, or fellow audience member. The sales representative joins with the prospect as they look at the screens and discuss them together. They explore how the brand story may apply to the prospects' goals and needs. The sales representative can then take advantage of one of the most powerful but least used elements of brand-building in a one-to-one presentation— building trust and credibility by listening to prospective customers and learning about their needs.

Source: Based on Cole and Lingle (1999).

In summary, the nature of sales management has changed dramatically due to emerging technological, behavioural, and managerial forces. To exploit the tremendous sales growth opportunities in the international marketplace, sales managers will not succeed merely by carrying out parochially defined roles and duties. They will need global perspectives and world-class skills to handle an eclectic array of sales and marketing functions.

International Sales Management Decisions

Multinational organizations that operate internationally are faced with the challenge of establishing and managing sales forces in economically and culturally diverse foreign markets. Market conditions abroad are often dissimilar to those in the home country of the organization's headquarters. While many Western European countries share some similarities with the USA in terms of infrastructures, cultures, and education levels, over four-fifths of the world is poor, have underdeveloped infrastructures, and are culturally diverse. It is easier to operate in a bilingual or trilingual country (e.g. Canada and Malaysia) than in those with 200 or more dialects (e.g. India, Zaïre, and Indonesia). Linguistic and cultural fragmentation make sales territories difficult to design, and overall coordination of sales policies and procedures becomes frenetic. Similarly, corporate elements such as sales force size, sales level, and organizational culture can influence the structure of a selling

MINI-CASE ILLUSTRATION **The need to optimize sales force efficiency**

Having an effective sales force is a critical factor for success in every pharmaceutical company. According to the research conducted by Reuters:

- In 2002, the top 50 companies globally spent an estimated US$28 billion on sales and marketing activity, representing almost 15% of their combined revenues. The sales force, on average, accounts for 11% of a company's total revenues. This highlights the importance of sales and marketing activities to the success of a company.

- 'Physician detailing' (i.e. sending sales representatives to doctors with information and samples) is estimated to account for 70–75% of the sales and marketing spend of an average pharmaceutical company. Therefore, maximizing the efficiency of detailing is vital to improve cost-effectiveness in the face of increasing pricing pressures, generic competition, and spiralling research and development costs.

- Primary research indicates that detailing is perceived to have a relatively high ROI (return on investment) in comparison with other marketing methods. Around 70% of doctors are influenced by representative visits. In contrast with only 20% influenced by patient requests.

- It is estimated that, on average, doctors currently see representatives for only seven minutes per day, in comparison with 12 minutes per day in 1995. With sales forces having more than doubled over the same period, increased competition is negatively impacting on ROI.

- Increasing the efficiency of the sales function is vital to the success of pharmaceutical companies, as almost 80% of the

40 companies in the research plan to enlarge their sales force by 2005 and so will drive greater competition for doctors' time.

As the pressures of an increasingly competitive market impact on the revenues of pharmaceutical companies, the expense associated with a sales force is growing. Companies need to keep pace with their competitors by increasing sales force numbers. As a consequence, maximizing field force productivity is paramount. By developing the most effective sales force structures and strategies, pharmaceutical companies can significantly enhance return on investment.

Source: Reuters (2002).

function regardless of geographic country-market (Hill and Still, 1990). Top management of organizations are often uncertain about how much they should influence their overseas sales forces. Clearly, management benefits from knowing which sales decisions are amenable to home-office input and, just as importantly, which are not (Hill et al., 1991).

The effectiveness of international sales management decisions has a direct impact on the success (and profitability) of an organization seeking to operate in foreign markets. In general, according to Hill et al. (1991), these decisions can be categorized into three areas (see Fig. 15.2):

Sales force administration

A decision has to be made on whether to employ a single sales force for multiple markets or a separate sales force for each market. The more culturally similar the markets are, the more a single sales force is able to be employed. This has the advantage of economies of scale and consistency. If the markets are culturally dissimilar, a separate sales force for each market may be a better option.

Sales force structuring

Depending on the complexity of the products, sales force structure may be either geographical, product-based, or matrix-based. With consumer goods, geographical and product-based

Fig. 15.2 International sales management decisions

Factors affecting sales force organization

Source: Based on Hill et al. (1991).

structures, may be more feasible, whereas with complex goods, such as medical equipment, a matrix structure may be more suitable.

Resource deployment

Decisions on sales force administration and structuring will depend on the company's resources. Where sales volumes are low in developing markets, an independent sales force may be used. The higher the market potential and the higher the volume, the more likely an 'owned' sales force will be employed or used in combination with an independent sales force.

International sales management decisions are generally affected by a number of industry factors (such as nature and intensity of competition, costs of market entry), environmental factors (mainly developed–developing market differences), and resource availability (depending upon the level of commitment to a market). In order to formulate sales policies that reflect the idiosyncratic needs of a country-market, organizations must, first, examine the factors that affect the decisions of sales force planning and management.

Environmental factors affecting sales force organization decisions

In their studies on sales policies and practices in 14 multinational corporations (MNCs) in four industries (i.e. general consumer, pharmaceutical, industrial, and EDP) with a combined market coverage of 45 countries, Hill et al. (1991: 22–4) identify the following as the main environmental factors which influence the decisions on sales force organization:

Geographic and physical dimensions: The larger the market size and sales potential, e.g. the USA, the easier it is to specialize selling responsibilities and structure the organization by territory, product, and customer. In smaller markets, however, it is more cost-efficient to consolidate, for example, a product structure with sales administration, e.g. selling a broad range of products as well as providing after-sales care.

Degree of market development: The more the market is developed, the easier it is to recruit and deploy a sales force. However, the higher the educational attainment, the more likely it is that selling, as a profession, will be viewed as unattractive. In Singapore, for instance, where a sales job is perceived as low in social status, many companies fill their sales functions with foreign nationals.

The lack of developed infrastructures and distribution structures in some developing countries can be problematic for companies that rely on these facilities. Adjustments in the selling operations may need to be made. For example, Electrolux (www.electrolux. com) sells 85% of its vacuum cleaners through retail dealers in its European markets but relies on traditional door-to-door personal selling in its South East Asian markets.

Differing political and legal structures: Compensation packages may vary from country to country due to differing political and legal structures. For example, EU legislation recognizes general benefits, including statutory pay holidays; other regions do not. These differences lead to adjustments in the proportion of the total remuneration packages, i.e. fixed to variable elements.

Human relations aspects of personal selling and sales management: Differences in social class systems, ethnic divisions, and business practices may force alterations on a global marketer's home-country practices. Commission, as an element of a salesperson's remuneration package, has a different status in different countries. For example, a strict salary may confer more respect and status than commission. Multinational marketers should adjust compensation practices, recruitment policies, and evaluation methods to reduce the difficulties which may arise from these social differences.

Local market circumstances: Local market conditions may afford opportunities to capitalize on customer preferences and sales presentations. For example, in Thailand and Vietnam, air conditioning is essential and communication emphasizing the availability of this product in cars and homes would be a major selling point. Differences in climatic conditions may also impact on working hours and behaviour and this should be taken into account.

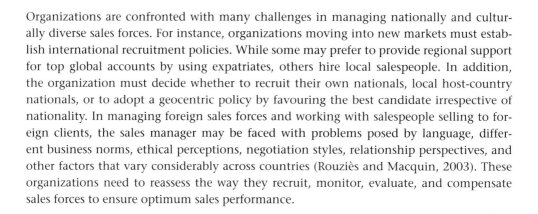

Cultural Impact on International Sales Force Management

Organizations are confronted with many challenges in managing nationally and culturally diverse sales forces. For instance, organizations moving into new markets must establish international recruitment policies. While some may prefer to provide regional support for top global accounts by using expatriates, others hire local salespeople. In addition, the organization must decide whether to recruit their own nationals, local host-country nationals, or to adopt a geocentric policy by favouring the best candidate irrespective of nationality. In managing foreign sales forces and working with salespeople selling to foreign clients, the sales manager may be faced with problems posed by language, different business norms, ethical perceptions, negotiation styles, relationship perspectives, and other factors that vary considerably across countries (Rouziès and Macquin, 2003). These organizations need to reassess the way they recruit, monitor, evaluate, and compensate sales forces to ensure optimum sales performance.

Recruitment and selection

The best organizations select sales personnel with the specific talent and characteristics conducive to building and maintaining profitable long-term customer relationships. There are numerous differences between the home and foreign markets that may complicate the process of hiring suitable sales personnel (Hill and Birdseye, 1989). In general, there are four cultural elements affecting sales force recruitment in a foreign market:

(1) Education—the level of education may be more variable in some countries. This may create difficulty in recruiting high-quality individuals into sales.

(2) Ethnic composition—in culturally and linguistically diverse markets (e.g. India, with 1,000 dialects and sub-cultures), the recruitment of sales personnel who speak the language and understand the culture can be complex and costly.

(3) Religious orientation—religious orientation can have a direct impact on salespeople's behaviour on a day-to-day basis. In Malaysia, the working hours and workplaces within all public sector organizations, which employ predominantly Muslims, are organized to facilitate the five daily prayer times. The religion of Islam generally exerts significant influence on the daily lives of its followers, in comparison with, for example, Protestantism.

(4) Social class environment—in the USA, there is a relatively simple social class system based on economic criteria, e.g. income, wealth, and possessions. Other countries may base their social class distinctions on seniority (e.g. Japan), hereditary criteria (e.g. India, and to a lesser extent Western Europe), or ethnic criteria (e.g. Malaysia). The differences in the social class environment can impact on the recruitment, selection, and promotion of salespeople in the host-country market.

In their empirical study of 652 bank managers employed in over 50 local banks in six European countries, Rouziès et al. (2003) sought to identify the key determinants of staffing decisions in international sales organizations. The findings suggest that the sales personnel international staffing decisions are affected by: (1) regional culture; (2) sales personnel characteristics; and (3) the organization's control variables. These determinants affect sales force management decisions on recruitment (i.e. whether to hire expatriates from the home-market or local nationals), and promotion (i.e. whether to promote internal or external candidates). This is illustrated in Fig. 15.3.

Fig. 15.3 Determinants of sales personnel international staffing decisions

Source: Based on Rouziès et al. (2003).

WHOSE RESPONSIBILITY IS IT? **Does nationality affect people's ethical perceptions and behaviours?**

As more companies establish sales subsidiaries overseas in response to globalization of competition, expatriate sales managers are confronted with situations that necessitate making decisions concerning what is right and wrong. They need to know how to assist sales personnel in reducing such conflict. A failure to help salespeople (both expatriate and local) address these dilemmas may leave them without the ability, knowledge, and judgement necessary to deal effectively with these problems. Performing in an unethical or inappropriate manner may lead to customer dissatisfaction, unfavourable word-of-mouth publicity, as well as reducing sales and profits for the company.

It is believed that nationality affects people's ethical perceptions and behaviours. Differing values, norms, and rules between nations can lead to diverse ethical beliefs and, consequently, there is no single standard of ethical behaviour for all business decisions across all countries. Should companies implement home-country or host-country standards?

In a comparative study of the ethical perceptions of salespeople within the computer-related product/service industry in the USA, Japan, and Korea, Dubinsky et al. (1991) found that nationality influences salespeople's beliefs about the ethics of selling practices and the need to have corporate policies to guide salespeople's behaviour. The participants were asked about their perceptions of a number of selling practices that could create an ethical dilemma, such as gift-giving, free trips, circumventing the purchasing department, exaggerating the seriousness of the client's problems, preferential treatment, and gaining unfair advantage by asking purchasers for competitors' pricing information.

Findings showed that salespeople from different countries have different perceptions of what constitutes ethical and acceptable behaviours in selling practices. US companies are more likely to have policies addressing gift-giving and free entertainment than their Asian counterparts. US salespeople view giving gifts to a purchaser as more of an ethical question than do Korean and Japanese sales personnel, who see this as a way of establishing personal connections—an ingredient necessary for business success in these countries.

These findings suggest that when marketers move into foreign countries and employ host-country nationals as sales personnel, the transfer of established policies regarding ethical issues may not be appropriate. Management needs to assess the ethical issues confronting the host-country market. Simply transferring domestic company policies to foreign markets does not appear appropriate or beneficial, nor does adapting automatically to local customs seem to be a foolproof solution.

Regional culture

Persistent cultural differences and similarities among Europe's major economies play an influential role in general recruitment and promotion practices. For instance, when making recruitment decisions, German managers, due to their less individualistic culture, may place more weight on group cohesiveness, while managers in individualistic cultures, such as the UK, might place more emphasis on individual characteristics related to performance. Managers in less individualistic cultures might also be more likely to hire and promote compatriots rather than foreigners out of concern for group cohesion.

Sales personnel characteristics

There are no simple, universal guidelines for matching salespersons' characteristics with the job specification. Best practice in organizations suggests that a good international sales force is highly adaptable to new situations, sensitive to different cultures, and has the required language skills and ability to work in international teams for positions dealing with international clients.

Rouziès et al. (2003) have identified five important sales personnel characteristics: (1) international openness (e.g. foreign market knowledge, foreign training); (2) acquired skills/competences (e.g. selling skills, communicational skills); (3) personality characteristics associated with career potential (e.g. ambition, personality type, growth potential); (4) objective/quantitative personal characteristics (e.g. age, gender, education/training, experience, assessment test scores); and (5) team spirit (e.g. ability to work with others, cooperation level). Organizations should prioritize one or a set of characteristics in order that a good match is made between the salesperson's characteristics and the job requirements.

Organization's control variables

Apart from regional culture and personal characteristics, there are other organizational characteristics which influence international staffing decisions. First, the international openness (i.e. exposure to other cultures) influences the general internationalization of the organization. An organization with a greater international outlook is more likely to have a higher level of foreign sales (in proportion to domestic sales), a wider geographic spread of sales, or more culturally mixed clients. Secondly, the size of the organization often influences the available financial and human resources, which may impact on the choice of staffing policies, level of training, and pay packages.

Performance, pay, and job satisfaction

Performance of a sales force is commonly measured by the value (or volume) of sales, self-ratings, and/or managerial evaluations. Although value of sales provides a clear and quantifiable measure of performance, it is insufficient to account for other equally (if not more) important performance indicators. Self-ratings and managerial evaluations should be used in conjunction with the values of sales to reflect evaluations of the sales personnels' discharge of activities that define their role in the organizations. These measurements include product knowledge, report filing, territory coverage, route planning, attainment of sales objectives, expense control, prospecting for new accounts, servicing customers, and maintaining satisfactory business relationships (Money and Graham, 1999).

Job satisfaction is influenced by pay level and performance. It is desirable to create and maintain a high level of job satisfaction among all employees. In general, when employees' values are consistent with those of the organization, they are more likely to (a) perceive membership in the organization as conducive to the attainment of personal goals; (b) be comfortable with the work environment and peers; and (c) satisfied with the job in general (Money and Graham, 1999). In a context in which the sales force is charged with responsibility to interact directly and maintain good customer relations with customers, it is critical to ensure a high level of job satisfaction in the sale force.

What motivates a sales force and how it should be rewarded may vary in different country-markets. Conventional wisdom in many Western countries suggests that financial compensation is the main motivator. In Japan, Johansson and Nonaka (1996, in Money and Graham, 1999) observe that most US companies use a combination of salary and commission to motivate, and the ratio between the two components often varies from year to year, depending on management policy and environmental changes. While both Japanese and US companies include bonuses as part of the compensation packages, those in Japan are based on company performance rather than individual performance.

Developing Customer-oriented Personal Selling

In the traditional sale-oriented model, the skills of closing the sale are considered more important than those of understanding or matching customer needs. Heavy usage of sales commission as an incentive and emphasis on 'closing the deal' were (and still are) pervasive in many organizations. In the new customer-oriented model these priorities are reversed (Fig. 15.4). Brooksbank (1995: 62) posits that:

> customer-oriented selling is all about investing the time and effort necessary to uncover each customer's specific needs and wants, and then matching to them, as closely as possible, the product/service benefits on offer, thereby creating the conditions for a relatively straightforward close. This is in sharp contrast to the sales-oriented selling which emphasises closing skills almost to the exclusion of all else. The role of interviewing and matching is minimized, and it relies instead on using a range of sophisticated and highly manipulative closing techniques designed to persuade, even manipulate, the customer to say 'yes'. Therefore the key difference between the old and the new model lies not so much with the selling process itself as it does with the way the salesperson chooses to apply.

Brooksbank (1995) argues that selling, in essence, is 'micromarketing' in action. The three phases in the new model of selling are identical to the three phases of the marketing strategy process, namely: (1) *analysing*—researching the SWOT profile facing the company; (2) *strategizing*—defining marketing positioning strategy and competitive advantage; and (3) *implementing*—activating the chosen strategy by assembling the 7Ps of the marketing mix.

(1) Interviewing phase

This involves interviewing customers to determine their specific needs and wants, and the range of options the customer has for satisfying them. This is similar to the marketing process of 'analysing' where marketing research techniques are used to provide answers to a series of questions about potential customer groups and competitors.

(2) Matching phase

This involves 'matching' what the organization can offer and what the customer wants. This is similar to the marketing process of 'strategizing' where the marketer aims to create a perfect 'fit' between what the organization can do and is good at doing (internal capabilities and core competences) and external opportunities (market needs and trends). In both cases, this is achieved through completing the matching process in such a way

Fig. 15.4 The traditional vs. the new model of personal selling

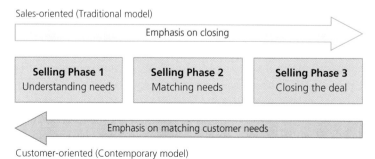

Source: Based on Brooksbank (1995: 62).

Fig. 15.5 The selling mix

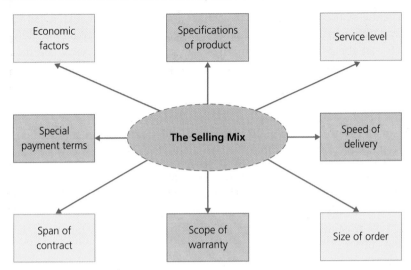

Source: Based on Brooksbank (1995: 65).

that the customer perceives a competitive advantage is to be gained by having a clear preference for the organization's offer.

(3) Closing phase

Stimulating action is common to both the selling and marketing. For the marketer, this involves assembling the various elements of the 7Ps marketing mix in a way which appeals to the target market. The salesperson attempts, on the other hand, to close the deal through a process of negotiating all the elements of the '7Ss selling mix' (Fig. 15.5), in order to arrive at a mutually satisfactory agreement with an individual customer.

In summary, personal selling is one of the most expensive but highly effective tools in marketing in both domestic as well as international markets. The success in international personal selling involves 'the matching of seller's product, knowledge and culture with the buyer's needs, knowledge and culture' (Mühlbacher et al., 1999: 702). International personal selling, in particular must be customized and carefully managed to create the perfect 'fit' between seller and buyer.

Sales Negotiations and the Effect of Culture

Chapters 2 and 4 considered the effects of 'culture' on global planning and operations. To reiterate briefly, the elements that make up culture are social organization, religion, language, aesthetics, law and politics, technology, material culture, education, and values and attitudes. When it comes to selling on a global scale, the practices which relate to the 'norms' and mores of a culture will be more acceptable than those which do not. According to Tenbrunsel (1998: 330): 'Negotiations are asserted to be the breeding grounds for unethical behaviour.' Bluffing, manipulation, and misrepresentation of information are considered unethical behaviour in normal life but may be seen as acceptable in the context of international negotiations. Salespeople need to know how culture functions in a country so that they can adapt their practice to make it acceptable. In order to be able to offer value to the market, it is essential that the seller knows which values are important to the culture and how cultural mores influence the selling process. Culture, though, is not easy to understand. Made up of both abstract and material elements, it can vary in importance and influence from one culture to another. The stage of economic development of a country can affect material culture, therefore products and services commonplace in one country may not be in another. There ought to be a market in Southern Africa, for example, for rainwear given that it rains heavily from November to March. However, the rainy season coincides with warm weather and rainwear is superfluous. A stout umbrella, on the other hand, could sell well.

Salespersons need to develop good cultural empathy skills to enable them to relate to cultures even if they are not aware of the individual nuances of a culture. Cateora and Graham (1998) suggest that people with good cultural skills can:

- convey respect and communicate, both verbally and non-verbally, a positive attitude and interest in people and their culture;
- cope with the frustrations and ambiguity that sometimes occur when faced with an unfamiliar culture;
- show empathy by understanding other people's needs and viewpoints;
- avoid judging people by their own value systems;
- control the use of self-reference criteria where assumptions are made based on one's own culture and values;
- use humour astutely to negate the rise in frustration when things do not go to plan.

In some cultures, selling is an occupation that does not have a high social standing, and it can be difficult to recruit salespeople. In other countries there may be different time values. In India and Africa, the salesperson may be left waiting for an appointment. The West is used to deadlines but in the Middle East this can be seen as insulting. The West is used to 'business lunches', but in India this is a violation of hospitality. The West rely on contracts and try to enforce them on other cultures, generally, but in the Middle East and parts of the Far East, the 'word' is the bond. The Chinese take time to build personal rapport between buyer and seller before a sale takes place, and it is essential that a Chinese person does not lose 'face'. Culture is an ever-changing phenomenon and it is essential to keep up with changes if the product or service is not to be made obsolete. Nowhere is this better exemplified than in the worlds of popular music and fashion. The strategic challenge is to pick up these changes and respond appropriately.

Preparing for Selling and Negotiating

Jobber and Lancaster (2000) suggest that a number factors need to be in order before successful negotiation can take place (see Fig. 15.6).

Product knowledge and benefits: Because people buy products for the benefits they confer, either 'objectively' or 'subjectively', it is insufficient for salespeople to have product knowledge only. Product features need to be related to consumer benefits. For example, wheel-locking nuts on a car wheel are a product feature and this translates into prevention of stolen wheels, a consumer benefit. A salesperson needs to know, in every situation, how a product benefit translates into a consumer benefit, and needs to be able to communicate this to the customer. In global marketing this is particularly important. The 4 × 4 (or sports utility vehicle, SUV) fashion phenomenon in the UK is different from its use through necessity in Africa, South America, or the Middle East. Salespersons in showroomes selling

Fig. 15.6 Factors affecting successful preparation for sales negotiations

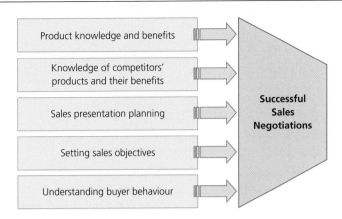

Toyota (www.toyota.com), Nissan (www.nissanusa.com), Mitsubishi (www.mitsubishi.com), and Isuzu (www.isuzu.com) 4 × 4s in the UK have to promote different customer benefits from those in Africa.

Knowledge of competitors' products and their benefits: This allows a salesperson to counter the mention of a competitor's product features by a customer. In B2B selling, a knowledge of a potential competitor's products may enable a technical engineer to work closely with a customer to solve a problem which leads to the customer choosing the company for whom the technician works. Competitor knowledge can be gained from many sources, e.g. salespersons.

Sales presentation planning: Sales presentation planning can augment versatility and the ability to think on one's feet. Important customer benefits will not be forgotten and visual aids add considerably to the power of a verbal presentation.

Setting sales objectives: Call objectives need to be related to sales cycles. Retail call cycles may be relatively short but in capital goods, such as oil rigs, they may be long. The temptation to set sales objectives in terms of what the salesperson wants the customer to do rather than the requirements of what the customer wants is a potential danger.

Understanding buyer behaviour: Consumers, while influenced by a number of social and economic factors, may have to be sold to in different ways from B2B and government customers, where there are multiple influences and, importantly, where the person who pays for the goods and services may be different from the one who orders them. In the latter case, care and time have to be taken to find out who are the influencers and other key people in the decision-making process. For example, BAe Systems (www.baesystems.com), the UK military jet manufacturer, in prospecting for orders overseas, may have to find the key purchase decision-makers as well as engaging 'sales personnel' in the process, such as current users and home government officials, who may perform a key role as influencers.

Preparation for Sales Negotiations

As well as the factors discussed above, sales negotiators may benefit in preparing the following (see Fig. 15.7):

Assessment of the balance of power: In the negotiation process, seller and buyer will each be looking to seal a deal most beneficial to themselves. This will depend on their negotiating

Fig. 15.7 Factors affecting successful sales preparation

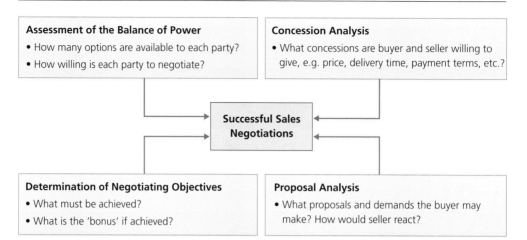

skills and the balance of power between them. The balance will depend on the number of options available to each party, the quantity and quality of information held by each party, the need for negotiation, and satisfaction of pressures, real or perceived, on the parties. The need, therefore, is to make a full balance of power assessment before entering into the negotiating situation. Of course, most of this depends on the options open to the buyer and seller. The more choice the buyer has to purchase goods and services, the more the balance of power is in his/her favour. A good example of this is a United Nations project based in a developing country. Holding a US dollar account in a country which has an unstable or depreciating currency gives the UN project great power. Linked with its diplomatic status, it could buy locally or anywhere in the world, and demand and get the best possible deal. However, if the host government withdraws or limits its diplomatic immunities, the balance of power may shift in favour of the domestic suppliers.

Determination of negotiating objectives: Setting objectives in advance prevents the likelihood of being influenced by the exigencies of the negotiating situation. Two types of objective are useful: those which must be achieved, such as the minimum price; and those which would be a bonus, such as the maximum price that can be extracted from the situation. The price eventually agreed may depend on the balance of power situation.

Concession analysis: This is a form of scenario-planning, where the seller attempts to assess in advance what may have to be conceded by the buyer in the negotiating process. The concessions envisaged may be price, product specification, delivery time, and payment terms.

Proposal analysis: Another step in the preparation process may be to estimate the proposals and demands the buyer may make and the seller's likely reaction.

In global marketing, sales negotiation may be informed by the marketing intelligence system, which is on either a routine or an *ad hoc* basis, collecting vital information on customer needs and wants and competitor data. For example, one of the key factors in the bidding process of Rolls-Royce's (www.rolls-royce.com) (UK) naval propulsion operations and also in Bombardier's (www.bombardier.com) (Canada) rail vehicle manufacturing operations, is the ability to assess 'teaming' arrangements, i.e. which grouping of suppliers and financiers the opposition is fielding for the bid.

The Transactional Sales Negotiation Process

Jobber and Lancaster (2000) suggest a seven-stage process in the personal selling and negotiation process:

(1) The entré or opening.

(2) Customer need and problem identification.

(3) Sales presentation and demonstration.

(4) Dealing with objectives/clarification and/or solution suggestion.

(5) Negotiation.

(6) Closing the sale.

(7) Follow up.

In global marketing, the process outlined above can be quite difficult and time-consuming. The entré or opening process can vary from culture to culture. To shake hands on meeting for the first time may be acceptable in Western culture but not India, where the traditional Namaste, with both hands steepled upwards, is more polite. We saw earlier that the negotiating process may be spread over several days in some cultures, e.g. Japan and China, whereas in the West, where 'time is money', it can be a fairly intense process. Of course, the time taken to complete the sale will be related to the size of the contract and type of business—selling a warship to an overseas buyer will not be completed in a matter of hours. The people involved in the process are also important. The more 'influencers' who are involved, the more drawn out the process. And, it is probably fair to say that where cultural influences play a part in the process, the longer the process is likely to take.

The Relationship Approach to Sales Negotiation

The approach used by Jobber and Lancaster (2000) could be interpreted as a 'transactional' approach to selling. This approach to both marketing and selling has its critics (Grönroos, 1994), primarily because it takes a more short-term view of the marketing transaction, as opposed to the long-term view or 'relationship' approach (see The Relationship Perspective on Pink Cadillac for an illustration). The relationship approach presumes the long-term objectives of seller and buyer are best met when a mutual relationship is developed. This in turn has its critics (Fontenot and Wilson, 1997) because, particularly in consumer marketing, who wants to build a relationship with a company? Relationship marketing, to date, has been long on theoretical development but short on empiricism.

Guenzi (2003) suggested that relationship marketing is a strategic choice for companies aimed at obtaining competitive advantage (Hunt, 1997). He argues that little attention has been paid to the role played by the sales force in the adoption and implementation of the relationship approach. Salespeople are often the only contact a buyer has with a firm and they can therefore, shape sellers' perceptions of a company's reliability and be key influencers in developing long-term relationships. Literature is scarce on the nature, objectives, components, and results of relationship selling behaviours and even more scarce on the factors capable of influencing the adoption of relationship selling on the part of companies. Guenzi (2003) argued that the role of the salesperson has changed in the last few years. Salespeople are now seen as value creators, customer partners, sales team managers, market analysts, and planners (see Wotruba, 1991; De Vincentis and Rackham, 1998; Weitz and Bradford, 1999). In a transactional approach, salespeople are supposed to shift rapidly from a hard selling technique to a smart approach (Kohl et al., 1998, in Guenzi, 2003). In this regard, the sales management approach has to change in terms of sales force selection, training, motivation, and reward and control systems. Guenzi attempted to explore which factors (internal or external) influence a firm's selling orientation (FSO) towards a preference for a transactional or a relationship approach. He identified external and internal factors as antecedents of the FSO. The external factors were characteristics of the customers (requests for customization, heterogeneity of buying and consumption needs, and the costs of switching to competitors) and of the competitive environment (entry frequency of new competitors, aggressiveness of competition). The internal factors were the characteristics of the offer (including variables related to the product sold—industrial or consumer. Guenzi found that contrary to many empirical and theoretical contributions that suggest the relational approach to selling is the best from an economic and competitive advantage point of view, it is necessary to investigate more deeply under which circumstances and conditions it is appropriate and advantageous to favour the relational over the transactional approach. This is of particularly interest to those sales managers who have goals set, like turnover targets and sale volumes, in a traditional way. Turnover can be increased by acquiring new customers or by selling more to existing customers or

THE RELATIONSHIP PERSPECTIVE The 'Pink Cadillac' phenomenon

When Mary Kay Ash brought her cosmetic compact to her local Cadillac dealer in the late 1960s and asked him to match the shade for her new car, he thought she was crazy. No one could imagine that the coveted pink Cadillac would become one of the most recognized brand symbols in the world—Mary Kay Cosmetics.

In mid-1963, after a successful career in direct sales, Mary Kay Ash retired and wrote a book aimed at women in the male-dominated business world. Then, with her life savings of US$5,000 and the help of her 20-year-old son, Mary Kay, Inc. (www.marykay.inc) was born.

Mary Kay Cosmetics now boasts a product range that includes more than 200 premium products in facial skincare, colour cosmetics, nail care, body care, sun protection, and fragrances to dietary supplements and men's skincare products. It has become one of the largest direct sellers of skin and colour cosmetics. The company's vision was to offer women unprecedented opportunities for financial independence, advancement, and personal success—opportunities that Mary Kay felt were often unavailable to women.

Mary Kay owed its ultimate success to unique relationships with its independent sales force as much as the quality and popularity of its products. Women are the primary audience and the face of the company. Apart from ensuring the high quality of its products, the company invests the majority of its marketing resources on recruiting, teaching, and motivating the independent sales force. The focus on developing and managing a motivated

and 'educated' sales force is what distinguishes Mary Kay from the competition.

Every sales force member is encouraged to inspire and mentor other sales force members as part of the company's business philosophy. The company's annual award is the 'Go-Give Award', which is presented at the company's annual convention to an independent sales force member who has demonstrated an outstanding achievement in helping other women succeed in their own Mary Kay businesses (i.e. widening the sales network). Over 50,000 independent sales force members attend the company's five conventions in Dallas each summer for three days' business-building classes, leadership education, and motivational speeches by top salespeople and company executives.

In addition, training sessions are held throughout the year to enable the independent sales force members to learn about Mary Kay's new products, leadership skills, and new ways to motivate their own team members. At headquarters events, the independent sales force members are made to feel valued, e.g. being greeted at the door (often by name) and being recognized publicly for their achievements, etc. They mingle with company executives and have their picture taken in Mary Kay's office. Even as its sales force approaches 1 million worldwide, this personal attention remains an important part of the company's culture and a critical success factor for the brand.

Source: Based on Shasteen (2002).

a combination of both. This proves the case that circumstances or conditions may dictate a relational or transactional strategy. The operating environment and factors specific to the firm can also govern the strategy adopted. Frequency of entry of new competitors may force a transactional approach, but where there are few competitors a relationship approach may prevail.

Developing a relationship approach to sales management and sales negotiation is a strategic challenge when operating across borders and cultures. Continental Europe is only a short distance away from the UK but the cultures are different. Primarily, there are language differences. While there has been a growing interest in relationship approaches over the last few years, there has been equal interest in examining the role of 'trust' and 'satisfaction' (Crosby et al., 1990) between salespeople and their customers. Tam and Wong (2001) suggest that although there have been numerous studies focusing on understanding the business-to-business exchange relationships between individuals who represent the firms and their customers, there has been little research on individual factors such as trust, customer orientation, personal disclosure, and the negotiator's skills and experience. Their research focused on the insurance services industry, particularly foreign insurers into China. The plan is to open up China in its entirety to foreign insurers by 2005 but, to date, the progress has been slow. In 1990, the Chinese government allowed only a few multinationals to open in Shanghai and Guanzhou. Of these, three were from the USA—Aetna (www.aetna.com), John Hancock (www.jhancock.com), and Chubb Life (www.chubb .com). In order to succeed in the expanded Chinese market, multinational life insurance companies must adapt to local customs and culture, requiring the ability to develop a mutual understanding and trust between sales professionals and customers. The Chinese may not understand the complexities of 'insurance', which means that effective management of the agent–client relationship is important.

Tam and Wong (2001) attempted to develop a framework to address this relationship. They started their research by examining the conceptualization that 'relationship quality' is manifested in the constructs of 'trust' and 'satisfaction'. 'Trust' is the reaction to exposure to potential losses. The trust in a salesperson depends on the perception of risk and uncertainty, which is perceived differently by an individual compared to an organization. 'Satisfaction' is an emotional response to the buyer–seller interaction experience. The high or low quality image of the organization that the seller represents helps in this regard. Successful sales experiences and, therefore, future sales depend on relationship quality brought about by a reinforced trust/satisfaction relationship. In selling insurance, the seller may face the dilemma of meeting sales quotas from his employee with selling a product, which is seen as a distress purchase by the buyer. Both will have an effect on the way a salesperson communicates and behaves. The need to 'stay in touch' with the potential customer is a tenant of insurance selling (Crosby, 1984, in Tam and Wong, 2001). Across cultures, these three factors have to be balanced to achieve the desired long-term effect. Tam and Wong carried out a survey of potential insurance product buyers of a large UK insurance company in Hong Kong to ascertain general demographic characteristics and information on life insurance policies, perceptions of the salesperson's selling behaviour, the salesperson's self, and company disclosure, levels of the satisfaction towards the service provided, level of trust towards the salesperson, and future buying intentions. The statistical analysis revealed six important factors in the relationship:

- customer-orientation;
- sales-orientation;
- agent's self-disclosure;
- relation-orientation;

- transaction-orientation;
- agent's company disclosure.

Interpretation of the findings suggested that customer orientation was important in insurance sales. The 'hard sell' was inappropriate. Satisfaction was influenced by the salesperson's personal disclosure and customer- and relationship-oriented behaviours. Buyers would like to develop a stable, ongoing relationship with the insurance provider, particularly when the perceived risk is high. In this study, in support of Guenzi's (2003) findings about industry-specific factors, it was important for companies to switch from a sales strategy to a relation strategy as referrals accounted for a high proportion of new business. Intentions to recommend the firm to others or do further business depended on customer satisfaction, the salesperson's relation orientation and self-disclosure.

Tam and Wong (2001) concluded that the employee is key in establishing relationships with customers. A 'happy' salesperson will be motivated to build long-term lasting relationships with customers rather than one driven by the need to meet short-term profit targets. They suggest that organizations adopt a 'three Es' approach:

- **Empathy with employees**: This is an essential element to help the company build a mutual concern and trust by showing confidence in their salesperson's ability and recognizing his/her contribution. Prudential Assurance Hong Kong Ltd (www .prudential.com.hk) do this by allowing some employees to take six months' leave of absence for studying while continuing to share in company profits during that period.
- **Empowerment**: Giving employees skills, tools, flexibility, and a desire to serve the customer.
- **Ethical problems can erode trust**: Organizational culture must not motivate a salesperson to act unethically.

Fostering the three Es will lead to achieving the goals of an enduring relationship, especially when dealing with the new Chinese life insurance market.

Ethical Considerations in Global Negotiations

In so far as building relationships based on trust and satisfaction is desirable, especially across international cultures, there are limits to which salespeople can go in their behaviour: their ability to anticipate their counterpart's actions and reactions and understand the motivations behind them. In sales negotiations, 'ethics' are paramount. As Zarkada-Fraser and Fraser (2001) point out, international marketers are business negotiators, who constantly discuss deals across borders with a variety of people (see also Ghauri and Usunier, 1996). Yet the focus of most of the international marketing literature is still on strategy, systems and processes rather than people. They point out that even under the relationship-oriented paradigm it is the firm, as instigator of the relationship process, which is still dominant. They further suggest that the field of international negotiations remains sparse, especially the role of the individual, yet 'negotiation' is a key managerial task. This becomes particularly relevant when negotiating across cultures where costly mistakes can be made. The authors addressed the question of the 'atmosphere' of a relationship developed during the negotiation process and suggested that it is of paramount importance. Perceptions of each member towards the other in the process is crucial, especially if these perceptions involve negotiation tactics that one party perceives as immoral.

Zarkada-Fraser and Fraser (2001) examined perceptions of ethicality in negotiation tactics employed in international sales negotiations and linked these to decision-making frameworks. The study looked at the context of international sales negotiations and was based on the premise that the more one party knows about the other party's expectations, possible courses of action, and decision-making mechanisms, the more likely that party is to adopt an appropriate strategy and find ways to implement it successfully. When faced with difficult moral issues, one party cannot simply apply the solution dictated by their own culture, as this may not be acceptable to the other party. Zarkada-Fraser and Fraser's research adds to the growing body of literature on anthropocentric analysis in international marketing, highlights the cross-cultural context in the negotiation process, and provides a much needed dyadic and meta-ethical perspective in the marketing ethics literature.

In building and maintaining effective buyer–seller relationships, nationality, communication difficulties through language, linguistic differences, and culturally different negotiation styles added to the lack of trust and could be mitigating factors in the process. This is compounded by the external environment, which has an impact on the moral decision-making process. Factors in this environment include the legal framework, cultural environment, ethical environment, and the organization within which a person works. In their research, Zarkada-Fraser and Fraser (2001) attempted to account for these factors when they studied 332 marketing or sales managers of exporting firms in six countries—Japan, the USA, Greece, Russia, the UK, and Australia. Respondents were given 11 negotiation tactics and were asked to indicate their moral evaluation in terms of the degree of moral content they perceived in each and how likely they would be to employ the tactics to gain advantage. For the decision-making variables the respondents were asked to reflect on the moral evaluation of the tactics and indicate how important each one was in selecting the respondents.

The results showed that for Greeks, management should be aware of the high degree of orientation to one's superior and the company. Therefore, in negotiations it would be prudent to obtain intelligence on the relationship between negotiators and superiors as well as organizational culture and strategy. For Russians, there appeared to be no room for intuition in negotiations, this being a legacy of the central bureaucratic days. Intelligence for negotiations should concentrate on an understanding of company procedures and their application through historical data. It would appear immoral to open a negotiation which appeared to undermine the other party as well as to convey an impression that there was no hurry to closure. The Japanese assign high importance to company-related concerns, such as relationships with other organizations and the strategic objectives of their firms. Unlike the Greeks, who display compliance to the micro-level organization of the firm only, the Japanese imply compliance to the macro-level organization, which includes not only the internal organization, but the industry as a whole. They also complied with professional codes of behaviour rather than legal frameworks, reflecting the non-litigious nature of Japanese society. Intelligence for negotiations should concentrate on past, current, and potential business relationships. They also appeared to be the least tolerant of unethical behaviour. Clear and unambiguous detail of the goods and services on offer is essential. They were also the least likely to engage in opportunistic negotiating behaviour. The Americans, British, and Australians revealed similar behaviour. Process issues, such as objectives of the negotiation and a time frame, were important and these cultures were found to be the most likely to engage in 'game playing', i. e. misrepresenting the process issues. Intelligence for negotiations should, therefore, concentrate on 'oneupmanship'. These cultures also placed greater emphasis on the law, particularly reflected in the USA, so negotiations involving these cultures should include a comprehensive knowledge of the law.

MINI-CASE ILLUSTRATION Ethics in global marketing

The Iraq war of 2003 revealed that the Iraqis were using weapons sold to them by the very countries that they were fighting against—the USA and the UK. Sold as a means for Iraq to put down insurrection years before, they were subsequently used to commit atrocities on a religious section of the Iraqi population opposed to the country's dictator. Selling military arms raises ethical issues. India purchased field guns from France in the 1980s. Later it emerged that a number of Indian politicians had accrued substantial financial gain from the purchase. Arms sellers have always walked a fine line, especially in sales to Third World countries. So-called 'conflict' diamonds are another example. Mined from war-torn countries like Angola and the Democratic Republic of the Congo, and sold or given in exchange for arms or military help, they have caused instability in a trade known for its tight regulation. In a different vein, there

still remain unscrupulous 'time share' or property sellers, preying on unsuspecting tourists in such places as Spain and Cyprus. Skillfully, and sometimes aggressively, tourists are negotiated into parting with sums of money only to find out later that they have gained little or nothing. The internet has been a tremendous tool for global selling. Yet, unless the product or service sold is well known, there is always the risk that the product will not live up to expectations. Sometimes, this can be hard to rectify.

Thankfully, through the efforts of global 'conscience-raisers', like Amnesty International (www.amnestyinternational) and government 'watchdogs' like the US Ethics Committee, organizations are becoming very aware of their global responsibilities. In fact, most multinationals, these days have codes of conduct built into their corporate culture.

While the research has its limitations, the challenge is clear for global negotiators, particularly in the selling situation. The expectations of the other party's behaviour are very important. Culture is a key factor in accounting for differences in expectations, perceptions, and evaluations. The challenge for the global marketer is to unearth the specific underlying societal values of each country as predictors and determinants of the prevailing ethicality norms. See mini-case illustration for examples of ethics in global selling.

The Role of Training

One of the keys to successful negotiation and the recognition of the need for cultural empathy is training. Perversely, when negotiators belong to different cultures training can either reinforce or diminish the differences and so increase or decrease the likelihood of building long-term relationships. Roman and Ruiz (2003) addressed the issue of training in a European context. It would be easy to fall into the trap of believing that a single negotiation style would be acceptable across Europe. But differences in negotiation styles are not determined only by different conditions and values, as there is a strong relationship between sales training and sales negotiation too. Sales training equips the salesperson with the concepts, rules, and skills to be in a better position to do the job. In the international environment, sales training enables salespersons to be better prepared to carry out the sales negotiation process. In line with cultural variations, different types of sales training may produce different business performance results. Roman and Ruiz (2003) contend that the literature on cross-cultural sales negotiations is mainly focused on studying cultural differences rather than looking at sales training, as an antecedent of negotiation, which differs within cultures. Europe has two different cultures—north and south. Companies in either culture will adopt sales training methods that are relevant to the culture to which they belong. There should be cross-cultural differences, therefore, in negotiation methods. Roman and Ruiz (2003) looked at the degree to which sales training practices differed

Fig. 15.8 Differences in sales training: Northern vs. Southern Europe

Southern Europe	Northern Europe
Degree of subsidization: high	Degree of subsidization: low
Investment in training: low	Investment in training: high
Training content: customer or market knowledge	Training content: company policy, product knowledge, teamwork, customer/market knowledge
Training methods: externally run (but training methods similar to those in Northern Europe)	Training methods: internally run, on-the-job training
Training effectiveness: on-the-job, in-house training more effective; sales-related performance weaker	Training effectiveness: in-house training negatively affect sales; sales-related performance effective

Source: Based on Roman and Ruiz (2003: 7–8).

between the north (Finland, the Netherlands and the UK) and the south (Portugal and Spain), and the degree to which the effect's of sales training on salespeoples' performance differed between northern and southern European countries. Ancillary research addressed whether sales training could be transferred between the two cultures and whether one approach to sales training was better.

In Hall's (1983) low-context, high-context approach to the study of culture, northern and southern Europe clearly differ. The north prefers schedules, time deadlines, etc., while the south prefers to build relationships first. In sale negotiations, salespersons in the north do not like to be kept waiting, but it is common in the south. So the first cultural difference is in relation to 'time'. In terms of training, open and distance learning methods are often used in the UK, Finland, and the Netherlands, where rules and regulations are acceptable, but southern Europe prefers more personal interaction. Northern Europe also prefers in-house trainers to external consultants. Roman and Ruiz (2003) obtained data from 555 SMEs in the three northern and southern countries. The results showed considerable differences between training in northern and southern Europe (see Fig. 15.8).

In today's global society, a monocultural approach to sales training is insufficient. The need to understand different cultures is essential in international business negotiations, as a method acceptable in one society may not be acceptable in another. The study by Roman and Ruiz (2003) showed that differences in sales training methods were more important than differences in content. The research concluded that the contemporary sales negotiator needs to have knowledge of product, customer/market, the company, and sales techniques to be successful. Further, international companies should be aware that although basic sales skills are the same around the world, training must be tailored to individual cultures and caution must be exercised when attempting to transfer sales training methods from one culture to another. This is particularly relevant where local salespeople are hired to sell in those markets. These companies may believe that in-house training is more effective when implemented in a polychronic culture than in a monochronic culture. It remains to be seen whether global companies operating in many countries adapt their sales training practice in each of the countries in which they operate.

Chapter Summary

1. The nature of personal selling and sales management is undergoing dramatic change. Organizations are increasingly looking to new ideas, sales channels, and technologies to sell products, manage buyer–seller relationships, and restructure the sales functions in response to the changing business landscape. New ways are being explored to provide greater value-added service and to develop mutually profitable, ongoing partnerships with customers.

2. In order to develop and manage an effective international sales force with an accomplished ability to adapt and evolve in this new business landscape, it is important for a marketing/sales manager to understand and account for the forces impacting on personal selling and sales management. These forces can be categorized into behavioural, technological, and managerial.

3. Multinational organizations that operate internationally are faced with the challenge of establishing and managing sales forces in economically and culturally diverse foreign markets. The effectiveness of international sales management decisions has a direct impact on the success (and profitability) of an organization seeking to operate in foreign markets.

4. In managing foreign sales forces and working with salespeople selling to foreign clients, the sales manager may be faced with the problems posed by language, different business norms, ethical perceptions, negotiation styles, relationship perspectives and other factors that vary considerably across countries. The best organizations recruit sales personnel by selecting individuals with the specific talents and characteristics that are conducive to building and maintaining profitable long-term customer relationships.

5. What motivates a sales force and how it should be rewarded may vary considerably in different country-markets. Conventional wisdom in many Western countries suggests that financial compensation is the paramount motivator of salespeople. Approaches to motivate salespeople can vary in other countries.

6. The three phases in the new model of selling are identical to the three phases of the marketing strategy process, namely: (1) *analysing*—researching the SWOT profile facing the company; (2) *strategizing*—defining marketing positioning strategy and competitive advantage; and (3) *implementing*—activating the chosen strategy by assembling the 7Ps of the marketing mix.

7. Negotiations are said to be the breeding ground for unethical behaviour. Bluffing, manipulation, and misrepresentation of information are considered unethical in normal life but may be seen as acceptable behaviour in the context of international negotiations. Salespeople need to know how culture functions in a given country so that they can adapt their practice to make it acceptable.

8. Transactional approaches to marketing and selling take a more short-term view of the marketing transaction, as opposed to the long-term view or 'relationship' approach. Developing a relationship approach to sales management and sales negotiation is a strategic challenge to global marketers operating across borders and cultures.

9. Differences in negotiation styles are not determined only by different conditions and values, as there is a strong relationship between sales training and sales negotiation. Sales training equips the salesperson with the concepts, rules, and skills to be in a better position to do the job. In the international environment, sales training enables salespersons to be better prepared to carry out the sales negotiation process. In line with cultural variations, different types of sales training may produce different business performance results.

END-OF-CHAPTER CASE STUDY Developing an effective sales force structure

It is estimated that the top 50 pharmaceutical companies spend about US$20 billion globally on sales and marketing, representing 14% of their combined revenues of US$200 billion (Reuters, 2002). Of this, approximately 70–75% of the sales and marketing budget is allocated to cover the costs of the sales force and managing relationship with doctors. These costs have led some companies to re-evaluate their sales forces. For example, in May 2008, Merck and Co. Inc. announced plans to cut the size of its sales force by 1,200. Pfizer and Glaxo also feel that doctors are now overloaded with sales 'clutter'.

Determining the size of the sales force is a key decision and is closely related to the market success of pharmaceutical companies. Many companies have increased the size of their sales force in recent years due to the need to cover new product launches. Indeed, pharmaceutical companies have increased the size of their sales force by approximately 70% over the past five years, significantly increasing the level of competition between sales personnel to gain sales visits. There is, however, substantial variation in the size of companies' sales forces in different countries. The sales forces structures in UK and Japanese companies are given below.

UK sales force structures

The sales forces of UK pharmaceutical companies grew by between 12% and 33% in the period 1999–2001, reflecting efforts to adapt to the changing environment in the UK National Health Service (NHS) and the growth of primary care groups. The main UK pharmaceutical companies are Glaxo Smith Kline (GSK, www.gsk.com), Bristol-Myers Squibb (www.bms.com), Wyeth (www.wyeth.com), Merck KgaA (www.merck.com), Schwarz Pharma AG (www.schwarzpharma.com), and Solvay (www.solvay.com). The sales forces range in size from approximately 65 reps for Schwarz Pharma to 420 reps for Wyeth. The sales forces of these companies are typically structured by target audience, with little specialization by therapy area. Primary care and hospital sales forces are split on a regional basis. One widespread variation between UK sales forces and others in Europe is the considerable focus on monitoring changes in the NHS. Many companies employ NHS development teams to monitor changes in the UK healthcare system and report findings either to sales reps or to primary care groups. The importance of this role in the changing UK healthcare market is exemplified by Merck KgaA, which increased its number of regional development managers eightfold over the three years to 2002.

Japanese sales force structures

The Japanese sales forces for all major pharmaceutical companies (e.g. Saiichi, Eisai, Fujisawa, Shionogi, Tanabe, Dainippon) range from 660 to 1,350 reps, with very little variation between companies. The similarity in sales force size correlates with the similarity in sales force structure.

Typically, Japanese sales forces are structured on a regional basis with little specialization by either customer type or therapy area. Reps are divided into regional and local sales forces and generally detail the company's entire marketed portfolio to a wide range of hospital, specialist, and primary care doctors. Such a structure reflects the importance of customer relations in Japan, as it ensures that doctors will be visited by only one rep from any particular company, allowing the rep to build a strong relationship with the doctor. However, such a structure will compel the rep to focus only on the best-selling products, as it is not possible to detail the entire product range in a single visit. This may partly explain why many Japanese companies are reliant on a small number of products to drive growth, with the majority of the remaining portfolio in slow decline.

Optimizing sales force structures is vital to ensure that a company's operations within a national market are as effective as possible. The most appropriate structure will depend on the nature of the regional market. For instance, UK companies focus on target audience (hospital or primary care), whereas in Japan a regional split with all sales reps promoting the same products is most popular. Moreover, the sales force structure will depend on the therapeutic focus of the company as this will determine whether a single mass-market sales force is more effective or whether therapeutic area-specific sales forces would be more productive. Finally, the overall size of a sales force will determine the most efficient system. Small sales forces are necessarily forced to rely on a territorial sales structure because it is not possible to specialize further if the number of doctors visited is to be maximized. As sales force size increases, so does the need to structure a sales force to maximize efficiency.

Source: Based on selected extracts from Reuters (2002 and 2008).

Case discussion questions

1 What are the differences in the sales force structures of UK and Japanese pharmaceutical companies? How do you think this affects the nature of personal selling, and the relationship between the sales rep and the doctor?

2 Discuss the determining factors in the planning of sales force structure within a national market for a pharmaceutical company. Can these factors be applied to the planning of sales force structures for other types of product or service? If so, provide examples.

END-OF-CHAPTER EXERCISES

1   What are the behavioural, technological, and managerial forces which are shaping the changing nature of personal selling and sales management?

2   What are the decisions involved in international sales management and planning?

3   Identify and briefly discuss the environmental factors affecting sales force organization decisions?

4   Discuss the cultural impact on sales force recruitment and selection.

5   Explain what is meant by customer-oriented personal selling.

6   Name the seven elements of the 'selling mix'?

7   What is the difference between the 'transactional' and 'relationship' approach to selling?

8   How does 'culture' affect the sales negotiation process? What must an organization do to take into account the effect of 'culture' in sales negotiations?

9   Explain the ethical considerations of international selling and negotiating.

DISCUSSION AND EXAMINATION QUESTIONS

1   'The nature of personal selling and sales management is undergoing dramatic change. Organizations are increasingly looking to new ideas, sales channels, and technologies to sell products, manage buyer–seller relationships, and restructure the sales functions in response to the changing business landscape.' Discuss.

2   What are the decisions involved in international sales management? How are these decisions affected by environmental factors in the international marketplace?

3   With relevant examples, evaluate to what extent cultural differences affect sales personnel international staffing decisions.

4   What fundamental differences in sales training must an organization consider when choosing a 'transactional' or 'relationship' approach to global selling?

5   Citing relevant examples, discuss the relevance of 'culture' in the preparation of global sales negotiations.

FURTHER READING

Calvin, R. J. (2000), *Sales Management*, The McGraw Hill Executive MBA Series, New York: McGraw-Hill.

Guenzi, P. (2003), 'Antecedents and consequences of a firm's selling orientation', *European Journal of Marketing*, 37(5/6), 706–27.

Jobber, D. and Lancaster, G. (2007), *Selling and Sales Management*, 7th edn., London: Pearson Education.

Zarkada-Fraser, A. and Fraser, C. (2001), 'Moral decision making in international sales negotiations', *The Journal of Business and Industrial Marketing*, 15(4), 274–93.

REFERENCES

Anderson, R. E. (1996), 'Personal selling and sales management in the new millennium', *Journal of Personal Selling & Sales Management*, XVI(4), 17–32.

Brooksbank, R. (1995), 'The new model of personal selling: micromarketing', *Journal of Personal Selling & Sales Management*, XV(2), 61–6.

Cateora, P. R. and Graham, J. L. (1998), *International Marketing*, Maidenhead: Irwin/McGraw-Hill.

Cavusgil, S. T. and Nevin, J. R. (1981), 'The State of the Art in International Marketing: An Assessment', in Enis, B. and Roering, K. (eds.), *Review of Marketing*, Chicago: American Marketing Association.

Cole, E. and Lingle, M. (1999), 'Building your brand with laptop sales presentation: how multimedia can help increase sales force effectiveness', *The Advertiser*, October.

Crosby, L. A., Evans, K. R., and Cowles, D. (1990), 'Relationship quality in services selling: an interpersonal influence perspective', *Journal of Marketing*, 54, 68–81.

De Vincentis, J. R. and Rackham, N. (1998), 'Breadth of a salesman', *The McKinsey Quarterly*, 4, 32–43.

Dubinsky, A. J., Jolson, M. A., Kotabe, M., and Lim, C. U. (1991), 'A cross-national investigation of industrial salespeople's ethical perceptions', *Journal of International Business Studies*, Fourth Quarter, 651–70.

Fontenot, R. J. and Wilson, E. J. (1997), 'Relational exchange: a review of selected models for a prediction matrix of relationship activities', *Journal of Business Research*, 38, 5–12.

Ghauri, P. N. and Usunier, J.-C. (1996), *International Business Negotiations*, Oxford: Pergamon.

Grönroos, C. (1994), 'From marketing mix to relationship marketing: towards a paradigm shift in marketing', *Management Decision*, 32(2), 4–20.

Guenzi, P. (2003), 'Antecedents and consequences of a firm's selling orientation', *European Journal of Marketing*, 37(5/6), 706–27.

Hall, E. T. (1983), *The Dance of Life*, New York: Anchor Press/Doubleday.

Hill, J. and Birdseye, M. (1989), 'Salesperson selection in multinational corporations: an empirical study', *Journal of Personal Selling & Sales Management*, IX(Summer), 39–47.

Hill, J. S. and Still, R. R. (1990), 'Organising the overseas sales force: how multinationals do it', *Journal of Personal Selling & Sales Management*, X(Spring), 57–66.

——, ——, and Boya, Ü. O. (1991), 'Managing the multinational sales force', *International Marketing Review*, 8(1), 19–31.

Hunt, S. (1997), 'Competing through relationships: grounding relationship marketing in resource-advantage theory', *Journal of Marketing Management*, 13, 431–45.

Jobber, D. and Lancaster, G. (2000), *Selling and Sales Management*, 5th edn., Harlow: FT/Prentice Hall.

Money, R. B. and Graham, J. L. (1999), 'Salesperson performance, pay, and job satisfaction: test of a model using data collected in the United States and Japan', *Journal of International Business Studies*, 30(1), 149–72.

Mühlbacher, H., Dahringer, L., and Leihs, H. (1999), *International Marketing: A Global Perspective*, 2nd edn., London: Thomson.

Reuters (2002, 2008), *The Pharmaceutical Sales Force Outlook: Structures and Strategies to Maximize ROI and Boost Product Intake*, Reuters Business Insight: Healthcare.

Roman, S. and Ruiz, S. (2003), 'A comparative analysis of sales training in Europe', *International Marketing Review*, 20(3), 7–8.

Rouziès, D. and Macquin, A. (2003), 'An exploratory investigation of the impact of culture on sales force management control systems in Europe', *Journal of Personal Selling & Sales Management*, XXIII(1), 61–72.

—— Segalla, M. and Weitz, B. A. (2003), 'Cultural impact on European staffing decisions in sales management', *International Journal of Research in Marketing*, 20, 67–85.

Shasteen, R. (2002), 'Mary Kay: inspiring beauty, enriching lives', *The Advertiser*, October.

Tam, J. L. M. and Wong, Y. H. (2001), 'Interactive selling: a dynamic framework for services', *Journal of Services Marketing*, 15(5), 375–96.

Tenbrunsel, A. E. (1998), 'Misrepresentations and expectations of misrepresentation in an ethical dilemma: the role of incentives and temptation', *Academy of Management Journal*, 4(3), 330–40.

Weitz, B. A. and Bradford, K. D. (1999), 'Personal selling and sales management: a relationship marketing perspective', *Journal of the Academy of Marketing Science*, 27(2), 241–54.

Wotruba, T. R. (1991), 'The evolution of personal selling', *Journal of Personal Selling & Sales Management*, 11(3), 1–12.

Zarkada-Fraser, A. and Fraser, C. (2001), 'Moral decision making in international sales negotiations', *The Journal of Business and Industrial Marketing*, 15(4), 274–93.

online resource centre

Visit the companion website to this book for lots of interesting additional material, including self-assessment questions, internet exercises, and links for each chapter:

http://www.oxfordtextbooks.co.uk/orc/lee_carter2e/

CHAPTER SIXTEEN

Organizing and Controlling Global Marketing Operations

Chapter overview

Chapter Introduction	520
Philosophy of Management	521
Ethnocentrism	521
Polycentrism	521
Regiocentrism and geocentrism	521
Planning for Global Marketing	521
Global Control Mechanisms	525
Factors affecting control	526
The elements of an international marketing control system	528
The global marketing audit	528

Specific control methods	529
Organizing for Global Marketing	535
Functional	535
Geographical, functional, or strategic business unit approach	536
Product organizational structures	537
Matrix organizational structures	538
'Hub and spoke' organizational structures	539
Virtual organizational structures	539
Issues in Global Organizational Structures	540
Chapter Summary	543

Learning objectives

After studying this chapter, the reader will be able to:

- describe the pattern of global organizational development;
- understand the different forms of global organization and their advantages and disadvantages;
- discuss the different types of global planning and control and examine the merits and demerits of each type;
- discuss the variables that can affect the control mechanism;
- examine some of the critical strategic considerations in organizing and controlling global marketing operations.

Management issues

The management issues that arise from this chapter include:

- With reference to the increasing importance of organizing and controlling global marketing operations, what are the implications of this development on your business?
- What are the specific problems in global marketing planning, control, and organization, and how can these be overcome?
- What are the global strategic implications of having an inappropriate global organization, and control structures and procedures?

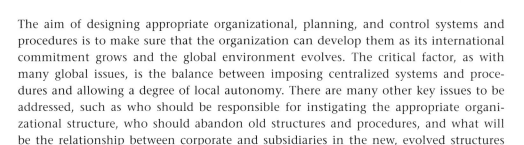

Chapter Introduction

The aim of designing appropriate organizational, planning, and control systems and procedures is to make sure that the organization can develop them as its international commitment grows and the global environment evolves. The critical factor, as with many global issues, is the balance between imposing centralized systems and procedures and allowing a degree of local autonomy. There are many other key issues to be addressed, such as who should be responsible for instigating the appropriate organizational structure, who should abandon old structures and procedures, and what will be the relationship between corporate and subsidiaries in the new, evolved structures and procedures. Harvey and Novicevic (2002: 525) showed the importance of addressing some of these issues when they identified that the globalization of organizations necessitated the development of a network organizational configuration and managers who could become 'boundary spanners' between the various organizations aligned in the global business network.

There never will be an 'ideal' organizational structure, or planning and control system. At one extreme are 'organic' structures, which afford flexibility in administrative systems, informal control, and authority by dint of situational expertise, and at the other extreme are 'mechanistic' structures, characterized by formality, bureaucratic values, rigidity of administrative systems and tight control (Slevin and Covin, 1990). The important thing is to create a structure which enables people to 'get on with each other' and to exchange ideas. Indeed, Picard (1980) suggested that personal contacts between headquarters and subsidiary staff at all levels would reduce misunderstandings and help to ensure that the subsidiary received the right form of assistance. With the growth of the intranet as well as internet, new organizational forms are evolving. The 'knowledge economy' has seen the rapid growth of the 'knowledge-based' organization. The Swedish insurance company, Skandia (www.skandia.com), acknowledges that its growth is partly due to a sophisticated employee knowledge-sharing intranet which enables it to share ideas and product knowledge worldwide. The growth of the 'virtual organization', based on internet technology, has spawned new and evolving organizational forms, e.g. Amazon.com (www.amazon.com) in online book retailing and Broadspeed.com (www.broadspeed.com) in online car retailing. These all require new approaches to organizational forms, e.g. the highly complex prescriptional requirement for an organizational form and control procedure for turnkey projects, such as the design and installation of an oil refinery, with project managers and engineers from a variety of organizations all working on site with hundreds of suppliers and numerous sources of finance.

Academic writers such as Mintzberg, Peters, Senge, Ohmae, and Porter have expressed differing approaches to organizational structures. Some authors (e.g. Peters and Waterman, 1982) believe that 'structure' is very important for effectiveness, whereas others (e.g. Porter, 1991) believe that 'strategy' is all-important and 'structure' must be designed to match the strategy. What matters is that those in charge of evolving global organizational structures, plans, and controls must design them to gain maximum strategic gain for all stakeholders. Coordination is essential to that performance as 'structure plus conduct equals performance'. The key strategic challenge is to achieve the balance of operational activity and efficiency, efficient resource allocation, and long-term organizational development, with excellent marketing service delivered at the lowest transactional cost. This is a significant strategic global challenge.

Philosophy of Management

Before describing the different global planning and organizational forms, a brief discussion of the different management orientations in global marketing is necessary, because these help to determine the organizational forms. These orientations are known as the EPRG framework—Ethnocentrism, Polycentrism, Regiocentrism, and Geocentrism (Perlmutter, 1969: 9–18).

Ethnocentrism

In this type of management style, the domestic market is seen as supreme and the overseas market as secondary. Wherever an opportunity arises overseas that is similar to the domestic one, the company will seek to exploit it. This is typical of companies which export on a minor scale, maintaining a home base as the major activity. Honda (www.honda.com) had this orientation in the early days of motorcycle exports.

Polycentrism

This is the opposite of ethnocentrism. This management style sees each host country as unique and sees real differences between these countries and the domestic one. These assumptions may not be always correct. General Electric (www.ge.com) is an example of a geocentric organization.

Regiocentrism and geocentrism

A regiocentric management style sees regions as unique but seeks to achieve an integrated approach. Such an orientation would be ideal in the European Union where there are many cultures but also many similarities between those cultures. Advertising agencies such as WPP (www.wpp.com) would be aware of these similarities but would have to abide by different regulations in different countries with regard to copy and media use. The geocentric management style is an amalgam of ethnocentric and polycentric styles. It is a global view, which accepts differences and similarities and seeks to develop appropriate strategies.

Each of these management approaches has an influence on the type of organizational structure that can be developed. The ethnocentric company is centralized in its marketing management, the polycentric is decentralized, and the regiocentric and geocentric companies are integrated on a regional or global scale. Each style has a different view of the importance of the home and overseas markets, hence its views on planning and control and the use of local and expatriate staff. These differences will become more apparent in the sections below.

Planning for Global Marketing

Before deciding on the appropriate organizational form for marketing internationally, it is appropriate to decide on the marketing and control plan, as the plan can often dictate the most effective organizational form. Fig. 16.1 shows the sequence in the planning and control process.

Fig. 16.1 The global planning and control process

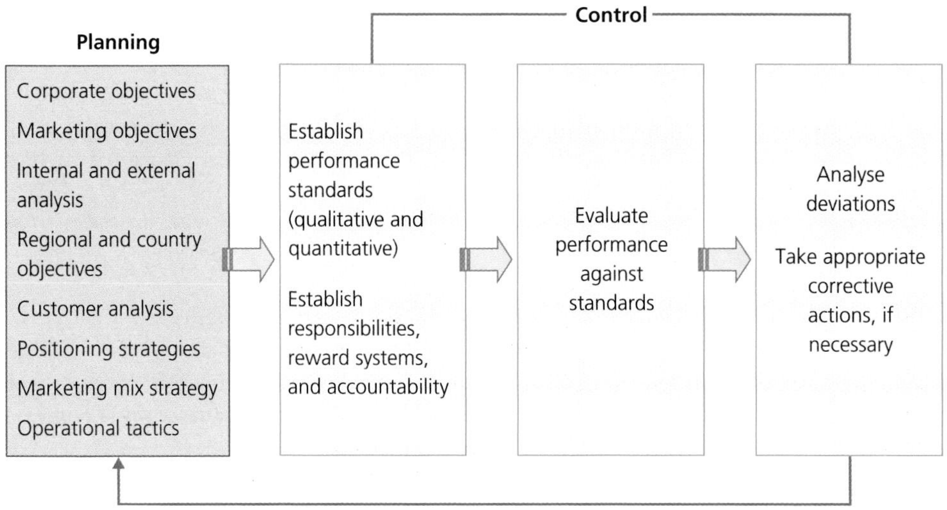

Having decided on the appropriate marketing objectives for each region/country, which are informed by the corporate objectives, an organization then has to decide on the necessary marketing strategy and operational tactics to carry out the plan. This will inevitably involve an allocation of appropriate resources, including a budget for the planned activities, a time frame, and the personnel, to carry them out. These could be headquarter's personnel, in-country personnel, or a mixture of both. Having decided on the plan, the plan must be carried out and controlled by establishing quantitative or qualitative standards or benchmarks, against which the activities and success of the plan are measured. If the plan is executed to anticipated outcomes, then appropriate rewards are conferred on the responsible personnel and the cycle is repeated. If the plan is not executed to anticipated outcomes, then appropriate accountability (or 'punishment') is meted out or the planned objectives and activities are revisited to see if they were too ambitious or unworkable.

Good planning relies on effective forecasting of many things, including environmental changes, which are often difficult to anticipate. A historical monitoring of the environment may assist in the process. However, getting competitive data, for example, can be very difficult and costly, as can obtaining reliable in-country statistics. However, in reality, marketers have to rely on assumptions that the changes in the environment can be anticipated and planned for, and that, internally, all actions can be anticipated and controlled. These assumptions can be dangerous as decision-making is often shrouded in uncertainty and complexity. Future changes are never wholly predictable, and sub-cultures and 'informality' within organizations often make concrete decision-making difficult. It is a universal truism that 'planning' is infinitely easier than 'implementation'. This complexity, and the fact that practice never really matches reality, can be borne out by the disastrous opening of Heathrow's Terminal 5 by British Airways in April 2008.

Initially, when going international, planning may be rudimentary, where there is more of a 'crisis management' approach. As the organization gets more international experience, 'budgeting' is usually the next stage, followed by 'annual business plans' and, finally, with ever more increasing sophistication, 'strategic planning', where the centre begins to exert a more directed approach. Whatever method is used, there are many benefits from effective planning. Fig. 16.2 illustrates the major planning benefits.

Fig. 16.2 Benefits from planning global operations

Systematic process of internal and external analysis	Leads to clear statement of objectives and policies
Identifies strengths and weaknesses	Quicker reaction to environmental changes
More focused thinking	Integrated action
Helps establish priorities	Helps performance and aids standards setting
Co-ordination of activities	Increased ownership of plans
Reduced internal conflicts	Standardised information
Leads to old and new market proactivity	Each player knows their part

In the planning and implementation process, different levels of management play different parts:

Strategic management: identifies stakeholder requirements and plans to meet them. This level of management scours the world looking for global opportunities and evaluates them for potential exploitation. It marshalls resources and sets performance standards.

Middle management: sets the individual business unit objectives to meet the corporate ones. Middle management plans for and gathers data for international opportunity analysis and makes strategic plans.

Operational management: sets budgets and carries out the strategic plans and tactics at the operational/functional level.

Each level provides feedback to the level above in order to assess how well the plan is being implemented, if there are any deviations from the planned activity, and the application of any corrective actions.

McKinsey and Company (www.McKinsey.com) provided a framework, the 7S framework, which depicted the essential activities necessary to implement a marketing plan. This showed the interrelatedness of the necessary activities in order to reduce the risk of the failure in the implementation of a marketing plan.

- **Shared organizational values**: all players must share the same company values and vision.
- **Strategy**: must be understood and owned by all players.
- **Style**: the management must adopt the most appropriate style to make the plan work and motivate all players to carry it out effectively.

Table 16.1 International marketing activity checklist

Activity	Yes/No
Environmental analysis—SLEPT, STEEPLE, etc.—to identify threats and opportunities	☐
Internal analysis to identify threats and weaknesses	☐
Forecasts of environmental factors to consider and markets	☐
Long- and short-term aims, objectives, and strategies	☐
Competitive position in each market	☐
Country-by-country forecasts and targets	☐
Country-by-country marketing plan	☐
Country-by-country marketing controls	☐
Organizational structure	☐
Centralized vs. decentralized responsibilities	☐
Resources in place—physical, human, and financial	☐
Activity GANTT chart in place	☐
Appropriate training carried out	☐
All 'permissions' agreed and in place	☐

- **Staff**: must be of the right calibre, trained, know what to do, motivated, and know the consequences of doing it.
- **Skills**: every player must have the necessary skills to carry out their assigned task or be able to acquire then quickly.
- **Systems**: whether machine of man-based, systems must be appropriate, understandable, and manageable.
- **Structure**: normally structure comes after the strategy has been decided and must be relevant, appropriate, and not detrimental to carrying out the marketing plan.

In carrying out a global marketing plan, it is always a good idea to have a checklist of activities so that no essential activity is missed out. Table 16.1 exemplifies such a checklist, which must be completed before the global marketing plan is operationalized.

There is often a debate on whether the use of expatriate staff or locals should be used in carrying out the marketing activity in-country. Arguments centre around issues of different cultural attitudes, sufficient training, and understanding of the processes involved. There are pros and cons on each side. Table 16.2 shows the planning problems at both central (headquarters) and subsidiary (overseas) levels.

International marketing planning is never easy. There are potentially major issues around language, fragmented rather than homogeneous markets, data availability, currencies, stability of the business environment, and different rules of 'engagement'. However, organizations can learn more the deeper they get into international marketing activity, although it is no guarantee of success. Tesco's (www.tesco.com) entry into the Thai market should, on the surface, have been easy given their international experience in many markets, including the USA and Canada. However, they were ill-prepared for the local small traders' outcry against the supermarket giant for threatening their livelihoods.

Table 16.2 Planning problems, headquarters, and subsidiary levels

Headquarters		Subsidiary	
Management	Processes	Management	Processes
Authority and responsibility unclear	Non-standard evaluation measures	Resistance to planning	Lack of top–down control
Lack of cultural empathy	Lack of ITC and support	Lack of training, qualifications, and skills	Incomplete or outdated information
Unattainable expectations	Limited feedback and control procedures	Information misinterpretation	Procedures unclear
Market myopia	Excessive bureaucracy	Unclear on objectives and requirements	Too little communication with HQ
Guidelines ambiguous	Excessive financial restraints	Resentment at top–down involvement	Incomplete and inaccurate data returns
Insensitive to local decisions	Top–down management processes	Lack of leadership and strategic skills	Little multinational marketing expertise
Witholding of information	Insufficient participation of subsidiaries in process	Lack of expertise	Excessive marketing and financial constraints

Source: Based on Wiechmann and Pringle (1979).

Global Control Mechanisms

Controlling the global marketing plan is an essential part of the planning and evaluation process. Depending on the type of planning process used, the control mechanism will be developed accordingly. We can define 'control' as:

> A process by which managers can ensure that resources are used in the most effective and efficient way in the attainment of organizational goals and objectives.

Management control and coordination between functions is attracting more attention in marketing (Jaworski et al., 1993; Oliver and Anderson, 1995). While there are a number of approaches to 'control', the main ones centre on the 'behavioural' (doing right things) to outcomes (sales results) continuum. Most traditional approaches to marketing control are transactional or outcome led, whereas non-traditional approaches are more behaviourally oriented. Data collected in the process of effecting controls can be used to inform the planning process. Collecting data via a marketing audit is one such process, but it must include 'hard' (e.g. sales) and 'soft' (e.g. competitive teaming arrangements) elements if both behavioural and transactional control mechanisms are to be operationalized. In the international marketing context this is by no means easy. According to Czinkota and Ronkainen (1996), controls can be 'bureaucratic' (formal), as typified by Western organizations, or 'cultural' (shared), as typified by Japanese organizations. The bureaucratic view is somewhat outdated as most performance and evaluation systems are now based on 'consensus' (360 degree) management philosophies. This issue was directly addressed by Baldauf et al. (2001) in a study on whether effective sales management was as important to managers of international organizations spanning many countries as it was to managers of local organizations. The research on Austrian- and UK-based organizations concerned management control from a behavioural control perspective compared with an outcomes-based perspective. The research concentrated on the role of the field sales manager compared with the salesperson and the chief sales executive. A major conclusion was the robustness of the behaviour-based control approach, tending to suggest that traditional transactional-oriented control approaches were less effective.

Despite the movement towards a more behavioural approach, many control systems are still based on traditional measurement tools such as budgets and manuals (Connell and Teare, 2000: 129). More enlightened organizations are introducing training programmes to enable employees to see the value of adopting behaviour which will lead to the achievement of the corporate mission and values of the organization. Chapter 15 expands on this issue in a sales context. Transactional approaches to control may be more appropriate for standardized products/market offerings. 'Coercive' sources of power and control, advocated by agency theory (Eisenhardt, 1988), may be legitimate where there are clear plans and concepts, but they can be counter-productive where such conditions are not present. In this case, 'non-coercive' sources of power may be more applicable. Quinn and Doherty (2000) describe the recent research interest in franchising as a form of retailing internationalization. The paper highlights the importance of power and control in the international retail franchise relationship and the ability of the marketing channels and agency theory literature to explain these issues. They conclude that where there is a well-defined concept and brand, e.g. McDonald's (www.mcdonalds.com), coercive sources of power, as advocated by agency theory, can explain power and control in the international retail franchise relationship, but not where the concept and brand are weak.

In a different setting, Connell and Teare (2000) studied franchising of higher education by British institutions overseas. Like Quinn and Doherty, they found that franchising offered significant potential for rapid and low-cost expansion of higher education programmes but the risks and uncertainties in this sector were greater than in other sectors. Significantly, Connell and Teare (2000: 129) discovered a similar phenomenon to that of Quinn and Doherty, in that, although the franchiser may have formal authority to ensure standards are observed, there is never certainty that a request for compliance or improvement will be followed. They further conclude that if the franchisee measures profitability purely on the basis of revenues and costs within a single or narrow range of programmes, franchise influence may be particularly constrained. They suggest why higher education institutions may err on the side of transactional or 'coercive' forms of control: in many sectors where franchising is utilized, the need for standardization and control is determined by market demand and the system-wide need for efficiency and effectiveness. In higher education, however, franchisers face additional regulatory pressures not only to achieve consistency but to demonstrate it to external bodies. This is certainly true of British higher education, where the government's Quality Assurance Agency (QAA, www.qaa.ac.uk) imposes its universal standards on all British higher education institutions wishing to do business in overseas markets. Monitoring costs are, therefore, likely to be greater than in sectors where agreements are judged mainly upon internally devised marketing and financial criteria. It is interesting that these authors believe that, in sectors outside education, transactional techniques predominate.

Factors affecting control

A marketing control system can be affected by a number of factors. These are illustrated in Fig. 16.3.

- **Domestic practices and values**: Organizations new to exporting, or exporting in a limited way, may be influenced by the customs and practice operating in the home market. These procedures can be ideal if the emphasis is on centralized and

Fig. 16.3 Factors affecting marketing control

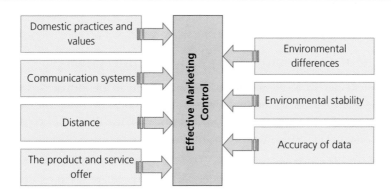

standardized procedures, but they may be inappropriate when operating in economies where less formal controls are used, e.g. Malaysia.

- **Communication systems**: Communication systems have a major influence on control mechanisms. However, not all organizations have the technology or the integrity of operating performance. It is not uncommon in developing countries to experience system shutdown due to lack of funds for spares and maintenance, or power failures and connectivity problems. It is imperative, especially if an organization spans many countries, that control mechanisms are based on appropriate and sustainable communications.

- **Distance**: The greater the distance, the bigger the physical and psychological barriers. This is particularly true with global operators and organizational structures which are more polycentric in nature. Video-conferencing and e-mail are enabling more organizations to overcome these obstacles, as are standard operating procedures.

- **The product**: It is easier to implement a uniform standard of control for more technologically advanced and complex products. Manufacturers of airliners, computers, and cars, and service providers for market research, insurance, and shipping find it easier to implement global standards of quality control and reporting as these types of product and service have a 'global currency', are well known, and are enforced by both regulatory and voluntary bodies.

- **Environmental differences**: The greater the environmental differences, the greater the delegation of control and the more limited the control process. This is particularly true where extremes of climate and diversity of commercial and economic development exist. For example, enforcing uniform standards of reporting in Germany would be easy when compared to Russia, where different climate, customs, and culture prevail within the confederate states.

- **Environmental stability**: A standardized measure of performance is less relevant in an unstable country. In Zimbabwe, for example, where inflation is running at over % millions per annum, turnover revenue would look excellent on a balance sheet but expenditure would be out of control as the inflationary effects seep through into costs.

- **Data**: Performance and reporting depend on the accuracy of consumer, business-to-business (B2B) and economic data. It is essential that this is checked for reliability and that the units of measurement are the same when comparing data. One example, from 1995, was the proud boast by one prominent government official that the Tanzanian horticultural industry had exports of produce which exceeded that of Kenya and Zimbabwe by a factor of ten. At that time Kenya was acknowledged as the industry leader in exports in eastern and southern Africa. On closer investigation the official discovered that for the previous five years his secretary had been typing the decimal point in the wrong position!

The elements of an international marketing control system

A control system has three elements: the establishment of performance standards, the measurement of performance, and the analysis of deviations. It is one thing to state what is needed, but another to carry it out in practice and give the illusion of control. The elements of a marketing control system are as follows.

- **Establishment of standards**
  Standards should be set by staff at headquarters and subsidiaries. They should be precise, clear, and accepted by all to be workable. They should be directly related to corporate goals, objectives, and strategy, and be clear as to the performance required, whether behavioural and/or outcome-oriented.

- **Performance evaluation**
  Performance evaluation can take place at various levels in the organization—strategic, operational, and tactical. Most international performance is judged by financial standards, return on investment, budgets, and historical performance. The problem of which standards to use is universal, as is the comparability of standards. Cost reduction strategies may be good for the bottom line but at the expense of market share. In multinational organizations the problem is compounded when related to rewards for performance. It can be argued that different criteria should apply and a mix of performance, both qualitative and quantitative, should also apply. In the case of BP (www.bp.com), for example, should managers be appraised on the same basis in Zimbabwe, with its % millions annual inflation rate, as in the UK with 1.5% annual inflation? In these situations, non-quantitative measures such as market share and good customer relations must be paramount.

- **Analysis of deviations and corrective action**
  When performance deviates from the expected standard, corrective action needs to be taken. This may take the form of improving the standard or changing the performance standard if unachievable, or both. This will not necessarily be easy, given cultural and geographical differences.

The global marketing audit

A global marketing audit is a technique aimed at evaluating and improving an organization's global marketing operations. It is formal and systematic, working as a diagnostic activity, conducted at periodic intervals. It may be conducted as a fully or narrowly focused activity and may be carried out by an independent or internal body. An independent body has the advantage of being impartial but lacks intimate knowledge of the organization and may take longer to conduct than an internal body. An internal audit has the advantage of knowledge of the industry but may suffer partiality as a result.
  An audit consists of:

- setting objectives and the extent of the audit, including coverage, data sources, and time period;
- gathering the appropriate data from documents, personal interviews, and other sources by the auditing team. Audit trails are necessary, as is the triangulation of information;

Fig. 16.4 Components of a global marketing audit

- preparing and presenting the report, covering some or all of the components presented in Fig. 16.4.

Auditing is not without its difficulties. Given the dynamics of the international environment any new data that emerges should be incorporated. Changes as a result of the audit should be communicated sympathetically and implemented with everyone's knowledge.

Specific control methods

There are a number of marketing control methods, either traditional (outcome) or non-traditional (behavioural). Some of the major methods are shown in Fig. 16.5.

Traditional methods

Strategic control: The objective of strategic control is to assess whether the organization has achieved its strategic objectives in quantitative (financial and otherwise) and/or qualitative terms. Generally, this control is activated via the marketing audit and the responsibility lies with senior management.

Efficiency control: The objective of this control is to ascertain whether marketing can be done more efficiently, that is whether more outputs can be gained from the inputs, e.g. increased sales to sales force ratio or advertising awareness to advertising budget inputs. The responsibility usually lies with line and staff management.

Annual plan control: The objective is to assess whether annual operating plans have achieved what they set out to do, e.g. market share gains or new market penetration. The prime responsibility lies with functional managers or the marketing manager.

Fig. 16.5 Traditional and non-traditional methods of international marketing control

Traditional Control Methods

Strategic control	Financial control
Efficiency control	Profit control
Annual plan control	Brand equity metrics

Benchmarking and best practice	Balanced scorecard
Self-assessment	Stakeholder value
Double-loop learning	

Non-traditional Control Methods

Financial control: Financial control is one of the main types of control and comes in a variety of guises, including return on investment, return on sales, earnings per share, cash flow, profitability, etc.

Profit control: Profit control comes in various guises. Comparing the budget with actual performance is the basic stage. Desegregating data down to the levels of product, channel, or area can also be a useful analysis. Techniques such as the Pareto analysis (80/20 rule) can be used to assess individual market, customer, or area performance. Responsibility generally lies with the marketing manager.

Brand equity metrics: Mars (www.mars.com), Nestlé (www.nestle.com) and IBM (www .ibm.com), for example, have spent much time and money over the years investing in the brand to build global recognition. It is only relatively recently that these efforts have been recognized in the balance sheet. The purpose of brand equity metrics is to assess the 'equity' represented in the brand and ascertain whether it is increasing or decreasing. A variety of techniques can be used, including consumer, end-user, innovation and trade/ retailer metrics. A full discussion of these techniques is given in Ambler and Styles (2000).

In recent years, market share as a quantitative metric of both success and control has become a rather old-fashioned measure. Slepian (2003) stated: 'Market share is yesterday's strategy, because market share is no longer a guarantee of profitability. Customer share is the metric to watch.'

The issue is how to maximize customer value, and this can mean more than a sale. It may involve total customer value analysis (CVA). CVA goes beyond, and enhances, customer satisfaction. Customer value measurement aims to improve the productivity of marketing activity and the profitability of the business by identifying the value of different customer segments and aligning marketing strategies, plans, and resources accordingly. Satisfied customers do not keep their experience to themselves; they talk to others. These others may include business colleagues, social contacts, family, and friends. This referred value may be worth more than the original sale. Capturing total customer value may mean sacrificing market share and, to the horror of some traditionalist marketers, may mean deliberately shedding customers. The mobile phone companies soon discovered that prepaid phones were less profitable than contracts and actively persuaded customers to change. Carnelsen (2003) gives a fascinating insight into how Mercedes-Benz (www.mercedes-benz.com) seeks to maximize customer value and devise a marketing strategy accordingly. The mini-case on the aftermarket illustrates what happens when an organization fails to control all its global operations effectively, giving rise to consumer dissatisfaction.

WHOSE RESPONSIBILITY IS IT? The aftermarket in less developed countries

It is the desire of every global marketer to ensure that all elements of the organization are in unison with the corporate mission, vision, and values, but it is very easy to get things wrong. Claims of an 'excellent' or 'world-class' organization can quickly be put to the test. Take the example of distribution and maintenance of consumer durable goods in less developed countries. The aftermarket in spare parts, e.g. for cars and electrical goods, is traditionally an area where good profits can be made by the original equipment manufacturer. This market can be severely affected by a country's lack of foreign currency as distributors will have to source foreign currency by other means. This leads to the manufacture and fitting of 'pirate' spare parts, often without the customer knowing. The manufacturer's warranty can be invalidated with subsequent consequences for the customer. No world-class organization can possibly control every single activity in every outlet for its product. Whose responsibility is it to ensure that this practice is controlled and the consumer is protected?

The distributor and the manufacturer certainly, but what about the government and suppliers?

Non-traditional methods

Benchmarking and best practice: The objective of these techniques is to measure the organization on a variety of bases, against like or similar business. Many UK banks and building societies conducted this activity in the 1990s and early 2000s to see how they performed against each other and to devise industry benchmarks for comparison. Armed with the industry 'average', organizations can compare whether they are above or below the norm.

Benchmarking should involve high-level executives and may be carried out by internal or external personnel. Many international airlines benchmark against each other in comparing customer service performance. It is not unusual for travellers at London's Heathrow Airport (www.baa.com.uk/main/airports/heathrow/) to be confronted by researchers canvassing opinion on the quality of the flight. British Airways (www.ba.com) constantly carry out customer service surveys onboard their aircraft in an attempt to improve their customer offering.

Self-assessment: This is similar to benchmarking in many ways. Industry sectors may set their own checklists/standards. For example, retailing and companies within the sector may tick off their individual performance on a five-point scale.

Double-loop learning: The purpose of this control is to make sure that feedback from performance is not only assimilated but applied. An example is where customer feedback is requested, acted upon, and then becomes enshrined in company policy. Acting is not enough, it requires that, once assessed for universal applicability, it becomes policy.

Balanced scorecard: Since its introduction by Kaplan and Norton (1992), the balanced scorecard has gained credence and acceptance as offering a balanced approach to strategy and control. The technique centres on the principal measures that drive business performance. It addresses the debate on whether financial measures (or any other single measure) are adequate for measuring the 'whole health' of a company. By balancing various stakeholder objectives and making sure that performance achieves them, it is deemed an infinitely more

Fig. 16.6 The balanced scorecard

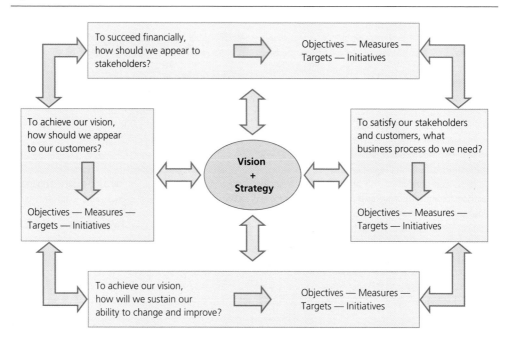

positive approach. The scorecard addresses four elements: the financial, customer, internal business, and the innovation and learning perspectives. The technique addresses the objectives, measures, targets, and initiatives needed to achieve these perspectives in a balanced way. The advantage is that it seeks to address and integrate many goals and measures which a single technique may be unable to do. The net result should be a balanced measure of the achievement of the organization's vision and strategy to realize it. Fig. 16.6 gives a summary of the method.

The balanced scorecard is widely used as a tool to help organizations to become strategy focused. The Mobil Oil Company launched the balanced scorecard project in 1994 (www .maaw.info/ArtSumKaplanNorton2001.htm). However, others have abandoned it due to the high costs of implementation.

Stakeholder value: The need to maximize stakeholder value has become a priority with the marketing profession (see *Marketing Business*, September 2003: 16–18). This might mean that instead of trying to satisfy all customers in the portfolio and choosing broad marketing strategies, organizations might concentrate their efforts on the most potentially profitable products and services in the product mix. Cadbury (www.cadbury.com) found that spreading the marketing budget everywhere did not generate the desired results. The best way was 'to create robust and sustainable regional positions'. It was a painful, but overall, profitable route.

The starting position for this form of control is the quantification of the organization's mission, vision, and values. Then appropriate strategies can be devised to reach the quantified targets. This process involves all management and stakeholders. It may mean hard decisions on the number and types of product and service to support, with some falling by the wayside in the process. For a more detailed description of this approach to marketing control, see Doyle (2000).

THE DIGITAL IMPACT Westpac—technology and global operations and control

Westpac Banking Corporation (www.westpac.com.au) was founded in Australia in 1816 as the bank of New South Wales and became Westpac in 1982. It services 7.5 million customers across more than 1,300 service points. It has branches and affiliates throughout Australia, New Zealand, and the Pacific region. It maintains offices in key financial centres around the world and provides a broad range of banking and financial services to personal, business, and institutional customers. Its market capitalization is AU$25 billion and total assets are AU$191 billion. It employs 26,131 people and has a net operating income of AU$7263 million.

In the late 1990s, competition in the financial services sector meant Westpac had to find efficiency and productivity savings to drive profitability and shareholder returns. It also faced challenging customer demands. The solution lay in an e-business infrastructure, provided by Oracle (www.oracle.com), the internet service solutions provider. Fuelled by the need to adopt international accounting standards (AS) by 2005, and Australian government plans to strengthen the financial reporting framework, accurate and timely information was vital. Westpac also recognized the need for good corporate governance to maintain transparency and accountability. Westpac turned to Oracle to meet these important standards. However, Westpac further recognized that corporate governance went beyond regulatory compliance by driving broader business effectiveness. For the past few years, Oracle systems have enabled Westpac to have a consolidated view to help meet this objective.

Oracle provided Westpac with a solution to integrate global operations. Westpac's objective was to deliver productivity and operational efficiency via more integrated systems and processes.

Applying an e-business approach was central to this strategy. The Oracle system developed a global perspective which enabled substantial efficiencies in work practices. Less time is spent on reporting and more on consolidated financial management. Before Oracle, Westpac was operating 13 different ledgers and book closure took 15 days. Staff spent valuable time on data entry, correction, reconciliation, and report consolidation. In 1996, Westpac adopted Oracle's Financials suite, a suite of applications designed for good governance through streamlined processes, consolidated business information, and support for a real-time enterprise. The result was the reduction of the ledgers into one single consolidated view and a reduction in month-end closure time from 15 to eight days. In 2000 this was further reduced to six days with an upgrade. This facility, not only helped executives to control the operation more effectively, but they were better equipped to make value-added business analysis and informed decision-making.

The introduction of Oracle e-business-based technology has given Westpac numerous benefits, including a 376% return on investment, which was achieved through cost reductions and productivity improvements; 13 ledger charts consolidated into a single global view; millions of transactions summarized to 1 million journal entries and posted to the ledger daily; speed of batch processing improved by 40% and month-end closure time was reduced by over 50%.

Source: www.oracle.com.

Many of the above controls are now implemented through ICT solutions, giving executives a global view of operations and efficiencies/deficiencies on a real-time basis (see mini-case on Westpac as an illustration).

Setting up the most appropriate and relevant organizational form and devising the most effective control procedure is never easy. Cultural differences and norms and physical distances conspire to thwart the best-laid plans. The solution is not to try to devise a system which will cater for every situation or contingency, but one which will deliver the desired outcomes in a way that is challenging, transparent, and comfortable to all employees. Many authors have suggested that organizing, implementing, and controlling marketing operations are some of the most difficult activities to perform, and that there is often a large gulf between theory and reality. Piercy (1997: 574–6), for example, argues that some authors believe that implementation is strategy, while others believe implementation is different from strategy. He suggests the following reasons for implementation failure:

- planning is often done by those who are not responsible for carrying it out;
- perhaps because of the isolation, the plans are based on 'hopeless optimism';
- implementation is recognized too late;
- management deny the problems which occur in implementation;

Fig. 16.7 Screening strategies for implementation problems

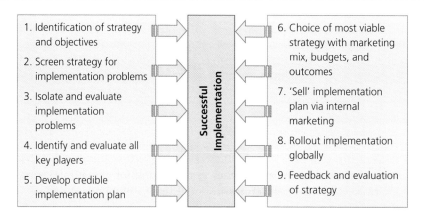

- implementation is bolted on at the end;
- implementation is a black box, divorced from all preceding activities and often left to sort itself out.

Clearly, these are serious issues and management, who are responsible for developing strategy and plans to implement it, must take all reasonable care to avoid them. Piercy suggests ways to implement strategy in a more effective way, taking early account of the many problems which may beset implementation (Fig. 16.7). This process includes having a team of people who possess interactive, allocating, monitoring, and organizing skills. In addition, there is a need to identify key players, whom Piercy (1997: 590–1) categorizes as influential supporters, influential opposition, non-involved supporters, and non-involved opposition, all of whom have important roles to play. One activity which can help to cement the key players, and ensure everyone takes ownership of the implementation activities, is 'internal marketing'. Just as external marketing requires a marketing mix for implementation, so does internal marketing. In brief, those responsible have to 'sell' the company plan and implementation (product), by communicating (promotion) to internal employees and other relevant stakeholders (place) and extolling the virtues and rewards of the plan (price).

It is simple to talk about control mechanisms in general, but difficult to develop and enforce them in practice. Equally, it appears from research evidence that the larger the organization grows globally and the more it becomes involved in outsourcing and network activities, the more 'relaxed' is the control mechanism. More importantly, rigid planning and control systems, based on transaction cost analysis, have ignored the importance of, and the role of, marketing managers in the governance of inter-organizational exchange. Klein et al. (1990), among others, argue that more work is needed into how individual boundary-spanning members can enhance or impede inter-organizational outcomes. Taking up this theme, Harvey and Novicevic (2002) highlight the importance of the strategic global staffing decision for global organizations where marketing managers were concerned. While addressing a channel of distribution context, the importance of their work in a strategic context is that sub-optimal performance and control may be achieved if marketing managers are not selected according to whether integrative (relational) and/or market (transactional) modes of control are required.

Organizing for Global Marketing

Having decided on the global marketing and control plan, the final stage is to decide on the most appropriate organizational structure to implement the global plans. There are a number of types of organizational structure, including product, international divisional, geographic, regional, matrix, and virtual, the latter being facilitated in recent years by the 'networking' phenomenon and technology.

Most organizations develop from an 'export' division to a more sophisticated structure as they grow and diversify. The development of the most appropriate form depends on a number of factors (Fig. 16.8). Most of these elements will be addressed in the sections below. There are many different approaches to organizing for global marketing, and the intention is not to explore all structures in detail but to highlight the major ones and discuss their strategic implications. The major global structures are based on functional, divisional, geographical (area), matrix, or virtual lines.

Functional

Many international organizational structures are based on a functional corporate structure with a mainly 'domestic' focus and have a small international division (Fig. 16.9). In the early stages of internationalization, the overseas division may not be so large and the strategic decisions rest with the corporate headquarters. Emphasis is mainly on producing products and services for the domestic market with the export division simply 'finding' orders to enable the organization to add to its revenue and profits. Few administrative problems should exist at this stage. This format may be suitable for small and medium-sized organizations operating in few markets. The width and nature of the product and service may be limited. It is relatively a risk-free structure. This format may be less appropriate when the above conditions are not met, as the demands of local markets and the complexity of the distribution system may demand a more appropriate organizational structure.

Fig. 16.8 The factors that determine the most appropriate global organizational structure

Fig. 16.9 Function-based organizational structure

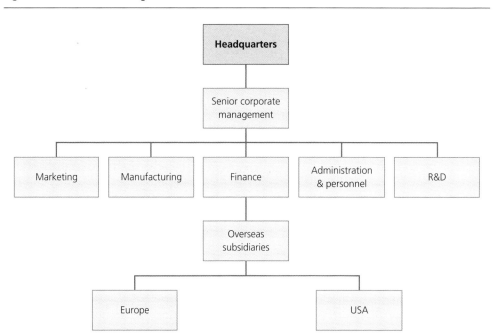

Fig. 16.10 Area- or region-based organizational structure

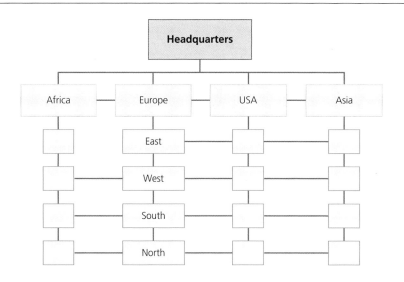

Geographical, functional, or strategic business unit approach

As the organization continues to evolve, the international division may be replaced by a variety of structures, such as a geographical, product, function, or strategic business unit approach. The geographic (or area)-oriented approach is used by highly market-oriented organizations with stable products (Fig. 16.10). Typical of this organizational structure is a tractor manufacturer such as John Deere (www.deere.com), a heavy plant manufacturer such as Caterpillar (www.caterpillar.com), or oil distribution companies such as BP

MINI-CASE ILLUSTRATION **BP's management structure**

BP (www.bp.com) is a large organization by any measure. Its total replacement cost operating results in 2002 were US$14,720 million. The way it organizes its business is based on a mixture of polycentric and ethnocentric management and its control system is based on organizational learning and stakeholder value. The way BP organizes and delivers its performance is called 'our system of internal control'. The system describes how executive management expects the organization to work, covering all the underlying systems through which it meets its core values, manages risks, and delivers on its promises.

BP has four businesses: Exploration and Production; Gas, Power and Renewables; Refining and Marketing; and Chemicals. Each business has an executive committee (ExCo) headed by the business chief executive. The chief executive of each business, the deputy group chief executive, and the heads of function (finance, etc.) make up the group chief executive's committee, under the leadership of John Browne, the group chief executive.

Operations in the businesses are made up of separate business units (BUs) sometimes organized along strategic lines into Strategic Performance Units (SPUs). SPUs are effectively separated from the company's executive management by the single layer of the business ExCo. In this way, the BU leaders can operate as though they are running their own businesses, subject to compliance to group policies and absolute accountability for the fulfilment of annual

performance contracts, which they negotiate with the ExCo of their business. Performance contracts, are drawn up annually between each ExCo and all its SPUs and/or BUs, including key financial and operational data. Non-financial objectives are included, such as safety and environmental performance. Performance contracts exist at various levels, including one between the group chief executive and the board.

Performance contracts are subject to regular monitoring and assessment, with the aim of ensuring achievement of performance objectives. They are challenging, drive results, and are one of the main ways of achieving performance improvements. Within this framework, BU leaders can manage as they see fit. Each BU can be significant and be further divided into a number of performance units, each headed by a performance leader.

The system allows for rapid and innovative responses to new situations without the barrier of red tape or the need for constant referral upwards, all in the context of scrutiny and performance challenge. The system allows the organization to act 'as one' if necessary. The management process begins with context and strategy. Medium- and long-term plans are derived from these and refined into performance contracts. Through measurement, learning, and constant improvement, delivery is sustained.

Source: www.bp.com (accessed 09/09/2003).

(www.bp.com), which split their global operations into geographical regions (see mini-case illustration on BP).

Strategically, this structure of organization encourages the growth of regional groupings, thus allowing a degree of autonomy (polycentric or regiocentric). It also allows a degree of management expertise to grow with each regional grouping, as knowledge of the areas begins to grow. Finally, such a structure enables a freer flow of information between the regional groupings, thus enabling a more responsive communication system. There are disadvantages. While encouraging a freer flow of communication within regions, communications between regions may not be as good. Duplication of systems and procedures may also ensue. The main drawback may be in the sub-optimal product and functional expertise allocation. Trying to match products and expertise to different locations may be market friendly but costly and not without considerable risk.

Product organizational structures

Another popular organizational structure is the product-based organizational structure (Fig. 16.11). This offers the firm a lot of flexibility as different divisions can develop regional, product, and management expertise to suit the region (a truly regiocentric view). This autonomy helps to reduce the risk and cost of failure. However, product divisionalization may mean that the organization could miss opportunities for cross-marketing and lead to a number of uncoordinated marketing activities. It is essential that company and marketing goals are clearly understood by all executives and employees in this type of organization, or dysfunctionality could occur.

Fig. 16.11 Product-based organization structure

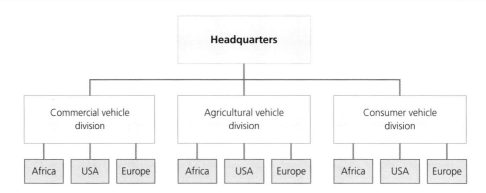

Matrix organizational structures

Matrix organizations are complex and sophisticated. They bring together the four competences of geographic knowledge; product knowledge and know how; functional competences in fields such as R&D, marketing, production, and finance; and a knowledge of customers and their needs (see Fig. 16.12).

Management's task in a matrix organization is to bring together all the perspectives (price, distribution, advertising, etc.) and skills to achieve particular objectives. These organizational structures require a sea-change in management thinking, behaviour, culture, and technical systems. Company goals have to be clear and disseminated to all functions in order that all personnel in the matrix are clear as to their role in the achievement of corporate goals. Matrix structures are typical of larger organizations operating in multiple markets. Often these organizations have long experience in global markets and the elements of the marketing task can be dealt with on a cross-market/product basis. With this type of structure, it is advisable to remember that 'structure should always follow strategy'. If not, then problems can occur. What is likely is that greater product sophistication and proliferation will result in an organization that is broken into more product divisions worldwide. Matrix structures have their critics—the 'one size fits all' approach can lead to inefficiencies in communications between the functions inside the matrix and those outside.

'Hub and spoke' organizational structures

The mini-case on BP illustrates an organizational structure adopted by a number of organizations, including Cummins, (www.cummins.com), the engine and power manufacturer. In this structure, the world is divided into a number of regions, according to a variety of criteria, such as potential sales, geographic location, etc. A central headquarters (hub) is established in the region. It has full strategic and operational capability and is responsible only to central HQ for its contribution to the overall group objectives (see Fig. 16.13). Countries, or regions, then report into this hub and take their strategic and operational guidelines from it. This form is used by many multi- and bilateral donor agencies, such as the Food and Agriculture Organization of the United Nations (www.fao.org) and the British Council (www.britishcouncil.org).

Fig. 16.12 Matrix organizational structure

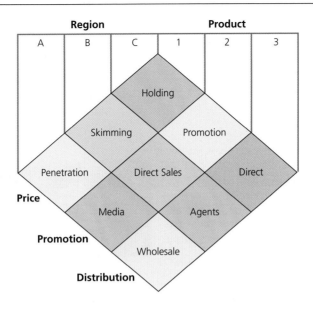

Fig. 16.13 The 'hub and spoke' organizational structure

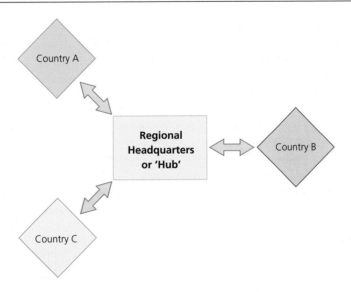

The advantage of this type of structure is that it overcomes most of the difficulties associated with a centralized HQ, which can be unaware of, or insensitive to, all of the management and process issues in its overseas subsidiaries. However, it does depend heavily on the quality and abilty of the 'hub' staff, and this in itself can be controversial if expatriate staff are preferred to locals.

Virtual organizational structures

A virtual organizational structure is a temporary or permanent network of company functions which come together to serve a specific purpose and then become permanent or disappear.

The growth of the internet and intranet has led to a plethora of functions, goods, and services being made available internationally. This technology has enabled organizations of any size, type, or form to bypass the need for a formal, recognizable organizational structure. Low-cost, high-quality communications technology, such as video-conferencing, has enabled even small firms to carry out order soliciting and progressing anywhere in the world without a formal organizational structure. This has been a positive driver in reducing their costs. Service industries have similarly benefited. An international freight forwarder, however big or small, can drive the whole of its operations from a central office using a number of interlinked services to shipping companies, couriers, etc. Although the freight forwarder may split the world into regions or geographic areas for the sake of convenience, the software and technology can be operated by one person sitting in front of a computer.

These organizational structures have the advantages of cost savings in physical space, flexibility, and responsiveness. Many products or services can be dealt with simultaneously, depending on the marketing task. Geographical boundaries can be crossed, giving relatively easy access to natural and human resources. They are, therefore, relatively risk-free. In order to be competitive, the astute selection of partners is essential and the organization must be able to exploit its core competences to the full.

Virtual organizations are the ultimate in the 'flattened organization' and those staff within them have to engage in a different 'mind-set' from the more 'physical' structure. Rather than the traditional approach to marketing management of planning, organizing, implementation, and control, virtual organizations depend very much on the 'people' aspect, with standard organizational procedures and a culture of competence and leadership. Amazon (www.amazon.com) is a classic example of a virtual organization with its HQ relatively small, but with huge fulfilment facilities and on-line customer order process.

Issues in Global Organizational Structures

There are a number of issues associated with global organizational structures. These include:

- the impact of different time zones on communications;
- the decision-making and managerial style;
- access to human, physical, and financial resources;
- the level and stage on international commitment;
- the stage of country development and its impact on ICT;
- the flexibility of the structure and responsivemess to evolutionary changes;

- the availability, concentration, or dispersal of suppliers, distributors, and customers; and

- access to 'commercial services' and infrastructure.

Linked to the concept of the virtual organization, are the notions of partnering, outsourcing, and networking (for a more detailed discussion, see Keegan and Schlegelmilch (2001: 537–45)). Outsourcing occurs where certain elements of the business may be provided by other organizations, e.g. car exporters may use specialist shipping firms for their sea transport logistical needs (the mini-case illustration highlights the relationship perspective on downsizing and outsourcing). Such is the growth of outsourcing that there is an Outsourcing Institute (www.outsourcing.com). Gartner Inc (www.gartner.com) (2003) estimated that the value of business process outsourcing (BPO) was US$110 million in 2002 and CBS (www.cbs.com) (2004) estimated that 400,000 jobs in the USA had been lost to China, Russia, and India through outsourcing in the early part of the twenty-first century. In order for both parties to benefit there must be a financial gain on both sides, a predisposition and commitment to make the process work, and the necessary linkages and knowledge of each other's business to ensure the smooth running of operations. However, outsourcing is not without its problems. While it can give economies in production and a reduction in costs, a survey by Educause (2002), for example, found that the supplier's lack of understanding of the outsourcer's needs may lead to outsourcing failure and result in long-term damage to the company's core competence. The survey revealed that the negative impacts were:

- opportunity cost;

- hidden/additional cost;

- lack of flexibility/control;

- human resource problems;

- vulnerability and dependence; and

- issues over privacy/confidentiality.

Similar to outsourcing, but on an internal scale, organizational networking aims to break down internal barriers in order to promote person-to-person communications and

 THE RELATIONSHIP PERSPECTIVE Downsizing and outsourcing

In the mid-1990s and at the beginning of the twenty-first century, a common feature in a number of organizations has been 'downsizing'. Advertising agencies are a typical example of this. In the heyday of the 'full line service' agency in the 1970s and 1980s, large agencies such as J. Walter Thompson (www.jwt.com) and Lintas (www.lintasimag.com) had nearly all the production and media-buying facilities in-house. This provided clients with a full range of services. As costs of overheads and wages began to soar in the 1980s and 1990s, it became too expensive to maintain the full range of services and much cheaper to have specialist services, e.g. media buying, 'bought out'. This was also true on an international scale. Employing local providers was often far cheaper than flying central staff all over the world. As local expertise has grown,

e.g. in location film production for advertisements, it has made even greater sense to employ local facilities. This 'network' or 'relationship' phenomenon is quite typical of the global advertising industry today, where only a few giants, like WPP (www.wpp.com) and Saatchi and Saatchi (www.saatchi.com) remain.

With downsizing, has come outsourcing. Many 'in-house' functions have now been oursourced. The growth of the Indian call-centre phenomenon is just one example, where giants like British Telecom have relocated much of their customer help and technical expertise. This has brought mixed results. In some cases it has worked well, but in others not so well, where customer frustration has resulted in companies relocating back to the UK.

provide a better service to the customer by shortcutting internal politics and red tape. The 'knowledge organization' is a further incarnation of the network organization.

Competition can have a major effect on the type of organizational structure which best serves the customer and helps leverage core competences. Vertical structures may be 'picked off' by specialist providers in the value chain. Computer and photocopier companies are typical of this. IBM and Rank Xerox (www.xerox.com) found a number of their activities were being picked off by smaller specialist organizations which could concentrate on an activity, do it cost effectively, and with the requisite customer quality. This has given rise to specialist stationery companies, computer peripherals, disk manufacturers, etc., all able to compete effectively in the value chain. In global terms, the vertical organization is more prone to being 'picked off' by companies than the flatter horizontal organizations, unless there are large entry barriers, e.g. in oil and petrol refining and distribution. The challenge is to develop a responsive organization which gives the maximum flexibility, yet achieves the correct balance of central control and devolution that is satisfactory to all parties. Anecdotal evidence suggests that successful firms in international markets are those which adopt a flexible approach. McClenahan identified this as far back as 1998. The higher the growth rate of the company, the more flexible it is likely to be (Child, 1975). Accelerated globalization from companies of Japanese, Western European, and North American origin has challenged their capability to manage subsidiaries overseas. The challenge is how to manage complex network, production, and outsourcing beyond domestic shores (Noria and Ghosal, 1997).

It is easier to design appropriate global structures in theory than it is in practice. How can theoretical organizational structures be made appropriate? What are the strategic decisions which have to be made in order to achieve an effective organizational structure? Decentralization has been offered as the most appropriate structure where there are great national differences, where the environment is unpredictable, and where local government pressures are strong (Farmer and Richman, 1965). The following research provides examples seeking to address the issues, both structural and managerial. Yeung et al. (2001), describing research conducted in Singapore, offer a framework for analysing the role of regional headquarters in the globalization strategies of transnational corporations (TNCs). They argue that regionalization of TNC activities increases the demand for regional control and coordination functions away from global headquarters. Regional headquarters are often set up to penetrate emerging markets but this puts a strain on central coordination. They conclude that three independent variables play a role in shaping the strategic decision by TNCs in establishing regional headquarters: geographical distance, strategic necessity, and the availability of business services. Not only does this provide empirical evidence for some of the factors identified in Fig. 16.8 as being important in the development of the most appropriate organizational structure, but, more importantly, it confirms Ohmae's argument (1990) of 'think global, act local'.

For an organization internationalizing for the first time, the establishment of regional offices or a more informal structure may be the most cost-effective way to penetrate a region. In a study on European entry strategies of newly industrialized East Asian firms, Chen and Wong (2003) identified that while firms may be acquainted with the domestic market, and therefore the most appropriate strategies and structure, when it comes to internationalization, structural changes may be necessary to ensure sufficient control of foreign subsidiaries and their communication with headquarters. Stopford and Wells (1972) view structure and strategy as interrelated. A strategy of diversification can lead to organizational problems and therefore to the evolution of a new corporate structure. According to Lam and White (1999), structural choices include the organizational structure of the subsidiary, control and communication modes with the foreign subsidiary, and the degree of influence of the headquarters on subsidiary decision-making. Chen and Wong's (2003) study suggested that, in a group of South Korean, Taiwanese, Hong Kong, and Singaporean firms in Europe, that the key to success was to have clear and ambitious goals and actively search for growth opportunities. They conclude that such actions are facilitated by informal organizations that do not adhere strictly to formal rules and procedures for getting things done. Finally, successful firms adopt a long-term view, are more committed to the market, and are prepared to spend time and effort investing in relationships with marketing intermediaries and customers. Confirming Yeung et al.'s (2001) study, Chen and Wong (2003) found that successful firms maintain informal and close relationships with their overseas subsidiaries.

While the textbooks rightfully identify various organizational structures for the internationalizing and global corporation, flexibility and a 'light corporate touch' appear to be the most appropriate strategic positions for the structure of the growing global organization. The BP case study cited above adds credence to this assertion.

In conclusion, one of the more recent trends is that modern consumers are demanding the highest quality product/service at the lowest possible price (Sculley and Fawcett, 1994; Avery, 1998). Competition is one of the leading catalysts of this phenomenon. This has raised a major strategic challenge. Manufacturers face trying to fight off the competitive challenge as well as satisfy ever-demanding customers. The main response has been the rationalization of global manufacturing strategies as a cost control method and, at the same time, seeking greater internal operating efficiencies through cross-functional process integration. Fawcett et al. (2000) site the example of General Motors (www.gm.com), which operates production facilities in over 28 countries while selling vehicles in 140 countries. While economies may be gained in production, often these savings are offset by higher logistical costs. This presents a challenge for manufactures and service deliverers. Fawcett et al. (2000) examined the cross-functional development of quality and cost competences in an international production setting. The study found that information and planning capabilities were vital antecedents to cost and quality competences. The impact of cost on a firm's performance was direct, while the impact of quality was indirect, through production enhancements. The Westpac case confirms the importance of information for planning, as found by Fawcett et al. (2000), and their study shows that merely cutting costs as a control mechanism is insufficient in itself. Global marketers need not only to seek efficiencies but need to be fully aware of the consequences of this in the marketplace.

Chapter Summary

1. Planning, control, and organizational structure are essential for managing and controlling global operations.

2. Organizational structures may be influenced by the philosophy of management, known as the EPRG framework—Ethnocentrism, Polycentrism, Regiocentrism, and Geocentrism.

3. Global marketing planning can evolve from a basic and rudimentary structure to a more strategically-oriented structure. Planning operates at different levels, i.e. top management, middle management, and operational management.

4. There are a number of factors affecting international controls, including the ease and availability of communications, the availability of accurate and timely data, the degree of stability in the environment, organizational culture, and the size of the global operation.

5. Global control essentially involves four activities: setting standards of performance, measuring actual performance against standards, analysing variances, and taking appropriate corrective action. This can be facilitated through conducting a global audit.

6. Control mechanisms may be based either on traditional or non-traditional methods, i.e. strategic control, efficiency control, annual plan control, financial control, and brand equity. Non-traditional methods include benchmarking and best practice, self-assessment, double-loop learning, the balanced scorecard, and stakeholder value.

7. Organizations may be structured on a functional, product, geographic, strategic business unit, matrix, 'hub and spoke', or virtual basis. The chosen structure will depend on the degree of internationalization, type of product or service, and resources of the organization.

END-OF-CHAPTER CASE STUDY **Anglo American—a global mining conglomerate**

Anglo American (www.angloamerican.co.uk) aims to become the leading global mining company, focused on adding value for shareholders, customers, employees, and the communities in which it operates. In 2007, the Group achieved an operating profit of US$10.1 billion and has a range of high-quality, core mining businesses including platinum, diamonds, coal, base and ferrous metals, and industrial minerals. The Group is geographically diverse, with operations and developments in Africa, Europe, South and North America, and Australia. It operates in some 45 countries in all and employs 100,000 people. Currently it has US$12 billion invested in ongoing projects. It has 21 Group offices in the countries in which it operates, with headquarters in the UK. One of its principal rivals is BHP Billiton (www.bhpbilliton.com), a giant Australian conglomerate.

Anglo's strategy centres around achieving world-class performance in all areas of the business. Companies in its portfolio include household names like De Beers, Tarmac, Debswana and Namdeb. Anglo's businesses are involved in a multitude of value adding products and services, some products of which go through the whole chain from mining producer to the ultimate consumer.

Anglo American's strategy centres around achieving world-class performance in all areas of the business, including:

1. Continuous improvements in operating efficiencies.

2. Investment to add value to expand the balanced portfolio of world-class assets.

3. Acquisition and business development based on leveraging core competences rather than alignment to any asset class or geography.

4. Provision of a safe and healthy environment for employees, acting ethically, demonstrating a commitment to the environment, and acting in a socially responsible way.

5. An aim to become the employer of choice through a culture of meritocracy.

6. Openness and empowerment to attract the best talent, helping employees to realize their full potential in driving superior business performance.

7. Efficiency optimization of the supply channel and improving the focus on marketing and customer relationships to drive value by anticipating and responding to changing customer needs and operating trends.

Anglo's businesses are both geographically diverse and cover a wide range of products.

Platinum

Anglo American's managed subsidiary, Anglo Platinum, mines, processes, refines, and markets the entire range of platinum group metals (platinum, palladium, rhodium, ruthenium, iridium, and osmium) and is the world's largest primary producer of platinum, accounting for 37% of global supply. All Anglo Platinum's current operations are located in South Africa.

Gold

Anglo American has reduced its holding in gold with the long-term goal of exiting.

Diamonds

Anglo American owns De Beers, the largest producer and marketer of gem diamonds by value in the world. Mines include those in South Africa, Botswana (Debswana), and Namibia (Namdeb). De Beers' expertise extends to all aspects of the diamond industry, including prospecting, mining, and recovery and, through the Diamond Trading Company, sorting, valuing, and selling rough gem diamonds.

Coal

Anglo American's coal interests are held through its wholly owned Anglo Coal business, one of the world's largest private sector coal producers and exporters. Anglo Coal has mining operations in South Africa, Australia, Colombia, and Venezuela. Anglo Coal produces thermal and metallurgical coals for international customers in the Med-Atlantic and Indo-Pacific markets as well as local customers in South Africa and Australia. Anglo American now has a significant presence in Australia's coal industry. In Asia, China is a significant market for their businesses. Anglo American opened its first corporate representative office in Beijing in September 2002.

Base metals

Anglo Base Metals comprises copper, zinc, nickel, and mineral sands operations and projects in South America, Southern Africa, and Ireland.

Industrial minerals

Anglo Industrial Minerals has two subsidiaries: Tarmac and Copebrás. Tarmac is a leader in the construction materials business in the UK, continental Europe, the Middle East and Far East. It is principally involved in the production of crushed rock, sand and gravel, asphalt, concrete and mortar, concrete products, lime and cement. Copebrás is a leading Brazilian producer of phosphate fertilizers, phosphoric acid, and sodium tripolyphosphate (STPP).

Ferrous Metals and Industries

Anglo Ferrous Metals and Industries is a leading producer of iron ore, vanadium, manganese, and carbon steel. It has operations in South Africa, with manganese operations in Australia, and grinding media operations in North and South America and Australia.

Anglo American is a truly global giant in the mining industry with a diversified product base and world-class operations.

Source: www.angloamerican.co.uk (accessed 14/05/2008).

Discussion questions

1 Describe the basis on which Anglo American organizes its business.

2 Explain how you think Anglo American coordinates its strategy and balances local versus global interests across 45 different countries.

3 Currently, Anglo American has seven areas of business activity. What impact might changes in the global marketing environment in the next decade have on these groupings and how might Anglo American deal with these changes organizationally?

END-OF-CHAPTER EXERCISES

1 What factors dictate the most appropriate form of global marketing organizational structure and control mechanism?

2 Identify and discuss the various types of global marketing organizational structure.

3 Identify and discuss the various types of global marketing control methods.

4 What are the personnel and financial implications of the different types of global organizational structures?

5 What would dictate the use of more traditional or less traditional methods of global marketing controls?

6 Identify three organizations which have different structures of global marketing organization and discuss why they have these structures.

DISCUSSION AND EXAMINATION QUESTIONS

1 Discuss the importance of having the most appropriate structure of global marketing organization.

2 Discuss the financial, organizational, and personnel implications of different types of global marketing organizational structure.

3 What is required to make different methods of global marketing control work effectively for an organization?

4 What are the strategic considerations for choosing a global organizational structure and control mechanism?

FURTHER READING

Doyle, P. (2000), *Value Based Marketing*, London: John Wiley & Son.

Hollensen, S. (2007), *Global Marketing: A Decision-oriented Approach*, 4th edn., Harlow: FT/Prentice Hall, Chapter 19.

Pascale, R. and Athos, A. (1981) *The Art of Japanese Management*, London: Penguin.

REFERENCES

Ambler, T. and Styles, C. (2000), *The Silk Road to International Marketing*, London: FT/Prentice Hall.

Avery, S. (1998), 'Buyers want suppliers that can reduce costs', *Purchasing*, 125(8), 36–8.

Baldauf, A., Cravens, D. W., and Piercy, N. F. (2001), 'Examining the consequences of sales management in European field sales organizations', *International Marketing Review*, 18(5), 474–508.

Carnelsen, J. (2003), 'What is the Customer Worth? Customer Value Analyses in Relationship Marketing on the basis of Car Buyers', *Yearbook of Marketing and Consumer Research*, Vol. 1, 27–46.

CBS (2004), www.cbsnews.com/stories/2003/12/23/60minutes/main590004.shtml (accessed on 11/11/2004).

Chen, I. S. N. and Wong, V. (2003), 'Successful strategies of newly industrialised east Asian firms in Europe', *European Journal of Marketing*, 37(1/2), 275–97.

Child, J. (1975), 'Managerial and organizational factors associated with company performance—Part 1', *Journal of Management Studies*, 11(May), 165–89.

Connell, J. and Teare, R. (2000), 'Power and control in the international higher education franchise relationship', *VUJ Journal*, 3, 122–31.

Czinkota, M. R. and Ronkainen, I. A. (1996), *Global Marketing*, Fort Worth, TX: Dryden Press.

Doyle, P. (2000), *Value Based Marketing*, London: John Wiley & Son.

Educause (2002), www.educase.edu/ir/library/pdf/ers0201/ers02013.pdf (accessed on 14/3/2004).

Eisenhardt, K. M. (1988), 'Agency- and institutional-theory explanations: the case of retail sales compensation', *Academy of Management Review*, 14, 50–62.

Farmer, R. N. and Richman, B. M. (1965), *Comparative Management and Economic Progress*, Homewood, IL: Richard Irwin.

Fawcett, S. E., Calantone, R. J., and Roath, A. (2000), 'Meeting quality and cost imperatives in a global market', *International Journal of Physical Logistics and Logistics Management*, 30(6), 472–99.

Gartner Inc. (2003), www3.gartner.com/5_about/press_releases/pr10june2003a.jsp (accessed on 10/3/2004).

Harvey, M. and Novicevic, M. M. (2002), 'Selecting marketing managers to effectively control global channels of distribution', *International Marketing Review*, 19(5), 525–44.

Jaworski, B. J., Stathakopoulaos, V., and Krishnan, S. (1993), 'Control combinations in marketing: conceptual framework and empirical evidence', *Journal of Marketing*, 57(January), 57–69.

Kaplan, R. S. and Norton D. P. (1992), 'The Balanced Scorecard—measures that drive performance', *Harvard Business Review*, Jan./Feb., 71–9.

Keegan, W. J. and Schlegelmilch, B. B. (2001), *Global Marketing Management*, Harlow: FT/Prentice Hall.

Klein, S., Frazier, G. L., and Roth, V. J. (1990), 'A transaction cost analysis model of channel integration in international markets', *Journal of Marketing Research*, May, 196–208.

Lam, L. W. and White, L. P. (1999), 'An adaptive choice model of the internationalisation process', *International Journal of Organizational Analysis*, 7(2), April, 105–34.

McClenahen, J. S. (1998), 'How US entrepreneurs succeed in world markets', *Industry Week,* 2(May), 47–9.

Noria, N. and Ghosal, N. (1997), *The Differentiated Network: Organizing Multinational Corporations for Value Creation*, San Francisco: Jossey-Bass.

Ohmae, K. (1990), *The Borderless World*, New York: Harper Business.

Oliver, R. L. and Anderson, E. (1995), 'Behavior- and outcome-based sales control systems: evidence and consequences of pure-form and hybrid governance', *Journal of Personal Selling & Sales Management*, 15(Fall), 1–15.

Perlmutter, H. (1969), 'The torturous evolution of the multinational corporation', *Columbia Journal of World Business*, Jan.–Feb., 9–18.

Peters, T. J. and Waterman, R. H. (1982), *In Search of Excellence*, New York: Harper.

Picard, J. (1980), 'Organizational structures and integrative devices in European multinational corporations', *Columbia Journal of World Business*, 15(1), April, 30–5.

Piercy, N. (1997), *Market-led Strategic Change*, 2nd edn., Oxford: Butterworth-Heinemann.

Porter, M. E. (1991), *Competition and Strategy*, Boston: Harvard Business School.

Quinn, B. and Doherty, A. M. (2000), 'Power and control in international retail franchising: evidence from theory and practice', *International Marketing Review*, 16(4/5), 354–72.

Sculley, J. I. and Fawcett, J. (1994), 'International procurement strategies: opportunities and challenges for the small firm', *Production and Inventory Management Journal*, 35(2), 39–46.

Slepian, J. H. (2003), *Finding Profits in Customer Behaviour*, www.destinationcrm.com/articles (accessed on 06/03/2004).

Slevin, D. P. and Covin, J. G. (1990), 'Juggling entrepreneurial style and organizational structure—how to get your act together', *Sloan Management Review*, 31(2), 58–9.

Stopford, J. M. and Wells, L. T. Jr. (1972), *Managing the Multinational Enterprise*, New York: Basic Books.

Wiechmann, U.E. and Pringle, L. G. (1979), 'Problems that plague multi-national marketers', *Harvard Business Review*, July–August, 118–24.

Yeung, H. W.-C., Poon, J., and Perry, M. (2001), 'Towards a regional strategy: the role of regional headquarters of foreign firms in Singapore', *Urban Studies*, 38(1), 157–83.

online resource centre

Visit the companion website to this book for lots of interesting additional material, including self-assessment questions, internet exercises, and links for each chapter:

http://www.oxfordtextbooks.co.uk/orc/lee_carter2e/

PART THREE CASE STUDY Oxfam International—Famine Relief or Pressure Group?

Oxfam International (www.oxfam.org.uk) is a confederation of 13 organizations working with over 3,000 partners in more than 100 countries to find lasting solutions to poverty and injustice. The Oxfam International secretariat leads, facilitates, and supports collaboration between the Oxfam affiliates to make Oxfam International's impact on poverty and injustice much bigger, through advocacy campaigns, development programmes, and emergency response. In-country programmes are delivered on a 'project' basis, many of which have been running for several years.

Oxfam was originally founded in England in 1942 as the *Oxford Committee for Famine Relief* by a group of Quakers, social activists, and Oxford academics. It was one of a number of local committees formed in support of the National Famine Relief Committee. Their mission was to persuade the UK government to allow food relief through the Allied blockade for the starving citizens of Nazi-occupied Greece. The first overseas Oxfam was founded in Canada in 1963. The first minutes of the Oxford Committee for Famine Relief, from a meeting organized by University Vicar, Canon Milford, in 1942 to help Greek civilian victims of war, is contained in a historic book. Although most similar groups closed down after World War II, Oxfam kept going. The Oxford Committee for Famine Relief changed its name in 1965 and is now known as Oxfam Great Britain. It is still based in Oxford, UK.

Oxfam's specific objectives are:

to prevent poverty and to relieve poverty, distress and suffering in any part of the world (including starvation, sickness or any physical disability or affliction) and primarily when arising from any public calamity (including famine, earthquake, pestilence, war or civil disturbance) or the immediate or continuing result of want of natural or artificial resources or the means to develop them and whether acting alone or in association with others; and in particular but without prejudice to the generality of the foregoing for that purpose to provide food, healing, clothing, shelter, training and education and to undertake or assist in work calculated directly to achieve that purpose; and in connection therewith to educate the public concerning the nature, causes and effects of poverty, distress and suffering as aforesaid and to conduct and procure research concerning these and to publish or otherwise make the results thereof available to the public. (The Charity Commission, June 2008)

Its area of operations are national (UK) and overseas. The overseas countries in which it operates number some of the poorest and neediest in the world, ranging from Afghanistan to Liberia and Zimbabwe, where it has just had to suspend its operations at behest of the government. However, it also operates in rich countries such as Israel and South Africa. In overseas countries, it operates as a non-governmental organization (NGO) and is therefore invited by governments to operate within those countries. It is not an arm of government, although it may help governments to achieve its agenda—poverty alleviation.

Oxfam's work is both varied and diverse, from combatting the cause of famine, to operating charity shops and clothing and shoe banks. Oxfam International's accounts for the period 2000–06 are shown in Table 1.

Though Oxfam's initial concern was the provision of food to relieve famine, over the years Oxfam has developed strategies to combat the causes of famine. In addition to food and medicine, Oxfam also provides tools to enable people to become self-supporting and opens markets to international trade where crafts and produce from poorer regions of the world can be sold at a fair price (Fairtrade) to benefit the producer.

Oxfam's programme has three main points of focus: (1) development work, which tries to lift communities out of poverty with long-term, sustainable solutions based on their needs; (2) humanitarian work, assisting those immediately affected by conflict and natural disasters, which often leads in to longer-term development work, especially in the field of water and sanitation; and (3) lobbying, advocacy, and popular campaigning, trying to affect policy decisions on the causes of conflict at local, national, and international levels.

Oxfam works on and a wide and diversified agenda, including trade justice, fair trade, education, debt and aid, livelihoods, health, HIV/AIDS, gender equality, conflict (campaigning for an international treaty to ban arms trading) and natural disasters, democracy and human rights, and climate change. It is part of the 'Make Poverty History' coalition.

Table 1 Oxfam International's accounts, 2000–06

Financial year start	Financial year end	Gross income	Total expenditure
01 May 2000	30 Apr 2001	£187,336,000	£196,126,000
01 May 2001	30 Apr 2002	£189,398,000	£186,668,000
01 May 2002	30 Apr 2003	£188,970,000	£182,195,000
01 May 2003	30 Apr 2004	£172,200,000	£176,500,000
01 May 2004	30 Apr 2005	£237,500,000	£211,900,000
01 May 2005	30 Apr 2006	£293,100,000	£282,700,000
01 May 2006	30 Apr 2007	£290,700,000	£297,200,000

Source: Figures from the Charities Commission, UK (www.charitycommission.gov.uk).

The first permanent Oxfam gift shop opened in February 1948 on the ground floor of 17 Broad Street, Oxford, England. This was one on the world's first charity shops. This innovative fundraising idea attracted donations ranging from false teeth, various stuffed animals, to a houseboat. Today Oxfam operates approximately 750 shops throughout Britain as well as a number in other countries. Over 70 of the organization's shops in the UK are specialist Oxfam Bookshops, making them the largest retailer of second-hand books in the United Kingdom. Oxfam Canada sold off its Bridgehead fair-trade business, which in 2000 became the Bridgehead Coffee (www .bridgehead.ca) chain, which continues to promote Fairtrade coffee and related products. Oxfam shops also sell Fairtrade products from developing communities around the world. Today, Oxfam's shops raise millions of pounds.

Oxfam has a number of successful fundraising channels in addition to its shops. Over half a million people in the UK make a regular financial contribution towards its work, and vital funds are received from gifts left to the organization in people's wills. While traditional tin-shaking techniques are still effective, Oxfam pioneered lots of new fundraising ideas, such as a table box from the 1960s that was passed around at family mealtimes. Other original ideas include regular giving, pledges, and the charity gift catalogue, *Oxfam Unwrapped*.

Many London Marathon competitors run to raise money for Oxfam, and Oxfam also receives funds in return for providing and organizing volunteer stewards at festivals such as Glastonbury. In conjunction with the Gurkha Welfare Trust, Oxfam also runs several Trailwalker events in Hong Kong, Australia, New Zealand, the UK, and Japan.

Oxfam has also been active in the 'co-branding' arena as a medium for fundraising. In 2007, it joined with Zeta 8 (www.zeta8 .com), the Australian-based nutrition and network marketing agency, and now 10% of all member joining and renewal fees received by Zeta 8 go to Oxfam.

Oxfam has a thriving publication arm, producing Oxfam policy papers, campaign reports, and news on policy developments as well as teaching and educational materials. The Oxfam press office deals with all media enquiries.

Although, strictly speaking, it would be difficult to class organizations in the same or similar kind of work as 'competitors' (given the fact that they are all working to achieve the same ends, rather than at the expense of each other), Oxfam has 'competitors' in Christian Aid, The Evangelical Alliance Relief fund (TEAR Fund), War on Want, Save the Children, World Vision, and Cafod, to name but a few. Each operates on a similar basis as Oxfam, but may specialize, as Save the Children does, on a specific market segment internationally. Each competes for the 'donor £/$' in similar ways to Oxfam.

Oxfam has not been short on courting controversy, nor has it been lacking in a fair amount of criticism. It has been accused of championing campaigns of little impact. But Oxfam counters that it wouldn't bother campaigning if it didn't work, from helping Ethiopia's coffee farmers get a fair deal with Starbucks (www .starbucks.com), to securing billions more in aid and debt relief for poor countries, as part of the Make Poverty History campaign. The following are some specific examples which have been widely discussed in the international media:

The Starbucks' affair

On 26 October 2006, Oxfam accused Starbucks of asking the US National Coffee Association (NCA) to block a trademark application from Ethiopia for two of the country's coffee beans, Sidamo and Harar. They claimed this could result in denying Ethiopian coffee farmers potential annual earnings of up to £47 million.

Robert Nelson, the head of the National Coffee Association, added that his organization initiated the opposition for economic reasons: 'For the U.S. industry to exist, we must have an economically stable coffee industry in the producing world. . . . This particular scheme is going to hurt the Ethiopian coffee farmers economically.' The NCA claims that the Ethiopian government was being badly advised and this move could price them out of the market.

Facing more than 90,000 letters of concern, Starbucks placed pamphlets in its stores accusing Oxfam of 'misleading behaviour' and insisting that its campaign needs to stop. *The Economist* derided Oxfam's 'simplistic' stance and Ethiopia's 'economically illiterate' government, arguing that Starbucks' (and Illy's, www.illy.com) standards-based approach would ultimately benefit farmers more.

Nonetheless, on 20 June 2007 representatives of the government of Ethiopia and senior leaders from Starbucks Coffee Company announced that they had concluded an agreement regarding distribution, marketing, and licensing that recognizes the importance and integrity of Ethiopia's speciality coffee designations.

Arms control

In 2006, Oxfam helped to persuade the United Nations to begin work on the first ever treaty on global arms controls. Its development continues.

Political affiliations

Another controversy has surrounded Oxfam's perceived political affiliations. Oxfam Great Britain has been strongly criticized by other NGOs for becoming too close to Tony Blair's New Labour government in the UK, and getting involved in other political activities.

In 2005, the website 'New Internationalist' described Oxfam as a Big International Non-Government Organization (BINGO). The website criticizes such organizations for being undemocratic while wielding enormous financial and economic clout.

On 28 April 2007, two academics in Melbourne, Australia, representing a right-wing think tank, lodged a complaint with the Australian Competition and Consumer Commission, accusing Oxfam of misleading or deceptive conduct under the Trade Practices Act in its promotion of Fairtrade coffee. The academics claimed that high certification costs and low wages for workers undermine claims that Fairtrade helps to lift producers out of poverty. These claims were subsequently dismissed by the Commission.

In 2003, Oxfam Belgium produced a poster with a picture of a dripping blood orange. The poster read: 'Israeli fruits have a bitter taste . . . reject the occupation of Palestine, don't buy Israeli fruits and vegetables.' Oxfam was widely criticized because of the poster's perceived anti-Israel political message and its allusion to traditional, anti-semitic blood libel rhetoric. Following publicity and pressure from *NGO Monitor*, Oxfam removed the poster from their website and Ian Anderson, the chairman of Oxfam International, issued a letter of apology (*NGO Monitor*, 2007). However, Oxfam maintained its support for a boycott of products grown in the West Bank and Gaza. Oxfam was criticized for its policy of what has been termed 'selective morality'.

Too much donor money goes on Oxfam's administration

One major criticism that Oxfam has always had to weather is that it is accused of spending too much money on administration and other overheads. Oxfam vigorously denies this. Oxfam claims to spend just 11p in every £1 donated to Oxfam on support and running costs—money that is vital in keeping an effective, professional organization going, running efficient projects, getting people, equipment, supplies, and funds to the places where they are needed.

Support of 'lazy' poor people

Other criticisms are that the money collected is spent of 'lazy' poor people who cannot be bothered to help themselves and have become 'aid dependent'. Oxfam denies this one too as it suggests that no one chooses to live in poverty.

Support of corrupt governments

Oxfam is accused of supporting corrupt governments in poor countries and so wasting money. But Oxfam does not give money to governments. It sometimes works with governments, but the money is spent on its own projects, run by its own staff, and Oxfam is committed to accounting for every penny. Oxfam's recent expulsion from Zimbabwe by the Zimbabwean government testifies to the fact it does not support corrupt governments.

Sources:

BBC News (2006), 'Starbucks in Ethiopia coffee row', 26 October.

Charity Commission, UK (www.charitycommission.gov.uk)

NGO Monitor (2007), 'Oxfam's apology', 16 July.

Overington, C. (2008), 'Oxford coffee harms poor farmers', *The Australian*, 28 April.

Oxfam (www.oxfam.org.uk)

The Age (2007), 'Not free, but fair: Oxfam cleared of coffee chicanery', 28 June.

Zeta 8 (www.zeta8.com).

Discussion questions

1 (a) Describe the contributing factors creating a 'credibility gap' between Oxfam's poverty, distress, and suffering alleviation objectives and its perceived foray into political/lobbying activities.

  (b) What can Oxfam do to narrow the perceived 'credibility gap'?

2 Accusation of a lack of transparency (e.g. too much spending of donor money on administration) is a common criticism of Oxfam, and other charities in general.

  (a) Discuss how an effective marketing control system can benefit Oxfam in addressing this issue.

  (b) Construct a balanced scorecard (see Chapter 16, Fig. 16.6) for Oxfam, showing clearly how its objectives can be achieved to the satisfaction of all stakeholders.

GLOSSARY OF MARKETING TERMS

Absolute advantage One country enjoying total lower costs of production than another country(ies).

Adaptation Goods or services adapted in either product, distribution or advertising form to take account of unique local conditions in any one country.

Advertising Any form of marketing communication in the paid media.

Agent A channel intermediary contracted to represent the interests of one or more suppliers for a fee.

Anthropology The discovery of beliefs, motives and values through the study of a society's overt and covert behaviour.

Area organization A geographically based form for organizing international operations.

Attitudes and values A predisposition towards a person or object based on cultural mores and values which is a precursor of behaviour.

Balance of payments An economic measure of imports minus exports.

Barter The direct exchange of goods and services of equivalent values between two parties, without cash considerations.

Bill of lading The receipt given by the shipping company to the shipper for goods accepted for carriage by sea (as opposed to an airway bill of lading for goods carried by air).

Bills of exchange An unconditional order in writing, addressed by one person (drawer) to another (drawee), signed by the person giving it (drawer), requiring the person to whom it is addressed (drawee) to pay on demand, at a fixed or determinable future date, a certain sum in money to, or to the order of, a specific person (payee) or to bearer.

Broker A channel intermediary which puts a specific buyer(s) and seller(s) in contact with one another in one or more commodity(ies) or service(s) with a view to achieving a sale or benefit.

Brussels Nomenclature An international convention aimed at grouping articles, mainly according to their material composition, into a simplified classification system for tariff administration.

Budget An amount of money set aside to cover the total cost of a marketing campaign or functional marketing activity(ies).

CIF A contract of sale 'cost, insurance, freight' of the documents of title, not the goods, whereby the buyer is under an obligation to pay against the shipping documents irrespective of the arrival of the goods.

Cluster analysis A technique for grouping similarities or differences between a set of objects or persons.

Comparative advantage One country enjoying a lower production ratio (i.e. inputs to outputs) than another country.

Comparative analysis Comparing the same set of statistics within a category of one country with another for the purpose of estimating potential demand.

Competition A product, organization or individual, in either the same or another category which can be directly substituted one for the other in fulfilling the same needs or wants.

Competitive strategy The adoption of a unique position in the marketplace through targeting a specific market and marketing mix.

Cooperative A collection of organizations or individuals, pooling their resources in order to gain commercial or non-commercial advantage in buying, selling or processing goods and/or services.

Countertrade An agreement by the customer to buy goods on condition that the seller buys some of the customer's own products in return.

Culture The sum total of learned behavioural characteristics or traits which are manifest and shared by members of a particular society.

Currency swaps A method to gain access to foreign capital at favourable rates in order to offset fluctuations in currency exchanges.

Decentralized plans Marketing plans which are prepared on a country-by-country basis to take into account local market conditions.

Demand pattern analysis A technique for analysing patterns of a country's growth rate in different stages of its development.

Devaluation The reduction in the value of one currency *vis-à-vis* other countries.

Diffusion theory A conceptualization of the adoption of innovation(s) which is characterized by a normal distribution.

Distribution channel An intermediary, linking the participants in the supply chain, through which goods or services are marketed and distributed.

Dumping The selling of goods or services in a buying country at less than the production unit price in the selling country, or the difference between normal domestic price and the price at which the product leaves the exporting country.

Ethnocentrism A home-country orientation but with export of surplus production.

Exchange rate The ratio of exchange of one currency to another.

Export credit guarantee fund A facility, provided by government treasury, to guarantee the development costs of exports or legal claims arising therefrom.

Export processing zone A zone, designated within a country, enjoying tax privileges or other status, where goods and services can be brought into, reprocessed and re-exported.

Exporting The marketing of goods and services produced in one country into another country.

Expropriation The annexation or seizure of national assets by a government.

FAS A contract of sale 'free along side' whereby the seller undertakes to place the goods alongside a ship ready for boarding and carry all charges up to that point.

FOB A contract of sale 'free on board' whereby the seller undertakes to place the goods on board a named ship at a named port and berth and carry all charges up to delivery over the ships rail.

Foreign exchange Facilities business across national boundaries, usually expressed in foreign currency bought or sold on the foreign exchange market.

Forward rates A mechanism whereby the risk of changes in exchange rates can be covered by obtaining a new rate quote for a future exchange of currencies.

Future A legally binding contract to deliver/take delivery on a specified date of a given quality and quantity of a commodity at an agreed price.

Geocentrism A global orientation with marketing strategies adapted to local country conditions.

Global environment All semi- or uncontrollable factors which a marketer has to account for in carrying out global operations.

Global marketing Marketing on a worldwide scale reconciling or taking commercial advantage of global operational differences, similarities and opportunities in order to meet global objectives.

Global products Products and services designed to meet global equivalent market segments.

Gross Domestic Product (GDP) The value of all goods and services produced by a country's domestic economy in one year.

Gross National Income (GNI) GNI equals Gross National Product, except that it is the income earned from the sale of products and services.

Gross National Product (GNP) The market value of all goods and services produced by residents of a country in one year, including income from abroad.

Hedging A mechanism to avoid the risk of a decline in future market prices of a commodity.

Hierarchy of needs The ordering of a person's needs into a hierarchy of relative potency such that, as lower order needs are fulfilled, higher unfulfilled order needs emerge, which require fulfilment.

High-context culture Cultural contextualization where there is minimum reliance on explicit verbal or written communications.

Ideology A philosophical stance, adopted by an individual, organization, or country, which has direct implications on the way of doing business.

Income elasticity measurements A description of the relationship between the demand for goods and changes in income.

Income per capita The market value of all goods and services produced by a country divided by the total number of residents of that country.

Inflation A condition where demand outstrips supply or costs escalate, effecting an upward change in prices.

Interactive plans A planning system whereby headquarters sets a policy and framework and subsidiaries interpret these under local conditions.

International Monetary Fund (IMF) A fund, with worldwide country membership, (United Nations) which lends money to countries on a short-term basis to assist them with balance-of-payments problems.

International product life cycle A conceptual model that suggests high-income, mass-consumption countries go through a cycle, over time, from exporting products and services to the importation of the same due to changes in domestic production costs.

Joint ventures An enterprise in which two or more investors share ownership and control over property rights and operations.

Letter of credit A method of international payment whereby the buyer instructs his own country bank to open a credit with the seller's own country bank specifying the documents which the seller has to deliver to the bank for him/her to receive payment.

Levy A tax imposed by government on imported goods and services.

Licensing A method of cooperation whereby an organization in one country agrees to permit an organization in another country to use the manufacturing, processing, trademark, know-how or some other skill provided by the licensor.

Low-context culture Cultural contextualization where there is high reliance on explicit verbal or written communications.

Market entry mode The method by which an organization enters a foreign market either by direct and/or indirect exporting, or by in-country production.

Market entry strategy A marketing strategy adopted by an organization to enter a foreign market.

Market holding price The charging of a price at what the market can bear in order to hold market share.

Market positioning The adoption of a specific market stance, either leader, challenger, follower, flanker, or adopter, *vis-à-vis* competition.

Marketing Planning, executing, and controlling the conception, pricing, promotion, and distribution of ideas, goods, and services in order to build lasting, mutually profitable exchange relationships satisfying individual and organizational objectives.

Matrix organization A complex form of organizing international operations bringing together the competencies of geographic knowledge, product knowledge, and know-how, functional competencies and knowledge of the customer, industry, and its needs.

Media Any form of communication channel between the seller of goods and services and consumers.

Media scheduling A schedule for the allocation of advertising messages in the media over a given time horizon.

Message An informative communication about a product or service placed in a communication channel.

Multiple factor indices A measure for estimating potential demand, indirectly, using as proxies, variables that either intuition or statistical analysis suggest can be closely correlated with the potential demand for the product or service under review.

Nationalism The assertion of indigenous culture by an individual, organization, or country.

Non-tariff barriers Non-monetary measures, public or private, imposed by a given country, which cause the restricted distribution of internationally traded goods or services.

Option A bilateral contract giving its holder the right, but not the obligation, to buy or sell a specified asset at a specific price at or up to a specified date.

Outsourcing A decision to have certain components in the value chain manufactured out of the organization on the grounds of economic or other necessity.

Penetration price The charging of a low price in order to gain volume sales conducted under conditions of undifferentiated products and elastic demand patterns.

Physical distribution The act and functions of physically distributing goods and services, including the elements of transport, warehousing, and order processing.

Polycentrism A host country orientation adapting all aspects of the marketing to local conditions.

Price ceiling The maximum price that can be charged bearing in mind competition and what the market can bear.

Price escalation The difference between the domestic price and the target price in foreign markets due to the application of duties, dealer margins and/or other transaction costs.

Price floor The minimum price that can be charged bounded by product cost.

Primary data New data collected for research purposes.

Product A good or service offered by an organization which affords a bundle of benefits, both objective (physical) and subjective (image), to a user.

Product organization A form of organizing international operations on a product basis.

Product strategy Decisions on the management of products or services reflecting a set of conditions in a given market.

Promotion The offer of an inducement to purchase, over and above the intrinsic value or price of a good or service.

Purchasing power parity (PPP) The base rate at which one unit of currency will purchase the same amount of goods and services, despite differential rates of inflation.

Quota A specific quantity imposed by one country on another, which once filled cannot be exceeded within a given time.

Regiocentrism A regional market orientation with marketing strategies adapted to regional differences.

Regression analysis A method of estimating market demand by projecting forward two correlated variables.

Retailer A channel intermediary that acts as the final player in the value chain, providing a range of utilities to end users.

Revaluation The increase in the value of one currency *vis-à-vis* other currencies.

Secondary data Published accessible data from a variety of sources for research and other purposes.

Self-reference criterion Perceptual distortion brought about by an individual's own cultural experience.

Skimming price The charging of a high price in order to gain maximum revenue conducted under conditions of differentiated products and inelastic demand patterns.

Standardization A global marketing strategy for the provision of standaridized goods or services unchanged in any one country.

Standardized plans A uniform planning system applied globally, based on economies of scale and consumer uniformity.

Strategic business unit (SBU) An independent grouping of organizations, products, or technologies within a parent organization, with complete resource and profit responsibility for serving an identified market(s).

Strategic equivalent segment A global market segment displaying similar characteristics or responses to products or services, irrespective of country.

Surveillance An initial screening of markets for market entry purposes using readily available information.

Tariff A revenue instrument, normally the imposition of a single or multiple excise rate, used by goverments on imported goods and services.

Terms of access The conditions imposed by one country which apply to the importation of goods from another country.

Transfer pricing The price at which goods or services are transferred between one country and another within the same organization.

Wholesaler A channel intermediary which purchases and sells in bulk from either original suppliers and/or other channel intermediaries, charging a margin for its services.

World Bank (known also as the International Bank for Reconstruction and Development) A bank with worldwide country membership, which provides long-term capital to aid economic development.

INDEX

Notes: *for Global marketing see Marketing, etc.; definitions of terms may be found in the Glossary (pages 551–554)*

A

Aablo 388
Abu Dhabi Investment Authority 48
Access to markets 79–80
  entry strategies 193–4
  modes 230–4
  opportunities of globalization 79–81
  shower/waterfall 192
  terms of access 475–7
Acculturation 119
Acer 471
Acquisitions 253
Adidas 153, 396
Advertising 350–9
  appeal 353–4, 357
  banner advertising 371–2
  creative strategy 350–1, 352(fig.)
  e-commerce and 371–3
  format 356–7, 358
  interactive TV advertising 372–3
  music 33, 357
  positioning 351–3, 357
  sponsorship 366–8
  tone 354–6, 358–9
  wireless devices 373
Aesthetics, culture and 111–12
Aetna 509
Africa
  growth 11
  Maize to Africa 41
  poverty 86–9, 95
  UEMOA (West African States in
    Economic and Monetary Union) 52
Aftermarkets 530, 531
Ageing population 5, 12–13, 56, 194
  grey customer effect 57, 194
  silver-haired surfers 57, 59
Agency theory 225
Agilent 347
Agriculture 87
Aid programmes 86
Air New Zealand 40
Airbus Industries 260
Aldi 237, 238
Amazon 53, 86, 437, 520
American Airlines 24, 67, 196
American Express 316
Amnesty International 148, 512
Analogy estimation 176
Anglo-American 544–5
Annual plan control 529
Ansoff product/market matrix 288, 292
Anti-globalization protest 86–9
  Korean farmers 87
AOL 59

Apple Computers 27
  iPod 59
Arcelor 431
Argentina 11
  cumulative services export growth 314
Ariel 252
Arms trade 512
Asda 474
ASEAN 23, 52–3
Asia
  East Asia
    European entry strategies 542
    financial crisis 466
  East Asian Vision Group 23
  population 8
  poverty 86–9, 95
Asia Pacific Economic Community (APEC) 52
Association of South East Asian Nations
    (ASEAN) 23, 52–3
AT&T 4
Attitudes *see* Values and attitudes, consumer
    behaviour
Auction, international business models 228
Audi 61
Audit
  environmental audit 211
  global marketing audit 528–9
Australia 113
Automobile Association 463
Avis 257

B

Balanced scorecard 531, 532(fig.)
Banana Republic 262
Bang & Olufsen 262
Banner advertising 371–2
Barclay's Bank 48, 421
Bargaining power theories 221–2
Barter 473
Bear Stearns 64
Behavioural forces 494
  buyer behaviour 132–4, 505
  culture and consumer behaviour 113–18
  culture and value patterns 125–9
  social behaviour 108
Ben & Jerry's 164, 426
Benchmarking 531
Benetton 111, 237, 329, 415, 428
BERI Index 44
Bertolli 357–9
Best practice 531
BhS 237
Bills of exchange 478
Black and Decker 292
Blogging 60

Bluetooth 257
BMG 83
BMW 62, 353
Body language 109
Body Shop 162, 164, 189, 237, 267, 287, 328
Boeing 61, 158, 163, 261, 287, 452
Bolivia 11
Boo.com 59
Born global, theories of globalization 223–4
Bosnia 43, 44
Boston Consulting Group
  growth-share matrix (BCG) 288,
    290–1(fig.)
  learning curve 452
BP 26, 133
Brands 415–20
  architecture of international brand
    298–302
  brand equity metrics 530
  co-branding 229
  corporate social responsibility 300
  dimensions of global brand 299(fig.)
  global myth 300
  local vs global brands 297
  most admired international brands
    294(table)
  quality 300
  social responsibility 300
  strategic international branding 293–7
  top ten global brands 294(table)
Brazil 11, 13, 49, 50, 427
  cumulative services export growth 314
Bribe Payers Index (BPI) 144
Bribery 144, 147
BRIC economies 50
British Airways 187, 426, 531
  and Go 302
  Terminal 5, 339–40
British American Tobacco 433
British Home Stores (BhS) 237
British Telecom 256, 362–3, 452
British wine 198
Broadspeed 520
Brundtland Report (1987) 97
BSkyB 25
BT 256, 362–3, 452
Burma 148, 433
Business Environment Risk Index (BERI) 177
Business models 226–9
  auction 228
  clicks and mortar 228
  collective business system 229
  cutting out the middleman 227
  industrialization of services 229
  low cost carriers (LCCs) 229
  monopoly 227

Business models (*Cont.*)
  multi-level marketing 226
  network effect 219(fig.)
  online auction 228
  razor and blades 226
  service quality 228
  subscription business model 226
  transformational 229
Business process outsourcing (BPO) 541
Business for Social Responsibility 96, 97
Business-to-business (B2B)
  buyer behaviour 132–4
    culture and 133–4
    models 132–4
  customer (vertical downstream)
    relationships 427–8
  relationship management 416, 427
Business-to-consumer (B2C) *see* Customers/
    consumers
Buyback 473
Buyer behaviour
  business-to-business (B2B) 132–4
    culture and 133–4
    government and state 132

C

CAD/CAM (computer aided development/
    manufacture) 292
Cadburys 268
Cadillac phenomenon 508
Canon 257
Capability building 264
Capability leverage 264
Capital
  corporate social responsibility and 164–5
  portfolio capital 81
Carrefour 256
Cartels 431–2
Cathay Pacific 67
Chaebols 22, 259
Challenger Technologies 14
Champagne Glass Phenomenon 88
Child labour 150–3
Chile 11
China 4, 8, 23, 44, 113, 133, 432
  accession to WTO 55–6
  accumulated reserves 48
  business ethics 130
  business strategy approach 225
  Coca-Cola 345
  consumer behaviour 118
  cross-culture theory 127–30
  and CSR 396
  culture 123
    Confucian dynamism 123, 125, 127–8
  cumulative services export growth 314
  emergence of economic powerhouse
    9–10, 23, 75
  Euro 2004 236
  evolution of middle class 136–7
  joint ventures 394

McDonald's 394
  Matsushita 395–7
  quanxi 423
  R&D 395–7
China Development Bank 48
Chubb Life 509
CIF (cost, insurance, freight) 478
CIGNA 351
Cisco 270, 428
Citigroup Bank 48, 165
Clicks and mortar, international business
    models 228
Climate change 5, 87, 93–6, 355
  components 93(fig.)
  and energy security 94–5
  and food security 94
  greenhouse gases 92–4
  Kyoto Protocol 87, 96
Cluster analysis 177
Co-operative Bank 161
  ethical policy 161
Coca-Cola 25, 29, 79, 105, 262, 414, 452, 461
  in China 345
  Dasani 185, 304
Code of Ethics 329
Code of Practice (CoP)
  ethics and 429
  supermarkets 428
Codes of Conduct 159
Codes of Ethics 155–8
Colgate 85, 431
Collaboration
  joint ventures 133, 233, 253, 394
  price cooperation 481
  relationship management with
    competitors 431–3
  supply chain management
    COMECON 52
    commodity markets 47, 130–1
    common markets 51(*table*)
    communication 344–80
    exhibitions and trade fairs 368–71
    globalization and 81
    horizontal 394
    integrated marketing communications
      (IMC) 347–50
    lateral 395
    moving beyond 'standardize or
      localize' debate 344–50
    nature of 349–50
    public relations (PR) 359–62
    relationship management and 416–23
    sponsorship 366–8
    technology and 347
    vertical 393
    see also Advertising; Direct-response
      marketing; Telecommunications
Collaborative partnership 392
Collective business system, international
    business models 229
COMECON 52
Commitment, marketing 420

Commodity markets 47, 130–1
  ethics 134–5
  supply chain management 47
Commodity trading 130–1
Communication process, Consumer-driven
    349(fig.)
Communications
  costs 82
  employee 360
Comparative advantage, theory of 5
Compensation trading 473
Competition 251–2
  assessment 63
  changing nature of 13–16
  globalization and 85–6
  growth factors 248–54, 249(fig.)
    changing microeconomic business
      environment 249–52
    sophistication of business operations
      and strategy 252–3
  relationship management with
    competitors 431–3
Competitive advantage 246–7
  absolute or relative 258
  anatomy of 255–60
  cause of 259
  corporate social responsibility 160–5
  creation of through generic routes 260–3
  direct or indirect 258
  discrete vs compound advantages 257
  effect of 258
  expression of 257
  generic competitive strategies 261(fig.)
  global 25–6
  homogeneous vs heterogeneous
    advantages 257
  individual-bound vs firm-bound vs
    virtual-bound advantages 258
  knowledge as transformation agent
    268–9
  knowledge/information 26–7, 268–9,
    330–2
  locale of 258
  national competitiveness and global
    competition 246–7
  new sources of 266–71
  positioning vs kinetic advantages 256–7
  resource-based theory 263–6
  strategy and 254–6, 260
  substance of 256–7
  tangible vs intangible advantages 257
  time-span of 260
Competitive analysis, 5-force 63
Competitive environment of global
    marketing 62–3
Competitor intelligence gathering 253–4
Complete solutions 5
Computer Misuse Act 1990 59
Computers 4
Computers *see* Information and
    communications technologies (ICT)
Concession analysis 506

Concorde 434
Confucian dynamism 123, 125, 127–8
Consumers see Customers/consumers
Contingency theory 224–5
Control mechanisms 525–34
    bureaucratic (formal) vs cultural
        (shared) 525
    coercive vs non-coercive sources of
        power 526
    elements of 528
    factors affecting marketing control
        system 526–8
        communication systems 527
        domestic practices and values 526
        environmental differences 527
    global marketing audit 528–9
    methods 529–34
Core business 4
Corporate social responsibility (CSR) 28–9,
        29, 64–5, 153–65, 266–7, 396, 429
    brands 300
    and capital 164–5
    and competitive advantage 160–5
    towards sustainable development 95–7
    see also Ethics
Corporate transparency 19
Corruption 143–7
    business and 145–6
    impact of 144
    indices of 143–4(table)
    legislation against 146–7
Corus 431
Cost, insurance, freight (CIF) 478
Costs
    cost leadership 260–1
    reduction strategies 253
Counter-purchase 473
Counter-trade 473–4
Country endowment factors 386
Creative plan 350–2
Credibility, reputation management 160–3
Credit Lyonnais 165
Credit restrictions and blacklisting 147
Cross-border financial transactions 318–19
Cross-border services
    defining 319–24
        by using multi-variant classification
            systems 321–4
        degree of consumer–producer
            interaction 320–1
        degree of intangibility 319–24
    drivers for growth 314–19
    strategic options for marketing
        333(fig.), 334
    value 313
    see also Service sector
Cross-cultural analysis 120–30
    applying cross-cultural frameworks
        129–30
Cross-sector partnerships and human
        rights 149
Cross-selling see Cross-cultural analysis

Crown Cork and Seal 109
Cuba 43
Cultural globalization 77–9
Culture 56–7, 104–13
    and aesthetics 111–12
    approaches to study of 57
    behaviour and value patterns 125–7
    business-to-business (B2B) buyer
        behaviour and 133–4
    communication and 344–5, 346
    components of culture 107, 108(fig.)
    consequences of mistakes with 105
    consumer behaviour and 113–18
    cross-cultural analysis 120–30, 500
    cultural products 78
    cultural services 78
    dimensions 122–3
    education and 109–10
    and ethics 134–5, 500
    four layers 107(fig.)
    globalization and 77–9
    high vs low context approach 120–2
    iceberg model 106(fig.)
    managing cultural differences 118–20
    market variable 38
    meaning of 107–13
    sales management 498–503
    socio-cultural environment of global
        marketing 56–7
    time values 504
    uncertainty avoidance (UA) 123
Currency environment of global marketing
        63–4
Customer relationship management (CRM)
        271, 435–41
    criteria for 440
    internal relationships add value across
        conventional functions 436(fig.)
    potential complexity 439–41
    technology 438
    see also Relationship management (CRM)
Customer value analysis (CVA) 530
Customer (vertical downstream)
        relationships 393, 425–8
    B2B 427–8
    B2C 425–7
    criteria for evaluating strategic
        relationships 427(fig.)
Customers/consumers
    building customer loyalty 415
    communication process 349(fig.)
    culture and consumer behaviour
        113–18
    customer-oriented selling 502–3
    customer-specific segmentation,
        internet 187
    demographics and expectations 12–13
    fad attitudes 110, 249–50
    global 169
    homogenization 316
    market differences 346
    profiles, data 187

    relationship management see
        Relationship management
    tastes 249–50
    trends 13–15, 24–5, 41
    types of need and consumer behaviour
        117–18
    understanding consumer behaviour 113
    value system and 114, 116–17
Customization 332–3
Customs clearance, Dagang Net, Malaysia 84
Customs unions 51

D
Daewoo 212, 259, 450
Dagang Net 84
Daimler-Chrysler 6, 202–5, 415
Danone 56
Dasani 185, 304
Data
    building consumer profiles 187
    competitor intelligence gathering 253–4
    direct marketing 364–6
    Extended Common Log Format
        (ECLF) 187
    primary 181
    protection 365
    reactive data collection technologies 187
    research 171–2
        analysis 184
        collection 174, 180, 183
    secondary 181
Decision-making process 174(table), 193
    environmental factors 212(table), 497–8
    factors affecting global pricing decisions
        449–52
    factors affecting supply chain 386–91
    international market environment, effect
        on market entry 211(fig.)
    sales management 495–8
    supply chain management, distribution
        systems 386–91
Deforestation 92
Delivery
    order 479
    services marketing and 334–5
Dell Computers 86, 154, 417
Demand pattern analysis 176
Demographic trends 5, 13–15, 24,
        89–90, 186
Deregulation and liberalization of trade in
        services 314–15
Design Tex 97
Devaluation 469
Dia 237
Diageo 63
Diamond factors 247
Diamonds
    Anglo-American 545
    Kimberley Process Certification
        Scheme 149
Differentiation strategy 262

Direct marketing
data 364–6
Internet and e-commerce 362–5
telecommunications 235
Disintermediation 62
Disney 25, 46, 78, 111, 150, 196, 285, 435
Disruptive technologies 61
Distribution systems 40–1, 386–91
ICT 18
risk management 384
supply chain management
collaboration in 391–7
country characteristics 386–8
factors affecting supply chain decisions
386–91
see also Supply chain management
Documentation, international trade
478–90
Domestic law 45
Domestic marketing 6
Double Taxation Convention 44
Double-loop learning 531
Downsizing 541
Dreamworks 257
Drug companies, and WTO 87–8
Dumping 472
DVD technology 373
Dynamic incremental pricing 457–8
Dyson 249

E

E-commerce see Internet and e-commerce
E-health 429
E-mails 371
E-tailing 329
East Asia
European entry strategies 542
financial crisis 466
East Asian Vision Group 23
EasyJet 294, 457
eBay 58, 59, 218
Eclectic theory 224–5
Economic blocs 47–53
Economic facilitators 53
Economic globalization 72–5
Economic growth and development
classification of economies 47(table)
competition and 251
corruption and 145
emergence of economic powerhouses
9–10, 23, 49, 75
nature of economies 50(table)
new economic architecture 23–4
sales management and 497–8
volatility 84–5
Economic poverty 86–9, 95
Economies
classification 48
Old vs New 85
Education 250
culture and 111

as export 250
international partnerships 107
Quality Assurance Agency (QAA) 526
sales force and 499
Egypt 235–6
Electrolux 256, 269, 498
Electronic Marketplace 235
Employees
communications 360
incentives 316
job satisfaction 501
labour practices 150–3
recruitment and selection, sales force
498–501
recruitment standards 316
relationship management with 434–5
sales see Sales force
satisfaction 163
Emulation 25
Enculturation 119
Energy consumption, and economic
income 95(fig.)
Energy and extractives, cross-sector
partnerships and human rights 149
Energy security 94–5
Ennovation 257
Entry strategies see Market entry strategies
Environmental analysis, PEST vs SLEPT 39
Environmental factors, in decision-making
497–8
Environmental issues 5, 92–7, 153, 287
climate change 5, 87, 93–6, 355
decision-making process 212(table)
degradation 89
Hartman Group traditional segmentation
189
pressure groups 64–5
sustainability 89, 92–7
Equity dilution 44
Ericsson 256, 435
Estonia, cumulative services export
growth 314
Ethical Trading Initiative (ETI) 267
Ethics 142–65
business ethics in China 130
codes of 65–6, 155–8
commodity markets and 134–5
competition and 251
corporate practices, transparency 19
corporate social responsibility 28–9, 65,
95–7, 266–7, 396, 429
ethics training 158–60
and cross-cultural analysis 500
culture and 134–5
fair trading 466
globalization and 86–9
Institute of Business Ethics 159
international franchising and 329
Internet and 61
investment 164–5
marketing research 184
pressure groups 64–5

sales management and 510–12
social issues 142–65
see also Corporate social responsibility;
Fairtrade
Ethnic composition 250
sales force and 499
Ethnic conflict 23
Ethnocentrism 521
Euro 2004, and China 236
Europe, second homes 177
European Bank for Reconstruction and
Development (EBRD) 55
European Convention on Corruption
(1997) 147
European Court of Justice 51
European Monetary Union (EMU) 474
European Round Table (ERT) 434
European Union 4
Council of Ministers 51
culture 107
cumulative services export growth 314
expansion 43, 45, 52
institutions 51–2
laws and regulations, economic effects 45
legislation against corruption 147
single currency 39, 64, 468, 474
Evian 29
Ex works/warehouse (EXW) 477
Exchange rates 63
currency fluctuations 466–9
Exhibitions and trade fairs 368–71
Experian 195
Experiential needs 118
Export financing, international trade 480–9
Export order process 475
Export payments 478
Exports
documentation 478–90
export order process 475
financing 480–9
payments 478–50
Expropriation 44
Extended Common Log Format (ECLF) 187
Exxon 24, 64

F

Facebook 60
Facilitators 41, 53–5, 252
Failures 185
Fair trading, ethics 429
Fairtrade system 166–7
Famine 41
FAS (free alongside ship) 478
Federal Express 316
Federal Reserve 64
Fedex 86
Ferrous metals
Anglo-American 545
steel industry 431–2
Steelcase Inc 97
Fiat 248

Financial crises 12–13, 76, 84–5
    East Asia 466
Financial integration 81
    opportunities of globalization 81
Financial management
    cross-border financial transactions 318–19
    export financing 480–9
Financial system, globalization and 81
First Direct 257
FMCG 392, 422, 426
FOB (free on board) 458, 478
Focus strategy 262
Food, and culture 78
Food security, and climate change 94
Ford 248, 415
Foreign direct investment (FDI) 81, 235
Foreign divestment, exit from a foreign
    market 234
Forests 92–3
Formula One, and Bernie Ecclestone 306–7
Forward contracts 469
France
    culture 78, 106, 113
    Iraq war 44–5, 66
    outshopping in 450
Franchises 232, 233, 328–9
    ethics and 529
Free alongside ship (FAS) 478
Free on board (FOB) 458, 478
'Free market' 429
Free on rail/truck (FOR/FOT) 478
Free trade areas 51
Friends of the Earth 65, 287
Functional departments, relationship
    management with 435–6
Functional needs 118
Functional structures 535–6

G

Galileo 196
Gap 79, 150, 262
Gartner Inc 541
General Agreement on Tariffs and Trade
    (GATT) 53, 79–80
General Agreement on Trade in Services
    (GATS) 235, 315
General Electric 58, 133, 287, 315, 425
    market attractiveness–competitive
        position matrix 290
General Mills 413
General Motors 21, 25, 202, 415, 543
    Shared Savings partnership 96
Geocentrism 521
Germany 4
GIB 328
Glaxo-Smith-Kline 64, 248
Global competition, realities 14
Global economies of scale 317
Global engagement, new rules 22–3
Global migration 71, 89–92
Global population 9

Global sourcing 83–4
Globalization 5, 11–19, 17, 71–2
    cultural 77–9
    definition 72
    economic 72–5
    global consumers 316–17
    opportunities of 79–84
        financial integration 81
        market access 79–81
        reduction in communication and
            transport costs 82–3(table)
        sourcing, purchasing and production
            83–4
    technological 77
    theories of
        agency approach 225
        bargaining power approach 221–2
        born global 223–4
        business strategy approach 225
        eclectic or contingency 224–5
        Industrial network approach (network
            model) 219–21
        transactional cost analysis 224
        Uppsala or incremental model (stage
            model) 213–19
    threats from 84–9
        anti-globalization protest 86–9
        globalization of competition 85–6
        macroeconomic volatility 84–5
Globally integrated marketing
    communications (GIMC) 347
Glossary 551–4
GM, Monsanto 89
GO 302
Government and state
    as buyer 131–4, 133
    organizational (B2B) buyer behaviour 132
    protectionism and 17, 71
    relationship management with 434
    role in economy 43
    stability 43–4
Green Isle Foods 400–1
Greenhouse gases, climate change 92–4
Greenpeace 65, 360
Greens 189
Grey markets 471–2
Griffin Manufacturing 402
Gross national income (GNI) 48
Groupe Casino 328
Growth and development *see* Economic
    growth and development
Guinness 119

H

Halifax Bank 253
Harmonized tariff system (HTS) 475
Harrods 294
Hartman Group, traditional segmentation
    189
Health care, telemedicine 15
Hedging 469

Hewlett Packard 269, 315, 347, 413, 471
Hilton Hotels 449
HIV/AIDS 23, 111
Holiday homes 285
Holidays, pricing 454
Hollywood 78
    and branding 285
Home entertainment 20
    digital television 18
Honda 248, 258
Honeywell International 146
Hong Kong 16
    service sector 313
HSBC 421
Human rights issues 147–53
Human rights treaties 19
Hyundai 259, 449, 451

I

IBM 4, 25, 253, 261, 315, 461, 530, 542
ICA 431
Implementation problems, screening
    strategies 534(fig.)
IMRG 58
Incentives, employees, recruitment
    standards 316
Income gulf 86–9
Incoterms 477
India 42, 49
    cumulative services export growth 314
    emergence of economic powerhouse 10,
        23, 49, 75
    Johnson & Johnson 44
Individualism 124
Indonesia 44, 146
Industrial networks 219–20
Industrialization of services 229
Inequalities 86–9
Inflation 465, 470
Information *see* Knowledge/information
Information and communications
    technologies (ICT) 17–19, 46
    advertising 371–3
    costs 82–3
    as driver of change 269–70
    globalization and 77
    growth in service sector and 317–18
    law of unintended consequences 374
    marketing and 26
        communications 347–50
        reduction in costs of 82(table)
        sales management and 495
        technological environment of global
            marketing 57–62
    personal selling 374
    publicity 374
    sales promotion 373–4
Innovations 4
    corporate social responsibility and 164
    see also Information and
        communications technologies (ICT)

Inspection and sampling order 479
Institute of Business Ethics, Guide to Good
     Practice in Implementation of Codes
     of Conduct 159
Intangibility vs environmental sensitivity
     325(fig.)
Integrated marketing communications
     (IMC) 347–50
  defining 347
Intel 258
Intellectual property rights 46
  and drug companies 87
Internal partnership 41
International Bank for Reconstruction and
     Development (IBRD) see World Bank
International business models see Business
     models
International Finance Corporation (IFC) 54
International law 45, 45–6
International Monetary Fund (IMF) 11,
     45, 54
International relations 44–5
International strategies 288
International trade
  documentation 478–90
  export financing 480–9
  export order process 475
  export payments 478
  fairness 17
  Incoterms 477
  non-tariff barriers 88, 477
  protectionism 17, 71
  tariffs 475–7
Internationalization see Globalization
Internet and e-commerce 4, 18, 58–62, 293
  advertising and 371–3
  customer relationships 436–7
  direct marketing 362–5
  entry strategies 235–8
  ethics and 61
  Extended Common Log Format
     (ECLF) 187
  market segmentation and 187
  relationship management and 436–7
  usage 60(table)
Investment, ethics 164–5
iPod 59
Iraq war 23, 24, 43, 44–5, 66, 512
Islam 110
ISO 9000 standard, quality 282
ISO 14001 standard 96
  waste disposal 165
Israel, cumulative services export
     growth 314
Isuzu 505
ITT International, night-vision devices 96

J

J. Walter Thompson 541
Jack Daniels 376
Jaguar 304

Japan 4, 23, 218
  advertising 354, 356
  ageing population 5
  collaborative relationships 432
  culture 106, 111
  sales force structure 515
  whaling 64–5
John Deere 292
John Hancock 509
Johnson & Johnson 156
  India 44
Joint venture, market entry modes 233
Joint ventures 133, 233, 253, 394
J.P. Morgan-Chase 64
Just in Time (JIT) 40

K

Kall Kwik 329
Kelloggs 38
Kenya 268, 448
KFC 294
KFMG 257, 316
Kia 449
Kimberley, diamonds 149
Kingfisher 64
Kmart 494
'Knowledge-based' organization 520
Knowledge/information 330–2
  as competitive advantage 26–7, 268–9,
     330–2
  management 27, 330–1
     development 331(fig.)
     four levels 331–2
  sources 180–1
  spreading 27
  see also Data
Korea 20, 23, 239–40
  South 22, 86, 87, 114, 118
Korean farmers, anti-globalization
     protest 87
Kronenbourg 449
Kyoto Protocol on Climate Change 87, 96

L

Labelling 106
Labour practices 150–3
Language, culture and 106, 109, 122, 360
Lateral (horizontal) partnerships 394,
     430–2
Latin American economies 11
Leader Price 238
Learning curve, Boston Consulting
     Group 452
Leasing 472
Legal environment 45–6
  competition and 251
  sales management and 498
Lego 185
Letters of credit 478
Lever Faberge 431

Levi 474
Levi Strauss 150
Licensing agreements 232, 233
Lidl 237, 238, 286
Life expectancy 13
Lintas 541
Literacy 110–11
London's Heathrow Airport 339–40, 531
Louis Organization 335
Low cost carriers (LCCs) 229
Loyalty business model 228
Loyalty schemes 426, 442–3
Lufthansa 196

M

McDonald's 25, 79, 98–9, 263, 283–4, 286,
     332, 449
  China 394
  protests 98–9
McKinsey 7S Framework 523
Macro-survey analysis 177
Maize to Africa 41
Malawi 433
Malaysia 43
  culture 108, 109, 111
  Dagang Net 84
  economy 222
  financial crisis 76
  intellectual property rights, piracy 46
  language 109
  literacy 111
  pricing 474
  Proton 274–5
Management
  innovations 253
  levels 523
  operational management 523
  philosophy of 521
  see also Relationship management; Sales
     management
Managerial forces 494–5
Market agreements, different forms
     51(table)
Market entry modes 230–4
  agents and distributors 232
  comparison 234(table)
  contract manufacturing 232–3
  export mode entry 232
  franchising 233
  hierarchical modes of entry 233–4
  intermediate modes of entry 232
  involvement, risk, and control 231(table)
  joint venture or strategic alliance 233
  licensing 233
  management contracting 233
Market entry strategies 193–4, 213–25
  agency approach 225
  bargaining power approach 221–2
     born global 223–4
     transactional cost analysis 224
  business strategy approach 225

eclectic or contingency 224–5
effects of international market environment on market entry decision 211(fig.)
environmental audit 211
environmental factors in decision-making 212(table)
industrial network approach (network model) 219–21
theories 213(fig.)
Uppsala or incremental model (stage model) 213–19
Market penetration 292
Market penetration pricing 457–8
Market profile analysis 172(fig.)
Market segmentation 185–8
concentration vs diversification 191(table), 192
country vs global segments 188–9
customer-specific segmentation, internet 187
Hartman Group traditional segmentation 189
personas and 197
strategically equivalent segments (SES) 193
VALS lifestyle system 188
Market selection 169–99
concentration vs diversification 191(table), 192
expansion possibilities 191(fig.)
four-step process 190
Marketing 4–17, 6–7
4 types 418
currency environment 63–4
definitions 6, 7
direct-response marketing 362–5, 494
domestic marketing 6
failures 185
global see Global marketing
global marketing audit 528–9
Internet/e-mail and 362–5
market selection 169–99
need for new approach to 20–8
organizing for 30–1
planning and control 7, 521–5, 522(fig.)
structure 31
theories of 21(table)
see also Specific topics
Marketing control system
analysis of deviations and corrective action 528
brand equity metrics 530
efficiency control 529
establishment of standards 528
financial and profit control 530
performance evaluation 528
strategic control 529
Marketing environment 36–69, 40(fig.)
changes 7–19, 9(fig.)
competitive environment 62–3
currency environment 63–4

definition 37–8
economic environment 46–56
importance of accounting for 38–9
intermediate environment 39–42
legal environment 45–6
macro environment 42
market entry modes 230–4
permission marketing 60
political environment 42–5
socio-cultural environment 56–7
technological environment 57–62
Marketing information system (MKIS) 171–2, 181
Marketing relationship
alternative approaches to inter-organizational interaction 422(fig.)
dynamics of international operations 421–3
Markets
access to
entry strategies 193–4
modes 230–4
opportunities of globalization 79–81
shower 192
terms of access 475–7
waterfall 192
development 292
'free market' 429
growth rate 290(fig.)
market penetration pricing 457–8
potential 48
ranking (attractiveness and ability to compete) 179(fig.)
research see Research
screening 175–80
Marks & Spencer 194, 237, 281, 295
shareholder action 41
Marriott Hotels 316
Mars 530
Mary Kay Cosmetics 508
Masculinity, culture and 125
MasterCard 353
Matrices, to portfolio management 290–1
Matrix organizational structures 538–40
Matsushita 395–7
Mauritania 47
Mauritius, cumulative services export growth 314
Media
homogenization of global consumers 316
multimedia and sales 495
Mercedes-Benz 61, 106, 202–5, 249, 296, 303, 414, 454, 463, 530
Mergers 253
Methane, from food scraps 96
Mexico 11
financial crisis (1994–95) 12
Mexico City 25
Microeconomic business environment 247
Microsoft 25, 27, 46, 79, 252, 256, 257, 294
Middle East 45, 66–7
Middleman 227

Migration 71, 89–92
brain-drain problems 90–1
humanitarian crises 91
Mining, Anglo-American 544–5
Mitsubishi 222, 432, 505
Mobil Oil Company 532
Mobile telephones 39–40, 530
text messaging 112
Monopoly 227
Monsanto, GM 89
Monster 372
Morgan Stanley 165
Mosaic UK, customer segmentation 195
Mothercare 237
Motorola 461
Motors
Formula One and Bernie Ecclestone 306–7
SUV fashion 504
Multi-level marketing 226
Multiple factor indices 176
Music 28, 32–3, 59–60
merger of Sony and BMG 83
Music industry, merger of Sony and BMG 83
Mytravel.com 431

N

NAFTA 50–1, 434
Nano-technology 61
Napster 59, 361
National Health Service (NHS) 312
National Westminster Bank 253
Near environment, competition and 251
NEC 164
Needs
stakeholder needs analysis 254
types of 117–18
Negotiations
ethical considerations 510–12
preparation 504–5
relationship approach 507–10
transactional process 507
Nestlé 19, 152, 237, 530
local vs global brands 297
social issues 300
Netto 237, 238
Network effect, international business models 219(fig.)
Networks
industrial network approach 219–20
internationalization process and 219–21
relationship management and 424–5, 428
New product development (NPD) 302–5
New technologies 18
NFP organizations 433
Nicaragua 47, 433
Nigeria 16, 148
human rights 19
Nike 19, 25, 150, 152, 153, 293
Nintendo 25

Nissan 119, 295, 432, 463, 505
　Cube car 176
Non-governmental organizations (NGOs)
　19, 430, 433
Non-tariff barriers 80, 88, 477
Norma 237
North American Free Trade Area (NAFTA)
　50–1, 434
Northern Rock 64
NTL 361
Nu Skin 227, 304

O

Obesity 286
OECD, Convention on Combating Bribery
　of Public Officials in International
　Business Transactions 147
Offset 473
OnDemand Distribution 272
Operational management 523
Options trading 469
Oracle 257, 533
Order process 475
Organization for Economic Cooperation
　and Development (OECD) 44, 71
Organizational structures 520–50
　control mechanisms 525–8
　functional 535–6
　geographical, functional, or strategic
　　business unit 536–7
　hub and spoke 539(fig.)
　matrix 538–40, 539(fig.)
　product 537
　virtual 539–40
Outshopping 450
Outsourcing 4, 62–3, 462, 494
　negative impacts 541
　sales function 494
Outsourcing Institute 541
Oxfam 64, 272, 548–50
　fair trading 466
　objectives 548

P

P&O cruise liners 433
Pakistan, Sialkot football programme 153
Parallel markets 471–2
Pareto 80/20 rule 28
Partnerships, lateral (horizontal)
　partnerships 430–4
Penetration pricing 292, 457–8
Penny 237
Pepsi 42, 262, 413
Performance measurement, *see also*
　Control mechanisms
Perfume 482–3
Perishability, services 327
Permission marketing 60
Peru 11
PEST, vs SLEPT 39(fig.)

Philippines, expropriation 44
Philips 435
Piracy, intellectual property rights and 46
Pixar 252
Planning and control process 522(fig.)
　benefits from planning global operations
　　523(fig.)
　planning and control process 522(fig.)
　problems, headquarters and subsidiary
　　levels 525(table)
　see also Organizational structures
Platinum, Anglo-American 544–5
PlayStation 25
Plus 237
Poland 461–2
Political discourse 112–13
Political environment 42–5
　competition and 250–1
　globalization 75–7
　sales management and 498
Political risk 43–4
　assessment 44
Political unions 51
Polycentrism 521
Porsche 294, 454
Portfolio capital 81
Ports, Dagang Net, Malaysia 84
Postal services, direct-response marketing
　362–5
Pot Noodle 356
Poverty 86–9, 95
　migration 71, 89–92
Power
　bargaining power theories 221–2
　coercive vs non-coercive sources 526
　power distance 123
　relationship management and 428
Pressure groups 64–5
Pricing 448–87
　changes 464
　competitive bid or tendering pricing 456
　cooperation 481
　coordination across subsidiaries 474
　cost-oriented pricing 455
　counter-trade 473–4
　currency fluctuations 466–9
　discounts and allowances 459
　dumping 472
　dynamic incremental pricing 457–8
　economies of scale 451
　economies of size 452
　escalation 465–6
　factors affecting global pricing decisions
　　449–52
　geographical 458–9
　going-rate pricing 456
　grey and parallel markets 471–2
　inflation 465, 470
　leasing and 472
　market based pricing 456–7
　market penetration pricing 457–8
　market/use 460

　markup 455
　objectives 455(table)
　price-setting decision process 448, 463
　product mix 460
　promotional 459
　razor and blades 460
　skimming 454, 458
　standardization 449, 451
　steps involved 448(fig.)
　strategy 452–5
　transfer pricing 470–1
Procter & Gamble 85, 152, 301, 435
Production
　economies 49
　globalization and 83–4
　process innovations 252–3
Products 282–7, 280–310
　components of international product
　　280–2
　development of new products 302–5
　differentiation 262
　growth strategies 292(fig.)
　international product management
　　282–7
　ISO 9000 282
　knowledge and benefits 504–5
　knowledge of 504–5
　life cycles 253, 289–90
　product strategy 288–93
Profit control 530
Promissory notes 479
Protectionism 17, 71
　international trade 17, 71
　non-tariff barriers 80, 88, 477
Protest
　anti-globalization protest 86–9
　Korean farmers 87
　McDonald's 98–9
　Seattle meeting 86
Proton 248, 274–5
Public relations (PR) 359–62
　planning in a cross-cultural context
　　362(fig.)
Puma 293
Purchasing, globalization and 83–4

Q

Qantas 196
Quality 420
　ISO 9000 standard 282
　services 228, 315–16, 336–7, 420
Quanxi relationships 394

R

Radio frequency identification (RFID) 62
Rank Xerox 542
RCA 4
Recruitment and selection, sales force
　498–501
Recruitment standards 316

Reebok 150, 153, 293, 396
Refugees 91–2
Regiocentrism 521
Regional development banks 55
Regional economic blocs 50–3
Regression analysis 177
Relationship management 28, 133,
    271–2, 413
  classification of relationships 424–5
  customer relationship management
    (CRM) 271, 435–41
  drivers for growth in relational
    perspectives 414–20
  importance of 413–18
  internal partnerships 434–6
  Internet and 436–7
  lateral (horizontal) partnerships 394,
    430–4
  marketing 416–19
    developmental stages 419(fig.)
    key characteristics 419–21
    managerial implications 421–3
    social reponsibility 429
  measuring success 437–9
  network perspective 424–5, 428
  outsourcing 337
  and power 428
  problems with 439–41
  sales negotiation and 507–10
  suppliers 428–30
  vertical downstream relationships 393,
    425–8
  vertical upstream relationships 428–30
Religion
  culture and 109–10
  missionaries 433
  sales force and 499
Rema 1000 237
Renault 248
Reputation management 160–3
Research
  data analysis 184
  data collection 174, 180, 183
  design of 174(table), 183
  ethics and 184
  information sources 180–1
  international marketing research 172–6
  marketing information system (MKIS)
    171–2
  objectives 182
  process 173(fig.)
  report writing and presentation 184
  screening international markets 175–6
  value of information 182–3
Research and development 28
Research process agreement 181–2
Resource economies 49
Resource-based theory of competitive
    advantage 263–5
Retail, Christmas sales 58
Retail franchises 328–9
Revaluation 469

Risk assessment 44
Risk management
  corporate social responsibility and 163
  supply chains and distribution 384
Robinsons 302
Role models 117
Rolls Royce 62, 109, 269
Romania, cumulative services export
    growth 314
Royal Selangor 248
  3 Es 510
RS Components 429
Russia 10, 49
Ryanair 457

S

S & A Asian Foods 250
S. C. Johnson 165
Saatchi and Saatchi 541
SADC (Southern and Eastern Africa
    Development Community) 52
Saga 24–5, 196, 250
Sales
  consignment basis 478
  forces affecting the nature of selling and
    sales management 493(fig.)
  open account 478
Sales force 495
  administration 496–8
  cultural empathy skills 504
  culture and 498–501
  customer-oriented selling 502–3
  personnel characteristics 501
  recruitment and selection 498–501
  sales negotiations 503–12
  structure 515
  training 512–13
Sales management 386–97
  changing nature of 387–95
  culture and 498–503
  customer-oriented selling 502–3
  decisions 495–8
  environmental factors in decision-
    making 497–8
  ethical considerations 510–12
  negotiations and culture 503–4
  training 512–13
Sales negotiations
  and power 428
  preparation 505–6
  relationship management and 507–10
  sales management 503–4
Samsung 20, 239–40, 257, 259
Sarcophagus 293
SARS 66–7
SARS (severe acute respiratory disease) 66–7
Saturn car 426
Scale economies 317
Scenario planning 66–7
Schwartz Value Inventory (SVI) 127, 128
Scottish arts and crafts businesses 223

Screening international markets 175–6
  assessing incipient markets 176
  fine 178(fig.)
  rough 175
Screening strategies, implementation
    problems 534(fig.)
Sears 494
Second homes 177
SELECT framework 256
Self-assessment 531
Self-reference criterion (SRC) 57, 118,
    119(fig.)
Serbia 44
Service packages 5
Service sector 312–42
  categories of service 323(fig.)
  cross-border services, drivers for growth
    314–19
  customization vs standardization
    332–4
  defining global services, by intangibility
    324–5
  delivery 334–5
  deregulation and liberalization of trade
    314–15
  franchising 328–9
  global economies of scale 317
  heterogeneity 325–6
  information-processing services 323–4
  marketing challenges 324–8
    intangibility 324–5
  multi-variant classification systems
    321–4
  people-processing services 323
  perishability 327
  possession-processing services 323
  provider and customer interaction 327
  quality, international business
    models 228
  relationship management 428–30
  role of technology 336
  scale of 312–13
  service quality and standards 228,
    315–16, 336–7, 420
  six-sector service taxonomy 322(fig.)
  socio-cultural differences 335–6
  strategic considerations for marketing
    330–8
  world trade in commercial services by
    category 313(table)
Services economy 16
SERVQUAL 337
Severe acute respiratory disease (SARS) 66–7
Shareholders, pressure groups 64–5
Shell 19, 26, 64, 163, 394
  Nigeria 148
Sialkot football programme 153
Siemens AG 10, 471
Singapore
  economy of 251
  outshopping from 450
  sales management 497–8

Singapore Airlines 262
Single European Payments Area 474–5
Skandia 253, 520
Skimming price 454, 458
SLEPT analysis 39, 42
Smart cars 202
SMEs (small and medium-sized enterprises),
    globalization process 215–17, 284
Social behaviour 108
Social changes 5
Social class, sales force and 499
Social issues 142–65
Social needs 118
Social organization, culture and 111
Social responsibility, brands 300
Socio-economic blocs 50–3
Socio-economic factors, competition
    and 250
Sogo-shoshas 401
Solace 461, 462
Sony 133, 256, 458
    Group Code of Conduct 65–6
    merger of Sony and BMG 83
Sourcing 83–4, 399–401
    domestic 398–9
    global 83–4, 399–401
    outsourcing 4, 62–3, 462, 541
        sales function 494
    purchasing and production 83–4
South Africa 41
Sovereign Wealth Funds (SWFs) 48
Spain, second homes 177
Speedo 418
Sponsorship 366–8
Spot trading 469
Stage models of globalization 213–19
Stakeholder value 532
Stakeholders 41
    needs analysis 254
Standard of living 247
Standardization 344–5
    factors preventing standardization of
        marketing communications 346(fig.)
    market differences 345–6
    prices 449, 451
    vs adaptation, in international markets
        283(fig.)
    vs customization 332–4
    vs localization 344–5
Star Alliance 196, 258, 259, 414
Starbucks 73, 164
Steel industry 431–2
Steelcase Inc 97
Stella Artois 449
Stock, FIFO vs LIFO 470
Stock market indices 165
Strategic alliance, market entry modes 233
Strategic architecture, economic growth
    and development 23–4
Strategic management 523
Strategically equivalent segments (SES) 193
Structural adjustment programmes 43

Subscription business model 226
Sun Microsystems 262
Sunkist 431
Sunsplash 289
Suppliers 40
    relationship management 428–30
Supply chain management 382–411
    collaboration 391–7
    country characteristics 386–8
    developing 397–406
    exhibitions and trade fairs 368–71
    factors affecting supply chain decisions
        386–91
    global competitive advantage 408–9
    global sourcing 399–401
    horizontal, lateral, vertical 393–5
    industry characteristics 388
    information sharing 404–5
    integrated policies and processes 403–4
    international supply chain 383(fig.)
    market responsive manufacturing 401–3
    nature of 349–50
    performance measurement 406
    risk 384
    sponsorship 366–8
    strategic relationships 385–6
    strategies 389–91
    technology and 347
    trade-offs 384
    web-based 390, 405
Sustainability, and development 89, 92–7
Sweatshops 151–2
Swissair 24
Switch deals 473

T

Taiwan 4
Tariffs
    harmonized tariff system (HTS) 475
    international trade 475–7
Tarmac 545
Taxation 41–2
Team Domino 60
Technological forces 494
Technology
    culture and 112
    customer relationship management
        (CRM) 438
    disruptive technologies 61
    DVDs 373
    globalization and 77
    nano-technology 61
    reactive data collection technologies 187
    sales management and 493
    services marketing and 336, 347
    standardization and 346(fig.)
    video-conferencing 540
    see also Information and
        communications technologies (ICT)
Telecommunications
    costs 82

direct marketing and 235
    mobile telephones 39–40, 112, 530
    text messaging 112
Telemedicine 15
Television, digital 18
Terrorism 8, 24
Tesco 229, 426, 436–7
    loyalty schemes 426, 442–3
    in Thailand 524
Texas Instruments 160
Text messaging 112
Thailand
    financial crisis 12
    intellectual property rights piracy and 43
Third World, poverty 86–9, 95
Tiger economies 4
TimeWarner 59
Tokyo 25
Toshiba 471
Tourism
    and 9/11 67
    tourist industry 196
Toyota 6, 27, 62, 119, 326, 452, 505
Toys 'R' Us 392, 494
Trade preference agreement 51
Training
    ethics 158–60
    sales, Northern vs Southern Europe 513
    sales management 512–13
Transactional cost analysis (TCA) 224
Transactional marketing, 4Ps mix,
        model 416
Transactional relationships 392–3
Transactional sales negotiation process 507
Transatlantic Business Dialogue (TABD) 434
Transformational business models 229
Transparency International, Corruption
        Perceptions Index 143(table)
Transport
    Dagang Net, Malaysia 84
    globalization and 82–3
    services and travel 313(table)
Travel and tourism industry 196

U

UEMOA (West African States in Economic
        and Monetary Union) 52
Uncertainty avoidance (UA) 123
Unilever 21, 85, 157–8, 164
    Bertolli 357–9
    Code 157–8
    local vs global brands 297
United Kingdom 23
    e-commerce 53
    education 526
    EU single currency and 37
    GDP, growth in service sector 313
    immigrants 45
    Internet in 59
        banking 21
    obesity 286

outshopping from 450
service sector 8
text messaging 112
wine drinking 198
United Nations 42, 50
  Conference on International Trade Law
    (UNCITRAL) 46
  Draft Norms, new standards for
    corporations and human
    rights 151
  Global Compact 149–50
  global laws 45
  organization 54
  Universal Declaration of Human Rights
    147–8
United States of America 4
  ageing population 5
  born global organizations 223–4
  cumulative services export growth 314
  as economic superpower 23
  Foreign Corrupt Practices Act 147
  GDP, growth in service sector 313
  international relations and 42
  music industry 28, 32–3
  protectionism 17
  service sector 8
  sub-prime market (mortgages) 64
  telemedicine 15
  terrorist attack on 8
Universalism vs particularism 125
Unocal, Burma 148
Urbanization 25
  shift to 57

V

VALS lifestyle system 188
Value system 114, 116–17
Values and attitudes, consumer behaviour
    114, 116–17, 125–9
  achievement vs ascription 126
  communitarianism vs individualism 126
  culture and 110, 125
  customer value analysis (CVA) 530
  diffuse vs specific cultures 126
  human–time and human–nature
    relationships 126
  neutral vs emotional 126
  superior vs inferior perceived values
    255(fig.)
Verifone 96
Video-conferencing 540
Virtual marketplace 61
Virtual organizational structures 539–40
Vivendi Universal 53, 59
  merger of Sony and BMG 83
Vodafone 112
VW group 6, 62, 292

W

Wal-Mart 152, 237, 494
Walkers Crisps 268
Warner Bros 78
Waste management 96–7, 165
  ISO 14001 165
Water shortages 94
Westernization 111

Westinghouse 4
Westpac 533
Wireless devices, advertising 373
World Bank 23, 47, 49–50, 54, 430
  Atlas classification of economies
    48, 49(fig.)
  Development Indicators in 2002 13
  fraud and corruption provisions 148
World population 9
  ageing population in 5, 12–13, 56, 194
  median ages 10
World Trade Organization (WTO) 17, 41,
    43, 49, 51, 86
  non-tariff barriers 80, 88, 477
  Seattle meeting 86

X

Xerox 326, 542

Y

Yves Rocher 236, 328

Z

Zambia 41, 45
  horticultural produce 221
Zimbabwe 23, 41, 43, 45, 50, 51, 55
  exchange rate fluctuations 467
  MMD 113
  Sunsplash 289